1 MONTH OF
FREE
READING

at

www.ForgottenBooks.com

By purchasing this book you are eligible for one month membership to ForgottenBooks.com, giving you unlimited access to our entire collection of over 1,000,000 titles via our web site and mobile apps.

To claim your free month visit: www.forgottenbooks.com/free923117

ISBN 978-0-260-02640-8
PIBN 10923117

ANNUAL REPORT

OF THE

STATE BOARD OF CHARITIES

FOR THE YEAR 1901.

IN TWO VOLUMES,

WITH STATISTICAL APPENDIX TO VOLUME ONE BOUND SEPARATELY.

VOLUME ONE.

WITH STATISTICAL APPENDIX BOUND SEPARATELY.

TRANSMITTED TO THE LEGISLATURE MARCH 17, 1902.

ALBANY

J. B. LYON COMPANY, STATE PRINTERS

1902

STATE OF NEW YORK.

No. 30.

IN SENATE,

MARCH 17, 1902.

THIRTY-FIFTH ANNUAL REPORT

OF THE

STATE BOARD OF CHARITIES.

STATE OF NEW YORK:

OFFICE OF THE STATE BOARD OF CHARITIES,

THE CAPITOL, ALBANY, *March* 17, 1902.

To the Hon. TIMOTHY L. WOODRUFF,

Lieutenant-Governor and President of the Senate:

Sir—By direction of the Board, I have the honor herewith to transmit to the Legislature the thirty-fifth annual report of the State Board of Charities.

Yours very respectfully,

WILLIAM R. STEWART,

President.

MEMBERS AND OFFICERS
OF THE
STATE BOARD OF CHARITIES
1902.

MEMBERS APPOINTED BY THE GOVERNOR, BY AND WITH THE ADVICE AND CONSENT OF THE SENATE.

DISTRICTS.	Names and addresses.	Date of appointment.
First Judicial.................. (New York county)	William R. Stewart, President, 31 Nassau street, New York city.	May 31, 1882
New York county..............	Mrs. Beekman de Peyster, 101 West 81st street, New York city.	October 4, 1890
New York county..............	Stephen Smith, M. D., 640 Madison ave., New York city.	*March 29, 1898
New York county..............	Michael J. Scanlan, 56 Pine street, New York city.	May 20, 1901
Second Judicial .... (Counties of Richmond, Suffolk, Nassau, Queens, Kings, Westchester, Orange, Rockland, Putnam and Dutchess.)	Edward H. Litchfield, 2 Montague Terrace, Brooklyn, New York city.	January 16, 1893
Kings county	John Notman, 136 Joralemon street, Brooklyn, New York city.	January 17, 1899
Third Judicial................ (Counties of Columbia, Sullivan, Ulster, Greene, Albany, Schoharie, and Rensselaer.)	Simon W. Rosendale, 57 State street, Albany, N. Y.	March 8, 1899
Fourth Judicial .... (Counties of Warren, Saratoga, Washington, Essex, Franklin, St. Lawrence, Clinton, Montgomery, Hamilton, Fulton and Schenectady.)	Newton Aldrich, Gouverneur, St. Lawrence Co., N. Y.	April 3, 1896
Fifth Judicial................ (Counties of Onondaga, Oneida, Oswego, Herkimer, Jefferson and Lewis.)	Dennis McCarthy, 219 S. Salina street, Syracuse, N. Y.	March 8, 1899
Sixth Judicial............... (Counties of Otsego, Delaware, Madison, Chenango, Broome, Tioga, Chemung, Tompkins, Cortland and Schuyler.)	Peter Walrath, Chittenango, Madison Co., N. Y.	April 7, 1886
Seventh Judicial .... (Counties of Livingston, Wayne, Seneca, Yates, Ontario, Steuben, Monroe and Cayuga.)	Enoch Vine Stoddard, M.D., Vice-President, 62 State street, Rochester, N. Y.	January 1, 1894
Eighth Judicial............. (Counties of Erie, Chautauqua, Cattaraugus, Orleans, Niagara, Genesee, Allegany and Wyoming.)	William H. Gratwick, 877 Ellicott square, Buffalo, N. Y.	April 17, 1901

OFFICERS.

WILLIAM RHINELANDER STEWART...PRESIDENT.
ENOCH VINE STODDARD, M.D..VICE-PRESIDENT.
ROBERT W. HEBBERD ....SECRETARY.
BYRON M. CHILD .............SUPERINTENDENT OF STATE AND ALIEN POOR.
WALTER S. UFFORD............................SUPERINTENDENT OF INSPECTION.

*Previously a commissioner.

ATTENDANCE OF COMMISSIONERS UPON MEETINGS OF THE BOARD HELD DURING THE YEAR 1901.

P. Present.   A. Absent.

COMMISSIONERS.	Years of service.	Stated meeting, Jan. 9.	Adjourned stated meeting, Jan. 24.	Special meeting, Feb. 28.	Stated meeting, April 10.	Special meeting, June 6.	Stated meeting, July 16.	Stated meeting, Oct. 2-16.
William R. Stewart, First Judicial District	20	P.	P.	P.	P.	P.		P.
Mrs. Beekman de T .... Mr. New York County	11	*A.	A.	A.	A.	A.	A.	A.
Stephen ... th, M. D., New York County	8	P.	P.	P.	P.	P.	P.	P.
Michael J. Sca ... lan, New York unty ‡	9					A.	A.	P.
Edward H. .... Mel. Second Judicial District	2	†A.	A.	†A.	†A.	A.	†A.	‡A.
John Notman, Kings ... ty	2	P.	P.	P.	P.	P.	P.	P.
Simon W. Rosendale, Third Judicial District	6	P.	P.	P.	P.	P.	‡A.	P.
Newton Aldrich, Fourth ... ial District	2	†A.	†A.	P.	P.	P.	P.	P.
Dennis ... ly, Fifth Judicial District	16	P.	P.	P.	A.	P.	P.	P.
Peter ... th, Sixth Judicial District	8	A.	P.	P.	A.	P.	P.	P.
... deh Vine Stoddard, M. D., Seventh Judicial District	4	A.	A.	A.	A.	P.	P.	P.
Harvey W. Putnam, Eighth ... ial §at f.								
William H. Gratwick, Eighth Judicial District			P.	.....	P.	P.	P.	P.
		7	8	8	7	10	8	10

* Commissioner de Peyster was absent because of illness.
† Commissioner Scanlan was appointed May 20, 1901.
‡ Commissioners Notman and McCarthy were granted leave of absence.
§ Commissioner Putnam resigned.
‖ Commissioner Gratwick was appointed April 17, 1901.
The Board consists of twelve members, and the average attendance during 1901 was eight.

ELECTION OF OFFICERS.

At the Board's stated meeting of April 10th, the annual election of officers was held, as provided by the by-laws. President William Rhinelander Stewart and Vice-President Enoch Vine Stoddard were unanimously reëlected, the former for the eighth and the latter for the seventh consecutive term, to their respective offices for the ensuing year. The other officers were continued subject to the pleasure of the Board.

STANDING COMMITTEES OF THE BOARD.

Stated Committees.

On Publication:

The President, Commissioners Stoddard, Smith and Scanlan.

On Finance:

The President, Commissioners Walrath and Rosendale.

On Inspection:

Commissioners Stoddard, Smith and Scanlan.

On State and Alien Poor:

Commissioners McCarthy, Walrath and Litchfield.

Additional Committees.

On Reformatories:

Commissioners Litchfield, Stoddard and de Peyster.

On Idiots and Feeble-Minded:

Commissioners Stoddard, Walrath and McCarthy.

On Soldiers and Sailors' Homes:

Commissioners Rosendale, Walrath and Gratwick.

On Craig Colony:

Commissioners Stoddard, Smith and Walrath.

On Thomas Asylum:

Commissioner Gratwick.

On the Blind:

Commissioners Smith and Gratwick.

On the Deaf:

Commissioners Notman, Aldrich and Scanlan.

On Almshouses:

Commissioners Walrath, Rosendale and Aldrich.

On Orphan Asylums:

Commissioners Notman, McCarthy and de Peyster.

On Hospitals:

Commissioners Smith, Notman and McCarthy.

On Legislation:

Commissioners Rosendale, Notman and Scanlan.

On the Construction of Buildings:

Commissioners Smith, Litchfield and McCarthy.

On Placing Out Children:

Commissioners Stoddard, Walrath and Gratwick.

On Dispensaries:

Commissioners Smith, Stoddard and Rosendale.

On Sanatoria for Consumptives:

Commissioners Smith and Stoddard.

On Legal Questions:

Commissioners Notman and Scanlan.

On State Hospital for Crippled and Deformed Children:

Commissioner Smith.

APPROPRIATIONS TO THE BOARD BY THE LEGISLATURE OF 1901.
APPROPRIATION BILL.

The appropriation bill, chapter 644 of the Laws of 1901, made the following appropriations for carrying on the Board's work:

For the salary of the secretary, $3,500.

For compensation of twelve commissioners as provided by chapter 546 of the Laws of 1896, $3,000, or so much thereof as may be necessary.

For superintendent of inspection, $2,500; chief clerk, $1,500; clerk, $1,400; statistician, $900; one stenographer, $900; one stenographer, $720; clerk, $600; junior clerk, $480. For temporary help at the Albany office, $500, or so much thereof as may be necessary.

For traveling expenses of the commissioners and secretary while engaged in the discharge of their official duties, $3,500, or so much thereof as may be necessary.

For traveling expenses of the employes of the Department while engaged in their official duties, $2,500, or so much thereof as may be necessary.

For rent, printing, stationery, and other expenses of the office, $5,000, or so much thereof as may be necessary.

For postage, and expense of transportation of all letters, official documents or other matter sent by express or freight, including boxes or covering for same, $1,200, or so much thereof as may be necessary.

State and Alien Poor.

For salary of the superintendent, $3,000; for the deputy superintendent in New York city, $1,500; for inspector, $1,500; for assistant inspector, $1,200; for transfer agent, Kings county almshouse, $900; for transfer agent, Monroe county almshouse, $180; for transfer agent, Erie county almshouse, $900; for stenographer, $720; for messenger, $300; for traveling expenses of superintendent and inspectors, $3,000; for incidental office expenses, $500; for maintenance, transportation and removal of State, alien and non-resident poor, $26,300, or so much thereof as may be necessary.

New York Office.

For superintendent, $1,500; two inspectors, $1,200 each; two inspectors, $900 each; stenographer, $720.

Rochester Office.

For inspector, $1,200, and stenographer, $600.

SUPPLY BILL.

The supply bill, chapter 645 of the Laws of 1901, made the following additional appropriations to the Board:

For messenger and clerk at the Albany office for the fiscal year ending September 30, 1902, $720.

State and Alien Poor.

For clerk and stenographer for the fiscal year ending September 30, 1902, $600.

APPROPRIATIONS DESIRED FROM THE LEGISLATURE OF 1902.

For the secretary of the Board, for salary, $3,500.

The compensation of twelve commissioners as provided by chapter 546 of the Laws of 1896, $2,000, or so much thereof as may be necessary. (This is reduced from $3,000 because of a balance on hand at the end of the last fiscal year.)

For superintendent of inspection, $2,500; chief clerk, $1,500; clerk, $1,400; statistician, $900; one stenographer, $1,200; one stenographer, $720; messenger, $720; clerk, $600; junior clerk, $480. For temporary help, $300, or so much thereof as may be necessary. (This item is reduced from $500 because of a balance on hand at the end of the last fiscal year.)

For traveling expenses of commissioners and the secretary while engaged in the discharge of their official duties, $2,500, or so much thereof as may be necessary. (This item is reduced from $3,500 because of a balance on hand at the end of the last fiscal year.)

For traveling expenses of the employes of the Department while engaged in the discharge of their official duties, $2,500, or so much thereof as may be necessary.

For rent, printing and other expenses of the office, $5,000, or so much thereof as may be necessary.

For postage, and expense of transportation of all letters, official documents or other matter sent by express or freight, including boxes or covering for same, $1,200, or so much thereof as may be necessary.

State and Alien Poor.

For salary of the superintendent, $3,000; for the deputy superintendent in New York city, $1,500; for inspector of State charitable institutions, $2,000; for inspector, $1,200; for inspector, $1,200; for transfer agent Kings County Almshouse, $900; for transfer agent, Monroe County Almshouse, $180; for transfer agent Erie County Almshouse, $900; for clerk and stenographer, $720; for stenographer, $600; for messenger, $300; for traveling expenses of superintendent and inspectors, $3,000; for incidental office expenses, $500; for maintenance, transportation and removal of State, alien, non-resident and Indian poor, $26,300, or so much thereof as may be necessary.

New York Office.

For superintendent, $1,500; one inspector, $1,400; one inspector, $1,200; two inspectors, $900 each; stenographer, $720.

Rochester Office.

For inspector, $1,200, and stenographer, $600.

The Board also wishes to employ an examiner of schools at a salary of $1,800 a year, in order that the inmates, estimated to number 15,000 annually, of institutions for children under the Board's jurisdiction, not now examined by any independent authority, may be regularly examined. This is desired to insure them a sufficient and suitable education. This important duty is clearly imposed upon the Board by law, but owing to lack of means heretofore it has been unable to give it attention.

CHARITABLE LEGISLATION, 1901.

The existing statutory provisions relative to the public and private charities of the State were but slightly affected by the legislation of 1901, as will appear from the following brief review of this class of general legislation which was enacted into law.

Amendments to the Poor Law.

Two sections were added to chapter 225 of the Laws of 1896, known as the Poor law, constituting chapter 27 of the general laws. The first of these sections relates to the medical care and treatment of indigent persons in counties of the State in which there are not adequate hospital accommodations, or in which no appropriations of money are made for this purpose. The new section is embodied in chapter 103, Laws of 1901, and reads as follows:

" § 30. In all counties of this State in which there are not adequate hospital accommodations for indigent persons requiring medical or surgical care and treatment, or in which no appropriations of money are made for this specific purpose, it shall be the duty of county superintendents of the poor, upon the certificate of a physician approved by the board of supervisors, or of the overseers of the poor in the several towns of such counties, upon the certificate of a physician approved by the supervisor of the town, as their jurisdiction over the several cases may require, to send all such indigent persons requiring medical or surgical care and treatment to the nearest hospital, the incorporation and management of which have been approved by the State Board of Charities, provided transportation to such hospital can be safely accomplished. The charge for the care and treatment of such indigent persons in such hospitals, as herein provided, shall not exceed one dollar per day for each person, which shall be paid by the several counties or towns from which such persons are sent, and provision for which shall be made in the annual budgets of such counties and towns."

Chapter 664, Laws of 1901, entitled "An act to amend the Poor Law, relative to poor persons owning real or personal property," amends such law by inserting therein a new section to be known as section 57, which reads as follows:

"If it shall at any time be ascertained that any person, who has been assisted by or received support from any town, city or county, has real or personal property, or if any such person shall die, leaving real or personal property, an action may be maintained in any court of competent jurisdiction, by the overseer of the poor of the town or city, or the superintendent of the poor of any county which has furnished or provided such assistance or support, or any part thereof, against such person or his or her estate, to recover such sums of money as may have been expended by their town, city or county in the assistance and support of such person during the period of ten years next preceding such discovery or death."

A provision intended to remove the "dead hand" from charitable bequests is embodied in chapter 291, Laws of 1901, entitled "An act to amend chapter 701 of the Laws of 1893, entitled 'An act to regulate gifts for charitable purposes,'" which reads as follows:

"Section 1. Section two of chapter seven hundred and one of the laws of eighteen hundred and ninety-three is hereby amended so as to read as follows:

"§ 2. The supreme court shall have control over gifts, grants, bequests and devises in all cases provided for by section one of this act and, whenever it shall appear to the court that circumstances have so changed since the execution of an instrument containing a gift, grant, bequest or devise to religious, educational, charitable or benevolent uses as to render impracticable or impossible a literal compliance with the terms of such instrument, the court may, upon the application of the trustee or of the person or corporation having the custody of the property, and upon such notice as the court shall direct, make an order directing that such gift, grant, bequest or devise shall be administered or expended in such manner as in the judgment of the court will most effectually accomplish the general purpose of the instrument, without regard to and free from any specific restriction, limitation or direction contained therein; provided, however, that no such order shall be made until the expiration of at least twenty-five years after the execution of the instrument or without the consent of the donor or grantor of the property, if he be living. The attorney-general shall represent the beneficiaries in all such cases, and it shall be his duty to enforce such trusts by proper proceedings in the court.

"3. This act shall take effect immediately."

A Children's Court for the City of New York.

In the revised charter for New York city, adopted by the last Legislature, provision is made by section 1399 of the charter for the establishment of a court for children's cases in the boroughs of Manhattan and the Bronx. The section reads as follows:

" The board of city magistrates of the first division shall assign a separate part for the hearing and disposition of cases now within the jurisdiction of said magistrates involving the trial or commitment of children, which part may for convenience be called the children's court; and in all such cases the magistrate holding said court shall have all the powers, duties and jurisdiction now possessed by the city magistrates within said first division. Said children's court shall be held by the several magistrates in rotation in such manner as may be determined by said board, and shall be open on such days and during such hours as the said board shall in its rules provide. Whenever, under any provision of law, a child under sixteen years of age is taken before a city magistrate in the first division sitting in any court other than the children's court, it shall be the duty of such magistrate to transfer the case to the children's court, if the case falls within the jurisdiction of said court as herein provided, and it shall be the duty of the officer having the child in charge to take such child before that court, and in any such case the magistrate holding said children's court must proceed to hear and dispose of the case in the same manner as if it had been originally brought therein. The board of city magistrates shall appoint a clerk for the children's court and such assistants as may be necessary, whose salaries shall be fixed by the board of aldermen on the recommendation of the board of estimate and apportionment. The said court shall be held, if practicable, in the building in which the offices of the department of public charities for the examination of dependent children are located, or if this shall not be practicable, the court shall be held in some other building as near thereto as practicable, to be selected by the commissioners of the sinking fund. Nothing herein contained shall affect any provisions of law with respect to the temporary commitment by magistrates of children charged with crime or held as witnesses for the trial of any criminal case, or the existing jurisdiction of the court of special sessions."

The friends of this measure believe that the establishment of such a children's court, marks a distinct advance in the disposition of children's cases falling within the provisions of the Penal Code. Hitherto such cases have been heard in the various magistrates' courts throughout the city. By the new plan, the children's court will be able to coöperate more promptly and

effectively with the department of public charities, which is
charged with the examination and commitment of destitute and
dependent children. For the first time, by the new arrangement, it will be possible to keep the children brought into court
from mingling with adults charged with the commitment of
crime. The Board gave its formal approval to the principle of
establishing children's courts in the city of New York by resolution adopted October 10, 1900, and communicated to the Charter Revision Commission.

An Amendment to the State Constitution.

The Senate and Assembly adopted a concurrent resolution.
which had been referred by the Legislature of 1899, pursuant to
statute and the Constitution, amending section 18 of article III.
of the Constitution, relative to cases in which private and local
bills shall not be passed. The addition to this section prohibits:
" Granting to any person, association, firm or corporation, an
exemption from taxation on real or personal property." The
adoption of this amendment has since been ratified by the people
at the polls. The effect of the amendment will be to relieve the
Legislature of further consideration of local bills introduced on
behalf of individual charitable societies asking to be relieved of
taxation. The question of non-taxation of charitable societies
as a whole by general legislation is not involved in the adoption
of the constitutional amendment, as seems to have been supposed,
judging by the opposition which developed in the course of the
discussions as to the merits of the amendment.

Proposed Legislation Which Failed of Enactment.

The session of 1901 was noteworthy for the general and full
discussion relative to the proposed abolition of the State Board

of Charities as at present organized and the substitution therefor of a commission to be composed of a president who should
receive a salary of $2,500 and who should give his entire
time to the duties of the office, and two other commissioners,
who might be State officers, and who should serve without
pay. A joint hearing on the proposed legislation embodied in Assembly bill No. 169 and Senate bill No. 114,
472 was given by the respective committees of the Senate and
Assembly, to whom the bills were referred. This hearing was
held in the Senate chamber on February 12, and was attended
by a large number of delegated representatives of the public and
private charities of the State. But one sentiment was expressed at the hearing. This was in favor of the continuance
of the policy adopted in 1867, namely, that the State Board of
Charities should be a body of considerable size, composed of
citizens representative of the charitable and correctional interests
of the various sections of the State, and knowing neither creed
nor political preferences in the administration of the public and
private charities intrusted to the visitation, inspection and general supervision of such Board. Neither the Senate nor Assembly bills embodying the proposed reorganization of the Board
were reported by the respective committees having the matter
in charge.

The Jurisdiction of the State Hampered.

The Board is impelled to bring again to the attention of the
Legislature the following facts contained in its report to the
Legislature of 1901:

Unfortunate conditions continue to exist in consequence of
the decision of the Court of Appeals in the case of The
People of the State of New York ex rel. The State Board of

Charities *v.* The New York Society for the Prevention of Cruelty to Children, handed down January 9, 1900, and reaffirmed April 17, 1900. By this decision those institutions only which receive public moneys are declared to be within the authority vested in the Board by section 11 of article VIII. of the state Constitution which says: "The Legislature shall provide for a State Board of Charities, which shall visit and inspect all institutions, whether State, county, municipal, incorporated or not incorporated, which are of a charitable, eleemosynary, correctional or reformatory character, excepting only such institutions as are" subject to the visitation and inspection of the State Commission in Lunacy and the State Commission of Prisons.

Briefly stated some of these unfortunate conditions are:

1. For the first time in a quarter of a century the Legislature and the public are prevented from having any definite knowledge annually of the amount of dependency which exists in the State. For example, the total number of dependent children in institutions cannot now be definitely known through any official source.

2. The State is prevented from having any definite knowledge of the work of many of the charitable corporations it creates, not a few of them having authority to stand in the place of parents or guardians of dependent childhood.

3. The protection which the State has hitherto extended to the inmates of such exempted institutions is removed.

4. The protection to trust funds, left by will or otherwise bestowed, for the use of the poor, amounting in some cases to hundreds of thousands of dollars, is also removed.

NEED OF FURTHER PROVISION BY THE STATE FOR THE CARE OF THE FEEBLE-MINDED, THE IDIOTIC AND THE EPILEPTIC.

The State of New York, in the course of the evolution of its local and general relief agencies from their primitive beginnings toward better forms, decided to care for the feeble-minded, the idiotic and the epileptic, in separate institutions maintained from the State treasury. This is shown by,

1. The establishment, in 1851, of the Syracuse State Institution for Feeble-Minded Children, intended for the education and training of children of this class. It now has a population of 536.

2. The establishment, in 1878, of the State Custodial Asylum for Feeble-Minded Women. This institution is designed to receive and protect feeble-minded women of child-bearing age. There are now 456 inmates at the asylum.

3. The establishment, in 1893, of the Rome State Custodial Asylum, which is intended to provide for the less teachable class of idiots. The population now numbers 539.

4. The establishment, in 1894, of the Craig Colony for epileptics who are not insane. The colony has 750 patients.

5. The enactment of the following provision of the Poor Law, chapter 225 of the Laws of 1896: "Section 6. Idiots and lunatics.—The superintendents of the poor shall provide for the support of poor persons that may be idiotic or lunatics, at other places than in the almshouse, in such manner as shall be provided by law for the care, support and maintenance of such poor persons."

Thus far, the State has provided only partially for these classes.

Feeble-minded Children.

1. There are now a large number of feeble-minded children in various private institutions for children, where they are being supported at public expense. Over seventy of these cases have been found by the Board's inspectors. Such children are out of place with those of normal minds, and should have the benefit of training in the Syracuse State Institution for Feeble-Minded Children. Beside these, a considerable number of the same class, approximately about eighty, are forced to remain in the county, city and town almshouses, owing to the lack of room for them at Syracuse.

Legislature has attempted to delegate powers possessed by it, and so the line of authorities cited to establish the proposition that the Legislature cannot delegate its powers do not apply. The Constitution itself provides, in section 14 of article 8: "No such payments" (that is, payments of public moneys to charitable, eleemosynary, correctional and reformatory institutions), "shall be made for any inmate of such institution who is not received and retained therein pursuant to rules established by the State Board of Charities." That is the direct and controlling mandate of the Constitution of supreme authority over the courts no less than executive officers. In discussing that section of the Constitution, the Court of Appeals said, in People ex rel. Inebriates' Home v. Comptroller, 152 N. Y. 407: "We entertain no doubt that this prohibition operated presently; that is to say, that from the time rules should be established by the State Board regulating the reception and retention by charitable institutions, no payments would be justified for the care, support and maintenance of inmates received or retained in contravention of the rules of the Board." Again the same court said, in People ex rel. N. Y. Inst. for Blind v. Fitch, 154 N. Y. 15: "This declaration of the organic law is plain and unambiguous and expressly forbids the appropriation of money by the counties and cities of the State, unless the inmates are received and retained in the manner stated. Its manifest purpose is to make all appropriations of public moneys by the local political divisions or municipalities of the State to institutions under private control subject to the supervision and rules of the State Board of Charities." While it is true that the precise point involved in the matter at bar was not before the court in either of the cases cited, still, as the expression of the opinion of the court of last resort discussing the general purposes of the new constitutional provisions applicable to the case now here, I must regard said cases as controlling on this motion. The evil aimed at by the constitutional convention and by the people in accepting its work is the precise evil sought to be perpetuated by this petitioner in this proceeding; namely, compelling public funds to be expended for inmates of private institutions without any examination by public authorities as to the necessity therefor. This, the Constitution says, shall not be done. Motion denied. Ten dollars costs.

This decision has been affirmed by the Appellate Division in the First Department, to which it was carried on appeal.

STATISTICS OF OUTDOOR RELIEF.

For the first time in the history of the State, so far as known to the State Board of Charities, the Board last year succeeded in collecting through the county superintendents of the poor and other like officials, statistics of outdoor relief from nearly every town and city in the State, as well as from the counties as a whole as heretofore. These statistics cover the year ending September 30, 1900, and are published in the statistical appendix to the Board's report to the Legislature of 1901. They show such great relative differences in the number relieved and in the amount expended for relief in the various localities of the State, and especially in the cities as will be seen by the following table for the fiscal year ending September 30, 1900 (and also for the fiscal year ending September 30, 1901, the statistics for which have since been collected), as to make careful examination on the part of the local authorities seem desirable, in order to make sure on the one hand that the poor are being properly relieved and on the other that pauperism is not in some cases being encouraged by the relieving officers:

OUTDOOR RELIEF IN CITIES FOR THE YEAR ENDING SEPTEMBER 30, 1900.

CITY.	COUNTY.	Population by census of 1900.	Number temporarily relieved.	Percentage of population relieved.	Expenditures for temporary relief.	Per capita expense for entire number relieved.	Per capita expense for entire population.
New York.........	New York...	3,437,202	*1,038	.0003	†840,221 00	$38 75	.01
Buffalo	Erie	352,387	12,034	.034	63,748 10	5 30	.18
Rochester	Monroe	162,608	7,642	.047	78,340 51	10 25	.48
Syracuse	Onondaga........	108,374	4,353	.010	29,483 29	6 77	.27
Albany	Albany	94,151	3,508	.037	9,595 84	2 73	.10
Troy	Rensselaer.......	60,651	1,614	.027	16,146 54	10 00	.27
Utica	Oneida	56,383	1,843	.033	6,648 63	3 63	.12
Yonkers	Westchester.....	47,931	327	.007	3,326 14	10 17	.07
Binghamton	Broome	39,647	1,449	.037	16 263 48	11 23	.41
Elmira	Chemung........	35,672	935	.026	4,199 00	4 49	.12
Schenectady.......	Schenectady	31,682	209	.006	5,817 15	27 83	.18
Auburn	Cayuga	30,345	1,854	.061	15,904 60	8 58	.52
Newburgh.........	Orange	24,943	1,052	.042	7,529 05	7 15	.30
Kingston	Ulster	24,535	2,127	.087	7,784 94	3 66	.32
Poughkeepsie	Dutchess	24,029	874	.034	3,884 39	4 71	.16
Cohoes	Albany	23,910	298	.012	6,187 75	21 63	.26
Jamestown	Chautauqua	22,892	436	.019	12,427 27	28 50	.54
Oswego...........	Oswego..........	22,199	1,089	.049	8,504 47	7 81	.38
Watertown........	Jefferson	21,696	‡	‡	2,537 01	‡	.12
Amsterdam	Montgomery.....	20,929	2,571	.123	15,562 00	6 05	.74
Mount Vernon.....	Westchester	20,346	350	.017	1,732 46	4 95	.08
Niagara Falls......	Niagara	19,457	226	.012	3,884 26	17 19	.20
Gloversville	Fulton	18,349	430	.023	5,014 90	11 66	.27
Lockport	Niagara	16,581	163	.010	1,683 57	10 33	.10
Rome	Oneida..........	15,343	441	.029	3,623 13	8 22	.24
New Rochelle.....	Westchester	14,720	312	.021	1,406 26	4 51	.10
Middletown.......	Orange	14,522	121	.008	3,272 61	27 05	.23
Watervliet........	Albany	14,321	1,750	.122	2,863 62	1 64	.20
Ithaca	Tompkins	13,136	360	.030	5,738 66	15 94	.44
Ogdensburg	St. Lawrence	12,633	576	.046	5,306 79	9 21	.42
Hornellsville	Steuben	11,918	161	.014	3,293 80	20 46	.28
Dunkirk..........	Chautauqua	11,616	170	.015	1,372 85	8 08	.12
Corning	Steuben	11,061	115	.010	4,134 65	35 87	.37
Geneva	Ontario	10,433	427	.041	6,708 04	15 71	.64
Little Falls	Herkimer........	10,381	§	§	§	§	§
Johnstown	Fulton	10,130	317	.031	2,841 55	8 96	.29
Hudson...........	Columbia	9,528	360	.038	2,054 90	5 74	.22
Olean	Cattaraugus	9,462	108	.011	3,169 08	29 34	.33
North Tonawanda..	Niagara	9,069	§	§	§	§	§
Cortland	Cortland	9,014	166	.018	2,200 68	13 26	.24
Rensselaer........	Rensselaer.......	7,466	129	.017	1,874 84	14 53	.25

* Of this number, 600 were blind persons and 438 G. A. R. veterans.
† Of this amount, $30,000 was for blind persons and $10,211 for veterans.
‡ No statistics.
§ No report.

OUTDOOR RELIEF IN CITIES FOR THE YEAR ENDING SEPTEMBER 30, 1901.

CITY.	COUNTY.	Population by census of 1900.	Number temporarily relieved.	Percentage of population relieved.	Expenditures for temporary relief.	Per capita expense for entire number relieved.	Per capita expense for entire population.
New York	New York	3,437,202	*1,161	.0003	$843,289 84	$37 24	.01
Buffalo	Erie	352,387	7,587	.022	48,101 32	6 34	.14
Rochester	Monroe	162,608	9,500	.058	75,775 00	7 98	.47
Syracuse	Onondaga	108,374	3,037	.028	29,829 21	9 76	.28
Albany	Albany	94,151	3,212	.034	7,369 35	2 29	.08
Troy	Rensselaer	60,651	1,665	.027	16,866 00	10 13	.28
Utica	Oneida	56,383	2,226	.039	7,993 55	3 59	.14
Yonkers	Westchester	47,931	342	.007	3,192 00	9 33	.07
Binghamton	Broome	39,647	1,309	.083	16,865 43	12 88	.43
Elmira	Chemung	35,672	535	.015	2,557 03	4 78	.07
Schenectady	Schenectady	31,682	234	.007	7,000 00	29 91	.22
Auburn	Cayuga	30,345	1,627	.054	16,607 13	10 21	.55
Newburgh	Orange	24,943	869	.035	6,446 17	7 42	.26
Kingston	Ulster	24,535	2,742	.110	6,975 83	2 54	.28
Poughkeepsie	Dutchess	24,029	915	.038	5,075 98	5 55	.21
Cohoes	Albany	23,910	123	.005	3,336 92	27 13	.14
Jamestown	Chautauqua	22,892	498	.022	11,034 32	22 16	.48
Oswego	Oswego	22,199	899	.040	8,349 23	9 29	.38
Watertown	Jefferson	21,696	410	.019	8,245 81	7 92	.15
Amsterdam	Montgomery	20,929	2,090	.100	16,776 42	8 03	.80
Mount Vernon	Westchester	20,346	349	.012	4,176 03	11 97	.21
Niagara Falls	Niagara	19,457	569	.029	6,612 70	11 62	.34
Gloversville	Fulton	18,319	508	.028	4,873 34	9 59	.27
Lockport	Niagara	16,581	190	.011	1,567 63	8 25	.09
Rome	Oneida	15,343	484	.032	2,781 69	5 75	.18
New Rochelle	Westchester	14,720	332	.023	1,798 00	5 41	.12
Middletown	Orange	14,522	407	.028	3,218 50	7 91	.22
Watervliet	Albany	14,321	648	.045	2,713 48	4 19	.20
Ithaca	Tompkins	13,136	249	.019	3,015 49	12 11	.23
Ogdensburg	St. Lawrence	12,633	626	.049	7,628 31	12 18	.60
Hornellsville	Steuben	11,918	148	.012	3,881 92	26 23	.33
Dunkirk	Chautauqua	11,616	98	.008	823 64	8 40	.07
Corning	Steuben	11,061	126	.011	4,542 20	36 05	.41
Geneva	Ontario	10,433	279	.027	6,120 35	21 94	.59
Little Falls	Herkimer	10,381	839	.080	5,888 83	7 02	.57
Johnstown	Fulton	10,130	472	.046	4,441 48	9 41	.44
Hudson	Columbia	9,528	431	.045	2,714 16	6 30	.28
Olean	Cattaraugus	9,462	66	.007	5,457 13	82 68	.58
North Tonawanda	Niagara	9,069	112	.012	2,108 46	18 82	.23
Cortland	Cortland	9,014	85	.009	1,441 19	16 95	.16
Oneida	Madison	7,538	309	.040	2,497 63	8 08	.33
Rensselaer	Rensselaer	7,466	37	.005	1,306 25	35 30	.18

* Of this number, 672 were blind persons and 489 G. A. R. veterans.

† Of this amount, $33,243.84 was for blind persons and $9,996 for veterans.

OUTDOOR RELIEF IN CITIES FOR THE YEAR ENDING SEPTEMBER 30, 1900.

CITY.	COUNTY.	Population by census of 1900.	Number temporarily relieved.	Percentage of population relieved.	Expenditures for temporary relief.	Per capita expense for entire number relieved.	Per capita expense for entire population.
New York.........	New York...	3,437,202	*1,038	.0003	$840,221 00	$38 75	.01
Buffalo	Erie	352,387	12,034	.034	62,748 10	5 20	.18
Rochester	Monroe	162,608	7,642	.047	78,340 51	10 25	.48
Syracuse	Onondaga..........	108,374	4,353	.010	29,483 29	6 77	.27
Albany	Albany	94,151	3,508	.037	9,596 34	2 73	.10
Troy	Rensselaer........	60,651	1,614	.027	16,146 54	10 00	.27
Utica	Oneida	56,383	1,843	.033	6,648 63	3 63	.12
Yonkers...........	Westchester......	47,931	327	.007	3,326 14	10 17	.07
Binghamton	Broome	39,647	1,449	.037	16 263 48	11 22	.41
Elmira	Chemung..........	35,672	935	.026	4,199 00	4 49	.12
Schenectady	Schenectady	31 682	209	.006	5,817 15	27 83	.18
Auburn	Cayuga	30,345	1,854	.061	15,904 60	8 58	.52
Newburgh	Orange	24,943	1,052	.042	7,529 05	7 15	.20
Kingston	Ulster	24,535	2,127	.087	7,784 94	3 66	.32
Poughkeepsie	Dutchess	24,029	824	.034	3,884 39	4 71	.16
Cohoes	Albany	23,910	296	.012	6,187 75	21 63	.26
Jamestown	Chautauqua	22,692	426	.019	12,427 27	28 50	.54
Oswego.........	Oswego...........	22,199	1,089	.049	8,504 47	7 81	.38
Watertown........	Jefferson	21,696	†	†	2,537 01	†	.12
Amsterdam	Montgomery......	20,929	2,571	.123	15,562 00	6 05	.74
Mount Vernon.....	Westchester	20,346	350	.017	1,732 46	4 95	.08
Niagara Falls.....	Niagara	19,457	226	.012	3,884 26	17 19	.20
Gloversville	Fulton	18,349	430	.023	5,014 90	11 66	.27
Lockport	Niagara	16,581	163	.010	1,683 57	10 33	.10
Rome	Oneida............	15,343	441	.029	3,623 13	8 22	.24
New Rochelle......	Westchester	14,720	312	.021	1,408 38	4 51	.10
Middletown........	Orange	14,522	121	.008	3,272 61	27 05	.23
Watervliet........	Albany	14,321	1,750	.122	2,863 63	1 64	.20
Ithaca.............	Tompkins	13,136	360	.030	5,738 66	15 94	.44
Ogdensburg	St. Lawrence	12,633	576	.046	5,306 79	9 21	.42
Hornellsville	Steuben	11,918	161	.014	3,293 80	20 46	.28
Dunkirk..........	Chautauqua	11,616	170	.015	1,372 85	8 08	.12
Corning	Steuben	11,061	115	.010	4,124 65	35 87	.37
Geneva	Ontario	10,433	427	.041	6,708 04	15 71	.64
Little Falls	Herkimer..........	10,381	§	§	§	§	§
Johnstown	Fulton	10,130	817	.031	2,841 55	3 96	.28
Hudson	Columbia	9,528	360	.038	2,064 90	5 74	22
Olean	Cattaraugus	9,462	108	.011	3,169 08	29 34	.33
North Tonawanda.	Niagara	9 069	§	§	§	§	§
Cortland	Cortland	9,014	166	.018	2,200 68	13 26	.24
Rensselaer.........	Rensselaer........	7,466	129	.017	1,874 84	14 53	.25

* Of this number, 600 were blind persons and 438 G. A. R. veterans.
† Of this amount, $30,000 was for blind persons and $10,241 for veterans.
‡ No statistics.
§ No report

Even the language of the statute which seems to give a supervisory power makes it questionable whether it was intended to give the Board managerial powers over the State institutions. To place the administration of the institutions in the hands of the State Board of Charities would be practically to deprive the State of the services of an independent and impartial board of inspection which the Constitution requires, inasmuch as such Board could not be expected to visit and impartially inspect the institutions it would manage and control.

Furthermore, the State Charities Law distinctly recognizes the fact that visitation and inspection and control and management are incompatible functions by providing as follows: "No commissioner shall qualify or enter upon the duties of his office, or remain therein, while he is a trustee, manager, director or other administrative officer of an institution subject to the visitation and inspection of such Board."

Local Boards of Managers.

The management and control of State charitable and reformatory institutions should be intrusted to individual boards of managers composed of philanthropic citizens of the State. Men and women of character and intelligence who have time and ability to give to the service of the State should be encouraged, as they are in other States and countries where charitable and reform work has reached a high state of development, to devote themselves to the service of the State, by acting as members of the boards of managers of its institutions. This course not only greatly benefits the institutions through the enthusiasm, the special knowledge and the disinterested and gratuitous service which such members bring to the work, but also keeps their management largely free from the semi-mechanical administration which a central board of control, having many institutions and diverse interests to care for, is able to give to each.

Besides helping to keep the institutions out of the undesirable routine liable to follow the administration of a central board of paid officials, it keeps their management in closer touch with the people.

This is not simply a commercial question. These institutions deal with men, women and children, and are the embodiment of the loftiest philanthropic sentiment of the State. Their work should not be carried on in a mechanical way. Philanthropic service and business ability combined in the management of these institutions should produce the best results. Competent boards of managers can always be obtained, and their powers can be properly regulated by the Legislature.

SUMMARY OF RECOMMENDATIONS FOR LEGISLATION.

The Board desires to renew the following recommendations for legislation contained in its report to the Legislature of 1901:

1. That all the special appropriations for the State institutions within the jurisdiction of the Board be included in one bill, with such provisions as will insure in every instance the most careful and economical expenditure of the moneys appropriated, in exact accordance with the intentions of the Legislature.

2. That the present site of the State Industrial School in the city of Rochester be sold, and a less costly site purchased in the country, to which the School can be removed.

3. That the House of Refuge on Randall's Island be also removed to the country, and that the girls' department of the institution be discontinued, the older girls being sent to the new

3

reformatory at Bedford, and the younger to the New York
Juvenile Asylum and the New York Catholic Protectory, or like
institutions.   Also, that this institution be placed under the rules
of the State Civil Service Commission.

To which is added this year the recommendation that this be
organized as a State institution as soon as practicable.

4. That legislation be enacted to prevent the continuance of the
fourteen liquor saloons at the gates of the New York State Soldiers and Sailors' Home, at Bath, which are supported by the
patronage of members of the Home, and are regarded as a source
of demoralization to its discipline.

To these recommendations the Board this year adds the
following:

5. That authority be conferred whereby it may cause the transfer of inmates of State institutions under the Board's jurisdiction,
particularly for the feeble-minded and the epileptic, to those
wherein such inmates may be most appropriately cared for or
dealt with.

APPROPRIATIONS MADE IN 1901, AND RECOMMENDED FOR 1902.

The following table shows the amounts appropriated for maintenance and for extraordinary expenses, respectively, by the
Legislature of 1901 to the various State institutions subject to the
Board's visitation and inspection, the amounts recommended by
the Board for appropriations to such institutions by the Legislature of 1902, and the pages of this report wherein the condition
and needs of the institutions are specifically set forth.   These
recommendations were agreed upon at a series of conferences
between representatives of the State Comptroller, the State

Architect and this Board, after careful inquiries had been made with relation to the needs of the various institutions.

NAME AND LOCATION OF INSTITUTION.	APPROPRIATIONS IN 1901.		RECOMMENDED FOR 1902.		Page.
	Maintenance.	Extraordinary expenses.	Maintenance.	Extraordinary expenses.	
State Industrial School, Rochester.............	$175,000 00	....	$180,000 00	$2,500 00	36-42
House of Refuge for Women, Hudson.......	65,000 00	$24,962 24	65,000 00	28,800 00	42-45
Western House of Refuge, Albion........	57,000 00	....	57,000 00	17,975 00	45-51
New York State Reformatory for Women, Bedford.................	47,500 00	34,715 00	58,000 00	14,800 00	52-57
Society for the Reformation of Juvenile Delinquents in the City of New York............	150,000 00	22,705 00	100,000 00	16,500 00	57-62
Syracuse State Institution for Feeble-Minded Children	82,000 00	11,146 50	81,000 00	6,000 00	62-65
State Custodial Asylum for Feeble-Minded Women, Newark......	58,000 00	56,858 26	60,000 00	57,350 00	66-70
Rome State Custodial Asylum.................	75,000 00	68,080 76	100,000 00	99,415 00	70-77
Craig Colony, Sonyea....	122,000 00	142,394 56	135,000 00	81,800 00	78-84
New York State Soldiers and Sailors' Home, Bath...................	345,000 00	45,609 27	*225,000 00	140,745 75	84-92
New York State Woman's Relief Corps Home, Oxford.........	24,100 00	52,228 18	25,000 00	45,465 00	92-97
Thomas Asylum for Orphan and Destitute Indian Children, Iroquois...................	25,000 00	26,350 00	25,000 00	52,500 00	97-101
New York State School for the Blind, Batavia..	60,000 00	6,546 00	38,000 00	10,250 00	101-104
New York State Hospital for the Care of Crippled and Deformed Children, Tarrytown.............	10,000 00	4,250 00	15,000 00	....	105-109
New York State Hospital for the Treatment of Indigent Pulmonary Tuberculosis, Raybrook	....	100,000 00	....	....	109-110
Totals	$1,175,200 00	$596,851 87	$1,197,000 00	$574,050 75	....

*The National government pays $100 a year towards the support of each member of the Home, thereby refunding to the State a large amount of the maintenance appropriation. During the last fiscal year this amounted to the sum of $155,000.25.

CLASSIFIED ORDINARY EXPENDITURES OF THE STATE INSTITUTIONS SUBJECT TO THE VISITATION AND INSPECTION OF THE STATE BOARD OF CHARITIES FOR THE FISCAL YEAR ENDING SEPTEMBER 30, 1901.

	State Industrial School, Rochester.	House of Refuge for Women, Hudson.	Western House of Refuge for Women, Albion.	New York State Reformatory for Women, Bedford.‡	Rockey for the Reformation of Juvenile Delinquents in the City of New York.	Syracuse State Institution for Feeble-Minded Children, Syracuse.	State Custodial Asylum for Feeble-Minded Women, Newark.	Rome State Custodial Asylum, Rome.
Average number of inmates								
Total ordinary expenditure								
Average annual cost of support								
Expended for salaries of officers								
Average annual per capita expenditure for salaries, wages and labor								
Expended for provisions								
Average annual per capita expenditure for provisions								
Expended for household stores								
Average annual per capita expenditure for household stores								
Expended for clothing								
Average annual per capita expenditure for clothing								
Expended for fuel and light								
Average annual per capita expenditure for fuel and light								
Expended for hospital and medical supplies								
Average annual per capita expenditure for hospital and medical supplies								
Expended for transportation and traveling expenses								
Average annual per capita expenditure for transportation and traveling expenses								
Expended for shop, farm and garden supplies								
Average annual per capita expenditure for shop, farm and garden supplies								
Expended for ordinary repairs								
Average annual per capita expenditure for ordinary repairs								
Expended for expenses of trustees or managers								
Average annual per capita expenditure for expenses of trustees or managers								
Expended for all other ordinary expenses								
Average annual per capita expenditure for all other ordinary expenses								

* Exclusive of amount returned to State Treasurer in accordance with chapters 572 and 580, Laws of 1894.
† Includes the value of home and farm products consumed.
‡ Institution opened to inmates May 11, 1901.

CLASSIFIED ORDINARY EXPENDITURES OF THE STATE INSTITUTIONS, ETC.—(Continued).

	Oneida County Hospital.	New York State Reformatory, Elmira.	Rome State Custodial Asylum for Unteachable Idiots.	State Custodial Asylum for Feeble-Minded Women, Newark.	Thomas Asylum for Orphan and Destitute Indian Children, Iroquois.	State Agricultural and Industrial School, Industry.	New York State Woman's Relief Corps Home, Oxford.	Totals and averages.
Average number of inmates								
Total ordinary expenditure								
Average yearly cost of support								
Expended for salaries of officers								
Average annual per capita expenditure for salaries, wages and labor								
Expended for provisions								
Average annual per capita expenditure for provisions								
Expended for household stores								
Average annual per capita expenditure for household stores								
Expended for clothing								
Average annual per capita expenditure for clothing								
Expended for fuel and light								
Average annual per capita expenditure for fuel and light								
Expended for hospital and medical supplies								
Average annual per capita expenditure for hospital and medical supplies								
Expended for transportation and travelling expenses								
Average annual per capita expenditure for transportation and travelling expenses								
Expended for shop, farm and garden supplies								
Average annual per capita expenditure for shop, farm and garden supplies								
Expended for ordinary repairs								
Average annual per capita expenditure for ordinary repairs								
Expended for expenses of management								
Average annual per capita expenditure for expenses of treatment or management								
Expended for all other ordinary expenses								
Average annual per capita expenditure for all other ordinary expenses								

* Exclusive of amount returned to State Treasurer in accordance with chapters 673 and 960, Laws of 1896.
† Institution opened to inmates December 1, 1900.
‡ Average for fourteen institutions.
§ Total expenditures for maintenance for fourteen institutions.

Table showing the number of inmates in the State institutions subject to the visitation and inspection of the State Board of Charities, October 1, 1901, arranged with reference to the representation from the several counties of the State.

COUNTIES.	State Industrial School, Rochester.	House of Refuge for Women, Hudson.	Western House of Refuge for Women, Albion.	New York House of Refuge for Women, Bedford.†	New York House of Refuge (of the Society for the Reformation of Juvenile Delinquents in the City of New York), Randall's Island.	Syracuse State Institution for Feeble-Minded Children, Syracuse.	State Custodial Asylum for Feeble-Minded Women, Newark.	Rome State Custodial Asylum, Rome.	Craig Colony, Sonyea.	New York State Soldiers' and Sailors' Home, Bath.	New York State Women's Relief Corps Home, Oxford.	Thomas Asylum for Orphan and Destitute Indian Children, Iroquois.	New York State School for the Blind, Batavia.	New York State Hospital for the Treatment of Crippled and Deformed Children, Tarrytown.	Total.
Albany	26	1			7	18	18	18	27	2			5		192
Allegany	27					7	2	2	9	18			1		66
Broome	22	2	1			7	5	2	9	28	1		1		85
Cattaraugus	29		1			4	2	4	3	29		47	2		122
Cayuga	20					9	3	3	12	31	6				85
Chautauqua	20		5			11	9	6	8	16	3				90
Chemung	14	3	10			10	7	4	2	57			5		125
Chenango	12		2			2	2	2	2	6					34
Clinton	3	11				3	5	4	3	4	2		1		58
Columbia	15	6			2	10	5	3	5	8					62
Cortland	9					2	4	1	2	5			1		38
Delaware	10	1				4	4	2	3	5					39
Dutchess	20	10			12	7	6	6	10	28			2		92
Erie	65		27			42	26	20	54	177	3	116	21		465
Essex	2	1				2	6	3	2	5					15
Franklin	16	2				1	9	4	4	4		•••			44
Fulton	9	4				12	3	2	4	7			2		49
Genesee	14		4			2	5	2	4	11			7		47
Greene		6			4	3	1	3		1	2		2		21
Hamilton										3					3
Herkimer	8	6				3	4	3	3	16					46
Jefferson	15	5				4	12	4	5	19	3		5		72
Kings		6		6	163	33	12	40	71	252	17			2	704
Lewis						5		2	1	3					12
Livingston	14					4	1	3	4	12	2		1		45
Madison	16		1			2	2	3	3	13					44
Monroe	21		19			31	21	24	50	160	6		11		420
Montgomery	18	2				7	4	4	5	8	1		4		50
Nassau	1					1	1	1	1	13					22
New York		7		15	526	69	79	100	282	205	13	†120		14	1,280
Niagara	28		10			7	8	12	26	28	1				117
Oneida	15	1	6			26	11	14	17	70	13	†110	3		162
Onondaga	45	10				30	9	13	15	78	6	‡121	2		224
Ontario	21		3			9	12	3	9	19	1		1		81
Orange	1	13			14	4	4	6	13	2		5	1	77
Orleans	16		5			1	1	1	6	9			1		40
Oswego	20	5				5	7	4	10	19	2		1		78
Otsego	9	4				14	9	4	4	1	1				46
Putnam							2	1	2	2					7
Queens		5			1	10	4	3	9	44					77
Rensselaer	57	8			4	17	6	15	9	27	1		3		154
Richmond	1	5		2	4	2	8	4	4	4					27
Rockland	7	5			8	3	1	1	5	4					41
St. Lawrence	34	30				6	6	6	16	12	2		1		112
Saratoga	34	3				4	5	4	8	9					70
Schenectady	21	9				4	2	2		18					35
Schoharie		1			2	1	1		3	6					15
Schuyler	3					2	1	1	5	6	1				19
Seneca	9		1			3	1	4	3	16			2		39
Steuben	15	4	11			3	5	6	11	65	5				130
Suffolk		2			11	1	6	5	4	21		2	3		52
Sullivan					2	5	3	3		5					18
Tioga	14	2	2			3	5	2	13	13			3		62
Tompkins	14	1	3			7	2	4	7	10			1		49
Ulster	8	5			18	13	8	3	8	14	1		2		77
Warren	16	3				2	2	4	5	4			2		36
Washington	10	3				2	3	4	2	4			2		34
Wayne	14					5	11	4	7	12					48
Westchester	20	30		4	41	12	10	8	17	48	2		1	177
Wyoming	6					5	2	2	7	10	1		2		41
Yates			5			2	4	3	4	9	4		1		23
State at large						2		3	1						5
From other states										79					79
Total	855	*235	†116	37	841	537	416	444	745	2,076	109	142	109	19	6,657

* Of these, 9 were infants.   † Of these, 6 were infants.   ‡ Opened May 11, 1901.   § Of these, 11 belong to the Allegany Reservation and 56 to the Cattaraugus Reservation.   ‖ Tonawanda Reservation.   ** St. Regis Reservation.   †† Tuscarora Reservation.   ‡‡ Oneida Reservation.   ‖‖ Onondaga Reservation.   ¶ Shinnecock Reservation.   *** Opened to patients December 1, 1900.

STATE INDUSTRIAL SCHOOL, ROCHESTER, MONROE COUNTY.

[Established 1846.]

This institution has capacity for 900 inmates. At the beginning of the fiscal year there were present 670 boys and 114 girls; total, 784. During the year 544 boys and 64 girls were admitted and 467 boys and 72 girls discharged, leaving a population, October 1, 1901, of 747 boys and 106 girls; total, 853—an increase of 69. The average number of inmates during the year was 827, and the average weekly cost of support, including the value of home and farm products consumed, $4.18; excluding the value of home and farm products consumed, $4.15.

The receipts during the fiscal year were: From cash on hand at the beginning of the year, $779.48; from special appropriations, $1,030.51; from general appropriations, $179,500; from other sources, $415.20; making the total receipts for the year, $181,725.19.

The ordinary expenditures were: For salaries of officers, $16,-419.78; for wages and labor, $61,732.45; for provisions, $39,503.83; for household stores, $4,144.90; for clothing, $7,827.57; for fuel and light, $24,195.62; for hospital and medical supplies, $1,406.49; for transportation and traveling expenses, $2,624.29; for shop, farm and garden supplies, $10,227.43; for ordinary repairs, $2,204.34; for expenses of managers, $711.35; returned to State Treasurer, $415.20; for unclassified expenses, $8,106.18; total, $179,519.43.

The extraordinary expenditures were $1,239.80, making the aggregate expenditures for the year, $180,759.23, and leaving, October 1, 1901, a cash balance of $965.96.

The outstanding indebtedness was $605.80, of which $209.33 was due for salaries of officers and employes and $396.47 for bills unpaid. The balance in cash was the only asset.

Of the ordinary expenditures during the year, 43.6 per cent.
was for salaries, wages and labor; 22.1 per cent. for provisions;
2.3 per cent. for household stores; 4.4 per cent. for clothing; 13.5
per cent. for fuel and light; .8 of 1 per cent. for hospital and medical supplies; 1.5 per cent. for transportation and traveling expenses; 5.7 per cent. for shop, farm and garden supplies; 1.2 per
cent. for ordinary repairs; .4 of 1 per cent. for expenses of managers, and 4.5 per cent. for all other ordinary expenses.

Chapter 644, Laws of 1901 (appropriation bill), appropriated
for maintenance, rewards to inmates, repairs and betterments of
tools, equipment and furniture, for repairs to buildings, for tools
to conduct the trades-schools and common schools for military
system and photographing inmates, $175,000.

This institution has presented no new questions for consideration during the past year. The ordinary discipline has continued without interruption. The technical sections, schools and
other departments have been conducted along the same lines as
during the past two or three years. Some changes are held in
abeyance pending the proposed removal of the institution to a
new location. The removal to the country will enable the School
to provide for instruction in general farming, horticulture, floriculture and similar pursuits, and secure the separation of boys
and girls. The change to a rural location is not only absolutely
demanded for hygienic and other reasons, but it is necessary to
meet the requirements of modern reformatory methods. The
change has been urged heretofore by the State Board of Charities,
and it is hoped that the Legislature during this session will make
the necessary appropriation and grant authority to purchase a
suitable farm in the vicinity of Rochester upon which to locate
the School. As the land now occupied by the institution is

valuable for city purposes, the proceeds of its sale should be
sufficient to purchase a suitable farm, as well as provide for the
erection and equipment of well-arranged buildings thereon for
the boys.

It is believed that public opinion in Rochester favors the
removal of the institution. This is evidenced by resolutions
adopted by public bodies in that city. The Board of Managers
of the institution believes the change should be accomplished.
A suitable location has been agreed upon by the commission
appointed under chapter 167 of the Laws of 1899, which was
authorized to select a new site for the institution, and action by
the Legislature is necessary to secure the removal desired and
recommended by this Board, as in accordance with the most
enlightened public sentiment. The Board recommends the sale
of the valuable site occupied by this School in the city of
Rochester and the purchase of a farm site in the country to
which it shall be removed.

The State Industrial School is intended for the reformation of
juvenile delinquents, and through reformation to save to the
Commonwealth those who would otherwise swell the ranks of
criminals and paupers. The School is for the training of those
sent to it, in habits of industry, morality and usefulness, and its
equipment should be ample to carry on its special work in the
best manner.

As this is a school, not a prison, it must be prepared to train
boys and girls for self-support. Its trades-schools should cover
the field of ordinary profitable industries, and in addition provide scholastic training at least equal to that within the reach of
youth living at home. The principal stress should be laid upon
industrial training, and this requires facilities for manual and

technical work. The boys should be thoroughly instructed so as to be capable of earning a good livelihood at a trade. It is not sufficient to give them a part of a trade; they should be under instruction long enough and have sufficient opportunity to master the trade in all its parts. This will make them skillful work-men, not afraid of competition, and acceptable to employers of labor. The industrial department of this institution should turn out finished workmen, and its facilities need to be increased to that end.

The Board recommends the following appropriations, or so much thereof as may be necessary, to this institution:

For improving economy of steam and electric plants and for pipe covering, $2,500; maintenance appropriation, $180,000; making the total appropriations, $182,500.

HOUSE OF REFUGE FOR WOMEN, HUDSON, COLUMBIA COUNTY.
[Established 1881.]

This institution has capacity for 311 inmates. The number of inmates October 1, 1900, was 268, and 79 were admitted and returned during the year, making the total number under care 347. During the year 25 were paroled to service, 2 died and 97 were discharged, thus leaving under care October 1, 1901, 223, of whom 9 were infants. The average number present during the year was 243, and the average weekly cost of support, including the value of home and farm products consumed, $4.97; excluding the value of home and farm products consumed, $4.86.

The receipts during the fiscal year ending September 30, 1901, were: From cash balance of the previous year, $480.01; from special appropriations, $11,246.63; from general appropriations, $62,000; from other sources, $238.98; total, $73,965.62.

The ordinary expenditures for the year were: For salaries of officers, $19,698.19; for wages and labor, $7,322.34; for provisions, $12,426.24; for household stores, $2,211.17; for clothing, $2,691.39; for fuel and light, $8,237.23; for hospital and medical supplies, $333.62; for transportation and traveling expenses, $1,646.81; for shop, farm and garden supplies, $1,712.63; for ordinary repairs, $401.41; for expenses of managers, $384.75; returned to State Treasurer, $236.20; for all other ordinary expenses, $4,330.43; total, $61,638.41.

The extraordinary expenditures were reported as $11,246.63, making the total expenditures for the year $72,885.04. The cash balance October 1, 1901, the only asset, was $1,060.58, and the outstanding indebtedness was $137.26 for bills unpaid.

Of the ordinary expenditures during the year, 44 per cent. was for salaries, wages and labor; 20.2 per cent. for provisions; 3.6 per cent. for household stores; 4.4 per cent. for clothing; 13.4 per cent. for fuel and light; .5 of 1 per cent. for hospital and medical supplies; 2.7 per cent. for transportation and traveling expenses; 2.8 per cent. for shop, farm and garden supplies; .7 of 1 per cent. for ordinary repairs; .6 of 1 per cent. for expenses of managers; and 7.1 per cent. for all other ordinary expenses.

Chapter 644, Laws of 1901 (appropriation bill), appropriated for the compensation of officers and employes, for the maintenance of the institution and for the transportation of the convicts, $66,000.

Chapter 324, Laws of 1901 (special act), appropriated for covering steam pipes, $1,000; repairs to cottages, $2,000; metal ceilings, $2,000; general repairs, $2,000; gymnasium equipment, $500; and for repairs to the steam plant, $5,000.

The sum of $400 appropriated by chapter 294, Laws of 1900, for a carriage shed near gate-house was reappropriated as an additional appropriation for building guard-house for confinement of refractory inmates authorized by chapter 294, Laws of 1900.

Of certain appropriations made by chapter 569, Laws of 1899, there were reappropriated as additional appropriations for building guard-house for confinement of refractory inmates authorized by chapter 294, Laws of 1900, the following unexpended balances: The sum of $444.54, an unexpended balance of an appropriation for flooring in cottages; the sum of $90, an unexpended balance of an appropriation for tile drain at boiler house; the sum of $27.80, an unexpended balance of an appropriation for fencing yard behind prison, leveling and graveling.

Of an appropriation of $13,500 made by chapter 294, Laws of 1900, for plumbing in cottages and administration building, $1,000 was reappropriated for plumbing and steam piping and connections of the guard-house for confinement of refractory women as authorized by chapter 294, Laws of 1900; and the remainder of said appropriation, namely, $12,500, was reappropriated for plumbing in cottages and administration building.

The special new appropriations amounted to $12,500, and the total appropriations available were $92,962.34.

When the present Board of Managers assumed charge of this institution the conditions which surrounded it were most disheartening. Through the intelligent and persistent efforts of the Managers, obstacles which at first interfered with the due and orderly progress of work in the institution have been largely overcome, and conditions now show great improvement. No important changes have been made to the buildings and grounds during the year, with one exception—a guard-house has been erected and is about ready for service. A number of repairs

have been made, but much remains to be done in the way of
betterment.

The disappearance of embarrassing traditions handed down
from former administrations indicates decided progress. The
introduction of more modern methods of discipline and the
change in the general atmosphere of the institution have
assisted in the improvement of conditions. Efforts are made
to encourage the inmates, and thus assist them to regain their
lost standing in society. This new and hopeful influence has
been observed by the Commissioners of the State Board of
Charities in their visits, and has been mentioned in the reports
of its inspectors.

In the report of the Board of Managers for the year ending
September 30, 1900, these words occur:

"In carrying out the work of reorganisation of this institution, it has been necessary to make many changes in the staff of
officers. * * * More and more we feel that the success of
the work in an institution of this kind depends upon the character of the officers directly in contact with the inmates. We
have seen our prison under one officer become thoroughly
demoralised in discipline, in housekeeping and in other
respects—a condition resulting finally in a riot; and we have seen
the same prison under another officer quickly brought into the
best of shape in all respects. We have seen a cottage considered
the best on the grounds rapidly deteriorate under the control of
an inefficient officer, and after her removal almost as rapidly
come back to the highest standard of good influence and discipline. Another cottage that was in a turbulent and most
unpromising condition was filled with many of the most disorderly and hardened inmates on the grounds and placed under

:harge of two promising officers. By hard work they have
e it as satisfactory a cottage as we have in the institution.
:r instances might be cited to show that the personality of
)fficer is an essential condition of success."

e introduction of a complete system of industrial training
 pressing need, for here as in similar institutions in the
: the instruction of the inmates in methods of self-support
i essential feature of the reformatory process. The young
en, during their period of custody, should be taught the
:ation of self-support by honest and respectable methods,
1at on leaving the institution they may not prey upon or
:wise become burdens to society.

 period of restraint unless it be accompanied by healthful
pline can reform character. The mind and heart must be
led, and they can be touched only through a training which
apted to the special needs of the individual. This House
:fuge is an attempt on the part of society to reclaim those
have gone astray. Its purpose is beneficent and its dis-
le should prove effective.

ne improvements to the present buildings as well as addi-
 to their number are considered desirable. Among these
onstruction of a hospital and the alteration of the present
nistration building are of prime importance. The building
used as a hospital is neither sanitary, commodious nor
:rly adapted for the care of the sick. One part of it has
arranged into isolation cells, and thus it combines the care
: patients suffering from acute diseases with the discipline
)se inmates who seriously transgress the rules of the insti-
1. The hospital should be separated as much as possible
the disciplinary feature, and be devoted solely to the care

of the sick. The building now used for a hospital can be converted into a gymnasium or into work rooms. A gymnasium is necessary, and the problem hitherto has been where to locate it. The construction of a hospital will thus serve two purposes.

The administration building is not adapted, in its present condition, for office purposes, as it combines under the same roof the general offices, dormitories for inmates and assembly rooms intended for general gatherings. It should be remodeled, and the reconstruction will necessarily prove expensive. The nursery building and some of the cottages are greatly dilapidated, making repairs necessary.

The Board recommends the following appropriations, or so much thereof as may be necessary, to this institution:

For renewing plumbing, and providing toilet rooms at the administration building, $2,500; for fire-escapes at administration building, $1,200; for fire-risers and hose for administration building, $600; for general repairs, making doorways in basement, and placing partition in superintendent's office, at the administration building, $1,000; for cleaning and painting interior cottage walls, $1,200; for repairs to coal shed and retaining wall, $300; for additional work at guard-house, $1,500; for hospital and equipment, $10,000; for gymnastic facilities in the industrial building, $1,000; for repairs and metal ceilings, cottages 5 and 6, and nursery, $4,000; for heating and plumbing for the reconstructed prison building, $2,500; for additional sewers, $3,000; making the special appropriations approved of, $28,800; also reappropriations of the sums of $9,000 for reconstructing the prison building, and $5,000 for sewage disposal plant, appropriated by chapter 294 of the Laws of 1900; maintenance appropriation, $66,000; making the total new appropriation, $94,800.

WESTERN HOUSE OF REFUGE FOR WOMEN, ALBION, ORLEANS COUNTY.

[Established 1890.]

This institution has capacity for 150 inmates. The number of inmates present October 1, 1900, was 129, and 49 were admitted during the year, making the total number under care 178. During the year 60 were discharged, leaving 118 present October 1, 1901, of whom 6 were children under 2 years of age. The average number present during the year was 130, and the average weekly cost of support, including the value of home and farm products consumed, $4.98; excluding the value of home and farm products consumed, $4.78.

The receipts for the fiscal year ending September 30, 1901, were: From cash balance of the previous year, $2,288.56; from special appropriations, $9,725.36; from general appropriations, $32,730.61; from all other sources, home and farm products, $1,392.08; total, $46,136.61.

The ordinary expenditures during the year were: For salaries of officers, $14,119.45; for wages and labor, $1,177; for provisions, $5,811.37; for household stores, $1,044.79; for clothing, $1,026.04; for fuel and light, $4,896.37; for hospital and medical supplies, $258.43; for transportation and traveling expenses, $499.45; for shop, farm and garden supplies, $1,141.15; for ordinary repairs, $490; for expenses of managers, $480.34; returned to State Treasurer, $58.68, and for all other ordinary expenses, $2,688.69; total, $33,691.76.

The extraordinary expenditures for improvements and other extraordinary expenses amounted to $12,013.92, making the total

expenditures for the year $45,705.68, and leaving a cash balance
of $430.93 at the close of the year. There was no outstanding
indebtedness, and the only asset was the balance in cash.

Of the ordinary expenditures during the year, 45.5 per cent.
was for salaries, wages and labor; 17.3 per cent. for provisions;
3.1 per cent. for household stores; 3 per cent. for clothing; 14.5
per cent. for fuel and light; .8 of 1 per cent. for hospital and
medical supplies; 1.5 per cent. for transportation and traveling
expenses; 3.4 per cent. for shop, farm and garden supplies; 1.5
per cent. for ordinary repairs; 1.4 per cent for expenses of managers, and 8 per cent. for all other ordinary expenses.

Chapter 644, Laws of 1901 (appropriation bill), appropriated
for the compensation of officers and employes, for the maintenance of the institution and for the transportation of those committed thereto, $35,000.

Chapter 645, Laws of 1901 (supply bill), appropriated for
deficiency on account of maintenance for the fiscal year ending
September 30, 1901, $2,000.

These were the only appropriations made, as the special act
carrying the appropriations for improvements and repairs failed
to pass the Legislature.

No changes of importance have taken place during the year.
Neatness, good order and discipline have been maintained, and
the usual routine of reformatory methods has been followed.

With the exception of the main building, all the dormitories
are of the cottage type, and afford opportunities for extensive
classification. The life in the cottages approaches the family
idea, and permits greater attention to the individual than is
possible in larger buildings.

The daily routine includes instruction in household work as

4

well as in the ordinary studies of the public schools. To make these women self-respecting they must be taught to be self-supporting, and be fitted to command honorable employment. The reformatory training should insist upon expert work, and should be sufficiently varied in character to provide for those of different degrees of ability and intelligence.

A house has been built for the coachman and a barn for the horses. Both are near enough to the administration building to be convenient, yet are outside the fences.

The hospital contains few inmates, as the general health has been excellent.

The Board wishes to take this occasion, very earnestly to call attention to the condition of the buildings of this institution, so far as possibilities of escape in the event of fire are concerned.

The staircases in all the dormitories are small; there is only one staircase from the second floor in each building, and all the windows are barred. There are no exits or fire-escapes of any description, and all the women in the so-called prison house are individually locked in their cells at night, and would consequently be almost entirely helpless should a fire break out.

Such a condition of affairs is, in the opinion of the Board, sufficiently serious to need very prompt and urgent consideration. The Board would recommend having the window gratings at the ends of the hallways on the second floors in each cottage on hinges, and fastened so that it would be possible to open them either from above or on the ground below, outside.

The Board would also recommend that, in case it is considered necessary or essential by the management of the institution to lock the women in cells at night in the prison-house, the system of locking be changed so that all the cells in each corridor can be unlocked by one lever.

No reformation of character will be lasting unless it is based upon sound principles. Many young mothers are sent here— their infants with them. If the mother is separated from her child her sense of responsibility is deadened and the restraining influence of a child's appeal to its mother is lost. The administration of the Refuge may be made easier, but the tendency toward reformation is decidedly weakened. It is false economy to sacrifice an important permanent interest for a minor temporary gain; hence the Board of Managers strives to keep together mother and child while in the Refuge, and to induce the mothers to undertake the support of their children after discharge, for it is felt that the development and deepening 'of mother-love will be a source of moral power when temptations again assail them.

The Board recommends the following appropriations, or so much thereof as may be necessary, to this institution:

For fencing, $350; for changes in the Refuge or main building, $1,200; for conduit and manholes, $2,000; for finishing off second story of hospital building and dividing it into rooms, $1,800; for spray baths and additional bath rooms in hospital, $750; for improvement to the electrical plant, $2,000; for safe, $300; for installing watchman's clock system, $125; for cement walks, $300; for carriage, harness and equipment and exchange of the horses now in use, $800; for spray baths, $2,500; for changing heating system in four cottages, $1,200; for fire protection, $2,500; for cell doors and locking devices, $2,000; for improving economy of steam plant, $150; making the special appropriations approved of, $17,975; maintenance appropriation, $37,000, making the total appropriation, $54,975.

NEW YORK STATE REFORMATORY FOR WOMEN, BEDFORD, WESTCHESTER COUNTY.

[Established 1892.]

This institution has capacity for 236 inmates. The institution was opened for inmates May 11, 1901, and 30 were admitted during the year. Three have been discharged, thus leaving 27 present October 1, 1901. The average number was 15, and the average weekly cost of support, including the value of home and farm products consumed, $25.77; excluding the value of home and farm products consumed, $25.

The receipts for the fiscal year ending September 30, 1901, were: From cash balance of the previous year, $261.18; from special appropriations, $29,734.66; from unexpended appropriations of former years, $17,739.32; from general appropriations, $14,307.18; total, $62,042.34.

The ordinary expenditures during the year were: For salaries of officers, wages and labor, $8,259.85; for provisions, $827.05; for household stores, $272.52; for clothing, $552.25; for fuel and light, $2,308.90; for hospital and medical supplies, $109.13; for transportation and traveling expenses, $68.02; for shop, farm and garden supplies, $557.04; for ordinary repairs, $416.70; for expenses of managers, $538.89; and for all other ordinary expenses, $712.65; total ordinary expenditures, $14,623.

The extraordinary expenditures for buildings and improvements, for repairs and general equipment, amounted to $47,-474.03, making the total ordinary and extraordinary expenditures $62,097.03, indicating a deficit of $54.69 at the close of the year.

Of the ordinary expenditures during the year 56.5 per cent. was for salaries, wages and labor; 5.6 per cent. for provisions; 1.9

per cent. for household stores; 3.8. per cent. for clothing; 15.8 per cent. for fuel and light; .7 of 1 per cent. for hospital and medical supplies; .5 of 1 per cent. for transportation and traveling expenses; 3.8 per cent. for shop, farm and garden supplies; 2.8 per cent. for ordinary repairs; 3.7 per cent. for expenses of managers; and 4.9 per cent. for all other ordinary expenses.

Chapter 644, Laws of 1901 (appropriation bill), appropriated for the compensation of officers and employes, for the maintenance of the institution and for the transportation of those committed thereto, $30,000.

Chapter 645, Laws of 1901 (supply bill), reappropriated the sum of $600, being a portion of the unexpended balance of the appropriation of $2,500 made by chapter 616 of the Laws of 1899, for farm and other utensils, for electric fixtures, and completing necessary electric work; and the sum of $1,835, being a portion of the unexpended balance of the appropriation of $2,500 made by chapter 616, Laws of 1899, for farm and other utensils, for the same purpose.

Chapter 72, Laws of 1901 (special act), appropriated for the maintenance of the institution for the fiscal year beginning October 1, 1900, and ending September 30, 1901, the sum of $10,000 in addition to the unexpended balance of $7,800.59 appropriated by chapter 420 of the Laws of 1900, for the maintenance of said institution to October 1, 1900.

The sum of $3,000 was appropriated for building an ice-house and cold-storage building.

Chapter 244, Laws of 1901 (special act), appropriated for facing and seeding embankments, $4,500; for galvanized iron vent ducts in attics, $750; sewage and water supply pumps, $1,700; heat connections in former prison building, now converted into cottage,

$1,000; elevator to kitchens in former prison building, $350; concrete floor under storage for coal in power-house and for shed
for storing coal adjoining said building, $750; entrance to base-
ment of administration building for taking in supplies, and for
shelving and otherwise preparing rooms in said basement for the
proper care of supplies of the institution, $1,000; miscellaneous
repairs, $1,500; fire apparatus, $1,000; covering steam pipes,
$1,500; interior furnishing for buildings, including iron bed-
steads, office and chapel furniture, carpets, window-shades and
rugs, $2,500, in addition to the appropriation of $6,250 under
chapter 616, Laws of 1899, for the same purpose, which was reappropriated; for a hospital building, $1,500, in addition to the bal-
ance of $4,980.90 of the appropriation of $5,000 for new disciplinary building under chapter 288, Laws of 1900, which balance
was reappropriated for hospital building.

The maintenance appropriations amounted to $47,800,59, the
special appropriations to $34,715.90, and the total appropriations
to $82,516.49.

The ice-house or cold-storage building, for which $3,000 was
appropriated, has been built under contract.

All the work provided for by chapter 244, Laws of 1901, has
been either finished or contracted for except the sewage and
water supply pumps, $1,700; the work of furnishing coal storage,
$750, and the construction of the hospital building, $6,480.90.

This institution was intended to provide custodial care for the
large number of young girls and women in New York and vicinity
who require the discipline of a reformatory institution. It was
opened for the reception of inmates on May 11, 1901. The number
of inmates admitted up to the present time is small, but enough
to insure the development of the institution along proper lines.

It is a matter of experience that all new efforts in this direction
should advance in accordance with the principles of humane and
scientific reformatory methods.   It is hoped that this institution
will develop distinctive lines of administration and discipline.
Already its internal administration is well organized, and it is
believed that the institution is fully prepared to meet its responsibilities.   The opening of this house of refuge suggests anew the
importance of a better system of classification of all the inmates
in our correctional institutions for women.   Inmates of these
reformatories should be grouped in such way as to assist in their
moral development.

Up to the present time about 70 girls have been sent to Bedford,
but the commitments have been made by a few only of the large
number of magistrates authorized to commit to the institution.
It is desirable that all the magistrates vested with the power of
commitment to Bedford avail themselves of the opportunity
afforded by the opening of the Reformatory to carry out the
beneficent object contemplated by the law.

It is recommended that instruction in market gardening be
made a feature of the training for such as are competent, as it
will open a new avenue for profitable employment after discharge.   This will require only a small building and its equipment, but the result will, it is believed, more than repay the cost
of the investment.

The location of this institution is so isolated that employes
must reside upon the grounds, and two cottages should be
erected for the accommodation of the men.

The present method of handling coal is awkward, expensive
and laborious.   At small cost the storage facilities can be
greatly improved, and the present wheelbarrow plan be aban-

doned. The cost of the extra help required to handle this coal will soon equal the cost of improvement.

An additional dynamo and engine are needed to complete the electric-light equipment. As the dependence of the Reforma-tory is upon a single dynamo, liable to get out of order at any time, it is apparent that there should be no delay in placing the second dynamo in position.

The hospital requires furniture, electric fixtures, sanitary floors, window guards, pipe covering, and other incidental work to com-plete it ready for use, and until these are provided it can do no service. The gate-house should be connected with the water service. It should have the plumbing and connections installed as soon as possible.

Owing to the exposed position of the Reformatory, the guards need occasional protection from storms. This can be given if sentry boxes are placed where needed. A small appropriation will be sufficient for this purpose.

The boilers have not been properly connected with the smoke-stack, and in consequence they are unable to do efficient work. They should be connected in a proper way as a measure of economy.

The Board recommends the following appropriations, or so much thereof as may be necessary, to this institution:

For 2 cottages for male employes, $2,500; for extension of coal shed, $750; for connecting boilers with smoke-stack and for new grates, $600; for plumbing and putting water into gate-house, $250; for sentry box, $150; for window guards, electric work, sanitary floors, pipe covering and incidentals for hospital, $1,500; for furnishing hospital, $500; for pipe covering in conduits, $1,500; for installing fire lines, $600; for duplicate engine and dynamo, $3,500; for equipment for instruction in market gardening and for propagation house, $3,000; making the special appropriations approved of, $14,850; maintenance appropriation, $50,000; making the total appropriation, $64,850.

SOCIETY FOR THE REFORMATION OF JUVENILE DELINQUENTS IN THE CITY OF NEW YORK, COMMONLY CALLED "THE HOUSE OF REFUGE", RANDALL'S ISLAND, NEW YORK CITY.

[Established 1824.]

This institution has capacity for 1,000 inmates. The number of inmates present October 1, 1900, was 827, and there were admitted during the year 498, making the total number under care 1,325. During the year 481 were discharged and 3 died, leaving present October 1, 1901, 841, of whom 748 were boys and 93 girls. The average number present during the year was 834, and the average weekly cost of support, including the value of home and farm products consumed, $3.83; excluding the value of home and farm products consumed, $3.81.

The receipts during the year ending September 30, 1901, were: From cash balance of the previous year, $6,128.06; from special appropriations, $34,806.31; from unexpended appropriations of former years, $4,356.15; from general appropriations, $139,500; from all other sources, including $19,546.96 from Board of Education, New York city, and $2,419.49 from fire insurance companies, $21,995.39; total, $206,785.91.

The ordinary expenditures for the year were: For salaries of officers, wages and labor, $71,850.25; for provisions, $37,395.19; for household stores, $5,607.36; for clothing, $12,691.57; for fuel and light, $14,847.92; for hospital and medical supplies, $705.14; for transportation and traveling expenses, $818.87; for shop, farm and garden supplies, $7,806.32; for ordinary repairs, $4,389.08; for all other ordinary expenses, $9,811.81; total ordinary expenditures,.$165,923.51.

The extraordinary expenditures were $38,195.84 for improvements, extraordinary repairs and all other extraordinary expenses, making the aggregate expenditure for the year $204,119.35. The cash balance at the close of the year, the only reported asset, was $2,666.56, and there was no outstanding indebtedness.

Of the ordinary expenditures during the year 43.3 per cent. was for salaries, wages and labor; 22.5 per cent. for provisions; 3.4 per cent. for household stores; 7.7 per cent. for clothing; 9 per cent. for fuel and light; .4 of 1 per cent. for hospital and medical supplies; .5 of 1 per cent. for transportation and traveling expenses; 4.7 per cent. for shop, farm and garden supplies; 2.6 per cent. for ordinary repairs, and 5.9 per cent. for all other ordinary expenses.

Chapter 644, Laws of 1901 (appropriation bill), appropriated for maintenance, rewards to inmates, repairs and betterments of tools, equipment and furniture, repairs to buildings and for necessary tools for the trades-schools and common schools, and military system and photographing of inmates, $150,000.

Chapter 497, Laws of 1901 (special act), appropriated for the establishment and equipment of a new trades-school and for supplies for the same and for those already established, $6,000; additions and betterments to steam plant and covering steam pipes, $7,500; constructing sewerage system and plumbing, $5,000; cadet guns, other military equipment and uniforms, $2,000; general electric repairs, $3,265, which amount was reappropriated from the $25,000 appropriated for additions and betterments to steam plant, new dynamos and motors, by chapter 282 of the Laws of 1900.

The special appropriations amounted to $23,765 and the total appropriations to $173,765.

The sum of $6,000 appropriated for a new trades-school and supplies for the same, under chapter 497, Laws of 1901, remained intact October 1, 1901, but arrangements for its expenditure have since been made. For additions and betterments to steam plant, $7,500 has been spent. The appropriation for reconstructing the sewerage system, $5,000, and the appropriation of $3,265 for general electric repairs have not been made.

During the past year some betterments in the buildings and facilities of the institution have been in progress. In some particulars its internal administration has improved. No special changes in discipline have been made, but the military drill has continued and the boys show its beneficial effect. In this institution a full development of drill exercises is desirable. In order to secure the greatest benefits from this training, it is suggested that an ample equipment of cadet guns should be provided for the military department.

In the girls' department the conditions remain as during previous years. Successful management of juvenile delinquents requires the separation of the sexes. It is therefore desirable that the girls be removed to some other and more suitable place where, apart from the boys, they may receive instruction and proper training.

The technical instruction undertaken by this institution is very limited. To fit these boys and girls for useful lives it is necessary that they receive sufficient instruction in industrial pursuits to be trained into habits of regularity and industry. The opportunities afforded by this reformatory do not give a training which will prepare the boys and girls for self-support. The equipment is limited; in consequence insufficient employment is provided, and the enforced idleness is destructive to morals. The trades, and the facilities provided by the institution should be such as to enable each boy and girl to work under instruction not less than four hours each day, the remaining hours to be given to the schoolroom, recreation and sleep.

As long as this institution retains its present character, remaining insufficiently equipped, and is continued in its present location, it will fail to accomplish fully its purpose in the reformation of juvenile delinquents. It is to the interest of the State to secure the transfer of this institution to a rural location and to provide ample opportunities for fuller instruction in profitable employment, so as to prepare these children for self-support.

The buildings are the property of a private corporation; the land upon which they stand belongs to the city of New York; the State therefore has no property right in either land or buildings. Nearly all of the buildings were erected many years ago, and annually, because of wear and tear, require extensive repairs. This Board does not consider it wise for the State to make appropriations from its funds to enlarge and maintain the property of any private charitable corporation. Additions and repairs to the buildings of this institution are imperatively needed to provide adequately for the wards of the State maintained therein, but the corporation in which the title to the property is vested is not in possession of an endowment, and therefore is unable to make repairs or additions.

The State Board of Charities urges the immediate consideration of some legislative enactment for the reorganization of the

Society for the Reformation of Juvenile Delinquents, and the transfer of the inmates of this institution to some suitable rural location which will be properly secured to the State by legal title as its own property, and which can be equipped with buildings and facilities necessary for their proper maintenance and instruction. As the State must maintain an institution of this character, it should have absolute control of it, and the Legislature is respectfully and urgently requested to undertake the proposed reorganization at the earliest practicable moment so that this juvenile reformatory may become a State institution in fact as well as in name, with managers appointed by the Governor and confirmed by the Senate in the same manner as the managers of all other State institutions.

In the opinion of this Board it would be an equitable arrangement for the city of New York, which owns the land upon which the institution is located, subject to the latter's right of occupancy so long as it continues its work in behalf of juvenile delinquents, to repay to the institution for the benefit of the State a considerable sum and receive in return the surrender of the Society's right of occupancy to the buildings which have been erected on the property at a cost of $500,000, mainly contributed by the State. The money thus obtained could then be used in purchasing property elsewhere and for the erection of new buildings thereon for the use of the institution. The demands upon the public charities of the city of New York are so great that they must be enlarged from time to time, and the surrender of these buildings would afford the city an opportunity for the extension of its hospital system.

It may be stated that while the State Board of Charities is opposed to the improvement of any property which is not

owned and controlled directly by the State, it is convinced
that pending the removal of this institution it is necessary to
provide for the proper carrying on of its work. As these extraordinary repairs to existing buildings are considered necessary
by the State Architect, under his advice the appropriations
required for them are approved.

The Board recommends the following appropriations, or so
much thereof as may be necessary, to this institution:

For the completion of new window frames, sash and casing,
$2,000; for changes in the plumbing system, $7,500; for completing the work of overhauling the steam plant and covering the
steam pipes, $5,000; continuing the work of establishing and
equipping the trades-schools, $2,000; making the special appro-
priations approved of $16,500; maintenance appropriation, $160,-
000; making the total appropriation $176,500.

SYRACUSE STATE INSTITUTION FOR FEEBLE-MINDED CHILDREN, SYRACUSE, ONONDAGA COUNTY.

[Established 1851.]

This institution has capacity for 546 inmates. The number of
inmates October 1, 1901, was 546, of whom 25 were absent on
vacation. There have been admitted during the year 63, making
the total number under care 609. During the year 56 were discharged and 16 died, leaving 537 on the rolls of the institution
October 1, 1901. The average number present during the year
was 515, and the average weekly cost of support, including the
value of home and farm products consumed, was $3.79; excluding
the value of home and farm products consumed, $3.37.

The receipts during the year ending September 30, 1901, were:
From cash balance at the close of the previous year, $123.33; from

special appropriations, $2,648.36; from general appropriations, $92,500; from sale of farm and garden produce, $911.06; from labor of inmates, $11.10; from counties and cities, $11,766; from individuals for the support of inmates, $2,472.37; from sources not classified, $176.23; total, $110,608.45.

The ordinary expenditures during the year were: For salaries of officers and teachers, $13,376.84; for wages and labor, $24,-067.04; for provisions, $23,123.42; for household stores, $3,102.89; for clothing, $5,923.57; for fuel and light, $9,813.63; for hospital and medical supplies, $876.60; for transportation and traveling expenses, $43.72; for shop, farm and garden supplies, $5,424.05; for ordinary repairs, $1,212.27; for expenses of managers, $52.61; returned to State Treasurer, $15,336.76; for all other expenses, $3,516.61; total, $105,870.01.

There was also expended for extraordinary repairs $2,648.36, making the total expenditures for the year $108,518.37. The assets were: Balance in cash, $2,090.08; due from counties and cities, $100; due from individuals, $490.04; a total of $2,680.12.

Of the ordinary expenditures during the year 41.4 per cent. was for salaries, wages and labor; 25.5 per cent. for provisions; 3.4 per cent. for household stores; 6.6 per cent. for clothing; 10.8 per cent. for fuel and light; 1 per cent. for hospital and medical supplies; 6 per cent. for shop, farm and garden supplies; 1.3 per cent for ordinary repairs, and 4 per cent. for all other expenses, including a small expenditure for transportation and traveling expenses and for expenses of managers.

Chapter 644, Laws of 1901 (appropriation bill), appropriated for maintenance and ordinary repairs $80,000.

Chapter 645, Laws of 1901 (supply bill), appropriated for maintenance to be paid from the moneys turned into the treasury of the State under section 37, chapter 580, Laws of 1899, $12,000.

Chapter 708, Laws of 1901 (special act), appropriated for installing watchman's clock system, $800; for brick corridor to connect
with the north wing to the boys' building, $1,000; the sum of
$6,546.50, being the unexpended balance of the appropriation of
$6,587 made by chapter 419, Laws of 1900, for the erection of a
building and connection of a corridor for a general bath-house,
was reappropriated for improving the plumbing and drainage system; the sum of $2,800, being the unexpended balance of the
appropriation of $2,800 made by chapter 419, Laws of 1900, for
plumbing, drainage and steam fitting for the bath-house, was
reappropriated for improving the heating system.

The special appropriations amounted to $11,146.50 and the total
appropriations to $103,146.50.

The brick corridor connecting the north wing with the boys'
building, for which $1,000 was appropriated, has been built. Con-
tracts have been made under the other appropriations.

This institution during the past year has continued as heretofore. The applications for admission continue to accumulate,
there being few opportunities for receiving new cases. A redis-
tribution of the inmates of the several institutions devoted to the
care of the feeble-minded class of dependents would result in
opening this school to many deserving children who are now
necessarily denied admission. There are many adults in this
school, men and women who have passed the age of improvement,
and who remain because there is no other place for them to go.
The removal of the men to Rome and the women to Newark will
be beneficial in many ways. For lack of room in this school,
feeble-minded boys and girls are growing up in ignorance without proper protection and to the ultimate detriment of society.
The power of transfer, when the public interests demand it,

should be lodged in a central authority covering these public institutions. This school for feeble-minded children is especially unfortunate because the compulsory presence of so many adults has practically changed the character of the institution. The work of the school will be benefited by the complete separation of the sexes.

In compliance with the request of the Board of Managers of this institution, the Board recommends the employment of a teacher of sloyd. This will necessitate an addition of $1,000 to the yearly allowance for maintenance.

Additional facilities should be provided for bathing, and the substitution of the spray bath system for that now in use will promote the health and cleanliness of the children.

The stairways in the central building are no longer safe. In case of fire their condition would certainly result in the loss of life. An appropriation for their reconstruction is necessary.

The stone wall surrounding the premises has been left unfinished on Grand avenue for a number of years. In order to protect not only the property but the children the premises should be surrounded by a safe fence, and the present fence should be extended.

The Board recommends the following appropriations, or so much thereof as may be necessary, to this institution:

For reconstruction of the stairways in the central building, $1,200; for extension of stone wall fence on Grand avenue, $3,000; and for the renewal of laundry machinery and repairs to laundry, $1,800; making the special appropriations approved of, $6,000; maintenance appropriation, $81,000; making the total appropriations, $87,000.

5

STATE CUSTODIAL ASYLUM FOR FEEBLE-MINDED WOMEN,
NEWARK, WAYNE COUNTY.

[Established 1876.]

This asylum has capacity for 400 inmates. The number of
inmates October 1, 1900, was 414, and 35 were admitted during
the year, making the total number under care 449. During
the year 24 were discharged and 9 died, leaving the number
present October 1, 1901, 416. The average number during the
year was 413, and the average weekly cost of support, including
the value of home and farm products consumed, $2.57; exclud-
ing the value of home and farm products consumed, $2.35.

The receipts during the year ending September 30, 1901, were:
From cash balance at the close of the previous year, $399.58;
from special appropriations, $36,834.89; from general appropria-
tions, $50,500; from all other sources, $31.68; total, $87,766.15.

The ordinary expenditures for the year were: For salaries of
officers and employes, $17,302.99; for wages and labor, $2,910.09;
for provisions, $12,871.60; for household stores, $3,133.65; for
clothing, $2,698.94; for fuel and light, $6,072.34; for hospital and
medical supplies, $575.69; for shop, farm and garden supplies,
$1,583.14; for ordinary repairs, $747.18; for expenses of managers, $371.02; for remittance to State Treasurer, $31.68; for all
other ordinary expenses, $2,310.35; total ordinary expenditures,
$50,608.67.

The extraordinary expenditures are reported as $36,834.89, of
which $33,308.46 was for buildings and improvements, $2,496.40
for extraordinary repairs, and $1,030.03 for all other extraordi-
nary expenses, making the total expenditures for the year
$87,443.56, and leaving as balance in cash at the close of the
fiscal year, $322.59. The outstanding indebtedness was $625 for
bills unpaid.

Of the ordinary expenditures during the year 40 per cent. was for salaries, wages and labor; 25.5 per cent. for provisions; 6.2 per cent. for household stores; 5.3 per cent. for clothing; 12 per cent. for fuel and light; 1.1 per cent. for hospital and medical supplies; 8.1 per cent. for shop, farm and garden supplies; 1.5 per cent. for ordinary repairs; .7 of 1 per cent. for expenses of managers, and 4.6 per cent. for all other ordinary expenses.

Chapter 644, Laws of 1901 (appropriation bill), appropriated for the services of the attendants, for other necessary expenses and the ordinary repairs of the asylum, $55,000.

Chapter 359, Laws of 1901 (special act), appropriated for new cottage dormitory to make provision for feeble-minded women of child-bearing age, $30,000; for sewage disposal plant and land for the same, $10,000; the development of water supply, $5,000; new boiler and connections, $3,500; painting, $500; walks and roads, $500; flooring, $500; removal of old building and grading and renewing grounds, $1,000; drainage, $500; retaining wall, $300; the sum of $1,846.26, being the balance of $3,000 appropriated by chapter 427 of the Laws of 1899, for extraordinary repairs, grading and improving grounds and walks, was reappropriated for the purposes specified; the sum of $1,407, being the balance of $2,500 appropriated by chapter 427 of the Laws of 1899, for grading and laying track to coal shed, and the sum of $300, being the unexpended appropriation for purchase of lands for railroad to coal shed, made by chapter 427, Laws of 1899, were reappropriated for general repairs and betterments; the sum of $1,500, being the balance of $12,000 appropriated by chapter 427 of the Laws of 1899, for boilers and boiler house, dynamos and electrical apparatus and engines for electrical plant, was reappropriated for the purposes specified.

The special new appropriations amounted to $56,853.26 and the total appropriation to $111,853.26.

Contracts have been made under the appropriation of $30,000 for a new cottage dormitory.

A contract has also been made for the new boiler and connections, for which $3,500 was appropriated.

The appropriation of $10,000 for sewage disposal plant and land for the same remains intact, as does that of $5,000 for the development of the water supply.

The other work for which appropriations were made has been contracted for, and some of it has been completed.

This institution was designed to meet the declared policy of the State, to remove from the almshouses and similar institutions all feeble-minded women of child-bearing age, and maintain them under humane custody where they may be protected and receive suitable training.

The capacity of the institution is now 450, which has been reached by successive additions to the original plant. During the past year a new cottage was erected which added room for 50 inmates, and a number of minor additions and improvements have also been made to the institution. It is now crowded.

The year has been a favorable one in the history and development of the Asylum, and in its various departments a satisfactory administration has been maintained. The applications for admission, however, have far exceeded the capacity, and at present there are many cases for which provision cannot be made. The necessity for additional cottages is urgent, there being no similar asylum in the State. The fact that most of the inmates are young women who must remain under custody for a long period, makes it apparent that the Asylum should be enlarged from time to time to provide shelter for the maximum number of feeble-minded women of child-bearing age resident in the State. The institution at Newark can be doubled in the number of its inmates at a minimum of expense for maintenance and administration. Another cottage is needed to make room for applicants whose papers are now on file. The enlargement should be pressed as rapidly as possible, and at least one more cottage be provided for by the Legislature of 1902.

This institution is very inadequately equipped for industrial and school training. The only rooms available are in the administration building, which is overtaxed to carry on the necessary administrative work. A new building to be used for industrial and educational work will make room for new patients in the present dormitories, as it will open the schoolrooms to dormitory service.

A residence for the Superintendent will add to the space devoted to administration by providing necessary offices for this growing institution. At present all the office work is done in a single room, in which books and records must be kept. There is no private consultation room, and all interviews must therefore be held in public to the great embarrassment of parents and friends of the inmates. By the erection of a house as suggested, the rooms now used by the Superintendent's family can be added to the offices and thus render administration easier. The Board approves the erection of a residence for the Superintendent for the foregoing reasons, and because it believes that while he should be required to live on the Asylum premises, neither he nor his family should be compelled to live in such close contact with the inmates of the institution as is now necessary because of the lack of a separate dwelling.

The present electric plant was installed with the intention to complete it as soon as possible. For this purpose a duplicate engine and dynamo are needed. With this the electric-light system can be extended to the new buildings and over the grounds, thus affording exterior light.

Cottage F will require furnishing in a short time, and pianos are needed for cottages B, C and E. An appropriation will also be needed for walks, grading, improving roads and grounds.

The Board recommends the following appropriations, or so much thereof as may be necessary, to this institution:

For the erection of cottage dormitory G, $32,000; for an industrial and school building, $10,000; for brick residence for Superintendent, $7,500; for duplicate engine and dynamo, $2,500; for extending electric-light system and for exterior lighting, $600; for walks, roads, grading and improving grounds, $1,000; for furniture for cottage F and 3 pianos for cottages B, O and E, $3,750; making the special appropriations approved of $57,350; maintenance appropriation, $60,000; making the total appropriation, $117,350.

THE ROME STATE CUSTODIAL ASYLUM, ROME, ONEIDA COUNTY.

[Established 1893.]

The Asylum has, at present, capacity for 550 inmates. The number of inmates October 1, 1900, was 352, and 119 were admitted during the year, making the total number under care 471. Of these 19 died and 8 were discharged, thus leaving 444 present October 1, 1901, of whom 313 were males and 131 females. The average number during the year was 399, and the average weekly cost of support, including the value of home and farm products consumed, $6.92; excluding the value of home and farm products consumed, $3.55.

The receipts during the year were: From cash balance of the previous year, $278.83; from special appropriations, $28,443.48; from general appropriations, $73,637.50; from all other sources, including $166.24 from sales of farm and garden produce and $583 from individuals for the support of inmates, $877.89; total, $103,237.70.

The ordinary expenditures were: For salaries of officers, $7,999.92; for wages and labor, $26,463.63; for provisions, $13,914.36; for household stores, $2,382.42; for clothing, $4,809.13; for fuel and light, $10,004.37; for hospital and medical supplies, $392.60; for shop, farm and garden supplies, $3,967.84; for ordinary repairs, $723.87; for expenses of managers, $360.30; returned to State Treasurer, $877.89; for all other ordinary expenses, $2,562.14; total, $74,458.56.

The total extraordinary expenditures were $28,443.48, of which $18,155.71 was for buildings and improvements, $440.36 for extraordinary repairs, $9,847.41 for all other extraordinary expenses, making the total expenditure for the year $102,902.04, and leaving a cash balance of $335.66 October 1, 1901. There was no outstanding indebtedness.

Of the ordinary expenditures 46.9 per cent. was for salaries, wages and labor; 18.9 per cent. for provisions; 3.2 per cent. for household stores; 6.5 per cent. for clothing; 13.6 per cent. for fuel and light; .5 of 1 per cent. for hospital and medical supplies; 5.4 per cent. for shop, farm and garden supplies; 1 per cent. for ordinary repairs; .5 of 1 per cent. for expenses of managers; and 3.5 per cent. for all other ordinary expenses.

Chapter 644, Laws of 1901 (appropriation bill), appropriated for the support and maintenance of the inmates, for the services of attendants and for other necessary expenses, $75,000.

Chapter 700, Laws of 1901 (special act), appropriated for heating and ventilating ward building G, $5,940; electric wiring and fixtures for ward building G, $2,000; plumbing and drainage for ward building G, $5,500; window guards, dividing doors, wall registers at ceilings and contingencies, $2,000; ice-house and cold-storage building, $6,000; addition to boiler-house, $6,800; installing night watchman's clock system, $750; fire-escapes in addition to $600 appropriated by chapter 420, Laws of 1900, $600; furniture and equipment for administration building, ward buildings F and G and other buildings, $5,000; dynamo and engine for 1,500 lights and all connections, $6,700; electric cable from switchboard to center of group of ward buildings, $2,160; changing switchboard connections, $530; one 150 horse-power boiler and connections, $3,500; feed-water heater, $1,800; painting, repairs and betterments, steel ceilings in wards 3, 7 and 9 of building D, $1,150; new floors, doors and windows throughout building B, except in administration portion, $3,500; steel beams, brick arch construction and new floors in bath-rooms of buildings B, C, D and E, $1,500; concrete floor in vegetable storehouse and cellar of farmhouse, $240; reimbursing maintenance account for moneys paid F. W. Kirkland, building inspector, on certificate of the State Architect, $437.50; the sum of $931.43, being the unexpended balance of appropriation of $2,000 made by chapter 620 of the Laws of 1899, for fencing, was reappropriated for the same purpose; the sum of $1,018.24, being the unexpended balance of the appropriation of $1,500 made by chapter 620, Laws of 1899, for stock and utensils for farm, was reappropriated for the same purpose; the sum of

$10,023.57, being the unexpended balance of $32,500 appropriated by chapter 620, Laws of 1899, for one dormitory building to house 150 inmates, was reappropriated for the same purpose.

The special appropriations amounted to $68,080.74 and the total appropriations to $143,080.74.

The appropriation for the work upon ward building G, $13,440, is being expended under contract, and the addition to the boiler house, for which $6,800 was appropriated, is under way.

Contracts have also been made for furniture and equipment for administration building, ward buildings F and G, and other buildings, $5,000.

No contracts have been made for the dynamo and engine for which $6,700 was appropriated, nor for the electric cable from switchboard, $2,160, and switchboard connection, $530, and the appropriation of $6,000 for ice-house and cold-storage also remains intact.

Contracts have been made for one 150 horse-power boiler and connections, $3,500, and feed water heater, $1,800.

For the other work in buildings B, C, D and E, plans have been made but no contracts let.

The sum of $10,023.57 reappropriated is under contract.

The other minor appropriations are mostly provided for by plans and work under way.

This institution was established by the State as the third in the plan for a complete classification of the feeble-minded. It is designed to receive and to care for those cases which are incapable of education or mental development, as well as for those who belong wholly to the idiotic class. Its development has been hampered by the fact that the property purchased by the State to use for asylum purposes was formerly

the Oneida county farm. It was incumbered by the almshouse
buildings, antiquated, dilapidated, and of comparatively little
value for custodial purposes. It was necessary to remodel, reconstruct and repair these old buildings, and this involved the loss
of much time and the expenditure of a very large amount of
money. The delay incident upon these changes and betterments
has prevented a rapid preparation of accommodations for this
class of cases; and hence, with a present capacity for but 550,
which is fully occupied, the necessity for new buildings to
increase the dormitory accommodations is very urgent.

The Managers of the Rome institution are and always have
been ready and willing to receive any patients for whom they
can provide. Their ability to add to the number of inmates,
however, is conditioned by the room at their disposal for dormitory or ward purposes. The pressure on this institution is
greater than upon any other in this State, not excepting Craig
Colony, where the applications for admission are numerous and
urgent.

It is the duty of the State to make proper provision for this
class of defectives, and a new group of buildings should be
provided for the institution at Rome as soon as possible, so as
to secure the removal to it of all the idiotic now kept in other
institutions, public and private, as well as those still cared for in
families owing to the lack of proper custodial resources. This
is demanded by the best interests of the younger members
of society, as well as by the needs of the unfortunates for whom
a custodial asylum is necessary.

To provide extended ward accommodations at the institution
at Rome by sufficient appropriation will decrease the pressure
upon the other two asylums for the mentally defective and

enable both Syracuse and Newark to transfer the idiotic now
held in these institutions to their proper place. It will open the
doors of the Syracuse school to the feeble-minded boys and girls
who are now denied admission for lack of room, and ultimately
the enlargement of the Rome Asylum will enable the State to
complete that plan of classification which it has undertaken for
the purpose of assuring humane and scientific treatment to its
defective wards.

As this Asylum is not located directly on a railroad, all supplies must be hauled to it on wagons a distance of two and a
half miles. The expense for this transfer is heavy, and the item
of freight is figured into every contract for building or general
supply, so that in the end the State pays not less than 50 cents
on each wagon load of material used at the Asylum. It is estimated that in the course of 10 years this expense will aggregate
$30,000. The inmates are idiots of low grade and cannot be used
to do this teaming. A railroad switch would do away with this
expensive hauling and permit the direct delivery of supplies
upon the grounds by the railroad company. The cost of such a
switch should be saved in a few years by the reduced charges
for freight, and it will be a wise investment of public funds to
secure its construction at once.

A mortuary building with facilities for laboratory work should
be added to the general equipment. This mortuary is needed
to replace an old shed that had been used by the county for
the dead awaiting burial. There should be better facilities for
preserving bodies in warm weather and for holding post-
mortems and doing other scientific work.

At the present time there are insufficient facilities for the
storage of vegetables, and as a consequence each year there is

more or less waste of the products of the farm and garden.
This will be remedied by the construction of an additional storehouse for vegetables.

The supply of ice furnished by the present ice pond is not
large enough to assure a full supply throughout the season. A
new ice pond can be made at a small expense. It is recommended that an appropriation be made for this purpose.

All the original buildings, having been used, as hereinbefore stated, for many years as county almshouse
buildings, require extensive repairs and alterations. By
reconstruction and repair they can be continued in use
for some years to come, but these repairs and alterations
cannot be postponed, for delay will greatly increase the ultimate cost. A liberal appropriation is needed for these repairs.
This should cover all the alterations in buildings B and E, as
well as the general painting, repairs, betterments and sanitary
floors in toilet rooms in B and C.

Additions are needed to the group of outbuildings. Silos and
a vegetable-propagating house will prove profitable to the State,
permitting the Asylum to preserve enough food for its large
dairy and also raise all the plants required to set out its vegetable gardens, thus escaping the annual loss incurred from frost,
rain or drought. There is need of stable room for additional
stock, and of a proper approach to the barn. The pig-pens
need a concrete floor, and the electric-light building one of
cement. The grounds should be graded and the walks extended
as the buildings are completed.

As this is a custodial Asylum, the safety of the inmates
depends upon the certainty of the custody. The locks of the
old buildings are worn out and do not hold the inmates, as

intended, within the buildings. New cylinder locks are needed in buildings D and E.

The Board recommends the following appropriations, or so much thereof as may be necessary, to this institution:

For mortuary building, $2,500; for ward building J to accommodate 210 men, $41,500; for heating and ventilating ward building J, $6,000; for plumbing and drainage in ward building J, $5,500; for lighting fixtures in ward building J, $2,000; for electric cable from switchboard to ward building J, $3,360; for silos, $425; for vegetable propagating house, $2,500; for additional stable for necessary stock, $3,000; for vegetable storehouse, $2,200; for painting, repairs and betterments in buildings B and E, including plastering and flooring in building B, remodeling north end of building E, and plastering, steel ceilings and sanitary floors in bath and toilet-rooms of building E, $11,400; for sanitary floors in four toilet and two bathrooms in building B, $1,600; for sanitary floors in four toilet-rooms in building C, $1,000; for steel flagstaff, $180; for concrete floor in pigpen, $400; for cement floor in electric-light building, $500; for approach to stable, $250; for grading walks and improving grounds, $2,500; for cylinder locks in buildings D and E, $800; for painting walls of administration building, $500; for railroad switch, $10,000; for fruit and shade trees, $500; for graveling ice pond, $300; for construction of new ice pond, $500; making the special appropriations approved of, $99,415; maintenance appropriation, $90,000; for deficiency in maintenance appropriation for the year ending September 30, 1902, $10,000; making the total appropriation, $199,415.

CRAIG COLONY, SONYEA, LIVINGSTON COUNTY.

[Established 1894.]

The Colony has, at present, capacity for 740 inmates. The number of inmates October 1, 1900, was 621, and 259 were admitted during the year, making the total number under care 871. Of these 92 were discharged and 36 died, thus leaving 743 present October 1, 1901, of whom 440 were men and boys and 303 women and girls. The average number present during the year was 676, and the average weekly cost of support, including the value of home and farm products consumed, $3.71; excluding the value of home and farm products consumed, $3.16.

The receipts during the year ending September 30, 1901, were: From cash balance at the close of the previous year, $686.95; from special appropriation, $82,622.74; from general appropriations, $111,084.39; from the sale of farm and garden produce and miscellaneous sales, $2,729.34; from all other sources, $2,930.78; total, $200,054.20.

The ordinary expenditures were: For salaries of officers, $10,400; for wages and labor, $39,898.99; for provisions, $27,696.96; for household stores, $3,773.38; for clothing, $5,131.88; for fuel and light, $13,357.56; for hospital and medical supplies, $1,753.67; for transportation and traveling expenses, $163.06; for shop, farm and garden supplies, $4,317.57; for ordinary repairs, $871.79; for expenses of managers, $995.60; remitted to the State Treasurer, $5,655.58; for all other ordinary expenses, $2,790.48; total, $116,806.32.

The extraordinary expenditures were: For buildings and improvements, $73,665.43; for extraordinary repairs, $4,060.78; for all other extraordinary expenses, $4,896.53; total, $82,622.74, making the aggregate expenditures for the year $199,429.06.

The cash balance at the close of the fiscal year was $625.14, and there was due from counties, cities and towns, $2,404.53; total, $3,029.67.

Of the ordinary expenditures, 45.2 per cent. was for salaries, wages and labor; 24.9 per cent. for provisions; 3.4 per cent. for household stores; 4.6 per cent. for clothing; 12 per cent. for fuel and light; 1.6 per cent. for hospital and medical supplies; 3.9 per cent. for shop, farm and garden supplies; .8 of 1 per cent for ordinary repairs; .9 of 1 per cent. for expenses of managers; and 2.7 per cent. for all other ordinary expenses, including a small expenditure for transportation and traveling expenses.

Chapter 644, Laws of 1901 (appropriation bill), appropriated for the salary of officers and employes, for the maintenance of the institution, and for ordinary repairs, $125,000.

Chapter 645, Laws of 1901 (supply bill), appropriated for maintenance, to be paid from the moneys turned into the treasury of the State under section 37, chapter 580, Laws of 1899, $8,000.

Chapter 330, Laws of 1901 (special act), appropriated for additional dormitories, $90,000; furnishing cottages and dormitories, $10,000; four cottages for employes, $4,000; water and sewerage connections, $1,500; steam pipe conduit to infirmary, $1,500; clearing and draining, fruit trees and vines, $1,200; hothouse and forcing beds for garden, $2,800; storage reservoir and storm-water drain, in addition to $800 appropriated by chapter 314, laws of 1900, $3,200; farm stock and implements, $1,000; two silos, $900; books and instruments, $1,500; graveling pond, $300; putting electric-light and telephone wires under ground, $3,750; feed-water heater, pump and fixtures, $550; finishing cold-storage and bakery building, in addition to balance of $100.11, $1,450; construction of third wing of trades-school building, in addition to unexpended balance of $4,199.62 under chapter 284, Laws of 1899, $2,000; brick conduit for steam heating pipes, $6,000; incidents of construction, infirmary buildings, $400; completion of dormitories provided by chapter 284, Laws of 1899, balance of $984.85; general repairs and improvements, $5,000; a total of $142,334.58.

Thus the total of all appropriations, special and general, was $275,334.58. .

The appropriations of $90,000 for additional dormitories and $10,000 for furnishing, remain intact.

For four cottages for employes, $4,000 was appropriated, and the lowest bids were $6,450, so the appropriation is intact.

For storage reservoir and storm-water drains, $4,000, the bids all exceeded the appropriation, and this appropriation also remains intact.

Plans have been made for putting the electric light and telephone wires underground, for which the sum of $3,750 was appropriated but no bids have been received; $6,199.62 was appropriated for third wing to trades-school building, and a contract has been made for the work.

The work of installing the conduit at the women's group, for which the sum of $6,000 was appropriated, is being done by days' labor, using the Colony teams and men.

All the other work provided for by chapter 330, Laws of 1901, has been done or is under contract.

The additional buildings intended to accommodate the "infirmary" class of epileptics have progressed toward completion during the past year, but are not yet ready for occupancy. It is promised, however, that they will soon be completed. They will constitute a very essential addition to the buildings of the Colony.

The delay in preparing the plans of the additional dormitory

buildings provided for by the last Legislature, has prevented
their commencement during the past summer. It was hoped and
expected when the appropriation was made that by the present
time they would have been well advanced toward completion.
The delay is unfortunate as it retards the development of the
Colony.

The Colony has made steady advancement in its work during
the past year. The number·of inmates has increased with the
opening of new buildings. A census of the dependent epileptics
in the almshouses and similar institutions in the State shows that,
on October 1, 1901, about 700 dependent epileptics were awaiting
transfer to the Colony. They can be taken into the Colony only
when it has the dormitory accommodations necessary for them.
The managers ask for an appropriation for this purpose, and it is
hoped that the plans for such additions will be ready for estimates
at an early date, that building operations may be expedited and
the almshouses be relieved of the care of epileptics.

The records of the Colony are being arranged in accordance
with a system which will make them readily available for study,
and assist in the classification of the important scientific facts and
other data which they contain.

The development of the several departments of this extensive
institution gives rise to many problems of administration; but as
indicated above, the most urgent need at the present time is for
sufficient dormitory accommodations for those dependents for
whom provision is still to be made. The second great need is
for the establishment of a greater variety of technical industrial
pursuits.

The agricultural feature of the Colony is a most important one,
as it has a direct bearing on the problem of self-maintenance,

6

but other occupations are required for those patients who are not
fitted for work in the gardens or on the farm. This need is even
more pressing in the winter season, when ordinary agricultural
employment must largely cease. In this direction it is proposed
to begin the manufacture of brooms, and a small appropriation is
asked for this purpose. This can be made a profitable industry,
even if the finished product be used solely for Colony work.
There are other similar light, safe industries which are well
adapted to the class of labor available in Craig Colony. Employment, properly regulated, is a curative agent, while enforced
idleness insures mental, moral and physical decay. It will,
therefore, be a wise expenditure of money to establish suitable
industries for the patients of the Colony capable of work; for
the effect of labor will supplement the scientific and remedial
efforts to cure the epileptic tendency.

When the buildings now under way and those provided for in
the appropriation of 1901 are completed, the Colony will be able
to accommodate 1,030 patients. As there are over 700 dependent
epileptics outside of Craig Colony, cared for in almshouses and
other institutions, it is apparent that provision must be made
for new cottages to receive them. Besides the epileptics actually resident in the Colony and comprising the number for whom
maintenance is required, there are patients who have been
relieved and discharged to attempt self-support, but in whom
the disease is so firmly seated as to make their need of future
care inevitable. Not less than 120 additional patients should
be provided for by an appropriation for new buildings.

The work of making roads and walks, and of grading the
grounds where required, must be continued to keep pace with
the building operations, and for this an appropriation will be
necessary.

The equipment of the Colony should be supplemented by a steam disinfecting plant. It will furnish an economical and sanitary method of sterilizing bedding, clothing and household goods, and should be installed at once.

An additional root cellar is needed for the proper storage of root crops. The present cellar cost $1,000, and holds 7,000 bushels. The large population requires much vegetable food, and for its storage another root cellar is required, and should be larger than the first.

The development of the Colony calls for more stock and additional teams, as well as farm implements to operate the new farm lands put under cultivation. At the present time teams have to be hired at a heavy expense.

More machinery is necessary for the dispatch of laundry work. Another washer and an extractor should be set up.

The Colony was established for the humane, scientific and curative treatment of epilepsy. To carry on scientific work requires a scientific equipment. Electricity, it is hoped, will be an effective agency in the control of epilepsy. An appropriation should be made for an electric machine and X-ray outfit.

The Board recommends the following appropriations, or so much thereof as may be necessary, to this institution:

For new buildings, making additional provision for the reception of the dependent epileptics of the State now in almshouses and other institutions, $60,000; for grading and making roads and walks, $6,000; for a steam disinfecting plant, $1,500; for fire alarm system, $1,000; for an additional root cellar, $1,200; for additional farm teams and equipment, farm stock and implements, $4,500; for additional machinery for the laundry, $750; for X-ray apparatus and electric machine, $400; for storm-water drains around the Village Green dormitory buildings, $2,000; for sheds and machinery at brickyard, $300; for balance to accept lowest bid for construction of four cottages for employes, $1,450, in addition to $4,000, appropriated by chapter 330, Laws of 1901; for new cottage for employe with sufficient room to provide accommodations for official visitors to the Colony detained over night, $2,500; making the special appropriations approved of, $81,600; maintenance appropriation, $135,000; making the total appropriation, $216,600.

NEW YORK STATE SOLDIERS AND SAILORS' HOME, BATH, STEUBEN COUNTY.

[Established 1878.]

This institution has capacity for 1,650 inmates. The number of members October 1, 1900, was 1,603, exclusive of 366 enrolled but absent; the admissions during the year were 978; total for the year, 2,947. There were 747 discharged and dropped out during the year; 124 died and 405 were absent, thus leaving at the close of the year 1,671 actually in the institution.

The average number present during the year was 1,596, and the average weekly cost of support, including the value of home and farm products consumed, $2.67; excluding the value of home and farm products consumed, $2.55.

The total receipts of the institution for the fiscal year ending September 30, 1901, were: Cash balance of the previous year, $85,640.67; from special appropriations, $50,932.74; from deficiency appropriations, $20,000; from unexpended appropriations of former years, $2,530.50; from general appropriations, $190,000; from all other sources, $770.66; total, $349,874.57.

The ordinary expenditures were: For salaries of officers, wages and labor, $64,773.05; for provisions, $76,636.85; for household stores, $7,514.29; for clothing, $21,549.90; for fuel and light, $17,964.73; for hospital and medical supplies, $4,135.80; for transportation and traveling expenses, $822.43; for shop, farm and garden supplies, $8,089.65; for ordinary repairs, $2,062.09; for expenses of trustees, $771.55; for remittance to State Treasurer, $770.66; for all other ordinary expenses, $8,210.16; total, $213,301.16.

The extraordinary expenditures were: $77,199.03, of which $58,958 was for buildings and improvements, $9,092.60 for extraordinary repairs, and $9,148.43 reverted to the State treasury, making the aggregate expenditures for the year, $290,500.19, and leaving a cash balance of $59,374.38.

Of the ordinary expenditures during the year, 30.5 per cent. was for salaries, wages and labor; 36 per cent. for provisions; 3.5 per cent. for household stores; 10.1 per cent. for clothing; 8.4 per cent. for fuel and light; 2 per cent. for hospital and medical supplies; .4 of 1 per cent. for transportation and traveling expenses; 3.8 per cent. for shop, farm and garden supplies; 1 per cent. for ordinary repairs; .4 of 1 per cent. for expenses of trustees; 3.9 per cent. for all other ordinary purposes.

Chapter 644, Laws of 1901 (appropriation bill), appropriated for support and maintenance, and for the transportation of applicants for admission, $225,000.

In addition to this chapter 645, Laws of 1901 (supply bill), appropriated for the deficiency on account of maintenance for the year ending September 30, 1901, $20,000, and reappropriated an unexpended balance of $1,278.87, which remained from $20,000 appropriated for the construction of the assembly hall by chapter 461, Laws of 1899, the said $1,278.87 to be used for the completion of the work on the assembly hall.

Chapter 709, Laws of 1901, appropriated the following amounts: For reconstruction and repair of the electric plant, $10,000; for reconstruction and repair of the steam plant, $5,000; and in addition the unexpended balance of appropriation made by chapter 395, Laws of 1900, $9,132.72; for reconstruction of boiler house and dynamo rooms, $15,000; for equipment of kitchen and annex, $250; for finishing 3 cottages, including cesspools, electric fixtures and walks, $1,600; for installing 3 kitchen ranges, $200; for general repairs to sanitary equipment, $950; for repairs to barracks 4 and 5 and hospital annex, $1,200; for general repairs to other buildings, $3,000; for filling and grading, $3,000; for reimbursing maintenance account, $2,530.50; for addition to headquarters building, $1,600; total, $50,473.24.

At the close of the fiscal year all the work provided for by chapter 709, Laws of 1901, had been contracted for, including the reconstruction and repair of the electric plant, and the reconstruction of the steam plant.

This Home is greatly overcrowded at the present time. It is supposed to have accommodations for 1,650 members, but it has been reported that already 2,134 members have been admitted to the Home. A number of these are away on furlough, but the maximum number for whom accommodations are provided has long been greatly exceeded; consequently members having no room in the dormitories are compelled to sleep in the basements. As a general rule the use of basements for dormitories or other living purposes is detrimental to health. In the Home at Bath this general principle is sustained by the fact that many of the basements are damp and ill-ventilated.

The members of the Home are now well fed, receive proper medical attendance, and have pleasant surroundings with opportunities for amusement. If in addition to these things there was ample barrack room, so that none of the members would have to sleep in basements, it could be said that the provision for these old soldiers is admirable. The Home maintains a band of music for the entertainment of the veterans, and has a library containing a large number of books sufficiently diversified in character to meet the wants of the men. With books, daily papers, magazines and various games, an amusement hall ready for other sources of enjoyment, the Home makes provision for the rational entertainment of its members.

The greatest need of the Home, after additional barrack room, is a suitably equipped hospital. The erection of such a building will enable the present hospital to be used for a barrack wherein the incurable class of cases can be domiciled. This will relieve the congested condition which prevails in the barracks, and will give opportunity for a better building with a more adequate equipment for the large number of sick which may be expected.

The State must continue to make provision for dependent veterans for many years to come. The time will probably not arrive when a home of this character will be no longer needed; but should such time come, the entire plant will continue in beneficent service for other uses of the State. Its equipment should be made satisfactory in order that the veterans whose strength and valor were devoted to patriotic service in the days of young manhood may not lack anything essential to comfort in their declining years.

The cemetery at the Home is now nearly filled, and it is necessary to prepare an adjoining tract of land for this purpose.

There is great need of a gate-house at the entrance to the grounds. The present structure has outlived its usefulness, and should be replaced by a suitable building.

The building now used for a place of detention within the grounds is entirely unfitted for such purpose. A new guard-house should take its place, and this, serving as it must as a lock-up, should be fitted with sanitary conveniences and be made comfortable for those who must be placed in it for infraction of the rules.

The enlargement of the main dining-hall this year has furnished room for dish-washing, but a further extension is needed for various purposes. This extension in the rear of the dining-hall would furnish ample room for storage, and also permit of toilet facilities.

As the dining-room is so very large, a number of entrances have been arranged by which the men may have ready access to their tables. They gather at these entrances long before the time for serving the meals. In order that they may have shelter during inclement weather it is desirable that a covered arcade or light colonnaded approach, extended from the main entrance toward the main road, be constructed. This will not only afford a desirable shelter, but also prove a favorite walk with many of the men.

For additional garden and farm land the adjoining Faucett farm, of 153¾ acres, has been selected by the trustees. This can be purchased for $45 per acre, which appears to be a reasonable price, and an appropriation should be made for this purpose. It is important for the Home to raise as large a portion of the vegetables consumed there as possible.

In nearly all of the buildings the ventilating system is

defective. This is especially true of the hospital. The basement is damp and the foul air is drawn directly from the cellars.
As a consequence the recovery of the sick is retarded, and the
health of the attendants is imperiled. A new system of ventilation should be installed by which pure air may be delivered into
the several wards and other parts of the hospital. The barrack
buildings should also receive consideration, and the ventilating
shafts be arranged so as to make it impossible to draw the polluted air of the basements, loaded with tobacco fumes, into the
dormitories.

One of the problems of a public institution of this character
is connected with the reception of new members. Many men
enter the Home with their clothing in very bad condition. For
the sake of the general health and to prevent the spread of
disease it is essential that a fumigating apparatus be installed
in the main laundry. This will permit of the sterilization of all
clothing and bedding.

For the same reason an additional wash-wheel is needed for
the hospital laundry. At the present time all the clothing of
the attendants and patients goes into the same washing-machine.
An additional wheel will enable the assistants in the laundry
to keep the clothing of the physicians, nurses and attendants
entirely apart from the clothing of the patients in the wards.

The sewerage, sinks and closets of the hospital are in need
of repairs, and an appropriation is asked for them. This is
apart from the general repairs necessary to the main barracks
and other buildings, for which a separate account is made.

The stables for the work horses of the Home and the wagon
sheds used by the details are now so dilapidated that new structures are needed.

The carriage house and stable of the Commandant are completely worn out. Located as they are where seepage from the hill passes under the floors, it is impossible to keep the floors dry. For this reason an appropriation is requested for a new carriage house and stable for the Commandant.

No matter what may be the ultimate use of the present hospital building, the several wards should have verandas, so that the patients may get out into the sun and fresh air. Several wards are equipped with such verandas, but it will be better if all are so arranged, and if the verandas are provided with sliding glass they can be used in the winter season as well as in the summer.

During the past year progress has been made in the laying of cement walks through the grounds, and this work should be continued until suitable walks are laid leading from the several barracks to all the other buildings and to the outlets from the grounds.

The present accommodations for the storage of second-hand clothing, the repair of uniforms and general tailor work are very poor. A small building arranged for these purposes should be erected and equipped. This will prove a good investment.

It is necessary that the chapel be extended. Its present arrangements are primitive, and at a slight expense the chapel can be made satisfactory.

A constant menace to the welfare of the Home is the presence of a large number of saloons at the entrance to the grounds. All the saloons on Belfast street are supported mainly by the pension moneys of the members of the Home. They are the source of almost every violation of the rules, and should be suppressed in view of the fact that a well-conducted canteen is maintained upon the Home grounds. In this the sale of drinks can be controlled, but these saloons are independent of the Home. A law should be passed making it il'egal to maintain a saloon within one mile of the Home grounds.

The Board recommends the following appropriations, or so much thereof as may be necessary, to this institution:

For carriage house and stable for the commandant, $2,500; for stable for work horses, and wagon sheds, $3,000; for gate-house at entrance to Home, $800; for house of detention or lock-up, $1,200; for cement walks, $2,400; for general repairs to barracks and other buildings, $5,000; for second-hand store, tailoring and repair shop, $2,400; for purchase of Faucett farm, 153¾ acres, at $45 per acre, $6,918.75; for grading and filling at new cemetery, $2,000; for sewerage, sinks and closets at hospital, $1,615; for ventilation system in hospital, $3,500; for electric fans for hospital wards, $912; for addition to chapel, $600; for new convalescent barracks, $45,000; for light arcade at main entrance to dining-hall as a shelter to the members of the Home, $5,000; for isolation pavilion for tuberculosis, $25,000; for enlargement of kitchen, $2,500; for fumigating plant in main laundry, $1,500; for additional machinery in hospital laundry, $250; for spring house on hill, $400; for completion of rearrangement of steam and power plant, $5,000; for pipe covering in assembly hall, $400; for fire protection, $3,000; for smoke stack at power house, $2,000; for steam-pipe conduit, pipes and covering, $10,500; for fire house, $900; for galvanized iron casings on heating stacks, $1,000; for hot water heater in laundry, $400; for plumbing improvements in barracks A, B and C, $250; for spray baths in hospital, $1,800; for telephone system, $1,000; for fire alarm system, $2,000; making the special appropriation approved of,

$140,745.75; maintenance appropriation, $225,000; making the total appropriation, $365,745.75.

NEW YORK STATE WOMAN'S RELIEF CORPS HOME, OXFORD, CHENANGO COUNTY.

[Established 1894.]

The Home has capacity for 150 inmates. The number of inmates present October 1, 1900, was 92, and 57 were admitted during the year, making the total number under care 149. During the year 8 died and 32 were discharged, leaving 109 October 1, 1901, of whom 32 were men and 77 women.

The average number for the year was 100, and the average weekly cost of support, including the value of home and farm products consumed, $3.93; excluding the value of home and farm products consumed, $3.68.

The receipts for the year ending September 30, 1901, were: From cash on hand at the beginning of the year, $306.16; from special appropriations, $51,777.11; from general appropriations, $19,500; total, $71,583.27.

The ordinary expenditures were: For salaries of officers, $1,500; for wages and labor, $5,838.76; for provisions, $4,615.98; for household stores, $590.32; for clothing, $623.04; for fuel and light, $2,510.73; for hospital and medical supplies, $579.05; for shop, farm and garden supplies, $1,394.59; for ordinary repairs, $98.41; for expenses of managers, $673.57; for all other ordinary expenses, $741.60; total, $19,166.05.

The extraordinary expenditures are reported as $51,838.49 for buildings and improvements, making the total ordinary and extraordinary expenditures for the year $71,004.54, and leaving $578.73 as balance in cash at the close of the fiscal year.

The outstanding indebtedness was $40 for bills unpaid.

Of the ordinary expenditures, 38.3 per cent. was for salaries, wages and labor; 24.1 per cent. for provisions; 3 per cent. for household stores; 3.3 per cent. for clothing; 13.1 per cent. for fuel and light; 3 per cent. for hospital and medical supplies; 7.3 per cent. for shop, farm and garden supplies; .5 of 1 per cent. for ordinary repairs; 3.5 per cent. for expenses of managers, and 3.9 per cent. for all other ordinary expenses.

Chapters 644 and 645, Laws of 1901 (appropriation and supply bills), appropriated for maintenance, furnishing and repairs, $26,800. (Maintenance, $24,100; furnishing, $2,000; repairs, $700).

Chapter 307, Laws of 1901, appropriated for the further enlargement and equipment of this Home: For dining-room building and corridor to cottage C, $19,600; for flooring and steel beams for coal shed, $505; for engine room floor, $135; for brick conduit for steam pipes, $4,500; for placing pipes in conduit, $700; for sheds, piggery, corn-crib and hen-house, $1,878; for developing water supply, $10,000; for wire fencing and gates, $300; for work horses (team of), $200; for furnishing, $2,000; for seeding and grading, $2,000; on account of cottage A, $220.18; for administration building (complete), $7,500; total, $49,538.18.

All the work for which appropriations were made by chapter 307, Laws of 1901, except placing pipes in conduit, for which $700 was appropriated, and for seeding and grading grounds and grading road to boiler house, $2,000, is either under way or under contract.

Since the last annual report, progress has been made in the building operations connected with this Home. The new dormitory has been completed and is partly occupied. A new administration building is rapidly approaching completion, and a large dining-room intended to accommodate all the members of the Home will soon be ready for occupancy.

The conduits for steam pipes are under way, and when the pipes are covered with asbestos this portion of the equipment will be practically completed.

The laundry building is too small for the work which has to be done. The machinery is crowded into the limited space until it is dangerous for the attendants to walk about. It is necessary to enlarge the building so as to provide room for the additional machinery required. Preparation was made for this enlargement when the laundry building was constructed, and an addition 25 feet square can be added at small expense. This should be done at once.

As this institution depends upon its own power for heating and lighting, it is essential that it be thoroughly equipped. The engine and dynamo which furnish electric light for the Home represent only one-half of the equipment intended. It may break down at any moment, in which case the Home would be left without light. An additional engine and dynamo, a duplicate of the present plant, should be added to the equipment immediately.

This institution has no resident physician. It is connected with Oxford by telephone, and the physician can be called at any moment day or night. It is desirable, however, that the hospital be under the supervision of a trained attendant. It has been found difficult to secure a competent trained nurse, but in time one will be found. Meanwhile it is fortunate that there is very little sickness in the Home.

This Home is fortunate also in the matter of its discipline. There is seldom an occasion to punish members for violation of the rules. Intoxication is rare, and there is no trouble experienced from the liquor habit.

The enlargement of the Home will enable it to receive applicants who now are necessarily denied admission, but another cottage is necessary to complete the plan of the Home. This will provide four connected cottages for the use of the Home, and will probably be sufficient to meet all its requirements for some years to come. A hospital will be needed, for although up to the present time the health of the inmates has been remarkably good, it is to be expected that with advancing age these men and women will require hospital treatment. At the present time the sick are cared for in their own rooms and in small wards in the several buildings. This distributes the sick over the entire group of buildings, and adds to the difficulty of waiting upon them. A properly equipped hospital building separated from the dormitories will be an advantage.

The completion of the dining-room building will provide comfortable sleeping rooms above it for the female help, and it is a source of satisfaction that consideration has been given to the need of recreation rooms for these attendants.

A residence is required for the farmer, for whom no provision of this kind has been made.

In the equipment of the buildings the lavatories have proven to some degree unsatisfactory. A small appropriation will remedy the defects and make them as intended.

A number of radiators are required to warm the corridors connecting the buildings. These with their fittings, when connected with the steam supply, will make the entire group of buildings comfortable for all the inmates. As the cor-

ridors furnish sitting rooms and are the favorite place of the
aged members of the Home, it is essential that they have sufficient warmth.

The cold-storage rooms are not entirely satisfactory. Some
defects have shown themselves, and it is desirable that the ice-
house connected with the cold-storage be made capable of better
service. A small sum expended upon this work will remedy the
defects and promote economy.

In the same interest the steam pipes in the basement should
be protected. Their exposure wastes the heat and makes the
basements unsuitable for storage of any kind. All these pipes
can be covered with asbestos for a moderate sum, and the cost
of the improvement will be repaid by the saving in the coal now
consumed for wasted heat.

The Board recommends the following appropriations, or so
much thereof as may be necessary, to this institution:

For the erection of cottage D and corridor, $30,000; for erec-
tion of a residence for the farmer, $1,500; to pay W. P. Buckley
for foundation stone furnished for laundry building, $40; for
flagging and grading, $500; for engine and dynamo, $1.750; for
steam radiators and making all connections in corridors, $100;·
for farming utensils and necessary supplies, $550; for erecting
veranda, $50; for extension of laundry building, $1,000; for
changes in lavatories, $150; repairs to ice-house and cold-storage
rooms, $300; for hood for kitchen range, $50; for covering steam
pipes, $1,400; for boiler and connections, $3,500; for piping and
pipe covering in conduit from power-house to buildings, $4,000;
for improving the efficiency of steam plant, $250; for wagon,
horse and sleigh belonging to the late Treasurer, Major Treadwell, and used by the Home, $325; making the special appropri-

ations approved of, $45,465; maintenance appropriation, $25,000; making the total appropriation, $70,465.

THOMAS ASYLUM FOR ORPHAN AND DESTITUTE INDIAN CHILDREN, IROQUOIS, ERIE COUNTY.

[Established 1878.]

The Asylum has capacity for 128 inmates. The number of inmates present October 1, 1900, was 126. During the year 29 were received and 13 discharged and transferred to other schools, leaving a population of 142, October 1, 1901, of whom 60 were boys and 82 girls. The average number during the year was 129, and the average weekly cost of support, including the value of home and farm products consumed, $3.98; excluding the value of home and farm products consumed, $3.57.

The receipts for the year ending September 30, 1901, were: From cash balance at the beginning of the year, $187.84; from special appropriations, $35,139.28; from general appropriations, $24,000; from other sources, $11.81; total, $59,338.93.

The ordinary expenditures were as follows: For salaries of officers, wages and labor, $11,530.95; for provisions, $3,186.76; for household stores, $594.81; for clothing, $1,254.77; for fuel and light, $4,177.04; for hospital and medical supplies, $53.48; for transportation and traveling expenses, $90.39; for shop, farm and garden supplies, $1,494.56; for ordinary repairs, $289.64; for expenses of managers, $304.80; for remittance to State Treasurer, $11.81; for all other ordinary expenses, $1,062.56; total, $24,051.57. The total expenditures were $59,190.85, the additional $35,139.28 being for buildings and improvements. The cash balance at the close of the year was $148.08, and there was no outstanding indebtedness.

Of the ordinary expenditures 47.9 per cent. was for salaries.

wages and labor; 13.3 per cent. for provisions; 2.5 per cent. for household stores; 5.2 per cent. for clothing; 17.4 per cent. for fuel and light; .2 of 1 per cent. for hospital and medical supplies ; .4 of 1 per cent. for transportation and traveling expenses; 6.2 per cent for shop, farm and garden supplies; 1.2 per cent. for ordinary repairs; 1.3 per cent. for expenses of managers, and 4.4 per cent. for all other ordinary expenses.

Chapter 644, Laws of 1901 (appropriation bill), for maintenance and for salaries of officers and teachers appropriated $24,000.

Chapter 645, Laws of 1901 (supply bill), for deficiency on account of maintenance for the fiscal year ending September 30, 1901, appropriated $2,000.

Chapter 642, Laws of 1901 (supplemental supply bill), for grading of grounds appropriated $7,500.

Chapter 707, Laws of 1901 (special act), made the following appropriations: For the erection of one brick dormitory building having capacity for 40 inmates (boys), $13,000; for steel tower and tank for water supply, $2,500; for repairs and alterations to hospital, $500; for fire apparatus, $350; for grading, $2,500. The special new appropriations amounted to $26,350, and the total appropriations to $52,350.

No contracts have been made for the erection of the brick dormitory building, for which $13,000 was appropriated, nor for the steel tower and tank for water supply, $2,500.

The work under the other appropriations has been contracted for.

Additional and improved accommodation provided by the new buildings has made it possible to do more satisfactory work, and as the Asylum assumes its final form it is taking rank with other successful institutions devoted to Indian education.

The appropriation of $13,000 for an additional dormitory has proven insufficient, owing to the increased cost of material. It will be necessary to add to this appropriation at least $3,000 to secure the immediate erection of this dormitory. Another building of the same size is needed for the accommodation of the boys. This will take the place of the dangerous frame building now used as a dormitory, and will complete the original plan for the dormitories adopted in 1896 by the State authorities and the Board of Managers.

An appropriation is also needed to build a new power-house, chimney stack, and connecting subways. The site selected for the power-house is sufficiently removed from the main group of buildings to diminish the danger of fire, and at the same time provide adequate room for the heating and power plants.

Conduits, tanks and fittings in connection with the new water tower are necessary, as is also an additional dynamo.

This Asylum is the only State institution which affords education and shelter to destitute and orphan Indian children, and should be thoroughly equipped to prepare these Indian wards of the State for the responsibilities of life. The time is, probably, not far distant when all Indians will be full citizens, and the State of New York owes it to itself to see that those for whom it is directly responsible shall be ready for the duties and privileges of citizenship. It is not enough that these children be fed, clothed and sheltered; they must be properly trained. An education which falls short of a full equipment for the duties and opportunities of the strenuous life of our modern civilization is incomplete. It tends to discouragement—to the loss of that heart and hope which is the mainspring of success. This is especially true of our Indian wards. They enter our competitive life under a heavy

handicap. They are easily discouraged by failure, and in addition must face the conscious or unconscious opposition of a
dominant race. Hence their education and training should be
such as will overcome the natural handicap under which they
labor, and furnish the means for self-support gained in honorable and profitable employment.

From another consideration this Asylum deserves hearty support. The children are gathered from all the Indian reservations of this State, and take back to these reservations the
spirit of modern civilization. Each Indian child, thoroughly
trained and educated, becomes a living force for good to the
older Indians. The work of the school is felt in the homes and
quickens a commendable ambition for better things. It thus
acts as a check to prevent an increase of pauperism, and promotes thrift and enterprise. Thus the Asylum does a double
work and exerts an influence on the adult Indians, as well as
upon the children in its care. It makes for the mental, moral
and physical welfare of all the Indians in the State of New
York, and is, therefore, an important factor in the promotion of
the general welfare.

The Board recommends the following appropriations, or so
much thereof as may be necessary, for the institution:

For one brick building, having capacity for 40 inmates (boys)
and attendants, $17,500; for additional appropriation to supple-
ment the appropriation of $13,000 for a brick building, made by
chapter 707, Laws of 1901, $4,500; for furnishing, $600; for conduit, piping, tanks, and fittings in connection with the new water
tower, $3,000; for additional dynamo, wiring and lights, $3,000;
for moving and converting " Nursery " into a laundry building,
$2,000; for flooring in basements of present dormitories, $400;

for labor of installing plumbing fixtures in hospital addition, $100; for power house, chimney stack and connecting subways, $15,000; for new boilers and connections, and removing plant to new power-house, $6,500; making the special appropriations approved of, $52,600; maintenance appropriation, $25,000; making the total appropriation, $77,600.

NEW YORK STATE SCHOOL FOR THE BLIND, BATAVIA, GENESEE COUNTY.

[Established 1865.]

This School has capacity for 120 pupils. The number of pupils October 1, 1900, was 100, and 34 were received during the year. The number in attendance October 1, 1901, was 109, of whom 60 were boys and 49 were girls. The average number during the year was 121, and the average weekly cost of support, including the value of home products ($277.89), $6.10; excluding the value of home products, $6.06.

The receipts of this institution for the fiscal year ending September 30, 1901, were as follows: Cash balance from the preceding year, $74.12; from special appropriations, $3,528.35; from general appropriations, $38,300.71; from all other sources, $1,403.57; total, $43,306.75.

The ordinary expenditures were: For salaries of officers, wages and labor, $23,922.27; for provisions, $7,027.01; for household stores, $355.75; for clothing, $501.88; for fuel and light, $3,483.22; for hospital and medical supplies, $175.58; for transportation and traveling expenses, $136.09; for shop, farm and garden supplies, $1,110.17; for ordinary repairs, $41.36; for expenses of trustees, $236.16; returned to State Treasurer, $1,403.57; for all other ordinary expenses, $1,279.96; total ordinary expenditures, $39,673.02.

The total extraordinary expenditures were $3,528.35 for improvements, making the aggregate expenditures $43,201.37. The only asset October 1, 1901, was the balance in cash, $105.38.

Of the ordinary expenditures during the year, 62.5 per cent. was for salaries, wages and labor; 18.3 per cent. for provisions; .9 of 1 per cent. for household stores; 1.3 per cent. for clothing; 9.1 per cent. for fuel and light; .5 of 1 per cent. for hospital and medical supplies; .4 of 1 per cent. for transportation and traveling expenses; 2.9 per cent for shop, farm and garden supplies; .6 of 1 per cent. for expenses of trustees, and 3.5 per cent. for all other ordinary expenses, including a small expenditure for ordinary repairs.

Chapter 644, Laws of 1901 (appropriation bill), appropriated for the maintenance and instruction of the inmates $38,000; and the supply bill, chapter 645, made a further appropriation for maintenance of $2,000.

Chapter 405, Laws of 1901 (special act), appropriated the following sums for the benefit of the school: For repairs and betterments (in addition to $1,500 appropriated by chapter 419, Laws of 1900), $1,500; for electric wiring and fixtures, $2,500; for lockers in gymnasium, $446; for library and apparatus, $1,000; for painting woodwork, walls and ironwork, $1,000; for fire extinguishers, $100; a total of $6,546.

Thus the total of all appropriations, special and general, was $46,546.

All the sums appropriated for extraordinary repairs for the State School for the Blind at Batavia have been either expended or the work is contracted for.

The general conditions which prevailed in this school at the time of the last annual report continue substantially unchanged.

The same methods in educational and industrial training have been pursued, the test of scholarship, so far as possible, being the Regents' examination papers. These tests, applied from time to time, have indicated fairly satisfactory results so far as mental discipline is concerned. The work of teaching has been facilitated by the use of machines for printing music and literature in the "New York" and "Braille" point systems. The use of the two systems of print does not conduce to satisfactory results. The efforts of the school should be concentrated upon one method. To compel pupils to learn the two points, results in a decided loss of facility. The simplest and the best method of point print, and that only, should be made use of in the State School for the Blind.

The range of industrial education is very narrow, the school confining its instruction to broom making, chair caning and piano tuning for the boys, with sewing as the main employment for the girls. It is an unwise policy for the State to maintain and but partially to educate this unfortunate class of its wards. The education should be sufficient to assure comfortable self-support if faithfully used. To limit the possible employments to the four industries named, is to make it certain that the majority of the blind educated at the expense of the State in this institution will continue either wholly or partially dependent upon public aid.

The President of the Board of Managers of this school has publicly expressed disappointment at the work accomplished by the school, his judgment being the result of nine years' observation. There is no good reason why this school should not make a large majority of its pupils self-supporting men and women. The State makes liberal appropriations; it has ample facilities;

and the number of pupils is not so great as to prevent individual attention on the part of the teachers.

The Superintendent of the school, Professor Gardner Fuller, having resigned his position at the close of the school term, his successor, Mr. Olin H. Burritt, formerly principal of the Franklin Academy at Malone, was chosen through competitive examination held by the State Civil Service Commission, to fill the vacancy.

The new gymnasium has been opened. It has a suitable equipment of apparatus, and under a competent instructor will prove decidedly helpful to the work of the school.

Owing to the fact that there are serious defects in the plumbing of the building, the general health of the school was seriously threatened during the year by the appearance of a number of cases of measles, mumps and typhoid and scarlet fevers. These cases compelled the employment of special nurses, and were fortunately controlled, but until the causes are removed it is feared similar outbreaks will occur again.

The Board recommends the following appropriations, or so much thereof as may be necessary, to this institution:

For fire-escapes from second and third floors of the school building and extension of fire-escapes in the court, $2,000; for fire-risers and hose in main building, $500; for improving economy of steam plant, $1,000; for steam cooking outfit, $750; for renovating plumbing, $3,500; for steel ceiling in main building, $1,000; for pianos to replace those worn out,$1,200; for team of horses, $300; making the special appropriations approved of, $10,250; maintenance appropriation, $38,000; making the total appropriation, $48,250.

NEW YORK STATE HOSPITAL FOR THE CARE OF CRIPPLED
AND DEFORMED CHILDREN, TARRYTOWN, WESTCHESTER
COUNTY.

[Established 1900.]

This institution has capacity for 25 patients. It was informally opened for the reception of patients on the 7th of December,
1900, when 5 patients were received, and formally opened with
appropriate ceremonies on the 17th of May, 1901.

During the year 14 boys and 10 girls were admitted and 2 boys
and 3 girls discharged, leaving a population October 1, 1901, of
12 boys and 7 girls. The average number of patients during the
ten months of the fiscal year was 13, and the average weekly
cost of support, including the value of home and farm products
consumed, was $11.25; excluding the value of home and farm
products consumed, $11.25.

The receipts during the fiscal year ending September 30, 1901,
were: From interest on deposits, $17.28; from general appropri-
ations, $10,012.31; total, $10,029.59.

The expenditures from the general appropriation were: For
salaries of officers, wages and labor, $1,868.44; for provisions,
$1,344.93; for household stores, $210.10; for clothing, $9.75; for
fuel and light, $399.50; for hospital and medical supplies,
$452.21; for transportation and traveling expenses, $120.95; for
shop, farm and garden supplies, $13.85; for ordinary repairs,
$15.88; for expenses of managers, $626.35; for all other ordinary
expenses, $1,371.74; total, $6,433.70.

The extraordinary expenditures were $3,290.39, for furnishing
and equipment, making the total expenditures for the year
$9,724.09. The cash on hand October 1, 1901, the only asset,
was $305.50.

Of the ordinary expenditures during the year, 29 per cent. was
for salaries, wages and labor; 20.9 per cent. for provisions; 3.3

per cent. for household stores; .1 of 1 per cent. for clothing; 6.2 per cent. for fuel and light; 7 per cent. for hospital and medical supplies; 2 per cent, for transportation and traveling expenses; .2 of 1 per cent. for shop, farm and garden supplies; .3 of 1 per cent. for ordinary repairs; 9.7 per cent. for expenses of managers; and 21.3 per cent. for all other ordinary expenses.

Chapter 369, Laws of 1900 (special act), appropriated $15,000 to establish the institution. The sum of $5,000 contributed by private individuals was expended in preparing the buildings for service as a hospital.

The Legislature of 1901, by chapter 701, made an appropriation of $4,250 for extraordinary expenses. This amount was to be expended as follows: For equipment of operating room, $2,000; for splints, braces, and other orthopedic apparatus, $500; for work bench, tools and accessories for repairing apparatus. $250; for isolation pavilion of wood construction for contagious diseases, $1,500; for maintenance the Legislature appropriated $10,000.

Of this appropriation, the item of $1,500 for an isolation pavilion has not yet been used.

The law establishing the hospital provides that it "shall be for the care and treatment of any indigent children who may have resided in the State of New York for a period not less than one year, who are crippled or deformed or are suffering from disease from which they are likely to become crippled or deformed. No patient suffering from an incurable disease shall be admitted to such hospital. No patient shall be received, except upon satisfactory proof, made to the Surgeon-in-Chief, by the next of kin, guardian, or a State, town, or county officer, under rules to be established by the Board of Managers, showing that the patient is unable to pay for private treatment. Such proof shall be by affidavit. If there was an attending officer before the patient entered the hospital, it shall be accompanied by the certificate of such physician, giving the previous history and condition of the patient."

This hospital is located in Tarrytown, upon a plot of ground fronting the Hudson river. The tract contains about four acres. Upon this a roomy private residence stood, which has been altered and repaired and is now in service as the Hospital. It is well located and, except that it is too small to permit of the reception of many patients, serves admirably for an experimental hospital. It is arranged to accommodate 25 children, but with this number and the necessary attendants the building is greatly crowded.

During the pleasant weather the children play on the Hospital grounds. Until the building formerly used as a carriage house was altered, the children were confined to the house on stormy days. Friends of the institution contributed funds to alter the carriage house and equip it as a playroom, and when the heating apparatus is installed the children will be able to use it as such.

Owing to the experimental nature of this institution nothing has been done in the way of providing occupation for the children; consequently their time is spent in efforts to amuse themselves. If this Hospital is to be a permanent institution, it will be necessary to provide facilities for their proper instruction.

In all, 58 applications for admission to this Hospital were received. Many of these applicants were not eligible on account of their incurable condition. Others who were eligible were not admitted because after application they did not report for examination.

There are in the institutions of the State, according to the reports of the inspectors of the State Board of Charities, 101 children afflicted with deformity or some form of disability, which with proper treatment should have been relieved or cured. Many of them are subjects for the good offices of this hospital.

The managers state that their future work requires that the objects of the hospital, and the class of patients received and treated by it, should be known better throughout the State. At present the tendency is to send to the hospital the semi-idiotic children, with the deformities of spastic paralysis and hemiplegia, whose condition, due to some brain lesion, is practically incurable. It does not seem to be known that patients with hip disease, spinal disease, white swelling, ankle-joint disease, club foot, knock knee, bowlegs, infantile paralysis and lateral curvature of the spine will be received and treated. These are all more or less curable, and with a few exceptions are eligible to the treatment of the hospital. All the patients received by the hospital need necessarily a prolonged treatment, sometimes for five or more years. These patients should receive mental instruction while under treatment, and to this end it is recommended that a competent teacher to undertake the industrial as well as the mental training of the children be employed at once. Ample school facilities are necessary, and ultimately an industrial school should be made an adjunct to the work.

The site of the hospital, while ample for the present needs, is not large enough to meet the demand of coming years. It will ultimately require a large tract of land, preferably among the Westchester hills, for a permanent site for its future buildings, and such buildings should be especially planned for hospital service. The Board recommends a maintenance appropriation of $15,000, or so much thereof as may be necessary, to this institution.

NEW YORK STATE HOSPITAL FOR THE TREATMENT OF INCIPIENT PULMONARY TUBERCULOSIS, RAYBROOK, ESSEX COUNTY.

[Established 1900.]

By chapter 416 of the Laws of 1900 the Legislature established the New York State Hospital for the Treatment of Incipient Pulmonary Tuberculosis. This act requires the appointment by the Governor of five Trustees, whose duty it shall be to select a site for such hospital, and after the approval of such site by the State Board of Health and the Forest Preserve Board, to proceed with the construction and equipment of suitable buildings upon plans adopted by them and approved by the State Architect and the State Board of Charities as soon as the necessary appropriation is secured.

In accordance with the provisions of the statute the Governor appointed as trustees Howard Townsend and Walter Jennings, of New York; Dr. Willis G. Macdonald, Albany; Dr. John H. Pryor, Buffalo, and Dr. Frank E. Kendall, of Saranac Lake. Mr. Townsend was subsequently elected President of the board.

By chapter 691 of the Laws of 1901 the sum of $100,000, or so much thereof as may be necessary, was appropriated for the construction of all the necessary and suitable buildings for this institution whenever the site shall have been chosen. These buildings are to furnish accommodations for at least 100 patients, besides the officers, employes and attendants of said institution, and the appropriation is intended to provide for the heating, lighting, plumbing, laundry fixtures, and water supply, as well as for the construction of roads leading thereto, and for the equipment and furnishing of the hospital with all the necessary fixtures, furniture and implements required for successful work.

At the close of the fiscal year for which this report is made no site had been selected by the Commission, composed of the Governor, the President *pro tem.* of the Senate, and the Speaker of the Assembly, intrusted with the location of the hospital. The one at Raybrook was, however, chosen before the assembling of the Legislature.

The State Board of Charities has no responsibility in connection with the location of the hospital. The duty of the Board begins with the approval of plans for the buildings. Until such plans are presented to the Board for approval, it is powerless to expedite the work of the hospital.

THE DEAF.

The following table gives the name and location of each institution in the State which is authorized by law to maintain and educate deaf pupils at public expense, and gives also the number and sex of the pupils in attendance October 1, 1901. All of the schools named receive both State and county pupils, the distinction being one of age and manner of compensation.

INSTITUTIONS.	Male.	Female.	Total.
New York Institution for the Instruction of the Deaf and Dumb, One Hundred and Sixty-third street, New York....	261	153	414
Le Couteulx St. Mary's Institution for the Improved Instruction of Deaf-Mutes, Buffalo	85	74	159
Institution for the Improved Instruction of Deaf-Mutes, Lexington avenue, New York.........	104	104	208
St. Joseph's Institute for the the Improved Instruction of Deaf-Mutes:			
Fordham Branch...	....	110	110
Brooklyn Branch...	....	69	69
Westchester Branch......	199	....	199
Central New York Institution for Deaf-Mutes, Rome	58	60	118
Western New York Institution for Deaf-Mutes, Rochester.......	83	93	176
Northern New York Institution for Deaf-Mutes, Malone.........	42	36	78
Albany Home School for the Oral Instruction of the Deaf, Albany	19	14	33
Total..	851	713	1,564

The above statistics show an increase of 2 over the total number of pupils in school on September 30, 1900. Last year's report showed a loss of 9 over 1899. In the latter year the reported attendance was 1,571, which statistics show to be the maximum reached in this State. This was an increase of 274 over the number of pupils present on September 30, 1892 (1,297). In the preceding decade the attendance remained stationary, the remarkable fact being noted that the attendance on the same date in 1882 was also 1,297. This was in spite of a 20 per cent. increase in the population of the State from 1882 to 1892.

It is evident that the existing school accommodations for the deaf in this State are entirely inadequate; that the increase in their attendance has been much below the normal increase to be expected with the general growth of population. There are no available figures as to the number of teachable deaf of school age not under instruction, but it would seem that this is quite small. The total includes the feeble-minded and under-average deaf children, who should be specially taught in a school set apart for their exclusive care. This should preferably be one of the existing schools.

The several schools have been visited and inspected once in each quarter by the Board's Inspector of State Charitable Institutions. His work has covered only the management and care of the property and general treatment of the pupils, as this Board discontinued its examination of the educational work on the assumption of that work in 1900 by the Superintendent of Public Instruction.

It is found that the pupils continue to be well cared for in general respects, and that the equipment of each school, with one exception, is adequate to the demands upon it. This exception

is the Albany school, where, with a notable increase in attendance, the building is extremely crowded and is in many respects
unsafe and unsuitable for the housing of children.

One matter concerning the welfare of the pupils deserves brief
mention here. This Board recommended in 1895 that each
school be equipped with a gymnasium suitably furnished for
systematic physical instruction of its pupils. After five years
it is noted with regret that but three schools have gymnasiums
worthy of the name, and that in two only is there regular physical instruction.

Attention is called to the lack of uniformity in the bookkeeping
systems of the several schools, and it is urged that the subject
be given consideration with a view to securing the advantages
of a common system in all.

NEW INCORPORATIONS.

During the year 1901 the Board approved the incorporation of
the following named institutions, societies and associations,
fifteen in number:

1.—" The Servants of Relief for Incurable Cancer;" principal
office, New York City. Formed for the " establishment of a free
home for persons suffering from incurable cancer, and the care
and nursing of such persons." Approved, January 24, 1901.

2.—" St. Faith's House;" principal office, Tarrytown. Formed
for the " rescue of women and wayward girls through the agency
of shelter, teaching and other means; the establishment and
maintenance of a house where women may be received, cared for
and treated during pregnancy or during or after delivery; the
boarding or keeping them and their nursing children, educating
and training them in religious teachings and exercises in accordance with the doctrine, discipline and worship of the Protestant
Episcopal Church." Approved, February 28, 1901.

3.—"The Benevolent Society of Divine Providence;" principal office, New York City. Formed for the "care and education of the orphan and other destitute children of Cuba." Approved, April 10, 1901.

4.—"Daughters of Abraham Friendly Relief Association;" principal office, Albany. Formed "to give assistance consisting mainly of friendly loans of money to be repaid without interest, in a specified time (usually in installments), to needy persons; and to render such pecuniary relief to deserving persons, such aid and assistance shall be rendered absolutely gratis, and without any charge whatsoever, from contribution and gifts of the members of such corporation and others." Approved, April 10, 1901.

5.—"Stony Wold Sanatorium;" principal office, New York City. Formed "to establish, maintain and carry on a hospital, infirmary or sanatorium for the reception, care and maintenance of, and the rendering of medical assistance to, women and children (including male children not over twelve years of age) who are suffering from or affected with tuberculosis or other thoracic diseases and such other diseases as may arise among the inmates while under the care of the institution." Approved, April 10, 1901.

6.—"Belknap Summer Home for Day Nursery Children;" principal office, Far Rockaway. Formed "to provide a summer vacation for day nursery children, primarily those of the Bryson and Sunnyside Day Nurseries." Approved, June 4, 1901.

7.—"Guild of the Infant Savior;" principal office, New York City. Formed "to receive, by surrender, commitment or otherwise, to support, care for or maintain destitute mothers and infants, and to place out and bind out, or cause to be placed out, bound out or adopted, destitute, abandoned, dependent, neglected or motherless infants in family homes or in such custody and care as may be permitted under or by virtue of any law of the State of New York, and to exercise an oversight over such infants who may have been so placed out or bound out; to secure or assist in

8

securing such mothers employment or shelter; and generally to assist and coöperate with the Department of Public Charities of the City of New York in helping, caring for and succoring such mothers or infants." Approved, June 4, 1901.

8.—"The Home Garden of New York City;" principal office, New York City. Formed "to maintain in the City of New York, a homelike place which shall always be open for temporary use to the children of the poor within said city and particularly for such children accustomed to wander upon the streets; the providing of opportunities at such place for work, study and play for such children; the cultivation of such influences as may tend to the betterment of such children and to the brightening and elevating of the homes of the poor within said city; the temporary care of such said children; the maintenance of religious services and schools of instruction which shall be open to such children and families; and the establishment and maintenance of all kindred forms of philanthropic endeavor." Approved, June 4, 1901.

9.—"Manhattan Maternity and Dispensary;" principal office, New York City. Formed "to erect, establish and maintain a hospital and dispensary and to render and furnish medical and surgical treatment therein to persons requiring the same, and especially the establishment and maintenance of a maternity hospital where women may be received, cared for or treated during pregnancy or during or after delivery; to provide hospital accommodations for obstetric cases and the surgery of women and children; to supply medical and surgical treatment to women of the poorer classes during their confinement in their homes; to provide facilities for the instruction of physicians and students of medicine; to establish and maintain a training school for nurses and to provide facilities for the instruction and training of women to be professional nurses." Approved, June 4, 1901.

10.—"Directorate of Neighborly Neighbors;" principal office, Yonkers. Formed "to provide homes for boys, assist them to find employment, provide for them evening instruction and aid them to become self-supporting." Approved, July 10, 1901.

11.—" The Beachonian Dispensary;" principal office, New York City. Formed "to establish and maintain in the city of New York a dispensary wherein poor persons, without regard to race, nationality, religion or sect, may receive free medical treatment and attendance, according to the Eclectic school or system of medicine." Approved, October 9, 1901.

12.—" Cosmopolitan Hospital Society;" principal office, New York City. Formed " to establish and maintain a hospital wherein the method or system of treating the sick shall be according to the Eclectic school or theory." Approved, October 9, 1901.

13.—" The Jewish Hospital;" principal office, Brooklyn. Formed " to erect, establish and maintain a hospital which shall afford medical and surgical aid to sick or disabled persons without regard to their creed or nationality." Approved, October 9, 1901.

14.—" Good Counsel Training School for Young Girls;" principal office, White Plains. Formed " to give industrial, mental and religious training to girls who, from ignorance, indolence or waywardness, may be in moral danger." Approved, October 9, 1901.

15.—" The Robins' Nest;" principal office, Greenburgh. Formed "to provide a temporary home in the country for children, between the ages of two and twelve years, from New York who need fresh air and good food." Approved, October 9, 1901.

DISPENSARIES LICENSED.

The following named dispensaries were licensed during the year:

Children's Mission, Dispensary of, 125 Eagle street, Brooklyn, N. Y., April 10, 1901.

Cohoes Hospital Association, Eye and Ear Department, 221 Main street, Cohoes, N. Y., April 10, 1901.

Lutheran Dispensary, corner East New York avenue and Powell street, New York city, October 9, 1901.

Nassau Hospital Dispensary, Mineola, Nassau county, N. Y., October 9, 1901.

St. Vincent's Hospital, Outdoor Department, Eleventh street and Seventh avenue, New York city, January 24, 1901.

Samaritan Hospital Dispensary, Eighth street, Troy, N. Y., April 10, 1901.

The University and Bellevue Hospital Medical College Dispensary and Clinic, 340 East Twenty-sixth street, New York city, January 24, 1901.

PLANS OF BUILDINGS APPROVED.

By the provisions of chapter 225 of the Laws of 1896 (the Poor law), and chapter 546 of the Laws of 1896 (the State Charities law), as amended by chapter 504 of the Laws of 1899, the State Board of Charities is required to approve or disapprove all plans for the erection of almshouses and State charitable and reformatory institutions. The duties imposed upon the Board by these laws have been performed in such manner as to secure the results which it is believed the Legislature sought to accomplish by their enactment. These objects are:

1. The more perfect adaptation of buildings to their purposes.

2. The most approved sanitary arrangements in the details of their plans.

3. Economy in the cost of construction.

All plans are first submitted to a special committee which has power to take such testimony as may be necessary to form a correct judgment, or to visit and inspect the location of a proposed new building, or the building to be improved. The plans for almshouses are generally made by local architects who are frequently unfamiliar with such institutions, and hence their details often require considerable modification. The plans of State institutions are now prepared by the State Architect, and they usually conform in detail to the established principles governing the architecture of such buildings.

It has been the policy of this Board, in the exercise of its duty to approve or disapprove the plans submitted for its action, to insist upon those general principles of construction essential to the adaptation of each building to its purposes, and to secure the best sanitary conditions, as well as economy of construction, and still to leave the local authorities ample opportunity to incorporate such peculiarities in the structure as they may prefer not inconsistent with these established principles.

The more important improvements which the Board has endeavored to secure in the new almshouses are as follows:

1. The complete separation of the sexes. The old almshouses usually consisted of a single building for the administration and for the inmates. This arrangement admitted of the free intermingling of the sexes, and gross immorality not infrequently resulted. The new almshouses provide an independent building for administration, and a separate building for each sex.

2. The abolition of the partially underground story generally known as the " basement." These structures were formerly very common and were usually devoted to kitchen and laundry purposes, but in institutions liable at certain seasons to be overcrowded they were converted into dormitories. Owing to this latter fact these basement stories have been discouraged by the Board and no plans of buildings devoted to the residence of inmates which provide basements are approved. The reasons for this action are twofold:

Partially underground rooms are unfit for living or industrial purposes, owing to the liability to dampness.

There is ample ground space for the construction of buildings, the living rooms of which are in the free air above the surface level.

3. The kitchen and laundry are removed to separate buildings. By this arrangement the living rooms of the inmates are entirely free from the emanations from these sources of impure air.

4. The isolation of the toilet-rooms and better bathing facilities. The toilet-rooms are required to be located in exterior rooms having corridors or ventilated halls and ample window space. They are thus effectually separated from living and sleeping rooms. The shower or rain bath is now employed instead of the tub, except in special cases.

5. The hospital is isolated and provided with all the necessary equipment for the proper care of the sick and for patients who have undergone operations.

6. Economy is secured by requiring simplicity of style of architecture and by the provision in the written certificate of approval of the Board that the cost of construction shall not exceed the appropriation. That there shall be no departure from the plans approved by the Board, it is required that the plans approved shall be filed in the office of the Board.

During the past year the Board approved plans and specifications for new buildings and improvements, with the proviso in each case that the expense should not exceed the appropriation therefor, as follows:

House of Refuge for Women, Hudson.—Plumbing cottages 2, 3, 4 and administration building; approved, February 28, 1901.

New York State Reformatory for Women, Bedford.—Constructing, plumbing, heating and ventilating, and. electric wiring and fixtures for hospital; plumbing kitchen of prison building; approved, July 10, 1901. Ice-house and cold-storage building; approved June 4, 1901. Repairs and additions to dam; heating and ventilating prison building and cottages; approved, October 9, 1901.

State Custodial Asylum for Feeble-minded Women, Newark.— Constructing, plumbing, heating and ventilating, pipe covering, electric wiring and fixtures for cottage " F; " approved, July 10, 1901.

Rome State 'Custodial Asylum, Rome.—Addition to boiler-house; concrete floors in vegetable storehouse and cellar of farm-house; fire-escapes for ward building " D; " approved, October 9,

1901. Constructing, heating and ventilating, plumbing, pipe covering, electric wiring and fixtures for ward building "G;" approved, July 9, 1901.

Craig Colony, Sonyea.—Brick church; approved, April 10, 1901. Constructing, heating and plumbing addition to trades school building; four cottages for employes; four dormitories for the Villa Flora group; finishing, plumbing and heating warehouse and cold-storage building; reservoir and drains for rainwater in the Villa Flora group; two silos; subway and approaches; approved, July 10, 1901. Greenhouse; sewers, drains and water supply for the men's and women's infirmaries; approved, October 9, 1901. Parochial residence for the Roman Catholic chaplain; approved, June 4, 1901.

New York State Woman's Relief Corps Home, Oxford.—Administration building; dining-room building; approved, June 4, 1901. Steel beams in coal shed; new floors in coal shed and engine-room; approved, July 9, 1901.

New York State School for the Blind, Batavia.—Electric wiring main building, laundry, hospital and barn; approved, July 9, 1901.

Department of Public Charities, Brooklyn.—Bakery building; approved, February 28, 1901. Brick observation pavilion; frame pavilion for male almshouse; piazza for main building; repairs to roof of almshouse; refrigerator at the Homeopathic hospital; tile floors and wainscoting for toilet-rooms in the Homeopathic hospital; approved, October 9, 1901. Repairs to Homeopathic hospital; approved, April 10, 1901. Steam laundry building and plant; approved, July 10, 1901.

Albany County Almshouse, Albany.—Hospital annex; approved, January 9, 1901.

Chautauqua County Almshouse, Dewittville.—Additions and alterations to hospital; approved, October 9, 1901.

Erie County Almshouse, Buffalo.—Consumptive hospital; approved, January 9, 1901.

Schenectady County Almshouse, Schenectady.—New almshouse buildings; approved, July 10, 1901.

Steuben County Almshouse, Bath.—Additions to women's building and hospital; approved, February 28, 1901.

Wayne County Almshouse, Lyons.—Dormitory for women; keeper's residence; approved, June 4, 1901.

THE CONSTRUCTION AND IMPROVEMENT OF ALMSHOUSE BUILDINGS.

The committee on the construction of buildings reports extensive structural improvements in almshouses during the year. New York and Kings counties have made extensive additions to their buildings. This is especially true of Kings county; the Flatbush Almshouse and Hospital has been repaired and added to until it has become a satisfactory institution. The almshouse of Onondaga county has added a hospital, new plumbing and other equipments. The new almshouses of Fulton and Montgomery counties are built in accordance with the plans approved by the State Board of Charities; the Albany Almshouse may be said to have undergone a complete transformation. These are instances of the improvements that have been undertaken throughout the State. Almshouses may be called hospitals; they are, however, hospitals intended for infirm, aged and disabled dependents. While they do not require the elaborate equipments of the general hospital, they do need careful attention in the matters of heating, lighting and ventilation. In no place is it more essential to have perfect sanitation, and yet few builders pay sufficient attention to the sanitary details in the construction of this class of buildings. It is difficult to make changes after buildings have been finished, yet it sometimes happens that even before a building is half completed its defects are apparent. In one building, erected under contract, the plaster began to crack and fall from the walls before the building was ready for occupancy, and within a week from the opening, odors from the sewer were plainly perceptible throughout the house. It is true that later the contractor was compelled to make changes, but the changes were not sufficient to remedy the evil, as the structure was radically defective.

The tendency toward separate hospitals is to be commended. It is impossible to give the aged sick such care as they need in the ordinary dormitories wherein other inmates are required to remain. It is essential that the sick be separated from the well, and the erection of a hospital building, removed to some distance from the other buildings of the almshouse group, is a necessity.

ALMSHOUSE INSPECTION.

The inspection of the almshouses of the State is one of the important duties of the State Board of Charities. This duty has been fully discharged during the past year. The several almshouses have been inspected at regular intervals by the almshouse inspectors appointed by the Board, and have also been visited by members of the Board in their respective districts, as well as in many instances by its committees. By these inspections and visitations the Board has maintained a close supervision over this class of our charitable institutions.

It is a matter of gratification that the Board is able to report a constant tendency toward improvement in the almshouses of the State. This improvement is especially manifested in more adequate provisions for the care of the sick, and in better methods of lighting, heating and ventilation.

Marked improvement has taken place in almost every almshouse within the past few years. It is not too much to say that

the almshouses of the State of New York will now compare
favorably with the best examples of this class of charitable institutions anywhere. It has been found that regular inspections
are helpful to the officers in charge of public institutions, and
bring to them a stimulus which promotes more efficient administration and conduces to the welfare of the inmates. Through
these inspections the county boards of supervisors are made
aware of the requirements of the almshouses, and are kept in
touch with the State Board of Charities. As the object of inspection is the welfare of the public charges, local authorities
recognize the fact that inspections secure economy, humanity
and efficiency. They are made in a friendly spirit with the single purpose of promoting the public welfare.

STATE ALMSHOUSES.

Under the law the almshouses which are designated as State
almshouses must be visited at least once each three months by
the Superintendent of State and Alien Poor or his representative. These receiving almshouses are located conveniently
throughout the State at central points, and receive poor persons
who are properly chargeable to the State. At the time of inspection each poor person is carefully examined to the end that the
State may not be burdened with the support of persons able to
care for themselves. The non-residents are sent to their homes
and the aliens are deported. In this way the numbers of State
Poor supported in the State almshouses are kept down, and the
State is thus relieved of what would otherwise become an excessive burden. In this way the inspection of the almshouses has
a direct effect by relieving the State and its political sub-di-
visions, of the support of persons properly chargeable elsewhere.

As these inspections are made at frequent intervals, they afford a basis of comparison by which to determine the improvements which are made, as well as to show if any of the inmates of almshouses are improper cases. The regular census of inmates shows the exact condition, physical and mental, of each inmate, as well as the residential locality to which such inmate is properly chargeable. By thus carefully examining into the condition of the inmates, the Board is enabled to enforce the proper administration of our poor laws and do much for the benefit of those who are dependent upon public relief.

STATE, ALIEN AND INDIAN POOR.

Chapter 225 of the Laws of 1896 places all State, Alien and Indian Poor under the direct supervision and care of the Superintendent of State and Alien Poor. Such persons as have not resided for sixty days in any one county of the State of New York within one year of the date of their application for relief are designated as State poor, and as such the law provides that they shall be removed to and be maintained in one of the State almshouses. Pauper aliens as well as non-residents have been attracted to the State of New York. The great work of tunneling under the city of New York has drawn to it laborers from other states as well as Europe. In other parts of the State public improvements have attracted transients in hope of employment. Added to this industrial activity the Pan-American Exposition brought many persons into the State with neither means to support themselves here nor the funds required to pay for transportation to their homes.

The Department of State and Alien Poor during the past fiscal year has been compelled to return 977 persons to their homes,

and its work has increased through the necessity for careful
investigation of all applicants for relief under this law.

Alien Poor.

The deportation of aliens who have not resided within the
United States for such period as serves to relieve the General
Government of responsibility for their return has been carried
on through the coöperation of the Department of State and
Alien Poor and the Immigration Commissioners of the United
States. The latter promptly responded to every request made
by the State Board of Charities, and returned to their homes in
foreign countries 12 persons from October 1, 1900, to the close
of the fiscal year.

In addition to those whose transportation has been undertaken
by the General Government, many aliens have become paupers
after the period during which the General Government arranges
for their deportation. All such persons have been returned by
the Department of State and Alien Poor, whether the aliens were
originally committed as poor persons to be supported by the
State or as charges upon a particular county. In either case the
fact that they were alien paupers has resulted in the return of 87
persons to their own country during the year ending September
30, 1901.

Indian Poor.

The relief of such Indians as may require assistance is a duty
undertaken by the State of New York. There are a large number
of Indians resident in this State, but comparatively few of these
are now public charges. Many require temporary relief, but
almost all contribute in some way to their own support. It is
only when sickness disables them that they make application for
removal to an almshouse or public hospital. The largest portion

relief fund is disbursed in temporary assistance.
that by the careful supervision of the Indians of
ey are encouraged to depend upon themselves, and
that every application for relief is carefully inves-
ts the abuse of public charity. In consequence,
elled to self-support who under less rigorous super-
come members of the pauper class.

b report of this Board contains statistical tables
o and to which attention is directed, showing the
he State Poor Law since it went into effect Octo-
id until the close of the fiscal year September 30,

s Resulting from the Removal of State and Alien Poor.
of State and Alien Poor is an economical plan to
:e from the burden of dependents for whose sup-
onwealth is in no way properly chargeable. From
he case direct financial benefits result. The pay-
t of transportation is made in order that the State
he cost of support during a long period of years.
:fully estimated that the class of persons admitted
ses survive for an average period of over fifteen
cost of support per capita is $104 per year, each
ed as a permanent inmate of a State almshouse
tate over $1,500. It is readily seen therefore that
sportation is very small when compared with the
, and that the removal of non-resident poor is a
nical enforcement of law.

nancial benefit which the removal of non-resident
upon the State, it is also apparent that anything.

which prevents the increase of the pauper class is a public benefit. Modern conditions are such that there must always be a certain proportion of incompetents and defectives who will have to be supported at public expense. The influence of pauperism is destructive. It assails the thrift, the morality and the intelli- gence of society; the more the number of paupers grows in any community, the more destructive this influence. The safety of society depends upon the encouragement of the wage-earners and taxpayers. No unnecessary burdens should be laid upon them. Everything possible should be done to decrease the number of voluntary dependents. All who have no just claims to public charity ought to be compelled to labor for their own support, and while the dependents of this State are entitled to help from the public, those who belong elsewhere should make their claim for relief in their own home localities.

During the past fiscal year the number of poor sent out of this State was 977, of whom 87 were returned as aliens to their homes in foreign countries and 890 were sent to other states. Some of those classed as State poor were returned to former homes in foreign lands.

In all cases of deportation an investigation was undertaken so as to make certain the fact that no injustice would be done by removal. More than twice the amount of the appropriation for the Department of State and Alien Poor would have been required had these persons who were removed from the State been per- mitted to remain in the State as public charges for a single year.

The whole number of removals since the State Poor act of 1873 and the Alien Poor act of 1880 went into effect has been 30,951. At the estimated term of fifteen years for each individual, the resulting expenditure, had these persons been permitted to remain in our almshouses, might have reached the enormous sum of $48,283,560. From this it is evident that the money expended in the removal of non-resident poor is a true economy and the result a permanent benefit to the State.

Expenditures.

On account of State poor.....................	$33,700 03
On account of alien poor......................	1,794 82
On account of Indian poor....................	1,883 13

DEPARTMENT OF INSPECTION.

All the institutions subject to visitation and inspection by the Board have not only been visited but thoroughly inspected during the past year.

In not a few instances, notably so in the case of hospitals, the last recorded general inspection was made in 1898. The reason why no inspection had since been made in such cases, is because so long as it was considered the duty of the Board to visit and inspect all charitable, eleemosynary, correctional and reformatory institutions in the State except such as were subject to the supervision of the State Commission in Lunacy and the State Commission of Prisons, the force of inspectors at the command of the department had been insufficient for the purpose. Under the recent decision of the Court of Appeals whereby the Board's jurisdiction was limited to institutions classed as charitable by the court, namely, institutions in receipt of public money for the support and maintenance of indigent persons, the number of inspectors has been found equal to the task of visiting each and every institution at least once during the year. In cases where an earlier inspection has revealed defects of a more or less serious

character, a reinspection has been made to learn whether such
defects have been remedied, in all such cases the findings of the
inspectors having been communicated by the Board to the managers of the institution with the request that proper remedies
be applied. Forty-one such reinspections were conducted during
the last fiscal year. It is gratifying to be able to report that, as
a rule, the response of managers to the recommendations and
suggestions of this Board has been both cordial and prompt. In
cases where defects are structural in character, so that radical
improvements are necessary, involving considerable expense,.
time will be necessary in which to secure the desired changes.'

Particular attention has been paid to the question of fire protection in charitable institutions subject to the inspection of the
department. The dreadful holocaust at the Rochester Orphan
Asylum on January 8, 1901, furnished a painful object lesson of
the necessity for providing every possible expedient for escape or
rescue in case of fire. The casual visitor to this particular institution would, in all probability, have pronounced the building.
fairly well safeguarded against such a catastrophe. The dormitory where the greatest loss of life occurred was but one story
and a half above the ground. Along one side of it ran a piazza
roof upon which several windows opened. Near by was a fire-
escape, accessible, unfortunately, only by passage through the
hallway in which the fire burned fiercest. So rapidly did the
flames spread that death from suffocation seems to have come
upon the inmates before they were aroused from sleep. The
employment of a night watchman, an additional means of protection which has since been put into effect at the Asylum, would,
in all probability, have led to an earlier discovery of the fire and
thus have prevented the terrible loss of life which ensued.

The importance of the most scrupulous care in such matters was again illustrated in the fire which broke out at midnight at the Shelter for Unprotected Girls, Syracuse, on July 21, 1901. As reported to the Board by its inspector who made careful inquiry into the origin and causes of the fire, " The apparent and generally accepted cause of the fire is that an attendant, subject to fainting spells, in one of these, overturned her lamp, setting fire to the furniture in her room or to her clothing." This accident cost the attendant her life. All the other inmates were rescued through the presence of mind of the matron and her associates. The President of the institution is quoted as saying: "Much relief is now felt that the bars have been removed from the second story windows in accordance with the suggestion of the State Board of Charities, although the inmates were not obliged to escape through these windows." It is quite possible that the knowledge that all possible egress was barred in this direction would have occasioned a panic with fatal consequences.

These instances are cited not because antecedent conditions made the danger from fire greater in these two institutions than in many others, but rather to emphasize the insistence which needs to be placed by this Department and boards of managers upon every possible precaution against fire, and in the event of such catastrophe upon every possible means of escape. While a single board of trustees may feel that the danger of loss of life from fire is comparatively small in its own institution, this Board, multiplying such chances in any given case by the sum total of institutions subject to inspection, realizes that no sug-gestion or recommendation on its part which will reduce the danger from this source to a minimum should be omitted. While the inspectors of this department are not experts on fire-proof

9

construction and kindred subjects, experience and training do
entitle the Board's agents to an opinion as to the adequacy or
inadequacy of fire protection. In all instances of reasonable
doubt, institutions are referred to the local authorities charged
with official responsibility in such matters.

There are, moreover, certain means of protection so valuable
as safeguards against the danger under discussion, that they
might well be made the subject of general legislation. One of
these is the erection of fire-escapes on orphan asylums and
similar institutions, as required in the case of hospitals by
chapter 381, Laws of 1895. Another safeguard might well be
furnished by means of an amendment to chapter 201, Laws of
1901, which at present relates only to educational institutions,
so as to make applicable to orphan asylums and all charitable
institutions for minors the requirement of that statute to the
effect, that it shall be the duty of the person in charge of any
such institution having more than a hundred inmates to instruct
and train them by means of drills, so that they may in a sudden
emergency be able to leave the building in the shortest possible
time and without confusion and panic. Such drills or rapid
dismissals shall be held at least once in each month. One other
provision which might well be embodied in a general law applicable to such institutions is a requirement that a night patrol
service be maintained, safeguarded by some system of official
registration by watchman's clock or similar device, such as is
the case in not a few institutions at the present time.

After the lessons of the past and previous years, it should
not be necessary to wait for further disasters before these
points are securely covered by general legislation. Reliance
upon local ordinances is valuable in matters of minor detail,

but questions of general utility, relating to the preservation of life and property, rightfully fall within the province of the State in the exercise of its police powers.

In the report upon the department of inspection, which appears in the 34th annual report of the State Board of Charities for 1900, occurs the following (vol. 1, p. 513):

"Two important duties remain to be more systematically performed by the Department. First, the examination of children, inmates of orphan asylums subject to the inspection of the Board, but not in receipt of public school moneys and consequently not inspected by the State or local school authorities. The education which these children receive bears so important a relation to their future welfare not only, but to that of the communities of which they are soon to become component parts, that more stress should be laid upon this subject by managers of children's homes. In many instances the Department has conducted examinations of the children of such institutions. The work which has been done in this direction has proven that such examinations are fruitful of result in awakening increased interest in an important subject and in creating an influence for better graded work in orphan asylums * * *."

Among the duties of this Board imposed by the State Charities law, scarcely one is more important than the following:

"§ 9. General Powers and Duties of Board.—The State Board of Charities shall visit, inspect and maintain a general supervision of all institutions, societies or associations which are of a charitable, eleemosynary, correctional or reformatory character, whether State or municipal, incorporated or not incorporated, which are made subject to its supervision by the constitution or by law; and shall * * *

"7. Aid in securing the establishment and maintenance of such industrial, educational and moral training in institutions having the care of children as is best suited to the needs of the inmates."

In the performance of this important task, clearly enunciated in the language quoted, a forward step remains to be taken by the Board. In order that the work may be done in an authoritative and expert manner, the Department requires the services of a school examiner, a man of practical experience as a teacher, and one whose training has been sufficiently broad to enable him to advise not only with reference to the secular education, such as is afforded by the public schools, but as to the introduction of manual and industrial instruction into reformatories and homes for juveniles. The inspectors of the Department are required to touch upon these subjects in the course of their general visitations and inspections of children's institutions, but the matter bears so important a relation to the preparation of the inmates of these homes, for self-support and intelligent citizenship, that a man should be appointed who can devote his entire time to this work.

For this purpose the Legislature is respectfully urged to appropriate the sum of $1,800, a salary which is deemed necessary to command the services of a trained school examiner. In support of such request, the following statistics are cited bearing upon the subject. There are in the State 121 homes for children which are under private control, but in receipt of public money. This number includes infant asylums. The latter in some cases retain children until seven or eight years of age, and maintain kindergarten and primary classes. Of these 121 institutions, there are several which conduct separate branches, one parent institution having no less than nine such branches. These 121 institutions, with their allied branches, have a school population of 23,781. Of this number 11,043 attend either the public schools or schools maintained in whole or in part by public school moneys, and subject to inspection and examination by the school authorities. The remainder, namely, 12,738 attend asylum schools which are privately organized. In addition to the per capita allowances for support and maintenance of the inmates in these institutions $129,477.80 are appropriated from school funds and in certain sections of the State, where no such direct appropriation is made, the teachers are furnished and their salaries paid by the school authorities.

In passing, it may be remarked that even in cases where children's institutions receive special appropriations for educational purposes, it does not necessarily follow in all cases that the local school authorities examine the institution or grade it as an integral part of the public school system; nor does such examination, when conducted, include within its scope the character of the industrial and moral training afforded by the institution apart from school instruction.

In conclusion, it may not be out of place to add that the corps of inspectors in this Department was reduced by one by the last Legislature at a saving of $900. Therefore, the number employed during the last fiscal year will not be increased, should the request for a special school inspector be favorably considered.

A subject which has received special attention during the past year in the inspections of the Department is the degree of compliance with the Public Health Law, chapter 661, Laws of 1893, so far as this statute relates to institutions for orphans, destitute or vagrant children, or juvenile delinquents. A special inquiry has been instituted and is now in progress for the purpose of ascertaining methods of compliance and the results obtained in safeguarding the institutions from the presence of infectious and contagious diseases.

It is hoped that the inquiry may be completed in season to print the results and conclusions as an appended paper to this report.

On June 4, 1901, the Board adopted the following preamble and resolutions:

"Whereas, The records filed with the Board relating to homes for children in receipt of public money, show that 5,000 such inmates or fully 20 per cent. have been retained five years or over in said institutions,

"Resolved, That in accordance with the recommendations of its Eastern and Western inspection district committees this Board direct that a systematic inquiry be instituted through the department of inspection to learn the causes of retention of all inmates who are supported as public charges in homes for children under private control, provided said retention has continued longer than five years.

" Resolved, That this inquiry be conducted in such a manner as to show the age, sex, religion, civil, physical and mental condition of said public charges, the causes for which committed or otherwise received, the authority under which received, the per capita amount received from public sources, and, furthermore, that the effort be made to ascertain whether the acceptance of each such public charge has been renewed annually as provided by the rules of the Board, as well as to obtain any other information on the general subject which may be of service to the Board."

Pursuant to the terms of the resolutions, the Department is now engaged upon a special inquiry relative to long term inmates in children's institutions. Much labor and time are being spent to make the examination thorough and its results trustworthy.

Inspection of Dispensaries.

In accordance with the provisions of chapter 368, Laws of 1899, which took effect October 1st of that year, this Board has issued licenses to 134 dispensaries. Of this number, 10 institutions have since surrendered their licenses and returned them for cancellation. In six other instances, dispensaries have closed, thus leaving 118 institutions which were operating under licensure from this Board at the close of the last fiscal year. No complaints have been received to indicate that any hardship is being suffered by the indigent sick through the reduction in the number of dispensaries. On the contrary, the number remaining seems sufficient, certainly in New York city, to meet the needs of this class of patients. On the whole, it appears that the law is serving its purpose in providing a wholesome check upon indiscriminate medical charity. The investigation of doubtful cases, as required by the rules of the Board adopted pursuant to the provisions of the statute, is not as generally observed as it should be. Every effort is being made to secure the coöperation of the institutions on this important point. The printed notices which are required to be posted in waiting rooms and printed upon admission and pass cards are believed to have a deterrent effect upon those who are able to obtain medical and surgical treatment at their own expense.

Department Statistics.

During the last fiscal year, the Eastern inspection district committee held ten meetings, and the Western inspection district committee, nine, for the purpose of considering the reports of inspections and making recommendations to the Board as to the disposition of such reports.

The following table shows the number of general inspectior special inspections, visits to societies, institutions and individua and the number of examinations and investigations conducted I the Department for the year ending September 50, 1901:

	Eastern district.	Western district.	Tot
General inspections	329	119	4
Special inspections	548	25	5
Visits to societies, institutions and individuals	721	194	9
Examinations and investigations......	18	8	:
Totals	1,616	346	1,9

A general inspection is one which "will secure a thorou inquiry into the operations and conditions of every departme of an institution." A special inspection is " a visit to an instit tion to inquire or examine as to some particular fact or co dition." Examinations and investigations pertain to childrer records, school work and books of account, or other matters whi demand particular inquiry. An examination of this charact frequently occupies several days.

Every general inspection is accompanied by a written ·repo describing in detail the conditions found to exist in the cour of the visitation and inspection. Where such reports record t presence of abuses, defects or evils in any given institutio copies are furnished to the trustees, directors or managers such institutions, in accordance with the provisions of section 1 Article I., chapter 546, Laws of 1896, known as the State Char ties law, as follows:

"Correction of evils in administration of institutions.—Tl State Board of Charities shall call the attention of the trustee

directors or managers of any such institution, society or association, subject to its supervision, to any abuses, defects or evils
which may be found therein, and such officers shall take proper
action thereon, with a view to correcting the same, in accordance with the advice of such board."

Frequently, where no "abuses, defects or evils" are found in
the course of inspection, the reports are furnished to the managers of charitable institutions by way of information and
suggestion.

The following tables show the number of reports which have
been written during the past year and the disposition made of
them:

REPORTS WRITTEN.

	Eastern district.	Western district.	Totals.
General	329	119	448
Special	173	6	179
Totals	502	125	627

DISPOSITION OF REPORTS.

	General inspection reports.	Special inspection reports.	Totals.
Filed with records	53	104	157
Referred to committees or Commission-ers of the Board	18	13	31
Sent to managers for information and suggestion	242	18	260
Sent to managers for correction of evils, abuses and defects	135	44	179
Totals	448	179	627

The inspectors of the Department, in the pursuance of their
several duties, have traveled 24,044 miles during the past fiscal
year, not including 7,864 miles traveled by the superintendent of
inspection.

In accordance with the provisions of the State Charities law, the chief subjects considered by the inspectors in the examination of institutions are (1) the nature and efficiency of the supervision exercised by boards of trustees, directors or managers; (2) the just, humane and economic character of the administration as shown in the conduct and efficiency of persons charged with the internal management; (3) the suitability and general condition of the buildings occupied and their sanitary condition; (4) the methods employed for the protection and preservation of the health of inmates; (5) the kind of industrial, educational and moral training afforded and its adaptation to the needs of the inmates; (6) the nature and accuracy of the financial and other records of the institution, and (7) compliance with the rules of the Board adopted pursuant to the provisions of the constitution, Article VIII., section 14.

The following table summarizes in a brief manner the conditions reported to exist in the private charitable institutions of the State subject to the visitation and inspection of the Board:

General conditions reported in the private charities inspected by the department for the year ending September 30, 1901.

	Excellent.	Good.	Fair.	Unsatisfactory.	Bad.	Not stated.	Does not apply.	Merged.
Supervision............................	24	193	139	22	1	1	11	57
Administration......	97	242	95	9	2	......	......,	8
Plant...................................	75	183	127	48	7	1	7	....
Sanitary condition	75	165	159	34	4	3	8	....
Records.........	49	241	140	22	4	10	2	....
General impression	48	247	131	21	1	......	....	....

Total general inspections, 448.

By the revised constitution of 1894, the State Board of Charities was made not only a constitutional body charged with the duty of visitation and inspection of the public and private charities of the State, but the Board was clothed with other important powers. The constitution, Article VIII., section 14, provides that:

* * * "Payments by counties, cities, towns and villages to charitable, eleemosynary, correctional and reformatory institutions, wholly or partly under private control, for care, support and maintenance, may be authorized, but shall not be required by the Legislature. No such payments shall be made for any inmate of such institutions who is not received and retained therein pursuant to rules established by the State Board of Charities. Such rules shall be subject to the control of the Legislature by general laws."

In accordance with the provisions of this section, the State Board is charged with the important duty of formulating rules and regulations governing the reception and retention of inmates of institutions in receipt of public money but under private control. These rules have been subject to amendment from time to time, as experience and circumstances have demanded. As at present formulated and administered, the rules require that every such institution having the care of children shall file with the Board a monthly statement showing the admissions and discharges for the preceding month and the total number of inmates remaining at the end of the month. Certain facts regarding each child so received or discharged are also requested. In this way the Board is enabled to keep a register of the inmates of all children's homes that are in receipt of public money. The following table shows the population of such institutions at the close of the fiscal years from September 30, 1896, to September 30, 1901:

Number of Inmates of Homes for Children in Receipt of Public Money.

September 30, 1896 (119 institutions)	27,769
September 30, 1897 (121 institutions)	28,380
September 30, 1898 (123 institutions)	29,967
September 30, 1899 (123 institutions)	29,440
September 30, 1900 (122 institutions)	28,649
September 30, 1901 (121 institutions)	29,241

The number of children present in these homes on September 30, 1901, shows an increase of 592 compared with the number present on September 30, 1900. Of this increase 109 represent two institutions which began to report during the year. The total increase was distributed by localities as follows:

	Increase in number of such children for year ending September 30, 1901.
Boroughs of Manhattan and the Bronx...........	24
Borough of Brooklyn...........................	278
Elsewhere in the State	290
Total	592

During the year St. Joseph's Home for Babies was merged with the Dominican Convent of Our Lady of the Rosary, New York city; the Shepherd's Fold was merged with the Children's Fold, New York city, and the children from St. Mary's Orphan Asylum, Canandaigua, were transferred to St. Patrick's Asylum, Rochester. The Brooklyn Children's Aid Society, and the New York Mothers' Home of the Sisters of Misericorde were added to the list of institutions which receive children and make monthly reports to this Board. The total of such institutions, therefore, was 121 as compared with 122 for the previous year.

During the fiscal year ending September 30, 1901, there were discharged from the homes for children under private control, but in receipt of public money, 15,217 children. The monthly reports made to the Board show the following facts regarding these children:

Facts Relating to 15,217 Inmates of 121 Homes for Children Discharged During the Year Ending September 30, 1901.

Sex.

Boys	9,305
Girls	5,912
Total	15,217

Age at Time of Discharge.

Less than 1 year of age	1,893
Between 1 and 5 years of age	2,765
Between 6 and 10 years of age	3,683
Between 11 and 16 years of age	6,086
Over 16 years of age	728
Not stated	62

Duration of Institution Life.

Less than 1 year	8,339
Between 1 and 2 years	2,057
Between 2 and 3 years	1,355
Between 3 and 4 years	943
Between 4 and 5 years	588
Between 5 and 6 years	458
Between 6 and 7 years	379
Between 7 and 8 years	300
Between 8 and 9 years	275
Between 9 and 10 years	165
Ten years or over	358

Method of Support at Time of Discharge.

Public charges 11,133
Private charges 4,079
Not stated 5

Method of Discharge.

To relatives 9,868
To friends or guardians 43
Placed out on trial.................................... 291
Placed in permanent homes.............................. 605
Adopted or indentured 760
Sent to hospitals 258
Sent to other institutions 215
Transferred upon approval of Commissioner.............. 211
Became self-supporting 598
Left by expiration of time............................. 319
Escaped 167
Died 1,439
Otherwise discharged 443

Of the 15,217 children reported as discharged during the year, 448 were afterward readmitted to the same institutions. If we add to this number those sent to hospitals or other institutions or transferred from one institution to another upon approval of a commissioner of the Board, we have a migration of 1,132 children, whose institutional life did not cease by reason of the discharge noted above.

Of the 1,439 children who died, 1,123 were inmates of infant asylums.

NEW YORK STATE CONFERENCE OF CHARITIES AND CORRECTION.

The Second New York State Conference of Charities and Correction was held in New York city November 19–22, 1901. The constitution adopted by the Conference at its inception in 1900, thus states the purposes of the organization:

"The objects of the New York State Conference of Charities and Correction are to afford an opportunity for those engaged in charitable and reform work to confer respecting their methods, principles of administration, and results accomplished; to diffuse reliable information respecting charitable and correctional work, and encourage coöperation in humanitarian efforts, with the aim of further improving the system of charity and correction in the State of New York. With this end in view, the Conference will hold an annual meeting in the State of New York, at a time and place to be agreed upon at the preceding annual session, at which addresses shall be made, papers read, discussions carried on, and general business transacted in accordance with the by-laws of the Conference.

"The Conference shall not, however, formulate any platform nor adopt resolutions or memorials having a like effect."

The second annual session of the Conference served to furnish ample proof that there is in this State need of just such a gathering as that provided for by the constitution of the Conference. There were in attendance upon the sessions of the Conference 539 delegates representing the departments of charities and correction of various counties and cities of the State, State institutions for the insane, feeble-minded and epileptics, State reformatories for women and children, private charities such as hospitals, dispensaries, homes for children, charity organization and kindred societies, social settlements and the like. The attendance upon the sessions taxed the capacity of Assembly Hall in the Unite:

Oharities Building, New York City. Not the least valuable feature of the Conference was the opportunity afforded for social interchange of views upon the papers and discussions of the Conference.

At the opening session of the Conference, Governor Odell extended a welcome to the delegates and invited guests on behalf of the State of New York, and in the course of his remarks urged the mutual coöperation of public and private agencies in advancing the charitable and correctional interests of the State.

The following is the list of the officers and committees chosen to organize the Conference of 1902, which it is proposed shall be held in Albany, in the month of November, unless other arrangements are made by the Executive Committee:

PRESIDENT.
WILLIAM R. STEWART, New York.

VICE-PRESIDENTS.
Rev. ISAAC GIBBARD, D. D., Rochester.   GEORGE B. ROBINSON, New York.
Rev. CAMERON J. DAVIS, Buffalo.

SECRETARY.
EDWARD T. DEVINE, New York.

ASSISTANT SECRETARIES.
Miss MARION I. MOORE, Buffalo.   Mrs. JAMES M. BELDEN, Syracuse.
W. FRANK PERSONS, New York.

TREASURER.
FRANK TUCKER, New York.

EXECUTIVE COMMITTEE.
Chairman, WILLIAM R. STEWART, President of the Conference, New York.
Hon. William P. Letchworth, LL. D.,   Dr. Lee K. Frankel, New York.
  ex-President of the Conference, Portage.   Thomas M. Mulry, New York.
Robert W. de Forest, ex-President of the   Robert W. Hebberd, Albany.
  Conference, New York.   Col. William G. Rice, Albany.
Prof. George F. Canfield, Peekskill.

COMMITTEE ON CARE AND RELIEF OF NEEDY FAMILIES IN THEIR HOMES.
Chairman, Thos. W. Hynes, Brooklyn.
Rabbi Israel Aaron, Buffalo.   Rev. Wm R. Huntington, D.D., New York.
R. C. Baker, Buffalo.   James F. Jackson, New York.
Nathan Bijur, New York.   Charles D. Kellogg, New York.
Rev. Samuel Bishop, Brooklyn.   Miss Maria M. Love, Buffalo.
Mrs. Herbert P. Bissell, Buffalo.   Dennis McCarthy, Syracuse.
John J. Fitzgerald, New York.   Charles Stern, Rochester.
Mrs. Frederick D. Hitch, Newburgh.   Frank Travis, Oyster Bay.
John R. Washburn, Watertown.

COMMITTEE ON DEPENDENT, NEGLECTED, DELINQUENT AND DEFECTIVE CHILDREN.

Chairman, Prof. F. H. Briggs, Rochester.

Frederic Almy, Buffalo.
Frederick A. Gaylor, New York.
Charles Loring Brace, New York.
Homer Folks, New York.
Prof. James H. Hamilton, Syracuse.
Rev. Thos. F. Hickey, Rochester.
Edward J. Hussey, Albany.

Rev. Thos. L. Kinkead, Peekskill.
Rev. Dr. Max Landsberg, Rochester.
Edgar J. Levey, New York.
Mrs. C. B. McGinnis, New York.
Charles F. McKenna, New York.
John E. Pound, Lockport.
Walter S. Ufford, Albany.

Mornay Williams, New York.

COMMITTEE ON RELIEF OF THE SICK POOR.

Chairman, Dr. S. A. Knopf, New York.

John J. Barry, New York.
Mrs. Tunis G. Bergen, Brooklyn.
John Crane, New York.
Mrs. August Falker, Syracuse.
Dr. George W. Goler, Rochester.
Robert W. Hill, D.D., Canandaigua.

Dr. Walter James, New York.
Dr. Alfred Meyer, New York.
Mrs. James E. Newcomb, New York.
Dr. John H. Pryor, Buffalo.
Dr. Francis J. Quinlan, New York.
Dr. M. A. Veeder, Lyons.

Rev. Wm. J. White, D.D., Brooklyn.

COMMITTEE ON INSTITUTIONAL CARE OF DESTITUTE ADULTS.

Chairman, Mr. Lafavette L. Long, Buffalo.

William H. Buck, New York.
Jason Dougherty, New York.
Michael J. Drummond, New York.
Dr. Jesse T. Duryea, Brooklyn.
Daniel C. Grunder, Angelica.
Mrs. Sarah H. Kulchling, New York.

Cyrus C. Lathrop, Albany.
Benton J. McConnell, Hornellsville.
B. B. McDowell, Van Etten.
Rev. Dennis J. McMahon, D.D., New York.
Levi A. Page, Seneca Castle.
Mrs. Ellen M. Putnam, Oxford.

Myles Tierney, New York.

COMMITTEE ON THE MENTALLY DEFECTIVE.

Chairman, Dr. John F. Fitzgerald, Rome.

Dr. Henry M. Allison, Matteawan.
Dr. Valentine Brown, Yonkers.
Miss Mary Vida Clark, New York.
Mrs. Charles S. Crouse, Syracuse.
Mrs. Mary C. Dunphy, New York.
Rev. Thos. A. Hendrick, Rochester.
Dr. Arthur W. Hurd, Buffalo.

Timothy E. McGarr, Albany.
Daniel B. Murphy, Rochester.
Dr. Frederick Peterson, New York.
Miss Florence M. Rhett, Rochester.
Miss Jane Rochester, Rochester.
Mrs. Leslie W. Russell, Canton.
Michael J. Scanlan, New York.

Mrs. Chas. W. Winspear, Newark.

COMMITTEE ON TREATMENT OF THE CRIMINAL.

Chairman, Prof. Herbert E. Mills, Poughkeepsie.

Rev. Samuel J. Barrows, New York.
Cornelius V. Collins, Troy.
Miss Alice E. Curtin, Albion.
Neuville O. Fanning, New York.
William H. Gratwick, Buffalo.
Patrick Hayes, Brooklyn.
Henry R. Hoyt, New York.

George A. Lewis, Buffalo.
Luke J. Lindon, Mt. Vernon.
Dr. Frank W. Robertson, Elmira.
Eugene Smith, New York.
Lispenard Stewart, New York.
Thomas Sturgis, New York.
Mrs. Annie M. Welsh, Auburn.

James Wood, Mt. Kisco.

COMMITTEE ON POLITICS IN PENAL AND CHARITABLE INSTITUTIONS.

Chairman, Eugene A. Philbin, New York.

Joseph T. Alling, Rochester.
Edward R. Annand, New York.
Michael E. Bannon, Brooklyn.
Edmund J. Butler, New York.
Bird S. Coler, Brooklyn.
John W. Keller, New York.
Prof. Morris Loeb, New York.

Mrs. Chas. R. Lowell, New York.
George McAneny, New York.
William Church Osborn, New York.
Herbert Parsons, New York.
Thomas Raines, Rochester.
Howard Townsend, New York.
Horace White, New York.

Ansley Wilcox, Buffalo.

10

The thirty-first annual convention of the County Superintendents of the Poor of the State of New York was held in the city of Buffalo on the 18th, 19th, 20th and 21st days of June, 1901, Superintendent Daniel C. Grunder, of Allegany county, presiding during the convention. This important association is the oldest conference of the kind in this country, and its beneficial influence on the administration of public charity is plainly discernible to those who have taken note of the annual gatherings.

The principal papers read during the sessions were: " Practical Charity," by George Blair, Superintendent of Outdoor Poor, New York city; " Classification of Inmates in Almshouses and Other Public Institutions," by Robert W. Hill, Inspector of Almshouses of the State Board of Charities, Albany; " Prevention in Small Communities," by Miss Marion I. Moore, Buffalo; " The Breaking Up of the Families of the Poor; Its Humanity, and Its Influence as a Whole on the Question of Pauperism, and the Duty of Officials in Such Cases," by William P. Constable, Commissioner of Charities, Yonkers; " Why Should Superintendents of the Poor Keep a Complete System of Records," by L. L. Long, Superintendent of the Poor, Erie county; " Dependency and Crime," by G. L. Mosher, Superintendent of the Poor, Cattaraugus county; " Concerning the Causes of Pauperism and Social Delinquency," by Dr. William O. Stillman, Albany, President of the Mohawk and Hudson River Humane Society.

Beside these papers, addresses to the convention were made by Mr. Charles F. McKenna, of New York city, on " The Catholic Home Bureau—Its History and Work;" by Rev. E. Trott, of the Children's Aid Society of New York, on the " Work of the Children's Aid Society;" and by Superintendent W. W. Mayo, of the

Berkshire Industrial Farm, Canaan Four Corners, on the "Care and Treatment of Wayward Boys." Dr. J. H. Pryor, of Buffalo, discussed the alarming increase of tuberculosis, and was followed by Senator Henry W. Hill in the advocacy of sanatoria. "The Work of the George Junior Republic" was presented by Mr. William R. George, its founder.

The papers were followed by interesting discussions, and the convention was greatly enjoyed by all in attendance.

The officers for the year 1902 are:

PRESIDENT.

A. W. WEBER..Otsego County.

FIRST VICE-PRESIDENT.

WM. P. CONSTABLE...Westchester County.

SECOND VICE-PRESIDENT.

P. REDMOND..Jefferson County.

SECRETARY AND TREASURER.

J. W. IVES..Wyoming County.

COMMITTEE ON ORGANIZATION.

J. W. Ives..Wyoming County.
Wm. P. Constable..Westchester County.
E. A. Barber..Yates County.
D. W. Hitchcock..Dutchess County.
G. L. Mosher..Cattaraugus County.

COMMITTEE ON LEGISLATION.

J. R. Washburn..Jefferson County.
C. R. Dean..Tioga County.
L. L. Long..Erie County.
Cortland Crossman..Genesee County.
Isaac Purdy..Westchester County.

COMMITTEE ON RESOLUTIONS.

Wm. P. Constable..Westchester County.
Homer Folks..New York County.
T. L. Stone..Livingston County.
W. W. Collins..Orange County.

COMMITTEE ON PLACE.

C. V. Lodge..Monroe County.
L. L. Long..Erie County.
C. M. Lane..Westchester County.
J. J. Kirkpatrick..Suffolk County.
D. C. Brooks..Tioga County.

COMMITTEE ON TOPICS.

H. C. Taylor..Chautauqua County.
Levi A. Page..Ontario County.
Mrs. G. L. Mosher..Cattaraugus County.
E. B. Kear..Westchester County.
Mrs. Robt. McPherson..Steuben County.

The next convention will be held in Yonkers, in June, 1902, the time to be determined by the officers of the convention.

THE TWENTY-EIGHTH NATIONAL CONFERENCE OF CHARITIES AND CORRECTION.

The twenty-eighth National Conference of Charities and Corrections with Mr. John M. Glenn, of Baltimore, President, was held at Washington, D. C., May 9 to 15. Over six hundred registered delegates were present, and the sessions of the conference were attended also by many of the residents of Washington and vicinity. Altogether the meeting was a pleasant and a profitable one.

Some of the subjects considered by the conference were: "Destitute and Neglected Children," "Legislation Concerning Charities," "The Insane," "Division of Work Between Public and Private Charities," "Needy Families in Their Homes," "The Care of the Feeble-Minded and the Epileptic," "Reformatories and Industrial Schools," and "Treatment of the Criminal."

A committee was appointed to coöperate with the Director of the United States Census in securing an amendment to the law which will permit the Census Bureau to collect throughout the United States uniform statistics with relation to dependency and crime.

This Board was represented at the conference by President William R. Stewart; Secretary Robert W. Hebberd; Superintendent of State and Alien Poor Byron M. Child, and Inspector Robert W. Hill. The delegates from the public and the private charities of New York State in attendance at the conference numbered 53.

The next conference is to meet in Detroit in May, 1902, with Hon. Timothy Nicholson of Richmond, Indiana, a member of the Board of State Charities, President.

THE STATE CHARITIES AID ASSOCIATION.

In compliance with chapter 546 of the Laws of 1896 the State Charities Aid Association—a voluntary association among whose objects are the visitation and improvement of charitable institutions maintained by the State, or by cities, counties, or towns, and placing destitute children in families—has submitted to the Board its twenty-ninth annual report, covering its work for the year ending September 30, 1901. The year's work is summarized in the report as follows:

1. The Association has maintained through its local committees, and from the central office, a visitation of the almshouses and public hospitals in forty-seven of the sixty-one counties of the State, including the frequent inspection of all the numerous institutions in the Department of Public Charities in New York city.

2. It has inspected eight State charitable institutions, through its eighteen local visitors.

3. It has appeared through its county committees before several county boards of supervisors, and before the board of estimate and apportionment in New York city, to state the needs of and to urge proper appropriations for public charitable institutions.

4. It has examined carefully all proposed legislation relating to charities, taking an active part by correspondence or by appearing before legislative committees, in furthering desirable measures, and in opposing several that were deemed to be detrimental to the public interest and to the welfare of the poor.

5. It has found permanent free homes in carefully selected families for seventy-two destitute children, nearly all of whom were received from public officials or institutions, and has exercised a careful supervision over these children, as well as over those placed out during the preceding two years and a half, a total of 182 being under oversight during the year.

6. It has maintained an oversight over dependent children placed out or boarded out in families by public officials in Queens, Nassau, Rockland, Richmond, Allegany, Lewis, Suffolk, Sullivan and Wyoming counties.

7. In many other ways it has labored for a wiser and more humane management of public charities through the development of an informed public sentiment, and through coöperation with public officials.

These results have been secured through the interest and coöperation of about one thousand volunteer workers residing in all parts of the State, with such paid service at the central office as has been necessary to give unity and continuity to the work.

The State Charities Aid Association.

In addition to the above, and supported by separate funds, are the following branches:

1. Committee on providing situations in the country for destitute mothers with infants, which secured 441 situations for homeless women with their babies during the year.

2. Newburgh Agency for Dependent Children, maintained by our committee in the city of Newburgh, which visited and maintained an effective oversight over 77 destitute children from that city placed in families, placed 11 children in carefully selected free permanent homes, and investigated 27 applications for the admission of children to the Children's Home.

3. Columbia County Agency for Dependent Children, which assists the superintendent of the poor of Columbia county in the investigation of the circumstances of children who are or are sought to be made a charge on the county. As a result of the work of this agency the number of children maintained by the county in private institutions has been reduced from 98 at the beginning of the year to 62 at the end of the year.

4. Joint committee (A. I. C. P. and S. C. A. A.) on the care of motherless infants, which, in coöperation with the Department of Public Charities, had under its care 99 motherless babies, received from Bellevue Hospital and the Kings County Hospital. Of these 99 babies, 43 were placed in permanent free homes for adoption during the year. The mortality rate among the foundlings has been reduced from an appallingly high rate to 17 per cent. among those under the care of the committee during the past year.

In all, 1,063 children placed in families, or with their mothers in situations, were under the oversight of the various branches and committees of the association on October 1, 1901. If these children were collected in one institution, the expenditure for site and buildings would certainly be at least $500,000, and the annual expenditure for maintenance not less than $100,000. Under the present plan there has been no expense for land or buildings, and only a few thousand dollars per year for placing out and subsequent supervision. The superior advantages of family life for these younger children are not less marked, and are far more important to the community than the incidental economy of the plan.

COUNTY VISITING COMMITTEES.

Forty-five of the association's 50 county committees have sent to the central office reports of their work during the past year. Nearly 300 visits have been made by members of these committees to 45 almshouses. This does not include the very large number of visits made by the members of the New York, Kings and Richmond county committees to public charitable institutions in New York city. Committees have been organized in the counties of Schoharie, Sullivan, Niagara, Wyoming, Clinton and Madison. Two of these, Clinton and Wyoming, are counties in which

The State Charities Aid Association.

the association has never before had committees. There are still five counties containing public charitable institutions where the association has no committee, and it is hoped that during the coming year committees will be organized in as many as possible of these counties, and that other committees which have fallen into partial inactivity will be reorganized. During the year the assistant secretary has visited the almshouses in the following 17 counties: Broome, Cattaraugus, Chautauqua, Chenango, Clinton, Columbia, Cortland, Herkimer, Livingston, Montgomery, Tompkins, Niagara, Orleans, Sullivan, Warren, Wayne and Wyoming. Committee meetings have been attended by the assistant secretary in the following 11 counties: Columbia, Herkimer, Livingston, Montgomery, Nassau, Rensselaer, Rockland, Tompkins, Ulster, Wayne and Westchester.

There can be little doubt that the almshouses all over the State have improved very markedly during the past few years. Eight years ago our report stated that "As a result of the visitation of all the county poorhouses and city almshouses, 62 in number, it may be said that the general condition of 38 is very good, of 16 moderately good, and that eight are so far below the present standard of efficiency in administration that their condition must be pronounced unsatisfactory." It is interesting to note that of the eight unsatisfactory almshouses one has been abandoned, one is being now replaced by a new institution, five are now in good condition and well managed, and only one of the eight is still unsatisfactory. Even in this case improvements will probably be made before long in accordance with promises made by the county board of supervisors to our local committee.

The defects of most of the almshouses seldom include overcrowding, which if present would exaggerate unhygienic conditions. Most of the almshouses have accommodations which are sufficient in quantity if not always satisfactory in quality. This is largely due to the fact that the almshouse population of the State is practically stationary. Dependents, defectives and delinquents are increasing, in some cases at a rate greater than the rate of increase in the general population, but owing to the gradual removal of certain of these classes from county to State institutions, the almshouse population is actually on the decrease. As an example of this, we may mention that in the case of 40 of the almshouses in this State, regarding which we have secured complete statistical returns both this year and five years ago, we found that while their total population on October 1, 1896, was 4,133, their census on October 1, 1901, is 3,965. Twenty-five years ago only about 10 per cent. of the State dependents, exclusive of the insane, were in State institutions. Now fully 30 per cent. are cared for by the State.

It is a noticeable fact that with few exceptions the best almshouses in the State are those where the keeper and matron have held office for the longest terms. At the Madison county almshouse the same man has acted as superintendent and keeper for 32 years; at the Oswego city almshouse the keeper has served for 21 years; at the Jefferson and Chautauqua county almshouses for 18 years; at the Suffolk county almshouse, 15 years. These almshouses have few equals in the State, and they are examples of the advantages that would follow the elimination of these positions from the influence of partisan considerations and their instatement in the civil service as positions where the qualifications for office are efficiency, fidelity and experience. To influence public opinion to this end might well be regarded as a part of the duty of our members in all sections of the State.

For many years we have been urging improvement in the care and accommodations of the sick, and from year to year have noted with satisfaction the steady though slow progress towards reform in this department. We have spoken with gratification of the erection of separate hospital buildings on almshouse grounds and the rearrangement and equipment for hospital uses of the buildings formerly used for other purposes. We wish to call attention to the fact that the setting apart of such rooms or buildings is not sufficient, that unless proper care is furnished, proper accommodation is of minor importance. A hospital where the sick are cared for by fellow-inmates under the occasional supervision of an over-worked matron, is not a hospital in any real sense of the term. In some cases it has been found that almshouse hospitals were not used for the sick on account of lack of nurses, but were filled with inmates who, though infirm, were considered able to care for themselves and one another; while those really ill were detained in their own rooms where the matron or attendants could more conveniently look after them. This is the case in Wayne county, where the association has long prided itself on having secured a cottage hospital, built on plans furnished by the association. Excluding Erie county, there are only five trained nurses employed at the ten county almshouses which have separate hospital buildings. These are at the hospitals in Broome, Niagara, Onondaga, Rensselaer and Westchester counties. At the almshouse hospitals in Chautauqua, Columbia, Steuben, Suffolk and Wayne counties the sick are cared for by untrained attendants or fellow-inmates.

Dutchess County.

As no improvements have been made during the past year, conditions at the county almshouse continue to be markedly unsatisfactory. The keeper and matron are the only paid employes, and on October 1, 1901, there were 108 inmates. This is at the ratio of one employe to 54 inmates. The average ratio of employes to inmates in other county almshouses is about 1 to 15. In our last year's report we described the almshouse in part as follows:

"The exterior of the buildings is very presentable, but inside they are worn out. The walls are cracked, the floors and staircases worn, the ventilation bad, and the whole arrangement and equipment unsatisfactory. It is difficult to think of any respect in which the almshouse is what it should be. * * * The bedrooms and dormitories are littered with the belongings of the inmates. There are only two bath tubs, and the inmates are not forced to bathe regularly. The inmates are obliged to use outside closets at a considerable distance from the buildings. For the women there is a good modern closet indoors, but this is kept locked, and is apparently not used, while the feeble old women are forced to use at all seasons of the year, and both day and night, the old closets at the end of their yard. This is entirely unnecessary and inexcusable. * * *

"It is probably unwise to spend much money repairing these worn-out old buildings, which should be abandoned for a new almshouse. It is difficult to understand how the people of Dutchess county can continue to be satisfied with one of the poorest almshouses to be found in the State. We wish that the people of the neighborhood, many of whom are noted for their public spirit, would disregard the deceptively creditable outward appearance of this institution, and would see from the inside its real condition and needs."

Erie County.

The committee reports that the improvements of the past year include a barn, a granary, and a vegetable cellar. A building for consumptives is being erected in connection with the county hospital. Among the needs are a new morgue, new bathrooms, and better food for the almshouse inmates. Neither the ventilation nor the drainage is what it should be, and the buildings are not kept perfectly clean and orderly. There is much room for improvement at the almshouse. The first and greatest need is that it should be put out of reach of political influence.

Livingston County.

The committee reports that the improvements of the past year are new bath-tubs and water-closets. The needs are said to be a hospital for the sick, a steam laundry, and a house for the superintendent and his family.

The almshouse was visited by the assistant secretary, June 15, 1901, in company with the secretary of the county committee and the chairman of the building committee of the board of supervisors. The institution was found in somewhat better condition than at the time of the visit from the central office four years ago. The appearance of the grounds had been improved by the removal of the sheds and outbuildings. The interior of the buildings had been painted, a concrete floor had been laid in the basement kitchen and dining-room, and modern plumbing had been introduced. None of the radical changes needed have, however, been made, and the necessity for a complete rearrangement of the buildings is still urgent. Happily, this reform is being considered by the board of supervisors. The plans under consideration include building a separate house on the grounds for the superintendent and his family, and reconstructing the main building for the exclusive use of the men inmates. One of the two buildings formerly used for the insane would then be occupied by the women inmates, and the other would be converted into a suitable hospital for the sick. At present sick men are cared for in a part of the building where there is no water connection, while the sick women are left in their own bedrooms or dormitories. A woman suffering from erysipelas was found in her bedroom attended by other inmates. A nurse for the sick is an urgent need. While the changes in the buildings are being made, dining-rooms and sitting-rooms should be provided on the ground floor, so that the use of the basement could be entirely abandoned except for storehouse purposes. Steam heat should take the place of the stoves now in use, and a steam laundry should be arranged for, with spray baths and clothes rooms adjacent. Now that the work of repairing this almshouse has been begun it should be done thoroughly. There is no reason why the institution should not become one of the best almshouses in the State, instead of continuing to be, as it has been for so long a time, one of the poorest both in construction and management.

Visitors to State Charitable Institutions.

During the past year the eight institutions of this class for which the association has visitors, have been inspected frequently by the eighteen visitors who have undertaken this important work on behalf of the association. The Craig Colony for epileptics and the Western House of Refuge for Women have also been visited by the assistant secretary, and the Syracuse and Rome institutions have been visited by our able visitors to the State Custodial Asylum for Feeble-Minded Women.

Of the eight State charitable institutions which we are now visiting, four are institutions for the feeble-minded, the epileptic, and the idiotic; two are reformatories for women, and two are institutions for children. With the exception of the last two these institutions are caring for only a part of those classes for whom they are supposed to make complete provision. This is due in the case of the four institutions for the feeble-minded and epileptic, to the failure of the Legislature to make sufficient appropriations for buildings; and in the case of the reformatories for women, to the failure of the courts to commit many who are eligible.

The four institutions for defectives have now a capacity for 2,400 inmates. With buildings now under way or already provided for by appropriations, this capacity will probably be increased in the course of a year by at least 300. In order that these institutions should do their work adequately they should be doubled in size.

An important feature in the management of these institutions is the fixing of rules for the admission, transfer and discharge of inmates. In our report of last year we said, " It is questionable whether the determination of the eligibility of persons for admission, discharge and transfer,

The State Charities Aid Association.

should be left to the managers and officers of the institutions, or whether it should not rather be controlled by an authority outside of the institutions whose interest is that of the State at large." As there is no obligation to receive a larger number of inmates than can be accommodated comfortably, the managers are not forced by the pressure of overcrowding to make strenuous efforts to secure appropriations for new buildings. An example of this is the cottage for sixty inmates at the Newark State Custodial Asylum, for which the appropriation was made in 1898, and which was opened for the reception of inmates in October, 1901. If the sixty inmates had been crowded into the institution during this time the authorities would probably have found some way to hasten the work.

At several of the State institutions applications for admission appear to be thrown out, not only because the person is described as "vicious" or "troublesome" or "bad-tempered," but often because the application papers are incompletely or inaccurately written. The occasional inability of the superintendent of the poor to make out an application in correct form is not a good reason for denying the benefits of the institution to needy cases. The State hospitals for the insane follow the custom of sending a physician to examine on behalf of the hospital every applicant for admission. Might not some such course be taken by the State charitable institutions with mutual benefit to the institutions and the community? If a central authority examined and passed upon the applications for admission to all these institutions there would not be found, as at present, so many inmates in each institution who properly belong in one of the others, who were either admitted because of misleading statements in the application papers, or have so changed after admission as to become unfit inmates suitable for transfer, but not transferred because of the lack of coöperation between different institutions in this group. The four institutions are so closely related in their work as to be interdependent, and if the needed coöperation among them cannot be secured by voluntary action on the part of the institutions in question, it should be brought about by the external pressure of a central authority.

State Custodial Asylum for Feeble-Minded Women, Newark.

Our efficient visitors continue to investigate the institution quarterly and to report regularly to us regarding its condition and needs. Of all the needed improvements mentioned in our report of last year, the only one which appears to have been made is the laying of new floors in the second and third stories of the main building. Retinting the walls and repairing the woodwork has further improved the dormitories and halls in this part of the building.

A new cottage which, by the terms of the contract, was to have been completed July, 1900, was actually completed July, 1901. Owing to the fact that in some respects the work was not done in accordance with the terms of the contract, the cottage was not opened for the reception of inmates until October. The plastering is already cracking. As the appropriation for this cottage was made in 1898, the prolonged delay in building and opening it is discreditable to the managers and the State officials responsible. Unfortunately it is not any of these persons who suffer for this neglect of duty, but the county officials and the community at large, who are not being relieved of the burden of caring for these defectives, as the State laws contemplate that they should be.

A house for the superintendent would probably be provided at less cost than a cottage for inmates, and as the space that could thus be vacated in the main building could be turned into dormitories and day-rooms for the women, an appropriation for this purpose would be of benefit.

An industrial building is also urgently needed. In July, the resident physician, having proved unsatisfactory, was dismissed, and since then a visiting physician from the village has taken charge of the sick. The visitors report the institution to be in its usual excellent condition and ably managed.

PLACING HOMELESS CHILDREN IN FAMILIES.

Our methods of investigating the character and circumstances of families applying for children, and of subsequent oversight through personal visits, correspondence with school teachers, foster parents and others were fully described in our report for 1899, with a detailed statement of several cases, and need not be repeated at length here. The work has been carried on with increasing interest and helpfulness on the part of all branches of the association, with gratifying appreciation and coöperation from public officials and institutions, and with most encouraging results.

The work of the past year may be briefly summarized as follows:

Number of children in families under our oversight, October 1, 1900. 110
Placed in homes during the year............................... 72

                                                                162
Passed from care during the year:
Returned to relatives who were found to be of good character,
    and able to care for their children......................... 2
Returned to institutions....................................... 2
Legally adopted 15
Died 2
                                                                —— 21
Remaining in families under our oversight, October 1, 1901........ 161

                                                                182

As the work has now been carried on for a period of more than three years, a fuller report of the work during the entire period may be of

The State Charities Aid Association.

During. From June 1, 1898, to September 30, 1901, a period of three years and four months, we received about 1,000 letters of inquiry from families who were considering the adoption of children. Of this number 609 supplied the information required by our formal application blank.

The results of our investigation of these 609 applications may be summarized as follows:

Investigated and approved.. 264
Investigated and disapproved.................................... 261
Withdrawn because the families decided not to take children or
   secured them elsewhere....................................... 63
Transferred to other societies.................................... 9
Still pending 12
                                        609

SUPERVISION OF CHILDREN PLACED OUT BY PUBLIC OFFICIALS.

In the counties of Allegany, Lewis, Sullivan, Suffolk and Wyoming, 138 children who have been placed in free family homes by superintendents or overseers of the poor, are under the friendly supervision of members of the association's committees in those counties. In Rockland and Nassau counties 125 children, who are boarded in families by public officials, are visited by members of the association's local committees. In most cases these children have been found to be in good homes, where they are being well cared for, sent regularly to school, and trained to be useful and self-supporting. In the few cases where children have been found in unsuitable homes the facts have been reported to the local officials or to the State Board of Charities, and steps have been taken to secure their removal.

SEVENTH ANNUAL REPORT OF THE AGENCY FOR DEPENDENT CHILDREN OF NEWBURGH.

The Agency for Dependent Children, established in October, 1894, by the Newburgh committee of the State Charities Aid Association, has continued during the past year its oversight of destitute children placed in families by the public and private charities of that city, and the finding of additional free homes in families for children becoming dependent. The average number under its oversight during the year has been more than twice the average number maintained in the City Children's Home. Though these children are in many different places and not known as objects of charity, they are as truly the wards of the city of Newburgh and the city was responsible for them as it is for the smaller number in the Children's Home. The primary object of this agency is to act for the city in the discharge of its responsibilities for the well being of these children. Besides the children received from the city, a certain number from the Home for the Friendless have been placed in families and a considerable number at the request of individuals. In many cases these children would have become public charges had not the agency provided for them. The number of children under the oversight of the agency October 1, 1900, was 69. Twelve have been added to the list during the past year, and four have passed from our care—of whom one has been legally adopted, another has become 18 years of age, and two were returned to parents or relatives— leaving 77 children under our oversight on September 30, 1901. Of these 77 children, 58 are in free permanent homes in families, 3 are being boarded in families at the expense of members and friends of the committee, 3 are in hospitals (2 of them boarded at the expense of friends of the committee), and 13 are in various institutions for the special training of those who are physically, mentally, or morally defective. Of these 77 children, 45 have been inmates of the City Children's Home, 14 of the Home for the Friendless, and 18 have been received at the request of individuals.

First Annual Report of the Columbia County Agency for Dependent Children.

This agency was established in January, 1901, for the purpose of assisting the superintendent of the poor in the investigation of the circumstances of children who are, or are sought to be made, a charge on Columbia county. All dependent children in this county are county charges, and must be passed upon annually by the superintendent of the poor. As this officer is also the keeper of the almshouse, it is impossible for him personally to make the investigations required by the rules of the State Board of Charities in pursuance of the provisions of the State Constitution. The association, desiring to assist the superintendent of the poor in the observance of the law, brought the matter to the attention of the board of supervisors, the assistant secretary appearing before the board in Hudson on December 5, 1900. The association offered to undertake the work of investigation, through its Columbia county committee, if the county board of supervisors would pay $500 to the county committee towards the salary and expenses of the agent. The offer was accepted, a member of the Columbia county committee was engaged to act as agent, and the work was initiated in January, 1901.

It was found that at the beginning of the year there were 98 children maintained by Columbia county in private institutions; at the end of the year the number was 62—a reduction of nearly 38 per cent. The bills presented to the county for the maintenance of children, which had in recent years amounted to between $9,000 and $10,000 a year, were between $2,000 and $3,000 lower for the present year, though the full effects of the reduction in the number of children maintained did not begin to be felt until the middle of the year.

The following reports and papers have been accepted by the Board for transmission to the Legislature:

APPENDED PAPERS.

Report of the Committee on Reformatories.

Report of the Committee on Idiots and Feeble-minded.

Report of the Committee on Soldiers and Sailors' Homes.

Report of the Committee on Craig Colony.

Report of the Board of Managers of Craig Colony.

Report of the Committee on the Blind.

Report of the Committee on the Deaf.

Report of the Committee on the Thomas Asylum for Orphan and Destitute Indian Children.

Report of the Committee on the New York State Hospital for the Care of Crippled and Deformed Children.

Report of the Board of Managers of the New York State Hospital for Crippled and Deformed Children.

Report of the Committee on the New York State Hospital for the Treatment of Incipient Pulmonary Tuberculosis.

Report of the Board of Trustees of the New York State Hospital for the Treatment of Incipient Pulmonary Tuberculosis.

Report of the Committee on State and Alien Poor; including annual report of the Superintendent of State and Alien Poor.

Report of the Committee on Inspection.

Report of the Committee on Orphan Asylums and Children's Homes; including report of the Superintendent of Inspection.

Report of the Committee on Placing-Out of Children.

Report of the Committee on Dispensaries.

Report of the Committee on Almshouses.

Your Committee on Reformatories would respectfully report that the several institutions of this class which come under the supervision of the State Board of Charities, have been duly visited by the members of this Committee, and inspected by the special inspector of this Board during the past year.

In reviewing the conditions existing in the several institutions, State and private, your Committee has the satisfaction of recording progress in some important particulars. This is more noticeable in some institutions than in others, but all have been striving to gain a position abreast with the most advanced sentiment and reformatory methods of the times. Some anticipated changes in the location of one of the State institutions of this class will, if accomplished, open questions relating to the establishment of certain technical pursuits and training for special occupation which have not heretofore found a place in the general scheme of our reformatory method. The necessity for the removal of one or more of these institutions, now situated in thickly populated centers, into a rural district where a sufficiently large section of land can be had for the development of agricultural and kindred pursuits, will present a new phase in the industrial resources for reformatory training. This is also to some extent anticipated for the new reformatory for women recently opened at Bedford, which institution has a considerable acreage of land included in its grounds and which can be devoted to such uses.

The addition to the State's resources for reformatory work among women in the establishment and opening of the institu-

REPORT.

To the State Board of Charities:

Your Committee on Reformatories would respectfully report that the several institutions of this class which come under the supervision of the State Board of Charities, have been duly visited by the members of this Committee, and inspected by the special inspector of this Board during the past year.

In reviewing the conditions existing in the several institutions, State and private, your Committee has the satisfaction of recording progress in some important particulars. This is more noticeable in some institutions than in others, but all have been striving to gain a position abreast with the most advanced sentiment and reformatory methods of the times. Some anticipated changes in the location of one of the State institutions of this class will, if accomplished, open questions relating to the establishment of certain technical pursuits and training for special occupation which have not heretofore found a place in the general scheme of our reformatory method. The necessity for the removal of one or more of these institutions, now situated in thickly populated centers, into a rural district where a sufficiently large section of land can be had for the development of agricultural and kindred pursuits, will present a new phase in the industrial resources for reformatory training. This is also to some extent anticipated for the new reformatory for women recently opened at Bedford, which institution has a considerable acreage of land included in its grounds and which can be devoted to such uses.

The addition to the State's resources for reformatory work among women in the establishment and opening of the institu-

tion at Bedford will give opportunity for more preventive work
than has yet been accomplished by providing for the commitment and care of a class of young girls who are wayward and
need to be removed during an important formative period of
their life from the great centers of population in which they
find those temptations which their environment is not of such
a character as to enable them to resist.

Much stress has been laid in previous reports of this Committee upon a classification of the inmates of these several institutions as far as possible based upon character, rather than
upon the age of the inmate. In some of the reformatories for
women very appreciable advance has been made in this respect
by the gathering into cottage families of certain classes of inmates, and of placing them under officers especially fitted for
the proper control and direction of such cases.

The changes made during the past two years in the several
boards of managers of the reformatories of this State have
resulted in marked advance for such institutions in important
respects. The introduction of new managers into such boards,
who represent the most advanced opinions and experience in
reformatory work, has accomplished a wide departure from the
long-cherished but unfortunate traditions of obsolete systems.

While congratulating ourselves upon the lines of development and advance, we are still compelled to recognize the existence of some important failures to develop, in a co-ordinate and
satisfactory manner, a system of technical instruction for the
male and female inmates of these institutions, which shall prove
to be the most desirable resource in securing to such individuals
a means of self-maintenance on their return to society after
their temporary absence from the same. While much has
already been developed along these lines in some institutions,
and a varied and extended course of technical instruction has
been established, the question whether the results obtained
from such instruction are the most satisfactory cannot at this
time be affirmatively answered. Technical instruction and labor
in such institutions are not only required to afford proper

mental development and education for the individual, but it is also demanded to afford to such individual those resources which will enable him or her to secure a sufficient and self-respecting maintenance in the life in society for which the reformatory effort has been invoked. This question is still a problem for whose solution the most earnest and efficient thought is demanded.

Another conspicuous lack noticeable in the results accomplished from year to year, is a failure to secure the contributions to our scientific knowledge, which these institutions present. In them are gathered a large number of defectives, who, though styled "delinquents," are mainly so because defective. These defectives are such either from hereditary entailment, or from defective early environment, or from a combination of both. Heredity, however, proves the less important factor in the problem, and we must look for an explanation of conditions which exist, to an early environment which has failed to provide for these unfortunates those circumstances which are essential to normal physical and mental development. This idea is rooting itself more and more deeply in the minds of students of sociology, and those who follow the development of our reformatory system with close observation will recognize this as an underlying consideration in the most important lines of reformatory effort as established in our several institutions of this character.

We would emphasize the importance of a general recognition of this fact. In these institutions are gathered a large number of defectives, and it is a necessity for their proper treatment that they should be considered *individually;* that is, instead of a general line of instruction and discipline, to which all are committed as a matter of course, each individual on entry should be examined by expert officers, who should make a careful and minute record of his or her physical or mental condition of all attainable information regarding the family history and the life history of the individual up to the time of coming under observation in the institution. These details, if systematically recorded, afford a basis for the proper treatment of such individual cases, as well as a source from which generalizations can be drawn, which will prove an invaluable contribution to scientific knowledge. At the present time no organized system of this character exists in the several institutions, and, hence, this valuable scientific information which might be accumulating, goes largely to waste. It is true that in some of these institutions an effort is made to obtain and secure some portion of this information, but such effort belongs to individual institutions and forms no part of a general plan established by the State and uniformly maintained in each institution of this class. One of the fundamental causes of failure in this respect is observed in a policy, seemingly unwise, of failing to employ the most competent medical service obtainable for such an institution. This fact is not due to parsimony on the part of the State and its officials, but to a failure to recognize the importance of the scientific aspect and needs of these institutions, and the erroneous tendency of regarding them as custodial efforts.

These institutions are, in one sense, a branch of the hospital work of society in that they have to do with the care of its defective members. In our hospitals for the treatment of acute diseases, a staff of the ablest, and best equipped physicians of the community is called into service. The same rule should be maintained throughout the entire system of reformatory effort.

We would urge, therefore, a recognition of the importance of an adequately compensated and carefully chosen body of medical officers for the necessities of these institutions and the establishment of a general system of observation and record which shall furnish to the State the information to which it is entitled in regard to its wards, and also shall secure and contribute for the benefits of the students of sociology, that knowledge and information of the causes of dependency and delinquency, in our communities, for the attainment of which earnest efforts are now being pushed in so many directions.

CONCLUSIONS.

In concluding this report, we feel that emphasis should be placed upon the importance of removing from our centers of population those reformatory institutions which are, at the present time, included within the boundaries of the same. This committee has, in previous reports, dwelt upon the importance of rural life and surroundings in their influence upon the mind and body of the adolescent. For the child, a close touch with nature is all important, and the crowded thoroughfare affords little during the plastic period of life which contributes to physical or mental development of a high order. The proposition, therefore, to remove certain of our reformatory institutions into rural surroundings is insisted upon in this report.

Your Committee feel that they should give equal emphasis to a matter which has been referred to in a previous portion of this report, involving a more perfect and extended scientific study of the inmates of these institutions. The causes of defect and delinquency being known, intelligent measures for their prevention and amelioration can be established. Without searching deeply into the causes of these conditions, any effort for their relief or removal must be partial. We would, therefore, recommend that the Committee of this Board upon reformatory institutions, be instructed to call the attention of the managers of the several institutions of this class within whose province such matters directly fall, to the importance of special consideration of these and kindred questions. This recommendation is made with the belief that, through such effort, steps may be initiated which will lead to the desired improvement in this respect.

A special report upon the special features of each institution is hereto appended.

Respectfully submitted,
                EDWARD H. LITCHFIELD,
                ENOCH V. STODDARD, M. D.,
                ANNIE G. de PEYSTER,
                                        Committee.

STATE INDUSTRIAL SCHOOL, ROCHESTER, N. Y.

[Established, 1846.]

President..............................Rev. Isaac Gibbard.

Secretary and Treasurer....................Andrew H. Bown.

Superintendent..........................Franklin H. Briggs.

During the past year the members of this committee have visited the institution individually, and the member from the Seventh district has visited the institution at various intervals. The inspector of State institutions of the State Board of Charities has frequently inspected the institution and its several departments.

POPULATION.

The census on November 1, 1901, was as follows:

Instructors	26
Teachers	23
Officials	12
Other employes	72
Total	133

BOYS' DEPARTMENT.

First division	146
Second division	229
Third division	204
Fourth division	192
Total	771

Of these 22 are colored.

INDUSTRIAL DEPARTMENT—TECHNICAL SCHOOLS.

Band	59
Bakery	24
Boiler room	17
Blacksmith shop	19
Carpenter shop	25
Electrical construction	20

Foundry 25
Floriculture 16
Laundry 45
Machine shop....................................... 27
Mason shop... 31
Pattern shop....................................... 16
Paint shop... 25
Printing office..................................... 45
Steam and gas fitting.............................. 10
Shoe shop.. 62
Tailor shop.. 29
Manual training.................................... 162
Police and yards................................... 37
Repair 27
Dining-rooms 27
Kitchen 8
Store room 5
Orderlies 9

    Total 770
                                                   ====

GIRLS' DEPARTMENT.

First division 47
Second division 64

    Total 111
                                                   ====

Of these 7 are colored.

TECHNICAL SCHOOLS.

Cooking school 28
Dress-making....................................... 12
Laundry 12
Millinery 12
Sewing 35
Kitchen 12

    Total 111

During the past year no notable changes have occurred in the lines of instruction and discipline followed in this institution. The system which has worked so satisfactorily for the past few years, has continued to yield corresponding results. No important changes have been made in the buildings or grounds of the institution, since many necessary changes in such direction are held in abeyance pending its prospective removal from the city to the country. The necessity for such a change becomes daily more apparent, and we feel that the time has arrived when such a transfer must be made in the interest of those for whom the institution was established. Modifications of lines of instruction, the addition of new and the discontinuance of some of the older methods are all dependent upon a change of the institution to a location where an ampler tract of land and freedom from the embarrassments of city surroundings will permit of their establishment and development. It is incumbent, therefore, upon the legislature of 1902, to make the necessary provision for such change.

Another urgent reason for this departure, is found in the combination, in a single institution, of a boys' and girls' department, an association which has been shown by experience to be an incompatible one under a single reformatory administration. The proposed removal of the institution to a new site, will, with the added facilities now available by the opening of the institution at Bedford, provide for the proper care of the girls now in the State Industrial School.

NEW YORK HOUSE OF REFUGE, RANDALL'S ISLAND.
[Incorporated, 1824.]

President ....Alexander E. Orr.
Secretary ....Evert J. Wendell.
Treasurer ....Edward M. Townsend.
Superintendent ....Omar V. Sage.

This institution has been visited and inspected during the past year by members of this Committee, individually, and inspected at intervals by the special inspector of the Board for State Institutions. All parts of the institution in such visits and inspection have been carefully examined.

POPULATION.

The total population on November 1, 1901, was:

BOYS' DEPARTMENT.

First division, white	312
Second division, white	269
Third division, white	91
Total	672
First division, colored	33
Second division, colored	24
Third division, colored	18
Total	75
Grand total	747

INDUSTRIAL DEPARTMENT—TECHNICAL SCHOOLS

	First division.	Second division.	Total
Tailor shop	25	23	48
Printing shop	25	14	39
Carpenter shop	....	8	8
Shoe shop	14	16	30
Machine shop	....	6	6
Bake shop	....	11	11
Paint shop	....	13	13
Blacksmith shop	5	9	14
Floriculture	10	7	17
Farm and garden	6	4	10
Masonry	5	6	11
Plumbing shop	....	3	3
Mattress wire-weaving shop	7	4	11
Electrician	2	1	3
Art of manual training	75	75	150
			374

Dining rooms	46
Kitchen	17
Hall duty	106
General duty	32
Yards	24
Carting	14
Quarantine	13
Steam and gas houses	14
Otherwise	59
	325

PRIMARY, BOYS.

Hall duty	22
Dining room	21
General duty	22
Tailor shop	22
Art manual training class	24
	111

GIRLS' DEPARTMENT.

White	75
Colored	18
Total	93

INDUSTRIAL DEPARTMENT.

Dormitories	12
Sewing room	35
Ironing room	12
Detailed duty	2
Cooking class	20
Wash room	12
Total	93

While no extensive changes have been made in or additions to the buildings of this institution, during the past year, improvements of considerable importance to facility of administration and the welfare of the inmates have been accomplished.

Chapter 282 of the Laws of 1900, appropriated for an addition to and improvements in steam plant and electric service, the sum of $25,000; for reconstructing the sewerage of the boys' department, $8,500. These appropriations, with others, providing for additional bathing and toilet facilities, equipment of the gymnasium and repairs to the building, have added greatly to the conveniences of administration, as well as to the health and comfort of the inmates.

The efforts of the superintendent to secure improvements in methods of discipline and a higher standard of service on the part of officers and employes, have been in many respects successful. An improvement is noted in the military discipline and in the movements of the boys in drill exercises. This department, however, still falls below what should be achieved from the fact that the development of the military system is limited. The boys are furnished with no arms of any kind, a means of considerable importance in securing interest and efficiency in military drill. This committee recommends the furnishing of the institution for its military department, with guns, to be used by the boys in their military exercises. In reviewing the boys during the past summer, the member of this committee so occupied, called attention of the superintendent to the fact that, though their system aimed at a regimental organization, neither the American flag nor the State flag was present in any of the military evolutions then witnessed. On inquiry it was learned that no such flag was in the possession of the institution. The national flag is important as a means of impressing youth with lessons of patriotism, loyalty and a high ideal of the province of the State, and should be kept constantly in sight. The attention of the Comptroller of the State was called to this deficiency and a prompt response was received that such a deficiency would be met on a requisition from the institution for such a flag.

Again your committee calls attention to the importance of the removal of this institution into a rural section, and the separation of the girls from the boys through the transfer of the former to an institution for girls solely.

HOUSE OF REFUGE FOR WOMEN, HUDSON.

[Established, 1881.]

President...........................Prof. Herbert E. Mills.
Secretary...............................Marcia C. Powell.
Treasurer...........................Thomas Wilson, M. D.
Superintendent.....................Hortense V. Bruce, M. D.

This institution has been visited by the members of this Committee individually, and has been frequently inspected by the Board's inspector of State institutions during the past year.

POPULATION.

The census on November 1, 1901, was 209 adults and 9 infants, who were distributed as follows:

	Inmates.	Infants.
Main building	14	......
Prison	44	......
Nursery	13	8
Hospital	16	1
Cottages	122	......
Total	209	9

Number of infants born in institution during year ending November 1, 1901	4
Age of oldest inmate	31
Age of youngest inmate	15
Number of officers	43
Number of employes	13

EMPLOYMENT STATISTICS.

For year ending October 31, 1901.

Inmates attending day schools................	92	
Inmates attending sewing schools..............	31	
Inmates attending dressmaking school.........	23	
Inmates attending cooking school.............	21	
Inmates attending laundry....................	33	
Total daily attendance...................	200	
Inmates attending two of above classes........	55	
Total number of inmates attending schools.......		145
Inmates training for nurses in hospital.........	2	
Inmates assisting storekeeper................	3	
Inmates who do general housework, kitchen and laundry work, knitting, sewing and mending..	40	
		45
Total number of inmates eligible to instruction...		190
Patients in hospital..........................	9	
Women with infants, unable to attend classes..	6	
Inmates admitted during previous month, who are still on probation......................	4	
		19
Total adult population, November 1, 1901........		209
Inmates who receive instruction in physical culture five days each week................................		190
Inmates who receive instruction in music two days each week		190

The progress made in reorganizing the several departments of the House of Refuge for Women at Hudson, and the establishment of an entirely different system of discipline by the present administration, has manifested gratifying development during the past year. The effort to secure a high grade of

officers and attendants and to establish an entirely different
spirit in the relations between the inmates and those under
whose supervision they were placed, have been productive of
notable improvement. In the cottages, in the prison and in
every department of this institution, this departure from obsolete resources and vindictive methods of discipline is everywhere
apparent. We feel that the managers have accomplished, in
the face of doubt and coolness on the part of some who cling
to old and discarded methods, a success in vindicating the correctness of newer views and methods. The steady disappearance of old traditions, of discontent and disorder, supports this
conclusion, and the managers have given an added corroboration
of the wisdom of substituting hopeful reformatory measures
for abitrary and vindictive, punitive resorts.

WESTERN HOUSE OF REFUGE FOR WOMEN, ALBION.

[Established, 1890.]

President..............................William J. Sterritt.
Secretary...................................Frederick Almy.
Treasurer............................Emily F. Swett, M. D.
Superintendent..............................Mary K. Boyd.

A formal visitation of this institution by the members of this
committee, individually, has been made during the past year.
It has also been inspected at intervals by the inspector of State
institutions of the State Board of Charities during the same
period.

POPULATION.

The census of inmates on November 1, 1901, was as follows:
Population, 119, 6 of whom are infants.

	Girls.	Infants.
Prison population	30	4
Cottage 1, population	22	
Cottage 2, population	20	
Cottage 3, population	20	1

Youngest girl, 15 years.
Oldest girl, 28 years.
Infants born in institution during year, 4.

Laundry class	11
Cooking class	18
General kitchen work	14
Sewing	20
Housekeeping and other departments	50
Infants	6
Total	**119**
School registry	65

While the number of inmates of this institution has slightly increased during the past year no important changes in its buildings or grounds have been made. The general condition of administration which has prevailed during the past three or four years continues. A quiet discipline and an atmosphere of content pervades the institution and no modification of the system previously followed has been considered necessary by its managers. While these statements may be made in general, regarding the system of discipline followed, this committee has considered it necessary in previous reports to call attention to the importance of keeping a more extended and accurate record of disciplinary measures. While in the main the superintendent considers the discipline of the institution not difficult, it is important that in this institution, as in no other similar institutions, an accurate daily record should be kept of all details of discipline and the disposal of such cases.

The addition of a farm house and stable has met a need which has proved embarrassing in the past.

A fuller development of technical instruction is desirable and an increase in the force of instructors in such departments is thought necessary. Some provision should be made by which the managers will be afforded facilities for the production of many articles used in the institution which can be made by the inmates with a reasonable amount of economy.

12

NEW YORK STATE REFORMATORY FOR WOMEN, BEDFORD.

[Established, 1892]

President..James Wood.

Secretary......................................Alice Sandford.

Treasurer.....................................Joseph Barrett.

Superintendent.....................Katharine Bement Davis.

This institution has been visited by the members of this Committee individually, and also by the Inspector of the State Board of Charities for State Institutions during the past year. Although opened but a short time, its administration is well established.

POPULATION.

The census of the officers, employes and inmates on November 1, 1901, is as follows:

Officers and employes................................... 25

Inmates... 53

Of the officers, 11 are men and are all employed outside the buildings. Fourteen are women and are occupied inside the buildings. Two additional employes, an assistant matron and the supervisor of the laundry have been asked for by the managers and granted to the institution. This completes the full number of officers required for the proper classification of its different departments.

Since the opening of the New York State Reformatory for Women, in April last, the commencement of an advanced reformatory system has been achieved. The more important official positions within the institution have been filled, and although the number of inmates is, at the present time, not large, such number has increased with sufficient rapidity to insure a continuous development of an efficient reformatory system. This institution starts with no embarrassment in initiating such systems of administration and discipline as are in accord with the most advanced ideas of the present time, and it is hoped that its development will proceed only so rapidly as is consistent with plans already outlined for its conduct. As is the case in the institution at Hudson, the Board of Managers at Bedford appreciate the importance of the selection of officials and employes possessing a high grade of character and fitness for the positions which they are to occupy. If this consideration is maintained unfaulteringly by the managers at Bedford, satisfactory results must follow.

The addition of the institution at Bedford to the State's resources for reformatory work, affords the means of doing more preventive work than has been possible in the past. In New York and its vicinity, are many girls whom the temptations of a great city are likely to lead astray. Such girls having slight or no home restraint or influences, during an impressible and formative period of their lives, need such instruction and training as the institution at Bedford, under a wise management, is capable of affording.

Among the valuable contributions from individuals for this institution, is the imposing flag-staff in the center of the group which, with its full set of handsome flags, is the gift of Mr. William H. Male, to the State.

Instruction in fine basket-making with all the materials therefor, is the gift of Miss Wood.

REPORT

Committee on Idiots and Feeble-Minded.

REPORT.

To the State Board of Charities:

Your committee on idiots and feeble-minded respectfully reports that the several institutions of this class have been visited by the members of this committee during the past year, and we desire to preface our detailed report upon each institution with some general statements which call for special consideration and early legislative action.

The policy of the State, in caring for its dependent and defective wards, is the outgrowth of an experience, which has gradually evolved a system of relief for certain classes of cases. The feeble-minded and idiotic have been separated from the several groups of dependents, among whom they were scattered promiscuously, and have been segregated into separate institutions specially adapted for their custody and care. They have been classified by the establishment of three custodial institutions, the Syracuse State Institution for Feeble-Minded Children who are teachable; the Rome State Custodial Asylum for idiotic and less teachable, and the State Custodial Asylum for Feeble-Minded Women at Newark.

In these institutions are gathered about fourteen hundred inmates, the Syracuse institution having over five hundred inmates, and each of the others over four hundred. This provision, however, falls far short of meeting existing demands, as there are still many feeble-minded children and adults in the several establishments for public relief, and in the private charitable institutions throughout the State.

In the State institutions for the care of the feeble-minded, a discriminating classification demands somewhat extensive changes. The capacity of each of these institutions is already fully taxed, and, consequently, additions and extensions to each are imperatively necessary. By a readjustment of the inmates, if increased accommodations are provided, a transfer of about one hundred and fifty adults from Syracuse can be effected. Of these, about one hundred men can be sent to Rome, and fifty women to the institution at Newark. This would provide for the reception of this number of young and teachable cases at the Syracuse institution. An extension of the institutions at Rome and at Newark is, therefore, urgently demanded.

Even this amount of additional accommodation will be insufficient to provide for the cases still under care in other public and private institutions. In nearly every community of the State, also, may be found children of teachable age who are more or less feeble-minded and who, in this early period, are capable of receiving and profiting by a special education, under favorable circumstances, which may prepare them for partial if not for full self-maintenance, and, at least, enable them to become harmless members of families in which they may be maintained.

The continuance of these feeble-minded cases in the community is an evil, and they should be promptly removed to a proper environment. In the family, in the school or in an institution, where there are children, the presence of the idiotic or feeble-minded is very pernicious. In his early years the child is imitative; he readily takes up peculiarities of manner or of speech. The mingling of normal children with the feeble-minded is of no benefit to the feeble-minded, but may be productive of lasting mental injury to the normal child. For this reason, therefore, provision should be made for the proper custody and care of all feeble-minded children separate from those of normal capacity.

The older cases of feeble-minded persons are a menace to society for the reason that, having little or no self-restraint and mental control, they are liable to increase the number of illegitimates in their communities, as well as to propagate a degenerate offspring. For this reason, the necessary provision should be made for their proper segregation.

A far larger number of such cases call for custody and care than is generally supposed. Indifference and failure to appreciate the important bearing of this question, tends to perpetuate a condition which is a menacing one. We, therefore, urge that this Board use all legitimate and reasonable efforts to secure such consideration of the subject by the next Legislature as shall secure the necessary appropriation for the extension of the institutions referred to.

We would call attention to another condition which this committee has considered in previous reports. The institutions of this class afford an extended field for scientific observation and research as to the causes of. defect and degeneracy. In thus gathering its dependents into special classes, the State not only provides for their humane treatment, but it also should require that such treatment be conducted on scientific lines, and that the results of such scientific observation shall be a matter of record, from which generalizations of great importance can be deduced. Thus, each individual ward, on entering an institution, should be made the subject of special study, and all facts of his family history ascertainable, and of his own individual life history and condition, should become a matter of record. If we are to lessen the conditions of dependency and defect in our communities, we must first seek and recognize the causes of such defect and degeneration. This can be done by the scientific study of these cases. Such observation and study and the generalizations drawn therefrom, can only be made by properly qualified medical officers.

The deficiency in this direction is very noticeable. The provision for medical officers is limited almost entirely to a custodial service. This has been especially the case at Newark. Here the superintendent is a layman, and the inefficiency of the medical department has been a source of almost constant embarrassment to the administration. The small salary paid secures a single resident medical attendant, of moderate professional capacity, and makes no provision for scientific observation or records. At Rome and at Syracuse, the superintendents, although able physicians, are almost exclusively occupied by the duties of supervision, with little opportunity for scientific work, and the assistant medical staff is too limited to admit of extended organization for such a purpose. We feel that a reorganization of this part of the administration of these institutions is essential, in order that the State may secure and make available the scientific data which this extensive field of observation will afford, if properly cultivated.

SYRACUSE STATE INSTITUTION FOR FEEBLE-MINDED CHILDREN.
Syracuse, N. Y.
[Established. 1851.]

This institution has a capacity for 546 inmates. The number of inmates present October 1, 1900, was 546. There were admitted during the year 63, making the total number under care for the year ending September 30, 1901, 609. The average number present during the year was 515.

Owing to inadequate provision for the large number of the teachable feeble-minded who are residents of this State, this institution has, unfortunately, been turned aside from its legitimate function as a school for the education of feeble-minded youth. This has been caused by the necessary retention of a large number of adult feeble-minded persons who, although originally admitted to the institution when young, have been retained for want of accommodations elsewhere. In addition to these, others were admitted too old to be improved by a course of training planned for younger and more susceptible cases. At the present time one-fourth of the inmates are above twenty-one years of age, and should be removed to give place to children who may derive benefit from the special instruction given in this institution. This change, however, will be impossible until provisions for the accommodation of such persons are established at the custodial asylums at Rome and Newark, to each of which a portion of this adult population should be removed. These institutions, however, are crowded to their fullest capacity, and the necessity for increased accommodations for this class of defectives is now very great.

It is desirable that immediate measures be taken to restrict this institution exclusively to the training and care of those feeble-minded youths who can be taken at as early a date as practicable and receive the benefit of such education as is afforded here.

Some important improvements are needed in this institution. A better system of baths should be provided by the removal of the old bathtub and the substitution of the spray bath. This change is urged on both economical and sanitary grounds.

The stairways should be arranged for the safety of the inmates in the event of fire. This has been proposed heretofore, but, owing to lack of funds, was not done.

Another important change should be effected by which a much more complete separation between the sexes can be secured than is at present the case.

STATE CUSTODIAL ASYLUM FOR FEEBLE-MINDED WOMEN.

Newark, N. Y.

[Established, 1878.]

This asylum has a capacity for 410 inmates. The number of inmates present October 1, 1900, was 411. Thirty-five were admitted during the year, making the total number under care 449. The average number present during the year was 413.

The improvements to the grounds have progressed favorably and a new building was completed during the past year. The work is of good character. The grading about the new cottages has improved the general appearance of that section of the grounds.

The electric light plant has been put in order for regular service, but the capacity of the dynamo seems to be insufficient for all the lighting that may be required. The improvements in the "A" building, in the main office and in other parts are completed and satisfactory.

The general condition of the property is good. The management of the gardens is especially commendable.

The laundry work is very much crowded for want of sufficient space. A great improvement could be made, at moderate expense, by converting the old power-house into a building to be used for laundry purposes.

The internal condition of the power-house is good. No provisions, however, for a retaining wall outside have been made and the bank has caved in some places. This should be remedied.

The excavation for the new cottage and for some new foundation work has progressed.

The pressure for admission of new inmates is constant and a new cottage dormitory is urgently necessary. In addition to this extension an industrial and school building is needed and should be considered in any extensions proposed for the coming year.

The general health of the inmates has been good, but little sickness having occurred during the past year.

The resignation of Dr. Benoit, late resident physician, causes a vacancy not yet filled. At the present time the medical service of the institution is provided for by the attendance of a physician from outside.

The new cottage, completed since last report, has room for 60 inmates. It contains two main floors and a basement devoted to service. The additional room afforded by this cottage is already discounted, and the pressure on the institution for admission of inmates remains as strong as ever, indicating the urgent necessity for enlargement.

During the past year several inmates who have been trained in the institution have been placed out in families, and reports thus far are encouraging for the continuance of such disposition of properly selected cases. While it cannot be expected that a large number of such cases can be so placed, the possibility of making even a limited number of these women self-supporting is an evidence of the value of such custodial training for such defectives.

ROME STATE CUSTODIAL ASYLUM.

Rome, N. Y.

[Established, 1893.]

This institution has a capacity for 550 inmates. The number of inmates present October 1, 1900, was 352. One hundred and nineteen were admitted during the year, making the total number under care 471. The average number present during the year was 399.

The general condition of the buildings occupied by the inmates is neat and the farm buildings also are generally in good order. The grading about the administration building is still incomplete and much additional work is required here.

Some important additions are required to the buildings. A proper mortuary building should be provided, as the present facilities are very poor and wholly inadequate and inappropriate.

An additional ward building for men is very essential, and provision should be made for not less than 150 additional beds.

Insufficient facilities for the storage of vegetables result in an actual loss to the State from inability to preserve all the products of the farm and garden.

A railroad switch would greatly facilitate the delivery and receipt of the freight required by the institution. This is now obtained by teaming, an expensive resort. Such a switch, entering upon the grounds of the institution, while a considerable item of expenditure in its establishment, would be paid for in three years by the amount now expended for teaming.

Somewhat extensive repairs, painting and betterments are required in some of the present buildings.

The rapid progress made on the new buildings gives promise that by the beginning of the new year one will be occupied and that the other will be ready before the close of the fiscal year. These will increase the capacity to 660.

The question of extensive additions to this institution for the accommodation of additional inmates is an important one. Each of the three State institutions for the care of the idiotic and feeble-minded is crowded to its fullest capacity. In the several almshouses maintained by the public, as well as in the private charitable institutions in the State, are many feeble-minded and idiotic persons who should be removed to some institution such as this at Rome or the one at Newark. The school at Syracuse for feeble-minded children should be relieved of about 150 adults, who ought to be transferred to the institutions at Rome and Newark. A considerable extension of the accommodations for inmates in this asylum is, therefore, necessary, and should be at once provided for by the enactment of the required legislation.

Respectfully submitted,

ENOCH V. STODDARD, M. D.,

Chairman.

REPORT

OF THE

Committee on Soldiers and Sailors' Homes.

REPORT.

To the State Board of Charities:

The committee of the Board, on Soldiers and Sailors' Homes respectfully reports:

The State of New York maintains two institutions of this character, one devoted exclusively to needy veterans, and the other intended to provide a home for veterans accompanied by their wives, and also for the mothers and widows of veterans. The first of these, the New York State Soldiers and Sailors' Home, at Bath, Steuben county, was established by chapter 48, Laws of 1878. The second, the New York State Woman's Relief Corps Home, located at Oxford, Chenango county, was incorporated by chapter 468, Laws of 1894. These two institutions are in every way independent of each other, and yet the establishment of both is due to the same desire to recognize the patriotic service of the soldiers and sailors who in early manhood gave themselves to their country.

THE NEW YORK STATE SOLDIERS AND SAILORS' HOME, BATH, STEUBEN COUNTY.

This Home was visited on the 20th of June by your committee, and also during the year at regular intervals by the Board's Inspector of State Institutions. On the 4th of December, 1901, the President of the Board also made a visit.

Since the last annual report there has been little in the way of radical change. The staff of officers, with one exception, remains the same. The vacancy which then existed in the surgical staff has been filled. Changes have taken place in the corps

of nurses and attendants, but the administration staff remains
substantially as before.

In the matter of general improvement: The three cottages
under way last fall are completed and occupied. The inspector,
the chaplain, and the chief engineer reside in them, and these
cottages, with those occupied by the adjutant, the quartermaster, and the surgeon, form a group near the main entrance to
the grounds.

The amusement hall has been completed, as also the new
canteen. The old canteen was converted into police headquarters. An addition to the main kitchen was built, but the kitchen
remains inadequate and another addition or extension from the
rear should be added to it. The ordinary repairs of the barracks
have been prosecuted throughout the year, and much of the
plumbing has been renewed. The addition of sanitary floors,
closets and lavatories has been beneficial. This change ought
to be continued until all the barracks are newly equipped. One
notable improvement has been the extension of cement walks,
and, when this extension is finished, these walks will greatly
promote the comfort of the members of the Home.

The renewal of the heat and power plant is now under way,
and when this is completed the complaint of inadequate heat
and light will be removed. Some improvements are needed in
the matter of drainage, for it was noted at the time of inspection
that there was much dampness in the basements of the buildings.

This Home is greatly overcrowded. With barrack room for
1,650 men, there are over 2,100 members on the roll. Some of
these are absent on furlough, but there are present, requiring
accommodations, over 1,900 men. To give beds to this number
it has become necessary to convert the basements into dormitories. As a result of this, the atmosphere in all the barracks
is rendered heavy and injurious. The air for the dormitories
is usually drawn from these basements in which men smoke
during the day and where they must sleep at night, thus not
only exhausting the oxygen but adding to the air the fumes of
tobacco.

Besides the veterans domiciled in this Home and those in the Oxford Home, there remains a large number of dependent veterans for whom there is no room. The enlargement of the Home is necessary. This can be accomplished in either of two ways: The first is by the construction of a hospital large enough to provide accommodation for all the sick, and making use of the present hospital as an overflow barracks into which shall be gathered convalescents and incurables who require a minimum of attendance. The second method is by the construction of new barracks with capacity for at least 300 inmates. It is the belief of this committee that a fully equipped hospital will have to be provided in the near future even though a temporary expedient be adopted for the present.

The Board of Trustees requests an appropriation for a convalescent hospital, and while this committee endorses the request, it does so without receding from the position that such provision ought not to take the place of the large hospital which the institution requires. The present hospital is entirely inadequate and is ill-arranged for convenience of administration. Its basements are damp, and from them foul air is drawn into the hospital wards. Every ward has cases of tuberculosis, although one ward is intended for the care of this class of patients. From the fact that it is not large enough and cannot well be separated from the ordinary work of the hospital, the germs of tuberculosis are spread throughout the building. It is advisable to have a separate structure for the treatment of patients suffering from this disease. Such isolation pavilion need not be costly, but should be equipped for the protection of the general hospital.

The present hospital ought to have verandas on each side of its wards. These now extend along the side and end of several, and furnish the patients the opportunity to enjoy the sun and air. They will give the patients relief from the air of the ward, as well as permit the wards to be more thoroughly ventilated than is possible under present conditions. This matter of ventilation is a very serious one. Pure air is so essential to the health and comfort of the men that too much stress cannot be laid upon the necessity for better ventilation. In the newer buildings ventilating shafts draw in pure air from without the buildings. The older ones, as has been said, draw their supply of air from the basements, and this should be remedied.

The laundry was found doing efficient work. In the general laundry the one great lack is for a steam fumigating plant in which the clothing of new comers may be sterilized. The hospital laundry requires two additional washing wheels, so that the bedding and clothing of the sick may not be washed in the same wheel which must cleanse the clothing of the well.

COLD STORAGE.

The appropriation for an addition to the ice house has secured a very necessary enlargement of that building. In the general kitchen the suggested addition would give ample room for an enlarged cold storage chamber. In the hospital kitchen, as well as in the main kitchen, the refrigerators are now inconveniently located. This is especially the case with the hospital kitchen. The ice for this refrigerator has to be delivered first in the basement from the wagon which hauls it from the ice house; then it must be taken through the basement to a place under the trap door in the refrigerator room, and be hauled up by rope to be placed in the ice chamber of the refrigerator. This entails a number of handlings of the ice before it reaches its final destination in the ice chamber of the refrigerator. This handling means hard work, altogether unnecessary and wasteful. Besides this the room in which the refrigerator is placed is surrounded by steam pipes, and the ice is consumed very rapidly.

COVERED COLONNADE.

As the dining-room is so very large, a number of entrances have been arranged by which the men may have ready access to their tables. The bugle blows for meals fifteen minutes before the dining hall is opened. The men begin to gather at the building even before the call of the bugle, and during the interval between the first call and the opening of the doors the men are grouped about the entrance. During pleasant weather they suffer no inconvenience, but in exceedingly warm weather as well as on rainy, cold or stormy days they suffer from the exposure. Several of the barracks are connected by covered ways with the dining hall, and these protect the men of such barracks. If a colonnade approach to the main entrance were made, covering the walk from the driveway to the main doors of the dining hall, it would afford shelter to the men at all times and would be of great service on stormy days. Besides this it would become a favorite promenade for infirm members, and could easily be arranged with seats.

ADMINISTRATION.

The general administration of the institution continues satisfactory. The officers appear capable, and a late expression from the members of the Home is that the veterans are contented with their treatment.

DISCIPLINE.

The discipline of the Home is mild and kindly. It is to be noted that the number of cases for discipline before the morning court is much less than at any time heretofore, which shows the beneficial effect of the present method. As drunkenness is the principal cause of the infractions of the rules, the lessening number of cases for trial shows a check upon the tendency to get drunk in the town, and either remain away from the Home all night, or return late and quarrelsome. The committee, repeating what has so frequently been said as to the evils of Belfast street, suggests that if it were possible to close up the large number of saloons on that thoroughfare, which is the main avenue to the grounds, the men would do their drinking in the Home canteen, and in consequence there would be little or no drunkenness. That little would be due to smuggling whiskey, which is punishable by expulsion. These saloons in proximity to the Home are its greatest bane, and legislative action should prevent the establishment of saloons within a mile or more of any soldiers' home in the State. Many men have been robbed in these places, and many more have lost their lives endeavoring to return to the Home while intoxicated. Many have died in the street who have been thrown out of the saloons after spending all their money, but the iniquity continues and will continue until legislative action sweeps the dives out of the street and makes it safe for the men.

RECORDS.

The method of keeping the records of the Home has been a development. As the system has grown it has become more and more perfect, and now the facts concerning individual members are always within easy reach in the adjutant's office.

The treasurer's department has hitherto occupied a room upon the second floor of the headquarters building. Last winter an appropriation was made to erect an addition to this building. This has been constructed and extends back of the rear office, and here the treasurer now does his work.

FOOD.

The variety, quantity and quality of food necessary for so many people makes the work of the quartermaster most exacting, and the efficient labor of this officer deserves commendation. Requisitions for food supplies are approved in the month preceding their issue. It may be said that the food supplied is of good 'quality and ample in quantity. The diet is varied as much as possible during the season.

Some complaint has been made locally that the Home does not purchase its supplies in Steuben county. It is to be borne in mind that the Soldiers and Sailors' Home is a State institution, and while located in Steuben county its maintenance must be provided for along lines of State policy. The quality of the meat and butter now supplied the Home gives no cause for complaint, and the economy exercised in the purchase of supplies is guaranteed by the watchfulness of the Comptroller's office.

CEMETERY.

The land used for cemetery purposes is now nearly filled, and it is necessary that additional land be prepared for cemetery purposes. To do this will require an appropriation.

NEEDS.

The present needs of this Home may be summed up as:

1. A new and completely equipped hospital.

2. Additional barracks.

3. Overhauling the ventilating system of the barracks and hospital.

4. The installation of a new heating and power plant in order that there may be adequate warmth and light for the institution.

5. The protection of life and property against the danger of fire.

6. The establishment of an isolation pavilion for the treatment of tuberculosis and other diseases requiring segregation.

7. The immediate enlargement of the general kitchen by the addition of a wing in the rear, and the use of screens for kitchen and dining-room.

8. The purchase of adjoining land for the enlargement of the cemetery.

9. The erection of a suitable guard house.

APPROPRIATIONS.

There was appropriated for maintenance and extraordinary expenses by the Legislature of 1901 the sum of $299,742.11.

The average number present during the year was 1,596, and the average weekly cost of support, including the value of home and farm products consumed, $2.67; excluding such value, $2.55.

The total receipts of the institution for the fiscal year ending September 30, 1901, were: Cash balance of the previous year, $85,640.67; from special appropriations, $50,932.74; from deficiency appropriation, $20,000; from unexpended appropriations of former years, $2,530.50; from general appropriations, $190,000; from all other sources, $770.66; total, $349,874.57.

The ordinary expenditures were: For salaries of officers, wages and labor, $64,773.05; for provisions, $76,636.85; for household stores, $7,514.29; for clothing, $21,549.90; for fuel and light, $17,964.73; for hospital and medical supplies, $4,135.80; for shop, farm and garden supplies, $8,089.65; for transportation and traveling expenses, $822.43; for ordinary repairs, $2,062.09; for expenses of trustees or managers, $771.55; for remittance to State Treasurer, $770.66; for all other ordinary expenses, $8,210.16; total, $213,301.16.

The extraordinary expenditures were $77,199.03, of which $58,958 was for buildings and improvements, $9,092.60 for extraordinary repairs, and $9,148.43 reverted to the State Treasurer, making the aggregate expenditures for the year $290,500.19, and leaving a cash balance of $59,374.38.

Chapter 644, Laws of 1901 (appropriation bill), appropriated for support and maintenance, and for the transportation of applicants for admission, $225,000.

Chapter 645, Laws of 1901 (supply bill), appropriated for the deficiency on account of maintenance for the year ending September 30, 1901, $20,000; and reappropriated an unexpended balance of $1,278.87 which remained from $20,000 appropriated for the construction of the assembly hall by chapter 461, Laws of 1899, the said $1,278.87 to be used for the completion of the work on the assembly hall.

Chapter 709, Laws of 1901, appropriating the following amounts: For reconstruction and repair of the electric plant, $10,000; for reconstruction and repair of the steam plant, $5,000, and in addition the unexpended balance remaining of appropriation made by chapter 395, Laws of 1900, $9,132.74; for reconstruction of boiler house and dynamo room, $15,000; for equipment of kitchen and annex, $250; for finishing three cottages, including cesspools, electric fixtures and walks, $1,600; for installing three kitchen ranges, $200; for general repairs to sanitary equipment, $950; for repairs to barracks 4 and 5 and hospital annex, $1,200; for general repairs to other buildings, $3,000; for filling and grading, $3,000; for reimbursing maintenance account, $2,-

530.50; for addition to headquarters building, $1,600; total, $53,463.24.

The chairman of your committee has had a conference with the president of the board of trustees of the Home on the subject of appropriations; while the trustees and officers of the Home recognize the propriety of a larger appropriation to meet more adequately its requirements, yet in conformity with the views of the Governor to reduce as greatly as possible all requests for appropriations for similar institutions, the amount to be asked of the Legislature has been reduced as far as is consistent with proper business administration. Your committee recommends that the appropriations asked for be approved, and that the State Board of Charities request for this institution the following appropriations, or so much thereof as may be necessary: For carriage house and stable for the commandant, $2,500; for horse stable for work horses and wagon sheds, $3,000; for gate house at entrance to Home, $800; for house of detention or lock-up, $1,200; for cement walks, $2,400; for general repairs to barracks and other buildings, $5,000; for second-hand store, tailoring and repair shop, $2,400; for purchase of Faucett farm of 153¾ acres at $45 per acre, $6,918.75; for grading and filling at new cemetery, $2,000; for sewerage, sinks, closets, etc., at hospital, $1,615; for ventilation system in hospital, $6,200; for electric fans for hospital wards, $912; for addition to chapel, $600; for new convalescent barracks, $45,000; for light arcade at main entrance to dining hall as a shelter to the members of the Home, $5,000; for isolation pavilion for tuberculosis, $25,000; for enlargement of main kitchen, $2,500; for fumigating plant, $1,500; for additional washing machinery for hospital laundry, $250; for spring house on the hill, $400; for completion of rearrangement and reconstruction of the steam and power plants, $5,000; for pipe covering in assembly hall, $400; for fire protection, $3,000; for smoke stack at power house, $2,000; making the special appropriations approved of $125,-595.75; maintenance appropriation, $225,000; making the total appropriation, $350,595.75.

NEW YORK STATE WOMAN'S RELIEF CORPS HOME, OXFORD, CHENANGO COUNTY.

The development of this institution proceeds rapidly along the lines approved by the Legislature. The Home has been visited during the year by the President of the Board. Your Committee on Soldiers and Sailors' Homes visited and examined it on June 19th. It has also been inspected by the Board's Inspector of State Charitable Institutions.

The situation of this Home is exceptionally fine. It is about 100 feet above the Chenango river, in the center of the valley, with the high hills overlooking it. The proximity to the river makes the drainage an easy matter.

The rules of the Home make veterans unaccompanied by their wives ineligible for admission. In the case of veterans and their wives or of widows of deceased veterans, the marriage must have taken place prior to 1880. The applicant must present a certificate of honorable discharge from the United States service, have resided one year in this State, be of good moral character and sound mind, and have no relatives in the State legally liable for his or her support under the law. In the case of those in receipt of a pension, it must be assigned to the treasurer of the Home. If a veteran with his wife, resident in the Home, is bereaved of the wife, the veteran must leave and seek admission to some other Soldiers' Home.

Of all pensions under $12 per month, assigned to the Home, $6 per month is paid to the pensioner and the balance is retained until his discharge or furlough, provided in the meantime he makes no other proper disposal of it. Of all pensions above $12, the Home reserves the excess of that sum for its own use.

On the 1st of October, 1901, the population consisted of 32 men and 77 women, there being more than twice as many women as men. Few of the men are able to labor, but a number of the women are capable of light forms of housework.

There is seldom occasion for penal discipline, as intoxication is very rare. The nearest saloon is in the town of Oxford, a mile and a half away, and the rules are exceedingly stringent in the matter of the introduction of intoxicants to the Home, expulsion being the penalty. For a number of months there has been no case of intoxication, and as a consequence the daily routine has gone on undisturbed.

The construction of connecting corridors between the several cottages of the group has given the members of the Home a number of convenient sitting-rooms, well lighted, well furnished now and with pleasant outlook. The installation of steam radiators of sufficient capacity in these corridors will make them very pleasant during the winter months. In the corridor connecting the small dining-room with the kitchen, two radiators were installed but have been discontinued and the fittings used in the new dining-room. It is necessary that these radiators be again connected with the steam supply, as this corridor is practically an annex of the kitchen, the baker using it as a place in which to set the dough over night in the bake pans, there being no heat in the kitchen at night.

The new dining-hall is rapidly approaching completion. It will be connected with the present kitchen by arched doorways and will have a table capacity for 120 persons. Its windows command pleasant views, and altogether it will be a grateful change from the present small and crowded room. The upper portion of this dining-hall is divided into rooms for the female help. These rooms are large and pleasant, and provision has been made for recreation, a very essential feature where the attendants are necessarily isolated from ordinary pleasures.

The new administration building is almost finished. The final touches, painting, installation of the plumbing and similar work, are under way. The connecting conduit carrying steam has been dug and the pipes are laid, so that as soon as the work of construction is finished the building can be occupied.

The steam for heating the Home is generated in the power-house under the hill, and much of the heat is lost by reason of the exposure of pipes. A new conduit is to be dug and the pipes properly protected, which will prove an economy. The pipes in the basements of the cottages are exposed and should be covered to save the heat that is now wasted.

Although this Home is not crowded at the present time, it is advisable to complete the plan which has received the sanction of the Legislature, and provide the additional building, thus giving to the Home a capacity which will suffice for the special cases which are eligible for admission.

It may well bear consideration whether these rules should not be altered so as to provide for the admission of needy veterans unaccompanied by their wives. This would to some extent relieve the present pressure upon the Soldiers' Home at Bath, and would give a suitable shelter for dependent veterans who are now excluded from the Soldiers' Homes because they are crowded.

The completion of the new barns and other outbuildings has been accomplished during the year, and the product of the farm and garden provided for.

It is recommended that the additional building which will complete the group be arranged for in the appropriations, and that the present laundry be extended so as to facilitate the work.

APPROPRIATIONS.

The special appropriations amounted to $52,238.18 and the total appropriations to $76,338.18.

Chapters 644 and 645, Laws of 1901 (appropriation and supply bills), appropriated for maintenance, furnishing and repairs $26,800. (Maintenance, $24,100; furnishing, $2,000; repairs, $700.)

Chapter 307, Laws of 1901, appropriated for the further enlargement and equipment of this Home: For dining-room building and corridor to Cottage C, $19,000; for flooring and steel beams for coal shed, $505; for engine-room floor, $135; for brick conduit for steam pipes, $4,500; for placing pipes in conduit, $700; for sheds, piggery, corncrib and henhouse, $1,878; for developing water supply, $10,000; for wire fencing and gates, $300; for work horses (team of) $200; for furnishing, $2,000; for seeding and grading, $2,000; on account of Cottage A, $220.18; for administration building (complete), $7,500.

RECEIPTS AND EXPENDITURES.

The average population for the year was 100, and the average weekly cost of support, including the value of home and farm products consumed, $3.93; excluding these, $3.68.

The receipts for the year ending September 30, 1901, were: Cash on hand at the beginning of the year, $306.16; special appropriations, $51,777.11; general appropriations, $19,500; total, $71,583.27.

The ordinary expenditures were: Salaries of officers, $1,500; wages and labor, $5,838.76; provisions, $4,615.98; clothing, $623.04; fuel and light, $2,510.73; hospital and medical supplies, $579.05; household stores, $590.32; ordinary repairs, $98.41; expenses of managers, $673.57; shop, farm and garden supplies, $1,394.59, and for all other ordinary expenses, $741.60; total, $19,166.05.

Th extraordinary expenditures are reported as $51,838.49 for buildings and improvements, making the total ordinary and extraordinary expenditures for the year $71,004.54, and leaving $578.73 as balance in cash at the close of the fiscal year. There is, however, an outstanding indebtedness of $40 for bills unpaid.

An interview between the chairman of your committee and a representative of the institution on the subject of the request for this year's appropriation disclosed the fact that the sum had been reduced to the lowest reasonable amount in view of the general desire for reductions in similar proposed appropriations.

The State Board of Charities recommends the following appropriations, or so much thereof as may be necessary, for this institution: For the erection of Cottage D and corridor, $30,000; for erection of a residence for the farmer, $1,650; to pay W. P. Buckley for foundation stone furnished for laundry building, $40; for flagging and grading, $500; for engine and dynamo connections, $1,750; for steam radiators and making all connections in corridors, $150; for farming utensils and necessary supplies, $550; for erecting veranda, $50; for changes in lavatories, $150; for changes in icehouse and cold storage rooms, $300; for hood for kitchen range, $50; for covering for steam pipes, $1,400; for extension of laundry building, $1,000; for boiler and connections, $3,500; for piping and pipe covering in conduit from power-house to the buildings, $4,000; for improving the efficiency of the steam plant,$250; for small wagon, horses and sleigh belonging to Major Treadwell's family, but used by this Home since November, 1898, $325; making the special appropriations approved of $45,665; maintenance appropriation, $25,000; making the total appropriation, $70,665.

Respectfully submitted.

S. W. ROSENDALE,

Chairman.

REPORT

OF THE

Committee on Craig Colony.

REPORT.

To the State Board of Charities:

Your committee on the Craig Colony respectfully report that this institution has been visited a number of times during the past year by this committee as a whole, and by the chairman and members of the committee individually.

POPULATION.

The census of population on October 1, 1901, was 743, of whom 440 were men and 303 were women, a gain of 131 during the year. There have been 295 admitted, of whom 198 were men and 61 women; 81 were discharged or died, and 13 transferred to insane or State hospitals, leaving 743 remaining on the above date.

The development of the Colony has continued during the past year, and the buildings under construction at the date of our last annual report, have been completed for occupancy, and provide for the accommodation of 120 additional colonists.

CONSTRUCTION.

The delay in obtaining completed plans for the new cottages has been unfortunate. The plans, as originally presented by the architect to this Board for approval, required several important changes and the delay in the receipt of the amended plans has prevented the letting of contracts for the construction of the same, thus disappointing the expectation that the cottages would be completed and available for occupancy during the current year.

One objectionable feature in the plans referred to has been a provision for basements under the cottages which were to be

14

used by the inmates and for purposes of the administration.
Your committee has been governed by what it believes to be the
opinion of the State Board of Charities, that no basements for
occupancy by inmates, for any purpose, should be constructed
in any State institution, and has, accordingly, expressed its positive disapproval of this feature of the proposed plans.

We have been unable to see any sufficient reason for the
adoption of a plan which is not in accord with the most
advanced sanitary opinion, and which is in conflict with that
generally held regarding institutional architecture. The broad
lands of the Craig Colony, with unlimited opportunity for the
location of new buildings, would alone prove sufficient objection
to plans which involve occupancy under ground, when life upon
the surface is more than amply provided for. Facility of administration is secured by surface construction. There are, therefore, no grounds upon which we can base an approval of such
plans. It has been suggested that such arrangement is more
economical and should be adopted for this reason. While we
believe in strict economy of expenditure in all administration
of the State institutions, such economy must be reasonable and
intelligently exercised. In all economical considerations, facility of administration and the welfare of the inmate should
never be lost sight of, and any attempt to lessen expenditure
at the cost of these considerations is an unwise economy. The
ease of administration and the convenience, comfort and health
of the inmate are more certainly secured by a building which is
as much as possible upon the surface level, and though such
plan may involve a slightly increased per capita cost for housing, such additional cost is in accordance with a judicious
economy.

ADMINISTRATION.

In presenting this report we desire to state that during the
past year, several important matters have required the presence
of the full committee at the Colony for special consultation
with its executive committee and superintendent. Every step
in the development of this institution is of importance to this

Board, in that, under statutory provisions, it shares with its managers the responsibility for all important measures adopted, touching constructive and administrative procedure. This special responsibility on the part of this Board, has led your committee to be solicitous regarding some questions which have arisen, affecting the interests of the Colony.

It frequently occurs that complaints from patients or their friends, are received by the State Board of Charities, which necessitate careful and thorough investigation. In this connection we would call attention to the fact that the epileptic is liable to be in more or less disturbed and unstable condition mentally, and that his sensations and mental impressions are susceptible of perversions which lead to irregular mental action. For this reason, he often becomes irritable and complains of others as being the cause of annoyances, or even of ill treatment, which are in reality the results of his own distorted fancy or ill-regulated actions. The care of these cases, therefore, calls for great forbearance and judgment on the part of officers, nurses and employes.

In the case of the epileptic, individualization of each case is specially important, and such persons must necessarily be kept under constant supervision, day and night. A larger proportionate number of attendants is required, therefore, for such an institution than for one where the character of the inmates demands less constant and skilled observation and attendance, on the part of officers and employes.

In all special investigations this committee has been accompanied by the Board's stenographer and a typewritten transcript of the notes taken in each inquiry, or special consultation, has been filed in the office of the Board at Albany.

TREATMENT.

The subject of the medical treatment of the patients presents some points of general interest. Diet, exercise in the open air, and medical treatment comprise the resources available in the Colony life. The relative importance of these measures is generally in the order given.

The dietary established at the Colony is a sufficiently liberal one, yet it is chosen with extreme care in order to avoid those foods which are rich in elements known to develop conditions of nutrition favorable to the development of the epileptic seizure.

The epileptic, usually, is lacking in self control and this is specially apparent in his inability to control his appetite either as to the quality or quantity of his food.

Most of the articles, if not all, which enter into this dietary are produced upon the grounds of the institution, and largely by the labor of the colonists.

TECHNICAL INDUSTRIES.

Employment, judicially adjusted, is a most important resource in the treatment of the epileptic. His disease leads him to be lethargic and sluggish, as regards physical effort and exercise. Employment in the open air which taxes his physical energy moderately, but continually, is of the greatest benefit. In the summer season, this can be found in farming, gardening and kindred pursuits, upon the Colony grounds; but the inclement seasons of the autumn and winter suspend such occupation, almost entirely, and it becomes necessary, therefore, to provide a variety of light technical pursuits for those who would otherwise be unemployed. Besides the physical and mental benefit thus ensured, many articles can be manufactured for use by the inmates of the Colony and contribute, in some degree, toward maintenance.

The manual dextrity manifested by some epileptics, is very considerable and to find a means of employing and developing this is a part of the scientific treatment required for such cases.

MENTAL INSTRUCTION AND DEVELOPMENT.

Aside from technical and other manual occupation, the treatment of the young epileptic, calls especially, for the consideration of possible mental development. The tendency of continued epileptic seizures is to favor the production of a mental inertia which condition is usually a progressive one in cases in which the seizures are frequent, severe or prolonged. Experience has shown that in connection with proper physical treatment, a mental therapeusis is also possible and beneficial.

Epilepsy thus develops in the individual that mental status which is manifest in a lack of initiative for mental or physical effort, as well as of continuity of such effort, when once set in motion. It is a noticeable feature of these cases that the manual dexterity, previously referred to as exhibited by many characteristic epileptics, is not associated with a corresponding mental condition, but that some cases which manifest much manual deftness and activity are very dull and slow in perception and other mental qualities. It has been the effort of the medical officers of the Colony, accordingly, to develop a system of school education, with a view to improving the arrested or impaired mental development of such residents as are capable of receiving benefit therefrom. For this work teachers specially qualified are required, since individualization of the several cases, is all important, and extension of this department will necessitate provision for additional skilled teachers.

DORMITORIES.

The ever present and foremost need of the Colony is for added dormitory accommodation. Nearly every resource of importance to the general establishment in administration otherwise, is now provided. The sewer and water system, the electric plant and agricultural departments are all in such condition that extension from time to time, to meet the needs of increasing numbers of colonists, are mainly what will be required in the future. The provision for housing resources for all the dependent epileptics now under care in various counties of the State, are, however, far short of actual requirements and a further extension must, accordingly, be provided for in the coming year and by the necessary legislative appropriation, in order that these cases may be received into the Colony.

It is to be remembered in the construction of cottage dormitories for these cases, that their external form and internal arrangement are modified to a greater or less extent by the necessities of the *class* of patients for which such provision is to be made. A proper classification of the epileptics requiring care, involves the gathering into separate groups of those presenting similar bodily and mental conditions. These vary in many grades from the quiet and comparatively simple case to the bed-ridden and disturbed or semi-voilent class. It is apparent, therefore, that separate and adequate dormitory provisions must be established for each such group. It is also to be borne in mind that the members of these general groups are by no means stationary in their conditions, but that many of them change, from day to day, and, consequently require a transfer from one group to another. The quiet case of to-day may, in a few days, become irritable or even violent. These facts cannot be ignored, in arranging the cottages for the reception of such cases, but demand consideration as to the extent and character of such accommodations. Uniformity of construction and arrangement cannot be rigidly followed in the buildings for the several classes.

It is evident, therefore, that some of the cottage dormitories can be arranged in a simple form with a very moderate per capita cost for housing quiet inmates, while for bed-ridden or disturbed cases ampler provisions, at an increased per capita cost, will be required. It is estimated that for the class requiring the smallest provision, $275 per capita for housing can be secured, while for the more complicated cases a per capita cost of as high as $450 is necessary. For other classes of cases a per capita cost, varying between these extremes, will be necessary.

One more point in this connection should be referred to, and that is that it is not the lowest possible per capita cost which is to be adopted, but such a per capita cost as shall secure the facilities for custody and care, which are required by the statutes regulating the administration of the Colony, in the care of its wards. That economy in construction is the wisest which fully meets the needs of the inmate and the requirements of a successful administration. This can be secured by such care in the perfection of plans as experience demands, and in this way only can those mistakes be avoided which are otherwise inevitable in so extended a provision for care as the Craig Colony presents.

In closing this report, your committee desire to express their conviction that the responsibility of the State Board of Charities in the development of the Craig Colony demands a continuous and scrupulous supervision of all efforts for development of these departments.

Respectfully submitted,

ENOCH V. STODDARD, M. D.,
STEPHEN SMITH, M. D.,
PETER WALRATH,

Committee.

EIGHTH ANNUAL REPORT

OF THE

Board of Managers of Craig Colony

TO THE

STATE BOARD OF CHARITIES

Adopted by the Board of Managers at a Meeting in Sonyea Hall at the
Colony. October 8, 1901.

CONTENTS.

Title and Address:

THE CRAIG COLONY FOR EPILEPTICS, SONYEA, LIVINGSTON COUNTY, N. Y.

[From the State Charities Law, chapter 546, Laws 1896, section 100.]

ESTABLISHMENT AND OBJECTS OF COLONY.

" The colony for epileptics established at Sonyea, Livingston county, is hereby continued and shall be known as the Craig Colony for Epileptics, in honor of the late Oscar Craig, of Rochester, N. Y., whose efficient and gratuitous services in behalf of epileptics, and other dependent unfortunates, the State desires to commemorate.

" The objects of such Colony shall be to secure the humane, curative, scientific and economical care and treatment of epileptics, exclusive of insane epileptics."

BOARD OF MANAGERS.

RESIDENT OFFICERS.

WILLIAM P. SPRATLING, M. D......Medical Superintendent.

L. PIERCE CLARK, M. D..........First Assistant Physician.

EDWARD A. SHARP, M. D......Second Assistant Physician.

EDWARD L. HANES, M. D.......Third Assistant Physician.

ANNIE M. TREMAINE, M. D..............Woman Physician.

HARRIET A. GIGNOUX, M. D..............Medical Interne.

WILLIAM T. SHANAHAN, M. D............Medical Interne.

TRUMAN L. STONE..............................Steward.

MISS B. M. FOX..................................Matron.

ADMINISTRATIVE ASSISTANTS.

ARCHIBALD C. McFETRIDGE.................Bookkeeper.

HARRY R. PORTER...........................Storekeeper.

JESSIE M. MURPHY.........................Stenographer.

MAUD J. PATTERSON.......................Stenographer.

CHAUNCEY TERWILLIGER...................Apothecary.

TEACHERS.

MARIETTA HITCHCOCK,   MARY TRACY.

JAMES A. GAFFNEY, *Sloyd Instructor.*

CHAPLAINS.

Resident Roman Catholic..................Rev. J. A. MALEY.

Resident Protestant...............Rev. ALFRED F. PRATT.

BOARD OF CONSULTING PHYSICIANS AND SURGEONS.
General Consultant.

FREDERICK PETERSON, M. D...............New York City.

Neurologists.

M. ALLEN STARR, M. D.....................New York City.

GEORGE W. JACOBY, M. D.................New York City.

HENRY HUN, M. D...........................Albany, N. Y.

JAMES W. PUTNAM, M. D...................Buffalo, N. Y.

Surgeons.

CHARLES McBURNEY, M. D.................New York City.

ROSWELL PARK, M. D.......................Buffalo, N. Y.

JOHN W. WHITBECK, M. D.................Rochester, N. Y.

NATHAN JACOBSON, M. D.................Syracuse, N. Y.

Physicians.

CHARLES CARY, M. D......................Buffalo, N. Y.

WILLIAM S. ELY, M. D....................Rochester, N. Y.

Orthopedic Surgeons.

HENRY LING TAYLOR, M. D...............New York City.

LOUIS A. WEIGEL, M. D...................Rochester, N. Y.

Ophthalmologists.

LUCIEN HOWE, M. D........................Buffalo, N. Y.

WHEELOCK RIDER, M. D.................Rochester, N. Y.

GEORGE M. GOULD, M. D.................Westfield, N. Y.

Gynecologist.

MATTHEW D. MANN, M. D...................Buffalo, N. Y.

Pathologist.

IRA VAN GIESON, M. D.....................New York City.

Bacteriologist.

HARLOW H. BROOKS, M. D................New York City.

Psychologist.

BORIS SIDIS, Ph. D........................New York City.

Dentist.

CHARLES J. MILLS.......................Mt. Morris, N. Y.

Board of Managers of the Craig Colony for Epileptics for the Fiscal Year Ending September 30, 1901.

To the State Board of Charities:

As required by statute, we beg to present the Eighth Annual Report of the Managers of the Craig Colony for Epileptics for the fiscal year ending September 30, 1901, including the reports of the Treasurer and Medical Superintendent to the Managers.

CHANGES IN THE BOARD.

Having been appointed President of the State Commission in Lunacy by Governor Odell, Dr. Frederick Peterson resigned the position of Manager and President of this Board last spring and Dr. Pearce Bailey, of New York city, was appointed by the Governor to fill the vacancy as Manager. At the quarterly meeting of the Managers held in July, Mr. George L. Williams, of Buffalo, was elected President of the Board. At the same meeting the Board was pleased to pass the following resolution bearing upon Dr. Peterson's work and services in connection with the Craig Colony:

"Whereas, Dr. Frederick Peterson, President of the Board of Managers of the Craig Colony since its first organization in 1894, has resigned his position as a Manager of the Colony in order to accept the position of President of the State Commission in Lunacy,

"Resolved, That the Board of Managers of the Craig Colony, while congratulating the State upon securing the services of Dr.

15

Peterson as a member and President of the State Commission in Lunacy, desire to express their profound regret at losing the official service and co-operation of one to whom, more than any one else, the State owes the establishment of this Colony on a humane and scientific basis.

"Resolved, That the Board extend to Dr. Peterson their sincere thanks for his long and fruitful labors in behalf of the work to which the Colony is dedicated and their sincere good wishes for equally beneficent results in his new field of labor."

The term of service of Judge O. P. Hurd, of Watkins, having expired, the vacancy was filled by the Governor by the appointment of Prof. E. W. Huffcut, who holds a Chair of Law at Cornell University. The Board was pleased to adopt a fitting resolution concerning the services of Judge Hurd to the Colony.

BOARD AND COMMITTEE MEETINGS.

All meetings of the Board and of its Committees have been held at the Colony, the full Board having met on the second Tuesday in October, January, April and July, an average of nine members attending each meeting. The Visiting Committee met at the Colony thirteen times during the year; while the Executive Committee had seven meetings.

CHANGES IN POPULATION.

On October 1, 1900, the Colony had 612 patients, 329 of whom were males, 283 females. During the year 259 were received; 198 males and 61 females; while during the same period 81 were discharged, 34 died and 13 were transferred as insane to State hospitals. This left the census on September 30th last, 743; 440 of whom were males, 303 females, making an actual gain of 131 for the year. Attention is called to the relatively low death rate for the year, it being less than 5 per cent.

We are pleased to note that the per capita cost of maintenance during the year was $7.62 less than the previous year. We feel that as the number of patients increase the per capita cost will correspondingly decrease. Your attention is also called to the low per capita cost of new construction, which is shown by the Superintendent's report to have averaged $425 per bed, exclusive of the hospital.

IMPROVEMENTS OF THE YEAR.

The two infirmaries under construction at the time of our last report are practically completed, and we are now awaiting the construction of water and sewer lines to them in order to occupy them. These are among the best buildings we have on the place. They are designed for the feeble and bed-ridden classes, and because of the increase in cases of this character these buildings should be enlarged in another year. There are enough suitable cases now on the premises to more than fill them as soon as they are ready for use.

We opened bids early in the season for the construction of four dormitories in the Villa Flora group for women, under the item of $90,000 in this year's appropriation; but we were unable to accept any of the bids because they exceeded the per capita allowance of $500 per bed. Preparations are being made to advertise for new bids for this work, for two additional dormitories on the Village Green and other dormitory accommodations for patients under the item of $90,000 mentioned above.

The Village Green buildings were opened early in the season and have proved very satisfactory indeed.

The two silos, for which we had an appropriation of $900, were built for $707.95. The two under grade crossings are completed, with the exception of paving and draining, both of which will be completed before the end of the year. The warehouse and bakery is being finished under the appropriation of $1,500 for that purpose. It is an excellent building and is greatly needed. The third wing to the trades school is under construction. The completion of this will give needed room for additional shop work for patients. Considerable delay was experienced in beginning work on the conduit to carry steam and hot water pipes in the women's group; but the work was commenced late in September and will be pushed to completion as rapidly as possible. It is thought that this conduit will result in considerable saving in fuel in heating this group.

Bids were also opened early in the season for four tenant houses under the item of $4,000 for same; but the lowest bid exceeded the appropriation by $2,450 and all were rejected. It will be necessary to secure an additional appropriation before these cottages can be built. At the same time, we ask for money for the fifth cottage, larger in size than the rest. We have accepted plans and specifications for a hothouse for the garden and are on the point of receiving bids for same. The State Architect has also completed plans and specifications for putting all wires underground, and it is expected that this work will begin at an early date.

NEEDS AND RECOMMENDATIONS FOR 1902.

The greatest need of the Colony continues to be for dormitories for patients. There are at present several hundred applications on file at the Colony for patients who cannot be received on account of lack of room. We also need money for furnishing. With the money the Colony has received for that purpose, it has been possible only for it to do the most necessary furnishing. We cannot but feel that the Colony should do more than this for a people who must find a home in the Colony for so many years. The houses in which patients live should be made a little more attractive.

We cannot impress upon you too strongly the necessity for building roads, for laying walks and for grading, and we ask for a fair appropriation for these purposes. It will be necessary either to build another pond from which to cut ice, or to install a refrigerating plant in the present cold storage building, and we believe the latter would be better.

Your attention is again invited to the necessity—a very great one we feel it to be—of a bridge over Kishaqua creek along the line of the new Dansville and Mt. Morris highway. We think this is one of the most urgent improvements that we should make. A steam disinfecting plant is also needed for purposes explained in the report of the Medical Superintendent.

An additional root cellar for garden purposes is one of our necessities, and we should also enlarge our facilities for making brick. It is necessary that we add to our farm stock and implements in order to meet the requirements of growing agricultural interests, and we ask for money for that purpose in addition to the sum requested for farm teams and equipment for same. Some improvements are also necessary in the laundry in order to do the extra work required by a growing population.

Our needs for an isolation pavilion for contagious diseases have grown since last year, and we again ask for a building for that purpose. The scientific work of the Colony requires a static electrical machine with X-ray outfit; while we should also have an appropriation of $7,500 for general repairs and improvements.

For maintenance for the year beginning October 1, 1901, we estimate that we shall require not less than $140,000.

In our last report we referred to the noble gift to the Colony by the Rt. Rev. B. J. McQuaid, Bishop of Rochester, of funds sufficient to build a Roman Catholic chapel and house for priest on the Colony grounds. Work was begun on both of these last spring and both are now nearly completed. The chapel is beautifully located on a bluff overlooking Kishaqua Creek gorge, and it makes a pleasant addition to the architecture of the place. We again most gratefully thank Bishop McQuaid for his practical, generous and timely gift.

We approve the recommendation of the Medical Superintendent that the law governing the admission of patients be changed to provide simply for the admission of epileptics without class distinction. We feel that such a change would be well for many reasons. Many patients are now received as indigents who should not come as such, yet, under the circumstances, we cannot require them to pay. We think all should be received on the same basis, then if it be found after proper inquiry that they can pay, require them to do so; if they cannot, then let them remain as indigents.

An effort has been made to collaborate and present in this report some useful data bearing upon epilepsy, its causes and treatment, to which we would call your attention. For details as to what has been done in this way, and for details of progress along industrial and other lines, we beg to refer you to the report of Dr. Wm. P. Spratling, Medical Superintendent.

We are gratified in being able to say that the work of the past year in caring for this most sadly afflicted class was successful in every respect.

SUMMARY OF APPROPRIATIONS WANTED FOR 1902.

For dormitories	$60,000
For furnishing	15,000
For roads, walks and grading	12,500
For installing a refrigerating plant in cold storage building	3,000
For bridge over Kishaqua creek on D. & M. highway, and for changing road to same	7,500
For a steam disinfecting plant for bedding, clothing and household goods	1,500
For root cellar for garden produce	1,200
For additional kiln, sheds over machinery, and other improvements to brickyard	800
For farm stock and implements	2,000
For additional farm teams and equipment for same.	2,500
For laundry machinery, including one 20 horsepower motor	1,500
For balance to accept lowest bid for construction of four cottages for employes and for an additional cottage, five in all (in addition to $4,000 appropriated by chap. 330, Laws 1901)	3,950
For isolation pavilion for contagious diseases	3,000
For static electrical machine and X-ray outfit	400
For general repairs and improvements	7,500
	$122,350
For maintenance, beginning October 1, 1902	$140,000

We were pleased to receive many visitors at the Colony during the past year who came to study the Colony system of care and treatment for epileptics, among them being Governor Odell and his party, and at various times members of the State Board of Charities.

GEORGE L. WILLIAMS, *President*.
HURLBERT E. BROWN, *Secretary*.
JAMES H. LOOMIS,
ANSON S. THOMPSON, M. D.,
PERCY L. LANG,
DANIEL B. MURPHY,
JEANETTE R. HAWKINS,
ABBOT L. DOW,
GEORGE E. GORHAM, M. D.,
MRS. EDWARD JOY,
PEARCE BAILEY, M. D.,
E. W. HUFFCUT.

SONYEA HALL, *October* 1, 1901.

Treasurer's Report.

To the Board of Managers of Craig Colony:

The Treasurer of Craig Colony respectfully submits the following annual report for the year ending September 30, 1901:

GENERAL FUND—MAINTENANCE.

1900.

Oct.	1. Balance, Treasurer's hands............	$686 95
	Balance, Comptroller's hands.........	6,400 00
	New appropriation	100,000 00
	Deficiency appropriation	6,000 00
	Clothing	2,436 04
	Private patients	490 00
	Miscellaneous earnings	2,729 64
	Refund	4 74
		$118,747 37

Receipts.

Balance, Treasurer's hands.	$686 95	
From Comptroller	111,084 39	
From clothing	2,436 04	
From private patients	490 00	
From miscellaneous earnings.................	2,729 64	
From refund	4 74	
Balance, Comptroller's hands................	1,315 61	
		$118,747 37

Disbursements.

Total disbursements for Colony	$111,150 94	
Disbursed to State Treasurer, as per section 37, chapter 580, Laws of 1899	5,655 68	
Balance, Treasurer's hands.	625 14	
Balance, Comptroller's hands	1,315 61	
		$118,747 37

GENERAL REPAIRS AND IMPROVEMENTS.
(Chapter 284, Laws 1899.)

Oct. 1. Balance, Comptroller's hands $282 23

Receipts.

From Comptroller	$246 13	
Balance, Comptroller's hands..	36 10	
		282 23

Disbursements.

Total disbursements	$246 13	
Lapsed	36 10	
		282 23

GRADING ROADS, WALKS AND PLANTING.
(Chapter 284, Laws 1899.)

Oct. 1. Balance, Comptroller's hands $0 40

Receipts.

From Comptroller	......	
Balance, Comptroller's hands..	$0 40	
		40

Disbursements.

Total disbursements	......	
Lapsed	$0 40	
		40

EXTENSION TO POWER HOUSE AND TWO BOILERS.
(Chapter 284, Laws 1899.)

Oct.   1. Balance, Comptroller's hands............ $61 28

Receipts.

From Comptroller	$60 75	
Balance, Comptroller's hands..	53	
		61 28

Disbursements.

Total disbursements	$60 75	
Lapsed	53	
		61 28

INDUSTRIES AND WING TO BUILDING.
(Chapter 284, Laws 1899.)

Oct.   1. Balance, Comptroller's hands............ $4,199 62

Receipts.

From Comptroller	......	
Balance, Comptroller's hands..	$4,199 62	
		4,199 62

Disbursements.

Total disbursements	......	
Reappropriated	$4,199 62	
		4,199 62

COAL FOR HEATING WOMEN'S GROUP.
(Chapter 572, Laws 1899.)

Oct.   1. Balance, Comptroller's hands............ $1 47

Receipts.

From Comptroller	......	
Balance, Comptroller's hands..	$1 47	
		1 47

Disbursements.

Total disbursements	......	
Lapsed.....................	$1 47	
		1 47

DORMITORIES.
(Chapter 284, Laws 1899.)

Oct. 1. Balance, Comptroller's hands............ $3,066 90

Receipts.

From Comptroller $2,304 87
Balance, Comptroller's hands..   762 03
                              ——————
                                          3,066 90

Disbursements.

Total disbursements $2,304 87
Reappropriated...............   762 03
                              ——————
                                          3,066 90

FURNISHING.
(Chapter 284, Laws 1899.)

Oct. 1. Balance, Comptroller's hands............ $146 56

Receipts.

From Comptroller $132 55
Balance, Comptroller's hands..   14 01
                              ——————
                                          146 56

Disbursements.

Total disbursements $132 55
Lapsed.....................   14 01
                              ——————
                                          $146 56

UNDERGRADE CROSSINGS.
(Chapter 419, Laws 1900.)

Oct. 1. Balance, Comptroller's hands............ $1,728 44

Receipts.

From Comptroller 1,728 44

Disbursements.

Total disbursements 1,728 44

DEFICIENCY IN CONSTRUCTION.
(Chapter 419, Laws 1900.)

Oct.   1. Balance, Comptroller's hands............ $33 67

Receipts.

From Comptroller	$30 58	
Balance, Comptroller's hands..	3 09	
		33 67

Disbursements.

Total disbursements	$30 58	
Unexpended balance	3 09	
		33 67

IMPROVEMENTS AND REPAIRS.
(Chapter 314, Laws 1900.)

Oct.   1. Balance, Comptroller's hands............ $625 99

Receipts.

From Comptroller	$610 83	
Balance, Comptroller's hands..	15 16	
		625 99

Disbursements.

Total disbursements	$610 83	
Unexpended balance	15 16	
		625 99

COLD STORAGE, WAREHOUSE AND BAKERY.
(Chapter 284, Laws 1899.)

Oct.   1. Balance, Comptroller's hands............ $5,964 56

Receipts.

From Comptroller	$5,822 45	
Balance, Comptroller's hands..	142 11	
		5,964 56

Disbursements.

Total disbursements $5,822 45
Reappropriated............... 142 11
                                      ————— $5,964 56

MACHINERY AND TOOLS FOR TRADE SCHOOL.
(Chapter 314, Laws 1900.)

Oct.   1. Balance, Comptroller's hands............ $339 75

Receipts.

From Comptroller $14 24
Balance, Comptroller's hands..   325 51
                                      ————— 339 75

Disbursements.

Total disbursements $14 24
Unexpended balance 325 51
                                      ————— $339 75

FARM STOCK AND IMPLEMENTS.
(Chapter 314, Laws 1900.)

Oct.   1. Balance, Comptroller's hands............ $341 20

Receipts.

From Comptroller $173 00
Balance, Comptroller's hands..   168 20
                                      ————— 341 20

Disbursements.

Total disbursements $173 00
Unexpended balance 168 20
                                      ————— 341 20

FURNISHING TWO INFIRMARY DORMITORIES.
(Chapter 314, Laws 1900.)

Oct.   1. Balance, Comptroller's hands............ $3,535 00

Receipts.

From Comptroller	$2,167 84	
Balance, Comptroller's hands..	1,367 16	
		3,535 00

Disbursements.

Total disbursements	$2,167 84	
Unexpended balance	1,367 16	
		3,535 00

TWO INFIRMARY DORMITORIES.
(Chapter 314, Laws 1900.)

Oct.   1. Balance, Comptroller's hands............ $59,980 96

Receipts.

From Comptroller	$49,978 70	
Balance, Comptroller's hands..	10,002 26	
		59,980 96

Disbursements.

Total disbursements	$49,978 70	
Unexpended balance	10,002 26	
		59,980 96

IMPROVEMENTS AND EXTENSION TO BRICKYARD PLANT.
(Chapter 314, Laws 1900.)

Oct.   1. Balance, Comptroller's hands............ $700 00

Receipts.

From Comptroller	$690 95	
Balance, Comptroller's hands..	9 05	
		700 00

Disbursements.

Total disbursements $690 95
Unexpended balance 9 05
                              ——————— $700 00

OUTSIDE ELECTRICAL LINE WORK AND POWER MOTORS.

(Chapter 314, Laws 1900.)

Appropriation $1,400 00

Receipts.

From Comptroller $1,301 92
Balance, Comptroller's hands.. 98 08
                              ——————— 1,400 00

Disbursements.

Total disbursements $1,301 92
Unexpended balance 98 08
                              ——————— 1,400 00

FIRE HOSE, REEL AND EXTINGUISHER.

(Chapter 314, Laws 1900.)

Appropriation $800 00

Receipts.

From Comptroller $685 00
Balance, Comptroller's hands.. 115 00
                              ——————— 800 00

Disbursements.

Total disbursements $685 00
Unexpended balance 115 00
                              ——————— 800 00

REPAIRS AT WEST GROUP, INCLUDING FIRE-ESCAPES.
(Chapter 314, Laws 1900.)

Appropriation $900 00

Receipts.

From Comptroller 900 00

Disbursements.

Total disbursements 900 00

SUPPLEMENTARY PUMPING STATION.
(Chapter 314, Laws 1900.)

Appropriation $4,000 00

Receipts.

From Comptroller $3,399 85
Balance, Comptroller's hands..   600 15
                              ———————   4,000 00

Disbursements.

Total disbursements $3,399 85
Unexpended balance 600 15
                              ———————   4,000 00

ADDITIONAL FILTER BED FOR SEWAGE.
(Chapter 314, Laws 1900.)

Appropriation. $1,500 00

Receipts.

From Comptroller 1,500 00

Disbursements.

Total disbursements 1,500 00

LAUNDRY MACHINERY.
(Chapter 314, Laws 1900.)

Appropriation.................................. $1,000 00

Receipts.

From Comptroller $995 00
Balance, Comptroller's hands..   5 00
                                ———————— 1,000 00

Disbursements.

Total disbursements $995 00
Unexpended balance 5 00
                                ———————— $1,000 00

FARM STOCK AND IMPLEMENTS.
(Chapter 330, Laws 1901.)

Appropriation $1,000 00

Receipts.

From Comptroller $700 00
Balance, Comptroller's hands.. 300 00
                                ———————— 1,000 00

Disbursements.

Total disbursements $700 00
Unexpended balance 300 00
                                ———————— 1,000 00

GENERAL REPAIRS AND IMPROVEMENTS.
(Chapter 330, Laws 1901.)

Appropriation......................... $5,000 00

Receipts.

From Comptroller $2,267 25
Balance, Comptroller's hands.. 2,732 75
                                ———————— 5,000 00

16

Disbursements.

Total disbursements	$2,267 25	
Unexpended balance	2,732 75	
		$5,000 00

DORMITORIES, REAPPROPRIATED.
(Chapter 330, Laws 1901.)

Balance, "Dormitories, chapter 284, Laws 1899"................................	$762 03

Receipts.

From Comptroller	$576 88	
Balance, Comptroller's hands..	185 15	
		762 03

Disbursements.

Total disbursements	$576 88	
Unexpended balance	185 15	
		762 03

Note.—According to chapter 330, Laws 1901, the amount re-appropriated is $984.85, which amount is $222.82 in excess of the actual funds available for reappropriation under "Dormitories, chapter 284, Laws 1899."

ADDITIONAL DORMITORIES.
(Chapter 330, Laws 1901.)

Appropriation	$90,000 00

Receipts.

From Comptroller	$22 12	
Balance, Comptroller's hands..	89,977 88	
		90,000 00

Disbursements.

Total disbursements	$22 12	
Unexpended balance	89,977 88	
		90,000 00

FEED WATER HEATER, PUMP AND FIXTURES.
(Chapter 330, Laws 1901.)

Appropriation $550 00

Receipts.

From Comptroller	$412 30	
Balance, Comptroller's hands..	137 70	
		550 00

Disbursements.

Total disbursements	$412 30	
Unexpended balance	137 70	
		550 00

STEAM PIPE CONDUIT.
(Chapter 330, Laws 1901.)

Appropriation $1,500 00

Receipts.

From Comptroller	$209 00	
Balance, Comptroller's hands..	1,291 00	
		1,500 00

Disbursements.

Total disbursements	$209 00	
Unexpended balance	1,291 00	
		1,500 00

MEDICAL BOOKS AND SURGICAL INSTRUMENTS.
(Chapter 330, Laws 1901.)

Appropriation $1,500 00

Receipts.

From Comptroller	$28 90	
Balance, Comptroller's hands..	1,471 10	
		1,500 00

Disbursements.

Total disbursements	$28 90	
Unexpended balance	1,471 10	
		$1,500 00

INCIDENTALS—COMPLETION OF INFIRMARY BUILDINGS.
(Chapter 330, Laws 1901.)

Appropriation $400 00

Receipts.

From Comptroller	$37 50	
Balance, Comptroller's hands..	362 50	
		400 00

Disbursements.

Total disbursements	$37 50	
Unexpended balance	362 50	
		400 00

BRICK CONDUIT.
(Chapter 330, Laws 1901.)

Appropriation $6,000 00

Receipts.

From Comptroller	$165 00	
Balance, Comptroller's hands..	5,835 00	
		6,000 00

Disbursements.

Total disbursements	$165 00	
Unexpended balance	5,835 00	
		6,000 00

GRAVELING POND.
(Chapter 330, Laws 1901.)

Appropriation	$300 00

Receipts.

From Comptroller	$26 88	
Balance, Comptroller's hands..	273 12	
		$300 00

Disbursements.

Total disbursements	$26 88	
Unexpended balance	273 12	
		$300 00

All of which is respectfully submitted.

JNO. F. CONNOR,
Treasurer.

We hereby certify that we have examined the foregoing report of John F. Connor, Treasurer, and compared the same with the Treasurer's books, bank accounts, vouchers and the books of the institution, and that such report is correct to the best of our knowledge.

H. E. BROWN,
JAMES H. LOOMIS,
DANIEL B. MURPHY,
Auditing Committee.

October 8, 1901.

Report of the Medical Superintendent for the Year Ending September 30, 1901.

SONYEA HALL, SONYEA, N. Y., *October* 1, 1901.

To the Board of Managers of the Craig Colony for Epileptics:

We are gratified in being able to report satisfactory progress in the continued recognition and extension of the true colony system during the year just passed.

Definite ideas as to what should constitute an ideal colony existed before the first blow was struck in the creation of this Colony, and we have not yet had cause to abandon or even to greatly modify any of the fundamental principles conceived at that time; including provision for classification, education, occupation and forms of treatment.

If there ever was an experimental stage in the development of this practical charity—and its work has ever been along new lines—it was passed long ago.

The Colony system rightly interpreted and created for the care and treatment of epileptics, is and must be an unqualified success.

NO THEORIES.

In making this report I have sought to include in it nothing theoretical, my aim being only to show something of what we are doing and how we do it.

Some epileptics taken in time and properly treated can be cured; some are being cured here. Many more, perhaps 60% to 70% of them all, if taken in time can be so improved as to make them capable of living in comparative comfort in a colony of this kind; while a few others must always remain beyond the aid of science to improve or to cure.

ADMISSIONS, DISCHARGES, DEATHS AND TRANSFERS.

A year ago we had 612 patients; 329 males, 283 females. Since then we have received 259 more; 198 males and 61 females. During the same period 80 were discharged, 36 died and 12 were transferred as insane to State hospitals, leaving our census on this date: 440 males, 303 females; total 743, a net gain of 131 for the year. The death rate for the year, based on the daily average number under treatment, 675.89, was less than 5%.

In the admission of new patients we endeavored to be impartial to all the counties of the State, as may be seen by referring to the county table in this report. New York county, for instance, which has nearly one-third of the entire population of the State, has contributed 309 cases, almost a third of the entire number received; while Greater New York alone has contributed 498 cases, nearly one-half of the entire number received.

Because of the disqualifications of an open colony system of this kind to care for persons having too great unsoundness of mind, we have to exercise constant care in the selection of new cases.

We have again omitted the statistical tables usually a part of such reports, feeling that the information they contain is not generally appreciated in such form.

COST OF MAINTENANCE.

As the population increases the per capita cost decreases.

Years.	Average daily attendance.	Annual per capita cost.
1897 and 1898	251	$300.02
1898 and 1899	355	216.51
1899 and 1900	502.413	172.04
1900 and 1901	676.41	164.42

COST OF NEW CONSTRUCTION.

The average cost of new construction for patients, including plumbing, heating and lighting, has been about $425. This does not include the hospital, which cost more.

The cost of building varies with the cost of labor and materials. Some of the buildings in the Villa Flora group for women should have had more money spent on them, by having cellars.

The average cost of furnishing for patients, with the necessary articles only, has been $30 a patient.

The Causes of Epilepsy in 1,070 *Cases;* 660 *Males and* 410 *Females.*

INHERITED CAUSES.	Males.	Females.	Total.	Per cent. Males.	Per cent. Females.	Total per cent.
Epilepsy	105	73	178	15	17	16
Alcohol	111	51	162	16	12	15
Insanity	49	42	91	7	10	8
Tuberculosis	101	50	151	15	12	14
Unknown	29	15	44	4	3	4
None	276	168	444	41	40	41

Epilepsy is essentially a disease of early life. The epileptic age begins with birth and terminates in nearly 85% of all cases before the 20th year; and in 16% of these the disease develops before the end of the third year.

To the question, "What causes its development so early in life?" there is but one answer, and that is, heredity and stress.

Under heredity we have as factors in the family that predispose to, or cause the disease in the offspring, in the order of their importance:

Epilepsy, alcoholism, insanity and tuberculosis, and in some cases to an extent not yet determined, syphilis when it affects the central nervous system, and possibly rheumatism.

Under stress we have the following, acting from within or without, and which do not require a soil prepared by heredity to cause the disease, but which makes its origin more certain if such preparation has been made:

External violence—such as a blow on the head.

Internal violence—such as hemorrhage in the brain, or on the brain.

Psychic—such as shock from any cause.

Chemical—such as the presence of toxins in the gastro-intestinal canal.

First taking up epilepsy itself in the parent as a cause of the disease in the child, we found that out of a total of 1,070 cases—660 males and 410 females—it was transmitted to 15% of the males and 17% of the females, or 16% all told.

Alcoholism was established as a family cause in the same 1,070 cases, in 111 males and 51 females—16% of the former and 12% of the latter, the aggregate for the two being 14%.

Dr. Paul Kovalevsky of St. Petersburg, stated in a paper read at the first annual meeting of the National Association for the Study of Epilepsy held in Washington last May, that the proportion of Epileptics to the population at large in Russia was 1 to 2,000; adding, " in the grape and wine making province of Caucausus, where the natives for centuries have been in the habit of quenching their thirst with large quantities of heavy wine, the rate is evidently much higher;" an opinion he had enjoyed abundant opportunity to confirm during 15 summers spent in practice in that locality.

Insanity in the parents in the same cases caused the disease in 49 males and 42 females; 7% of the former and 10% of the latter. It seems clear that more males acquire epilepsy as a result of alcoholism in the parent than do females, while more females acquire it as a result of insanity in the parent than do males.

Tuberculosis was definitely established in the immediate ancestors in 101 males, or 15%, and in 50 females, or 12%; the two combined giving over 13%.

Collectively, we found either epilepsy, alcoholism, insanity, or tuberculosis, and in some cases two or more of all these, to be hereditary factors in 56% of the 1,070 cases studied, leaving 44% not due to inherited causes.

Now besides the active and important part played by heredity in causing epilepsy, we must also consider the influence of stress, under the subdivisions laid down above.

As to the frequency with which external violence causes epilepsy, I present no figures at this time, and only make the general statement that trauma is sometimes responsible for the disease.

Children often get a blow on the head and nothing is thought of it until years after when, convulsions arising, the blow is recalled and the convulsions ascribed to it. We ought to be careful in accepting without challenge such a cause, especially in cases where heredity is bad.

A blow on the head that crushes the skull so that it injures brain tissue, and is followed by convulsions, in a case never before having convulsions, does not, at first, any more imply the presence of epilepsy, to my mind, than do the convulsive movements of the frog subjected after decapitation to the irritation of a galvanic current.

Convulsions alone do not constitute epilepsy; but in a case of brain injury, unless the irritation is removed within a reasonable time, the length of this time depending upon the stamina of the individual, the convulsions may become fixed and eventually acquire all the characteristics of and pass into true epilepsy.

Internal violence—hemorrhage within the brain or beneath its coverings was found to have caused the disease in 116 cases, or 11% of the entire number studied.

The brain palsies of early life that cause epilepsy are manifested later in life in the form of hemiplegia, paraplegia, or diplegia; the two latter being comparatively rare.

The seat of the lesion in these cases is to be found in the hemispheres, the central motor neurons being involved in that part of the direct motor tract which extends from the brain cortex to the spinal cord as far as the anterior horn.

Brain palsies oftenest occur during the first three years of life. About one-third of all cases are congenital; the rest being due to injuries received at birth, to the stress of dentition in favorable subjects, and to causes that lead to embolism and thrombosis; these being injuries and the infectious fevers, such as pneumonia, whooping cough, measles and scarlet fever.

Of the 116 cases, 47 were males and 49 females—62 suffering from left and 51 from right hemiplegia, three being diplegies.

We have seen many epileptics whose disease was caused by a cerebral palsy, and in which the cause had gone unrecognized, because the marks of the paralysis had become so indistinct.

It often requires the most careful inspection with the patient completely stripped, with accurate comparative measurements of the legs and arms, the testing of the muscular power and of the various reflexes, in addition to a close and systematic inquiry into the patient's early personal and family history, to bring the true cause to light.

The "stress" of psychic violence sometimes causes epilepsy. Three cases of the kind have recently come under our observation; the cause in two of them being fright from violence on the part of a drunken father; the other fright from attack by a vicious dog. In these cases shock acts on a nervous system predisposed to disease.

Chemical causes, in our opinion, play an important role in the production of epilepsy, and by chemical causes I mean all toxic agencies generated in the body or introduced from without.

It seems that there must be some local relationship between the gastric aura, which we find in nearly 20% of all cases, and the epilepsies due to gastro-intestinal poisoning; nor is it unreasonable to suppose that serum therapy may not some day be used to advantage in the treatment of cases of this kind. This is not surprising after the recent deductions by Dr. Ford Roberston, pathologist to the Scottish asylums, that "the larger number of cases of insanity are not primarily diseases of the brain, but are due to the action of toxins in the cortical neurons by disordering their metabolism, and often permanently damaging and even destroying large numbers of them."

NOTES ON METHODS OF CLASSIFICATION, OCCUPATION, EDUCATION AND TREATMENT OF COLONISTS AT SONYEA.

CLASSIFICATION.

Since the establishment of the Colony we have constantly maintained that no other single feature was so essential for the successful colonization of epileptics as proper classification. Coming as they do from all walks of life—some young, some old, some educated, some not, some having attacks daily, some being free from them for weeks or even months at a time, many retaining fair conditions of mind in spite of the disease, while others pass rapidly into idiocy, imbecility, or dementia; some having attacks mostly by day, others by night—it is easy to see that to classify them into suitable households means the greatest good to all concerned.

THE INFLUENCE OF ARCHITECTURE ON CLASSIFICATION.

Ruskin gave it as his opinion that a nation's character was expressed in its architecture; and certain it is that the architecture of a colony for people of this kind largely determines its success or its failure, for it alone makes proper classification possible, and proper classification is one of the indispensable requisites for success.

Having adopted a practical system of classification early in the development of the Colony, we are gratified at being able to make a brief exposition of the same in this report. The illustration of the Villa Flora group for women here presented shows a type of each building by which classification is secured. Buildings 8 to 15, inclusive—an illustration of one of which is also presented—are for the best class of female patients, each holding from 16 to 18 persons, each being complete in all its appointments for housekeeping, except for general bread making and laundry work, these being done in a central plant for the entire Colony. The general plan, arrangement, and capacity of these buildings have proved entirely satisfactory. Home-life, the one thing so very essential for our people, has been more nearly attained in these small cottages than in any others we have.

Buildings 4 to 7, inclusive, are occupied by the large number of persons making up the middle class. Each building holds from 28 to 30 patients, each having a cook and a nurse in charge, while the smaller cottages mentioned above have but one employe, nurse, cook and housekeeper combined. Prototypes of these buildings are on the Village Green and are occupied by 120 of the best male patients. An illustration of one of these cottages is also shown in this report.

Building 16 in the rear of the group is an infirmary for bedridden and helpless cases, and also has a special wing with isolation rooms for those temporarily mentally disturbed. This building holds from 40 to 50 cases, but might readily be made larger, for the reason that classification has less value in the care of such patients; the problem here being rather an economic one.

Of the 740 patients now at the Colony, approximately 200, or about 25%, live in the best buildings of class one; about 440, or 60%, live in buildings of class two, designed for the greater middle class; while the remaining 100, or 15% of the whole, live in the infirmary buildings for feeble and bed-ridden cases and comprise, under our classification, class three.

While our classification is not an elaborate one, it is practical and satisfactory; and in our opinion it is necessary to have buildings of each of these types in every colony for epileptics. We have observed that many patients who, on admission, may belong to the first class, in a few months, by reason of the progress of their disease, require to be placed in a building of the second class, and eventually become infirmary cases. On the other hand, many are admitted into buildings of the middle class, who, by reason of their great improvement, later on live in buildings of the first class.

OCCUPATION.

Wherever there is work to be done, and that is everywhere, in every department, indoors and out, epileptic labor is to be found; and this is as it should be. Our facilities for the useful employment of such labor are not yet adequate or complete, but we are developing them as fast as possible.

In the sewing-room in the women's group, by epileptic labor, is made practically all the clothing worn by women; while the tailor in the male department, with epileptic labor, begun some time ago to manufacture all clothing worn by men.

In the brick yard an average of twenty to twenty-five patients were employed during the past season to great advantage. On the farm and in the garden many more find regular work; while numbers have steady employment in the care of stock, in the poultry house, on the lawns and roads, in the power house, in the various furnace rooms, the carpenter shop, the bakery, the mattress shop, the plumber's shop, the engineer's department, the printing office, laundry, in the store and warehouse, in delivering supplies to the various buildings, in office work, as assistants to nurses in the care of sick, in dining-room and chamber work, and various other things too numerous to mention.

In our opinion the Colony will never be self-supporting. A community of sick folks like this can never do as well as a community of well folks. The chief handicap the epileptic bears as a factor in industrial life is that more than three-fourths of them acquire the disease in childhood, which deprives them of that early training the skilled laborer must have. We find that it takes many years to put our people in proper condition to perform useful labor and do it methodically. And many can never do it.

EDUCATION.

In our Third Annual Report we summarized the needs and indicated the lines along which epileptics should be educated, and our opinion has not changed since then.

In school work for epileptics we seek to attain two things. First: To inculcate certain principles. A few hours daily spent in the atmosphere of the school room, where order is enforced, discipline maintained, and continuity of action patiently taught, will in time instill into the students habits of industry and principles that can be applied to good advantage in the ordinary vocations of life. Second: To give them a common school education.

A great majority of the young people committed to our care have so long been afflicted that educational advantages have hitherto been denied them. The doors of ordinary institutions of learning are closed to them.

All the educational work of the Colony is now proceeding along these lines. It is all practical, designed to be useful, and we try not to make it of such a character as to put it beyond the power of the epileptic student to grasp and comprehend.

It is difficult to teach persons who have passed from childhood into young adult life, who yet retain the minds of children; difficult for two reasons: First, their powers of comprehension have never been exercised and they do not know how to learn. Second, what they may learn to-day is apt to be forgotten to-morrow. A seizure has occurred in the meantime and largely destroyed all that was recently acquired. This fact makes repetition necessary and also calls for the education of as many faculties or special senses as possible at the same time. That is why finger, hand and brain work combined is best for them. That is why manual and industrial training is preferable to that which is purely intellectual, remembering that in acquiring the latter they must always get some of the former.

We now have two teachers who devote their time to the girls. They instruct them in ordinary school branches, in manual work along kindergarten lines, and in exercises for the physical development of the body. The Sloyd school has recently been enlarged and continues to be the most useful agent we have in the education of the boys. Sloyd work is not all manual; to carry out its principles requires the constant exercise of the highest faculties of the mind.

NOTES ON TREATMENT.

THE VALUE OF EARLY ADMISSION.

Elsewhere in this report it is stated that more than three-fourths of all cases of epilepsy develop under the age of twenty years, making it essentially a disease of early life.

The time when the most promising results are more likely to be secured is when the disease is recent, for its tendency is to become quickly and firmly established. It is a matter for regret that the Colony receives very few cases in which the disease is not of long standing. The family physician has really the best opportunity for treating it when possibility of cure is greatest; but he is nearly always handicapped by a lack of needful facilities that it is difficult to command in the patient's home; for while the drug treatment of the disease is most important, we have learned that to be successful we must be in a position to use at the same time a large number of other agencies difficult to command in the patient's home.

DURATION OF EPILEPSY ON ADMISSION.

Out of 1,070 cases admitted to the Colony, only 15, or less than 1½%, had had epilepsy less than one year; 197 had been epileptics for from 1 to 5 years; 267 from 5 to 10 years; 405 from 10 to 20 years; 156 from 20 to 40 years; while 30 had had the disease 40 years and over.

AGE OF ADMISSION.

Only one person was less than 5 years of age when admitted; 33 were between the ages of 5 and 10; 422 between 10 and 20; 486 between 20 and 40; while 128 were 40 and over.

SURGERY IN EPILEPSY.

From the nature of the nervous disease which the Colony cares for, emergency and accident surgery constitutes a large part of the surgical work. During the seizures the patients frequently sustain severe lacerations and contusions of various parts of the body and the slighter wounds and bruises occasionally become infected from repeated trauma and abscess or cellulitis more or less extensive results. Fractures are common as a result of falling during attacks. These occur on almost all parts of the body and in the epileptic are particularly difficult to treat, owing to the difficulty in keeping the parts immobilized during epileptic convulsions. Dislocations of the shoulder and lower jaw occur occasionally in some epileptics as a result of the violent muscular contractions in the convulsions. Several cases that habitually have dislocations of the shoulder in seizures have been fitted with an apparatus devised for us by Dr. Charles McBurney of New York. The appliance consists of a canvas shoulder cap and jacket fitting closely about the chest to prevent the arm from abducting during the attack. When abduction can be prevented the dislocation will not occur. The apparatus has proven a very uesful appliance in such cases.

Numerous operations have been performed to correct deformities resulting from burns about the face and other parts of the body sustained during seizures; plastic operations and skin-grafting have been frequently resorted to in these cases.

Very little can be done at any time for the direct treatment of the epilepsy by surgical intervention and much less for cases of traumatic epilepsy admitted to the Colony in which the trauma has necessarily been of long standing. However, as a palliative measure, three cases that presented evidences of focal epilepsy have been trephined. In one case the dura was greatly thickened over a small area. This part was removed and a piece of gold foil inserted between the brain and the skull. No adhesion occurred between the scalp and the cortex after the healing was complete. All the cases trephined were temporarily benefited but they still continue to have infrequent seizures.

Three cases were operated upon for disease of the ovaries. The diseased organs were removed, but there was no permanent improvement in the character or frequency of the epileptic seizures as a result of the operations, although the general health of the patients was much improved. The uterus was removed

17

in another case and found to be a retention cyst. The patient
has had no attacks since the operation, a period of sixteen
months. Previous to the operation she had several attacks
daily.

Some of the operations that have been performed for surgical
conditions not directly connected with the epilepsy are: Circum-
cisions, varicocele, hernia, fistula in ano, resection of the rectum,
hemorrhoids, uterine polyps, appendicitis, tubercular perito-
nitis, amputations, ectropium, entropium, tenotomies of eye mus-
cles and various other minor operations.

MEDICAL TREATMENT.

While we have employed all the older remedies in the treatment of epilepsy, which are well known and too numerous to
mention here, we have relied chiefly upon the bromides to control the frequency and severity of the seizures. The potassium,
sodium and ammonium salts, either singly or in combination,
are those most preferred and frequently employed. The chief
difficulty in their use, as in all the bromide salts, has been to
combat bodily and mental intoxications resulting from the
necessarily continuous sedation. To accomplish this end tonics,
reconstructives, massage, gastro-intestinal antiseptics, eutro-
clysis, hypodermoclysis, baths and special dietetic principles
have been employed constantly.

In our further efforts to reduce the possibility of bromism,
some adjuvant principles to the bromide treatment have been
very successfully used, such as Toulouse hypochlorization or
salt starvation in the epileptic dietary. Briefly considered, the
plan is to undersalt or withdraw sodium chloride (table salt)
from the dietary, in order to induce the body tissues to take
up bromine in place of the deficiency of chlorine from any one
or a combination of the bromide salts. Ordinarily we use the
sodium salt, which is given on the patient's food in the prescribed doses, as it forms a very good substitute flavoring for
table salt. By this method the tissues store up and hold the
bromine for a much longer time than by the older methods.
Thus bromine substitutes chlorine physiologically and acts as

a therapeutic agent of sedation. As one-half the ordinary doses of bromide are necessary by this plan, its economy is obvious.

Notwithstanding the advantages of this plan, bromide intoxications have occurred to some extent while using the bromide salts, therefore we have endeavored to still further modify the bromide treatment by using organic bromine in a preparation known as *Bromipin*. The bromine is united in a 10 per cent. solution with ol. sessamum, thereby losing its characteristic odor, taste and irritating properties. While the expense of the preparation has precluded its extensive use, we have noted in conjunction with the hypochlorization dietary the general absence of gastro-intestinal irritation, constipation, mental hebetude and other well-known evidences of bromism. Bromipin has also been used to advantage in some cases of status epilepticus by hypodermic injections and also in the weak and feeble epileptics in the form of nutrient emulsion. Its usual dosage is about twice that of an equal volume of the bromide salts.

While these adjuvant principles of sedation are very great improvements on older lines of treatment, they undoubtedly reach their highest efficiency when carried out in conjunction with colonization principles of care. Indeed, the minute and painstaking application of general hygienic rules to every individual epileptic is rather more necessary than ever. The patient is a biological unit in which both the epileptic and the epilepsy must be given unremitting attention. Therefore special dietetics, exercise, educational occupation and special medicopedagogical plans for physical and mental development in colonies especially constructed to meet these requirements are absolutely essential.

THE EFFECTS OF EPILEPSY ON THE MIND.

We have made a systematic and careful study of the effects of epilepsy on the mind in 1,070 cases admitted to the Colony since its opening. These studies include in every case the sex, age, duration of the disease, the patient's mental condition on admission, hereditary causes and the subsequent mental condition, and we present a brief summary of the results of these studies for the following reasons:

First, to further illustrate the need for classification; second, to show that all epileptics are not proper subjects for our present system of Colony care; third, for the scientific interest that attaches to such a study.

(In explanation of the showing made by the mental condition in the following studies, it should be stated that it is due to the fact that the Colony has received large numbers of chronic cases from county poor and almshouses and from the homes of the poor, where the specialized care and treatment all epileptics need could not be applied. We hope in future to receive more patients less affected by the ravages of the disease, and in whom the possibility of improvement or cure will be greater.)

MENTAL CONDITION ON ADMISSION AND SUBSEQUENTLY.

	On admission.	Subsequently.
Good	31	29
Fair	267	211
Feeble minded	447	377
Imbecile	146	148
Idiot	40	40
Dementia (mostly partial)	124	212
Insane	15	53
Total (male and female)	1,070	1,070

In speaking of epilepsy and insanity in our report a year ago, we said: "Scientifically speaking, epilepsy and insanity are closely allied in so far as they affect the mind. In one, mental perversion is periodic, in the other continuous; both have an origin in common in the brain, both dependent on that organ for their manifestations. Unchecked or uncured, both tend to (impair or) destroy the faculties of the mind."

In the same report we stated that out of 845 epileptics admitted to the Colony in four and one-half years, twenty had been transferred to State hospitals as being legally insane, and

that we still had forty cases suffering from incomplete forms
of insanity. We took no account at that time of the large number who were feeble-minded or of imbeciles, idio-imbeciles, or
idiots.

From the data made in the 1,070 cases, it appears that 31 were
received whose mental condition at the time was regarded as
"good"—normal in every way—and that later on two of these
failed sufficiently in mental vigor to pass into a lower class.

Two hundred and sixty-seven were classed on admission as
"fair," being little less sound in mind than those marked good,
while later on 56 of these lost enough mentally to place them
in lower classes.

Four hundred and forty-seven were feeble-minded on admission, and this number later dropped to 377.

One hundred and forty-six were imbeciles on admission, and
this number was later increased to 148, a gain of 2 only.

Forty were pronounced idiots when received and later on the
same number belonged to that class.

One hundred and twenty-four were suffering from dementia,
complete or partial, when admitted, and it is notable that this
number was later increased to 212. The great majority of those
that passed out of the feeble-minded class went to swell the
number of those having epileptic dementia, or other forms of
insanity.

Fifteen were insane when admitted, and this number was
later increased to 53, a gain of 38.

Seven hundred and forty-five of the whole number admitted,
all included in the first three classes given above, were very
good cases for Colony life, there being little or nothing in their
condition unfitting them for the freedom so essentially a part
of such a life.

Because of the marked mental impairment in the remaining
325 cases—impairment due in most instances to the effects of
the disease, but in some congenital—we do not feel that an un-
modified system of Colony care, such as it seems this Colony
was designed to be, can give them the form of treatment and
close custody their condition requires.

PHYSICAL INFIRMITIES IN 1,070 CASES ON ADMISSION.

CEREBRAL PALSIES.

Many patients are admitted bearing clearly defined evidences of a former paralysis, about which the accompanying certificate is silent, and it not infrequently happens that the family or friends of the patient learn for the first time of a former paralysis, after the patient's rigid and systematic examination at the Colony.

One hundred and sixteen persons—67 males and 49 females—were suffering in some degree from some form of paralysis on admission.

Males.—Of the 67 males so affected, 6 were between the ages of 5 and 10 years; 37 between 10 and 20; 20 between 20 and 40; while 4 were 40 and over. Of the entire number 28 suffered from right hemiplegia, 38 from left, and 1 from diplegia.

In 35 of the 67 cases, the degree of helplessness was slight; in 16 partial; in 8 marked; and in 3 complete. Left hemiplegia out numbered those of the right side by 10%.

Females.—Of the 49 females, 5 were between the ages of 5 and 10 years; 21 between 10 and 20; 21 between 20 and 40; while 2 were 40 and over. Of this number 23 had right hemiplegia; 24 left; and 2 had diplegia.

The degree of helplessness in 26 of them was slight; in 14 partial; and in 7 marked; helplessness in two cases of diplegia being complete.

Although we had difficulty in trying to fix the age of onset of the paralysis, we were able to do so to the extent that led us to feel without reservation that practically all originated in infancy. This fact, if needed, would be additional proof that epilepsy is a disease of early life.

DISEASES OF THE HEART AND LUNGS.

The conclusion is forced upon us that epileptics are prone to diseases or disorders of the heart and lungs, the organs of blood and air.

Whether heart disease, pure and simple, or tuberculosis of the lungs, arising de novo in the individual, ever causes genuine epilepsy we are unable at this time to say; but there seems to be no room for doubt about the part played by tuberculosis as a family cause in the etiology of epilepsy.

Thorough physical examination in 1,070 cases on admission showed the following:

Heart.—Mitral regurgitation in 77; irregular cardiac force and rhythm in 75; cardiac hypertrophy in 50; roughened first sound in 13; systolic murmur apex in 10; aortic regurgitation in 9; mitral stenosis in 6; accentuation second sounds in 5; atheroma in 5; aortic stenosis in 4; fatty heart in 3; double mitral in 2; tricuspid regurgitation in 1; diastolic murmur apex in 1.

Lungs.—Defective breathing in 86; consolidation of the lungs (mostly partial) in 31; emphysema in 5; asthma in 2.

Showing causes of death in 95 cases at the Craig Colony in 5¾ years.

CAUSES.	Per cent.
Tuberculosis	24.210
Status epilepticus	23.158
Epilepsy, including accidents	16.849
Heart disease	10.526
Pneumonia	8.421
Epileptic mania, delirium, exhaustion	7.368
Meningitis	2.105
Bright's disease	2.105
Septicæmia	1.053
Brain tumor	1.053
Apoplexy	1.053
Peritonitis	1.053
Pleurisy	1.053
	100.000

The diagrammatic chart here presented shows that more epileptics die from tuberculosis than from any other single cause, every fourth death being caused by it, while status epilepticus, a very fatal condition to which every epileptic is liable, followed as a close second, it being the cause of death in over 23% of all cases. The very force and violence of the convulsions themselves sometimes produce death, while there are always accidental causes, such as asphyxiation during sleep, or mechanical violence, from which every epileptic having his freedom is at times unprotected. Ten of the 95 deaths were due to organic heart disease.

It is interesting to note the intimate relationship between the matter under the head of " Infirmities on Admission " in this report and the " Causes of Death " shown above.

SOME OF THE IMPROVEMENTS OF THE PAST YEAR AND OTHERS UNDER WAY.

INFIRMARIES.

The two infirmaries, one for either sex, each holding 40 to 50 cases, both designed with a view to future enlargement, are practically completed and we hope to occupy them by January first next, or as soon as the sewer and water lines to them are completed. The bids for this latter work were opened August 2d last, and were as follows: $1,920.50, $1,640.30 and $1,340. The appropriation for it was $1,500, and the contract was let at $1,340.

DORMITORIES.

Early in the summer, plans were made and accepted for four dormitories in the Villa Flora Group. On receiving bids it was found that they exceeded the per capita cost of $500 per patient and were all rejected. Preparations are under way at the present time for making plans and specifications for all buildings to be put up under the item of $90,000 given us this year for dormitories.

VILLAGE GREEN.

The four buildings for 120 male patients on the Village Green were finished early in the year and are now occupied. They each hold from 28 to 30 patients, each have a man and his wife in charge, and have proved to be very satisfactory homes for patients.

TWO SILOS.

Bids were opened on August 2d for two silos under the appropriation of $900 for same. The contract for their construction complete was awarded the Mt. Morris Lumber Company, at $707.95. The silos have been completed and filled with ensilage.

UNDERGRADE CROSSINGS.

The two undergrade crossings on the Pennsylvania Railroad are practically completed and will soon be opened for use. The bid for doing this work by contract was $1,591, while it will be finished by day's labor for less than $1,000. With these two crossings in use, and with the railroad track properly fenced, the danger of accidents to Colonists will be lessened.

WILLOW POND.

We have cleaned Willow pond by removing several hundred cubic yards of mud and silt and distributed it over the adjoining land as a fertilizer. All the ice we now use, amounting this year to 1,700 tons, was cut from this pond.

WAREHOUSE AND BAKERY.

The appropriation of $1,500 for finishing the warehouse and bakery is being expended for that purpose by contract, and we hope to occupy this building within six weeks or two months.

TRADES SCHOOL.

A contract was made on August 2d for the construction of a third wing to the trades school, and the work is now under way. The addition of this wing will give us the needed increase in the amount of room for shop and industrial purposes.

FILTER BED.

The new filter bed in connection with the sewerage system, an acre in extent, was completed last fall and is in successful use. We have found the intermittent filtration sewage system perfectly satisfactory in every respect.

CONDUIT FOR STEAM PIPES.

We are building a brick conduit, 3 x 4 feet, to carry steam heating and hot water pipes about the Villa Flora group, including the Roman Catholic chapel and priest's residence. It is regretted that work on this conduit was so long delayed, but every effort is now being made to complete it as soon as possible.

TENANT HOUSES.

Bids were opened in August last for four new tenant houses under the $4,000 appropriation for that purpose, but all were rejected as being in excess of the appropriation. An additional appropriation will be required before these cottages can be built.

HOTHOUSE AND WIRES UNDERGROUND.

Plans have been made and accepted for a hothouse of approved design, 20 x 100 feet, for garden and floral purposes, and its construction will be begun at an early date. Plans and specifications have also been made for putting all electric light, telephone and other wires underground, for which bids will be received at an early date.

FENCING.

About one mile of new wire fence has been built through the forest along the east line of the property. This completes the fencing around the entire estate, but some cross fences need yet to be built.

MINOR REPAIRS.

A large number of minor repairs have been made in all departments, including engineering, carpentry, plumbing, masonry and painting. The following buildings were painted outside, wholly or in part: Tallchief cottage, Hoyt cottage, Walrath, Gleaners, trades school, power-house, laundry, carriage house, some of the buildings of the West Group, the East Group kitchen, the farmer's house and the granary.

FARM AND GARDEN.

Your attention is invited to the Steward's report, which shows the value of the produce of these two departments. We commend the work of them both.

SPECIAL APPROPRIATIONS REQUIRED
FOR 1902.

FOR DORMITORIES, $60,000.

When the two infirmaries now nearing completion are occupied, and when the buildings authorized by the item of $90,000 in this year's appropriation are also finished and occupied, the Colony will have accommodations for 1,050 patients.

A great many patients are so much improved or cured by two or three years' treatment here that they are able to go away and earn their own living. On the other hand, there are many beyond recovery when admitted and whose disease is of such a nature that they grow worse in spite of everything that can be done for them, and these do not leave the Colony, the result being a gradually increasing accumulation of the helpless class. The infirmaries now building are for this feeble class and for those temporarily insane, and were originally planned with the idea that they should be made larger. If this item of $60,000 is secured, it should go for that purpose, one-half of it to be spent on each building.

FOR FURNISHING, $15,000.

The money given us from year to year "for furnishing" has not been sufficient for equipping the houses of patients with the very necessary articles of furniture, while it has always seemed to us that it would be desirable to do more than that and make the houses as home-like as possible for a people who must live in them so many years. The reasons given in former reports for the need for more money for furnishing apply with much force at this time.

FOR ROADS, WALKS AND GRADING, $12,500.

The great extent of the Colony estate—nearly 2,000 acres—the distance its buildings and groups of buildings are apart, the very bad condition of its roads and walks during the winter months, the constant damage to floors in the homes of patients from the freedom of patients running in and out, make it most desirable to construct three to four miles of substantial roadways and several hundred running feet of good walks as soon as possible.

FOR INSTALLING A REFRIGERATING PLANT IN COLD-STORAGE BUILDING, $3,000.

The cold-storage building, near the Pennsylvania Railroad station requires 600 to 700 tons of ice annually. We cut 1,700 tons of ice from Willow pond last winter, which was barely enough to last the year out. The pond is small and we were lucky last winter in being able to cut two crops of ice. The need for cold storage facilities is growing all the while. If the cold-storage building was fitted with a refrigerating plant we would then be able to cut from Willow pond all ice needed in the small refrigerators in individual houses. We must either put in a refrigerating plant or build another pond, and the former, we think, is the better plan of the two.

FOR BRIDGE OVER KISHAQUA CREEK ON D. AND M. HIGHWAY, AND FOR CHANGING ROAD TO SAME, $7,500.

The need for this bridge was spoken of in our seventh annual report. The necessity for it has grown greater since that time. As soon as possible we should divert the great amount of travel that now takes place over the public highway that passes through the Colony estate, so as to leave the present bridge and road between the male and female departments for the sole use of the thousand inhabitants of the Colony now living, about equally divided, on the two sides of Kishaqua creek. From all standpoints it would be a benefit to the traveling public to build this bridge, and a measure of safety to the epileptic population of the Colony.

FOR A STEAM DISINFECTING PLANT FOR BEDDING, CLOTHING AND HOUSEHOLD GOODS, $1,500.

We have no sort of a disinfecting plant at this time for clothing, bedding and household goods and we need one very much. We receive many patients from the tenement districts in the cities, where contagious diseases are always rife, and at any time we may stand in urgent need of an efficient disinfecting plant as a measure of checking the spread of disease. Such a plant is also needed for cleansing and purifying goods infected in other ways. The apparatus desired has a capacity for eight single bedsteads and mattresses at one time and operates under a steam pressure of 240 pounds. The disinfecting chamber alone, with appliances, will cost $1,250, the balance being required for steam connection with the power-house.

FOR ROOT CELLAR FOR GARDEN PRODUCE, $1,200.

We have one root cellar now, but it does not hold the potatoes alone raised on the place. We need another one, larger in size, in which to keep garden vegetables and fruits. Vegetables play an important part in our dietary, being especially valuable in the class of individuals the Colony cares for, and we need to preserve them as well as possible.

FOR ADDITIONAL KILN, SHEDS OVER MACHINERY AND OTHER IMPROVEMENTS TO BRICKYARD, $800.

In our opinion the Colony will never have a better paying or more valuable industry than brickmaking. Epileptic labor is well suited to it. The deposits of pure clay on the premises are practically without limit. An acre of clay one foot in depth will make one million bricks. We have more than one hundred acres of fine clay that might be used for brick. This wealth of raw material, the cheapness and abundance of labor and the certainty of a market always for the output of the plant, all combine to give this industry great value. Let us develop the plant, as I believe should be done, and we could not only make brick for our own use, but could supply other institutions, besides making other things that require clay of pure quality, such as drain tile, sewer pipe, etc. We can make brick for less than $2 a thousand, and we now sell them to contractors on Colony work at from $6 to $7 a thousand, or whatever the market price may be. The brickyard now clears from $2,500 to $3,000 annually. We ought to increase its capacity next year by building an additional kiln, which will cost about $550, and by building substantial sheds over all machinery.

FOR FARM STOCK AND IMPLEMENTS, $2,000.

Additional cows are constantly needed to keep the milk supply up to our requirements. New tools, implements and machinery are needed on the farm and in the garden. The value of farm and garden produce as given in the Steward's report, which is a part of this report, would seem to justify an appropriation of this kind.

FOR ADDITIONAL FARM TEAMS AND EQUIPMENT FOR SAME, $2,000.

We have never had enough teams to do the combined work of the farm, garden and miscellaneous hauling. In summer we always have large amounts of grading to do, and will spend this year alone, out of special appropriations, from $1,500 to $1,800 for such work. Out of the expenditures of one season we could pay for several teams and their equipment and own the teams afterwards.

FOR LAUNDRY MACHINERY, INCLUDING ONE 20 H. P. MOTOR, $1,500.

There is room now in the laundry for more machinery and we need it to do the additional work required by a constantly increasing population. Another washer, an extractor and a 20 H. P. electric motor will be installed if this item is secured.

FOR BALANCE TO ACCEPT LOWEST BID FOR CONSTRUCTION OF FOUR COTTAGES FOR EMPLOYEES AND FOR AN ADDITIONAL COTTAGE, FIVE IN ALL (IN ADDITION TO $4,000 APPROPRIATED BY CHAPTER 330, LAWS 1901), $3,950.

On July 6th last, bids were opened for four cottages for employees under the item of $4,000 in this year's appropriation. The lowest bid received exceeded the appropriation by $2,450, so all bids were rejected. The $4,000 will be available another year and an additional appropriation of $3,950 should be asked for, so that these four buildings, together with an additional cottage, five in all, the fifth to be a little larger in size, may be constructed.

FOR ISOLATION PAVILION FOR CONTAGIOUS DISEASES, $3,000.

We stand in great need of a plain, substantial building of some kind in which to isolate communicable diseases, should the necessity arise. At any time we may have diphtheria, smallpox, scarlet fever or measles, and we now have no place in which to care for such diseases. Our people all being free, and not confined to one or two buildings, and because of their free communication with each other, makes the danger of a general infection all the greater, and we should have means for promptly isolating infected cases. I would favor a wooden building for the purpose, at a cost of $200 to $300 a bed, with room for from twelve to fifteen persons.

FOR STATIC ELECTRICAL MACHINE AND X-RAY OUTFIT, $400.

It behooves us to keep pace with all that is new and of approved value in the treatment of all diseases, and epilepsy being one of the most obstinate and intractable of them all, we must take advantage of every agency or remedy that offers any hope whatever for good to the patient. Our equipment in a medical and scientific way would be more complete if we had the appliance here asked for.

FOR GENERAL REPAIRS AND IMPROVEMENTS, $7,500.

There are a multitude of little things constantly requiring to be done in every department of a great institution like this in the way of ordinary and extraordinary repairs that it is impossible to foresee and enumerate so far in advance, and a fund of the above amount should be secured for doing them as they arise. It is estimated that a sum equal to 3 per cent. to 4 per cent. of the whole value of a building must be spent on it annually to keep it in proper repair.

REGULAR APPROPRIATION FOR MAINTENANCE.

For the year beginning October 1, 1902, we estimate that the Colony will require for maintenance $140,000. This estimate is made on the belief that the average daily population for that year will be not less than 950.

SUMMARY OF APPROPRIATIONS WANTED FOR 1902.

For dormitories	$60,000
For furnishing	15,000
For roads, walks and grading....................	12,500
For installing a refrigerating plant in cold storage building	3,000
For bridge over Kishaqua creek on D. & M. highway, and for changing road to same..................	7,500
For a steam disinfecting plant for bedding, clothing and household goods	1,500

18

For root cellar for garden produce..................	$1,200
For additional kiln, sheds over machinery, and other improvements to brickyard......................	800
For farm stock and implements....................	2,000
For additional farm teams and equipment for same..	2,500
For laundry machinery, including one 20 horse-power motor	1,500
For balance to accept lowest bid for construction of four cottages for employees and for an additional cottage, five in all (in addition to $4,000 appropriated by chapter 330, Laws 1901).................	3,950
For isolation pavilion for contagious diseases......	3,000
For static electrical machine and X-ray outfit......	400
For general repairs and improvements............,	7,500
	$122,350
For maintenance, beginning October 1, 1902........	$140,000

ADMISSIONS, DISCHARGES, DEATHS, TRANSFERS AND NUMBER REMAINING BY COUNTIES SINCE OPENING OF COLONY.

County.	Admitted.	Discharged, died or transferred.	Remaining Sept 30, 1901.
Albany	24	7	17
Allegany	13	4	9
Broome	5	3	2
Cattaraugus..................	16	7	9
Cayuga	16	4	12
Chautauqua	13	7	6
Chemung	19	10	9
Chenango	4	1	3
Clinton	3	....	3
Columbia	6	1	5
Cortland	6	3	3
Delaware	5	2	3
Dutchess	13	3	10

County.	Admitted.	Discharged, died or transferred.	Remaining Sept 30, 1901.
Erie	90	36	54
Essex	4	2	2
Franklin	8	2	6
Fulton	9	5	4
Genesee	8	4	4
Greene	3	3	....
Hamilton	1	1	....
Herkimer	3	....	3
Jefferson	11	6	5
Kings	89	18	71
Livingston	15	9	6
Lewis	5	2	3
Madison	5	3	2
Monroe	73	23	50
Montgomery	9	4	5
Nassau	2	1	1
New York	309	87	222
Niagara	15	3	12
Oneida	22	5	17
Onondaga	25	10	15
Ontario	13	4	9
Orange	8	2	6
Orleans	11	5	6
Oswego	13	3	10
Otsego	5	1	4
Putnam	4	3	1
Queens	5	1	4
Rensselaer	15	6	9
Richmond	5	1	4
Rockland	5	....	5
St. Lawrence	30	14	16
Saratoga	9	1	8
Schenectady	2	2	....
Schoharie	3	1	2

County.	Admitted.	Discharged, died or transferred.	Remaining Sept. 30, 1901.
Schuyler	4	4	....
Seneca	7	4	3
Steuben	17	6	11
Suffolk	4	....	4
Sullivan	1	1	....
Tioga	17	4	13
Tompkins	9	2	7
Ulster	12	4	8
Warren	5	....	5
Washington	6	2	4
Wayne	3 .	1	2
Westchester	21	4	17
Wyoming	12	5	7
Yates	7	3	4
State at large	1	....	
Out of State	1	1	....
Totals	1,104	361	743

Eighth Annual Report of the Steward of the Craig Colony for Epileptics to the Medical Superintendent, September 30, 1901.

To the Medical Superintendent:

I have the honor to submit to you the eighth annual report of the steward of the Craig Colony for Epileptics, for the year ending September 30, 1901, in which are included summaries of the value of the work done in the printing office, carpenter shop, blacksmith shop, shoe shop, tailor shop, paint shop and sewing room, not including cost of material; also, the total of the debit and credit accounts of the brickyard, farm, garden and dairy, showing the value of products raised on the farm, garden and dairy, the cost of production, aside from patients' labor and the net proceeds for the same period of time.

There has been more advancement in the manner of utilizing patients' labor in the past twelve months than at any former period in the history of the Colony. Early in the spring of 1901 at a meeting of the medical staff, supervisors, and steward, a certain number of male patients were detailed for specific work: for instance, a list of twenty-five men were detailed to work on the farm; a list of twenty men to work in the brickyard; a list of twenty boys to work in the garden, and others as assistants in the various departments. Each head of department was furnished with a list of patients that were so detailed. This method aided each patient to become proficient in his work, and contented with Colony life; and he was thereby better enabled to contribute all that he was able for his support.

In years past there has been some trouble experienced in finding work that was congenial to patients. This was not due so much to the kind of work as it was to the fact that they were not employed at any one thing long enough to become interested in their work.

Heretofore patients have not generally wanted to work in the brickyard for the reason that it was heavy, hard work. The past summer the patients have gone to their work of their own accord, generally being on the spot ready for work before time and before the foreman had arrived.

I believe that this system of thorough organization of patients' labor and their systematic training by the heads of departments in which they worked has had much to do in making patients better help and more contented with Colony life.

I would suggest that, so far as possible, some attention be paid to employing for heads of departments persons who have tact, ability, and conscientious zeal in their work along the line of teaching patients how to help themselves.

BRICKYARD.

The brickyard was opened on May 10th and closed on October 1st. During this time there were only 41 dry days, consequently the season was very short. However, the down-draft kiln and dry racks erected in the yard last season enabled the Colony to make a superior quality of common hard brick.

During the season 250,000 No. 1 common hard brick were made. At $7 per thousand this would amount to $1,750. The cost for labor and coal was $697, or $2.78 per thousand. This leaves a net sum of $1,053 for the season's work.

I would suggest that an appropriation of $800 be asked to erect one more down-draft kiln, furnish material for building sheds over the clay crusher and for one more dry rack.

MAINTENANCE.

Total cost of maintenance with home product... $130,641 45
Total cost of maintenance without home product.   111,147 96

PER CAPITA COST OF ITEMS UNDER MAINTENANCE.

Average per capita cost of wages and labor	$74 42
Average per capita cost of expenses of managers ..	1 47
Average per capita cost of provisions	40 91
Average per capita cost of household stores	5 59
Average per capita cost of clothing	7 53
Average per capita cost of fuel and light.........	19 76
Average per capita cost of hospital and medical supplies..	2 60
Average per capita cost of shop, farm and garden..	6 44
Average per capita cost of ordinary repairs.......	1 31
Average per capita cost of transportation of inmates.....................................	26
Average per capita cost of miscellaneous.........	4 13
Total average per capita cost	$164 42

THE FARM AND GARDEN.

The value of the produce raised on the farm and garden and used as provisions, including canned goods, vegetables, hay, grain and coarse fodder now on hand is.............................	$21,615 87
Miscellaneous sales	3,356 21
Total value of farm and garden products and miscellaneous sales	$24,972 08

The cost of production, aside from labor of patients, is as follows:

Produce raised last year and used as food for live stock...............	$7,945 49	
Seeds, fertilizer, etc................	1,582 73	
Wages and labor...................	4,619 51	
Total cost of production........		$14,147 73

This amount deducted from the total value of farm and garden products gives a net value of........	$10,824 35

THE DAIRY.

The average number of cows milked during the year was 42.
The total number pounds of milk produced was 221,014.
The average per cow is 5,260 pounds.

I would suggest that you ask for a small appropriation to purchase extra milch cows to replace old cows.

INDUSTRIES.

Carpenter shop (work done by patients with one paid foreman)	$3,280 30
Blacksmith shop	553 30
Tailor shop (work done by patients with one paid foreman)	712 15
Painter's shop (work done by patients with one paid foreman)	1,213 19
Printing office (work done by patients)	526 16
Dressmaking department (work done by patients with one paid seamstress)	674 00
Shoe shop (work done by patients)	96 00
Brickyard, 250,000 bricks at $7 per M	1,750 00
	$8,805 10
Increase in value of live stock	$549 50

RECAPITULATION.

Farm and garden products, after paying all expenses, including miscellaneous sales	$10,824 35
Industries	8,805 10
Increase in value of live stock	549 50
Total	$20,173 95

INVENTORY.

The annual inventory made on October 1st, and presented with this report, shows an increase in real and personal property amounting to $27,480.62.

All of which is respectfully submitted.

TRUMAN L. STONE,
Steward.

Report of the Matron.

OCTOBER 1, 1901.

To Dr. WM. P. SPRATLING, *Medical Superintendent:*

I herewith tender my report as matron for the fiscal year ending September 30, 1901.

The fact that the Colony covers a very large area, and that the different groups of cottages and households are so widely separated from each other, some being almost one and one-half miles apart, as for instance the West House and Villa Flora groups, gives an idea of what my work consists of, inasmuch as it is necessary for me to visit the houses very frequently, though it is impossible for me to visit every one of them every day. The kitchens, dining and serving rooms call for a great deal of attention and supervision. However, I must say I have found, without exception, that the nurses and cooks in these departments, as well as in all the other parts of the households for the order and cleanliness of which the matron is always responsible, are conscientious and careful in performing their work. Of course they have a certain amount of assistance from patients who are considered capable, under their direction, of doing the work and to whom occupation is a benefit. But at times they have occasion to be discouraged, as the patients who usually assist them are apt to be physically unfitted for work, on account of the nature of their disease, and just when they are most needed. Still on the whole our employees succeed in getting their work done well and adapt themselves quickly to their surroundings, for we must frequently have new people on account of the increasing number of patients and the necessity for opening new houses. Since our last report, for instance, the Village Green group, viz., the Birch, Beech, Willow and Walnut cottages, accommodating about 120 male patients, has been opened.

I would reiterate what I said last year as to the advantage and advisability of having a distinct dining room for each cottage. There cannot possibly be any extravagance in the preparation or distribution of the food, as only the per capita allowance is sent out, and food can be much more tastefully prepared if done in small quantities. Besides, a small dining room is more homelike. It obviates the risk of having at times cold food, occasions less noise, and prevents quarreling, which is apt to occur where a vast number of patients is congregated. Everyone familiar with epileptics knows that some of them, at least, are apt to be irritable after an attack, and attacks will come on even in the dining room. The confusion necessarily following attacks at the table is infinitely lessened by having a small number seated in one room, where one can be easily removed and the meal allowed to proceed undisturbed.

In addition to the mending room which has previously existed in Bluet, the children's cottage, in which the girls of that house did all their own mending (and there is an average of 41 patients living there) and darned all the socks from the men's groups, we started this past year a mending room, under the direction of the seamstress, where a large number of adult female patients are employed. These patients, besides doing good work, seem to have become more cheerful from associating with and meeting their neighbors from other cottages.

In the sewing room, too, there has been quite an improvement, as we have more than twice the number of women employed that we previously had. A good deal of hand sewing is done in order to keep the patients supplied with occupation.

The number of articles made in the sewing room was as follows:

Aprons	393
Bags, broom	259
Bags, laundry	22
Bags, coffee	71
Bibs	57
Curtains, window	23
Corset covers	24
Drawers, pairs	217
Dresses	195

Dress waists	50
Dress skirts	8
Holders	91
Night dresses	248
Night shirts	21
Jackets, boys'	12
Operating gowns	3
Overalls, pairs	68
Pillow cases	14
Shirt waists	23
Silence cloths	11
Sanitary napkins	52
Table napkins	112
Table cloths	183
Ticks, bed	127
Towels, hand	679
Towels, roller	305
Towels, dish	41
Underskirts	181
Scarfs, dresser	9
Valances	8
Wrappers	24
Shirts, men's	85
Shirts, boys'	73
Stockings, pairs knitted	108
Total articles made	3,797
Total articles mended	6,768

I should have mentioned that since the beginning of summer the dining and sitting rooms have been plentifully supplied by the nurses and patients with flowers gathered in the fields, woods and garden.

In all the cottages an effort was made to can as much fruit as could be obtained to provide for the table in winter.

Respectfully submitted,

B. M. FOX,

Matron.

Report of the Protestant Chaplain.

October 1, 1901.

To Dr. Wm. P. Spratling, *Medical Superintendent:*

The following is the report of the work of the Protestant Chaplain from February 1 to October 1, 1901:

The regular preaching and Sunday school services have been conducted every Sunday afternoon, the combined service beginning at 2.45 p. m. Bible and song services have also been held. The House of the Elders and Bluet Cottage have been used. The musical instruments are a piano in the former and an organ in the latter, patients served alternately as organists.

Number under pastoral care, about 400. Attendance, preaching services, 125 to 150; Sunday school, over 100. Bible services, separate, 60 men, 60 women.

Pastoral visiting has been regularly conducted, calling at all the cottages of the patients every week.

The preaching and pastoral work was acceptably performed during July by Mr. William A. Aiken, a student from Auburn Theological Seminary.

The study of the Bible has been systematically encouraged, and Bibles and religious literature brought within reach of the patients. This intellectual element is found helpful in promoting courage, contentment and patience. Song also affords great pleasure and profit to the participants. Donations of religious literature will do great good and will be greatly appreciated by the recipients.

The endeavor is to make all feel a true Christian fellowship, and to use religious influences to banish homesickness and to overcome worry and temper, those foes of nervous sufferers. Thus, these influences build up faith and strengthen right character.

The strong feeling is expressed that fundamental, manual and intellectual training are urgently needed as proper bases for the religious and moral influences to have their full and proper effect in character building and helpfulness to health.

The work has been steady and of a healthy character, the ground being broken and good seed sown.

The above report is respectfully submitted.

REV. ALFRED F. PRATT,

Protestant Chaplain.

Report of the Catholic Chaplain.

OCTOBER 1, 1901.

To Dr. WM. P. SPRATLING, *Medical Superintendent:*

At the close of the present fiscal year, which also terminates my first year as Catholic Chaplain of Craig Colony, I have the honor to submit the following report:

During the year there have been nearly 300 Catholic patients at the Colony, 12 of whom have died. For varied reasons 18 have returned to their homes, some greatly benefited by the treatment here received. There are at present 261 Catholic patients at the Colony; 146 men and 115 women. Of this number about 50 are never able to attend public religious services, owing to physical or mental disability. All the others are free to attend the services provided for them on Sundays and certain other days throughout the year.

The following order of service is taken from the printed card given each Catholic patient:

Mass, Sunday, 9 a. m.

Sunday school for girls, Sunday, 3 p. m.

Sunday school for boys, Sunday, 4 p. m.

Confessions (men), second Saturday of month, 4 p. m.

Communion (men), second Sunday of month, 6.45 a. m.

Confessions (women), fourth Saturday of month, 4 p. m.

Communion (women), fourth Saturday of month, 6.45 a. m.

Mass at 7 a. m. on following days of year: New Years, Ascension day, August 15th, November 1st, December 8th and Christmas Day.

In arranging these services it has been my aim to give the patients ample opportunity to perform all the duties of their religion, and at the same time not to conflict with the established order that must necessarily be preserved in a large institution.

In visiting the cottages two or three times a week, and the hospital daily, I find that a chaplain may benefit the patients in many other ways besides conducting the above mentioned services.

Our religious services are now held in the House of the Elders, but will be transferred to the new Catholic chapel, which will be completed some time in November. This chapel (with adjoining cottage for the chaplain), which has been so generously donated by the Rt. Rev. Bishop McQuaid of Rochester, will have cost about $12,000 when ready for use. Much of this money is the personal gift of the Bishop.

Situated on the east side of Kishaqua creek and but a few feet from the gorge on an excellent site, it can be seen from all parts of the Colony. It is a brick structure, Romanesque in style, with blue stone and terra-cotta trimmings. Its full length is 85 feet by 40 feet wide, and has a seating capacity of 300. The tower, including a surmounting cross, is 52 feet high. In furnishing and decorating the interior, it is our aim to give a cheerful effect, and at the same time to preserve a thoroughly religious aspect. The stained glass windows, which the Bishop has already ordered from Germany, will contribute greatly to the interior beauty of the place.

And we feel confident that this chapel, when complete, will not only add one more desirable feature to the Colony plan on which the institution is founded, but that it will also serve as a haven of solace, where God's poor afflicted can commune with Him who never turns a deaf ear to human woes.

In concluding this report, I am prompted by feelings of personal gratitude to thank the officers and employees of the Colony from whom I have received so many helps and courtesies during the past year.

Respectfully submitted.

J. A. MALEY,
Catholic Chaplain.

Report of Dentist.

MT. MORRIS, N. Y., *September* 30, 1901.

To the Medical Superintendent of Craig Colony:

I have the honor to report to you my professional attendance upon the patients at Craig Colony as dentist for the fiscal year ending September 30, 1901.

Permit me to state that I have had this year, as during the preceding years, the valued co-operation of yourself and staff, which has been of great value to me in the prosecution of my work.

I have made during the past year one thousand and seventeen treatments, classified and described as follows:

Males treated		795
Females treated		222
Total number treated		1,017
Teeth filled, males	20	
Teeth filled, females	22	
Total number filled		42
Teeth extracted, males	699	
Teeth extracted, females	189	
Total number extracted		897
Special treatment of teeth, males	38	
Special treatment of teeth, females	27	
Total special treatments		65
Teeth scaled, males	8	
Teeth scaled, females	5	
Total teeth scaled		13
		1,017

All of which is respectfully submitted.

CHARLES J. MILLS,

Dentist.

DONATIONS.

The Colony is greatly indebted to the following for donations noted:

The Pennsylvania Railroad Company, through the courtesy of Mr. G. W. Creighton, General Superintendent, for the use of an excursion car for fifty persons to Portage.

Mrs. Elizabeth Warren	$2 00
John Belknap	5 00
Mrs. A. T. Speight	5 00
Carl Forndran	2 00
Geo. M. Bennett	10 00
Dr. and Mrs. Peterson and Madame Berg	20 00
Chas. A. Macy	25 00
Geo. M. Wirt	5 00
J. S. Haselton	60 50
Mrs. John Seder	5 00
Mrs. C. Brown	1 00
Mrs. Gottlieb	1 00
Hugo and Mrs. Emma Generlick	5 00
Mrs. Minnie Biele	2 00
J. Eisenberg	5 00
W. R. Brown	4 00
John Gutman	1 00
Mrs. Robert Ross	5 00
Theodore R. H. Hanne	5 00
Francis M. Jones	1 00
D. Szasz	10 00
Charles P. Olsson	2 00
Mrs. E. Meehan	1 00
Joseph Bader	2 00
Mrs. John Miller	1 00

Mrs. M. Applebone	$10 00
Mrs. Broseman	2 00
Mrs. Fred Baumgarten	1 00
Charles L. Adrian	20 00
Rev. D. M. Wilson	3 00
Leo P. Frohe	15 00
Mrs. Elvirah D. Winchell	2 00
Mrs. Michael J. Kerwin	1 00
Miss Emily Bell	10 00
Matthew Reilly	3 00
A. Meyer	10 00

Dr. W. Scott Hicks, reading matter.

C. L. Newton, papers and magazines.

Miss Julia F. Beebe, reading matter.

C. L. Carhart, magazines, papers, etc.

Seigel-Cooper Co., games, toys, etc.

Moulson Soap Works, pictures.

Leroy History of Art Club, papers.

Mrs. Anna Hardick, books.

William Pape, books.

G. D. Keeney, books, magazines, etc.

The College Settlement, New York city, toys, games and books.

F. M. Howard, one year's number Youth's Companion.

A. O. Bunnell and others, books, magazines, etc.

Levi Ellis, toys.

Montgomery County Committee State Charities Aid Association, reading matter.

Mrs. Ira Patchin, reading matter.

Mrs. E. C. Brocklebank, reading matter.

Miss Jennie B. Fillmore, reading matter.

Pittsford Women's Christian Temperance Union, papers and magazines.

Miss Jessie Gillender, books.

Mrs. Ellen H. Lovejoy, magazines and papers.

Mrs. J. P. Winters, reading matter.

Mrs. John Seder, box clothing.

Charles De Hart Brower, books.

Mrs. Ezra Clark, magazines.

Magazine Dispensary All Souls Church, Chicago, magazines.

Brooklyn Public Library, magazines.

Mrs. Harriet Morgan Pratt, magazines.

Mrs. E. Hook, chair and game board. ·

Mrs. Ludwig Larson, toys.

Dr. M. Bresler, books.

Junior Endeavor Society, Batavia, by Miss Jennie B. Fillmore, literature.

Mr. K. D. Lindsay, reading matter.

Emil V. Kohnstamm, magazines.

Murray Dunham, magazines.

Mrs. J. W. Swanton, three pieces furniture.

We are much indebted for copies of the following papers:

Caledonia Advertiser, Caledonia, N. Y.

Castilian, Castile, N. Y.

Christian Advocate, New York city.

Dalton Enterprise, Dalton, N. Y.

Dansville Advertiser, Dansville, N. Y.

Dansville Breeze, Dansville, N. Y.

Gazette and Independent, Ovid, N. Y.

Hammondsport Herald, Hammondsport, N. Y.

Holley Standard, Holley, N. Y.

Ithaca Democrat, Ithaca, N. Y.

LeRoy Gazette, LeRoy, N. Y.

Livingston Democrat, Geneseo, N. Y.

Livingston Republican, Geneseo, N. Y.

Livonia Gazette, Livonia, N. Y.

Mt. Morris Enterprise, Mt. Morris, N. Y.

Mt. Morris Union, Mt. Morris, N. Y.

Oakfield Reporter, Oakfield, N. Y.

Oakland Standard, Oakland, N. Y.

Oneida Despatch, Oneida, N. Y.

Ontario County Times, Canandaigua, N. Y.

Ovid Independent, Ovid, N. Y.

Penn Yan Express, Penn Yan, N. Y.

Rochester Herald (daily), Rochester, N. Y.

Rochester Post-Express (daily), Rochester, N. Y.

Rochester Post-Express (weekly), Rochester, N. Y.

Rochester Union and Advertiser (daily), Rochester, N. Y.

Rochester Union and Advertiser (weekly), Rochester, N. Y.

Rochester Presbytery News, Rochester, N. Y.

Union Springs Advertiser, Union Springs, N. Y.

Watkins Express, Watkins, N. Y.

Yates County Chronicle, Penn Yan, N. Y.

We have received a number of other donations, but not knowing from whom they came, we have to thank the donors collectively, which we take pleasure in doing.

Miscellaneous Notes and Recommendations.

A CENTRAL PLANT FOR HEATING.

At our request Mr. George L. Heins, State Architect, considered at length the advisability of heating the Villa Flora group, the East group and the Village Green group, in all of which 1,500 to 1,800 patients will eventually live, from the main power plant, but thought it would not be a matter of economy at this time. Fuel and light cost $19.76 per patient in the total per capita cost of $164.42 during the past year, and we are confident that the time will soon come when it will be more economical to heat all groups from one central plant.

LOCAL TRANSPORTATION.

A year ago we spoke of the problem of local transportation. We thought a system of electrical roads would be a good thing to have. We need a better and cheaper system than doing it by teams. If we could build good roads, it would enable us to do it by teams better than it is done now. The present cost of the service is close to $3,000 a year.

ECONOMY AND COMFORT IN HOUSES OF WOOD.

We have again to recommend the building of some houses of wood for patients. We illustrated this point last year with a picture of Tallchief Cottage, a wooden building forty years old, still good, and of excellent design and arrangement for epileptics. Such a building is as little exposed to fire, and, with our facilities for fire protection, would not be destroyed by fire any quicker than one of the new non-fireproof brick cottages on the Village Green or in the women's group. Homes like Tallchief Cottage could be built for $200 a bed, and judging by similar buildings now on the place they would be good for seventy-five years.

CHANGES IN LAW GOVERNING THE ADMISSION OF PATIENTS.

We feel that it would put the Colony on a broader basis to do good if that part of its organic law governing the admission of patients could be amended to provide simply for the admission of epileptics without class distinction. Once here, if they have no means, accept them as indigents and do not require them to pay; if they have means, then let them pay. This provision would not abridge in the slightest the consideration the present law evidently intended to bestow upon the indigents, while it would deny admission to many as indigents who now enter as such but who can afford and would like to pay.

NERVE NOSTRUMS.

Many epileptics in their eagerness to find relief from the disease, try all sorts of patent and quack nostrums, and in doing so run great risk of suffering evils more destructive than epilepsy. True, many of these quack remedies, so glowingly set forth in the public prints, do possess the power of suppressing the attacks for a time; but it is suppression only, not cure, and from repeated observations on the effects of such nostrums we have noted that the patients are always worse afterwards. Some of them are poisonous in unskilled hands and I have known death to result from their use. Others, though they temporarily suppress the fits, destroy the mind.

TRAINED NURSES.

Two candidates graduated from the Colony Training School for Nurses in June last. We have found the service of nurses especially trained in our school invaluable in the care of epileptics.

BISHOP McQUAID'S GIFT.

The very generous and noble action on the part of the Rt. Rev. B. J. McQuaid, Bishop of Rochester, in donating funds was noted in our last annual report, and the report of the Resident Catholic Chaplain shows that the Church of the Divine Compassion and priest's residence in connection with same are nearing completion.

MORE INDUSTRIES.

We are constantly training more patients to work and we need more industries. In summer we can find employment for all, but we have not enough shops and indoor forms of work to keep them busy during the long months of winter. The women, especially, need a building in which all the creative work by them could be carried on: a sort of useful arts building.

PRESERVATION OF SCIENTIFIC DATA.

After six months study and trial we determined upon a card index system to supplant the present system of keeping medical, surgical and scientific data, and hope to see the system in use at an early date. We are in a position to collect and preserve vast quantities of valuable data about epilepsy, and we would be at fault if we did not do so. Our records are now quite elaborate and complete, but the card index system would make them more so.

VISITORS.

Governor B. B. Odell and party, consisting of Congressmen James W. Wadsworth and Lucius M. Litthauer, State Senators Frank W. Higgins and T. E. Ellsworth, Hon. S. Fred Nixon, Speaker, Hon. Otto Kelsey and Hon. J. P. Allds, Assemblymen, visited and inspected the Colony August 29.

The President, Hon. Wm. R. Stewart, the Vice-President, Dr. E. V. Stoddard, Dr. Stephen Smith, Mr. Peter Walrath and Mr. D. McCarthy, Commissioners of the State Board of Charities, and Mr. Hebberd, Secretary, also made visits during the year.

We also had many visitors from this and foreign countries who came to see and study the Colony system; three commissioners from England coming during the past summer. Commissioners also came from Pennsylvania, Massachusetts, New Jersey and other states where the public care of epileptics is receiving attention.

APPOINTMENTS.

Dr. Annie M. Tremaine was appointed woman physician January 21, 1901. Dr. Harriet A. Gignoux was appointed medical interne March 7, 1901. Drs. Tremaine and Gignoux have since had charge of the entire women's group.

Dr. William T. Shanahan was appointed medical interne February 11, 1901. Rev. Alfred F. Pratt was appointed Resident Protestant Chaplain February 8, 1901. Miss Mary F. Tracy and Miss Marietta Hitchcock were appointed teachers on the respective dates of September 9 and 21, 1901.

RESIGNATIONS.

Dr. L. Pierce Clark, for five years first assistant physician, resigned the latter part of September and went to Europe to study general medicine in the schools of Berlin and Vienna. After a year's absence Dr. Clark expects to enter private practice in New York city. He was always ready and willing to give his best efforts to the work of the Colony during his period of stay, and with all his duties was an ardent student of epilepsy. His genial personality and example of industry will be greatly missed.

Dr. Edward L. Hanes, third assistant physician, resigned October first and went to accept a similar position in the Hudson River State Hospital, at Poughkeepsie, by request of the Superintendent of that institution.

THANKS TO ALL.

I most gratefully acknowledge the good work of the officers, administrative assistants and employees during the year. The undivided support and consideration I have always received from you, and for which I again thank you, have been pleasant and effective aids in doing the work required of me.

Very respectfully submitted,

WILLIAM P. SPRATLING, M. D.,

Medical Superintendent.

REPORT

Committee on the Blind.

REPORT.

Your Committee on the Blind presents the following report for the year ending September 30, 1901:

NEW YORK STATE SCHOOL FOR THE BLIND.

This institution, located at Batavia, has been visited by the committee and inspected by the Board's inspector of State charitable institutions on four occasions during the fiscal year, namely, in November, January, April and July.

The inspector has made careful inquiry, as required by the State Charities Law, in these particulars:

1. The proper and economical expenditure of public moneys received and the general condition of the finances.

2. The accomplishment of the objects of the institution with regard to its industrial, educational and moral training.

3. The methods of government and discipline of its inmates.

4. The qualifications and general conduct of the officers and employes.

5. The condition and care of the grounds, buildings and other property.

Summarizing the results of the inspections, and considering them along the foregoing lines, it may be stated:

1. The appropriations to the institution have been properly and economically expended through the medium of the Bureau of Charitable Institutions of the State Comptroller's office. The work performed under special funds was duly advertised for and awarded to the lowest bidder. With regard to maintenance funds, however, it was found that the steward appar-

ently does not seek the most advantageous markets for the purchase of general supplies, but confines his buying largely to the village of Batavia. The provisions, other than meats, are bought from any firm, in his discretion, without the desirable competition secured by inviting bids from month to month by the various merchants of the village. And concerning the financial records, failure to secure a bookkeeper resulted in the neglect of the general books for the long period of seven months, or from June, 1900, to February, 1901. It is also to be noted that the institution has maintained a private fund devoted to recreation and amusement of pupils, said fund being made up from admissions charged at concerts and sundry donations. Under a proper compliance with law this fund should have been reported to the State Treasurer, but such action does not appear to have been taken.

2. The industrial and educational training of the pupils has continued without special change, the test of scholarship in scholastic branches being the Regents' examinations, in which satisfactory results were obtained. The work of teaching has been facilitated by the employment of a woman to operate the machines for the printing of music and literature in the "New York" and "Braille" point-print systems. There is a diversity of views as to the utility of maintaining instruction in a dual system of print in one school.

With regard to the industrial education the school confines its attention to broom-making, chair-caning and piano-tuning for the boys and sewing for the girls. It is suggested that mattress making be again taken up, and that there be established a cooking school. Both of these subjects are included in the course at the New York city institution.

Physical instruction has been given during the last half of the school year in the new gymnasium, which has a suitable equipment of apparatus and shower baths. The teacher in charge is a man of experience, who could not have been secured at the salary offered, but for his securing other employment in the village in addition to his work for the State.

It is the opinion of your committee that the pupils have received insufficient instruction in the very important fire drill.

3. Concerning the government, discipline and general treatment of the pupils the methods in vogue have continued to be satisfactory in general respects. The food has been found always good and well prepared, but insufficient time, in our opinion, is allowed the children at table. The average time spent at dinner, the principal meal of the day, has averaged only fifteen minutes, which is far too little even for a seeing child.

During the year measles, mumps, typhoid and scarlet fever appeared, necessitating the employment of special nurses. These diseases were fortunately confined to scattering cases.

The policy of the superintendent has been to discourage, as far as possible, the practice of drawing on the counties for clothing supplies. Where a poor child has been in need of garments he has endeavored to secure contributions of cast-off garments or other donations. It is stated that during his term of office clothing requisitions on counties have been decreased by one third. His motive has been that the public supplying of garments, etc., was a pauperizing influence. It is considered by your committee that the results of this policy have been to keep many children in want of neat raiment, and that the general practice of schools for the deaf in drawing on the counties for clothing account should be the guide for procedure here. The custom is probably not as baneful in creating ideas of dependence as the soliciting of alms. It is a part of the State's general charitable policy in securing to the blind and the deaf *a home* during their education.

The population at the Batavia school has averaged 130 during the year, which is practically the normal capacity of the dormitories. It is noted that in 1892 there were the same number of pupils in attendance, so that a decade shows no increase. As attendance during the same period at the New York institution has decreased, the facilities for education of the blind in this State seem ample at present.

4. Concerning the officers and employes, the year was chiefly marked by the resignation of Superintendent Gardner Fuller, who has ceased his connection with the school after several years of conscientious work in its behalf. His successor had not been appointed at the opening of the new term in September, and Mr. Fuller kindly remained long enough to see that the work was resumed in an orderly manner.

There have also been several other changes in the teaching and housekeeping staff. The officers and employes in general have been faithful and competent. Some of them have become aged in the State's service here.

5. The property of the school has been well cared for; the grounds and buildings have always been found in a neat condition. It is proper, however, to again point to the unnecessarily large task falling to the school in being obliged to maintain its very extensive grounds and the approaches thereto. By the residents of Batavia these grounds are regarded as a public park.

The location and character of the general provision storeroom of the school are unsatisfactory, and the supplies should be removed to more desirable rooms, of which there are several in the basement of the main building.

New work accomplished during the year included electric wiring and fixtures, provided for by an appropriation of $2,500, under chapter 405, Laws of 1901; also general repairs and betterments.

Appropriations were made under the same law for gymnasium lockers, for library and apparatus, for painting walls and woodwork and for additional fire extinguishers. There was no expenditure during the fiscal year for any of these items.

The new cement walks have been completed under an appropriation of $1,000, in 1900, and there has been a partial expenditure under the 1900 appropriation for repairs to tin roofs, gutters and conductor pipes.

THE NEW YORK INSTITUTION FOR THE BLIND.

This institution, located at Ninth avenue and Thirty-fourth street, New York city, was also inspected by the Board's inspector of State charitable institutions, his visits during the fiscal year being made in October, December, March and June.

Inquiry was made along the same lines as at the Batavia School, and the findings are as follows, the arrangement being the same as in the foregoing report:

1. The financial condition of the institution is good. It is under private management, reporting to the State Comptroller with regard to expenditures in behalf of the public pupils received. Its relations with the State are on a per capita contract basis of $250 per pupil. This sum is not sufficient, even when supplemented by the clothing moneys paid by the counties, to enable the institution to provide for the pupils without drawing upon its own invested funds.

As the State pays a per capita allowance of $280 for each State pupil in a school for the deaf, it is manifestly unjust to reimburse this institution on a lower scale. Your committee recommends that the Legislature remedy this condition, which has continued to the detriment of this famous school for some years. Although it has a large endowed fund, the desire of the management to remove the school to its more desirable suburban site at Washington Heights, should be assisted by keeping these private funds intact.

2. The educational and industrial training of the pupils continue along proper lines, with excellent results, as shown by the examinations. The specialized instruction of the blind is here developed to its highest efficiency, and is assisted by an equipment of devices and apparatus that could not be readily improved upon. Such instruments as the " stereograph," for the duplication of literature in the " point-print " system (New York) and the " kleidograph " or typewriter for the blind person's use with point-print, are manufactured here under the direction of the inventor, the superintendent of the institution. They are of very general use in the instruction of the blind throughout the country.

It is proper to note that the work here in literary and musical branches is performed through the exclusive medium of the New York point-print alphabet and musical notation, and that the double system, as used at Batavia, does not obtain.

3. Concerning the government, discipline and general care of the pupils, observation has shown that the methods are humane and proper. The general health is good, the food satisfactory and clothing neat. There are limitations to the amount of open air exercise which the children can obtain in the heart of the city, and for their sake the removal of the institution to a less crowded locality is greatly to be desired.

The attendance at the opening of the new school year was 176, including 20 pupils from New Jersey. With dormitory accommodations for 225 pupils, the notable decrease in attendance during the last decade is very evident. On September 30, 1892, there were 207 pupils enrolled. In 1886, there were 216 pupils. A falling off is seen from year to year.

Prior to 1870, the buildings here were very much smaller, and although the Batavia School had been opened in 1868, the demand for admission of State pupils became so great that in 1870 large expenditures for additions were made from the investment funds.

The number of blind children of school age in the Greater New York territory has been gradually diminishing through modern surgical methods which operate to save large numbers of young children from blindness. The effect of this decrease is readily seen in the decreased attendance noted above. Having provided accommodations for such a number of pupils, there should be an adequate attendance to fully utilize the buildings and plant, and it is thought that enlargement of the territory from which pupils may be received will help to secure this.

Incidentally, the lowering of the average attendance is a further reason for an increase in the per capita compensation for State pupils.

4. Concerning the officers and employes of the institution, there are no changes to note, and the force is fully adequate to

meet the scholastic and housekeeping requirements. An assistant to the steward and bookkeeper would be desirable. At the time of the last inspection this gentleman reported that the arduous nature of his work had prevented his having a vacation during the past summer. He has no office helpers.

5. The grounds and buildings have been generally well kept. It is difficult, in so busy a portion of New York, to avoid dust and dirt, and constant care is necessary to keep the property in good order. Improvements should be made chiefly in the boys' water closets, which several inspections have shown to be unsanitary and far from neat, and in the arrangement of pupils' lockers. There should also be receivers and sewers for the interior court yards to care for surface and roof drainage and waste water thrown out by the help, which now passes down these courts in open gutters, evaporating and leaving the yards damp and dirty.

During the past summer the institution has been equipped with a chemical refrigerating system, with a system of electric signals for general school and emergency use, and with an electric power device to operate the large pipe organ.

All of which is respectfully submitted.

STEPHEN SMITH, M. D.,
Chairman Committee on the Blind.

Dated New York, October 25, 1901.

20

REPORT

OF THE

Committee on the Deaf.

REPORT.

To the State Board of Charities:

Your Committee on the Deaf has the honor to report as follows on the institutions subject to its special care:

There are at present in this State ten schools, counting as
separate schools the three branches of the St. Joseph's Institute. Five of the schools are situated in the interior part of
the State and five in Greater New York. The former are so
located as to be about at equal distances from each other and so
as to draw for pupils upon well-defined sections. It happens,
however, that very often pupils from one school's logical territory
attend some other. There are no school districts and the population is unevenly divided. A child has the choice of any one
of the eight institutions as his or her parents or guardians may
be moved by facilities offered or by other reasons.

A child is eligible for education as a "county" pupil at the
age of five years, and may be received by any one of the schools
on the certificate of a town overseer of the poor or of a supervisor of the county, whose duty it is to place such child in an
appropriate institution if, as the law declares, it is likely that
such child may "become a charge for its maintenance on any
of the towns or counties of this State."

At the age of 12 years the child becomes a "State" pupil, and
his or her instruction is continued to graduation, or to the
age of 25, on the yearly appointment of the Superintendent of
Public Instruction.

The county pupils are paid for by the several counties on the
basis of $300 per pupil, this sum covering board, tuition and
clothing. State pupils are paid for by the State on a per capita

basis that has varied from year to year. It has been as high
as $300, as low as $250 and is now $280. If a State pupil is in
indigent circumstances the county where he or she resides must
pay for his or her clothing not to exceed $30 per year.'

All of the schools receive both State and county pupils.

The following table gives the name and location of each institution in the State which is authorized by law to maintain and
educate deaf pupils at public expense, and also gives the number and sex of the pupils in attendance September 30, 1901:

Institutions.	Male.	Female.	Total.
New York Institution for the Instruction of the Deaf and Dumb, One Hundred and Sixty-third street, New York....	248	149	397
Le Couteulx St. Mary's Institution for the Improved Instruction of Deaf-Mutes, Buffalo......................	70	65	135
Institution for the Improved Instruction of Deaf-Mutes, Lexington avenue, New York...............................	108	102	210
St. Joseph's Institute for the Improved Instruction of Deaf-Mutes:			
Fordham Branch	...	110	110
Brooklyn Branch	...	67	67
Westchester Branch	197	...	197
Central New York Institution for Deaf-Mutes, Rome.......................	59	60	119
Western New York Institution for Deaf-Mutes, Rochester	85	93	178
Northern New York Institution for Deaf-Mutes, Malone	39	33	72
Albany Home School for the Oral Instruction of the Deaf, Albany........	19	14	33
Total	825	693	1,518

The above statistics show a decrease of 44 over the total number of pupils in school on September 30, 1900. The report of the same date in 1900 showed a decrease of 9 over the previous year, 1899, in which the attendance (1,571), seems to have reached the maximum. There had been a gradual increase each year from 1892, when the reports gave a total of 1,297 pupils.

President Stewart, of this Board, in reporting on an inspection of the schools for the deaf in 1892 stated: "On the 1st of October, 1892, the number was 1,297, by a singular coincidence exactly the same as on the same date in 1882. Thus, while the population of the State has increased 20 per cent. in the last ten years, the deaf-mute population, so far as shown by the attendance at the schools, has remained stationary, a gratifying fact. There is no reason to believe that there is a relatively larger number of deaf-mute children outside the schools now than there was in 1882."

During the past decade there has therefore been a total increase of but 274 over the number under instruction in 1882, which is also remarkable, in view of the growth of the population. This shows an almost stationary attendance for twenty years. The proportion of teachable deaf of school age now outside of the schools must be very small, by reason of the effective recruiting efforts on the part of some schools, and the fact that the grand special work of instruction of the deaf having become more widely known, has brought to the schools deaf children as soon as they have arrived at the age of five years, and often before, in which case they are considered as private pupils until the legal age is reached.

It is therefore evident that existing school accommodations in this State for the deaf are ample. Their past growth has not been so much from increase in the deaf population as from the recruiting agencies referred to. It is remarkable that at this late day there are still found teachable deaf children to whose parents the duty of providing for their neglected offspring has not been presented or to whom the existence of the schools is in fact unknown. In many of such cases a compulsory education law would apply with good results.

The number of deaf children without instruction also includes those feeble-minded or mentally dull children who, in justice to the great majority, cannot be received into the schools, yet who would greatly profit by careful instruction. This again suggests the wisdom of setting apart one school for their special and exclusive use, as recommended by this Board in 1898. There is no necessity for a new school. It would be better to utilize one of those now in existence.

The yearly graduation of deaf pupils into the various walks of life should be the commencement of a history of each child, showing his or her whereabouts and after life. The duty of each school towards its children does not end with the completion of the term of instruction, but they should lend encouragement thereafter and know most fully the fruits of their efforts in producing individuals sufficiently equipped to cope with world problems. But one school has undertaken to secure this valuable information, and having only recently inaugurated the system, finds that many old pupils are now unknown and beyond tracing.

The several schools have been visited and inspected once in each quarter by the Board's inspector of state charitable institutions. The inspection has covered only the management and care of the property and general treatment of the pupils, as this Board discontinued its examination of educational work on the assumption of that duty by the Superintendent of Public Instruction in 1900.

Summarizing the findings of the year's work, it can be stated that no abuses have been found, that the pupils are well cared for in general respects, and that the equipment and care of the buildings, in almost every school, continue adequate to the demands upon them. In all of these things the various boards of trustees are aided by the increase in the per capita compensation for State pupils from $260 to $280.

This Board recommended in 1895 that each school be equipped with a good gymnasium for the systematic physical instruction of the pupils. After a lapse of five years it is noted, with regret, that but three schools have given any serious efforts to this important subject.

Appropriations were made by the Legislature of 1901 for additions to the buildings at the Malone school and for improvements at the Rome school.

In connection with the fact that the most notable increase in attendance at any one school is at Albany, the Board calls attention to the very crowded condition of the building occupied and its dangerous construction.

There should be some action looking towards the adoption of a uniform system for keeping the accounts in the several schools. It is found that the financial records at the Malone school, approach what would seem an ideal set of books in adaptability to every need of a large or small population, and which are simple and easily kept. Similar books are in use in each of the State charitable institutions.

Very respectfully submitted,

JOHN NOTMAN,

Chairman Committee on the Deaf.

Dated Albany, October 26, 1901.

REPORT

ON

Thomas Asylum for Orphan and Destitute Indian Children.

REPORT.

To the State Board of Charities:

Your Committee on the Thomas Asylum for Orphan and Destitute Indian Children reports as follows:

This institution has been regularly inspected at frequent intervals during the past year. The Inspector of State Charitable Institutions noted the condition of the asylum, and the methods of administration as observed by him at different times. His reports were carefully examined by your committee, and, together with personal observation, are made the basis of this report. In addition to the regular inspections, your committee, accompanied by the Superintendent of State and Alien Poor, Mr. Byron M. Child, and Dr. Robert W. Hill, Inspector of the Board, made a special inspection of the asylum, and examined into its needs and work.

This institution is the only one of the kind in the State of New York. From a small beginning, as a purely private charity, it has grown to large importance as a State institution, and become a decided influence for the betterment of the remnants of Indian tribes resident in the State. According to the latest report there are now 5,265 Indians on reservations containing 87,677 acres, which are located in this State. The number seems to remain about the same as it has been for many years, which is an indication that with favorable environment the Indians can maintain themselves in association with the whites. It is true that the transition from barbarism to civilization has been slow and fraught with many perils to the red race, but out of them all there survives a people which has assimilated many of the habits of civilization, and which seems destined to continue and progress until, by a natural process of absorption, the Indian and the white become one people.

The Thomas Asylum represents a sense of duty as well as a charitable impulse of the commonwealth. It is proposed to care for orphan and destitute Indian children in this asylum, and thus save them from the consequences of a neglected youth. The forces of civilization are most effective when the children of the Indians are taken in hand early. If the natural propensity to a vagrant and idle life is permitted to obtain control, there is little hope that the Indian will ever develop into useful citizenship. The training in habits of thrift and industry must therefore commence while the character is unformed. For the 1,115 ordinary Indian children of school age the State provides, under the general provisions of the school law, 34 teachers in 30 day schools, at an annual expense of about $11,000. For the orphan and the destitute, this larger and more beneficent asylum provision is made.

The capacity of the asylum at present is sufficient to provide dormitories for 125 children, but when all the buildings of the institution are completed according to the original plan, there . will be room for 160 pupils and the necessary attendants. At the present time the main buildings are completed with the exception of one dormitory, and for this an appropriation is to be asked during the coming session of the Legislature. If granted, this will equip the asylum with a satisfactory group of dormitories, modern in plan, well built, with proper ventilation and sanitary plumbing.

It has been said by persons who have seen this asylum that because these orphans are of the Indian race, the State should not provide a good equipment for the institution. That they must go out from the asylum to cabin homes is no reason they should be deprived of the educational advantages of proper environment during the years they are in the care of the State. Not all will remain " cabin Indians "—some will be so strongly influenced during their school life that they will strive to make

better homes which will continue for them the pleasant associations of their early years. Even those who remain "cabin
Indians" will take to their cabins an impulse and ambition for
better things. Thus, although at first sight these substantial
buildings and their good equipment may seem unnecessary,
they are silent forces which mold Indian character. It must
also be remembered that this institution has a constant educational influence upon the adult population of the various reservations. The friends and relatives who visit the Indian children
are impressed by the buildings and the furnishing. The methods
of the asylum and its provision for the children are carefully
noted, and on remote reservations the memory of what the State
considers necessary for Indian youth stimulates the older
Indians to better their own condition.

At the present time the dormitories of the institution fitly
represent two periods in its history. The building known as
the "Nursery," now used as a dormitory for the boys, is one of
the first structures erected by private charity. Its small, ill
arranged, and poorly ventilated rooms show the difficulty of
securing funds from people who were doing all in their power
to carry on many charitable works. They show also the early
conception of what was thought to be a fairly satisfactory building for a reservation boarding school. The new brick dormitories, bright, roomy and well arranged, show a larger conception
of public duty as well as the change which years have wrought
in the plans for school buildings. Frame structures are unsuitable for dormitory purposes because they are so liable to destruction by fire. The cost for repair is greater than in brick
buildings, and the life of the structure is much shorter. It is
now proposed to move this old "Nursery" building to a proper
site in the rear of the new group, and convert it into a laundry.
It is also proposed to remove the power house to a more suitable
location, and, when these changes are made, the State of New
York will possess an institution well arranged and thoroughly
adapted to asylum purposes.

It is somewhat unfortunate that the asylum is at such a

distance from any of the main thoroughfares of the State. It is about three miles from the nearest railroad station, and to many of the thousands of travelers who pass by on the trains its very existence is unknown. Although it is within thirty miles of the city of Buffalo, it is safe to say that not one person in a hundred of those who reside in that city knows of its work. Interest is stimulated by observation, and an institution which is seen by a great many people arouses a sympathy and appreciation which is not awakened where the institution is isolated. This should have been considered when the State undertook the establishment of an asylum of this character.

THE COST OF THE BUILDINGS.

The original frame structures were built by the philanthropic Quaker, William E. Thomas, after whom the asylum is named, as a direct consequence of an interest awakened in the orphan and neglected young people of the Six Nations, by the Rev. Ashur Wright, D. D. When the State undertook the control and rebuilding of the institution, it appropriated $44,000 for three new buildings. The original appropriation of $22,000 for two brick dormitories, and of $10,000 for a school building, proved insufficient, and an additional appropriation of $12,000 became necessary. For all of the brick dormitories a total of $45,000 has been appropriated by the Legislature. Beside this amount, appropriations of $60,000 have been made for an administration building, a school building, the dining hall, kitchen, and assembly building. Thus, up to the present time, the total appropriations for the new buildings amount to $105,000.

It is proposed to ask the coming Legislature for an additional sum of $22,000 to complete all the dormitories. If this be granted, the total cost of the changes made necessary to provide suitable accommodations for 160 children and necessary attendants will be $127,000. This will make the gross per capita cost of the asylum $793.75. If, however, the cost of these administration buildings be deducted, and the actual expense for dormitories be considered, it appears that the net per capita cost will be less than $420.

Certain it is that this group of structures has not been burdensome to the State so far as its cost is concerned. The scope of the work has broadened with the change in the architecture. Now a liberal education is offered to the Indian children who are fortunate enough to be taken under the care of the State in this asylum. It is not a Hampton, nor a Carlisle, but in a modest way it seeks the intellectual advancement of the children committed to its care, and in some respects its work is better, for its discipline is mild and paternal rather than military.

The studies of the six grades are suited to the average of Indian children, and, while the school is in no sense a sectarian school, it is dominated by a religious influence.

Some of the pupils from this school have gone in past years to institutions of higher learning, and it is encouraging to note that the older pupils have regularly taken the Regents' examinations, meeting with much success. On the whole, your Committee is glad to be able to report favorably upon the work and prospects of this institution.

Respectfully submitted,

W. H. GRATWICK,

Committee on Thomas Asylum.

21

REPORT

OF THE

Committee on the New York State Hospital for the Care of Crippled and Deformed Children.

REPORT.

To the State Board of Charities:

Your committee on the New York State Hospital for the Care of Crippled and Deformed Children reports as follows:

The Hospital for Crippled and Deformed Children is located at Tarrytown, Westchester county, and was established by authority of chapter 369 of the Laws of 1900, which appropriated for the institution the sum of $15,000. As was stated in the last annual report, the board of trustees leased for a term of five years at an annual rental of $1,000, a private residence located on a plot of high ground fronting the Hudson river at Tarrytown.

The ground has a frontage of 300 feet on the river, going back 600 feet, and is bounded on one side by the main road leading north and south from Tarrytown.

Some improvements were made in the residence to fit it for the accommodation of patients, and it now has room for 25 children, beside the necessary attendants.

The hospital was informally opened for the reception of patients on the 7th of December, 1900, when five were received. It was formally opened with appropriate ceremonies on the 17th of May, 1901.

During the year ending September 30, 1901, 14 boys and 10 girls were admitted and 2 boys and 3 girls discharged, leaving a population October 1, 1901, of 12 boys and 7 girls. Since that time the institution has been filled to its maximum capacity.

Beside the appropriation of $15,000 made by chapter 369 of the Laws of 1900, $5,000 was contributed by private individuals. This was expended in preparing the buildings for service. The Legislature of 1901, by chapter 701, made an appropriation of

$4,250 for extraordinary expenses. This amount was to be expended as follows:

For equipment of operating-room, $2,000; for splints, braces and other orthopedic apparatus, $500; for work bench, tools and accessories for repairing apparatus, $250; for isolation pavilion of wood construction for contagious diseases, $1,500. In addition to this the Legislature appropriated $10,000 for maintenance.

All of the improvements thus provided for, with the exception of the isolation pavilion, have been made. Up to the present time plans for this pavilion are incomplete. Two sets of plans have been made, but of such character that it was impossible to secure the construction of a pavilion for the amount appropriated therefor. This pavilion is greatly needed and should be erected as speedily as possible.

The law establishing the hospital provides that it "shall be for the care and treatment of any indigent children who may have resided in the State of New York for a period of not less than one year, who are crippled or deformed or are suffering from disease from which they are likely to become crippled or deformed. No patient suffering from an incurable disease shall be admitted to such hospital. No patient shall be received, except upon satisfactory proof, made to the surgeon-in-chief by the next of kin, guardian, or a State, town or county officer, under rules to be established by the Board of Managers, showing that the patient is unable to pay for private treatment. Such proof shall be by affidavit. If there was an attending officer before the patient entered the hospital, it shall be accompanied by the certificate of such physician, giving the previous history and condition of the patient."

When this hospital was established the State Board of Charities furnished the board of managers with a list of more than 70 inmates of children's institutions who were reported as crippled and deformed. Unfortunately some of them have passed the age limit when they are eligible for treatment in this hospital, but the names of all such crippled children were furnished to the authorities of the institution in the hope that the new institution would be able to do something for the permanent benefit of some of these cripples.

The hospital is intended to minister to the needs of the children of the poor who may now be suffering from physical deformity in their own homes, as well as those who may be inmates of children's institutions.

Up to the present time a total of 32 persons have been under treatment. Several of these have been returned to their homes as permanently cured; others were taken out before the cure was effected, but the larger number still remain under treatment.

Owing to the character of the diseases for which this hospital is established it will be necessary for patients to remain a long time, hence the number of patients under care at any one time will not be great. If the institution is to be continued, it will ultimately require enlargement, and this enlargement must be in a new location where more land will be available.

Owing to the experimental nature of this institution nothing has been done in the way of providing occupation for the children. By the beneficence of private individuals a school is maintained three hours each day. If this hospital is to be a permanent institution it will be necessary to provide facilities for the regular instruction of the children under treatment.

Respectfully submitted,

STEPHEN SMITH, M. D.,

ANNIE G. DE PEYSTER,

Committee.

FIRST ANNUAL REPORT

OF THE

Board of Managers of the New York State Hospital for the Care of Crippled and Deformed Children, to the State Board of Charities.

Of the Albany Medical College.
A. VAN DER VEER, M. D.
SAMUEL B. WARD, M. D.

Of the Buffalo Medical College, Buffalo, N. Y.
ROSWELL PARK, M. D.
CHARLES G. STOCKTON, M. D.

Of the Long Island Medical College, Brooklyn, N. Y.
JARVIS S. WIGHT, M. D.*
JOHN A. McCORKLE, M. D.

Of the Syracuse University, Syracuse, N. Y.
JOHN A. VAN DUYN, M. D.
HENRY L. ELSNER, M. D.
REGINALD H. SAYRE, M. D., of New York city.
L. A. WEIGEL, M. D., of Rochester, N. Y.
RICHARD B. COUTANT, M. D., of Tarrytown, N. Y.

Attending Medical Staff.

Surgeon-in-Chief................NEWTON M. SHAFFER, M. D.
First Assistant Surgeon..........P. HENRY FITZHUGH, M. D.
Assistant Surgeon.....................HENRY SCOTT, M. D.

---

* Deceased.

HOUSE OFFICERS.

Superintendent................... THE SURGEON-IN-CHIEF.

Assistant Superintendent.................GEORGE M. WHITE.

Matron........................MISS GERTRUDE A. HOXIE.

Stenographer................MISS MARGARET F. BARRETT.

Trained Nurses.............. { MISS AUGUSTA STEINKOPF.
MISS MARIE SCHMIDLING.

LOCATION OF THE HOSPITAL.

The hospital building is located at Tarrytown, N. Y., about one mile south of the New York Central and Hudson River Railroad station, at Paulding avenue, on the banks of the Hudson river.

My Dear Sir:

With this I beg to transmit to you the report of the Surgeon-in-Chief of the New York State Hospital for the Care of Crippled and Deformed Children for the year ending September 30, 1901, said year being actually the ten months during which the hospital has been in existence.

This report, I would add, has been submitted to the Board of Managers and adopted and approved by them.

I am, dear Sir,

Very faithfully yours,

HENRY C. POTTER,

President.

The Hon. WILLIAM R. STEWART, *President,*

December 23, 1901.

REPORT OF THE SURGEON-IN-CHIEF AND SUPERINTENDENT.*

To the Board of Managers, New York State Hospital for the Care of Crippled and Deformed Children:

Gentlemen.—I submit for your consideration the following report of the hospital under your care for the ten months ending September 30, 1901.

As this is the first formal presentation of the work which will reach the public, it seems wise to refer to the early history of the hospital.

In the autumn of 1897 the Hon. William Rhinelander Stewart, then President of the National Conference of Charities and Correction, asked the writer of this report to make an address before the conference which met in May, 1898, " On the Care of Crippled and Deformed Children." An essay was prepared and presented on this occasion, in which the history of the work performed in this country and abroad among the crippled and deformed children was reviewed, and the following suggestion was made: "And why should not the State aid in such an effort? A strictly dependent, and even to-day a much neglected class is being only half cared for by the excellent medical institutions established for its relief. The educational and charitable systems of the State should be adapted to meet the demands of this class of crippled and deformed as fully as are those for the deaf, the dumb, the blind, or the insane. A child with a curable deformity demanding prolonged treatment should be treated as well as taught until he is fully recovered, and not, when convalescence is fairly established, and he is sure with proper care to recover, be sent out of the hospital to relapse after a few weeks or months, and to become ultimately a more or less useless member of society, perhaps a permanent burden upon the State."

*Read before the Board of Managers of the hospital at a special meeting held December 23, 1901. Approved and ordered sent to the State Board of Charities.

When this address was delivered its author did not know that in the winter of 1897 a bill had been introduced into and passed by the Legislature of Minnesota through the instrumentality of Dr. Arthur J. Gillette, of St. Paul, Minnesota, appropriating $5,000 a year for two years "for the relief of indigent crippled children of the State of Minnesota." It is a pleasure to report that Dr. Gillette's efforts have been most successful, and that at the last Legislature a sum of $15,000 was appropriated for the present year's work.

In the latter part of the year 1899 a bill incorporating the New York State Hospital for the Care of Crippled and Deformed Children was prepared by Mr. J. Adriance Bush and the writer and introduced into the State Legislature with the approval of Governor Roosevelt. These initiatory steps were fortunate in securing the cordial and impartial co-operation and wise counsel of the Hon. B. B. Odell, Jr. The act was signed by Governor Roosevelt on April 11, 1900. Fifteen thousand dollars was appropriated for the purpose of equipping the hospital and for the first year's maintenance. Under the provisions of the act the Governor appointed the following Managers: The Right Reverend Henry C. Potter, D. D., J. Adriance Bush, George Blagden, Jr., J. Hampden Robb and Dr. Newton M. Shaffer. At a meeting called for organization in the latter part of April, 1900, Bishop Potter was made president, Mr. Blagden was elected secretary and treasurer, and Dr. Shaffer was appointed chairman of the executive committee.

A commodious house on the banks of the Hudson river at Tarrytown, N. Y., was leased, and converted into a building arranged for hospital purposes. This was done with private funds raised by the writer. Over $5,000 was thus expended, the contributors being Mr. Edward Severin Clark, Mr. Joseph Milbank, Mr. George Blagden, Jr., and the surgeon-in-chief. Organization matters were pushed with much energy, especially by Mr. Bush, Mr. Blagden of the board of managers and Drs. Fitzhugh and Scott of the medical staff, and always with the hearty co-operation of the President of the Board of Managers and Mr. Robb. On December 5, 1900, the hospital was opened for the reception of patients, on which date four patients entered the hospital.

The Board of Managers appointed a consulting medical staff representing the professors of surgery and medicine in the following medical colleges of the State, viz., the College of Physicians and Surgeons, New York city; the Cornell University Medical College, New York city; the University-Bellevue Medical College, New York city; the Buffalo Medical College, Buffalo, N. Y.; the Long Island Medical College, Brooklyn, N. Y.; the Albany Medical College, Albany, N. Y., and the Syracuse University, Syracuse, N. Y. In addition, two prominent orthopaedic surgeons, one residing in New York city and one in Rochester, N. Y., and a prominent practitioner of Tarrytown, N. Y., were appointed on the consulting staff.

The active medical staff consists of three officers—a surgeon-in-chief, a first assistant surgeon and an assistant surgeon. The surgeon-in-chief is made superintendent by the act of incorporation.

One of the active medical staff visits the hospital daily, and any acute illness is attended by Dr. Coutant of Tarrytown, whose office is connected with the hospital by telephone.

The hospital will accommodate 25 patients with the necessary officers, and patients of either sex between 4 and 16 years are received.

During the ten months ending September 30, 1901, 24 patients came under treatment.* Of these, 5 have been discharged, leaving 19 under treatment on October 1, 1901. The average attendance was 13.

The 24 admitted were classified as to disease as follows:

Hip joint disease 13
Spinal disease (humpback)............................ 5
Knee joint disease (white swelling).................. 1
Infantile paralysis 3
Club foot 1
Rachitic deformity of spine.......................... 1

Total 24

---

* February 1, 1902.—The hospital has now 25 patients, all it can accommodate, and there are over 30 applicants on the waiting list.

Thirteen of these patients were boys and 11 were girls.

Four patients with spinal disease and one with hip joint disease were discharged. In each instance much benefit was received by these patients. In three cases, the patients after discharge were able to attend school. In the other two cases, the patients were too young to go to school. They were, however, enabled to walk about freely in their braces.

For the ten months ending September 30, 1901, 62 applications (see Table No. I) have been received for admission to the hospital. Of the 24 accepted for treatment, 16 came from New York county and 8 from the State at large, outside of New York county (see Table No. II). Of the 38 rejected, 25 were eligible, the majority being from New York county. The question as to the disposition of these applicants from New York county was submitted to the State Board of Charities, which advised as follows: " In the opinion of the Board it is desirable to have the entire State as equitably represented as possible by the patients who are received at the hospital." This opinion of the State Board clearly expressed the view of the Board of Managers in the matter. Hence, the hospital was not filled early in its history, as it might have been, with patients without discrimination as to their residence in the State. It is hoped that those interested will think a wise decision was made, as there have always been vacant beds kept for patients from the State at large. A hospital with over 40 beds, if it had existed, could have been filled with most deserving patients if no discrimination was deemed advisable in the matter of locality as a qualification for admission. In no case has a patient been received from New York county when there was a probability that such patient would be cared for by any New York city institution.

The vacancies that existed on October 1, 1901, would have been filled with applicants from the State at large, if the hospital and its work were more generally known. It is to be hoped that measures will be taken in the immediate future to bring the work of the hospital prominently before the public.

Experience proves that the objects of the hospital are not fully understood by the residents of the State at large. It is too apt to be regarded by the comparatively few who know of its existence, as a *home* or *asylum* rather than as a *hospital*, and on several occasions mentally defective children have sought admission on the ground that they had some form of paralytic deformity. The hospital is especially intended for children with the *deformities of hip joint disease, spinal disease, knee and ankle joint disease, club foot, bow legs, knock knee, infantile and other forms of paralysis, lateral curvature of the spine; and all other forms of the deforming diseases of childhood which are susceptible of relief or cure.* The fact that there are to-day over 100 children (see Table No. III) in the various institutions making monthly reports to the State Board of Charities, who are, or who have been, eligible to the hospital, points clearly to the demand for special and permanent work among this class by the State.

The length of time required for the treatment of this class of patients should be duly considered. If a patient with hip joint disease, or spinal disease, for example, is fortunate enough to have the disease discovered in the early stage, the treatment is not likely to be prolonged. But, generally, the disease reaches the stage of considerable deformity before surgical advice is sought. Treatment then demands not only relief of the deformity but the ultimate cure of the disease. This disease is almost always tuberculous and is located in the bones of the joints. It, therefore, can be readily seen that years may be consumed before the patient is cured. So also as to some other conditions. On the other hand, knock knee, bow legs, club foot, etc., which are not inflammatory conditions, and which can be operated on if necessary, may be greatly relieved oftentimes in a few months. But the majority of patients if properly cared for should remain in the hospital for years, for it is manifestly an unwise policy for the State to discharge a patient from the hospital who has been relieved of deformity, and who is fairly on the way to recovery from the disease which produced it, to meet with a certain relapse.

This prolonged residence in a hospital may be made most useful from an educational standpoint. All these patients can be taught not only mentally, but in the various industries to which their condition adapts them. This was the intention of the founder of the hospital, and a clause was introduced into the original bill of 1900 creating this educational work. In some way, this clause was omitted during the passage of the bill through the Legislature. After the hospital was opened, and the question of education came up, a friend of Dr. A. Alexander Smith, of the consulting medical board, gave the surgeon-in-chief $500, and another friend of the hospital gave $150, which enabled the surgeon-in-chief to employ a teacher and to purchase the necessary equipment. In carrying out this school project it was found necessary to remodel and fit up an old carriage house upon the premises. This, with the salary of the teacher, etc., has been thus far met with the fund above alluded to. It is to be hoped that the matter of education of the patients under treatment will receive the prompt attention of the Legislature.

A brief reference to the patients who have been received and treated seems necessary. They were all from the very poor class, and some were received from the almshouse. A few had formerly been patients of some hospital. These patients aptly illustrate the remarks made before the National Conference of Charities and Correction, for they had been only partly cured by the hospital which had treated them and then discharged to make room for others who, apparently, were in need of immediate attention. The inevitable relapse that followed undid all the good previously accomplished. Others, without treatment, too poor to pay for apparatus, even by installments, and who had no means even for car fare, had relapsed under dispensary care, and seemed hopelessly deformed. Still others, half starved and Illy-clothed, had been waiting for admission to some hospital for months or years. In two instances widows, unable to work, owing to the care which the crippled child demanded, have been self supporting since these children have been cared for in the hospital. In one case, the father of the patient was too ill to support his family and the child received no home care at all and was half starved when admitted.

The improvement in the patients has been remarkable. For many years the writer has been connected with some hospital for the treatment of crippled and deformed children, but they have all been hospitals in the *city*. This hospital is in the *country*, and the difference in the improvement in the patients, under the same treatment, in the country air, is very marked.

The future of the hospital is one which demands earnest attention. Soon after the hospital was opened, it was inspected by a prominent officer of the State Board of Charities. While stating his great satisfaction at the present condition of the work, he expressed the opinion that our little plot of four acres was wholly insufficient to meet the demands of the future. In his opinion, and this is shared by others familiar with the work, we need 50 acres or more somewhere, for example, among the Westchester hills, where a suitable modern hospital and administration buildings can be erected. It is not an exaggeration to say that before many years the hospital will provide for 500 patients.

The appended tables better express than I can, in words, the work performed and the results obtained. I desire to direct your attention to them.

In the work of organization, which at times has been very arduous and trying, the entire hospital staff has given the surgeon-in-chief hearty and unselfish co-operation. This is especially true of Dr. Fitzhugh and Dr. Scott, the assistant surgeons; Miss Hoxie, the matron; Miss Barrett, the stenographer; and Miss Steinkopf, the trained nurse. None of these officers have questioned the wishes or the orders of the superintendent, and all have given their whole energies to the work. The result is shown in the well equipped, if small, hospital, which I feel, as years go by, will become more and more an honor and a credit to the State.

And my thanks are especially due to the executive officers of the State Board of Charities, the Comptroller's office, and the Civil Service Commission. On all occasions, and under all circumstances, they have made the work of the chief executive of the hospital as easy as possible, and on several occasions they have been more than kind when a novel or difficult proposition in organization has confronted the chairman of the executive committee.

The hospital has been most kindly remembered by its many friends in donations of books, clothing, fresh vegetables, ice cream, etc.   A list of these kind donors is appended.   The rules and regulations governing the admission of patients, and blank forms of affidavits for the use of applicants are also appended to this report.

Respectfully submitted,

NEWTON M. SHAFFER, M. D.,

Surgeon-in-Chief and Superintendent.

NEW YORK, *December* 11th, 1901.

TABLE No. 1.

Summary of Applications for Admission.

DISEASE OR DEFORMITY.	AGE.			Total.
	Under 5 years.	5 to 10 years.	10 to 16 years.	
Hip joint disease..................................	2	7	10	19
Pott's disease of the spine.......................	1	8	3	12
Rachitic curvature of spine.......................	2	....	....	2
Club foot...	....	2	....	2
Infantile paralysis.................	4	4	2	10
White swelling of knee............................	....	1	....	1
"Crippled"..	....	1	....	2
Spastic paralysis.................	4	2	3	9
Knock knee..	1	....	....	1
Chronic hydrocephalus......................... ...	....	1	....	1
Ankle disease....	1	....	....	1
Cerebral hemiplegia...............................	....	1	....	1
Total	15	27	20	62

Summary of Accepted Patients.

Case number.	Date of admission.	Age, years.	Resident county.	DISEASE.	Condition on admission.	Application made and endorsed by affidavit of	Remarks.
1900							
1	Dec. 7	7	New York	Hip disease	Hip deformed and stiff	Father	Much improved. Joint motion good. General condition excellent.
2	Dec. 7	6	New York	Club foot	Rigid club foot	Mother	Improved.
3	Dec. 7	7	New York	Hip disease	Stiffness and deformity	Mother	Very much improved. Abscess disappeared without operation.
4	Dec. 7	10	New York	Hip disease	Thigh flexed and adducted	Mother	Great improvement. Abscesses healed.
5	Dec. 19	11	Kings	Hip disease	Very painful; abscess. Hip painful and stiff	Mother	Practically cured. Hip motion nearly normal. Walks without any apparatus.
1901							
6	Jan. 3	11	New York	Hip disease	Thigh flexed, pain and disability.	Father	Much improved. Discharged practically cured. Goes to school. Only slight shortening.
7	Jan. 5	13	New York	Hip disease	Deformity and pain	Father	Painful joint. Much improved.
8	Feb. 16	13	Westchester	Pott's disease of the spine. (Humpback.)	Pain and deformity	Father	Discharged—much improved. Only slight curvature which is under control. Goes to school.
9	Apr. 11	9	Westchester	Hip disease	Pain and extreme deformity.	Overseer of poor	Deformity. Abscess. Improved. Walks well with brace.
10	Apr. 17	16	New York	Hip disease	Great deformity, pain, abscesses. Unable to walk.	Aunt and guardian	Large abscesses which with the deformity are very much improved. Can walk about.
11	Apr. 17	12	New York	Hip disease	Great deformity. Unable to walk.	Mother	Rapid improvement. Walks about freely.
12	Apr. 17	9	New York	Chronic inflammation of knee joint. (White swelling.)	Pain, swelling and deformity	Mother	Cured. Under observation.
13	Apr. 17	6	Westchester	Infantile paralysis	Disability. Unable to walk.)	Father	With apparatus patient walks well.
14	Apr. 19	8	New York	Pott's disease of the spine.	Commencing humpback; pain.	Father	Patient much improved. Only slight deformity, which is arrested.
15	Apr. 23	9	New York	Infantile paralysis	Disability	Mother	Improved. Walks about.
16	Apr. 23	12	New York	Hip disease	Deformity and pain.	Mother	Has improved rapidly. Good motion at hip.
17	Apr. 23	5	Kings	Pott's disease of the spine.	Spinal deformity with pain. Abscess.	Mother	Discharged, much improved.
18	Apr. 23	5	New York	Pott's disease of the spine.	Spinal deformity and pain.	Mother	Deformity under control. No pain. General condition excellent. Discharged.
19	Apr. 23	12	New York	Hip disease	Deformity and stiffness.	Mother	Much improved. Slight deformity. No pain.
20	May 31	12	Ontario	Infantile paralysis	Disability	Superintendents of poor.	Improved.
21	June 21	11	Orange	Hip disease	Abscess. Deformity	Guardian	Great improvement. Two abscesses, both healed.
22	July 17	3	Kings	Rachitic spinal curvature	Very weak and unable to walk.	Mother	Spine straight. Patient walks without effort.
23	Sept. 4	4	New York	Hip disease	Hip rigid and deformed.	Guardian	Improving steadily.
24	Sept. 4		New York	Pott's disease of the spine.	Slight curvature and pain.	Mother	Discharged after a few weeks' treatment at parents' request.

TABLE No. III.

Summary of Reports made to the Managers of the Hospital by the State Board of Charities of Children Physically Defective in Institutions making monthly returns to the Board. Facts taken from the Records. Date of Reports, December 1, 1900, and February, 1901.

DISEASE.	Age.				Total.
	Under 5.	5 to 10.	10 to 15.	15 to 20.*	
Paralysis of one or more members...............	2	5	4	3	14
Crippled, condition not specified.....................	....	....	3	5	8
Deformed limbs..	1	11	10	6	28
Hip disease..	....	3	4	4	11
Spinal disease..	2	....	1	....	3
Spinal curvature...	....	4	4	....	8
Bow legs..	1	1	2	... .	4
Knock knee...	....	2	3	....	5
Congenital deformity.....................................	1	....	....	....	1
Rachitic deformity..	11	....	....	....	11
Club foot...	1	1	1	1	4
White swelling of knee..................................	... .	....	2	....	2
Dwarf...	....	....	1	1	2
Total.........	19	27	35	20	101

* Of these, eight were over 16 years.

DONATIONS TO THE HOSPITAL OF CLOTHING, MATERIALS, ETC.

Dec. 10. A friend, through Dr. Newton M. Shaffer, for clothing, $9.25.

Dec. 15. Mrs. Newton M. Shaffer, 5 games, 4 books.

Dec. 24. Mrs. Newton M. Shaffer, 1 cap, 1 pair gloves, 5 pairs stockings, 1 hat, dolls and clothes, games, bean bags, books, toys, paper soldiers, paper war ships, soap bubble pipes, crayons, work box, rubber balls, pencils and tablets, drawing books, painting books and brushes.

Dec. 24. Employes of the hospital, $2.50 for ornaments for Christmas tree.

Dec. 24. Mr. Engelke, 3 packages fancy crackers.

Dec. 24. Dr. Newton M. Shaffer, Christmas dinner for all the inmates.

Dec. 28. Mrs. Newton M. Shaffer, 3 pairs drawers, 2 woolen under vests, 3 night dresses.

Jan. 10. Mrs. S. C. Welsh, 6 pairs stockings, 4 waists, 2 knit caps.

Jan. 10. Dr. Richard B. Coutant, St. Nicholas Magazine for one year.

Jan. 10. Mrs. S. C. Welsh, 1 doz. handkerchiefs, 6 books.

Jan. 22. Miss Laura W. Hard, 1 box books, magazines.

Jan. 31. Mr. Carneth, 1 box magazines.

Feb. 1. Dr. Richard B. Coutant, $1.00 to buy materials for fancy work for patients.

Feb. 16. Miss Anna R. Bush, 2 shirts, 2 under vests, toys.

Feb. 25. Miss Anna R. Bush, 4 games, toy horse and wagon, 2 packages cards, 4 magazines.

March 31. Mrs. William H. Gunther, 9 games, paper dolls, ball, rattle, 1 pair slippers, toy automobile, bead purse.

April 6. Mrs. Newton M. Shaffer, Easter plants for children.

April 19. Dr. Richard B. Coutant, $1.00 to buy materials for fancy work for patients.

April 19. Mrs. W. Emerson Peck, 5 dresses, 1 outing flannel wrapper, 3 undervests, 3 corset waists.

April 20. Mrs. Francis A. Van Dyke, 32 bound books, 5 magazines.

May.   6. Miss Mabel Welsh, 1 dressing sack, 1 night gown, 3 dresses, 4 books.

May   11. Miss Adeline Fox, 1 hat, 1 sun bonnet, box of toys.

May   11. Mrs. Newton M. Shaffer, apron pattern.

May   15. Mrs. Frederick Edey, through Dr. Newton M. Shaffer, for clothing, shoes, etc., $100.00.

May   16. Mrs. A. W. Hard, box of books.

May   17. Mrs. William H. Gunther, flowers, fruit.

May   17. Mrs. Butler, box of toys.

May   20. A friend, through Dr. A. Alexander Smith, for employment of teacher, books, school room, etc., $500.00.

May   21. A friend, for teacher, etc., $150.00.

May   22. Mrs. Newton M. Shaffer, Bible.

May   22. Miss Isoline Geisse, scrap book, pictures.

May   24. Miss Anna R. Bush, 4 quarts ice cream.

May   29. Mrs. J. Sinclair Armstrong, 73 bound books.

June   3. Mrs. Lucy Thomas Guild, 2 scrap books.

June 13. Miss Anna R. Bush, 6 quarts ice cream.

June 24. Miss Anna R. Bush, 4 quarts ice cream.

June 24. Mrs. Newton M. Shaffer, scrap book.

July   1. Mrs. Frederick Snow, box of books and magazines.

July   1. Miss Coutant, 1½ dozen palm leaf fans.

July 11. Miss Anna R. Bush, 4 quarts ice cream

July 16. Miss Gould, box of paints, book.

July 18. Miss Jaggar, basket of apples.

Aug.   2. Miss Jaggar, basket of vegetables.

Aug. 14. Miss Jaggar, basket of vegetables.

Aug. 14. Mrs. Roswell Skeel, basket of sweet corn.

Aug. 16. Mrs. Roswell Skeel, basket of pears and apples.

Aug. 19. Miss Jaggar, basket of vegetables.

Aug. 28. Townsend Young's Son, 27 straw hats.

Aug. 31. Mrs. Isabella Russell, shoe and $5.00 for high sole shoe.

Sept. 2. Robin's Nest, Tarrytown, basket of vegetables.

Sept. 10. Miss Josephine Williamson, large box of toys.

Sept. 10. Misses Ida and Ruth Hilton, through Dr. P. Henry
          Fitzhugh, gave the children a sail on the Hudson.
          Supplied refreshments.
Sept. 13. Mrs. Roswell Skeel, basket of vegetables.
Sept. 23. Mrs. Roswell Skeel, basket of fruit.
Sept. 26. Robin's Nest, Tarrytown, basket of fruit and vege-
          tables.

For the information of those interested, the following rules
governing the admission of patients and the forms of affidavit
are appended. Affidavit blanks will be forwarded upon application to the Surgeon-in-Chief, New York State Hospital for the
Care of Crippled and Deformed Children, Tarrytown, N. Y.

RULES AND REGULATIONS

GOVERNING THE ADMISSION OF PATIENTS TO NEW YORK STATE
HOSPITAL FOR THE CARE OF CRIPPLED AND DEFORMED CHIL-
DREN.

The New York State Hospital for the Care of Crippled and
Deformed Children, established by the Legislature of 1900, is
now open for the reception and treatment of patients.

The hospital was established "for the care and treatment of
any indigent children who may have resided in the State of New
York for a period not less than one year, who are crippled or
deformed, or are suffering from a disease from which they are
likely to become crippled or deformed."

The following conditions are imposed upon all applicants:
"No patient shall be received except upon satisfactory proof
made to the Surgeon-in-Chief, by the next of kin, guardian, or a
State, town or county officer, under the rules to be established
by the Board of Managers, showing that the patient is unable
to pay for private treatment. Such proof shall be by affidavit.
If there was an attending physician before the patient entered
the hospital, it shall be accompanied by the certificate of such
physician giving the previous history and condition of the
patient."

Patients from four to sixteen years of age will be received
for treatment, and all applications will be acted upon in the
order of their reception. No patient will be admitted without
an examination by and a certificate from the Surgeon-in-Chief,
or in his absence, one of his assistants.

No patient whose condition is such that death is likely to occur in the immediate future, or whose condition precludes a reasonable amount of relief as the result of treatment, will be
admitted.

As this institution is a hospital, and not an asylum or home,
it should be clearly understood by each applicant that the patient, if received, may be returned to the committing institution,
parent or guardian at the discretion of the Surgeon-in-Chief.

It would aid the Surgeon-in-Chief very much in deciding upon the eligibility of a proposed candidate for admission, if, in addition to a written statement, giving the past history and present condition of the applicant, a photograph showing clearly the nature and location of the deformity should accompany the application.

Application for admission should be made to Dr. Newton M. Shaffer, Surgeon-in-Chief, No. 28 East Thirty-eighth street, New York, who will appoint a time and place for the examination of the patient. Patients living at remote points in the State are referred to the following gentlemen (out of town members of the consulting staff): Dr. A. Vander Veer and Dr. S. B. Ward, of Albany, N. Y.; Dr. Louis A. Weigel, Rochester, N. Y.; Dr. Roswell Park and Dr. Charles G. Stockton, Buffalo, N. Y.; Dr. Richard B. Coutant, Tarrytown, N. Y.; Dr. J. Van Duyn and Henry L. Elsner, Syracuse, N. Y.

Approved by the State Board of Charities and issued by order of the Board of Managers of the Hospital.

AFFIDAVIT BLANK FOR STATE, COUNTY OR TOWN OFFICERS.

To NEWTON M. SHAFFER, M. D., *Surgeon-in-Chief*,

No. 28 EAST 38TH STREET, NEW YORK.

STATE OF NEW YORK, } ss.:
·COUNTY OF................

.... being duly sworn, says that he
·is the.............officer, in the.............of............
.............., New York State; that he is acquainted with the
·position and circumstances of..................; that the said
.............is.............years of age; that.............
is suffering from..............; that......has resided in the
State of New York for over one year and that....is unable to
·pay for private treatment for....condition.

Name ....

Residence ....

....

And further this deponent says not.

·Sworn to before me this....day of.........190

AFFIDAVIT BLANK FOR PARENTS AND GUARDIANS.

To NEWTON M. SHAFFER, M. D., *Surgeon-in-Chief*,

No. 28 EAST 38TH STREET, NEW YORK.

STATE OF NEW YORK, } *ss.:*
COUNTY OF................

...................................being duly sworn, says that......is
the...............of.............aged......years; that the said
..............is suffering from...............; that......has
resided in the State of New York for over one year, and that
I as............am unable to pay for private treatment for the
said................

Name ....

Residence ....

....

And further this deponent says not.

Sworn to before me this....day of.........190

REPORT

OF THE

Committee on the New York State Hospital for the Treatment of Incipient Pulmonary Tuberculosis.

REPORT.

To the State Board of Charities:

Your Committee on the New York State Hospital for the treatment of Incipient Pulmonary Tuberculosis respectfully reports that by chapter 416 of the Laws of 1900 the Legislature made provision for a State hospital for the treatment of incipient pulmonary tuberculosis. Under this act the Governor was empowered to appoint a board of five trustees, whose first duty was to select the site for such hospital, and after its approval by the State Board of Health and the Forest Preserve Board, proceed with the construction and equipment of suitable buildings upon plans adopted by them and approved by the State Architect and the State Board of Charities. An appropriation of $50,000 was made to establish the institution.

In accordance with the provisions of the statute the Governor appointed as trustees Howard Townsend and Walter Jennings, of New York; Dr. Willis G. McDonald, of Albany; Dr. John H. Pryor, of Buffalo, and Dr. Frank E. Kendall, of Saranac Lake. Mr. Townsend was subsequently elected President of the Board of Trustees. The site chosen by the Board of Trustees was not approved, and new legislation was enacted in 1901.

By chapter 691 of the Laws of 1901 the sum of $100,000, or so much thereof as may be found necessary, was appropriated for the construction of the necessary buildings for this institution whenever the site should be determined. It is contemplated that these buildings shall furnish accommodations for at least 100 patients, besides the officers, employes and attendants of the hospital. The appropriation is intended to provide not only for the construction of the buildings but as well for the heating, lighting, plumbing, laundry fixtures, water supply,

As to the support of free patients the act provides:

Section 15. Support of free patients.—At least once in each month the superintendent of the hospital shall furnish to the Comptroller a list countersigned by the treasurer of the hospital of all the free patients in the hospital, together with sufficient facts to enable the Comptroller to collect from the proper local official having charge of the relief of the poor such sums as may be owing to the State for the examination, care and treatment of the patients who have been received by the hospital, and who are shown by the statement of such local official to be unable to pay for their care and treatment. The Comptroller shall thereupon collect from the said local official the sums due for the care and treatment of each such patient at a rate not exceeding five dollars per week for each patient.

In connection with this hospital it will be seen that the State has adopted the policy of caring for patients at the expense of the local authorities by whom they are sent to the institution, thus making a new departure, the outcome of which will be watched with interest.

Respectfully submitted,
STEPHEN SMITH, M. D.,
Chairman.

December 1901.

Second Annual Report

OF THE

BOARD OF TRUSTEES

OF THE

New York State Hospital for the Treatment of Incipient Pulmonary Tuberculosis, to the State Board of Charities.

REPORT.

To the Honorable the State Board of Charities of the State of New York:

The report of last year gave to your honorable body a statement of what had been done in connection with the State Hospital for Tuberculosis up to January 1, 1901.

In April, 1901, by chapter 691 of the Laws of that year, the sum of $100,000 was appropriated with the following provisions:

Section 4. No expenditures shall be made from appropriations under this act or from appropriations under chapter four hundred and sixteen of the laws of nineteen hundred until a determination of the proper location and site for suitable buildings has been made or approved by a commission composed of the governor, the president pro tempore of the senate and the speaker of the assembly, and their decision and the reasons therefor in writing filed with the comptroller.

During the summer the Commission appointed by the above act visited and examined various sites in the Adirondacks, including Lake Clear, Ray Brook, Dannemora and White Lake. The Commission then conferred with your Board and requested it to make a visit to White Lake. At the request of the Commission, the Board had previously presented to it in writing the reasons of its individual members for the selection of Ray Brook.

Finally, in December, 1901, the Commission approved as a site for the State Hospital, Ray Brook, already selected by this Board of Trustees, and filed a letter stating such reasons for its approval.

The contracts for the purchase of the property have been prepared, and it is hoped that the land will soon be acquired.

Out of the $50,000 appropriated at the session of 1900, $40,000 will be available for the construction of the hospital after payment of the purchase money for the site and of contingent expenses. The Board respectfully asks that this sum be reappropriated by this Legislature. The sum of $140,000 is therefore applicable to the construction of the hospital. Of this, from $10,000 to $20,000 will be necessary for the furnishing and equipment of it. We have therefore the sum of $120,000 to $130,000 for all purposes. This is probably not sufficient to enable us to build with brick, but we can build a frame or brick veneer.

It is the earnest hope of the Board of Trustees that the work of the hospital buildings can be begun this spring and pushed through as rapidly as possible to a termination.

All of which is respectfully submitted to your honorable body.

JOHN H. PRYOR,

Secretary.

December, 1901.

REPORT

OF THE

Committee on State and Alien Poor.

REPORT.

To the State Board of Charities:

During the fiscal year ending September 30, 1901, the Department of State and Alien Poor has been busy with the care, maintenance and removal of alien and non-resident poor persons who have no legal claim upon any of the counties of this State. Through investigations conducted by the Superintendent of State and Alien Poor and his assistants the State has been relieved of the burden of maintenance of a large number of paupers. Not only have many persons been removed from the State almshouses to their homes and friends, but many more from county and city institutions. It is not possible to prevent pauperism under present social conditions, but it is possible to curtail in some degree the evils incident thereto. The increase of the pauper class is a menace to the State, and the law which provides for the removal of non-resident dependents is intended to check the evil.

The State of New York attracts a large number of people who come in the hope of bettering their condition, but who are ill-fitted to cope with the strenuous competitions which they find. As a consequence many speedily sink into a condition of either partial or total dependence, become burdens upon charity and add to the difficulties of society. While the State of New York must bear its proper burdens, it is unfair to require it to carry the burdens of other communities. The State Poor Law has been enacted for the financial benefit of the public as well as to define methods of procedure in the distribution of public charity. It has its economical as well as humanitarian side. Under its provisions the Department of State and Alien

Poor is required to remove non-resident paupers whose proper residential localities can be determined, but to accomplish this removal with due consideration for the needs of the unfortunate poor person.

METHOD.

The Superintendent of State and Alien Poor, by a systematic inquiry into the merit of all applicants, endeavors to determine which are properly chargeable to the State. Many facts are developed through these investigations which prove that were it not for the operations of the law the charitable institutions of the State of New York would be filled with the undesirable dependents of other States and countries.

The steamship lines which land large numbers of immigrants in New York bring many alien paupers who, in a brief period of time, make application for public or private relief. Steamship lines landing their passengers at other ports in the United States or Canada bring over a similar undesirable class of immigrants who ultimately find their way to the State of New York. The railroad lines which thread the United States also serve for the transportation of the unfortunates who look to the State or city of New York as a final haven.

At the two main gates of the State, New York and Buffalo, the Department of State and Alien Poor has established offices wherein applications for relief, based upon the ground that they are proper charges upon the State, and not upon counties, are at once investigated. From these offices the meritorious applicants are promptly returned to where they belong, and those which are not chargeable to the State are dismissed or referred to the proper relieving officer. In addition to the work of these offices, each State almshouse is visited once in three months and all of its inmates examined. Whenever the county almshouses are inspected, due attention is given to all inmates whose settlement is doubtful. In this way, by constant examination, the number of paupers is kept from increasing. For a number of years past. in spite of the yearly increase of applications, the total number permanently supported has remained practically the same from year to year.

This check upon the growth of pauperism is largely due to the promptness with which investigations are made. It has been found that if any great length of time elapses between the admission of a pauper to an almshouse and investigation of his claim, it becomes exceedingly difficult to arrive at the truth, but if the case be examined into at the time of commitment, facts are developed upon which a safe conclusion may be based.

ADMISSIONS AND REMOVALS.

One reason why the number of paupers in State almshouses, chargeable to the State, has remained practically the same for several years is that the list is made up mainly of men and women who have been inmates of these State almshouses for many years. Since the present Superintendent of State and Alien Poor entered upon the duties of his office, June 1, 1899, 4,230 persons have been committed to State almshouses as State poor persons. On the 1st of July, 1899, there were 103 State poor persons in institutions supported at the expense of the State. At the close of the fiscal year, September 30, 1901, only 87 persons were maintained in almshouses at the expense of the State, and these, with ten children, represented the total number of dependents for whom the State must provide. Thus it will be seen that 4,236 persons, committed by county superintendents or commissioners of charity to the custody of State almshouses as State poor persons, have been disposed of by the Department of State and Alien Poor. All of these have been either sent to their homes in the United States or foreign lands, discharged as able to support themselves, or removed by friends upon notification of their condition and whereabouts by the Department of State and Alien Poor.

Before the present law went into effect the burden of support imposed upon the State by these non-resident dependents was very great. The average period of life of inmates of public institutions who fall within the provisions of this act has been carefully estimated at not less than fifteen years, and as the annual per capita cost for maintenance alone is $104, it will be readily understood that the tax upon the Commonwealth would become unbearable were it not for the present law. In fact, some of the 87 persons who are now inmates of State alms-houses have been there over this period of fifteen years, so that the estimate of ultimate expense is borne out by the experience of this Department. While the fundamental principle of the State Poor Act is economical, as has been said, it is also humane in its results. If it on the one hand protects the tax-payers of the State of New York, on the other hand it relieves those in distress, returns wanderers to their homes, and at the same time prevents an increase of our pauper population.

PAN-AMERICAN EXPOSITION.

One year ago it was anticipated that the opening of the Pan-American Exposition in the year 1901 would greatly increase the number of applications for public relief. It was also sup-posed that in the city of New York there would be an increase of applications for relief under the State Poor Law. Experi-ence heretofore has shown that enterprises of this character have attracted multitudes of people many of whom become impoverished. The Pan-American Exposition has proven no exception to the general rule. The number of applications for State relief in the city of Buffalo and in the counties immedi-ately adjoining has increased over 70 per cent., even though Buffalo has been compelled to relieve 90 per cent. of all appli-cations, owing to the fact that the majority of applicants resided more than sixty days in Buffalo. Were it not for the fact that an unusual degree of prosperity has prevailed in the manufac-turing towns and in the city of New York, which has caused a decrease in the number of applications at that point, the appro-priation for the maintenance and removal of State poor would have been insufficient. The decrease in applications in the city of New York has been so great, however, that in spite of the increase elsewhere the Department has been enabled to conduct its operations within the appropriation made for its work.

It may be said, however, that the end of the Pan-American is not yet, so far as its influence upon public charity is concerned. As long as work of any kind continues upon the Exposition grounds many persons who would otherwise become dependent can find employment. As the construction of the buildings gave opportunity for self-support, so their demolition gives labor to very many persons. It is hoped, however, that by the opening of spring the applications for relief which are directly due to the Pan-American Exposition will have ceased.

IMMIGRATION.

As has been said, many undesirable alien immigrants become dependent shortly after arrival in the State of New York. The laws of the United States are supposed to prevent the landing of paupers. The immigrants are landed at Ellis Island, where the United States Government, through its Department of Immigration, makes its examinations. All immigrants are required to declare the amount of money they possess and exhibit the money itself. If the sum is considered sufficient, or if they have friends who will become their sponsors, and if there be no charges against their character of a kind to debar them from landing, they are permitted to land, otherwise they are detained for a time pending further investigation or are at once returned to Europe. But experience has proven that the money in possession of immigrants is usually very small in amount, and if there be no friends to assist the immigrant the prospects are that application for charity will soon be necessary. Thus, recently, the landing of 800 immigrants was observed. The money in possession of many of these was noted, and it was found that the largest sum in the possession of any one of the number was only 250 marks. There were very many whose money did not exceed $2.50—a very small amount with which to begin life in a foreign land.

24

The United States Commissioner of Immigration has promptly
responded to applications of this department for the deportation of alien paupers who have been committed to State almshouses by local authorities.   There is no doubt, if the local
authorities were more active in causing the commitment of
aliens who are applicants for charity, that many more would
be returned to their native land, to the ultimate relief of the
State of New York. The Department of State and Alien Poor
can only return such persons to their homes as are properly
committed to State or county almshouses by local officers. If
there is an increase of beggary due to pauper immigration local
authorities are more or less responsible.

FOREIGN-BORN POOR.

In a recent public address the Commissioner of Charities of
the city of New York, whose duties are directly associated with
the enforcement of the Poor Law, has declared that one of the
greatest problems of almshouse administration is how to dispose of the foreign-born poor.   He gave a table showing
the nativity of persons admitted to the almshouse under his
management during the year 1900, and this table shows that
out of a total of 2,936 persons admitted to the almshouse only
554 were born in the United States. Of the 2,382 foreign born
1,617 were born in Ireland alone. He says: "There is a law
prohibiting the immigration of paupers to the United States.
It would appear from this table that that law is evaded." He
continues: "If so many immigrants actually in pauperism or
verging upon pauperism were not admitted to the United States
we should have a smaller census in the almshouses." While
Commissioner Keller's statement as to the evasion of the law
forbidding the immigration of paupers into the United States
is true, it is not justified by the tables in his address. Every
foreign-born person is not an alien, for the laws of the United
States provide for the naturalization of foreign-born persons.
Hence the statement that 2,382 foreign-born persons were admitted to the almshouse on Blackwell's Island in 1900 does not

prove that these 2,382 were aliens. On the contrary, the fact that they were admitted to the almshouse on Blackwell's Island is prima facie evidence that they were all citizens of the United States. Had any of them been aliens, under the law it would have been the duty of the commissioner of charities of the city of New York to have committed them as alien paupers, in which case steps would have been taken for their deportation by the Department of State and Alien Poor. It is a singular fact that many persons fail to distinguish the difference between aliens and foreign-born persons, and class as aliens all persons whose place of birth was in other lands.

It is unfortunately true that great numbers of foreign-born citizens become dependent, and it is a striking testimony of the beneficence of American institutions that comparatively few native-born citizens become paupers. It should not be forgotten, however, that in the city of New York the proportion of the foreign-born population to the native born is much larger than elsewhere, and we must expect that of those who seek the assistance of charity there the larger number will always be of foreign birth.

RESTRICTION.

It will be agreed by all who seriously consider the problem of immigration that there should be a greater restriction than is at present in force. We have practically closed the western gates and shut out immigration from Asia; the eastern gates remain wide open. They should be barred to such an extent that no person may enter who is not prepared for self-support. Some method should be devised by which the northern border of the United States, as well as the sea ports, may be closed against the undesirable immigrant. It is not desirable to impose undue restrictions upon any one who will be of service in our American communities, but it is in the line of self-protection to exclude all others. There is no reason why our working classes should not be protected and the wages of the laborer and the standard of living for his family be kept where they will minister to self-respect.

By such restriction the drift of the unfortunates of other countries to the overcrowded slums of our cities would be checked and the consequent draft upon the resources of charity lessened. At the present time our large cities have sections wherein poverty, vice and crime lower the moral tone to such an extent as to make the conditions of life almost unbearable. In so far as the restriction of immigration will mitigate such conditions and prevent the increase of vice, crime and pauperism, it is a right which American people are justified in demanding of Congress.

EFFECT UPON THE TREASURY.

Thus it will be seen that the operations of the State Poor Law are humane in the very highest degree, and that the State treasury is directly benefited. During the past year 977 persons were removed from the State. As has been said, the average duration of life of inmates of public institutions, falling within the provisions of the State Poor Law, is fifteen years. Had these 977 persons been permitted to remain inmates of our public institutions for a single year, they would have cost the State treasury $101,608. Had they survived for one-half of the estimated period they would have cost the State $762,060, and should they have survived the full period of estimated life (that is fifteen years) the State would have been compelled to pay the enormous sum of $1,524,120 for the support of the persons who, under the provisions of the State Poor Law, were removed by the Department of State and Alien Poor at a total cost of less than $40,000, which covered maintenance in almshouses, the cost of removals, and supervision.

The report of the Superintendent of State and Alien Poor, and statistical tables showing the work of the Department of State and Alien Poor are appended, and will be found of interest.

Respectfully submitted,

D. McCARTHY,
EDWARD LITCHFIELD,
PETER WALRATH,
Committee on State and Alien Poor.

REPORT OF THE SUPERINTENDENT OF STATE AND ALIEN POOR.

To the State Board of Charities:

The general work of the Department of State and Alien Poor was prosecuted diligently during the fiscal year ending September 30, 1901. The work of this department includes the inspection of State institutions, county and city almshouses, the investigation of special cases requiring attention, and the preparation of reports embodying the results of inspections and investigations. Besides these things, the care, maintenance and removal of State, non-resident and Indian poor are imposed upon the Superintendent by statute.

The reports embodying inspections and examinations show a general tendency toward improvement in the public institutions. The county boards of supervisors throughout the State are taking an intelligent interest in the welfare of the public dependents under their charge, and, as a consequence, repairs and betterments have been made in many of the almshouses. In two counties, plans have been perfected and appropriations made to provide new almshouses which will take the place of buildings in use at present but which are no longer satisfactory.

The care of the sick continues to receive special attention, and the officers in charge of public almshouses are endeavoring to provide better accommodations and attendance.

The removal of State and non-resident poor from the almshouses of the State to their homes in other states and countries is one of the chief duties of this department. A large number of dependent aliens in almshouses have been examined, and the causes of their pauperism investigated; most of them were subsequently returned to Europe.

The following statistics embody that portion of the work of the department during the year, which has to do with State, Alien and Indian Poor.

STATE POOR.

During the fiscal year ending September 30, 1901, the total number of State poor provided for pursuant to the provisions of chapter 225 of the Laws of 1896, was 1,760, as against 2,004 during the previous fiscal year, a decrease of 244. The changes during the year were as follows: Discharged as able to go out and provide for themselves, 678; absconded, 83; removed to their homes or places of legal settlement in other states and countries, 888; died, 24. This left 87 in State almshouses October 1, 1901, of whom 75 were males and 12 females. Ten children were at the same time in the custody of orphan asylums, making a total of 97 under State care October 1, 1901, as against 86 October 1, 1900. The expenditures for the fiscal year have been $23,-035.03, as against $27,588.17 the preceding year, as follows: For maintenance and care in State almshouses, $10,444.45; for maintenance and care in orphan asylums and homes, $1,139.39; for removals to State almshouses, $624.39; for removal from State almshouses, to their homes in other states and countries, $7,-387.21; for miscellaneous expenses, traveling expenses and printing, $3,439.59. The per capita expenditure was $13.09, as against $13.69 in 1900.

Twenty-eight years have elapsed since the State Poor Law became operative, during which time 42,570 persons have been committed to State almshouses, a yearly average of 1,520. Of these 32,936 have been males and 9,634 females. This large number has been disposed of as follows: Discharged as able to provide for themselves, 11,877; provided for by adoption or in families as self-supporting, 87; absconded, 2,032; transferred to State hospitals, 249; sent out of the State to their friends or places of legal settlement in other States and countries, 27,354; died, 884. This left 97 under care October 1, 1901, 87 in almshouses and 10 in homes, as follows: At the Albany State Almshouse, 4; at the Broome County State Almshouse, 19; at the Erie County State Almshouse, 7; at the Jefferson County State Almshouse, 4; at the Kings County State Almshouse, 29; at the Monroe County State Almshouse, 7; at the Oneida County State

Almshouse, 3; at the Onondaga County State Almshouse, 3; at the St. Lawrence County State Almshouse, 11; in the Albany Orphan Asylum, 5; in the New York Catholic Protectory, 3; in the New York Juvenile Asylum, 2.

ALIEN POOR.

During the fiscal year ending September 30, 1901, there were removed 87 alien poor to their homes in other countries. These were found in almshouses, asylums, hospitals and other charitable institutions in this State, and their condition at the time of landing in this country, as brought out by the inquiries, was as follows: Feeble-minded, 3; vagrant and destitute, 22; diseased, 27; children, 28; sick or disabled after landing, 7. These had been furnished transportation to this country as follows: By relatives, guardians and friends, 17; not known, 70. By their own statements they were found to have landed as follows: At the port of New York, 46; other United States ports, 2; Canadian ports, 14; not known, 25. After careful examination, these persons were returned to their homes as follows: To England, 19; to Ireland, 12; to Italy, 8; to Germany, 19; to Austro-Hungary, 8; to Sweden, 9; to West Indies, 6; to South Africa, France, Scotland, Denmark, Greece, Moldavia, each 1. The total expenditures for these removals was $1,794.82; the average per capita expenditure $20.60. Since this act went into effect in 1880, to September 30, 1901, there have been 3,595 removals made at a total expenditure of $80,579.74, an average per capita cost of $22.41.

INDIAN POOR.

The total number of Indian poor provided for in almshouses and asylums during the fiscal year ending September 30, 1901, was 25, of whom 6 were in custody at the beginning of the year and 19 were admitted during the year. Of these 8 have been discharged as able to provide for themselves; 3 transferred, 4 absconded and 4 died, leaving 6 remaining October 1, 1901, of whom 1 was in the Niagara County Almshouse, 3 in the Erie

County Almshouse, 1 in the Cattaraugus County Almshouse and 1, a small Indian boy, in the Western New York Home at Randolph. The expenditures during the year have been $1,883.13, as follows: For maintenance in the Cattaraugus County Almshouse, $93.25; for maintenance in the Erie County Almshouse, $318; for maintenance in the Niagara County Almshouse, $256.75; for maintenance in the Onondaga County Almshouse, $8.75; for maintenance in the Western New York Home, Randolph, $94.70; for outdoor relief, $1,111.68.

EXPENDITURES.

On account of State poor........................	$33,700 03
On account of alien poor........................	1,794 82
On account of Indian poor......................	1,883 13
	$37,377 98

Respectfully submitted,

BYRON M. CHILD,
Superintendent State and Alien Poor.

TABLE No. 1.

*Showing the name and location of the several State Almshouses,
the time at which the contract was entered into with the State,
and the present rate of support per week, respectively.*

STATE ALMSHOUSES.	Location.	Date of contract.	Rate of support per week.
Albany City	Albany	October 1, 1873	$2 00
St. Lawrence County	Canton	October 1, 1873	2 00
Erie County	Buffalo	October 1, 1873	2 00
Broome County	Binghamton	January 1, 1875	2 00
Jefferson County	Watertown	January 1, 1875	2 00
Onandaga County	Syracuse	January 1, 1875	2 00
Kings County	Flatbush	June 20, 1875	2 50
Oneida County	Rome	December 28, 1875	2 00
Monroe County	Rochester	December 4, 1877	2 00

TABLE No. 2.

Showing the changes which occurred in the several State almshouses during the year ending September 30, 1901.

STATE ALMSHOUSES.	Number of inmates October 1, 1901.	Number committed during the year.	Whole number supported.	Discharged.	Adopted.	Absconded.	Sent out of the State.	Died.	Remaining October 1, 1901.		
									Male.	Female.	Total.
Albany	5	57	62	7	......	17	32	2	3	1	4
Buffalo	7	258	265	93	......	25	186	4	7	......	7
Canton	11	7	18	4	......	1	......	2	10	1	11
Binghamton	17	26	43	12	......	4	6	2	17	2	19
Syracuse	3	3	6	2	......	1	......	......	2	1	3
Watertown	5	1	6	2	......	......	......	......	4	......	4
Flatbush	19	1,270	1,289	528	......	27	643	12	22	7	29
Rome	1	23	24	14	......	3	2	2	3	......	3
Rochester	7	40	47	16	......	5	19	......	7	......	7
Total	75	1,685	1,760	678	....	83	888	24	75	12	87

TABLE No. 3.

Showing the number and sex of the State paupers committed each year since the act went into operation, October 22, 1873.

	Male.	Female.	Total.
For the year ending September 30, 1874.........	513	50	563
For the year ending September 30, 1875.........	566	88	654
For the year ending September 30, 1876.........	514	119	633
For the year ending September 30, 1877.........	707	165	872
For the year ending September 30, 1878.........	930	190	1,120
For the year ending September 30, 1879.........	1,326	261	1,587
For the year ending September 30, 1880.........	1,023	320	1,343
For the year ending September 30, 1881.........	1,046	327	1,373
For the year ending September 30, 1882.........	1,024	368	1,392
For the year ending September 30, 1883.........	1,033	393	1,426
For the year ending September 30, 1884.........	1,378	514	1,892
For the year ending September 30, 1885.........	1,409	439	1,848
For the year ending September 30, 1886.........	1,252	354	1,606
For the year ending September 30, 1887.........	1,247	370	1,617
For the year ending September 30, 1888.........	1,317	348	1,665
For the year ending September 30, 1889.........	1,369	388	1,757
For the year ending September 30, 1890..	1,133	307	1,440
For the year ending September 30, 1891.........	1,026	339	1,365
For the year ending September 30, 1892.........	1,095	272	1,367
For the year ending September 30, 1893.........	1,057	349	1,406
For the year ending September 30, 1894.........	1,490	484	1,974
For the year ending September 30, 1895.........	1,669	502	2,171
For the year ending September 30, 1896.........	1,589	513	2,102
For the year ending September 30, 1897.........	1,448	539	1,987
For the year ending September 30, 1898.........	1,300	504	1,804
For the year ending September 30, 1899.........	1,582	467	2,049
For the year ending September 30, 1900.........	1,522	350	1,872
For the year ending September 30, 1901.........	1,371	314	1,685
Aggregate...............................	32,936	9,634	42,570

TABLE No. 4.

Showing the several almshouses to which State poor were committed and the changes occurring in the number under their care from October 22, 1873, to September 30, 1901.

ALMSHOUSES.	Whole number admitted.	Discharged.	Provided for by adoption or otherwise.	Absconded.	Transferred to State hospitals.	Sent out of the State to friends or places of legal settlement.	Died.	Remaining October 1, 1901.
Albany	3,464	1,111	7	505	20	1,730	87	4
Buffalo	8,479	1,886	33	452	31	5,937	133	7
Canton*	402	146	4	72	9	87	73	11
Delhi*	74	57	......	20	1	10	6	..
Yaphank*	1,110	76	5	85	1	987	6	..
Binghamton	740	310	8	74	10	262	57	19
Syracuse	839	380	3	117	15	283	32	3
Watertown	299	78	4	41	12	118	12	4
Flatbush	23,432	6,567	5	279	55	16,191	306	29
Rome	668	387	1	77	69	141	60	3
Waterloo*	513	345	......	88	5	54	21	..
Rochester	2,567	604	18	222	21	1,604	91	7
Total	42,570	11,877	87	2,032	249	27,354	884	87

* Discontinued.

TABLE No. 5.

Showing the ages of the State poor committed to the several State almshouses from October 22, 1878, to September 30, 1901.

STATE ALMSHOUSES.	Under twenty years.	Twenty years and under thirty.	Thirty years and under forty.	Forty years and under fifty.	Fifty years and under sixty.	Sixty years and under seventy.	Over seventy years.	Total.
Albany	570	818	728	552	354	274	173	3,464
Buffalo	2,491	1,979	1,498	952	736	525	298	8,479
Canton	42	59	80	51	46	66	58	402
Delhi	6	9	12	17	10	13	7	74
Yaphank	47	416	385	172	89	45	6	1,110
Binghamton	120	117	129	104	100	84	86	740
Syracuse	172	189	164	122	73	56	56	832
Watertown	74	48	61	24	23	20	19	269
Flatbush	5,216	7,112	4,826	2,983	1,821	1,039	436	23,432
Rome	40	150	204	113	90	67	34	688
Waterloo	10	40	73	78	101	128	83	513
Rochester	553	606	444	397	281	210	146	2,567
Total	9,341	11,543	8,548	5,495	3,714	2,527	1,402	42,570

TABLE No. 6.

Showing the years in which State poor in care of the several State almshouses September 30, 1901, were committed.

STATE ALMSHOUSES	1874	1875	1876	1877	1878	1879	1880	1881	1882	1883	1884	1885	1886	1887	1888	1889	1890	1891	1892	1893	1894	1895	1896	1897	1898	1899	1900	1901	Total
Albany													1								1							4	4
Buffalo																					3							6	7
Canton												1				1	2						1		1	1	4		11
Binghamton																													19
Syracuse																						1		1	3			11	3
Watertown																									1				4
Flatbush																						1		1	1			27	27
Rome					1																							2	8
Rochester						1																	1					2	7
Total						1			2			1	1			1	2		2		4	2	4	2	7	1	7	58	87

TABLE No. 7.

Showing the classified quarterly expenditures for the support, care and removal of State poor for the fiscal year ending September 30, 1901.

QUARTERS.	For removals to State almshouses.	For maintenance, clothing, medical attendance and care in State almshouses.	For maintenance in orphan asylums.	For removals from the State to other States and countries.	For miscellaneous expenses and printing.	Total.
Quarter ending December 31, 1900	$179 26	$3,001 14	$381 97	$2,598 42	$996 81	$7,057 60
Quarter ending March 31, 1901	141 63	2,990 76	266 81	1,858 90	765 19	5,983 29
Quarter ending June 30, 1901	146 18	2,246 78	312 37	1,894 88	916 85	5,517 01
Quarter ending September 30, 1901	157 37	2,265 77	278 24	1,035 01	760 74	4,497 13
Total	$624 39	$10,444 45	$1,139 39	$7,387 21	$3,439 59	$23,035 03

TABLE No. 4.

Showing the several almshouses to which State poor were committed and the changes occurring in the number under their care from October 22, 1873, to September 30, 1901.

ALMSHOUSES.	Whole number admitted.	Discharged.	Provided for by adoption or otherwise.	Absconded.	Transferred to State hospitals.	Sent out of the State to friends or places of legal settlement.	Died.	Remaining October 1, 1901.
Albany	3,464	1,111	7	505	20	1,730	87	4
Buffalo	8,479	1,886	33	453	31	5,937	133	7
Gon*	402	146	4	72	9	87	73	11
Delhi*	74	37	......	20	1	10	6	
Yaphank*	1,110	78	5	85	1	987	6	
Bingbamton	740	310	8	74	10	262	57	19
Syracuse	832	380	8	117	15	263	32	3
Watertown	269	78	4	41	12	118	12	4
Flatbush	28,433	6,567	5	279	55	16,191	306	29
Rome	688	387	1	77	69	141	60	3
Waterloo*	513	345	......	88	5	54	21	
Rochester	2,567	604	18	222	21	1,604	91	7
Total	42,570	11,877	87	2,039	249	27,354	884	87

* Discontinued.

TABLE No. 5.

Showing the ages of the State poor committed to the several State almshouses from October 22, 1873, to September 30, 1901.

STATE ALMSHOUSES.	Under twenty years.	Twenty years and under thirty.	Thirty years and under forty.	Forty years and under fifty.	Fifty years and under sixty.	Sixty years and under seventy.	Over seventy years.	Total.
Albany	570	818	728	552	354	274	173	3,464
Buffalo	2,491	1,979	1,498	952	736	525	298	8,479
Canton	42	59	80	51	46	66	58	402
Delhi	6	9	12	17	10	13	7	74
Yaphank	47	416	335	172	89	45	6	1,110
Binghamton	120	117	129	104	100	84	96	740
Syracuse	172	189	164	122	73	56	56	832
Watertown	74	48	61	24	23	20	19	269
Flatbush	5,216	7,112	4,826	2,983	1,821	1,039	436	23,432
Rome	40	150	204	118	90	67	34	688
Waterloo	10	40	73	78	101	128	83	513
Rochester	553	606	444	337	281	210	146	2,567
Total	9,341	11,543	8,548	5,495	3,714	2,527	1,402	42,570

TABLE No. 6.

Showing the years in which State poor in care of the several State almshouses September 30, 1901, were committed.

STATE ALMSHOUSES.	1874.	1875.	1876.	1877.	1878.	1879.	1880.	1881.	1882.	1883.	1884.	1885.	1886.	1887.	1888.	1889.	1890.	1891.	1892.	1893.	1894.	1895.	1896.	1897.	1898.	1899.	1900.	1901.	Total.
Albany												1								1	1							4	4
Buffalo													1				2		2		3							8	7
Canton																1									1	1	1	12	11
Binghamton																							1	1	3	1	4	13	12
Syracuse																									1			2	3
Watertown																							1	1	1			4	4
Flatbush																									1			27	22
Rome																								1	1		2	22	22
Rochester				1																								7	7
Total				1		1	2			3		1	1			1	2		2	2	4	2	1	2	7	1	7	63	57

TABLE No. 7.

Showing the classified quarterly expenditures for the support, care and removal of State poor for the fiscal year ending September 30, 1901.

QUARTERS.	For removals to State almshouses.	For maintenance, clothing, medical attendance and care in State almshouses.	For maintenance in orphan asylums.	For removals from the State to other States and countries.	For miscellaneous expenses and printing.	Total.
Quarter ending December 31, 1900	$179 26	$3,001 14	$381 97	$2,598 42	$996 81	$7,057 60
Quarter ending March 31, 1901	141 68	2,930 76	266 81	1,858 90	765 19	5,963 29
Quarter ending June 30, 1901	146 13	2,246 78	312 57	1,894 88	916 85	5,517 01
Quarter ending September 30, 1901	157 37	2,265 77	278 24	1,035 01	760 74	4,497 13
Total	$624 39	$10,444 45	$1,139 39	$7,387 21	$3,439 59	$23,035 03

·REPORT

Committee on Inspection.

385

REPORT.

The Department of Inspection

THE DEPARTMENT OF INSPECTION.

The Department of Inspection is charged with the visitation and inspection of the private charities of the State which are in receipt of public moneys. These philanthropies comprise dispensaries, eleemosynary educational institutions, fresh-air charities, homes for the aged, homes for children including infant asylums, hospitals, placing-out agencies, reformatories and temporary homes.

In addition to 573 special inspections and 915 visits to societies, institutions and individuals, made in the course of the performance of their official duties of inspection, 448 general inspections were conducted during the year ending September 30, 1901, by the agents of the Department. The conditions found to exist at the time of such general inspections have been noted and summarized under the headings "Supervision","Administration", "Plant", "Sanitary Conditions", "Training—Industrial, Educational and Moral", "Records" and finally "General Impression".

The following table is intended to indicate in a brief form the conditions reported as a result of these inspections. The entries under class A indicate that conditions on the subject under consideration were found excellent, while conditions under B are regarded as good; under C as fair; under D as unsatisfactory; under E as poor or positively bad.

Conditions Reported as a Result of the General Inspection of the Private Charities of the State in Receipt of Public Moneys Visited and Inspected for the Year Ending September 30, 1901.

	SUPERVISION.								ADMINISTRATION.									PLANT.						
	A.	B.	C.	D.	E.	Not stated.	Does not apply.	Merged with administration.	A.	B.	C.	D	E.	Not stated.	Does not apply.	Merged with supervision.	A.	B.	C.	D.	E.	Not stated.	Does not apply.
Dispensaries																							
Education—Eleemosynary																							
Fresh-air charities																							
Homes for aged																							
Homes for children, including infant asylums																							
Hospitals																							
Placing-out agencies																							
Reformatories																							
Temporary homes																							

Conditions Reported as a Result of the General Inspection of the Private Charities of the State, etc.—(Continued).

	SANITARY CONDITIONS.							INDUSTRIAL.							EDUCATIONAL.						
	A.	B.	C.	D.	E.	Not stated.	Does not apply.	A.	B.	C.	D.	E.	Not stated.	Does not apply.	A.	B.	C.	D.	E.	Not stated.	Does not apply.
Dispensaries	4	9	14	2										29							29
Education—Eleemosynary	14	6	11	1				3	28					1	10	18					9
Fresh-air charities	2	3	3	2						1				9							18
Homes for aged	31	11	66	30	3			9	62				1	17	25	28	1				117
Homes for children, including infant asylums	21	57	51	8	1					2				58	26	19	53			3	119
Hospitals		65		1			4							144							
Placing-out agencies		9		1				1		9				7	2	2	11	1			7
Reformatories		6	8					1		1				2	2	2		1			4
Temporary homes	2	4											1	5						1	5

Conditions Reported as a Result of the General Inspection of the Private Charities of the State, etc.—(Concluded).

	TRAINING. MORAL.						RECORDS.							GENERAL IMPRESSION.				
	A. B.	C.	D.	E.	Not stated	Does not apply	A.	B.	C.	D.	E.	Not stated	Does not apply	A	B	C	D	E.
Dispensaries	30					29	1	13	9	6				4	10	11	4	
Education—Eleemosynary	1	1				8	1	14	15	1		1		7	18	9	3	
Fresh-air charities		1				8		7	2					1	6	5	1	
Homes for aged						17		8	4	3	2			1	13	2	1	1
Homes for children, including infant asylums	44	45	4		2	14	23	91	52	3	1	5		18	102	51	8	1
Hospitals	2	2	2			142	20	71	47	5	1	3		16	79	47	4	
Placing-out agencies						7	1	5	9					1	6	7		
Reformatories	3	10	2	2		1	1	6	1	2		1	1		8	7	3	
Temporary homes	3	1	1	1		2		2				1		1	5	3		

SUPERVISION.

The subject of supervision has to do with the duties performed by boards of trustees, directors or managers. Such boards usually consist of professional or business men or charitably inclined women who serve without compensation. In many institutions, especially those in charge of various sisterhoods, there is practically no supervisory board as distinct from the administrative management, which is in the hands of the sister in charge and her associates. In other institutions there is frequently a double supervisory board consisting on the one hand of trustees charged with the care of the material interests of the charities, their financial management and the proper maintenance and improvement of their properties, while on the other hand is to be found a board of managers who exercise supervision over the internal administration such as the housekeeping affairs and the provisioning of the charities, and who periodically visit and inspect the several philanthropies. In certain cases, one of these boards acts in an advisory capacity to the other.

In homes for children the opportunities for service are limitless. Not only are the financial interests of this class of institutions to be promoted and the internal administration supervised, but there is the important duty of mothering the orphans and friendless children, many of whom are received in infancy and retained for years under institutional care.

Too much stress cannot be laid upon the necessity for close and constant supervision of their respective charities by those whose names appear upon the directorate of these institutions. The philanthropic public looks upon such members of boards of trustees or managers as guarantors that the work of the charities in which they are interested is conducted in a progressive and enlightened spirit.

The importance of official records, such as minutes of meetings and of all business transacted, of attendance upon such

meetings, and an official visitors' book in which shall be registered the names of officers and managers and members of committees on the occasion of their visits to the institution, as well
as frequent reports from special committees embodying the
statement of conditions found to exist from time to time and
recommendations or suggestions offered looking to the improvement of the administration of the charity—none of these things
should be overlooked as means to accomplish the end in view,
namely, the maintenance of the institution at such a level of
economy and efficiency as will merit and command the confi-
dence of beneficiaries and supporters alike. The embarrassment which may befall boards of managers through failure to
keep full official records of their transactions and visits has
received recent illustration in the experience of the late boards
of managers of State hospitals for the insane, who, when asked
by the Governor and certain legislators to give account of their
stewardship, were obliged to confess that the written records,
particularly of visits to the institutions under their care, did
but scant justice to their performance of duty for the reason
that they had frequently visited when they had failed to so
record themselves.

Of the 448 general inspections made during the year, which
include 41 duplicate or re-inspections, in but 24 instances has
the supervision exercised been of so marked and distinguished
a character as to be considered "excellent." On the other hand,
in but one instance was it positively poor, while in 193 cases it
is reported to have been good, in 139 cases fair, and in 22
cases unsatisfactory. As the inspectors of the Department
rarely meet members of boards of managers, the basis of judgment must be largely such written records as are accessible, the
evidence furnished by condition of properties, the domestic
atmosphere of the charities and other indices somewhat in-
tangible in kind but not altogether unreliable when considered
by one accustomed to institutional characteristics.

ADMINISTRATION.

The term "administration" as used in the table of summaries refers to the internal management of the institutions subject to inspection. In 97 instances such administration was characterized as excellent; in 242 others as good; in 95 cases as fair; in 9 of the charities as unsatisfactory, and in 2 as poor. On the whole this showing is a favorable one. In this connection it should be borne in mind that while official visits of inspection are not frequent, they are repeated from year to year and the judgments formed are based not upon a single inspection but upon a series of official visits each of which becomes a matter of written record and report. Comparison is therefore instituted between conditions reported as a result of earlier inspections and conditions found to exist at the time of the latest official visit. If therefore an injustice is done any institution on one occasion, this is quite sure to be corrected at a subsequent inspection, while the policy adopted by the Board, namely, that of sending copies of reports to the managers of the charities, insures a correction of the records should errors of judgment or statement occur.

From the foregoing table it will be observed that 179 of the inspections reported relate to homes for children, including infant asylums. It is gratifying that in but four of these homes is the administration considered unsatisfactory, while in but one is it characterized as poor. From year to year considerable improvement is observed in the conduct of this form of charity, than which none is more important.

However faithful may be the supervision exercised by voluntary boards of trustees or managers, it is the experience of the Department that the success or failure of a particular charity depends in no small degree upon the personality and executive ability of the resident head. This often finds illustration where there occurs a change of superintendents or matrons who have been notably successful or the reverse. Where marked improvement or retrogression is found in the administration of any given institution as contrasted with conditions

observed on previous visits, the presumptive explanation, based
upon experience, is that there has been a change of resident
managers. This is usually found to have been the case.

CONDITION OF PROPERTIES.

In 75 instances the condition of properties, including buildings and grounds, is reported as excellent; in 183 cases as good;
in 127 institutions as fair, and in 48 others as unsatisfactory,
while in 7 of the charities the plant is considered poor or un-
suited for its present use. When one considers how philanthropies are frequently organized from small and imperfect beginnings, making use of properties which have been donated
or rented for the purpose and which require radical improvements in order to adapt them for the uses to which they are
put, the showing is on the whole a good one. Material conditions, however, as is well known, do not always determine the
character of the work which is performed. Cleanliness and order
may persist even when properties themselves are old and inadequate, but the difficulties of the administration under such circumstances are greatly enhanced. On the other hand, the spirit
of true charity may be absent even where institution buildings
are of the most approved pattern. Such, however, is not usually
the case, for suitable housing facilities are usually the expression of a progressive administration.

It is once more worthy of note that the cottage system makes
but slow progress in homes for children within this State, although accepted elsewhere as a necessity for the proper conduct of this class of institutions. Only by the adoption of the
family-group system can our largest institutions best offer to
their inmates some degree of compensation for the lost advantages of individual and family life.

SANITARY CONDITIONS.

Special stress has been laid for some time past upon the question of fire protection. Scarcely a year goes by but that one
or more of the charitable institutions of the State are visited

by a disastrous conflagration. The recent destructive fires at St. Agnes Convent, Sparkill, the Shelter for Unprotected Girls, Syracuse, and the Rochester Orphan Asylum, the first and last mentioned of which were attended by serious loss of life, are still fresh in mind. The character of the population in certain of the institutions increases the danger from fire. The standards of protection differ in various localities, as indicated by the range of local ordinances on the subject. Appeal to the authorities of cities and towns has been found to meet with different responses, in some cases accomplishing little betterment; in others leading to radical improvements shown by the erection of iron fire-escapes, the installation of fire-alarm boxes connecting with fire headquarters, of electric signals, standpipes, fire extinguishers and the institution of a system of night patrol, none of which means of protection should be overlooked in institutions of any considerable size.

Reference to pages 128-131 of this volume will show that the Board has sought legislative action by which there shall be a uniform standard of fire protection established, especially for children's institutions, which include so large a proportion of the charities of the State. The revised charter of the city of New York, section 664, chapter 466, Laws of 1901, restrains the Commissioner of Public Charities of the city of New York from committing " any child to any institution not situated in the city of New York unless such institution shall have been certified by said Board (State Board of Charities) to be properly protected from fire and other dangers." There are no less than 18 institutions situated outside the limits of Greater New York to which dependent children are committed by the Department of Public Charities of that city. It would be of aid to the Board in making the required certification were certain existing statutory provisions on the subject of fire protection extended to include homes for children. The statutes referred to are chapter 535, Laws of 1895, entitled "An act to protect the lives of the inmates of public buildings of State institutions and to protect said buildings against destruction by fire ";

chapter 381, Laws of 1895, entitled "An act to protect human life," which requires the erection of iron stairways on the outside of hospital buildings, and chapter 201, Laws of 1901, entitled "An act providing for fire drills in the schools of this State."

Another subject which has received special attention has been the matter of compliance with sections 213, 214, 215 of the Public Health Law, chapter 661, Laws of 1893, as amended by, section 2, chapter 667, Laws of 1900. The particular sections of the law referred to relate to the better preservation of the health of children in institutions. The results of the inquiry of Inspector Mary E. Moxcey upon the subject are presented as a separate report.

The protection afforded in these and other matters pertaining to the life and health of the inmates of the charities under inspection may be summarized as follows: In 75 institutions the general sanitary conditions were regarded as excellent; in 165 as good; in 159 as fair; in 34 as unsatisfactory, and in 4 as bad.

TRAINING.

The subject of " training " in charitable institutions relates chiefly to homes for children and kindred asylums. In this class of charities the educational facilities afforded the inmates should form an important if in fact not the most important part of the advantages afforded by institutional maintenance and care. The industrial training usually consists of certain household tasks readily performed by young children and not unlike the duties which fall to children of corresponding age and sex in private families. The opportunity which is presented by institutional life to teach manual training or to give instruction in cooking and sewing to the girls and the use of tools to the boys is seldom fully utilized. Much improvement remains to be made in these directions.

Educational training or regular attendance upon institutional, parochial or public schools is a subject deserving of much more serious consideration than the Department of Inspection, with the force at its command, has been able to give to it. Statistics gathered by the Department and cited on pages 132 and 133 of this volume show that 121 institutions, several of which conduct separate branches, had last year a school population of 23,781, of which number 11,043 were attending either the public schools or schools maintained in whole or in part by public school moneys, while the remainder, namely, 12,738, were attending asylum schools which are privately organized.

An inquiry has recently been instituted by the Board looking to a more careful investigation than has hitherto been made regarding the educational equipment and facilities afforded by homes for children. Pending the completion of this investigation the report of conditions given in the table under the head of "Training" must be regarded as provisional.

The moral training afforded by this same class of institutions has to be judged by the emphasis placed upon the individuality of the child, the respect shown for his personal and property rights as indicated by such homely matters as use of individual toilet articles and the individual system of clothing, privacy accorded in bathing and toilet accommodations, the teaching of cleanliness and order, the means of discipline, inculcation of honesty, courtesy and unselfishness and the development of the child's powers of self-expression. It is in the last named respect that long continued institutional care of children most commonly breaks down. Shut away as such long-term inmates are from the common experiences of children in private families, it must necessarily result that the typical institution child will lose that virility of moral training which comes from the rough and tumble daily experiences of boys and girls trained in homes where self-denial is a necessity and where mutual helpfulness and unselfishness are fostered by circumstances, if not directly taught by parents.

RECORDS.

Among the provisions of the State Charities Law, chapter 546, Laws of 1896, defining the general powers and duties of the Board, are the following:

"Section 9. General powers and duties of the Board.—The State Board of Charities * * * shall, * * *

"8. Establish rules for the reception and retention of inmates of all institutions which, by section 14 of article viii. of the constitution, are subject to its visitation.

"11. Collect statistical information in relation to the property, receipts and expenditures of all institutions, societies and associations subject to its supervision and the number and condition of the inmates thereof * * * .

"Section 10. Visitation, inspection and supervision of institutions.—* * * Any member or officer of such board, or inspector duly appointed by it, shall have full access to the * * * books and papers relating to any such institution, and may require from the officers and persons in charge thereof, any information he may deem necessary in the discharge of his duties."

The "records" of charitable institutions include the "books and papers relating to any such institution" as provided by the statute.

In accordance with the provisions of the constitution, and subdivision 8 of section 9 of the State Charities Law, quoted above, the Board has provided that "no destitute child shall be retained as a public charge in any institution wholly or partly under private control, which shall fail to keep a book in which shall be entered the name and address of every person visiting such child, supported in whole or in part by public funds in such institution, which name and address shall be secured upon such visit". The purpose of this rule is clear, namely, to make the visitation of all public charges matters of official record so far as to show the frequency of such visits, the interest shown in the child by its parents, guardians, relatives and friends and the proper address of such relatives or friends. The latter is particularly important since it may become necessary at any time to find on short notice the legal guardians of the children. It has been found that many of the addresses because of long-standing or for other reasons have proven worthless when attempt has been made to verify them. By the new rule it is hoped that institutions will be constrained to keep on file the latest obtainable information as to the present whereabouts of those sufficiently interested in the welfare of the children to visit them. In this respect it is suggested for the consideration of boards of managers that the record of visits be kept by register so arranged that the names of children who are public charges shall be entered in alphabetical order, and that all visitors to such children shall be enrolled under the following titles:

Name of child visited.

Date of visit.   Name of visitor.   Relationship.   Address.

If sufficient space is left after the name of each new visitor, the registration of the date of each successive visit, together with note of any change of address, will form an adequate entry. This system if followed will save much clerical work and simplify the keeping of the records required.

If institutions for the reception and retention of inmates would adopt more generally the envelope and card system of registration their secretaries or other officials charged with the keeping of the records would find the clerical burden of their work much reduced. This would be found especially true in the case of children's institutions, where often complaint is made that the records required are unnecessarily detailed. In the envelopes, in which should be kept the record card containing the information called for by the monthly reports of movement of population made to the Board, there should also be placed the commitment papers, quarantine blanks and correspondence relating to any given case, together with any other information respecting the inmate which it is desired to place on file. Envelopes containing records of children who have left the under private control but in receipt of public moneys on September 30 of each year from 1896–1901, inclusive:

September 30, 1896 (119 institutions)................... 27,769
September 30, 1897 (121 institutions)................... 28,380
September 30, 1898 (123 institutions)................... 29,967
September 30, 1899 (123 institutions)................... 29,440
September 30, 1900 (122 institutions)................... 28,649
September 30, 1901 (121 institutions)................... 29,241

Reference to this table shows a marked increase in the population of children's institutions from 1896 to 1898, inclusive; a decrease in 1899 and 1900, followed by an increase during 1901. This movement of population may be represented by the following diagram:

Table Showing Movement of Population in Homes for Children under Private Control but in Receipt of Public Moneys, from September 30, 1896, to September 30, 1901.

1896	*1897*	*1898*	*1899*	*1900*	*1901*
Sept. 30	Sept. 30	Sept. 30	Sept. 30	Sept. 30	Sep.

30000

29000

28000

'769

27000

26000

The following tables are based upon statistics regarding the children present in private institutions in receipt of public moneys on September 30, 1901, as compared with the children present in similar institutions on September 30, 1900:

TABLE SHOWING NUMBER OF INMATES AND CHARACTER OF POPULATION IN HOMES FOR CHILDREN UNDER PRIVATE CONTROL BUT IN RECEIPT OF PUBLIC MONEYS AT THE CLOSE OF THE FISCAL YEARS 1900 AND 1901 RESPECTIVELY.

	Sept. 30, 1900.	Sept. 30, 1901.	Increase in 1901 over 1900.	Decrease in 1901 over 1900.
Sex:				
Male	16,154	16,645	491	......
Female	12,495	12,596	101	......
*Age classification:				
Under 2 years	1,886	2,108	222	......
Between 2 and 5 years	3,363	3,282	......	81
Between 5 and 10 years	10,537	10,711	174	......
Between 10 and 16 years	11,869	12,177	308	......
Over 16 years	827	832	5	......
Not stated	167	131	......	36
*Civil condition:				
Orphan	2,465	2,415	......	50
Half orphan	13,523	13,898	375	......
Parents living	9,355	9,787	432	......
Unknown	2,735	2,639	......	96
Not stated	571	502	......	69
*Physical condition:				
Healthy	24,246	24,755	509	......
Fair	2,281	1,748	......	533
Not healthy	1,939	2,057	118	......
Not stated	183	681	408	......
*Mental condition:				
Intelligent	24,280	24,857	577	......
Fair	1,570	1,658	88	......
Weak	224	295	71	......
Not stated	2,575	2,431	......	144
Duration of institutional life:				
Less than 1 year	8,900	9,645	745	......
Between 1 and 2 years	5,500	5,629	129	......
Between 2 and 3 years	4,222	3,880	......	333
Between 3 and 4 years	2,698	3,069	371	......
Between 4 and 5 years	2,045	1,979	......	66
Between 5 and 6 years	1,519	1,487	......	32
Between 6 and 7 years	1,219	1,091	......	128
Between 7 and 8 years	855	828	......	27
Between 8 and 9 years	657	595	......	62
Between 9 and 10 years	419	423	4	......

*The statistics represent conditions reported at time of admission.

Duration of institutional life—(Continued):	Sept. 30, 1900.	Sept. 30, 1901.	Increase in 1901 over 1900.	Decrease in 1901 over 1900.
Between 10 and 11 years.................	295	265	......	30
Between 11 and 12 years...............	130	166	36	......
Between 12 and 13 years...............	92	81	......	11
Between 13 and 14 years...............	46	44	......	2
Between 14 and 15 years...............	21	24	3	......
Between 15 and 16 years...............	10	7	......	3
Over 16 years........................	21	19	......	2
How supported:				
By institution	2,893	3,159	266	......
By relatives, guardians or friends.......	2,818	3,163	345	......
By counties	3,167	3,107	......	60
By cities	19,002	19,104	102	......
By towns	604	563	......	41
Otherwise	23	71	48	......
Not stated	142	74	......	68

	BIRTHPLACE OF CHILD.		BIRTHPLACE OF FATHER.		BIRTHPLACE OF MOTHER.	
	Sept. 30, 1900.	Sept. 30, 1901.	Sept. 30, 1900.	Sept. 30, 1901.	Sept. 30, 1900.	Sept. 30 1901.
Native born	25,388	26,216	8,857	9,475	9,193	9,815
England................	115	92	659	671	559	570
Ireland.................	207	180	4,571	4,628	4,913	5,048
Scotland	22	20	202	222	172	197
Germany	143	135	1,802	1,908	1,518	1,648
Austria	115	91	430	343	565	418
Russia	334	327	955	1,154	1,037	1,231
Italy	610	611	1,639	1,679	1,873	1,634
France	37	34	211	190	153	149
Switzerland	2	4	53	64	38	37
Norway and Sweden....	19	28	204	223	215	223
Canada	133	153	389	417	445	430
Cuba	22	21	52	40	26	34
Other foreign countries.	208	205	502	610	504	690
Unknown	847	725	6,205	6,672	6,807	5,474
Not stated	447	399	1,918	1,945	1,932	1,664

The statistics given above afford certain information concerning the character of the population in homes for children
under private control but in receipt of public money in this
State. Comparison between the years 1900 and 1901 shows that
conditions are materially the same for the two years under consideration. So far as the sex of the children is concerned, a
considerable preponderance is noted in favor of the male population, this constituting in 1901 nearly 57 per cent. of the entire
number of inmates. The ages of the children may be roughly
grouped into three periods: First, those five years or under;

second, those between 5 and 10 years of age; third, those between 10 and 16 years of age. The last group constitutes the
largest number, namely, in 1901, 12,177; while those between 5
and 10 years of age numbered 10,711, and those 5 years or
under, scarcely more than 5,000. These facts throw some light
upon the placing-out possibilities, since it is a recognized fact
that children are available for placing-out in proportion either
to their extreme youth or approaching maturity. In other words,
those wishing to receive children for adoption prefer to take
them when they are either in infancy or scarcely removed therefrom in order that they may become an integral part of the
household, while those who wish to take children for service
prefer those who are above school age. Thus the problem of
placing-out children between the ages of 8 and 12 is a somewhat
difficult one.

The facts given regarding the civil condition of the children
relate to such condition at the time when the children were
received in the institutions. In many instances, doubtless,
children who were reported at the time of admission as half-
orphan or with both parents living have since either been
abandoned by their parents or have lost them through death
so that such children practically belong in the orphan class. It
will be observed that in about a third of the cases the parents
were reported as living at the time when the children were
received, and in nearly half of the cases the children were
reported as having either father or mother living.

The facts regarding the physical and mental conditions of
the children when admitted to the institutions are of no little
moment. It is therefore interesting to note that notwithstanding the fact that many of the children are from homes of destitution and in some cases of neglect, about five-sixths of them
are reported as in good physical and mental condition at the
time of reception. In the case of many of the infants received
either at birth or soon thereafter, no note is available concerning the mental condition and therefore this item appears as
"not stated." In but 2,057 cases were the children reported

at entrance as not healthy and in but 295 instances was the mental condition given as weak. Doubtless in making up the record in not a few instances the child has been given the benefit of the doubt and has been declared "healthy" or "intelligent" when better acquaintance with the actual facts has proven that the record was too optimistic.

The duration of institutional life, as given above, is not to be understood as representing the extent of the institutional history of the children under consideration for the reason that their institutional career at the time indicated had not ceased. In order to ascertain the total duration of institutional custody we should need to follow the children until they were discharged. Of the 29,241 children present on September 30, 1901, just about one-third had been under institutional care for less than a year; one-third had been under such care for from one to three years, and the remaining third had been present in institutions for periods varying from three years to sixteen years or over.

The method of support is of interest as showing to what extent the inmates of the homes for children in receipt of public money are objects of private benevolence and to what extent they are supported at public expense. On this point the figures for 1901 indicate that of the 29,241 children present at the close of the year, 22,774 or 77 per cent. were maintained as public charges. These figures are supposed to represent conditions at the time specified for the reason that institutions are requested to notify the Board whenever any change occurs in the method of support of inmates; that is to say, when such inmates are taken off the public pay-roll on the one hand or are made public charges on the other.

The facts reported regarding the birthplace of the children and their parents indicate that while the majority of the parents are of foreign extraction, the majority of their children are American born. Thus, for example, in about one-third of the cases the parents are reported to have been born in this country, while 89 per cent. of the children are reported as native born.

Other statistical records gathered by the Department and general results of inspection are presented elsewhere in this volume, notably under the heads of Reports of the Committees on Dispensaries and on Orphan Asylums, as well as in the special report of inquiry regarding compliance with the provisions of the Public Health Law.

Respectfully submitted.

ENOCH VINE STODDARD, M. D.

Chairman Committee on Inspection.

under private control but in receipt of public moneys on September 30 of each year from 1896–1901, inclusive:

September 30, 1896 (119 institutions)..................	27,769
September 30, 1897 (121 institutions)..................	28,380
September 30, 1898 (123 institutions)..................	29,967
September 30, 1899 (123 institutions)..................	29,440
September 30, 1900 (122 institutions)..................	28,649
September 30, 1901 (121 institutions)..................	29,241

Reference to this table shows a marked increase in the population of children's institutions from 1896 to 1898, inclusive; a decrease in 1899 and 1900, followed by an increase during 1901. This movement of population may be represented by the following diagram:

Table Showing Movement of Population in Homes for Children under Private Control but in Receipt of Public Moneys, from September 30, 1896, to September 30, 1901.

1896	1897	1898	1899	1900	1901
Sept. 30	Sept. 30	Sept. 30	Sept. 30	Sept. 30	

30000

29000

7760

27000

26000

REPORT

OF THE

Committee on Orphan Asylums and Children's Homes.

REPORT.

To the State Board of Charities:

The Committee on Orphan Asylums and Children's Homes has, through the Department of Inspection, maintained its usual general oversight of the work of such of these institutions as come within the Board's jurisdiction, and submits the accompanying report of the Superintendent of Inspection, Mr. Walter S. Ufford, covering in considerable detail various important phases of the work of such institutions, with the recommendation that the report be printed in the Board's annual report to the Legislature.

That there has been during recent years much improvement in the administration of this class of institutions seems to the committee obvious. It seems equally clear that this is due in no small part to the systematic visitation and inspection by the representatives of the Board, as well as largely to the very general coöperation of the managers of the institutions where the Board has attempted to secure improved conditions upon its being made apparent that these were desirable. For this coöperation the managers of the institutions are entitled to much credit. Without their active assistance but little could have been accomplished. It is, however, not too much to say that, while generally speaking, these charities are in excellent condition throughout the entire State, there still remains much room for progress, and that efforts towards this end should be judiciously continued.

Among other things of greater importance it is desirable that the duration of institutional life be materially lessened where practicable. Dependent children should in many cases be earlier

Dining-Room.

Arrangements Common to Private Families.	Arrangements Observed in Certain Children's Institutions.
Chairs.	Benches with or without backs.
Tables, spread with cloths.	Tables with white enamel covering or without table-cloths.
Stoneware or chinaware.	Enamel ware.
Knives and forks (solid or plated).	Steel knives and prong forks or none at all, spoons being commonly used as a substitute.
Napkins.	No napkins nor substitute facilities.
Presence of members of family at table.	Inmates eat by themselves at long tables, supervised by attendants.
Exchange of conversation.	Silence.
Variety of diet.	Monotony as shown by the frequency of stews and absence of meat in a form requiring the use of knives and forks.

Fortunately many of the homes for children are to a greater or less degree adopting the arrangements which are usual in private families so far as the furnishing and equipment of their dining-rooms and the service and methods employed therein are concerned. Where such is not the case, the reply is frequently made that the children are much better off than they were in the homes from which they have come, and that they must not be unfitted for the life to which they inevitably are to return. The self-evident answer is that they should be treated like other children and the penalties of their former destitution and unfortunate environments should not be visited upon them, but they should receive that individual training and attention which will fit them for early restoration to wholesome family life.

The presence of large numbers of children under the same roof necessitates special precaution regarding the safety of health and life. Note has been taken elsewhere of the means employed to guard against fire and also concerning the degree of compliance with those portions of the Public Health Law relating to the better preservation of the health of children in institutions.

FIRE PROTECTION.

In respect to fire protection, the Board has placed itself on record as favoring complete and thorough-going facilities in all homes for children.

The following provisions have been regarded as constituting the necessary general equipment:

Iron fire-stairways.—Iron-fire stairway-escapes to which access may be had from every story above the ground.

The use of iron ladders sometimes found upon children's homes is not approved, nor can portable canvas chutes, with which some homes have been recently equipped, be regarded as a proper substitute for iron stairways.

Standpipes.—Standpipes with coils of hose sufficient in length to cover entire floor space.

Fire-drills.—Fire-drills to acquaint employes and older inmates with their particular duties in case of emergency and to accustom the inmates to the use of outside fire stairways.

Fire-extinguishers.—Fire-extinguishers or fire-pails on each floor.

Night patrol.—Employment of night patrol service in institutions of any considerable size and use of time detectors to register regularity of visits to different portions of building.

Fire-alarm connection.—Direct connection with fire-headquarters whenever possible.

Hose should be regularly tested at least once a quarter, and all chemical extinguishers should be emptied and recharged at least once a year and a record of such recharging should be made upon a tag attached to the extinguisher for the purpose.

COMPLIANCE WITH PUBLIC HEALTH LAW.

In regard to compliance with the Public Health Law, it is believed that the inquiry undertaken at the direction of the Board by Miss Mary E. Moxcey, an inspector of the Department, the results of which inquiry may be found elsewhere in this volume,* will prove to have had a beneficial effect in several important respects. Inspector Moxcey, in the discharge of her official duties, visited the attending physicians of the children's homes covered by the inquiry, and also the offices of the local boards of health. The particular object of these visits was to learn regarding the health of inmates for the period selected, namely, May 1, 1898, to May 1, 1901, both from the attending physicians and the records which said physicians are required to file in the office of the local board of health. Without repeating what is elsewhere reported upon, it will be sufficient to point out the important relation which the attending physician sustains to the children's institution to which he is assigned. Among his duties are the following:

DUTIES OF ATTENDING PHYSICIAN.

The attending physician is required by section 213 of the Public Health Law to examine every newcomer before such child can be admitted to contact with the other inmates.

He must give a written certificate stating whether or no the child has any contagious disease and specifying its physical and mental condition.

He must discharge every child from quarantine and endorse upon the certificate the length of quarantine and date of discharge therefrom.

Moreover, by section 214 of the same statute, such physician is required to examine and inspect the entire institution thoroughly at least once a month, and to report in writing to the managers and the local board of health the condition of the premises and the physical condition of the children, especially as to the existence of any contagious disease, particularly of the eyes or skin, and as to the children's food, clothing, cleanliness

*Vol. I., Thirty-fifth Annual Report.

and whether a sufficient number of attendants of proper ability are provided.

Finally, by section 215 he is charged with the duty of notifying the board of health and the board of managers of any violation of the provisions of such section relating to the cubic air space in the dormitories.

Much has been written concerning the duties of boards of managers and administrative heads of children's institutions, but the responsibility of the visiting physician under the requirements of the Public Health Law has not been hitherto properly emphasized. Many of these physicians are leaders in their profession in their respective towns. It is asking much of them to comply with the provisions of the statute in all its details, but such compliance is essential to the well being of the inmates of these homes. The inspectors of the Board visit these institutions once or twice a year. The attending physician is required to conduct a thorough monthly inspection touching the condition of premises and health of the inmates, the results of which inspections are to be made matters of public record by the filing of written reports in the office of the local board of health as well as with the managers of the institutions. Copies of these monthly records should be so accessible to the inspectors of the Department that they may be able to learn from a study of the records the exact health of the inmates for any given period. Perhaps no provision of the Public Health Law is more important than section 214 regarding the monthly examination of inmates and reports.

DURATION OF INSTITUTIONAL LIFE.

It is commonly agreed that the best place for a child is the family home. Institutions at most are but a substitute for family life. As temporary shelters, they have proven a necessity at least in this State, nor is it likely that they will be supplanted by other methods for the disposition of destitute and neglected children for many years to come. Meantime, the question of the average duration of institutional life is an important

27

one. While it may be admitted that the institution occupies
an essential place in the system of charities of the State, the
most enthusiastic champion of such homes for children will
scarcely contend that beyond a limited period of time retention
under institutional care is desirable. Certainly from the standpoint of the taxpayers, an indefinite continuance as public
charges of such children as may be eligible for placing in family
homes is not likely to be approved.

The following table is intended to show the population of
homes for children, not including infant asylums, which are
under private control but in receipt of public moneys. In this
table the total number present on September 30, 1900, and on
September 30, 1901, is given, and also the number present on
these respective dates who have been retained for upwards of
five years. The proportion which this latter class bears to the
entire population is also indicated under the heading " Percentage." In this connection attention should be called to the fact
that the Department is now engaged upon a special inquiry relative to long-term inmates who are public charges in children's
institutions pursuant to the resolutions of the Board adopted
June 4, 1901. A copy of these resolutions will be found on page
134 of volume I. of the Board's Thirty-fifth Annual report to the
Legislature.

RECORDS OF CHILDREN'S HOMES.

	No. present September 30, 1900.	No. present five years or over.	Percentage.	No. present September 30, 1901.	No. present five years or over.	Percentage.
Albany Orphan Asylum.............	470	127	27	509	110	21.6
American Female Guardian Society and Home for Friendless, New York	145	8	5.5	143	11	7.6
Asylum of Our Lady of Refuge, Buffalo	64	5	7.8	72	10	13.8
Asylum St. Vincent de Paul, New York	225	61	27.1	226	54	23.8
Asylum Sisters of St. Dominic, Blauvelt	406	185	45.5	383	153	39.9
Auburn Orphan Asylum............	139	31	22.3	129	19	14.7
Brooklyn E. D. Industrial School Association	301	7	2.3	305	10	3.2
Brooklyn Children's Aid Society...	....	....	....	29	....	....
Brooklyn Howard Colored Orphan Asylum	157	33	21	159	35	22
Brooklyn Industrial School, Association and Home...............	296	17	5.7	315	29	9.2
Brooklyn Training School and Home for Young Girls............	42	....	....	36	....	....
Buffalo Orphan Asylum...........	153	1	.6	138	3	2.1
Cayuga Asylum for Destitute Children, Auburn	48	7	14.5	65	4	6.1
Charity Foundation P. E. Church, Buffalo	67	12	17.9	76	9	11.8
Children's Fold, New York........	154	15	9.7	165	16	9.6
Children's Home, Amsterdam......	36	4	11.1	27	3	11.1
*Children's Home, Middletown....	15	....	....	25	....	....
*Children's Home, Newburgh......	29	1	3.4	33	1	3
Children's Home, Schenectady....	23	2	8.6	31	4	12.9
Church Charity Foundation of L. I., Brooklyn	65	18	27.6	56	23	39.2
Colored Orphan Asylum, New York.	293	72	24.5	294	69	23.4
Convent of the Sisters of Mercy, Brooklyn	530	160	30.1	550	159	28.9
Dominican Convent of Our Lady of the Rosary, New York...........	485	203	41.8	512	144	28.1
Evangelical Lutheran St. John's Orphan Home, Buffalo...........	83	46	55.4	78	45	57.6
Fairview Home, Watervliet........	101	9	8.9	110	10	9
Five Points House of Industry, New York	334	17	5.08	351	26	7.4
German Odd Fellows' Home and Orphan Asylum, Unionport......	65	5	7.6	69	12	17.3
German R. C. Orphan Asylum, Buffalo	203	28	13.7	235	28	11.9
Gustavus Adolphus Orphan Home, Jamestown	70	30	42.8	63	32	50.7
Hebrew Benevolent Asylum Society, New York....................	751	116	15.4	834	135	16.1
Hebrew Orphan Asylum, Brooklyn.	302	78	25.8	307	82	26.7
Hebrew Sheltering Guardian Society, New York...................	908	176	17.1	922	187	20.2
Home for the Friendless, Lockport.	39	1	2.5	40	2	5
Home for the Friendless of Northern New York, Plattsburg..	39	2	5.1	43	3	6.9
House of the Good Shepherd, Utica.	36	7	19.4	64	6	9.3
House of Nazareth, White Plains (Now Good Counsel Training School)	251	90	35.8	276	99	35.8
House of Providence, Syracuse.....	144	31	21.5	138	41	29.7
Hudson Orphan and Relief Association	62	14	22.5	45	4	8.8
Industrial Home of Kingston.......	34	2	5.8	37	2	5.4
Industrial School Sisters of Mercy, Rochester	60	7	11.6	48	3	6.2
Institution of Mercy, New York....	824	330	40	754	261	34.6
Ithaca Children's Home............	12	....	....	16	1	6.2
Jefferson County Orphan Asylum, Watertown	45	9	20	49	11	22.4
Jewish Orphan Asylum of Western New York, Rochester..........	30	5	16.6	30	3	10
'Madison County Orphan Asylum, Peterboro	44	5	11.3	46	4	8.6

* Under public control.

	No. present September 30, 1900.	No. present five years or over.	Percentage.	No. present September 30, 1901.	No. present five years or over.	Percentage.
Mission of the Immaculate Virgin, New York	1,374	269	19.5	1,362	255	18.7
Missionary Sisters Third Order of St. Francis, Peekskill	1,116	317	28.4	1,101	369	33.5
Mt. Magdalen School of Industry, Troy	52	9	17.3	33	10	30.3
New York Catholic Protectory	2,506	470	18.7	2,545	345	13.5
New York Juvenile Asylum	802	2	.24	896	7	.78
Nursery and Child's Hospital, Country Branch, S. I., N. Y.	262	60	22.4	190	44	23.15
Ogdensburg Orphan Asylum	158	22	13.9	163	19	11.6
Onondaga County Orphan Asylum, Syracuse	184	32	17.3	183	25	13.6
Ontario Orphan Asylum, Canandaigua	47	6	12.7	35	3	8.5
Orphan Asylum Society, Brooklyn.	305	27	8.8	298	38	12.7
Orphan Home and Asylum, Holy Trinity Church, Brooklyn	791	277	35	868	245	28.3
Orphan House of the Holy Saviour, Cooperstown	88	7	7.9	77	8	10.3
Orphanage and Home, Free M. E. Church, Gerry	26	....	....	42	....	....
Oswego Orphan Asylum	42	....	....	38	....	....
Ottilie Orphan Asylum, East Williamsburg	57	16	28	58	19	32.7
Poughkeepsie Orphan House	38	4	10.5	45	3	6.6
P. E. Church Home, Rochester	25	1	4	38	2	5.3
Rochester Orphan Asylum	98	2	2	53	2	3.7
St. Agatha's Home for Children, Nanuet	398	134	33.6	386	98	25.3
St. Ann's Home, New York	525	136	25.9	507	136	26.8
St. Benedict's Home, Rye	144	67	46.5	144	61	42.3
St. Colman's Orphan Asylum, Watervliet	139	29	20.8	129	27	20.9
St. Elizabeth Industrial School, New York	35	4	11.4	34	2	5.8
St. Francis Home, Oswego	63	....	....	68	12	17.6
St. James' Home, New York	110	27	24.5	115	20	17.3
St. John's Female Orphan Asylum, Utica	134	37	27.6	138	29	21
St. John's Home for Boys, Brooklyn	1,207	274	22.7	1,257	301	23.9
St. John's Orphan Asylum, Rensselaer	91	40	43.9	54	19	35.1
St. Joseph's Female Orphan Asylum, Brooklyn	493	97	19.7	489	64	13
St. Joseph's German R. C. Orphan Asylum, Rochester	86	23	26.7	84	23	27.3
St. Joseph's Male Orphan Asylum, West Seneca	181	37	20.4	216	37	17.1
St. Joseph's Orphan Asylum, Corning	3	1	33.3	3	2	66.6
St. Joseph's Orphan Asylum, New York	832	170	20.4	833	145	17.4
St. Malachy's Home, Brooklyn	645	65	10	701	89	12.6
St. Mary's Boys' Orphan Asylum, Rochester	154	34	22	144	25	17.3
St. Mary's Catholic Orphan Asylum, Binghamton	120	27	22.5	131	30	24.7
St. Mary's Orphan Asylum, Canandaigua	11	2	18.1	Closed		
St. Mary's Home and School, Dunkirk	60	19	31.6	81	22	27.1
St. Mary's Orphan Asylum, Port Jervis	141	20	14.1	143	18	12.5
St. Michael's Home, Green Ridge	159	14	8.8	175	21	12
St. Patrick's Orphan Girls' Asylum, Rochester	95	12	12.6	98	6	6.1
St. Patrick's Orphanage, Watertown	51	....	....	57	....	....
St. Vincent's Female Orphan Asylum, Albany	207	49	23.6	201	60	29.8
St. Vincent's Female Orphan Asylum, Buffalo	148	13	8.7	155	16	10.3
St. Vincent's Female Orphan Asylum, Troy	160	48	30	172	48	37.9

	No. present September 30, 1900.	No. present five years or over.	Percentage.	No. present September 30, 1901.	No. present five years or over.	Percentage.
St. Vincent's Industrial School, Utica	187	12	6.4	203	24	11.8
St. Vincent's Male Orphan Asylum, Albany	116	18	15.5	154	13	8.4
St. Vincent's Orphan Asylum, Syracuse	206	63	30.5	184	55	29.8
Sacred Heart of Mary Orphan Asylum, Buffalo	145	....	....	154	....	....
Sacred Heart Orphan Asylum, West Park	80	14	17.5	87	13	14.9
Saratoga Home for Children	21	....	....	16	....	....
Sheltering Arms Nursery P. E. Church, Brooklyn	57	3	5.2	68	4	5.8
*Shepherd's Fold, New York	25	1	4	*		
Society for Aid of Friendless Women and Children, Brooklyn	48	6	12.5	49	6	12.2
Society for Protection of Destitute R. C. Children, West Seneca	393	10	2.5	440	10	2.2
Society of United Helpers, Ogdensburg	24	....	....	32	....	....
Southern Tier Orphan's Home, Elmira	32	2	6.2	36	2	5.5
†Suffolk County Children's Home, Yaphank	47	1	2.1	45	2	4.4
Susquehanna Valley Home, Binghamton	141	16	11.3	147	26	17.6
Temporary Home, etc., Mineola	58	12	20.6	56	6	10.7
Troy Catholic Male Orphan Asylum	225	48	21.3	251	47	18.7
Troy Orphan Asylum	204	39	19.1	231	42	18.1
Utica Orphan Asylum	158	19	12	157	27	17.1
Western New York Home, Randolph	136	12	8.8	148	11	7.4
Westchester Temporary Home, White Plains	126	6	4.7	139	9	6.4
	25,372	5,159	20.33	25,950	4,864	18.74

*Merged with Children's Fold.

† Under public control.

	Sept. 30, 1900.	Sept. 30, 1901.
These homes may be classified as follows:		
Number of homes retaining over 50 per cent. of inmates five years plus......................	1	8
Number of homes retaining between 40 and 50 per cent. of inmates five years plus..................	6	.
Number of homes retaining between 30 and 40 per cent. of inmates five years plus..................	8	8
Number of homes retaining between 20 and 30 per cent. of inmates five years plus..................	26	23
Number of homes retaining between 10 and 20 per cent. of inmates five years plus.................	29	33
Number of homes retaining between 1 and 10 per cent. of inmates five years plus.................	29	31
Number of homes retaining no inmates five years plus	10	9

Respectfully submitted,

WALTER S. UFFORD,

Superintendent of Inspection.

REPORT

OF THE

Committee on the Placing-Out of Children.

REPORT.

To the State Board of Charities:

Your Committee on the Placing-Out of Children respectfully reports as follows:

Among the functions of the State Board of Charities, the prevention of evils and abuses in connection with the placing-out of children is not the least important. To safeguard the welfare of dependent childhood, and to see that such supervision be given as will prevent abuse and assure proper homes for such as may be placed out, is the object of chapter 264 of the Laws of 1898. This authorizes the Board to issue licenses to such persons or corporations as apply therefor and who, in the judgment of said Board, are proper agencies for placing out children. Under these licenses destitute children may be placed in approved homes by such persons and corporations, and it is made unlawful for unlicensed persons, except public officials to whom authority is given by statute, and who therefore do not require a special license, to engage in the business of placing-out dependent children. This act confers upon the Board full oversight of dependent children placed out by charitable societies or by individuals in family homes. It was passed in obedience to a public demand that there be a thorough supervision over children placed in homes. Prior to the passage of this act, many private individuals had engaged in the business of finding homes for destitute children, and for personal gain had frequently sacrificed the interests of the children. These abuses became so flagrant that the public demanded the passage of a law for their suppression, as it had been found that there was no other way to control these persons. They covered their practices by declaring that they were engaged in a work of charity, and, while often fostering crime, posed before the public as earnestly laboring for the benefit of society. Midwives, keepers of private lying-in asylums, and frequently individuals living principally upon the proceeds of immorality, were engaged in this business, and it became necessary to enact a law which would save the children from sacrifice to their cupidity.

The second section of chapter 264, Laws of 1898, makes it "unlawful for any person or corporation, other than a charitable or benevolent institution, society or association, or society for the prevention of cruelty to children, now or hereafter duly incorporated under the laws of this State, or a local officer charged with relief of the poor and placing out in the manner now provided by law, to place out any destitute child, directly or indirectly, unless such person or corporation shall be duly licensed as hereinafter provided, by the State Board of Charities, to place out destitute children. Nor shall any local officer charged with the relief of the poor, directly or indirectly, place out any child or children in a family not residing in this State." .

This section has gone a long way toward the prevention of abuses and evils which have existed in connection with the placing-out of children. Its provisions were deemed ample to prevent unlicensed persons and those not approved by the State Board of Charities from engaging in this work, but an experience of over three years has shown that there is a method by which its provisions are sometimes evaded. Authority is granted to local officers charged with the relief of the poor to place out destitute children, and some local poor authorities have taken advantage of this provision to employ as agents parties who have been refused license by the State Board of Charities. In some of the counties the superintendents of the poor have chosen careful and competent agents who are doing most excellent work. In other counties, however, it has been found cheaper to employ parties who cannot meet the requirements of the State Board of Charities for license. If all county poor authorities would undertake the work of placing out children as it is done in Erie, Essex, Monroe, New York, and some other counties, there would be little reason to fear that our dependent children would be placed in improper homes.

The law requires that " any person or corporation who shall place out a destitute child, shall keep and preserve a record of the full name and actual or apparent age of such child, the names and residence of its parents so far as known, and the names and residence of the person or persons with whom the child is placed. If such person or corporation shall subsequently remove such child from the custody of the person or persons with whom it was placed, the fact of such removal and the disposition made of such child shall be entered upon such record."

This provision of the statute is exceedingly important, as it enables the public authorities to follow the movements of the child. It has been found, however, in examinations made by inspectors of this Board, that these records are not kept with the completeness which the law requires. In many instances children have been placed-out, and the actual residence of the persons to whom these dependent wards of the State have been committed are not known. Children have been transferred from one family to another at the pleasure of the families, and without consultation with the county authorities who are responsible for the welfare of such public wards.

The books of record required by the statute should be made as complete as possible, and all essential facts concerning the child, as long as it is properly a public ward, should be recorded. A failure to keep such record in proper form is made a misdemeanor. Sometimes large interests depend upon records of this character. At the present time it is said that the disposal of a very large estate hinges upon the identification of certain children who were placed-out by a county superintendent of the poor.

The visitation and inspection of homes for dependent children should be carried on with thoroughness and frequency. The limited inspection force at the command of the Board at the present time does not permit as frequent visitation of such homes as is desirable. During the past year the inspectors of the Department of State and Alien Poor have made a large number of visitations. They have examined into the condition and environment of many of the children, and also have made investigations whenever complaints have reached the Board. From the result of these visitations your committee reports that, in the main, children placed out by public officials were found in satisfactory homes. If it were possible to have every child visited at least twice a year, it would be very desirable, but, with the other duties devolved upon the inspectors, this is not possible at the present time. Were the Legislature to realize the importance of this work, there is no doubt that ample provision would be made to carry it on in a proper way. Until such time as our appropriations warrant the employment of additional inspectors, we shall be obliged to continue, in connection with other work, the visitation of the homes of children placed-out, and as a rule can secure reports upon children placed-out under the authority of the county superintendents and overseers of the poor only.

Respectfully submitted,

ENOCH V. STODDARD, M. D.,

Chairman Committee on the Placing-Out of Children.

REPORT

OF THE

Committee on Dispensaries.

REPORT.

To the State Board of Charities:

The duties imposed upon the Board by the enactment of the "Dispensary Law" in 1899 were of such novel character as to require the most judicious use of the powers which that law conferred. The dispensaries have held an honorable position among our charities for upwards of a century, and it is only within the last two or three decades that abuses have crept into their management which required to be remedied by a legislative enactment. The most serious allegation against them was that they were no longer devoted solely to the treatment of the sick poor, but were patronized by those able to employ physicians. Though these abuses have long been recognized in other states and countries, the State of New York was the first to place dispensaries under legal control. The medium selected through which that control was to be exercised is the State Board of Charities, and the authority given the Board was discretionary to the extent of empowering it to revolutionize the management of every dispensary in the State. But in the preparation of the rules governing the future management of the dispensaries as required by the "Dispensary Law", the Board endeavored to accomplish the purpose of the statute with as little disturbance of their operations as possible. These rules have now been in operation for a period of two years and upwards, and the results are on the whole distinctly favorable. The dispensaries have gradually conformed more and more completely to the regulations of the Board until, with but few exceptions, the rules are so generally observed as to secure the more important reforms which the law was designed to accomplish.

In the present report the committee has endeavored to present in a concrete form the work of the dispensaries of the State under the "Dispensary Law", constituting chapter 368 of the Laws of 1899.

Mr. John B. Prest, the Board's inspector of dispensaries, has prepared the tables submitted below with accompanying explanations.

THE DISPENSARIES OF NEW YORK STATE AND WHAT THEY ARE DOING—WHAT ATTENDANCE FIGURES SHOW.

A statistical table has been carefully prepared and is the basis of this report by which it is intended to show the number of applicants for relief at the licensed dispensaries in the State, the number of times such applicants have been treated and the number of prescriptions given. One of the principal objects of this tabulation has been to present as a basis for future dispensary statistics definite figures to show what has been done in the past, so that comparison may be made from time to time when future figures are obtained. It has been intended also to indicate with the use of this table and the accompanying report what effect the dispensary law of 1899 has had upon the dispensaries.

In the following summary the first subdivision represents the number of persons or individuals who have applied for treatment at the dispensaries during three years. The second subdivision is intended to show the whole number of treatments or visits and the third subdivision shows the number of prescriptions given.

The figures in parentheses indicate the number of dispensaries, while the attendance is shown by the figures alongside. The words "in operation" indicate the dispensaries which were doing business in 1899 and were still doing business in 1900 and 1901. Included with these figures are reports from three new dispensaries which have been established since 1899. The words "since closed" indicate the dispensaries which reported in 1899 and 1900 but have since discontinued business. It is only fair to include these in the totals, but for comparison such figures have been kept separate. It is also fair to state that according to the printed annual report of this Department for

1899 there were fifteen other dispensaries then in operation, but from which no reports were obtained. Had these fifteen reports been made, the totals for 1899 would have been further increased in the following table.

SUMMARY TABLE.

NUMBER OF PERSONS TREATED.	Year ending Sept. 30, 1899.		Year ending Sept. 30, 1900.		Year ending Sept. 30, 1901.	
New York city.						
Dispensaries in operation, Manhattan..........	(57)	735,006	(58)	745,178	(59)	755,750
Dispensaries since closed, Manhattan	(6)	6,972	(2)	970		0
Total, Manhattan.....................		741,978		746,148		755,750
Dispensaries in operation, Brooklyn	(24)	141,422	(24)	111,634	(26)	102,622
Dispensaries since closed, Brooklyn	(12)	39,127	(2)	5,825	(2)	1,442
Total, Brooklyn.....................		180,549		117,459		104,064
Dispensaries in operation, Bronx, Queens and Richmond.....................	(4)	10,060	(4)	12,463	(4)	12,179
Dispensaries since closed, Bronx, Queens and Richmond.....................		0		0		0
Total, Bronx, Queens and Richmond.......		10,060		12,463		12,179
Total, New York city.............		932,587		876,070		871,993
Outside New York city.						
Dispensaries in operation	(24)	38,391	(26)	34,883	(28)	34,577
Dispensaries since closed		0		0		0
Total, outside New York city..............		38,391		34,883		34,577
Grand total, entire State.................		970,978		910,953		906,570

NUMBER OF TREATMENTS.						
New York city.						
Dispensaries in operation, Manhattan..........	(57)	2,022,508	(58)	2,099,759	(59)	2,151,455
Dispensaries since closed, Manhattan..........	(5)	14,067	(2)	7,839		0
Total, Manhattan		2,036,575		2,107,598		2,151,455
Dispensaries in operation, Brooklyn	(24)	344,281	(24)	281,622	(26)	261,549
Dispensaries since closed, Brooklyn	(11)	46,460	(4)	13,386	(2)	5,734
Total, Brooklyn.....................		390,741		295,008		267,283
Dispensaries in operation, Bronx, Queens and Richmond	(4)	19,905	(4)	19,656	(4)	22,438
Dispensaries since closed, Bronx, Queens and Richmond		0		0		0
Total, Bronx, Queens and Richmond.......		19,905		19,656		22,438
Total, New York city.....................		2,447,221		2,422,262		2,441,176
Outside New York city.						
Dispensaries in operation	(24)	119,015	(26)	105,241	(28)	109,849
Dispensaries since closed		0		0		0
Total, outside New York city..............		119,015		105,241		109,849
Grand total, entire State		2,566,236		2,527,503		2,551,025

SUMMARY TABLE—(*Concluded*).

NUMBER OF PRESCRIPTIONS DISPENSED.	Year ending Sept. 30, 1899.		Year ending Sept. 30, 1900.		Year ending Sept. 30, 1901.	
New York city.						
Dispensaries in operation, Manhattan	(57)	1,686,725	(58)	1,741,769	(59)	1,903,676
Dispensaries since closed, Manhattan	(5)	15,622	(2)	9,475		0
Total, Manhattan		1,702,357		1,751,244		1,903,676
Dispensaries in operation, Brooklyn	(24)	252,075	(24)	225,220	(26)	181,181
Dispensaries since closed, Brooklyn.............	(11)	52,378	(4)	6,656	(2)	150
Total, Brooklyn		304,253		231,876		181,331
Dispensaries in operation, Bronx, Queens and Richmond	(4)	15,972	(4)	17,424	(4)	15,907
Dispensaries since closed, Bronx, Queens and Richmond		0		0		0
Total, Bronx, Queens and Richmond.......		15,972		17,424		15,907
Total, New York city		2,022,382		2,000,544		2,060,914
Outside New York city.						
Dispensaries in operation	(24)	74,777	(26)	72,862	(26)	72,949
Dispensaries since closed		0		0		0
Total, outside New York city ... ,........		74,777		72,862		72,949
Grand total, entire State...................		2,096,059		2,073,406		2,076,863

It will readily be seen from an examination of these figures that the grand totals for each year since 1899 have been less than they were when dispensary figures reached high-water mark in that year. It is also noticeable that the whole number of patients treated in 1900 was about 60,000 less than in 1899 and in 1901 only about 4,000 less than in 1900. The same ratio, however, is not borne out by a comparison of the number of treatments, or by the number of prescriptions. For example, the whole number of treatments at dispensaries was about 39,000 less in 1900 than during 1899, but during 1901 recovered about 24,000 of the losses shown by the 1900 figures. The number of prescriptions dropped about 25,000 in 1900 but recovered about 3,000 of the losses in the following year. In regard to both treatments and prescriptions the totals have not reached the record established in 1899, but indications point to a gradual recovery of the enormous figures recorded in that year. So much for aggregate results.

The figures become more interesting. when the totals in the different boroughs of New York city and those elsewhere in the State are taken up. In New York city the number of persons treated as well as the number of treatments and the number of prescriptions, have been increasing rapidly in Manhattan borough, and an increasing tendency is shown at the dispensaries located in Bronx borough. It is noticeable that the number of treatments given has increased much faster than the number of individual applicants, and this leads to the conclusion that when once a person has commenced going to a dispensary such person continues the practice rather than go to a private physician thereafter. A very marked falling off is shown by the dispensary figures representing Brooklyn, and a corresponding decrease is noted in Queens and Richmond boroughs. All of this goes to show that the movement of population at dispensaries has a strong tendency toward Manhattan borough, where the large hospital and medical school dispensaries have been established in considerable numbers.

Still closer comparison of the figures obtained shows that, generally speaking, the most material increase in dispensary attendance has been found at the large and magnificent dispensary institutions, such as those of Cornell University, Gouverneur Hospital, New York Eye and Ear Infirmary, Presbyterian Hospital, University and Bellevue Hospital Medical College and the Vanderbilt Clinic, all in Manhattan. To this list might be added Harlem Hospital Dispensary in Manhattan, which shows a phenomenal increase.

Those dispensaries which show the most noticeable decrease n attendance are all in Brooklyn, and include the Brooklyn Central, Brooklyn City, Brooklyn E. D. Homeopathic, Brooklyn Orthopaedic, Brooklyn College of Physicians and Surgeons, Gates Avenue Homeopathic, Brooklyn Hebrew and the Twenty-ixth Ward Homeopathic dispensaries.

To any one familiar with conditions, and particularly to lose who have studied the situation, it does not appear strange lat the attendance at the dispensaries in Manhattan borough is been found increasing. One reason for this condition lies the acute competition for cases, regardless, when generally speaking, of the question whether the applicant is worthy of free treatment or not.

The large medical schools create a tremendous demand for material for clinical instruction. This demand must be met for the success of the institution, and the question of ability to employ a physician does not enter into the problem to the extent generally supposed.

On the other hand, doctors will be found in considerable numbers who will say that they want to continue to practice at dispensaries whenever they can spare the time from their private practice, because in doing so they are able to keep themselves "brushed up" and "abreast of the times" in their profession. This enlivens the competition for cases.

Close observation shows that a comparatively small number of the persons who apply leave the institution without paying something. The number of so-called "free" dispensaries "which charge" is increasing.

According to the figures at hand, it is apparent that the proportion of increase in Manhattan borough is not so great as the proportion of decrease in the residential boroughs of Brooklyn, Queens and Richmond. Satisfaction may be found in this condition, for such may be taken to indicate less sickness and poverty, assuming, however, that the increase in Manhattan is due to a considerable extent to the fact that persons go from all localities to the institutions in Manhattan with the belief in mind that more expert treatment is to be found at the larger institutions which exist in the business borough.

In this connection the following summary, which is explained below, may be found interesting:

	1900 AS COMPARED WITH 1899. NUMBER OF DISPENSARIES WHICH SHOW—		1901 AS COMPARED WITH 1900. NUMBER OF DISPENSARIES WHICH SHOW—		1901 AS COMPARED WITH 1899 NUMBER OF DISPENSARIES WHICH SHOW—	
	Gains.	Losses.	Gains.	Losses.	Gains.	Losses.
New York city.						
Manhattan	36	22	37	22	35	24
Brooklyn.............	10	14	12	14	10	16
Bronx	2	0	2	0	2	0
Queens	0	1	0	1	0	1
Richmond	0	1	0	1	0	1
	48	38	51	38	47	42
Outside New York city	10	16	15	13	15	13
Entire State...........	58	54	66	51	62	55

There were three new dispensaries established in New York city and two elsewhere in the State during 1901. This will account for the increased number of dispensaries as shown in the table.

In Manhattan borough there were 36 dispensaries which show an increase and 22 dispensaries which show a decrease in attendance in 1900 as compared with 1899. In 1901 there were 37 dispensaries which showed an increase and 22 which showed a decrease as compared with 1900, and in 1901 there was one more dispensary in the borough, but when compared with 1899 it has been found that 35 of them had increased and 24 had decreased in attendance.

In Brooklyn borough it has been found that at 10 dispensaries the attendance increased and at 14 dispensaries the attendance decreased in 1900 as compared with 1899. In 1901 there were 12 dispensaries which showed an increase and 14 which showed a decrease as compared with 1900, but the increase is accounted for by the fact that there were two new dispensaries opened in 1901. When comparing 1901 with 1899 it may be seen that 10 dispensaries increased and 16 decreased in attendance.

In Bronx borough both dispensaries show an increased attendance each year, and in Queens and Richmond boroughs the dispensaries show continuing decreased attendance.

The figures obtained show that in the State outside of New York city 16 dispensaries had a smaller.attendance and 10 dispensaries had a larger attendance in 1900 than in 1899. In 1901 the falling off in attendance shown the.previous year did not continue but there was an increase instead. The aggregate attendance however was not so great, but the number of dispensaries reporting was greater, and only 13 showed losses while 15 institutions reported gains. In 1901.there were 13 dispensaries which showed losses and 15 which showed gains as compared with 1899.

Comparison of the figures obtained from the institutions, one with another, shows that the attendance has been increasing at the large dispensaries, while at the small dispensaries it has been decreasing. There is, however, no uniform standard for comparison.

A study of the statistics relating to five of the largest dispensaries in Manhattan borough shows that in the case of Bellevue, for example, the dispensary gave 12,000 more treatments in 1900 than in 1899, but in 1901 fell off 39,000 treatments as compared with 1900. The Good Samaritan Dispensary gave 5,000 more treatments in 1900 than in 1899, but in 1901 fell off 10,000 treatments as compared with 1900. The New York Dispensary increased 300 treatments in 1900 over 1899, but in 1901 fell off 9,000 treatments as compared with 1900. The New York Eye and Ear Infirmary shows an increase of 13,000 treatments in 1900 as compared with 1899, but in 1901 the figures are increased only 200 over 1900. The Vanderbilt Clinic shows an increase of about 4,000 treatments more in 1900 than in 1899, but in 1901 the figures are increased less than 100 treatments over 1900.

In the following statistical tables the dispensaries are arranged in alphabetical order, according to localities, those in the several boroughs of the city of New York being grouped separately from those outside New York city:

	NUMBER OF DIFFERENT PERSONS TREATED AT THE DISPENSARY DURING THE YEAR ENDING SEPTEMBER 30.			TOTAL NUMBER OF TREATMENTS AT THE DISPENSARY DURING THE YEAR ENDING SEPTEMBER 30.			TOTAL NUMBER OF PRESCRIPTIONS DISPENSED DURING THE YEAR ENDING SEPTEMBER 30.		
	1899.	1900.	1901.	1899.	1900.	1901.	1899.	1900.	1901.
Amity, 313 W. 54th street									
Babies, 657 Lexington avenue									
Bellevue, foot E. 26th street									
Beth-Israel, 206 E. Broadway									
Bloomingdale, 201 W. 99th street									
Calvary, 316 W. 130th street									
Columbus, 226 E. 20th street									
Cornell, 1st avenue and 28th street									
Demilt, 2d avenue and 23d street									
East Side, 334 E. 2d street									
Eclectic, 250 E. 16th street									
French, 330 W. 34th street									
General Cancer, 8th avenue and 106th street									
German, 137 2d avenue									
German Polyclinic, 50 E. 7th street									
Good Samaritan, 75 Essex street									
Gouverneur, Gouverneur slip									
Harlem, 105 E. 128th street									
Harlem Eye, 144 E. 127th street									
Harlem Hospital, 538 E. 120th street									
Homeopathic of Harlem, 63 W. 130th street									
J. Hood Wright, 131st street and Amsterdam ave									
Lincoln, 104 W. 40th street									
Manhattan Eye, 103 Park avenue									
Memorial Baptist, 3d and Thompson streets									
Metropolitan, 349 E. 23d street									
Metropolitan Throat, 351 W. 34th street									
Mt. Sinai, 151 E. 67th street									
New York, 137 Centre street									
New Amsterdam Eye, 220 W. 38th street									
New York Eye, 2d avenue and 13th street									
New York Infirmary for Women, 321 E. 15th street									
New York Medical, Women, 19 W. 101st street									
New York Ophthalmic and Aural, 44 E. 12th street									
New York Ophthalmic Hospital, 201 E. 23d street									

I. Licensed Dispensaries on September 30, 1901—Borough of Manhattan—(Concluded).

	NUMBER OF DIFFERENT PERSONS TREATED AT THE DISPENSARY DURING THE YEAR ENDING SEPTEMBER 30.			TOTAL NUMBER OF TREATMENTS AT THE DISPENSARY DURING THE YEAR ENDING SEPTEMBER 30.			TOTAL NUMBER OF PRESCRIPTIONS DISPENSED DURING THE YEAR ENDING SEPTEMBER 30.		
	1899.	1900.	1901.	1899.	1900.	1901.	1899.	1900.	1901.
New York Orthopaedic, 126 E. 59th street									
New York Polyclinic, 214 E. 34th street									
New York Post Graduate, 303 E. 20th street									
New York Skin and Cancer, 3d ave. and 19th st.									
New York Society (or Ruptured), Lex. ave., 42d st.									
New York Throat, 241 E. 19th street									
North Eastern, 222 E. 59th street									
Northern, Waverly place									
North Western, 408 W. 36th street									
Out-Patient Dept. (Flower), 409 E. 23d street									
People's Home Church, 543 E. 11th street									
Presbyterian, Madison avenue and 70th street									
Roosevelt, W. 59th street									
St. Bartholomew's, 221 E. 42d street									
St. Christopher's, 630 7th avenue									
St. Luke's, W. 113th street									
St. Mark's, 177 2d avenue									
St. Vincent's, 7th avenue and 11th street									
Trinity, 209 Fulton street									
University and Bellevue, 1st avenue and 26th street									
Vanderbilt, 10th avenue and 60th street									
West Side German, 328 W. 43d street									
Willard, 489 9th avenue									
Woman's, Lexington avenue and 49th street									
Fifty-nine institutions	735,006	745,178	765,786	2,922,508	2,099,709	2,151,405	1,895,785	1,741,769	1,905,975

A. Estimated by managers; no records kept or records incomplete.
B. Not in operation during that year.
C. Not in operation part of that year.
D. No prescriptions given.
E. Report for calendar year.
F. Orthopaedic braces, etc.

II. Licensed Dispensaries on September 30, 1901—Borough of Brooklyn.

	NUMBER OF DIFFERENT PERSONS TREATED AT THE DISPENSARY DURING THE YEAR ENDING SEPTEMBER 30.			NUMBER OF TREATMENTS AT THE DISPENSARY DURING THE YEAR ENDING SEPTEMBER 30.			TOTAL NUMBER OF PRESCRIPTIONS DISPENSED DURING THE YEAR ENDING SEPTEMBER 30.		
	1899.	1900.	1901.	1899.	1900.	1901.	1899.	1900.	1901.
Bedford, 315 Ralph avenue									
Brooklyn Central, 39 Third avenue									
Brooklyn City, 11 Tillary street									
Brooklyn, E. D., Dispensary, and H., 109 S. 2d st.									
Brooklyn, E. D., Homeopathic, 191 S. 3d street									
Brooklyn Eye, 54 Livingston street									
Brooklyn Hospital, Raymond street									
Brooklyn Orthopedic, Raymond street									
Bushwick and E. Brooklyn, 106 Myrtle avenue									
Central Homeopathic, 366 Howard avenue									
Children's Mission, 125 Earle street									
College of Physicians and Surgeons, Prospect pl									
East New York, 129 Watkins street									
Fifteenth Street, 13th and 4th avenue									
Gates Avenue, 13 Gates avenue									
Helping Hand, 188 Lawrence street									
Jewish Hospital (Brooklyn Hebrew) 70 Johnson av.									
Kings County, Clarkson street									
Long Island College Hospital Dispensary, Henry st									
Long Island Throat, 55 Willoughby street									
Lutheran, East New York avenue									
Memorial Women, 311 Bedford avenue									
Memorial Hospital Women, Clarence avenue									
Methodist, 6th street and 7th avenue									
Polhemus Memorial, Henry street									
St Catherine's, 260 Bushwick avenue									
Twenty-sixth Ward Homeopathic, 100 Bradford st									
Williamsburg, Bedford avenue									
Twenty-eight institutions									

A. Estimated by managers; no records kept or records incomplete.
B. Not in operation during that year.
C. Not in operation part of that year.
G. Revised by the managers.
H. Not doing dispensary work.

III. Licensed Dispensaries on September 30, 1901—Boroughs of the Bronx, Richmond and Queens.

	NUMBER OF DIFFERENT PERSONS TREATED AT THE DISPENSARY DURING THE YEAR ENDING SEPTEMBER 30.			NUMBER OF TREATMENTS AT THE DISPENSARY DURING THE YEAR ENDING SEPTEMBER 30.			TOTAL NUMBER OF PRESCRIPTIONS DISPENSED DURING THE YEAR ENDING SEPTEMBER 30.		
	1899.	1900.	1901.	1899.	1900.	1901.	1899.	1900.	1901.
Fordham, Bronx	2,308	2,994	3,164	6,908	5,113	7,147	7,112	7,114	8,167
Lebanon, Bronx	6,082	7,840	8,480	9,740	11,480	18,440	7,560	8,990	9,990
S. R. Smith, Richmond	A G 1,008	A 839	951	A 1,505	G 1,988	966	A 900	A 150	A G 180
Flushing, Queens	722	780	344	1,752	3,085	888	A 1,100	1,200	800
Four institutions	10,000	12,468	13,179	19,905	19,656	99,488	15,972	17,494	18,907

A. Estimated by managers; no records kept or records incomplete.
G. Revised by the manager.

IV. Dispensaries which had discontinued business prior to September 30, 1901.—New York city.

	NUMBER OF DIFFERENT PERSONS TREATED AT THE DISPENSARY DURING THE YEAR ENDING SEPTEMBER 30.			NUMBER OF TREATMENTS AT THE DISPENSARY DURING THE YEAR ENDING SEPTEMBER 30.			TOTAL NUMBER OF PRESCRIPTIONS DISPENSED DURING THE YEAR ENDING SEPTEMBER 30.		
	1899.	1900.	1901.	1899.	1900.	1901.	1899.	1900.	1901.
Abigail Free School, Manhattan	168			184			184		
Atlantic Avenue, Brooklyn	8,458			12,408			11,371		
Bethesda Sanitarium, Brooklyn	5,367	2,560			5,190				
Brooklyn Eclectic	6,002								
Brooklyn Homeopathic							6,275	5,149	
Bushwick, Brooklyn	4,006			10,181			13,500		
Central Hospital and Polyclinic, Brooklyn							4,383		
Columbus, Manhattan									
Hahnemann, Manhattan	3,892			1,157			1,068		
Homeopathic of Dutch Reformed Church, B'klyn	763								
Homeopathic Hospital Association, Brooklyn				787	904		785	904	
McDonough, Manhattan	588	152							
Manhattan Hospital, Brooklyn									
Montefiore Home, Manhattan									
Mothers and Babies, Manhattan	912	818		7,996	7,085		5,986	9,271	
New York Frauen Klinik, Manhattan	1,467	1,761	1,282	5,850	6,406	5,282	8,775		
North Brooklyn Eye							608	185	100
Norwegian Lutheran, Brooklyn	1,196								
Old Marion Street, Manhattan			210			608			
St. John's Hospital, Brooklyn	265	918		780	656		20	45	
St. Lazarus, Brooklyn	658			1,045			1,008		50
St. Mary's Free, Brooklyn	6,301			12,408			8,850		
St. Peter's, Brooklyn	1,318			1,446			1,580		
Southern Dispensary, Brooklyn	5,331	1,896		7,097	1,804		3,565	1,394	150
	46,090	6,795	1,449	60,587	21,325	5,734	67,900	16,181	150

V. Licensed Dispensaries on September 30, 1901 — Outside of New York city.

	TOTAL NUMBER OF PERSONS TREATED AT THE DISPENSARY DURING THE YEAR ENDING SEPTEMBER 30			TOTAL NUMBER OF TREATMENTS OR CONSULTATIONS AT THE DISPENSARY DURING THE YEAR ENDING SEPTEMBER 30			TOTAL NUMBER OF PRESCRIPTIONS DISPENSED DURING THE YEAR ENDING SEPTEMBER 30		
	1899	1900	1901	1899	1900	1901	1899	1900	1901
Albany City Free Disp. Association, Albany									
Albany City Homeopathic Hosp. Disp., Albany									
Albany Hospital Dispensary, Albany									
Buffalo Eye and Ear Infirmary, Buffalo									
Charity Eye, Ear and Throat Hosp. Disp., Buffalo									
City Mission Dispensary, Albany									
City Mission Branch Dispensary, Albany									
Cohoes Hosp. Ass'n Eye and Ear Dep't, Cohoes									
Emergency Hosp. of Sisters of Charity, Buffalo									
Fitch Accident Hospital Dispensary, Buffalo									
Fitch Providont Dispensary, Buffalo									
German Hosp. of City of Buffalo Free Disp., Buffalo									
Good Samaritan Dispensary, Yonkers									
Homeo. Hospital and Disp. Ass'n, Mt. Vernon									
Hospital Ass'n City of Schenectady, Schenectady									
Mt. Vernon Hospital Dispensary, Mt. Vernon									
Nassau Hospital Dispensary, Mineola									
N.York Hospital Dispensary, N.York									
Ossining Hospital Dispensary, Ossining									
Rochester City Hospital Dispensary, Rochester									
Rochester Homeo. Hosp. Free Disp., Rochester									
St. John's, Riverside Hospital Disp., Yonkers									
St. Joseph's Hospital Dispensary, Yonkers									
St. Peter's Hospital Dispensary, Albany									
Saratoga Hospital Dispensary, Troy									
Saratoga Free Dispensary, Saratoga Springs									
Syracuse Free Dispensary, Syracuse									
Troy Hospital Association Dispensary, Troy									
University of Buffalo Dispensary, Buffalo									
Utica Dispensary, Utica									
Total	26,361	24,685	24,677	118,045	105,241	129,040	74,777	72,588	72,949

A. Estimated by managers; no record kept or records incomplete.
B. Not in operation during that year.
C. Not in operation part of that year.
D. Revised by the managers.

Many of the figures given above have been verified, and in several instances they were carefully revised. Where the records were found incomplete the statistics presented have been closely estimated. The results have been generally satisfactory, and it is believed that the figures which now appear in the above tables represent very nearly the exact work accomplished by the dispensaries. It should also be observed that in the large tables, figures appear opposite the name of every institution except in the case of dispensaries which were not in operation. Thus the work has been made more valuable because it is complete.

On the whole, experience has shown that the figures given by the larger dispensaries are the most reliable, while at the small dispensaries, where only one or two doctors serve, the figures are less trustworthy. Almost without exception medical men seem to detest figures, and accurate records at the smaller dispensaries are the exception rather than the rule. There is still a lack of uniformity at the various dispensaries concerning statistical records which efforts should be made to improve.

COMPLIANCE WITH THE BOARD'S RULES.

In conclusion, it may be said that after the dispensary rules have been in operation two years and upwards it is found that they are being generally observed except in certain particulars indicated below. Perhaps the most important provision of the rules, and that which is yet not strictly complied with in many instances, is rule III., section c, which reads as follows:

" Every applicant, either personally or by the parent or guardian of such applicant, in regard to whose ability to pay for medical or surgical relief, advice or treatment, medicine or apparatus, or either, in whole or in part, the registrar is in doubt, shall be admitted to a first treatment on signing a card containing the 'representation' or statement of the applicant, but the registrar shall forthwith cause an investigation of his or her ability to pay either personally or by parent or guardian; the results of such investigation shall be filed among the permanent records of the dispensary. Any such applicant who declines to sign the required ' representation ' or statement shall be refused admission."

It will be observed that the above regulation calls for both an investigation of doubtful applicants and also requires that the results of such investigation shall be kept on file. In a majority of instances the investigation has consisted of simply questioning the applicant. Something more than this, however, is clearly contemplated by the rule. In certain parts of the State private organizations, such as the Charity Organization Societies in New York city and Buffalo and the Bureau of Charities in Brooklyn, have indicated a willingness to co-operate with the dispensaries by investigating doubtful cases referred to them. These offers have not, however, been taken advantage of by the managers of dispensaries as extensively as might have been the case.

A more general and frequent use of the representation cards with which the dispensaries have provided themselves is urged, together with a subsequent investigation relative to the ability to pay of all doubtful applicants who are admitted to a first treatment under the rule.

Rule VIII. requires that

"The managers of dispensaries shall comply with the ordinances and orders of the local board of health, and shall annually make a minute showing compliance therewith upon their official records on or before September 30th in each and every year."

This rule has evidently not been clearly understood by certain of the institutions concerned. Its intention and purpose is that the managers of dispensaries shall at least once a year indicate upon their official records that there are no ordinances and orders of the local board of health uncomplied with.

The following is a form of minute approved by the Board:

Minute of Compliance.

The following minute is made in compliance with rule VIII. of the rules and regulations governing licensed dispensaries in the State of New York, made pursuant to chapter 368, Laws of 1899, which rules were amended October 10, 1900:

New York, ..., 190

This is to certify that to the best of my knowledge and belief
the .... Dispensary has complied with all of
the ordinances and orders of the local board of health, and that
since September 30, 190 , no orders of the local board of health
have been issued against this institution which still remain
unsatisfied, or which are not now complied with fully.

(Signed) ....

(Title of official) ....

The " separation of the sexes in both waiting and treatment
rooms, except in cases of family groups, or of infants," as required by rule IX., is not always as faithfully observed as it
should be.

On the whole, however, the rules of the Board have
received respectful consideration and there has been manifest
an increasing co-operation between the Board and managers
of dispensaries,.including the physicians directly in charge, with
a view to remedying the abuses which the Dispensary Law is
designed to check. The annual reports printed by many of the
dispensaries take occasion to refer to the law and its results,
and serve to emphasize the wisdom and timeliness of the enactment of such a statute.

Respectfully submitted,

STEPHEN SMITH, M. D.,

Chairman.

REPORT

OF THE

Committee on Almshouses.

29

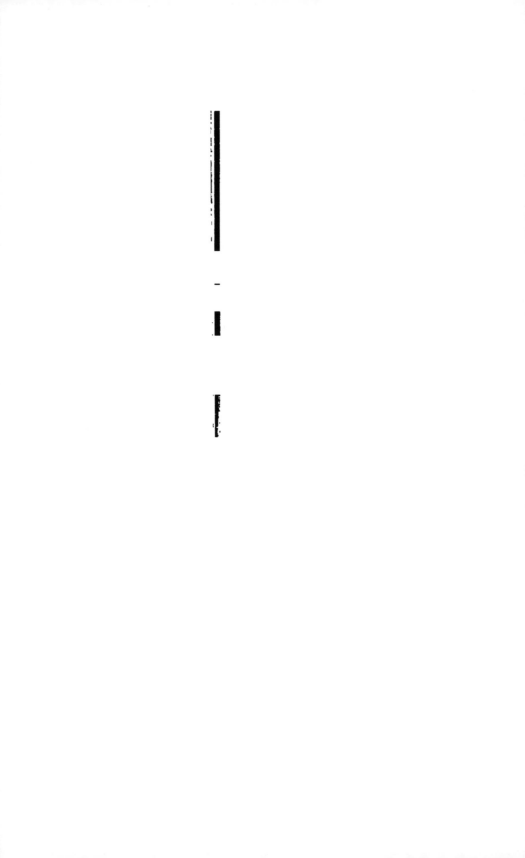

REPORT.

To the State Board of Charities:

Your committee on almshouses respectfully submits the following report upon the almshouses of the State:

The inspection of these institutions has been carefully made at regular intervals during the past year by the two inspectors of almshouses. Beside these inspections they have been visited by the commissioners in their several districts, and by the Superintendent of State and Alien Poor. These examinations have been frequent enough to enable this committee to keep in touch with the officials of the almshouses in the several counties, and to furnish full information as to the management of the buildings, grounds and equipments, the administration and discipline, as well as the physical and moral condition of the inmates.

A decided tendency toward improvement has been manifested, and the reports submitted during the past year are remarkable or the testimony they bear to this general trend. It is a matter f congratulation that our almshouse officials are imbued with he desire to improve the conditions which surround the dependnt poor of the State. That they have such a laudable desire r the welfare of those under their charge and for the improveent of the buildings is an indication to your committee that e people appreciate the necessity for an intelligent and humane administration of public charity.

THE DIFFUSION OF KNOWLEDGE.

There can be no doubt of the fact that the almshouses of the ite have greatly improved within the last few years. That ch of this improvement is due to frequent inspection will not be questioned, but beside this stimulus, the influence of greater and more general knowledge of sociological problems must be recognized. The wider the spread of knowledge, the more intelligent the administration of public trusts.

Abuses in almshouses cannot withstand the light of publicity. The people of the State desire that public charity shall be administered in accordance with the dictates of humanity, and the authorities who have the almshouses in charge recognize this desire and seek to have the methods of to-day accord with the principles of kindliness, sanitation and economy.

ECONOMY.

Early in the nineteenth century the last of these three administrative principles was considered as first in importance; to-day it has taken the third place because the people have been educated to a general acceptance of the doctrine that charity is first of all humane. It is true, economy is essential to successful administration. The taxpayers who bear the public burdens deserve and must receive consideration, but they do not desire to be relieved of the care of dependents properly chargeable to them in order to decrease the tax rate, nor is there need, under present conditions, to curtail the reasonable expenses of the almshouses. The cost of maintaining a county almshouse adds very little to the sum which must be raised by taxation in the county. It cannot be denied that an almshouse administration should be as economical as is consistent with proper care of the poor. There is no need of unduly elaborate buildings, nor should waste of any sort be permitted. The end aimed at should be a maximum of comfort at a minimum of cost.

Fortunately for the dependent poor, an intelligent interest on the part of boards of supervisors makes ample provision to meet this requirement. Some of the almshouses are true homes in their provision for the care of inmates, and from one end of the State to the other the public insists that the unfortunate, the aged, the sick, the defectives, sheltered in almshouses shall receive a full measure of humane and considerate attention.

SANITATION.

The inspections during the year show that in almshouses of
the State greater attention is paid to the essentials of sanitation
than ever before. Pure air, pure water, proper drainage and
sewage disposal, are matters which concern not only the comfort but the very life of the inmates of public institutions.

Ninety per cent. of those who are cared for in almshouses are
infirm, and consequently have little vitality to withstand the
inroads of disease. For this reason the sanitary conditions
must be far above those which prevail in the dwellings of the
poor. The association of so many people of weakened constitution makes it essential that all things which promote disease
be removed as quickly as possible.

Ventilation of a proper character is difficult to secure where
the flues, windows and transoms through which fresh air must
come are within the control of inmates. In their weakened
condition they fear the cold, and prefer to breathe impure air
over and over again rather than permit the opening of a door
or window. Ventilation should therefore be automatic, or at
least entirely within the control of attendants. In some
of our almshouses systems of ventilation have been introduced
similar to those which are used in the best modern hospitals.
By these systems the pure air is warmed before it is distributed,
and the arrangements for the change of air in the dormitories
or rooms is such that it is accomplished at short intervals. It
will be to the advantage of other almshouses when similar
systems are introduced into them.

Few of these institutions now retain the distinctive institu-
ional odor. Cleanliness and ventilation have combined to
estroy it. When every almshouse is properly ventilated, this
isagreeable odor will be a thing of the past.

The sanitary conveniences of the institutions are also greatly
nproved. In most of the almshouses the betterment of the
ater supply has enabled the authorities to introduce flush
ater closets. The plumbing in the lavatories and the general
rangements for drainage have removed a great menace to the

health of the almshouse inmates. A problem still remains for many almshouses in the method of disposal of the wastes. Several have erected furnaces for their destruction by fire. It is not possible for all almshouses to build these furnaces, and the compost heap is not always a good disposal. Where there is proper sewerage the problem is generally an easier one; in other cases more complicated. Fortunately, especially in the rural almshouses, the farm provides a quick and profitable place to utilize all these things, and by this disposal of wastes the farm itself is enriched. It is a sign of improvement that questions of sewage and waste disposal receive such consideration as they do.

CARE OF THE SICK.

In several counties of the State the care of the indigent sick has received greater attention than ever heretofore. Perhaps the general dissemination of knowledge as to certain forms of contagious diseases and the enforcement of the health laws have had much to do with awakening the interest of the people. Certain it is that the condition of the sick inmates of public institutions has been a matter of anxious thought, and county boards of supervisors, as well as the officials of almshouses, have planned better care than has heretofore been possible.

Many counties have erected separate hospitals for the sick inmates of almshouses, and others are making arrangements to do the same. A commendable instance of this interest is the completion of the fine hospital connected with the Onondaga county almshouse. The building committee of the board of supervisors of this county has worked intelligently and zealously to better conditions which had become intolerable. As a consequence of these efforts a fine large building has been erected for the sick; the entire almshouse has been put into repair, and the general conditions so improved that the result may be called a renovation. Smaller counties have made similar improvements, and, with few exceptions, the condition of the sick inmates is better than ever before.

In some almshouses, like that in Monroe county, the board of supervisors has failed to make proper provision for the sick. They are crowded together, under most uncomfortable and unsanitary conditions, in dormitories where the minimum of six hundred cubic feet of air for each inmate is not possible, and are compelled to linger in pain because the supervisors have failed to agree upon a new location for the almshouse.

RECORDS.

For many years the present method of keeping records seems to have prevailed throughout the State. The law requires that almshouses shall make full record of the antecedents, history and condition of all persons admitted. Transcripts of such records are forwarded to the State Board of Charities. An examination of the record books in the several almshouses shows that, with few exceptions, it is almost impossible to obtain the information called for by the law. The difficulty lies with the primary committing officer. When an indigent person applies to an overseer of the poor for relief, all of the facts required by the law could and should be obtained by such overseer. When a poor person is removed from the locality wherein he has resided for a longer or shorter time, the difficulty of obtaining the information is greatly increased, and it is no wonder that almshouse records are often merely skeletons. If the information desired were combined with the commitment now in use it would be possible to have better records. Some of the almshouses have satisfactory systems, but all should be able to make records of statistical value.

Especially is there a lack in the matter of records concerning the sick. Usually the sick inmate is examined by the attending physician and prescribed for, but no record is made. Each almshouse should have a regular form for use in connection with a hospital or sick ward, and this form ought to embody all those things which will make the record a true history of the case.

ABLE-BODIED PAUPERS.

The almshouse is intended for those who are unable to care for themselves by their own efforts. Modern society has developed a class of able-bodied persons who are determined to live without work. Many of this class are criminals by profession; others remain within the law and obtain their livelihood by practices which, while legal, are morally wrong. Still others fasten themselves upon charity, and in our almshouses are numbers of this class who have there settled down to live without work, at public expense.

What to do with the able-bodied pauper is a grave problem. How to know him even is sometimes a matter of difficulty, for every able-bodied pauper will complain that he is afflicted with all the diseases known to the medical profession. Something should be done of a "work-test" character to rid the almshouses of able-bodied paupers who can earn their own living.

POLICE JUSTICES.

One of the difficulties in decreasing the number of able-bodied paupers in our almshouses is due to the seeming unwillingness of committing officers to exercise the right conferred by law. Vagrants taken before police justices are sent to the almshouse, when in ninety-nine cases out of every hundred they should be sent to the penitentiary. Your committee believes in the exercise of charity toward the unfortunate, and would go as far as any in relieving distress, but it does not believe that society should permit itself to be imposed upon by the vagrant and disorderly characters of both sexes for whom some justices of the peace have such tender consideration.

It is unjust to the worthy poor that such persons are placed in an almshouse. They subvert discipline, promote immorality, are quarrelsome and impose upon those whom the law had in contemplation when it made provision for a public almshouse.

The last Legislature passed a bill through both houses which was intended to correct this evil. The Governor withheld his approval, and it died in his hands after the Legislature adjourned. It is hoped that further consideration of the necessities of the case will secure such legislation as may in a large measure cure this evil. To this end the definition of vagrancy as embodied in the code should be enlarged so as to make it equivalent to tramping, and a crime punishable by hard labor for an indeterminate period of not less than six months. The law at present provides for the commitment of "tramps" to prison; it should do the same for able-bodied vagrants of sound mind. This should not be left to the discretion of police justices, for discretionary power may nullify the law.

In every county jail and penitentiary this vagrant and tramp class could be profitably employed in breaking stone for the highways, and if the daily task were sufficient to tax the strength and tire the arms, one term of six months would be enough for very many of the vagrants. They would either go to work on their discharge and thus earn their own living, or else leave the State. In either case the public would be relieved of their support. In order to save the taxpayer and the hard-working citizen from imposition, it is hoped that legislation of this character will be enacted without delay.

CIVIL SERVICE.

The administration of the Civil Service Law has not hitherto covered county almshouses. It is hoped that the constitutional provision will be extended, through legislative enactment, so as to cover the employes in this class of public institutions. The beneficent provision which insures tenure of office to the competent has a tendency to improve the service. Men and women feel that there is much to work for, and with the assurance of continued employment exert themselves to improve the condition of the institutions in which they serve.

In one way the people of several counties are recognizing the principle of civil service. They continue capable officials in office term after term. Some county superintendents have been in service for twenty years or more, many for a shorter period, and few for only a single term. This popular approval of faithfulness is sometimes overridden by the supposed needs of political parties. If it were possible to assure superintendents and others charged with the administration of the poor laws of a long period of service regardless of changes of political control, there can be no doubt the almshouses of the State would be greatly benefited. In the same way, if the minor officials connected with these institutions, the keepers and matrons, could have an assurance of permanency during efficiency and faithfulness, much more might be expected from them than at present.

Our whole system of supervising and administering public charity should be beyond the control of partisans, and be safeguarded by the strongest application of the laws governing the civil service. This would secure the retention in office of competent and deserving men and women whose work deserves the highest commendation.

THE DEFECTIVE CLASS.

The intention of the State as expressed in its laws is to relieve the several counties of the support of all indigent members of the defective class. For this purpose it has established asylums, schools, hospitals and colonies in which, classified according to disability, the defectives may be gathered and receive humane, scientific and curative treatment.

As a general thing these defectives are very difficult to manage when inmates of almshouses. The idiots and the feeble-minded are subject to abuse from other inmates, and in turn are prone to mischief, often immoral, and, because of their lack of mental power, generally filthy and destructive. The epileptics, owing to the peculiar character of their disease, the suddenness of the seizures and the dangers attendant thereon, are most unfortunate when their only refuge is the ordinary almshouse.

All of these people require scientific treatment, and the State institutions which have been established for their reception ought to be enlarged so as to make provision for all dependents of this class in the State. The moral danger connected with the care of the feeble-minded and idiots requires that for their own sake and for the future welfare of the State they be closely guarded in custodial institutions. The increase in the number of idiots and feeble-minded persons is largely due to the liberty which has been accorded this class of unfortunates in the past. The females are liable to abuse when away from the oversight of friends, and oftentimes even their own families are negligent of this duty. Every idiot and all male persons of feeble mind, incapable of self-protection, should be maintained in a custodial asylum during life; and all females of feeble mind be kept in a similar asylum during the child-bearing period.

EPILEPTICS.

The facilities for the care of this class of dependents are taxed to the utmost in Craig Colony, and as a consequence large numbers of epileptics are compelled to find refuge in the almshouses of the State. The resources of the almshouses, the character of the attendants, and the nature of the disease from which these persons suffer are such that almshouses are altogether unfitted for them. ."That terrible form of insanity which precedes, is coincident with, or follows an epileptic convulsion", known as "epileptic mania", is a form of disease most dangerous in an almshouse. The violent character of its victims, their destructiveness and irritability, require restraint and control which can only be provided in an institution especially equipped for the treatment of epilepsy.

For this reason the enlargement of Craig Colony should be pushed as rapidly as possible. The almshouses of the State must be freed from all those who are not proper inmates, and the process of classification continue until the almshouse assumes its true form of a home for the aged dependents who may find therein an expression of the sympathy and charity of society.

CHILDREN.

The law which prohibits the commitment, to the almshouses of the State, of children between the ages of two and sixteen years has been generally complied with. There are few instances where children of the prohibited age have been maintained for any length of time in an almshouse. It happens sometimes that a child is temporarily kept in an almshouse because of difficulty in arranging for its future. Instances of this character are infrequent, and the reports during the year show a purpose on the part of superintendents to comply with the spirit and letter of the law. The only instances which indicate an evasion of the spirit of the law is where it has been necessary to make provision for idiotic children or those suffering from some disease.

In one instance a county superintendent has maintained a child in an almshouse for several years contrary to law, and for no apparent reason other than that it would cost the county a considerable sum to maintain the child in a hospital where he would receive proper treatment. In another county an idiot child of seven years is maintained at the present time. In neither of these instances is there good excuse for the retention of the children. The first instance has deprived the child of all hope of recovery. Had he been taken in time it is possible he might have been helped, but associated for several years with the inmates of the county almshouse, dependent to a large measure upon their attention, he has reached a condition where it is impossible now to give him any permanent relief.

HOMES FOR CHILDREN.

The county superintendents of the poor have generally taken a decided interest in securing homes for such children as become county charges. In some counties placing-out agents are employed; in others the superintendent makes all arrangements. An instance of commendable work in this direction is shown by a recent letter from Mr. Alberti D. Smith, Superintendent of the Poor of Essex county, who reports that during the year 1900 he placed in homes, for adoption, eight children who had been committed as county charges, and for the year 1901, fifteen children, making a total of twenty-three, of whom twenty-two were placed in homes without any expense to the county beyond the cost of transportation. The saving to this county by the work of Superintendent Smith in thus finding homes for these children amounts to $30.50 per week, or $1,586 per year.

If the retention of children in almshouses contrary to law deserves rebuke, work of this character deserves commendation.

PASSING ON PAUPERS.

The officials of each county are anxious to lessen the cost of maintaining public dependents as much as possible. Sometimes this anxiety leads to illegal methods. Those who are properly chargeable to a particular town or county are "passed on" to some other town or county. They are furnished transportation, told to apply to another officer, and thus sent from place to place. This adds to the difficulty of almshouse administration by making it necessary to return persons of this character to their proper residential localities. They usually proceed at once to the almshouse, and, although they may be returned to their homes in due time, pending removal are a source of annoyance.

Section 50 of chapter 225 of the Laws of 1896, makes this practice a misdemeanor punishable by a fine of $50, and it would be well if some of the parties who violate the statute were punished.

DIET.

The diet for the inmates of almshouses involves a serious problem. In spite of the fact that almshouse inmates are usually of enfeebled vitality, they insist upon the most substantial forms of food. The food is not only of substantial character, but they insist that it shall be furnished in large quantities. Their mental condition is such that they do not appreciate the folly of over-feeding. As a consequence, owing to the character of the food supplied, there is more or less suffering from indigestion and allied troubles.

Some of the institutions, to lessen the labor connected with the preparation of food, prepare only two meals each day, the breakfast usually about eight o'clock in the morning, and the dinner about three oclock in the afternoon. The result of this is that the inmates, knowing they will receive no food after three o'clock, eat as much as they possibly can at the afternoon meal and suffer in consequence all night.

It would be well if the county authorities could be induced to adopt a standard of diet which, while ample in quantity, would be better adapted to the real needs of the inmates of the alms-houses than that which at present obtains. It would be eco-nomical, healthful, diversified, and, in the end, more nourishing and useful.

In one almshouse, in the month of December, for the third meal of the day, the bill of fare included corned beef, mashed turnips and potatoes, bread, butter, tea, sugar and milk. For the other two meals equally hearty food was provided. As most of the persons who partook of this food were in the neighbor-hood of seventy years of age, did no work, and went to bed immediately, it is apparent the diet was not suited to actual needs. All over-feeding is waste. While inmates ought to have enough, it should be of the right kind and not in wasteful quantity.

One other defect in the matter of diet is its monotonous character. There are almshouses which supply the same fare practically throughout the year. All breakfasts are alike, all suppers contain the same things, the only variety being in the principal article of the noonday meal and changes in vegetables due to the season. The fare ought to be as diversified as is con-sistent with health, economy and the needs of the inmates. The cost will be no greater than at present, and in a short time the inmates will prefer lighter forms of food than those now in use.

PROTECTION.

Owing to the infirm character of the inmates of the almshouse, its protection from the dangers of fire is of prime importance. Most of our almshouses are equipped with fire-escapes; all of them have some form of chemical extinguishers or other fire fighting devices, and except in a few instances the buildings may be said to be fairly equipped to meet an emergency.

One of the problems in effectively providing for the safety of the inmates in case of fire is due to the difficulty experienced by infirm people in descending fire-escapes; consequently the form of escape adopted should be suitable for all the classes of people usually found in the almshouse. Ladders will do for the young and athletic, but are unsuitable for the higher stories of an almshouse where inmates must depend upon their own efforts for escape to the ground. The iron stairways attached to some of the almshouses are almost as unsuitable as the ladders. The form most serviceable is the tubular, in which inmates can slide from the upper entrance to the ground without danger to themselves or interference with the escape of others. This form may be a little more costly than outside stairways and ladders, but it is the safe fire-escape. The fire-escapes on these institutions should be planned for a helpless and infirm population. It will be better to pay a greater price for a perfect fire escape to assure safety, than to put up a set of scaling ladders because they cost little, and through them endanger the lives of the inmates of the institution.

WATER.

During the past year most of the almshouses have paid particular attention to the water supply. The drought which prevailed during the preceding season had shown the reliance which could be placed upon the provisions made for the institutions, and, where it was found deficient, steps in most instances were taken to remedy the defect. As the health and safety of the inmates depend upon an abundant supply of water, too much stress cannot be laid upon this necessity.

Where the present water supply is not of the best character it should be improved, and where experience has proven the possibility of failure in an emergency, steps should be taken to add to the capacity of wells and reservoirs so as to insure a sufficiency for every need.

IN GENERAL.

It may be said in conclusion that the present condition of the almshouses of the State is exceedingly gratifying. This is mainly due to the officials who are in charge. They are as a body, zealous in their work, have the welfare of the inmates at heart, and are desirous to have their administration merit the approval of the State Board of Charities. The improved conditions due to their administration gives promise of further advance in the almshouses of the State, and an ultimate condition which will be a source of pride to all who are connected with the administration of public charity.

Respectfully submitted,

NEWTON ALDRICH,
PETER WALRATH,
Committee on Almshouses.

REPORT

OF

Visitation of Public Hospitals and Almshouses

IN THE

FIRST JUDICIAL DISTRICT.

30

As an introduction to this report it is proper to say that all the public hospitals and almshouses in the First Judicial District have been visited during the year by the President of the State Board of Charities, Hon. William R. Stewart, as Commissioner of the First Judicial District; and, further, that he directed the inspection of these institutions by Dr. Robert W. Hill, Inspector of Almshouses, and requested the Inspector to write the report upon these public hospitals and almshouses which follows, and that the same has been submitted to him. read and approved.

IN GENERAL.

The public hospitals and almshouses of the First Judicial District, which comprises the boroughs of Manhattan and the Bronx, may be said to have remained in statu quo since the last report. The several hospitals and almshouses, the Department of Outdoor Poor, the pavilions for the insane and idiots, and the schools for feeble-minded children have been inspected at frequent intervals so that their operations might be thoroughly studied before the preparation of this report.

With one or two exceptions little except minor repair has been done in the way of extension or improvement during the past year. The exceptions are the Metropolitan Hospital and the Asylums and Schools for Feeble-Minded Children on Randall's Island. To both of these institutions additions in the way of buildings have been made, so that accommodations are increased and preparations made for even better work than in the past.

The great struggle for political supremacy which has occupied the attention of the people of the city of New York has been felt to a greater or less degree in provision for the maintenance of the public institutions. The desire to go before the people with a record for economical management has prevented the appropriation of sufficient funds to carry out the betterments absolutely necessary for the welfare of the public dependents.

At the time of last inspection, in the closing days of December, 1901, in most of the institutions the shelves were found swept bare of supplies. Many things which should have been done long before election time had been postponed awaiting the result of the ballot at the polls. As a consequence of this desire to make an appeal to the people on the ground of an economical administration, the institutions have been crippled where they most needed assistance.

The total amount available for supplies was $825,623.97, which was only reached by a transfer of a large sum from the fund appropriated for alterations, additions and repairs. This transfer stopped much necessary work and reduced an already depleted fund to a point where nothing of importance could be undertaken. Of the net decrease of $64,206.76 in the appropriation for the Department of Charities, as compared with the preceding year, $63,500 were taken from the estimate for alterations, additions and repairs, which, as before stated, was further reduced by a necessary transfer to eke out the supply fund. With an average population in the institutions of about 7,500 to be provided for, the appropriation made the annual per capita cost for supplies about $107.

In spite of this apparent desire for economy, where economies could have been well made (that is, in the employment of assistants), none were practised. Heretofore in these institutions election times have witnessed large additions to the roll of employes. The last campaign was an exception to this rule, and although no additions were made to the roster of attendants, many incompetents and inefficients were retained in the city service, to the detriment of the institutions which thus were compelled to carry an unnecessary burden.

The total amount appropriated for the support of the Department was $1,413,033.21, and, with the estimated average population of 7,500 to be maintained, the annual per capita cost was $188. As $459,316 was paid for salaries and wages, the annual per capita cost for this purpose alone was $61.24. On the first of October, 1901, the total number of employes was 1,928, and it can easily be believed that many of this number were worse than useless to the Department service, and will have to be dismissed by the new administration as soon as possible.

The outgoing administration accomplished one good thing in its last months of service. It made the necessary appropriation for the building of the Harlem Hospital, and during the coming

year, doubtless, that structure will be erected and new conditions prevail where they have been so sadly needed for many
years.

This affords an opportunity to secure a properly planned hos
pital for the city. Heretofore public buildings of this character
have not represented the best ideas in the arrangement of wards,
work and service rooms, quarters for help, ventilation and sanitary equipment. The new administration can have, if it will,
the benefit of special study of hospital problems, and in these
buildings introduce an arrangement of the several departments
of service which will make the new Harlem Hospital a model
institution. This may be done within the appropriation of
$275,000.

The general approval which the public has accorded to the
proposal for a new Bellevue Hospital, an approval voiced unanimously by the press of New York city, gives assurance that in
time the city of New York will add to its general receiving hospitals an edifice in every way worthy of the greatest city of
the western continent, an institution equipped with all that
modern science can provide for the alleviation of sickness, and
so managed as to reflect credit upon the business ability and
humane spirit of the administration.

The more frequent the inspection of this institution the more
forcibly is it borne in upon the mind that nothing other than a
new hospital can meet the demands of the city. Although the
basements have been largely cleared of occupants, the cellars
remain damp and wet, the walls are in a state of dilapidation,
the floors are more or less worn, and the various dark rooms,
diet kitchens, air shafts and closets continue breeding places
for the germs of disease. A new hospital on a larger area, preferably to the north so as to abate the nuisance now maintained
by the electric light and power company, whose smokestacks
belch torrents of smoke and gas which pour into the windows
of the hospital wards, will give opportunity for a properly
planned hospital of the most modern type.

In his annual estimate of necessary appropriations to the
Board of Estimate and Apportionment, Commissioner Keller

presented an item of $2,000,000 for a new hospital, but, probably owing to the fact that in a short time there was to be a change in the administration of city affairs, this item was not embodied in the final appropriation. It therefore remains for the new administration to do what the old failed to do, and make provision for Bellevue commensurate with the importance of the work to be done therein.

The new board of trustees which is to be vested with the management of Bellevue and its allied hospitals is composed of the Commissioner of Charities (ex officio) Homer Folks and the following appointees of the mayor:

Dr. John W. Brannan, James K. Paulding, Howard Townsend, Theodore E. Teck, Martin Stine, Samuel Sachs, Myles Tierney.

Of these Dr. Brannan has been chosen president and Mr. Paulding secretary of the board.

In making the appointment the mayor addressed these gentlemen as follows:

"Under the revised charter, on February 1, 1902, the jurisdiction of the Department of Public Charities ceases over Bellevue Hospital and over the Fordham, Harlem, Gouverneur and Emergency hospitals. These five hospitals thereafter are to be committed to your care as the Board of Trustees of Bellevue and allied hospitals.

"The charter made it my duty to call upon the United Hebrew Charities of the City of New York, the Particular Council in New York of the Society of St. Vincent de Paul and the New York Association for Improving the Condition of the Poor to present to me a list of not less than twice the number of persons to be appointed. I have not been constrained by the charter to make these appointments from this list, but I have been glad to do so, first, because I believe you are all well equipped for the sacred trust to be committed to your care, and, second, because in making my selections from this list I hope to secure for you, in the management of the hospitals, the potent support of the great and strong societies that have placed you in nomination.

"The removing of these hospitals from the jurisdiction of the Department of Public Charities and their committal to the care of a separate board of trustees is another of the new departures of the revised charter. The purpose of it undoubtedly is to remove the administration of these hospitals, as far as possible, from the baleful influence of politics in the baser sense of that word. But it is not in any sense to be interpreted as indicating that the city's interest in the management of these hospitals is to be lessened. On the contrary, the change itself is intended to be significant of the fact that the city's sense of responsibility for the care that it gives to its own sick and wounded has grown, and that it will hold you and your successors to a strict account for the manner in which you discharge your trust. The city in its corporate capacity stands for all that is strong and powerful. It is the glory of the strong to be gentle, to be pitiful, to be tender with the weak and the helpless.

"In conferring these appointments upon you I ask you to remember that the city commits to your keeping its own good name as toward its sick and injured poor."

The two points emphasized in this address are, first, the purpose to relieve these hospitals of the political incubus which has hindered their proper work, and, second, the expression of the duty of the city toward the sick poor. The good name of the city requires ample and proper hospital facilities, and the new board of trustees must, therefore, labor for a new Bellevue.

TWENTY-SIXTH STREET DOCK.

Some painting and minor repairs were made to the buildings on the charity dock during the past year. A part of the building which forms the gateway was fitted up for a waiting room. Passengers intending to visit the island hospitals or almshouses are now kept separated from those making application for admission to institutions or applying for other relief.

One portion of this building, however, is set apart for the temporary shelter of prisoners to be transferred to the penitentiary or the workhouse. The Department of Corrections jointly with the Department of Charities has the use of the dock and, in consequence, the criminals are brought more or less into contact with the sick poor and other dependent wards of the city. To this dock must go women and children seeking assistance from the Bureau of Outdoor Poor, and other persons having business at the hospitals or with the department, and for their sake the use of this dock by the Corrections Department should be given up. The fact that many paupers have at some time been under the charge of the Corrections Department is no reason why the burdens of poverty should be made heavier by enforced association with criminals. Such association is enforced when the two departments use the same dock and when the landings are made at the same places on the island. It would be advisable for each department to have its own dock and its own service, as well as separate landing places on the island. This would keep the Charities apart from the Corrections, and have a tendency to improve the moral atmosphere.

In the main building at the end of the wharf, occupied by the administrative offices of the department, no changes were made during the year. It has room enough for the service and does very well for an administration building, and until such time as one more centrally located shall be established this, must serve the purpose. The enlargement of the department, through consolidation of the heretofore separate boroughs departments, will require greater space than this building affords. In the matter of work of the Outdoor Poor Department it is possible to make a number of improvements and thereby secure some classification of applicants for relief. The present method of receiving nearly all applicants in one large room is productive of harm. The children were sent out of this room more than two years ago, but men and women must assemble there for examination of their cases by the Superintendent of Outdoor Poor. The women receiving a weekly allowance of alimony are compelled to push their way through crowds of men in order to get to the desks where payment is made, and the fact that they are on such business too often subjects them to remark. If nothing else were done, the room might be divided into three parts, with separate entrances, one of which could be devoted to women, the central portion to administration, and the other part to the reception of men who have business with the bureau.

In connection with the Outdoor Poor Department, the steamer service is worthy of note. The principal boat is the "Brennan," which, with the "Fidelity" and one or two small boats, makes all the transfers between the city and the island. The "Brennan" is the largest but is often out of repair, and is also much more difficult to maintain and handle than any of the smaller boats.

The landings at the island have not room enough for two boats at one time, which is the frequent cause of delay. If the Corrections Department boats all landed on the east side of the island and all supplies intended for the workhouse or penitentiary were sent to that side, leaving the west side landings for the hospital boats, delays would be avoided and these landings be freed from the presence of convicts.

Complaint has been made that the arrangement of pilot service is made to work injustice to some of the men employed. It is said that certain of the pilots have comparatively short daily hours and neither night nor Sunday duties, while others are compelled to work at night and also almost every Sunday. A service of this kind could be easily classified, so that pilots doing similar work would receive the same wages and have by rotation the same hours and the same duties.

One matter heretofore spoken of is the necessity for a steam launch from the foot of One Hundred and Twentieth street to Randall's Island. The open rowboat now in use is not adequate, nor is it right to put women and children into a boat of this character, especially in stormy or winter weather. A small steam launch should be placed in service; one which would be ample for the needs could be purchased for a comparatively small sum.

BELLEVUE HOSPITAL.

(Foot of East Twenty-sixth Street, New York City.)

Dr. GEORGE TAYLOR STEWART, *Superintendent.*

Last inspection December 20, 1901.

With the exception of a new crematory built during the year, and some minor improvements, Bellevue Hospital remains substantially in the condition reported one year ago. The wards and halls have been painted, the water towers and pavilions repaired, and a new operating room completed and fully equipped. These are all important, but make little change in the appearance of the buildings.

In the matter of management the year has witnessed many changes, owing to the discovery of abuses in the treatment of patients sent to the pavilion for the insane. The several departments of the hospital were investigated by the commissioner, and many removals and transfers followed. The former superintendent was transferred to Metropolitan Hospital, and the present superintendent, who had for years been in charge of that institution, was assigned to duty as the head of Bellevue and the hospitals associated with it.

The staff of male nurses, mostly pupils of the Mills' Training School, was changed greatly by resignation and the admission of new students. A resident physician is now in charge of the pavilion for the insane, and graduate nurses instead of pupils are assigned to duty there. From the general force of employes there were many discharges. Inefficients were weeded out to some extent, and those addicted to intoxication discharged. A new set of rules was adopted for the government of the hospital, and the hearty co-operation of the medical board promised the commissioner. Since the time when these changes were made, the hospital has continued its general work as heretofore. A careful observation has shown that the new rules are not in effect; in fact, the only copy in existence is that originally drawn, and so far as the new rules or even the older rules are concerned, the medical staff and employes of the hospital are unacquainted with their provisions. As there were 570 emplóyes in the hospital on the first of October, which number has not been diminished, it is essential that these general regulations should be in an accessible form for the instruction and guidance of this large corps of employes.

At the present time, as in the past, these men and women follow precedent, having no other guide. As a consequence some of the things which investigation showed to be detrimental to the welfare of the hospital have continued without change in spite of the adoption of a new code of rules. The members of the medical staff, both visiting and resident, are supposed to be governed by these rules, and it would be advisable therefore to have them printed in such form that each member of the staff may have a copy.

GROUNDS.

The grounds of the hospital are kept in good condition. Since the walks and driveways were laid out and covered with asphalt, the grounds have presented an attractive appearance and been free of the former annoyances—mud and dust. The sidewalks on the streets bordering the hospital grounds are not in good repair. This is especially noticeable in rainy weather when water collects in pools, to the great discomfort of all pedestrians, and the serious jeopardy of thinly shod women and children necessarily compelled to use these sidewalks. The sidewalks fronting the hospital grounds on Twenty-sixth street is the main thoroughfare to the Department of Outdoor Poor on the wharf and to the department boats, and consequently should be kept in good condition as a protection to the health of the poor compelled to use this street.

BUILDINGS.

With the exception of the changes indicated above, and the construction of a rear entrance to the phthisis pavilion, the buildings remain as heretofore, and all that has been said suggesting a new hospital gathers force by the lapse of time. The building used formerly by Cornell College, one portion of the lower part of which is devoted to dispensary purposes, was arranged for the accommodation of some of the female help, but as funds were not available the alterations which had been planned were not accomplished and the upper portion remains unoccupied and unfit for service. Something should be done with this building. It stands apart from the general group so that it can be made available for a dormitory, and, pending all other changes in the hospital, this building should be renovated and put into this service. The dispensary, which occupies a portion of the ground floor, needs many improvements, and the entire upper portion of the college ought to be rearranged for the emergency maternity service now carried on in the small and ill appointed Emergency Hospital further up the street.

The crematory has been doing good service since its construction. Something of the kind was greatly needed. It affords a means for the destruction of much dangerous material that heretofore has passed out of the hospital and been lost sight of. Now everything of this character is destroyed in the crematory. The fire burns day and night, and there are no accumulations of rubbish permitted.

THE LAUNDRY.

The laundry requires enlargement. It is unfortunate for Bellevue Hospital that there is not sufficient space for a laundry large enough to do easily the amount of work which has to be done there. The inclosure does not permit of open air drying, and the only way in which there can be exposure of the washings to the open air is to add another story to the laundry building and arrange for roof drying. The objection to this plan, under present conditions, is that clothing exposed in the open air is immediately soiled. The Electric Light and Power Company consumes soft coal in its plant, which bounds the hospital on the north. The wind wafts the dense smoke from this plant over the hospital grounds, and clothing exposed for a short time must be returned to the wash wheels. As has been suggested heretofore, if new ground be purchased for the extension of the hospital, the laundry can be removed from its

present place and relocated to advantage. Pending any extension of the grounds, as the present laundry building is inadequate for all the work which must be done, it should be enlarged
and its equipment be increased.

INEFFICIENT HELP.

At a late inspection the deputy superintendent of the hospital
was found in his shirt sleeves directing the laudry work. The
same thing had happened on a number of previous visits. Inquiry developed the fact that the employes are not competent
to get the work done properly and promptly when left to themselves. Every little while affairs in the laundry are tangled up,
and the deputy superintendent is compelled to give his whole
attention for a time to this part of the hospital work. The
remedy is the employment of competent help to do the work in
the laundry. Surely the deputy superintendent of so great a
hospital as Bellevue ought to have duties of more importance
than supervision of the men and women engaged in washing.
The wages paid should be sufficient to secure the services of
good men and women for this work. It is false economy to
have this important department stalled from time to time because the wages paid are insufficient to attract a competent and
faithful class of help.

PAVILIONS.

Heretofore it has been the practice to send patients suffering
from alcoholism to a pavilion arranged with a large number of
small rooms, each of which was intended to accommodate a
single patient. Many serious accidents have happened in these
rooms, and it was suggested that the open ward was preferable,
for in the open ward all the movements of the patients would
be under the constant observation of the nurses. In the small
cells or rooms patients might endanger their lives without it
being known until too late, but in the open ward immediate help
could be given to any patient requiring assistance, for the nurse
or another patient would be sure to see the necessity for relief.
Consequently during the year the male patients suffering from

alcoholism were transferred and now occupy the lower portion of the pavilion intended for tuberculosis patients, the latter retaining only the upper floor. Since the use of this pavilion there have been no accidents of a serious nature in connection with the alcoholics.

THE PAVILION FOR THE INSANE.

The insanity pavilion, constructed on the plan of the one formerly used by the inebriates, has witnessed a number of serious accidents since the Hilliard case of November, 1900, and the question has been raised whether many of these accidents are not due to the fact that the patients are frequently shut off from observation while in a condition of restraint. The last accident of a serious character, it was claimed, occurred while the patient was in restraint, and the evidence indicated that he had been left to himself for too long a time. To this pavilion 1,340 male and 1,169 female patients were committed during the year.

HARSHNESS.

It was stated last year that male nurses were frequently inclined to harsh methods in their treatment of patients in the insane and inebriate wards. Trained nurses are now employed for this service, but even trained nurses sometimes forget their duty toward patients. Constant watchfulness on the part of the physicians in charge can alone prevent abuse. During the year, nurses in the insanity pavilion have been changed a number of times, and always the change has been made because serious allegations of abuses were preferred against them.

The relatives who make calls upon the patients should be received with the greatest kindness by the attendants, and whatever can be done to relieve their anxiety and distress should be done. Complaint has been made that they have not received due consideration, but frequently have been brusquely dismissed by nurses and other attendants.

The presence of Dr. Schultz, the medical inspector of the department, has been beneficial to this pavilion during the past year. Many of the patients and their friends can speak English imperfectly only, and Dr. Schultz has therefore been of assistance to the examiners and a comfort to the friends of the patients by his ability to converse in several languages.

RESIDENT PHYSICIAN.

The employment of a resident physician has proven wise. Without such an officer constantly in the pavilion there would always be trouble. As said before, it requires constant vigilance to prevent abuses, and this has been illustrated during the year, and resulted in the discharge of the first physician employed for the service.

Another source of gratification was that the investigation conducted by the commissioner proved the kindness and efficiency of the female nurses throughout the hospital. No charges were made by any person reflecting in any way upon the young women serving in the wards as nurses, either graduate or pupil. They seem to have been of a much better class than the men at that time under training in the male training school.

THE PRISON WARDS.

Every year a large number of persons are committed to the prison wards of the hospital. These are located on the ground floor of the main building, that for men being most primitive in its arrangements, small and cumbered with much unnecessary litter. It is dark, unsanitary, and ill-ventilated. The ward for women is much larger and cleaner, but it, too, is dark and unsanitary. There is no reason why the superintendent of Bellevue Hospital should be compelled to act as a prison warden, but in practice he is responsible for the safekeeping of all the prisoners who are committed to these wards. They usually arrive in bad condition, suffering from wounds or bruises, and, no matter how crowded the ward is at the time, room has to be made for the new patients. This works great hardship upon those confined in the male ward. These wards ought to be removed, even if the hospital continues to be required to keep prisoners. A small outside pavilion could be fitted for custodial purposes, but it should be equipped so as to be sanitary and comfortable. Many of the prisoners are received into these prison wards laboring under temporary mental aberration, and others have been seriously injured.

The records of the prison wards show that during the past year 608 males and 367 females were under treatment, of whom 63 died, 36 males and 27 females, the large mortality indicating the serious condition in which the prisoners were received.

During the same period in the alcoholic ward there were 4,677 males and 1,433 females. Of these 150 of the men died and 42 of the women, a total of 192, the percentage being very much less than that in the prison ward.

KITCHENS.

These were usually found in good order when visited. The same criticism as to the inadequacy of the facilities for the ward kitchens can be repeated, but as they occupy the only space now available for this purpose there is no probability that better conditions will prevail until such time as a new hospital with adequate accommodations shall be provided.

CELLARS.

Bellevue stands with its feet in the mud and slime. Consequently all the cellars are damp. Some of them have been flooded with water at sundry times during the year. Fortunately the use of the basements as dormitories has been discontinued, and none of the cellars are now occupied except one which is used for storage.

The ground floor dining-room for employes, and the halls, reception offices, store and similar rooms upon the ground floor are more or less affected by the dampness from the cellars. Where employes have quarters on the ground floor, as happens in a few instances, they must expect rheumatism and similar troubles as a consequence of the dampness.

DISPENSARY.

This is a very important adjunct of Bellevue Hospital. The records show that 62,786 persons were treated in it during the past year. With three visits to the dispensary by each person, which is the probable average, this record shows its great service to the sick poor who are not proper cases for admission to the wards of the hospital.

The dispensary is always crowded during the hours when it is open, and the visiting staff of physicians and surgeons is kept exceedingly busy. Its ventilation has been somewhat improved, but it should be fitted up with sanitary conveniences for the physicians and the patients if it is to continue. It does not compare favorably with the dispensaries connected with the medical colleges in the vicinity.

SUPPLIES.

The supplies are usually of good quality, but serious complaint has been made from time to time that they are insufficient in quantity. For example, to show how ordinary supplies are depleted, on a recent inspection it was found impossible to obtain a small piece of rubber tubing required for use in connection with a small gas stove by which water was heated for a patient whose throat had been cut.

Sheets, towels, clothing supplies, crockery, in fact, all the articles needed for the hospital with the exception of drugs, were in very limited quantities. It is hoped that under the new management the city will make ample provision for everything necessary in Bellevue and the other hospitals.

MORGUE.

Nothing has been done to this building during the year. Sixty-three hundred and seventy-six bodies were consigned to it during that period, and frequently it was taxed to such an extent that bodies had to be removed before the usual period for identification had elapsed. Under the new arrangement this building

31

is to continue in charge of the commissioner of charities of the
city, who will therefore be responsible for the disposal of the
bodies from all the public institutions. If the same death rate
continues a larger building will be required.

STABLES.

It was suggested a year ago that provision for the comfort
of the men employed in the stable be made, so that during the
cold weather they may not suffer as they now do from cold.
This suggestion is renewed. A large number of drivers and
attendants are required for the ambulance service, and as this
is trying work, the men should be made as comfortable as
possible.

FINANCIAL.

An abstract of the ledger of Bellevue Hospital for the last
fiscal year is exceedingly interesting. The salaries for the
period amounted to $106,609.11, and the provisions to $131,332.15.
For the same period drugs cost $43,670.32; liquors, $2,065.46.
while surgical instruments to the value of $7,477.15 were pur-
chased. Fuel cost $16,031.28; light, $15,878.04; clothing.
$12,198.59, but bedding received an outlay of only $2,287.14.
For furniture $829.80 was expended, but paints, oils and glass
required $1,301.68, and soap and soap material cost more than
twice as much as the paint, $2,609.55. Much of the clothing
for the women is evidently included in the term "dry goods,"
which cost $6,342.95; $585 were spent for new horses, $913.54
for harness, and $1,310.06 for horse feed. It required $1,229.76
to shoe the horses and $3,527.10 for ambulances, wagons and
other repairs.

The total cost for the maintenance of the hospital during the
fiscal year was $369,282.51, none of which amount was for the
special repairs and new work carried on during the year.

It will be noticed that for ambulances, wagons and repairs
$3,527.10 was spent. Of this $2,309.43 was disbursed between
the 1st of January and the 30th of September. The ambulance
service is exceedingly important, for during the year 6,693 calls

were made, requiring each wagon to make about twenty trips a day.

The garbage crematory cost $2,598.75; the hoisting apparatus for discharging coal cost $2,590.35, and the alterations in the laundry $3.343.75.

STATISTICAL.

At the end of the last fiscal year 644 patients were under treatment in the hospital. During the year there were admitted 23,721; total under treatment, 24,365, of whom 21,738 were discharged and 1,871 died, leaving in the hospital 756.

The census on October 1, 1901, was as follows:

	Males.	Females.	Total.
Officers...............................	3	2	5
Officer's family	1	2	3
Medical staff	38	0	38
Chaplains.............................	3	0	3
Nurses................................	82	84	166
Other employes	164	152	316
Patients..............................	506	223	729
In the general drug department........	10	1	11

GOUVERNEUR HOSPITAL.

(Gouverneur and Water Streets.)

Miss JESSIE A. STOWERS, *Supervisor.*

Inspected November 29, 1901.

Gouverneur Hospital has occupied this new building for a little over a year, and the general conditions have improved steadily during that time. When the hospital was first opened some time had to be spent in adjusting the old work to the new environment, but one by one the features which had worked against the old hospital were removed.

What has been said heretofore about the water-closets could be repeated at this time without a change of word, as nothing has been done to make a proper separation of the sexes.

Fire-escapes have been added during the past year, and the steps leading down to the dispensary made safer by railings.

The ambulance service is provided for in the same rented wooden stable, and there is great complaint of the discomforts of the men engaged. A new stable is greatly needed, and an appropriation should be made to remodel the building so long used as a hospital and remove it where it could serve as the ambulance house.

One very satisfactory change has been accomplished during the year—the removal of the "Goose Market" which, with its noise, and smells, and flying feathers, had so long been a public nuisance. The market was removed from this section altogether and is now located a mile or more distant, on the water front.

CENSUS.

Number of patients—males, 54; females, 25; total, 79.

HARLEM HOSPITAL.

(East One Hundred and Twentieth Street, near the East River.)

Miss S. A. GAINSFORTH, *Supervising Nurse.*

Last inspection December 20, 1901.

The city of New York is to be congraulated that the days of this temporary hospital are about ended. Plans have been suggested and an appropriation of $275,000 made for the new Harlem Hospital to be erected on the block between One Hundred and Thirty-sixth and One Hundred and Thirty-seventh streets, fronting on Lenox avenue. While many believe that the location of the buildings now occupied by the hospital is the best to meet the needs of the Harlem district, the selection of the Lenox avenue site has settled the matter, and it only remains to push building operations as rapidly as possible.

This hospital occupies an important position as one of the emergency hospitals of the city. It ministers to the needs of a very populous district, and the value of its work to Harlem cannot be overestimated. For this reason the new hospital will be a much larger building and have accommodations for about 150 patients. It will be possible, also, to retain patients for a longer period than is practicable in the present building. This will lessen the death rate. All that can be done now is to give first aid and, as soon as the patient is able to bear transportation, send him to either Bellevue or one of the island hospitals.

At the time of inspection the wards were found packed to their utmost capacity, and the records show that this has been the case during the whole year. A patient may be removed, leaving a bed unoccupied, but within an hour the ambulance, in response to a call, will usually have returned with a new case, so the nurses and attendants are taxed to their utmost ability in receiving, attending and transferring patients.

Several wards were ceiled with metal during the year, new floors were laid in the operating rooms, and the laundry received a new roof.

Because of the cramped and unsuitable quarters, there can be no opportunity to classify the patients, except upon the broad line of sex. Children badly burned or suffering from some other dreadful accident have to be placed in the female ward, where patients are lying with various acute forms of disease. In the male wards the consumptive, the fever-stricken and the mangled must lie side by side. Hence the urgent necessity for quick work in the construction of the new buildings.

The lack of bathing facilities still continues. One tub does for all the patients—and this in the great city of New York. Fortunately the prospect brightens with the assurance of the new building, in which it is hoped science and sympathy will unite to secure a proper equipment for the care of the sick and injured.

The ambulance service at this hospital is very important. Between five and six thousand ambulance calls are answered during the year, and the members of the staff on this service find their time fully occupied.

The dispensary service is also important. When the Gouverneur Hospital was completed, a small wooden shanty, which had

Fire-escapes have been **added** d...
steps leading down to the dispens...

The ambulance service is provid...
wooden stable, and there is great ...
of the men engaged. A new stable...
appropriation should be made to ren...
used as a hospital and remove it w...
ambulance house.

One very satisfactory change has ...
the year—the removal of the " Goos...
noise, and smells, and flying feathers. ...
nuisance. The market was removed fro...
and is now located a mile or more distan...

CENSUS.

Number of patients—males, 54; female...

HARLEM HOSPITAL.

(East One Hundred and Twentieth Street, no...

Miss S. A. GAINSFORTH, *Supervi...*

Last inspection December 20, ...

The city of New York is to be congraulat...
this temporary hospital are about ended. ...
gested and an appropriation of $275,000 mad...
lem Hospital to be erected on the block betw...
and Thirty-sixth and One Hundred and Thir...
fronting on Lenox avenue. While many believe...
of the buildings now occupied by the hospital i...
the needs of the Harlem district, the selecti...
avenue site has settled the matter, and it only...
building operations as rapidly as possible.

This hospital occupies an important positi...
emergency hospitals of the city. It ministers...
very populous district, and the value of its wor...
not be overestimated. For this reason the new...

served as an outside dispensary and was no longer needed there, was sent to the Harlem dispensary to make an addition to the shanties formerly used. This addition has provided shelter for certain work which before had no room, but even with this addition the Harlem Hospital dispensary is a forlorn and unsuitable structure. It has neither sanitary conveniences nor opportunity to separate the sexes. There are two general rooms, one for each sex, but both have entrance to the examination and dispensing rooms into which men, women and children are called. The wonder is that disease is not communicated more frequently, for under present conditions there is no possibility of separating the sick from the well. All of these conditions point to the importance of larger, more sanitary, and properly appointed arrangements for dispensary purposes.

CENSUS.

Number of patients—males, 17; females, 18; total, 35.

FORDHAM HOSPITAL.

(St. James Street and Aqueduct Avenue.)

Miss CARRIE GRAY, *Supervisor.*

Last inspection December 21, 1901.

With the exception of some minor repairs and painting, no improvements have been made in this hospital since last report. The new walks and the new floors which were made last year are a decided improvement, as is also the better arrangement for entrance into the dispensary.

One serious complaint heretofore made at this hospital has been the difficulty of getting a sufficiency of supplies, but at the time of inspection there was an abundance of all kinds, so that the hospital is much better equipped than at other times.

The great need of the hospital continues as before—the matter of water supply. Owing to the somewhat remote and high location of the institution, it has not been able to secure an adequate service. From time to time, during periods of drought, the hospital has been seriously crippled by its limited water supply. As long as the hospital remains where it is and depends upon its present service, it will be impossible to have a sufficient and certain supply of water. When the reservoirs are filled, after heavy rains, the hospital has ample for all daily needs, but as soon as the reservoirs diminish in quantity the hospital suffers. Last year, in consequence of this, there was more or less of typhoid fever. Under the new administration, steps will be taken, doubtless, to make the supply satisfactory at all seasons of the year.

The ambulance service of this hospital, like that of Harlem and Gouverneur, is exceedingly important. This hospital has the long drives are very wearying to the attendants as well as the long drives are very wearying to the attendants as well as dangerous to the patients. This ambulance service covers the city from its northern boundary to One Hundred and Thirty-eighth street, and from the Hudson river to City Island. The long drive is too often fatal to the chances of a patient's recovery, but under present circumstances is unavoidable. The only way to obviate these drives is to provide minor emergency hospitals to which patients remote from Fordham may be taken temporarily for treatment until able to bear the fatigue of transfer. In spite of every inconvenience, however, the ambulances, like the other service of the hospital, have done most excellent work.

The dispensary connected with Fordham Hospital is also an important agent for the relief of the sick poor. It, too, has cramped quarters and rather limited opportunities to respond to demands, but this is true of all departments of the hospital and of all the staff, for from the supervisor to the lowest on the roll of attendants, every hour is required to dispatch the work. Perhaps, when the city has grown into a better financial condition, the whole subject of emergency hospital service will be newly considered.

Last winter a bill was introduced into the Legislature to provide for a centrally located hospital for the borough of The

Bronx, large enough to meet all the requirements of this rapidly growing section. That such a hospital is needed is beyond dispute, and the fact that the present buildings are leased for a comparatively short term of years would suggest the advisability of taking steps to secure a suitable site for a new and enlarged hospital to be erected at the earliest possible moment.

CENSUS.

Number of patients—males, 27; females, 9; total, 36.

THE CITY HOSPITAL.

(Blackwell's Island.)

Joseph Schilling, *Superintendent.*

Last inspection December 31, 1901.

This is one of the largest public hospitals in the city, and serves as one of the overflow institutions to which transfers are made from all of the other public hospitals in the boroughs of Manhattan and The Bronx. The principal improvements during the year were the renovation of the delivery room of the maternity pavilion and the thorough repainting and repairing of the solarium. Some minor improvements were made from time to time throughout the institution. In one of the wooden buildings set apart for epileptics and paralytics new floors were laid; in other wards repairs to the ceilings and walls and a little painting.

Unfortunately the funds for alterations and additions in the department were insufficient to allow for the major improvements necessary in the City Hospital. A new heating plant could not be installed, nor the present plant repaired. A much needed addition to the nurses' home, for which a small appropriation was made some time ago, could not be undertaken. Neither could the leaky roofs of the main entrance be thoroughly repaired, to say nothing about new and properly equipped pavilions to take the place of the group of shanties which are now in service for the special cases requiring isolation. For the same reason—lack of available funds—another greatly needed improvement, the erection of a shelter on the dock, has had to be postponed. In rainy weather visitors waiting for the boats to the city are dangerously exposed, while the patients transferred to and from the hospital have no protection from the rain or cold or heat. A shelter of some kind is greatly needed, and when the improvement of the dock is undertaken should not be forgotten. The dock itself has not sufficient facilities for a landing place, where oftentimes two or more boats should be at one time. An extension of the dock will afford much needed room.

While upon the subject of the dock it may be well to say that here all the coal used by the boats of the Departments of Charities and Corrections is unloaded and distributed to the boats as they require it for consumption. The transfer of the coal often takes considerable time, during which boats are delayed. If, as elsewhere suggested, the Corrections Department boats made their landings upon the eastern side of the island, and there discharged and received freight, including coal, it would be an improvement on the present arrangement.

The use of ferry boats intended for the transportation of sick in many of the rooms for the help, dining-rooms and lavatories. The sewing rooms and storerooms are still crowded; the drug and dispensing rooms as well as the other offices upon the ground floor have no room to spare; but, considering conditions some time ago, there is much more comfort.

THE WARDS.

The wards throughout the hospital were found, as a general thing, clean and in order, although there were instances where a lack of thoroughness in this respect was manifest. One trouble with these wards is the limited number of helpers available to do a large amount of work. Perhaps if the character of the help were improved, much more work would be done, but the tendency in many instances now is to try to cover the ground by slighting the work. This was not so noticeable upon the female side of the hospital. The female nurses were found to take greater interest in the cleaning of their wards than the male nurses. This, however, is true of all the hospitals, and is to be expected. Women are naturally expert housekeepers while men are inclined to overlook the little details upon which success depends. For this reason the nursing in this hospital is far more successful upon the women's side than upon the men's. In fact, in this as in other things, the standard of efficiency is much higher among the female nurses, and the patients express greater satisfaction at their ministrations.

NURSES.

As the problem of nursing the sick in public hospitals is studied, it becomes apparent that, with the exception of two or three special wards, female nurses are more satisfactory than male nurses, and the hospital must eventually depend upon the class which has done and will continue to do the best work. However, it is not to be understood that the male training school is not graduating capable and efficient male nurses. The contrary is true, and at the late inspections of this hospital it was a pleasure to see that the standard of service on the male side had greatly improved. Certainly the superintendent in charge of the male training school, who has supervision of the work in the wards, is faithful in her efforts to secure satisfactory results, and it is no fault of hers that some of the men seem out of their sphere or seem harsh in their handling of patients.

THE MATERNITY PAVILION.

A large number of cases pass through this pavilion each year, and the nurses in charge have much work to perform. The accommodations are rather primitive, better than at Emergency Hospital in the city, but not what they should be in a city institution.

This old pavilion has served its day and should be replaced by a commodious, well-appointed structure in which the women, both before and after accouchment, could have the comforts they need. The stove still does service for heating water in the delivery room, and the dormitories for the waiting women are cold and cheerless. The chief point in favor of this pavilion is the complete separation of the several departments, the pavilion being arranged with radiating wings. It is fairly well ventilated; in fact its construction is such that the wind forces its way through the sides and for this reason is conducive to good results. It should, however, be replaced by a new pavilion as soon as possible.

OTHER PAVILIONS.

The isolation pavilions and buildings intended for special cases have long since passed the stage where it would be possible to repair and make them useful for any length of time. They should be removed, the ground on which they stand be thoroughly cleaned, and new pavilions built which will be larger, located with some degree of order, and be properly fitted for the special work to be done in them.

TRANSFERS.

There are a number of cases in the pavilion for paralytics who could well be transferred to the hospitals of the almshouse, and there are a number of cases in the almshouse who ought to be

transferred to the care of a hospital. All the epileptic patients of the several institutions on the island should be
gathered together in one pavilion rather than remain scattered
as they are now in the several hospital departments. The construction of a pavilion for cancer cases and other contagious
diseases of similar character will be beneficial. In this connection it is suggested that as soon as possible the phthisis cases
in several wards of the hospital be removed to the tuberculosis
hospital, which it is promised will be established in one of the
buildings lately vacated by the insane. When these changes
are accomplished it may be possible to reclassify some of the
wards of the main hospital and arrange a better grouping than
prevails at the present time. The fact that patients of several
types are in the same wards is prejudicial to their recovery. The
removal of all the consumptives will be a great relief to the
general wards. As most of the skin diseases applying for relief
are sent to this hospital, it will then be possible to permanently
set apart a special isolated section wherein patients afflicted
with this class of disease may be treated.

SUPPLIES.

At the time of inspection the supplies for this hospital were
greatly depleted. The bedding had run down, the stocks intended for special diets were very slim, and medical and surgical
supplies required large additions. It is difficult to keep much
of a surplus on hand in these public hospitals, but there are
certain standard supplies which are always necessary to keep
in quantity. It is no economy to permit these things to become
exhausted. Paints, oils, carpenters' and plumbers' supplies
must be kept on hand that the repairs needed from day to day
be made. These things cost double when work accumulates.
Many minor repairs were left unmade because supplies of this
character were not to be obtained.

The food was in general satisfactory. It is usually furnished
in fair variety, although in the winter time the vegetables
dwindle to two or three standard forms. A great improvement

has been made in the service of the food, especially in the way in which the hospital help is fed.

The clothing furnished has not been altogether satisfactory, especially that provided for the female patients, but here again improvement was seen and it is believed the commissioner has succeeded in getting a better quality than was possible before.

ADMINISTRATION.

The superintendent has undertaken the duties of the steward for the past year, and, although this has involved considerable extra work, with the help of the clerical assistants in the office he has managed to oversee both departments, so that the commissioner has not found it necessary to detail a steward for this hospital.

The grounds have been maintained in good order, and the work has been dispatched promptly.

CENSUS.

Number of inmates—males, 384; females, 268; total, 652.

METROPOLITAN HOSPITAL.

(Blackwell's Island.)

WM. B. O'ROURKE, *Superintendent.*

Last inspection December 30, 1901.

At the time of the preparation of the last annual report this hospital was under the superintendency of Dr. George Taylor Stewart, who for many years had it in charge. His transfer in January to Bellevue left the hospital for a time without a superintendent. One of the members of the house staff took charge temporarily, and in February Mr. Wm. B. O'Rourke, who for a number of years was the superintendent of Bellevue Hospital, was transferred to this institution as its superintendent. He found the hospital with some repairs and improvements initiated by Dr. Stewart unfinished, but otherwise in a commendable condition.

The long experience of Mr. O'Rourke in hospital management had prepared him for the responsible duties in connection with this institution, and although his appointment was looked upon with disfavor it is justice to him to say that when the last inspection was made, after he had been in charge for nearly one year, the hospital was found, in all its departments, in a highly commendable condition. The improvements begun by Dr. Stewart were carried through by Mr. O'Rourke, to the decided advantage of the hospital.

ALTERATIONS.

When the transformation of this institution from an asylum for the insane into a hospital for the sick began, a great many necessary alterations were made. Some, however, could not well be undertaken at first. These have been made one by one, the last, the erection of the two water towers, completing the sanitary equipment. By their construction the lavatories and toilets originally located in the heart of each wing were rendered unnecessary, and the space occupied by them transformed into ward rooms. The towers themselves are well fitted up, having sanitary floors and modern plumbing. This improvement was finished by the new superintendent, and, although begun by his predecessor, its successful issue remains to his credit.

Great changes have been made in the ground floor of the hospital, and the dining-rooms for the help and other adjacent rooms have been completely renovated. Metal ceilings, paint, and good furniture make these rooms pleasant and desirable, and the orderlies and help now have satisfactory quarters.

KITCHEN.

Another improvement has been the renovation of the kitchen. Heretofore the kitchen has been the one dingy place in the institution. It is now in thorough repair, and, with a fresh coating of paint, looks bright and cheerful. When examined the equipment was clean on the outside, but the interior of the urns and vessels used for cooking was found in a dangerous condition, the tin lining having worn off, leaving the copper to come into immediate contact with the food. There is great danger of wholesale poisoning from the use of vessels in such a condition, and these should be relined immediately. The superintendent had reported the matter and was awaiting the necessary authority to send them away for repair. With this exception the equipment was satisfactory.

The several wards of the hospital were clean and cheerful, the patients apparently receiving all necessary attention. The great trouble with these wards is the inability to classify the patients, owing to the fact that a large number of tuberculosis cases are sent to the hospital.

TUBERCULOSIS PAVILION.

The surrender of the buildings heretofore used as an asylum for the insane gives an opportunity to the department to establish a tuberculosis pavilion. This is absolutely necessary for the welfare of all the other patients, not only upon the island but in all the public hospitals of the city. With patients of this class removed from Metropolitan, City, Bellevue, and other hospitals, the recovery rate of ordinary patients will largely increase. At the same time the general comfort of the wards will be improved. Another improvement in the classification may be accomplished by the removal of all cases of a filthy character or of a contagious nature from this hospital to some pavilion or wing connected with the City Hospital, so that Metropolitan may be devoted entirely to surgical work and acute cases of a non-contagious character, in addition to the maternity patients who can be properly cared for in this well-equipped hospital.

CONVALESCENT HOSPITAL.

On the 7th of November, 1901, the buildings used by the Manhattan State Hospital under lease were turned over to the city. Some of them immediately adjoin this hospital and can easily be made a part of it. What disposition shall be made of all the buildings is a question for the immediate future. The establishment of a tuberculosis pavilion upon the island is a necessity, as also a hospital for convalescent patients, for whom nothing is required save food and shelter until their strength has been fully recovered. It is unfortunate that the crowded condition of the public hospitals compels the authorities to send out patients before they are strong enough to again undertake self-support. These persons have been kept in the public hospitals until they no longer need medical aid, although not really fit to go back to work. The large number of acute cases needing immediate hospital attention requires that beds shall be surrendered as soon as a patient no longer needs special medical treatment. A convalescents' hospital or home would provide for such patients and in the end save many lives now lost through relapse brought on by the necessity for work before strength is fully recruited.

LAUNDRY.

The laundry of this hospital does a very large amount of work each day. The general work department is well managed and satisfactory in its results, but the work in the laundry can be improved by the employment of better help.

NURSES.

The nursing standard of this hospital has been high since the training school was first established. It maintains its character of thoroughness and efficiency. The entire hospital is carefully scrutinized by the supervisor each day, and the instruction given to the pupil nurses is of such a character that they rapidly become efficient. The Home is pleasant and has enough room for a school of the size of this. If the suggestion to connect the almshouse hospitals with the training schools for a supply of nurses be adopted, probably the Nurses' Home building will have to be enlarged to accommodate the increased number of pupils rendered necessary by the additional work.

On the 1st of October, 1901, the roster of officers, nurses and employes numbered 201 persons. Besides these there were 16 unpaid helpers and 18 workhouse women detailed for work in the laundry. These workhouse women and unpaid helpers are the worst feature of the hospital. The women detailed in the daily gang to the laundry and other places lower the quality of work performed. They expect to get through the day with as little labor as possible. They have no desire to do it well, and hence the paid helpers soon form habits of shirking. It would be economy to introduce paid help instead of these workhouse women. The greater care which paid employes would exercise together with diligence and pride in good work would pay in the end.

Taken altogether, the hospital is in a very satisfactory condition and should be continued in the same state of efficiency.

CENSUS.

Number of patients—males, 250; females, 135; total, 385.

EMERGENCY HOSPITAL.

(223 East Twenty-sixth Street.)

Inspected December 30, 1901.

The ill-appointed and unsuitable building on East Twenty-sixth street, formerly used by the fire department, still serves as the Emergency Maternity Hospital of the Department of Public Charities of the city of New York. The necessity for different quarters has been pointed out time and again, and that necessity has not diminished during the past year. The location is bad, the street dirty and noisy.

On a late visit the street from Third avenue to First, especially in front of the hospital, was in as foul condition probably as any in that section of the city. At 3 o'clock in the afternoon the ashes placed for removal early in the morning had not been removed and one can had been upset by mischievous boys at the hospital door. The whole exterior presented an ill-kept and uninviting appearance.

The interior of this hospital has been repaired and painted, but continues practically unchanged; in fact, the nurses on duty

32

are kept so busy with their special work that they cannot give much time to other things nor make much impression upon the crowded interior. Usually the women who are received in this hospital are too far advanced to be able to render assistance even in the ordinary housework, consequently the most of it falls upon the over worked nurses, and they have no time for this extra work.

This emergency service should be removed to a better place. It was proposed by Commissioner Keller to fit up a portion of the "College building" on the Bellevue grounds for it, but nothing has been done so far. By the removal as thus proposed, the present building could be turned over to the City Lodging House, to be used for homeless women, and both services would be benefited by the transfer.

CENSUS.

Mothers, 5; babies, 5; waiting women, 6; total, 16.

THE ALMSHOUSE.
(Blackwell's Island.)
Robert Roberts, *Superintendent.*
Inspected December 13–14, 1901.

The almshouse now on Blackwell's Island is the largest institution of the kind in the State of New York, if not in the United States, and was in all probability the first institution of the kind established in Colonial times. It has had at least four different locations, and from it all the public hospitals of the city may be said to have developed. To this day it retains a hospital character, for although its ordinary dormitories are filled with aged and infirm people, it has a hospital department wherein blind, paralytic and other incurable patients are cared for. Thus it is closely allied to the hospital system of the city. In fact, many of the convalescents sent out of the hospital, being indigent, complete their recovery in the almshouse. For this class, however, there should be other provision, as commit-

STATE BOARD OF CHARITIES.

ment to an almshouse is destructive of self-respect, owing to enforced association with degraded characters.

Since the last report the management has been in the same hands and the general discipline has followed the same lines as heretofore. With such a large population, where so many admissions and discharges take place, vigilance on the part of the superintendent and employes is necessary to keep things running smoothly.

The improvements in the general equipment have been few, although many repairs were made. A long shop building was completed. This has taken the place of an unsightly lot of old shanties which stood on the east bank of the island. The bakery destroyed by fire last year has been rebuilt, and the new building is well fitted for the large amount of work which must be done in it. This bakery supplies bread to other institutions as well as the almshouse, and it is therefore necessary that it have ample room and sufficient help. Most of the help is drawn from the workhouse, where many bakers are always to be found. Perhaps the time will come when this workhouse labor can be dispensed with, but at present this help is all that is available to do the bread making.

Pavilion R and S was thoroughly renovated and all of the wards and dormitories in the other buildings were painted. All the roofs of the hospital buildings are what are known as tar and gravel roofs. These are good when new and well laid, but become leaky in a comparatively short time. This has happened on the island, and although retarred this year, the only permanent remedy will be found in new roofs of metal.

During cold weather the main building for women is not sufficiently warmed. This is due to the plan for heating—the "indirect" system—and to the fact that the piping is old and worn out. There is a sufficiency of steam, and with a modern system of distribution into the several wards they would be warm enough.

The crematory used for the destruction of garbage and rubbish has not worked satisfactorily at all times. The stack

seemed to be choked at the time of last inspection, and, as a
consequence, the smoke filled the workroom and poured out of
the doorways. Something should be done to improve this plant,
as upon its successful working the disposal of all refuse depends.

BATHING FACILITIES.

The large population of the almshouse makes demands which
the present arrangements for bathing are not able to meet. It
will be well to erect two larger bathhouses—one for each sex—
and arrange them so that all the inmates can be bathed with
comfort and rapidity. While some tubs are necessary, the
larger number of the inmates should have the spray bath for
their own protection. The present bathhouse could be converted into an additional shop, of which there is great need,
especially for the sewing and tailoring departments.

FOOD.

The food supplied to the inmates of the almshouse is usually
of good quality and in ample quantity. The chief criticism is
as to the lack of variety, especially in the winter season. This
uniformity of diet is unnecessary with the per capita for maintenance allowed by the city. The markets have an abundance
of cheap foods, especially vegetables, at all seasons, but the tendency is to get such supplies as can be most easily cooked and
be served with least trouble. The large numbers to be fed make
it difficult to have a satisfactory table service, but even this
can be improved by effort.

HELP.

The superintendent is fortunate in having a working staff of
assistants who are generally satisfactory. This is especially
the case with the steward and office force. Some of the employes filling minor positions should be discharged as incompetent, and with a larger measure of liberty in this matter than
heretofore the superintendent will probably make changes.

As a rule the nurses in the hospitals are satisfactory, although
they are not well paid, nor is the standard of qualification high.

If the almshouse hospitals can be united in one system with the others on the island an immediate benefit will be the better service such change would introduce. The nurses could then be drafted from the two training schools, and would take to the incurables the skill and attention now given to other patients.

NURSES' HOME.

In this connection the recommendation that a nurses' home be established in connection with the almshouse is renewed. These nurses have no place to go for rest—they are in the hospital atmosphere day and night. Something should be done for them in this direction, although if the suggestion to get them from the training schools be adopted a separate home will be unnecessary, as in that case they can go to the homes at the hospitals on the north and south ends of the island when off duty.

CLASSIFICATION.

The establishment of the several hospitals for the incurables has been in the line of classification. The blind have gone into these hospitals, the paralytics, epileptics and others, but save in two of the dormitories the problem of classification remains to be attempted. Now that the almshouses at Flatbush and on Staten Island are under one commissioner a systematic grouping of all the paupers in these institutions should be attempted. To one of these almshouses it may be possible to send, for example, all the blind and other incurables in the other two institutions, so that in the special hospital they may have the benefit of the expert medical and surgical attention freely given by the college staff.

Some of these people are capable of productive labor. If Richmond be selected for their abode, they can be utilized on the farm or in the gardens, or at other profitable employments adapted to their strength, training and intelligence. Thus the problem of classification might be attacked, and from the tentative groupings the best methods be discovered.

In this connection, as well as in illustration of the methods of this almshouse, the following notes of a statement made by the superintendent while the last inspection was in progress are appended. The statement was not intended for publication, but an examination of the notes made at the time show them to be of value, especially as proving the possibility of utilizing alms-house inmates in many ways.

"Vigilance and unremitting labor are necessary to conduct an institution of this description in a proper manner. On assuming charge my first endeavor was directed towards the classification of inmates in so far as separating, when practicable, the idle and good-for-nothing rounder and ex-prisoner from the worthy poor. For instance, in the case of women inmates who appear respectable and are obliged to become public charges through sickness or reverses of fortune, they are placed in the South Pavilion, also known as the Old Ladies' Home, and the crippled, blind, paralytic and epileptic put in separate wards. This rule also applies to the men.

"The labor at one time performed by the prison help is now done by our own inmates. They were formerly allowed to loiter and roam around the grounds in summer and collect in gangs to smoke and gossip in the wards in winter. Now, those who are physically able are obliged to work at some occupation during all or some period of the day, and I have found this plan conducive to judicious discipline.

"There is an average of 600 men daily employed at painting, tailoring, tinsmithing, carpentry, laboring; also as cooks' helpers, coal passers, etc.; and an average of 400 women at sewing, scrubbing, bed-making, laundry and dining-room work, etc.

"Under my personal direction the men have reclaimed two large tracts of waste ground and converted them into parks, equipped with comfortable settees, so that inmates unable to work may spend the time out of doors when the weather permits.

"The old roads have been drained and regraded, new ones cut, and these, together with the lawns, are kept in good condition and regularly attended to by a gang of inmates in charge of a paid attendant.

"Part of the seawall near the boathouse crumbled away, and

although it required skilled labor to make the necessary repairs, we were obliged to do the work ourselves, and made a pretty good job of it.

"The old iron bedsteads which were lying in an unsightly heap for years have been utilized for fencing and railing, and with the aid of a few coats of paint present as good an appearance as if done by contract.

" New picket fences have been made and put up around the ' Old Maternity ' building, bakery and south pavilion.

" The conservatory, which was almost wiped out by fire last winter, has been rebuilt and supplied with steam heat instead of stoves, as formerly.

"A new shingle roof has been put on the old laundry and a new washing machine and mangle placed in the building.

"A stone sidewalk and stoop were made at the administration building, equipped with two modern gas lamp posts and lamps.

"A brick footpath has been made between the south pavilion and the boiler house.

"The wards throughout the institution have been completely renovated and painted, as well as the drugstore and office.

"Small tables for each patient have been supplied in the hospital wards, and are much appreciated by the patients, and fill a long-felt want.

"The roofs of the north and south pavilions have been painted and those of the six hospital buildings re-tarred.

"I have frequently urged the necessity for metal ceilings in all the wards, and particularly the hospital wards, and it is to be hoped that the coming year will see this much-desired innovation adopted.

" New shops are now under way and nearing completion, and as soon as they are ready for occupancy the old ones, which have long been an eyesore, will be removed.

"A new system of steam heating has been introduced in the north and south pavilions.

"All or nearly all the buildings were in need of paint and kalsomine. They have been attended to during the year.

"The food question, which to my mind is one of the most important features to handle, receives my personal supervision. Heretofore good supplies were improperly handled, badly cooked and served up cold. We have been fortunate in securing the services of a first-class cook, who takes the greatest interest in his work and special pride in making soups and stew. There is always ample quantity and generally sufficient variety. New cans, with tight-fitting covers, have been provided so as to ensure the meals being served hot to the different wards."

CENSUS.

	Males.	Females.	Total.
Officers	6	3	9
Officers' families	7	7	14
Medical staff	7	0	7
Chaplain	1	0	1
Other employes	84	91	175
Incurable hospital patients	58	54	112
Inmates	968	920	1,888
Inmates (blind)	59	70	129
	1,190	1,145	2,335

THE CITY LODGING HOUSE.

(First Avenue, near Twenty-third Street.)

GEORGE T. STEWART, M. D., *Superintendent.*

Last inspection December 31, 1901.

The Municipal Lodging House of the city of New York has undergone no important change since the report made upon it one year ago. The change in the general superintendency of Bellevue and allied hospitals, and the removal of Mr. W. B. O'Rourke from Bellevue to Metropolitan Hospital, have placed the general oversight of the lodging house in charge of Dr. George T. Stewart, the new superintendent of Bellevue and its allied hospitals.

The working force necessary to manage the lodging house is the same, and the methods for caring for homeless men and women are substantially as before. One great improvement in these methods, however, is a more complete separation of the sexes, by which the women's department is entirely disconnected from that set apart for the men.

At each of the inspections during the year the several dormitories were found clean and well cared for. The crowded condition of the building prevents the allotment of sufficient space to the lodgers, but with this exception they are made comfortable and are well provided for. The food was examined frequently and carefully and always found of good quality and ample in quantity.

The water-closets and lavatories on the upper floors are inconvenient and not suited to a public institution, but, under the circumstances, as this is a leased building, there is no opportunity to make the necessary changes. Until the city has its own building it is not to be expected that radical alterations will be made. It is therefore necessary that special attention be given to the water-closets and lavatories so as to minimize the dangers incident to their present location.

The erection of a large stable in the rear of the lodging house has cut off some of the light and air which formerly entered through the rear windows. This is another consequence of the location, and emphasizes the importance of a city lodging house disconnected from surrounding buildings. Fortunately the recipients of shelter do not remain for any length of time, and what would be a serious evil under ordinary circumstances, may be borne without damage for one or two nights. Next to air and sunlight come baths and laundry. The bathing facilities are taxed to their utmost, as is the laundry. These, with the machinery, are located in the basement where the cramped quarters make walking about dangerous. In this basement the fumigator is located, and the storage nets in which the clothing of lodgers is placed after being taken from the fumigator. In the small available space the machinery is necessarily crowded together to make room for bathing and storage. More than twice the amount of space could be used for the work done in this basement.

The recommendation heretofore made for a complete separation of the sexes is renewed at this time, and the suggestion is again presented that until better arrangements can be made the use of the emergency hospital for women and children will be a solution of the problem. Although the women are separated from the men by partitions, and have a separate entrance also, they are necessarily brought in contact with the male lodgers. The common rendezvous for both sexes is the office, and only by the establishment of a separate lodging house for the women will this undesirable contact be prevented. Thus, for both sexes, the importance of a new home increases with each year of the municipal lodging house work. While the general location is probably as good as can be found, it is desirable to have a house for each sex, arranged differently and, if possible, detached from its neighbors.

The new administration of public affairs for the city of New York may take up this matter in due time. Until then this lodging house must continue as it is now arranged.

The largest number sheltered on any one day was 561. As the total capacity is only 323, the overflow had to be sent to the rooms on the dock, foot of East Twenty-sixth street, thus converting the dock building into an annex of the lodging house. On another occasion 83 were sheltered, but the same day there were 23 unpaid helpers. Between these figures the daily census fluctuates, but the average taxes the capacity of the building, especially when the 19 employes and the unpaid help are added to the average.

STATISTICS.

	1900.	1901.
Males	57,150	63,018
Females	6,977	7,764
Total	64,127	70,782

RANDALL'S ISLAND INSTITUTIONS.

Mrs. M. C. DUNPHY, *Superintendent.*

Last inspection December 20, 1901.

The institutions on Randall's Island form a distinct but most important group in the public charities of the city of New York. All the other institutions are intended mainly for adults, but Randall's Island is primarily for the care of children. On this island are located the hospital for infants, the children's hospital, and the hospitals and schools for the feeble-minded. The first of these institutions cares for destitute infants, whether foundlings, orphans, or accompanied by their mothers. The children's hospital receives destitute children for medical treatment when it is not deemed advisable to send them to any of the larger hospitals under the management of the Commissioner of Charities.

Since the last report a number of changes have been made upon the island. The pavilion destroyed by fire in 1900 has been rebuilt and is now occupied, and Pavilion F, for feeble-minded children, has been improved, giving to the defective wards of the city better accommodations than they have hitherto enjoyed. The steam heating has been improved by the installation of new heating plants, so that the hospitals are now prepared to withstand any ordinary degree of cold and are comfortable at all times. The hospital pavilions have been painted, which makes them more cheerful, and a bathing crib intended for the children and made safe for them is now in use.

Some minor repairs were made during the year, which was to be expected, as on this island repairs of some kind are always in progress under the direction of the superintendent. Additions were made to the equipment in the kitchen, and, as a whole, the service has been kept up to the standard.

infancy, is one which greatly interests charitably disposed
people, the statement of continued progress in the reduction of
the death rate is a matter of general interest.

In the infants' hospital 1,028 children were under treatment
during the year ending December 31, 1901, a decrease of 43 from
the number treated in 1900, and of this number 186 died, or
18.09 per cent. Of the children who died, 29 were with their
mothers in the hospital at the time of death, and 157 were
orphan children. The total number of children who were accompanied by their mothers was 554, of whom 260 were boys
and 294 girls, and as 29 of this class died the mortality was only
5.23 per cent. Of orphan children 474 were under treatment.
239 boys and 235 girls, and as 157 of this class died the mortality
was 33.12 per cent.

It is interesting to note that from the number received at the
hospital, 41 were boarded out by the Guild of the Infant
Saviour, 15 boys and 26 girls, all of the 41 being foundlings.
Nine were taken from the hospital to homes by the State Charities Aid Association, 6 boys and 3 girls, these also all being
foundlings except one.

Of the foundling class but 88 were treated during the year.
Thirty of these were in the hospital on the 1st of January,
1901, and 58 were received during the year. Of this class 13
died, or 14.77 per cent., 41 were boarded out by the Guild of the
Infant Saviour, 8 were boarded out by the State Charities Aid
Association, 23 were adopted, 1 returned to friends, and there
remained at the hospital on the 31st of December, 1901, only 1
of this class.

An interesting tabulation is that of the foundlings boarded
out by the two societies during the year 1901. The State Charities Aid Association took from the infants' hospital 8 foundlings
and from Bellevue Hospital 43, a total of 51 of the foundling
class. Of these 13 died. The Guild of the Infant Saviour took,
during the same time, from the infants' hospital 41 and from
Bellevue 2, a total of 43; 6 of these died. From these figures it
is seen that while the percentage of deaths of the orphan

children, not foundlings, was 39.9 per cent., the mortality among the foundlings boarded out in homes was 20.2 per cent.

Besides the infants, 441 women were in the hospital during the year, none of whom died. Of this number 61 were inmates of the workhouse. The total of those treated in the hospital was 1,557, of whom 529 were adults.

The foregoing figures are from the copy of the records made by the bookkeeper on the island. The following tabulation of the results with 100 infants is from the records in the office of the Commissioner. The period is substantially the same but not exactly. The children are all foundlings and assigned to the two societies.

GUILD OF THE INFANT SAVIOUR.

Sent to free homes....................................	12
Sent to boarding homes..............................	23
Died in boarding homes.............................	6
	41

STATE CHARITIES AID ASSOCIATION.

Sent to free homes....................................	14
Sent to boarding homes..............................	27
Died in boarding homes.............................	4
	45

In addition to the 86 foundlings thus accounted for, 4 others died in Bellevue, 8 in the hospital on Randall's Island, 1 in the New York Eye and Ear Hospital, and 1 was discharged to the mother. Total 100 foundlings, of whom 10 died in homes provided by the societies and 13 in the hospitals. The foundling death rate from these figures was 23 per cent., but only 11.6 per cent. among the infants actually placed in homes, showing the greater chance for life given to the infant for whom a home is found.

These figures are even more interesting when it is remembered that the foundlings are usually abandoned when very young, and are consequently handicapped in the struggle for life as compared with the other children cared for in the infants' hospital. With this in mind the figures become much more favorable, and the death rate of the whole group of foundlings may be considered low.

A careful analysis of all the names of the infants treated in the hospital might show that many were registered as received and discharged from two to five times, which would greatly increase the number of apparent survivals and diminish the death rate. If the "repeaters" were taken out of the rolls whenever they appeared more than once, the total number of infants would probably be nearly 100 less but the deaths would remain the same, hence the death rate as thus obtained would be much higher. This true hospital rate compared with the foundling death rate of 23 per cent. would serve to show the relative probability of life in the two environments.

If the comparison only included the deaths among infants actually placed in homes (11.6 per cent.) the greater probability of life for the child in the home is apparent. As it is estimated that 10 per cent. of all children born under ordinary conditions die before they reach the age of one year, the fearful handicap of the foundlings is shown to have been almost overcome when the death rate is kept as low as 11.6 per cent., and the hospital rate, including all classes treated, was 18.09 per cent., taking the list of children reported without excluding "repeaters," while if these be deducted as they should be the comparison will show much more favorably. This is proven beyond question by an examination of the list of 859 admissions to the infants' hospital furnished by the commissioner.

Of this number were reported:

Discharged	624
Died	158
Remaining	77
	859

On this list 247 names were duplicated, making the actual number of children treated 612, the actual death rate then being 25.82 per cent. instead of 18.39 based on 158 deaths and 859 admissions.

IDIOTS.

The large number of idiots heretofore cared for on Randall's Island has been reduced during the year by transfers to State care. The enlargement of accommodations at Rome gave opportunity to receive all the non-epileptic idiots, but the others are forced to remain under care of the city because the Custodial Asylum does not receive idiots afflicted with epilepsy. It is suggested that the scattered groups of this class of defectives now maintained by the city in its three almshouses be combined on Randall's Island.

The new pavilion F, which was finished last year at a cost of $40,000, has been opened during the year and has accommodation for 100 of these idiots. Their quarters are so much better than heretofore that the rebuilding of pavilion F is a decided advantage.

Formerly these defectives had dormitories heated by stoves; now the new steam plant furnishes ample heat and there are no stoves in use. This is in the line of greater safety. Not only was there danger of fire destroying the buildings as a consequence of the use of stoves, but the patients were always in danger of burning themselves even though each stove was protected by wire guards.

The new pavilion has outside stairs which serve as fire-escapes, but unfortunately these outside stairs are of wood.

THE FEEBLE-MINDED.

In addition to the unteachable idiots on the island, there are large numbers of the feeble-minded under care. Schools are provided and instruction given to them in such things as sewing, basket-making, tailoring, tinsmithing, the making of shoes and rugs, as well as in gardening and similar out-of-door pursuits. A strong effort is made by the superintendent to increase the

light industries suitable for this class, as well as to develop
their powers through instruction in the common English
branches.

The school on the island has to provide instruction not only
for the feeble-minded but also for the children of normal mind
sent to the Children's Hospital. As the latter are seldom on
the island for any great length of time, the task of the teacher
is exceedingly difficult so far as their instruction is concerned,
but with the feeble-minded the several industries thrive and the
children take pleasure in their work.

EPILEPTICS.

There are a large number of epileptic children on the island
beside those included in the idiot class. All the epileptics who
can be benefited by the transfer should be sent to Craig Colony,
and it would be well were a definite plan adopted by which those
suffering from double defects, as idotic epileptics or epileptic
feeble-minded, could be transferred to a suitable institution.

NEEDS.

Many new trees have been set out on the grounds during the
past year, and this plan of providing fruit and shade should be
continued, as in all probability Randall's Island will always remain the seat of some of the large public charities of the city.

One special need is that a nurses' home be provided for this
system of hospitals. In 1899 the Board of Estimate and Apportionment appropriated $15,000, which amount was deemed in-
sufficient. There may be use for a larger sum, but the need
of a nurses' home grows greater from year to year, and the
necessary steps should be taken to provide such a building.

There is need of a crematory for the several institutions on
the island. Doubtless one could be built which would serve as
a destructor for the House of Refuge and the children's institutions, and the expense could be divided equitably.

A new ice house is required and also a better dormitory for
the male help employed. Necessarily there are a number of

men who work upon the island, and these should be properly housed. A good dormitory should be provided for them.

One other improvement greatly needed is a better shelter on the dock at One Hundred and Twentieth street. To this dock all visitors to the island go and wait until a boat is able to convey them across. In stormy weather women and children are exposed, and a shelter of some kind, large enough to accommodate the crowd which makes use of the dock, should be provided. Then a steam launch is a necessity as a ferry between the island and the dock. At present the transfer is made by open rowboat. When it is remembered that hundreds of infants are taken to the hospital on the island, and that numbers of sick children must be transferred, it will be apparent that protection should be provided. The cost of a steam launch will not be very great, but even if such a ferry were to cost $5,000 or $6,000 the money would be well spent if it save the lives of some of the children whose death may be traced to exposure.

CENSUS.

CHILDREN'S HOSPITAL.

	Boys.	Girls.	Total.
Remaining last report..............	224	172	396
Admitted	222	194	416
Total	446	366	812
Died	15	19	34
Discharged	229	182	411
Eloped	2	......	2
Remaining	200	165	365
	446	366	812

33

IDIOT ASYLUM.

	Males.	Females.	Total.
Remaining last report..............	308	160	468
Admitted	77	70	147
Total	385	230	615
Died	15	9	24
Discharged	106	47	153
Remaining	264	174	438
	385	230	615

Statistics of Hospitals.

	Capacity.	Patients treated.	Transferred.	Discharged.	Died.	Ambulance calls.	Dispensary calls treated.	Persons treated in dispensary.
Bellevue	938	24,523	23,805	17,422	1,932	6,740	152,753	62,786
&ar	DO	3,385	1,423	1,573	310	4,613	63,274	4,613
Harlem	40	8,366	1,529	1,544	270	4,102	61,157	26,508
Fordham	44	1,386	202	988	180	1,728	7,147	3,485
City	750	7,469	122	6,032	683	...	...	...
Metropolitan	425	3,913	50	3,166	312	...	...	...
Emergency	15	336	...	298	10	...	...	...
ine	2,750	4,884	...	2,430	414	...	...	...
Infants'	300	1,580	...	1,150	195	...	...	...
Children's	100	830	...	417	26	...	...	...
Feebl eMinded School	500	602	84	60	27	...	...	...

CENSUS OF OFFICERS, EMPLOYES AND PATIENTS.
October 1, 1901.

	Officers and paid employes.	Unpaid help.	Workhouse help (daily gang).	Patients.
Central office..........	21	......	......	......
Bellevue	570	......	......	700
Gouverneur	85	......	......	79
Harlem	49	......	......	28
Fordham	41	......	......	41
City	224	54	......	591
Metropolitan	201	36	20	353
Almshouse	204	......	......	2,035
Infants'	169	2	......	208
Hospitals and schools..	242	18	......	819
Lodging-house	19	23	......	83
Outdoor Poor Department	49	2	......	......
Steamboats	46	......	......	......
Storehouse	13	47	45	......
Training School.......	79	......	......	......
Total............	2,012	184	65	4,937

NUMBER OF EMPLOYES IN THE DEPARTMENT.
October 1, 1900, and October 1, 1901.

	1900.	1901.
Officers and paid employes....................	1,698	2,012
Unpaid employes...........................	198	184
Workhouse helpers..........................	14	65
	1,910	2,261

a decrease of 14 unpaid helpers, and an increase of 51 workhouse helpers and 314 paid employes.

This required an appropriation of $459,316 for salaries.

ALMSHOUSE, BLACKWELL'S ISLAND.

INCLUDING ALMSHOUSE HOSPITALS, HOSPITALS FOR INCURABLES
AND BLIND ASYLUM.

	Males.	Females.	Total.
Number of inmates October 1, 1900.....	886	888	1,774
Admitted during the ensuing year......	1,744	1,366	3,110
Total	2,630	2,254	4,884
Number discharged during year........	1,559	1,071	2,630
Died	213	231	444
Transferred to City Hospital...........	....	......	......
Transferred to Metropolitan Hospital...	....	......	......
Transferred to other institutions.......	....	......	......
Number remaining October 1, 1901......	858	952	1,810
Total	2,630	2,254	4,884
Capacity of almshouse (inmates only), including all departments.............	1,439	1,313	2,752
Of those admitted to the almshouse during year ending October 1, 1901, there were admitted for first time..........	685	538	1,223
Number of cases of phthisis in almshouse on October 1, 1900..................	41	43	84

BLIND ASYLUM.

	Males.	Females.	Total.
Number of inmates remaining October 1, 1902	50	70	120
Admitted during ensuing year..........	124	5	129
Total	174	75	249
Died	....	......	......
Discharged	120	5	125
Number remaining October 1, 1901......	54	70	124
Total	174	75	249

HOSPITAL FOR INCURABLES.

	Males.	Females.	Total.
Number of patients October 1, 1900.....	58	54	112
Admitted during ensuing year..........	17	22	39
Total	75	76	151
Died	8	12	20
Discharged	10	10	20
Remaining October 1, 1901.............	57	54	111
Total	75	76	151

ALMSHOUSE HOSPITALS.

	Males.	Females.	Total.
Number remaining October 1, 1900......	155	156	311
Admitted during ensuing year.........	741	733	1,474
Total	896	889	1,785
Died	213	231	444
Discharged	525	509	1,034
Remaining October 1, 1901.............	158	149	307
Total	896	889	1,785

Respectfully,

ROBERT W. HILL,

Inspector.

JANUARY 15, 1902.

REPORT

OF

Visitation of Almshouses

IN THE

SECOND JUDICIAL DISTRICT.

519

REPORT.

For the purposes of inspection the Second Judicial District is divided into two parts, one of which covers Kings and Queens counties, now incorporated in the city of New York, and the other the several counties of the district outside the city. Since the organization of Greater New York the public charities of Kings county, while operated independently of the other boroughs, have been provided for by the common treasury. In the original charter of the greater city, Brooklyn was organized as a borough with its own commissioner of charities and staff of officials, and the several borough commissioners were united in one general department of charities, the president of which was the commissioner for the boroughs of Manhattan and the Bronx.

Under the revised charter, which became operative on the 1st day of January, 1902, the public charities of the several boroughs are united in one department, a single commissioner of charities having the management and control of the public charitable institutions in all the boroughs. Brooklyn and Richmond have deputy commissioners who are responsible for the proper management of the almshouses and hospitals in their respective boroughs. Kings and Queens counties, therefore, should be considered hereafter in connection with the public charities of the city rather than as counties maintaining independent institutions.

IMPROVEMENTS.

A number of improvements were made in the Flatbush institutions during the past year, and gradually the almshouse and hospital are being brought to a satisfactory condition. This is especially true of the hospital. Within the year changes have taken place which are calculated to promote the comfort of all the patients. Wards which in the past were dark and gloomy are now light and cheerful. The sanitary conditions have been improved, and a better classification conduces to the welfare of all the patients.

In the almshouse the crowded dormitories and general lack of accommodations have worked against the welfare of the inmates. At all seasons of the year this almshouse has been crowded, and in stormy weather—especially during the cold season—the large number of inmates has made the wards very uncomfortable. These conditions are to be changed. The construction of pavilions for work and recreation will afford the inmates opportunities for change of air, which lack of room heretofore has made impossible. Hereafter they can use the pavilions for shelter when it is undesirable to have them in the open air. By the use of the pavilions during the day the general dormitories can be aired, and thus the health of the inmates will be promoted.

In the counties outside of the city of New York, conditions have shown a tendency toward improvement. One county is engaged in the erection of an entirely new set of buildings for its almshouse. In the other counties attention has been given to repairs and to improvements calculated to promote safety. The matters of fire protection, water, hospitals and classification have been considered more or less, and, on the whole, throughout the Second District, it may be said the year has been fruitful, and there is a clear indication of a purpose on the part of the authorities to make ample provision for the welfare of the public dependents under their charge.

DUTCHESS COUNTY ALMSHOUSE.
Millbrook, N. Y.

At the date of writing this report plans have been approved and contracts let for the construction of a new almshouse for Dutchess county. For years the old wooden buildings have been unsatisfactory for many reasons. The sanitary conditions have jeopardized health; the construction of the dormitories and the lack of help have prevented proper care of the inmates.

The location of the old almshouse is bad, being very near, and all the drainage of the institution discharging into, a tract of swampy ground. It was originally intended to have the new buildings erected on higher land and at a considerable distance from this spot, but the last report of inspection indicates a purpose to build on the site now in use. The buildings are to be removed, and pending the erection of the new almshouse, the inmates will be transferred to the Amenia Seminary, which is at some distance from the county farm.

It is to be regretted that an opportunity to relocate the almshouse has not been embraced. All the sanitary conditions could be improved by building on the higher ground, miasmatic exhalations from the swamp be avoided, and it would be possible to keep the ground in much better condition as the natural drainage would carry off storm water.

At the time the plans were approved the architect stated that the buildings were to be located on the higher ground, but some influence has been brought to bear upon the supervisors, and the old site is now substituted for that recommended in former reports.

The general plan of the proposed buildings is similar to that recommended by the State Board some years ago; the dormitories are to be placed on each side of a central work and service building, the administration building forming the front of the group. All the buildings are to be connected by corridors which will afford protection to the inmates in stormy weather, and comfortable places for sun, rest and air at other times.

It is likely that the present power house will be retained for service in connection with the new buildings. It is hardly large enough, and if this was the principal reason for location upon the old grounds the county could have well afforded the cost of a new power house rather than have lost the opportunity of properly placing this important institution, which is intended to serve for a century.

At the time of the last inspection the almshouse was found in a generally clean condition; the grounds were orderly; the premises have been kept fairly free from vermin, although the practice of hanging wearing apparel upon the walls furnishes opportunity for vermin to harbor. It was noted, however, that the store rooms were in a disorderly and unclean condition.

Complaint has been made that the physician employed to visit the almshouse has not made visits with such regularity as is necessary. He is said to give ample attention in cases of acute attacks and to be very prompt in his service whenever special cases require attention, but at other times his visits are very irregular. A physician who could devote more time to the service of the almshouse would probably be more useful.

The food in the main has been satisfactory, although during the winter but two meals are served daily, and the meals have little variety from day to day.

CENSUS.

The census was as follows:

	Males.	Females.	Total.
Number of inmates	119	24	143
Children under two years	1	0	1
Children between two and sixteen years	0	0	0
Number of blind	1	0	1
Number of deaf-mutes	0	0	0
Number of feeble-minded	3	1	4
Number of idiots	2	0	2
Number of epileptics	0	1	1
Persons over seventy years old	26	13	39

POUGHKEEPSIE CITY ALMSHOUSE.
Poughkeepsie, N. Y.

This institution is one of the best almshouses not only in this district but in the State. Its management is satisfactory, the inmates are contented because well cared for. It has a fine group of well located brick buildings, with the several parts connected by inclosed corridors. At the time of the several inspections it was reported in excellent condition throughout, clean, well furnished, and in arrangement up-to-date.

Recently a new brick storehouse and carriage barn, with a fine cellar underneath, has been added to the group; new floors have been laid in some of the buildings. These with outside stairs as fire-escapes from the rear buildings, and steel ceilings and general repairs, constitute the recent improvements.

In the matter of fire protection, stand pipes and hose connections have been installed on all the floors, so that as far as ordinary foresight can provide protection it has been made. It is expected that more fire-escapes will be placed on the main buildings. Although there is very little danger of a fire, in view of the height of the buildings and the character of the inmates it is deemed essential to have this provision for escape in time of danger. The abundant supply of water furnished by the Poughkeepsie city water system is a great protection.

The bathing facilities are the same as at the report of the committee a year ago, consisting of four zinc tubs, two of which are intended for each sex. It is hoped that spray baths will be installed in a short time, and when this is done it is proposed to put in a sterilizer to make complete the laundry equipment.

The board of charity of the city of Poughkeepsie, which manages this institution, has worked on broad lines and endeavored to make this almshouse a model, so far as equipment and liberal support can do it. The almshouse is a credit to the city and shows what can be done when an intelligent commission undertakes to solve the problems of the almshouse.

The last step taken by the superintendent, under the direction of the Board of Managers, is in the direction of classification of the sick. All suffering from special forms of communicable disease are now isolated. Owing to the frequent presence of many persons afflicted with contagious diseases, it might be well to have a special hospital building as an annex to the almshouse.

CENSUS.

The census was as follows:

	Males.	Females.	Total.
Number of inmates	35	39	74
Children under two years	1	0	1

Children between two and sixteen years	Males.	Females.	Total.
Children between two and sixteen years	0	1	1
Number of blind	0	1	1
Number of deaf-mutes	0	0	0
Number of feeble-minded	0	4	4
Number of idiots	0	0	0
Number of epileptics	0	0	0
Persons over seventy years old	17	18	35

HEMPSTEAD TOWN ALMSHOUSE.

Hempstead, N. Y.

In addition to the several inspections of the year 1901, a special inspection of this almshouse was made on the 15th of January, 1902, in time for the annual report.

The conditions, from a sanitary standpoint, were found to have improved during the year. Two modern shower baths have been installed, and the water supply is greatly increased. A caloric engine lifts the water to a steel tank capable of holding 1,000 barrels. This tank is in the attic of the main building. The shower baths are practically useless, however; the construction work was poorly done, and the rooms in which the baths are placed are not large enough.

An effort to classify the sick is now made. The ordinary patients are looked after in their own rooms, but men suffering from contagious forms of disease are placed in a small cabin somewhat removed from the main building.

The old tramp house has outlived its usefulness, and should be razed. If it is found necessary to maintain a tramp house, a good building with sanitary equipment should be erected. The present building is not clean, and its general condition unfits it for tenancy. The same is true of the small hospital building, and both these structures should be thoroughly cleansed and then be kept in such condition. The main building was found clean throughout, everything being in an orderly condition.

Food is served only twice a day during the winter months. It was found well cooked and abundant, but two meals may entail a hardship upon those who have been accustomed to breakfast, dinner, and supper. This is especially true in the winter season, when the inclement weather makes greater demands upon the system than are made at other seasons.

The chief needs of this almshouse are in the line of greater fire protection. Like all large frame buildings, this is in constant danger from an outbreak of fire. It is hoped the authorities having it in charge will take steps to make it as safe as possible.

CENSUS.

The census was as follows:

	Males.	Females.	Total.
Number of inmates..................	27	13	40
Children under two years old........	0	0	0
Children between two and sixteen years	0	0	0
Number of blind....................	1	0	1
Number of deaf-mutes...............	0	0	0
Number of feeble-minded............	3	1	4
Number of idiots....................	1	1	2
Number of epileptics................	0	0	0
Persons over seventy years old......	12	7	19

NORTH HEMPSTEAD AND OYSTER BAY TOWN ALMSHOUSE.

East Norwich, N. Y.

This almshouse remains in practically the same condition as it was at the time of the last annual report. An number of improvements were suggested, plans have been approved for them, and it was expected that they would have been finished long ago. Owing to failure to secure an appropriation, nothing has been done. This almshouse is endowed. It has two funds invested, the revenue from which is used to support the institution. One amounts to $30,000 and the other to $18,000. Besides the interest from the invested funds, the moneys derived from excise are applied to the support of the almshouse, and there should have been enough to make all the repairs and enlargements suggested.

The sanitary conditions do not conduce to the welfare of the inmates. Bath tubs, flush water-closets and better drains are needed, but everything waits for necessary action by the town board.

One great need of this institution is better protection against the dangers of fire. Three barrels filled with water, located in different parts of the main building, are the only available means of fire defence. For a building of such rambling combustible character, having three inside stairways and no fire escapes, greater protection is needed.

The housekeeping department is to be commended. The residence building was found clean throughout.

Two meals a day are served during the winter months. The food provided is well cooked and abundant, but there is probably little economy in the plan of having only two meals each day.

CENSUS.

The census was as follows:

	Males.	Females.	Total.
Number of inmates..................	36	8	44
Children under two years............	0	0	0
Children between two and sixteen years	0	0	0
Number of blind.....................	2	0	2
Number of deaf-mutes..............	0	0	0
Number of feeble-minded............	0	0	0
Number of idiots....................	0	0	0
Number of epileptics................	0	0	0
Persons over seventy years old......	9	4	13

Of this number, 12 men (3 of whom are over 70 years of age) are maintained at the expense of Nassau county.

THE DEPENDENT POOR OF NASSAU COUNTY.

At the time of the division of Queens county, the almshouse on Barnum's Island, in which the county poor of Queens had been maintained for many years, was turned over to the new county of Nassau. It had a large number of buildings, an electric light and heating plant, and could have provided accommodation for many more persons than were usually dependent in Nassau county.   It was thought wise to sell this almshouse; it was considered too large for the county's needs, as well as too expensive.   When the almshouse was sold the county made arrangements with the two town almshouses in the county and with the Brunswick Home, at Amityville, to care for the county adult charges.   The conditions in the town almshouses have already been presented.   It remains necessary to speak of those in the Brunswick Home.   This is a private corporation.   It is used for the purpose of receiving patients from cities, towns or counties which have to maintain patients as public charges, and from guardians, parents and others who desire to place defective or afflicted wards in an institution.

Nassau county maintains 14 persons in this home.   Of this number, 2 are epileptics; 5 are idiots (2 of whom are blind); 4 are feeble minded; and 3 are cripples, whose only means of getting about is the wheel chair.   One of the feeble-minded patients is a dumb boy of seven years; two of the cripples are young men, one 21 and the other 28 years of age; the third is a young woman of 26 years.   Of those classed as feeble-minded, two are men 63 and 73 years of age respectively, and therefore are suffering from senility.   Two of the idiots are females, one 31 years of age and the other 15; the three males are aged respectively 30, 25 and 36.   Both the epileptics are males, their ages being 27 and 39 years.

It will be seen from this enumeration that the institution receives all classes of patients.   Its facilities for the care of these defectives are better than those of the ordinary alms-house.   This is due to the larger number of attendants employed, and to the further fact that the institution is fitted up as a custodial asylum.

It is doubtful expediency for the county of Nassau to make contracts with a private corporation for the care of its dependents of this class.   Of course the crowded condition of the State institutions may render such a step necessary as a temporary expedient, but as a final solution of the problem of the care of defectives such contracts will hardly prove satisfactory.

An institution of this kind is run for profit, and, while the managers will give a measure of care, they expect to make a profit.   This home is intended to return a regular profit to its

34

owners. While nothing may be said adverse to the treatment of patients, it is against public policy to make the maintenance of paupers or defectives a matter of private gain. The temptation is always present to push economies to such an extent as to deprive patients of the attention and treatment they should receive.

It would be better for Nassau county to combine in one the two almshouses now maintained by the public. and. placing it under the charge of the county authorities. make provision for all the public dependents in a satisfactory way. The income from the several endowments set apart for the maintenance of the poor will be ample to pay all the expenses of a well equipped modern almshouse. These endowments need not be lost by a transfer to the county. for all the conditions attached to the endowments could be carried out by the county itself. At the present time the division of the endowments into three parts entails an unnecessary expense of administration which could be saved were the county to maintain this almshouse. The poor in the two almshouses would have better treatment, and the last vestige of the contract system disappear. This is not merely a matter of economy—the vital interest is that of humanity. Where the contract system prevails, no matter how carefully guarded its provisions may appear, there is always danger that the effort to profit by the contract may result in abuse of the inmates. It may be further urged in favor of this plan that. while giving full credit for the changes which have been made in the two town almshouses of the county, it is a fact that neither can be considered entirely satisfactory. A county almshouse built on modern plans and properly equipped will prove economical and assure more satisfactory results.

ORANGE COUNTY ALMSHOUSE.
Orange Farm, N. Y.

This almshouse consists of a group of three residence buildings, in addition to the barns and outbuildings. Two of these buildings are of stone, and the other of brick. Of the stone structures, one contains quarters for the men and the work and service department. In the other two are located the hospital and the dormitories for the women.

In general the buildings are in good condition, although the basement and upper floors of the brick dormitory need new plumbing and painting. Recently fire protection has been added by the introduction of a fire riser to carry water to the third floor of the men's building. Connected with this are four swinging hose brackets with hose and all connections. This gives adequate protection; with the hydrants near the several buildings, and water under heavy pressure from the village supply system, it may be said the institution is as well guarded as is here possible.

One other improvement should be added—an outside iron fire-escape upon the brick building for women, but no appropriation was made for the further repairs or improvements at the last session of the board of supervisors. A steam laundry is also necessary. The present hand appliances are inadequate, and as a consequence there is never a certainty that the laundry work is well done.

By a resolution of the supervisors, the system of having three superintendents of the poor for the county is to be discontinued. One superintendent will be retired each year until the last of the three remains, and he and his successors will thereafter reside at the almshouse and act as both superintendent and keeper.

CENSUS.

The census was as follows:

	Males.	Females.	Total.
Number of inmates	94	47	141
Children under two years	2	0	2
Children between two and sixteen years	0	2	2
Number of blind	6	1	7
Number of deaf-mutes	0	0	0
Number of feeble-minded	5	5	10
Number of idiots	2	0	2
Number of epileptics	1	4	5
Persons over seventy years old	28	15	43

NEWBURGH CITY ALMSHOUSE.
Newburgh, N. Y.

Some interior improvements have been made at this institution. These include sanitary plumbing and the introduction of fire extinguishers. It is intended to build a water tower in connection with the men's building. At the time of inspection all the buildings were found in good order, and the inmates cared for in a satisfactory manner.

CHILDREN'S HOME.

As a part of the charitable work of the city of Newburgh, a Children's Home is maintained by the commissioners of charity. This is entirely distinct from and has no connection with the almshouse. The building is located in the heart of the town, where the children have all the advantages of the public school. This Home was found in a satisfactory condition, with 15 boys and 15 girls under care. Here, as well as in the almshouse, the diet was carefully examined and found satisfactory.

CENSUS.

The almshouse census was as follows:

	Males.	Females.	Total.
Number of inmates..................	64	40	104
Children under two years old.........	1	1	2
Children between two and sixteen years	0	0	0
Number of blind....................	1	1	2
Number of deaf-mutes...............	2	1	3
Number of feeble-minded............	3	1	4
Number of idiots....................	1	0	1
Number of epileptics................	2	0	2
Persons over seventy years old.......	17	16	33

PUTNAM COUNTY ALMSHOUSE.
Carmel, N. Y.

Here the main building is a frame structure, two stories high, with finished attic and basement. In this both men and women are housed. A one-story wooden cottage in the rear is used as a hospital for the men. These buildings are generally in good repair, but the fact that they are built entirely of combustible material renders it necessary that great precautions be taken against fire. There are five liquid chemical fire extinguishers, which are the main dependence. As means of escape there are inside stairways and two rope fire-escapes from the third floor. The simple statement of a rope fire-escape from the third story indicates the utter worthlessness of the arrangement for the safety of decrepit aged people. Structures of this character, when so poorly equipped, are exceedingly dangerous, and would probably be fire-traps for all who are on the upper floor.

During the year the water supply has been greatly improved, and flush water-closets connected with soakage cesspools were installed. In fact, the plumbing throughout the almshouse has been overhauled. Three porcelain-lined steel bath tubs are now in service, and the kitchen is equipped with a new range.

The dietary was found satisfactory so far as quality, variety, and quantity of food are concerned.

CENSUS.

The census was as follows:

	Males.	Females.	Total.
Number of inmates..................	35	7	42
Children under two years old........	0	0	0
Children between two and sixteen years	0	0	0
Number of blind.....................	1	0	1
Number of deaf-mutes...............	0	0	0
Number of feeble-minded.............	2	0	2
Number of idiots.....·...............	0	0	0
Number of epileptics................	0	0	0
Persons over seventy years old.......	8	3	11

ROCKLAND COUNTY ALMSHOUSE.

Viola, N. Y.

This almshouse is in good repair, the buildings being of brick with roofs of slate and tin. Each of the residence buildings is three stories high. No improvements have been made recently, nor are any in contemplation. The precautions against fire are not adequate. There are only three small dry chemical extinguishers, some garden hose upon a reel kept in the laundry building, which is near the one occupied by the women. As there are no outside fire-escapes, the fire risk is increased. Fortunately the two inside stairways are located one at each end of the building.

In this almshouse there is no special accommodation for the sick. Whatever their ailment may be, the sufferers must be cared for in their rooms. This jeopardizes the health of all the inmates, and it would be well were a suitable hospital erected. Some adverse criticism may properly be made of the housekeeping department.

CENSUS.

The census was as follows:

	Males.	Females.	Total.
Number of inmates..................	79	31	110
Children under two years old.........	0	1	1
Children between two and sixteen years	1	1	2
Number of blind.....................	2	1	3
Number of deaf-mutes...............	0	0	0
Number of feeble-minded.............	4	3	7
Number of idiots....................	1	0	1
Number of epileptics.................	0	0	0
Persons over seventy years old.......	29	12	41

SUFFOLK COUNTY ALMSHOUSE.

Yaphank, N. Y.

The general condition of this institution is very satisfactory. The buildings are in excellent repair, the grounds attractive. This almshouse has a separate building for the sick. In this the men have wards upon the main floor, and women upon the second. This building will accommodate 26 sick persons. There are three paid hospital attendants to look after the patients.

Under the supervision of the county superintendent, on a farm adjoining the almshouse property, is located the Suffolk County Children's Home. Mr. and Mrs. Waldemar Bapst have charge of the 24 boys and 22 girls who are at present maintained in the Home. The teacher gives the children daily instruction, and they are carefully watched over until homes are found for them.

CENSUS.

The census was as follows:

	Males.	Females.	Total.
Number of inmates	71	65	136
Children under two years old	1	2	3
Children between two and sixteen years	0	0	0
Number of blind	4	1	5
Number of deaf-mutes	1	1	2
Number of feeble-minded	13	22	35
Number of idiots	1	1	2
Number of epileptics	2	2	4
Persons over seventy years old	23	27	50

WESTCHESTER COUNTY ALMSHOUSE.
East View, N. Y.

This is a large institution, the several buildings used for dormitories being connected. The main building is of stone, and of the four additions three are stone structures and one concrete. The hospital is a new building three stories high, with a basement. This has been occupied only a year, and it was found necessary to build a pest house in addition, for patients suffering from contagious diseases. The almshouse has been visited by small-pox several times lately, and in consequence a rigid quarantine has been in force for some time.

Electric lighting should be introduced into the almshouse and an elevator into the hospital. At the time of visitation the institution was in good order, clean in all its parts. The removal of a number of small outbuildings has opened the grounds in front of the main building and improved the general appearance.

One matter which should be remedied here is the lack of sufficient quarters for the dining-room. These are so small that it necessitates setting the tables a number of times to accommodate all the inmates.

CENSUS.

The census was as follows:

	Males.	Females.	Total.
Number of inmates................	176	78	254
Children under two years old.........	2	7	9
Children between two and sixteen years	1	2	3
Number of blind.....................	2	0	2
Number of deaf-mutes...............	0	0	0
Number of feeble-minded............	3	3	6
Number of idiots...................	1	0	1
Number of epileptics...............	2	2	4
Persons over seventy years old........	38	15	53

RICHMOND COUNTY ALMSHOUSE.
Port Richmond, N. Y.

Since the county of Richmond was made a part of the city of New York, under the name of "The Borough of Richmond," the control of the almshouse at Port Richmond has been assumed by the Department of Charities of the city. Its maintenance is provided for in the general budget, and such matters as are necessary from time to time are now ordered by the department. This change of relations has worked to the advantage of the almshouse itself. The city of New York is better able and more willing to appropriate funds for repairs and betterments than was the county. One other and perhaps even a greater advantage is the coördination with the other charities of the city. It is now possible to classify the almshouse inmates, and send to other places those whom it is not desirable to keep in this institution.

There are seventeen buildings, one of them about one hundred years old, the others more or less modern, but all somewhat out of date for almshouse purposes where a population is as mixed as it has been in this institution. The transfer of some of the inmates now kept here, to Blackwell's or Randall's Island will be advantageous, for these buildings can be turned to good account in the final distribution of the wards of the city.

Probably because the plan of classification has not been decided upon, no improvements to these buildings have been attempted. They are still lighted by kerosene lamps and heated by hot air furnaces and stoves. The ventilation is by doors and windows only, and the bathing facilities are inadequate. When the classification plan is elaborated, changes must be made in these conditions as well as in the general sanitation and means of escape in event of fire.

The care of the sick is somewhat primitive, so far as accommodations are concerned. A two-story frame building, originally designed for the laundry, is now used as the hospital for women; however, only the first floor is in service, and on this are eight beds. The men are cared for on the first floor of the men's building, and on this floor the hospital consists of a room which contains twelve beds. The ventilation is poor, and the sick are not at all comfortable.

The general care of the grounds and outbuildings, as well as those devoted to residence, is excellent. The food was pronounced abundant and satisfactory by the inmates. It is hoped that steps will be taken to coördinate all the almshouses and public hospitals of the city, that there may be soon a proper classification of all public charges, in which event the Richmond almshouse will have an appropriate place.

CENSUS.

The census was as follows:

	Males.	Females.	Total.
Number of inmates.................	64	42	106
Children under two years old........	0	1	1
Children between two and sixteen....	0	0	0
Number of blind....................	1	0	0
Number of deaf-mutes..............	0	0	0
Number of feeble-minded............	9	17	26
Number of idiotic	0	1	1
Number of epileptic................	2	3	5
Persons over seventy years old......	23	10	33

KINGS COUNTY ALMSHOUSE.

Flatbush, N. Y. .

Including the employes, who numbered 52, the population of the Kings County Almshouse at Flatbush on the 31st of December, 1901, numbered 1,321 persons. Of this total, 732 were adult males and 589 were adult females. On the same day, in the Kings County Hospital there were under treatment 361 male adults, 156 female adults, 31 male children and 40 female children. Besides these there were in the hospital 77 unpaid male helpers, 7 unpaid female helpers, 83 male employes and 90 female employes, a total of 845 persons. The unpaid help were all convalescents who were retained to assist in the work until completely recovered.

In the Neurological Hospital there were 66 male adults and 58 female adults under treatment, 3 male employes and 4 female employes, a total of 131 persons.

In the pavilions for feeble-minded there were 15 male children, 24 female children, 22 male adults, 42 female adults, 3 male employes, and 7 female employes, a total of 113, making a grand total for the Flatbush institution of 2,410.

This number covered the administrative as well as the pauper population. It included the training school for nurses, the resident medical staff, the mechanical department, stable and transportation helpers, storehouse, bookkeeping and drug departments. The total number of employes and assistants of all kinds was 326, of whom 190 were connected with the hospital service and 136 with the almshouse.

The buildings used by these institutions have been greatly improved within the last three years, and now are in a markedly better condition than ever before. The additions, extensions, and new buildings have not only changed the general appearance but increased the efficiency of all departments. However, in spite of the improvements which have been made, these buildings are not yet adequately equipped for the great service they are called upon to perform each year. For example, the heating plant, which might have been sufficient for the buildings as they stood four years ago, is not sufficient for the institution as it stands with all the recent new buildings and additions. At the present time there are two heating plants, each independent of the other, one at the almshouse and the other at the hospital, and both are very old, the one at the hospital being in a very dilapidated condition. If there were a consolidation of these heating plants, and a proper installation of the additional boilers necessary to furnish all the heat and power required, several economies could be practiced which are now impossible.

At the present time the electric light is furnished by the Flatbush Gas Company, and in 1901 this cost the city $10,869.17, yet during the same time the cost of the coal for the heating plants was $16,170.98. Two years ago a new heating and lighting plant, centrally located and arranged to supply all the buildings, was recommended by the State Board of Charities. This is still the only economical method to provide proper facilities for the institution. Such a plant could be built for an estimated cost of $125,000, and as a result there could be a saving of $10,000 for electric light, $6,540 in the cost of labor rendered unnecessary, while the new plant would burn at least twenty per cent. less coal, so that a heat and power plant, properly constructed, would result in a total saving of nearly $20,000 per annum. The need of such a plant is imperative, as something must be done to increase the resources of the institution in this direction.

The almshouse buildings have had a number of improvements made during the year. The plumbing was entirely overhauled, many of the buildings refurnished, and the workrooms and dining-rooms located in the basements repainted and receiled. As the buildings are all quite old, it is necessary to provide extensive repairs from year to year.

There is not sufficient room to accommodate the large number of people who are committed to and maintained in this institution, so that it has been necessary to transfer the care of the State poor committed from the city of New York from this institution to the almshouse on Blackwell's Island. Even this relief is not sufficient to meet the need for room. At least two additional pavilions are required to furnish adequate accommodation for the population. The fact that there are no day rooms in the almshouse buildings, the entire space being required for dormitory purposes, has been keenly felt, especially in stormy weather, when men have crowded into one room and the halls to find shelter from the inclemencies. Such pavilions as were proposed heretofore would provide not only sitting, or day rooms, but also work rooms, and enable the dining-rooms to be removed from the dark, ill-ventilated basements, for location above ground, where they could be made light, cheerful and comfortable. Under present circumstances it is impossible to do the work which ought to be done in this institution, as there is no place for work other than in poor dark rooms below the surface of the ground.

THE FEEBLE-MINDED.

Besides these pavilions, the provision made for the feeble-minded has not been found adequate. The distribution of this class of public charges in the several almshouses of the city makes it necessary to have sufficient accommodations at Flatbush for a large number of persons. As is shown above, 113 persons must be accommodated in the two pavilions now set aside for the use of the feeble-minded. If the suggestions heretofore made to the Commissioner of Public Charities of the city of New York are adopted, and a regrouping of all of this class of defectives be accomplished, these two pavilions will find proper employment in connection with the hospital work itself, and the removal of the feeble-minded will relieve some of the present strain. All the feeble-minded ought to find domiciles in the State institutions, but until the State institutions are enlarged sufficiently to accommodate all of this class now in the almshouses of the State, it will be necessary to provide for a large number in the institutions of the city of New York. It is not required, however, that they be retained in the scattered groups of the present time. All the feeble-minded below adult age could be sent properly to Randall's Island. It would be inexpedient, perhaps unwise, to send any of the adults of this class to that island. There the feeble-minded are in school under instruction and employment in various industries suitable to their powers. The presence of a large number of adults would interfere seriously with the course of instruction. But while the adults ought not to be permitted to interfere with the work on Randall's Island, there are other places in the city where they could be well cared for. Until these persons can be removed to State institutions, it is incumbent upon the city to make adequate provision for their proper care.

THE HOSPITAL.

The hospital has been doing more efficient service during the past year. The appended statistics will show that, measured by the number of cases sent to it from week to week, it is one of the most important in the city. It therefore should be properly maintained, and have such additions made as will enable it to continue and extend its beneficent work.

A new general store house is needed. At the present time the inadequate store houses are scattered and are hardly suitable for the large business which has to be transacted. A new store house is a necessity, and by erecting one large enough all of the steward's department could be under one roof.

In three years from now the State will be compelled to vacate the buildings occupied by the insane on the adjoining tract, and then the hospital work will probably be extended to embrace wards thus left at the disposal of the city. To provide for this extension of work, and to make it possible to conduct the several store departments with economy, it will be necessary to erect new buildings.

LABORATORY.

The clinical laboratory and morgue is a small building. There are accommodations for only nine bodies. It is unwise as well as impracticable to attempt to convey bodies from this hospital to the central morgue at the foot of Twenty-sixth street, therefore there should be a mortuary building large enough to accommodate at least three times the number of bodies which can now be cared for. This would enlarge also the clinical laboratory and greatly enhance its usefulness.

WATER.

One other matter has been referred to in previous reports as deserving consideration, that is, the water supply. Last year, as in times past, this was furnished by a private water company, and the cost to the city was $8,932.32, which seems a very large price for the city to pay for water for these institutions,

when it can obtain a supply by the expenditure of a comparatively small amount. The entire cost of a private plant would
not exceed the amount which the city pays to the Flatbush
Water Company for a single year.

LAUNDRY.

One important improvement has been the consolidation of
the laundry work. A central laundry has been erected at a cost
of nearly $15,000. This will be , ready for use in the early
spring, and greatly lighten the labor in the laundry as well as
facilitate it. Last year a small frame pavilion was erected at
the almshouse for a smoking and sitting room, which will be
used in 1902. The total cost of this was $4,964.

OTHER IMPROVEMENTS.

The front of the hospital has been changed also, a new portico
having been constructed to take the place of the old dilapidated
one which had outlived its usefulness.

THE INSANE.

Heretofore the suspected insane have been kept in two wards
in the basement of the hospital building. These wards were
dark and inconvenient. A contract has been made for the erection, at a cost of $30,000, of a special pavilion for the observa-
tion of such cases. This will enable the hospital to transfer
the insane from the two small buildings originally intended for
hospital help, into which they have been lately removed from
the basement wards. Work has not yet been begun on this
pavilion, but as the contract is let it will be under way in a
very short time.

ALLIED HOSPITALS.

Beside the buildings at Flatbush, the city is about to open a
new hospital in another part of the city. The Brooklyn Homeopathic Hospital, turned over to the city, has been undergoing
repairs, alterations and improvements for a number of months,
at an expense of $45,000. It is said that it will require at least
$20,000 more to put the building in a satisfactory condition, and
to equip it for work. As this emergency hospital is greatly
needed, there should be no delay in furnishing its equipment.

During the summer time an emergency hospital is maintained at Coney Island. This is strictly for emergency cases; these are treated and transferred as soon as able to bear the long journey to the main hospital at Flatbush. Last season the Coney Island hospital did most acceptable work.

THE HELP.

One complaint of a serious nature has been made against the character of the help who are employed. A large number of convalescents are used in the hospital, but many permanent employes must be maintained, and in the minor positions the wages allowed by the city are not sufficient to attract the most satisfactory people. A slight addition to the wages now paid would remedy this, and secure to the public service, people willing and qualified to do satisfactory work.

SUPPLIES.

During the past year there was a considerable shortage in clothing, bedding and other supplies, especially during the last six months. This was in consequence of the appropriations being too small, and the necessity therefore of stopping the purchase of necessaries. It is hoped that there may be no future trouble on this score.

The total salary list on the 31st of December, 1901, was $35,662.50. For the month of January, 1902, about $15,000 additional has been asked for.

The following statistics of the general service in the borough of Brooklyn will be of interest.

Respectfully submitted,

ROBERT W. HILL,

Inspector.

NAME OF INSTITUTION.	Average daily census 1900.	Average daily census 1901.	Increase per cent. in average daily census 1901 over 1900.	Decrease per cent. in average daily census 1901 less than 1900.	Total expenses of institutions from January 1 to December 31, 1901.	Add increase per cent. in census to meet requisitions for 1902.	Deduct decrease per cent. in census to meet regulations for 1902.	Departmental estimate 1902.
Kings County Hospital	836	852	.0191	......	$106,794 66	$2,038 63	....	$108,773 29
Kings County Almshouse	1,420	1,373	......	.0331	98,769 14	....	$3,269 25	95,499 89
Cumberland Street Hospital. Estimated average census of 281 for 306 days at $0.34322 per diem								29,512 11
Reception Hospital, Coney Island. Estimated average census of 30 for 150 days at $0.34322 per diem								1,544 49
Bradford Street Hospital. Estimated average census of 35 for 183 days at $0.34322 per diem								2,198 32
Necessary increase per capita for 407,871 hospital days								21,120 19
Necessary increase per capita for 501,145 almshouse days								14,752 01
Central Office and City Morgue								10,000 00
								$283,400 30

Brought forward.......................... $283,400 30

Furnishings and equipment for Cumberland Street
    Hospital 15,000 00

1,000 iron beds for Kings County Almshouse, at
    $3.75 each.................................. 3,750 00

(Most of the beds now in use are of the old strap
    iron variety, with straw ticks. They are difficult
    to keep clean, uncomfortable, and the constant
    refilling of the ticks with straw is an expense
    that should be abolished.)

Total for supplies and contingencies........ $302,150 30

MISCELLANEOUS APPROPRIATIONS.

Additions, alterations and repairs, as per list.....	$41,500 00
Clothing for insane............................	4,000 00
New ambulances, horses, stable supplies, etc......	10,000 00
Rents	4,300 00
Burial of pauper dead.........................	2,000 00
Transportation of paupers.....................	1,300 00
Poor adult blind..............................	15,000 00
Burial of veterans	10,000 00
Donation to Grand Army veterans..............	10,000 00
Clothing for patients at Craig Colony...........	1,000 00
	$99,100 00

EXPENSES FOR 1901.

Central Office.

BOROUGH OF BROOKLYN.

Capacity.	Pay-roll Dec. 31, 1901.
One commissioner ....,........	$7,500 00
One deputy commissioner......................	5,000 00
One chief clerk................................	2,500 00
One bookkeeper	2,000 00
One secretary	2,400 00

35

	Pay-roll Dec. 31, 1901.
One private secretary	$1,500 00
One clerk	2,500 00
Two clerks, $1,800 each	3,600 00
One clerk	1,500 00
Two clerks, $1,200 each.......................	2,400 00
One clerk	1,000 00
One superintendent outdoor poor................	1,800 00
Two examiners in lunacy, $1,800 each...........	3,600 00
One warrant officer...........................	1,200 00
One investigator	1,120 00
Three investigators, $1,000 each..............	3,000 00
One messenger	1,000 00
One stenographer	1,200 00
Three physicians, $1,000 each.................	3,000 00
One janitress	840 00
Five examiners of charitable institutions, $1,000 each	5,000 00
One examiner of charitable institutions.........	1,200 00
One morgue keeper.............................	1,500 00
One telephone operator	480 00
	$56,840 00

KINGS COUNTY HOSPITAL.

Capacity.	Pay-roll Dec. 31, 1901.
One general medical superintendent.............	$4,000 00
One deputy superintendent	1,200 00
One steward	1,800 00
One clerk	1,000 00
Three clerks, $360 each.......................	1,080 00
One apothecary	1,200 00
One apothecary	780 00
One apothecary	600 00
Three enginemen, $3.50 per day................	3,832 50
Three stokers, $720 each.....................	2,160 00
One laundryman	660 00
Two laundry laborers, $600 each..............	1,200 00
One laundry laborer	420 00
One laundry laborer	480 00

	Pay-roll Dec. 31, 1901.
One laborer	$600 00
One laborer	720 00
One watchman	480 00
One watchman	420 00
One butcher	420 00
One baker	300 00
One morgue keeper	480 00
One elevator attendant	300 00
One stenographer and typewriter	750 00
One doorman	300 00
One barber	480 00
One attendant	240 00
One attendant	300 00
One supervising nurse	600 00
Five trained nurses	3,000 00
Five trained nurses, $360 each	1,800 00
One nurse	300 00
Two nurses, $360 each	720 00
One orderly	600 00
Three orderlies, $300 each	900 00
Three hospital helpers, $240 each	720 00
Four hospital helpers, $264 each	1,056 00
Eight hospital helpers, $300 each	2,400 00
Five hospital helpers, $360 each	1,800 00
Five hospital helpers, $216 each	1,080 00
One hospital helper	168 00
Eleven hospital helpers, $144 each	1,584 00
Eleven hospital helpers, $192 each	2,112 00
One cook	720 00
One cook	300 00
Three cooks, $240 each	720 00
One matron	540 00
One seamstress	216 00
One teacher	720 00
One waitress	240 00
One waitress	216 00
One waitress	180 00
Two waitresses, $192 each	384 00
One laundress	216 00

	Pay-roll Dec. 31, 1901
Three laundresses, $240 each.....................	$720 00
One superintendent, training school..............	1,200 00
Two supervising nurses, $480 each...............	960 00
One operating room nurse......................	420 00
One nurse	240 00
One nurse	216 00
Forty-three pupil nurses, $120 each..............	5,160 00
One pupil nurse...............................	144 00
	$58,554 50

KINGS COUNTY ALMSHOUSE.

Capacity.	Pay-roll Dec. 31, 1901.
One steward.....................................	$1,500 00
One chief engineer.............................	1,800 00
Three engineers, $3.50 per day...................	3,832 50
One stoker	780 00
Two stokers, $720 each.........................	1,440 00
One watchman.................................	420 00
One laundryman................................	600 00
Two chaplains, $450 each.......................	900 00
One cook......................................	360 00
One cook......................................	600 00
Three orderlies, $360 each......................	1,080 00
Two hospital helpers, $300 each.................	600 00
One hospital helper............................	720 00
One hospital helper............................	288 00
Three hospital helpers, $216 each...............	648 00
Three hospital helpers, $192 each...............	576 00
Two hospital helpers, $180 each.................	360 00
Four hospital helpers, $144 each................	576 00
Three hospital helpers, $240 each...............	720 00
One waitress	192 00
Two matrons, $540 each........................	1,080 00
Two nurses, $240 each.........................	480 00
One baker.....................................	720 00
One baker.....................................	600 00
Eight drivers, $720 each.......................	5,760 00

	Pay-roll Dec. 31, 1901.
One driver	$840 00
One driver	900 00
One foreman	1,800 00
Three carpenters, $3.60 per day each.............	3,240 00
One plasterer, $4 per day.......................	1,200 00
One plumber, $3.50 per day.....................	1,050 00
	$35,662 50

KINGS COUNTY HOSPITAL.
HOUSE DIET IN DECEMBER, 1901.

	Sunday.	Monday.	Tuesday.	Wednesday.	Thursday.	Friday.	Saturday.
Breakfast	Bread. Butter. Coffee. Hominy.	Bread. Butter. Coffee. Farina.	Bread. Butter. Coffee. Indian meal.	Bread. Butter. Coffee. Oatmeal.	Bread. Butter. Coffee. Farina.	Bread. Butter. Coffee. Hominy.	Bread. Butter. Coffee. Oatmeal.
Dinner	Bread. Beef soup. Boiled beef. Potatoes.	Bread. Veg. soup. Corned beef or mutton. Cabbage.	Bread. Coffee. Mutton or corned beef. Potatoes.	Bread. Thick soup. Beef. Sweet potatoes.	Bread. Corned or fresh beef. Potatoes. Beans.	Bread. Salt fish. Potatoes. Tea.	Bread. Veg. soup. Beef. Potatoes.
Supper	Bread. Butter. Tea. Baked apples. Stewed prunes.	Bread. Butter. Tea. Potatoes. Stewed apples.	Bread. Butter. Tea. Stewed prunes.	Bread. Butter. Tea. Potatoes. Stewed apples.	Bread. Butter. Tea. Stewed prunes.	Bread. Butter. Tea. Stewed apples.	Bread. Butter. Tea. Stew'd prunes.

The house diet has been the same for December and January. The supply of prunes and dried apples was exhausted about November 30, and with the exception of these items the entire list has been filled. The per capita quantity used is as follows:

	Ounces.
Tea	.088
Coffee	.2
Cereals	.5
Meat (fresh)	7.0
Corned beef	5.0
Salt pork	4.0
Potatoes	7.0
Butter	1.0
Beans	2.0
Salt hake	6.0
Dried fruits	'1.5
Fresh apples	4.0
Cabbage	4.0
Bread	ad libitum

The diets at the hospital are under the following captions:

"House Diet," as above.

"Half House Diet," as above except 1 quart milk substituted for the meat.

"Milk Diet," 3 quarts milk daily.

"Special Diet," 1 quart milk, 2 eggs, gruel, 1 pint; beef tea, 1 pint.

"Extra Diet" consists of the following list; any one or more of the articles may be ordered by attending physician, in addition to any one of the regular diets. for special cases: Sherry wine, egg nog, milk punch, Valentine's meat juice, Liebig's extract, malted milk, eggs, peptogenic milk, chicken soup. barley water, toast, custard.

The average number of patients on "Half House," "Milk" and "Special" diets for December, 1901, was 240, and for January, 1902, was 243.

The regular almshouse dietary is as follows:

	Sunday.	Monday.	Tuesday.	Wednesday.	Thursday.	Friday.	Saturday.
Breakfast	Bread. Butter. Coffee. Oatmeal.	Bread. Butter. Coffee. Hominy.	Bread. Butter. Coffee. Farina.	Bread. Butter. Coffee. Oatmeal.	Bread. Butter. Coffee. Hominy.	Bread. Butter. Coffee. Corn meal.	Bread. Butter. Coffee. Farina.
Dinner	Mutton stew. Potatoes. Bread.	Beef stew. Bread.	Salt hake. Potatoes. Bread. Coffee.	Boiled beef. Soup. Bread.	Beef. Beans. Bread.	Hake. Potatoes. Bread. Coffee.	Boiled beef. Soup. Bread.
Supper	Tea. Bread. Butter. Crackers.	Tea. Bread. Butter. Crackers.	Tea. Bread. Butter. Dried apples.	Tea. Bread. Butter. Bologna.	Tea. Bread. Butter. Prunes.	Tea. Bread. Butter. Eggs.	Tea. Bread. Butter. Prunes.

The per capita quantities allowed are as follows:

	Ounces.
Bread	ad libitum
Fresh meat.....................................	8
Butter	1
Coffee	$\frac{5}{8}$
Tea	$\frac{1}{8}$
Hake	8
Dried fruits....................................	$1\frac{1}{2}$
Cereals	$1\frac{1}{2}$
Eggs	1
Crackers	3

The dried fruits have not been furnished during December or January, otherwise the dietary has been fully carried out.

The average number of "Special Diets" in the almshouse during December, 1901, was 99, and during January, 1902, 121. The "Special Diet" consists of 1 egg, 1 quart milk, 1 pint of beef tea daily in addition to regular diet, and has not been changed since December 1, 1901.

The "White Table" at the almshouse is used by an average of 250 inmates, who are regularly employed on the grounds, stables, laundries, etc. In addition to the regular diet they get meat every day for supper.

STATISTICAL SUMMARY.

COUNTIES.	INMATES.			Children under 2 years.	Children between 2 and 16.	OVER 70 YEARS OLD.			Epileptics.	Feeble-minded.	Idiots.
	Male.	Female.	Total.			Male.	Female.	Total.			
Dutchess	119	24	143	1	0	26	13	39	1	4	2
?ie city	35	39	74	1	1	17	18	35	0	4	0
Kgs	826	656	1,482	0	9	184	144	328	35	114	4
?d town	27	13	40	0	0	12	7	19	0	4	2
*North ?d and ?er Bay	24	8	32	0	2	6	4	10	2	0	0
*Nassau	21	5	26	0	2	3	1	4	2	4	5
?ange	94	47	141	2	0	28	15	43	5	10	2
?urgh city	64	40	104	2	0	17	16	33	2	4	1
?	35	7	42	0	0	8	3	11	0	2	0
?nd	64	42	106	1	0	23	10	33	5	28	1
?nd	79	31	110	3	2	29	12	41	0	7	1
Suffolk	71	65	136	9	0	23	27	50	4	35	2
Westchester	176	78	254	9	3	38	15	53	4	6	1
Total	1,635	1,055	2,690	20	19	414	285	699	58	220	21

* As the Nassau County Almshouse has been discontinued, these dependents are cared for in the Brunswick Home, Amityville, with the exception of 12 men (3 of whom are over 70 years of age) who are at the North Hempstead and Oyster Bay Town Almshouse.

*² In addition to this number there are 12 men (3 of whom are 70 years of age) who are cared for at the expense of Nassau county.

REPORT

OF

Visitation of Almshouses

IN THE

THIRD JUDICIAL DISTRICT.

REPORT.

To the State Board of Charities:

Your commissioner presents his annual report upon the almshouses of the Third Judicial District, and is gratified to be able
to state that throughout the district conditions are much
improved, and that the general tendency is toward betterment.
During the year he has visited the several institutions and
examined into their condition.

IMPROVEMENTS.

The Albany almshouse has passed into the hands of a new
administration. The work and service building, which was
begun two years ago, has been completed and occupied. This
is a fine brick structure, roomy and well appointed. The hospital has been enlarged and remodeled, a new equipment of beds
and other necessary furniture installed, which, with sanitary
plumbing, makes this building very satisfactory, excepting as
to the new floors, which are in unsatisfactory condition. Other
improvements in the way of repairs were made to the dormitories, and the grounds were put in order.

A number of changes were made also in the Schoharie County
Almshouse, so that it is much better than at any time in its
history. In the almshouse of Greene county the chief recent
improvement is an increase of the water supply.

THE CARE OF THE SICK.

From what has been said, under the head of improvements in
Albany county, it will be seen that the care of the sick is a
matter of concern with those who have charge of these institutions. Throughout the entire district greater attention is now
paid to the proper care of inmates who are suffering from sickness. The work of the physician is more constant, the accommodations provided for patients increased, and the necessary
supplies suitable for the sick are furnished in abundance.

ADMINISTRATION.

It is a matter of satisfaction to the commissioner to be able to state that the administration of the several almshouses is not deteriorating. The officials generally are intelligent, zealous, and efficient, and, as a consequence, the management of these almshouses has due regard to the welfare of the poor, as well as that of the taxpayers.

The tables appended to the reports on the several counties will serve to show the general character of the inmates.

Respectfully submitted,

SIMON W. ROSENDALE,

Commissioner, Third Judicial District.

ALBANY ALMSHOUSE.

Albany, N. Y.

WILLIAM H. STORRS, *Superintendent.*

(Frequently visited by the commissioner during 1901.)

In addition to the regular inspections made during the year by the inspectors of almshouses, this institution was visited by the commissioner, in company with the Superintendent of State and Alien Poor, as well as on other occasions, and its condition observed from time to time.

At the time of the last annual report, important building operations were under way. These have been completed, and, as a result, the almshouse is in better condition than for many years. The new building for work and service is large and well arranged; the hospital is practically a new building; and all of the dormitories have received important repair. In the extension of the hospital, as well as in the older portion, the new floors are in very unsatisfactory condition; the attention of the superintendent has been called thereto, and it is hoped that they will be remedied.

Situated close to the business part of the city of Albany, there is constant inducement for inmates of this almshouse to seek permission to spend the day in the town, but, under the new commissioner, an effort is made to prevent such wandering about the streets. In the past, one great source of trouble has been the facility with which inmates could obtain intoxicants. It required diligent oversight to prevent indulgence, but a determined effort of the new superintendent is directed toward the prevention of this evil.

At the time of the inspection the institution was found clean throughout. all things apparently in order, and the inmates contented.

CENSUS.

The census was as follows:

	Males.	Females.	Total.
Number of inmates..................	125	66	191
Children under two years...........	0	0	0
Children between two and 16 years..	0	0	0
Number of blind....................	2	2	4
Number of deaf-mutes...............	0	0	0
Number of feeble-minded............	8	11	19
Number of idiots...................	0	0	0
Number of epileptics...............	0	0	0
persons over 70 years old...........	26	25	51

COLUMBIA COUNTY ALMSHOUSE.

Ghent, N. Y.

J. H. RIVENBURGH, *Superintendent.*

(Visited by the commissioner August 31, 1901.)

All the buildings of this almshouse are in good repair, and, at the time of inspection by the commissioner, were in excellent condition, well appointed, and the walls well whitened.

There have been no improvements made recently beyond the ordinary casual repairs. The matters of a steam laundry and of electric lighting were considered at a meeting of the board of supervisors, and it is possible that during the year these may be introduced.

The food supplied to the inmates is of good quality and in sufficient quantity. The officials seem to have the interest of the inmates at heart.

CENSUS.

The census was as follows:

	Males.	Females.	Total.
Number of inmates..................	101	37	138
Children under two years old........	2	0	2
Children between two and sixteen years	0	0	0
Number of blind....................	0	2	2
Number of deaf-mutes..............	0	0	0
Number of feeble-minded...........	6	9	15
Number of idiots...................	3	3	6
Number of epileptics...............	4	0	4
Persons over seventy years old......	40	15	55

GREENE COUNTY ALMSHOUSE.

Cairo, N. Y.

A. V. DECKER, *Keeper*.

(Visited by the commissioner September 21, 1901.)

These buildings are in good condition. Some minor repairs have been made, and others are in progress. The almshouse is lighted by kerosene oil lamps, which are dangerous. The water supply has been improved since the last report; the main supply is now received from the Cairo water works.

While precautions against fire have been improved, there is still a lack of outside fire escapes. This almshouse has a large number of feeble-minded and defective inmates, there being no less than 13 who are classed as idiotic or feeble-minded, besides 4 blind persons and 3 epileptics. Twenty-seven of the inmates are over seventy years of age.

The food is supplemented by the butter and milk from the dairy, and the inmates gave evidence, by testimony, of having been well cared for.

CENSUS.

The census was as follows:

	Males.	Females.	Total.
Number of inmates..................	45 .	32	77
Children under two years old........	0	0	0
Children between two and sixteen years	0	0	0

	Males.	Females.	Total.
Number of blind	. 2	2	4
Number of deaf-mutes	1	0	1
Number of feeble-minded	5	6	11
Number of idiots	2	0	2
Number of epileptics	1	2	8
Persons over seventy years old	13	14	27

KINGSTON CITY ALMSHOUSE.

Kingston, N. Y.

OSCAR ADDIS, *Superintendent.*

(Visited by the commissioner September 13, 1900.)

This is quite an extensive building for a town the size of Kingston. The residence building is of brick, two stories high, with basement and attic. The central part contains the administration and work and service departments and rooms for men. The superintendent's quarters are in the wing to the east, and the women have dormitories upon the main floor of the western wing. The whole second floor in the main building and the western wing are used by the male inmates. Beside this main building there is a two-story detached house for tramps, and two small isolation wards.

There have been no recent improvements. At the time of inspection the premises were found in good order, but the buildings not adequately protected from the danger of fire. There is neither fire hose nor connections. A city hydrant is 500 feet from the building, but the nearest engine house is one mile distant. There are one liquid and 25 dry chemical extinguishers.

As the precautions are not adequate, neither are the means of escape. There are two exits for men and women from the parts which they occupy, to the main floor. Upon the ends of the second floor occupied by men there are two winding stairways, which, by reason of their spiral form, are unsafe.

The second floor of the tramp house is used as a medical ward for repulsive or infectious male cases. There are also two pest

36

houses for contagious diseases. The other sick are cared for in the ordinary dormitories.

The house throughout was found clean and in excellent order; the food good, well prepared, and in sufficient variety.

CENSUS.

The census was as follows:

	Males.	Females.	Total.
Number of inmates...................	39	18	57
Children under two years old........	0	0	0
Children between two and sixteen years	0	0	0
Number of blind....................	3	0'	3
Number of deaf-mutes...............	0	0	0
Number of feeble-minded............	0	2	2
Number of idiots....................	1	0	1
Number of epileptics................	0	0	0
Persons over seventy years old.......	15	7	22

RENSSELAER COUNTY ALMSHOUSE.

Troy, N. Y.

JOHN D. KITTELL, *Keeper.*

(Visited by the commissioner, September 5, 1901.)

This almshouse affords shelter and support to a large number of able-bodied men who ought not to be retained in an almshouse. At the time of inspection the institution was found in fair order and in good repair. Recently an ice house was built, which contains a large cold storage room. This is of brick, and is connected with the kitchen by an inclosed passage.

Although located in the city of Troy, where there are ample facilities for electric lighting, the almshouse depends upon kerosene oil lamps for its light at night. This is one instance of failure to keep up with the times. Another instance is in the matter of laundry appliances. As has been stated before, although Troy is known all over the United States as the home of the steam laundry, this institution continues to do its laundry work by hand. Fortunately, wooden tubs were discarded long

ago, and stationary slate tubs introduced. It would be well for
the institution were steam washers put in. There is a steam
drying rack in use at the present time and also a soap caldron.
It would cost comparatively little to equip the laundry in a
proper manner.

THE CARE OF THE SICK.

At present the hospital accommodations are not sufficient to
meet the needs of the institution. There are two small hospital
additions connected with the dormitories. These are of brick
and located at the extreme ends of the main building. The one
for the men has two main wards, containing twenty-one beds,
and one isolation ward containing four beds. Two rooms are
also taken from the adjoining end of the main dormitory; these
are used for convalescents and chronic cases, and in them are
accommodations for thirteen more patients. The women's hospital has two wards, containing twenty beds, and a lying-in ward
with two additional beds. As on the men's side, so here two
rooms are set apart from the main dormitory for the overflow
of the women's hospital. These are used for convalescent,
chronic, and infectious cases, and have accommodations for
twelve patients. The tax upon the hospital accommodations is
so great that the patients are uncomfortably crowded together,
and, as has been said, the hospital overflows into the main dormitory. The hospital should be enlarged and made separate,
so that the ordinary dormitories might be relieved of all patients.
The introduction of infectious cases into the main building, and
the consequent endangerment to the general health, should be
guarded against by a suitable provision in the way of an isolation ward.

At the time of inspection the food was examined and found
to be good and served in abundance. The hospital, however, having so many patients, suffers from a lack of milk in sufficient
quantity. This should be remedied.

The new ice house and cooler is a valuable improvement, and
will prove economical. The old one was located in a dark cellar,
and was small, inconvenient, and unsatisfactory.

CENSUS.

The census was as follows:

	Males.	Females.	Total.
Number of inmates..................	209	67	276
Children under two years old........	0	0	0
Children between two and sixteen years	0	0	0
Number of blind....................	3	3	6
Number of deaf-mutes................	0	0	0
Number of feeble-minded............	3	1	4
Number of idiots...................	0	0	0
Number of epileptics...............	0	0	0
Persons over seventy years old......	40	22	62

SCHOHARIE COUNTY ALMSHOUSE.
Middleburg, N. Y.

IRVIN SPICKERMAN, *Superintendent.*

(Visited by the commissioner, September 18, 1901.)

The farm connected with this almshouse contains sixty acres, and greatly assists in the support of the institution. The almshouse itself consists of a two-story brick building, with attic and basement, together with barns and necessary outbuildings. The buildings are in good repair and well appointed inside and outside. It is intended to have a new laundry and full equipment of machinery, including a mangle; and the supervisors are talking of putting in a shower bath also.

This is one of the almshouses in which acetylene gas is used for illuminating purposes, and it has been found to work satisfactorily. The heating is by hot water.

The one serious criticism to be made is that which concerns the accommodations for the sick. These consist of two rooms, one on each of the floors devoted to men and women, each room containing three beds. There are no means for isolating cases or tuberculosis cases, and, therefore, the hospital service should be improved. A small addition, properly arranged, connected with the main building by a corridor, would solve the problem of providing for the sick.

On the whole, this institution is a good example of a well constructed and well administered rural almshouse.

CENSUS.

The census was as follows:

	Males.	Females.	Total.
Number of inmates...............	19	15	34
Children under two years old.........	0	1	1
Children between two and sixteen years	0	1	1
Number of blind...................	1	1	2
Number of deaf-mutes..............	0	0	0
Number of feeble-minded...........	2	4	6
Number of idiots..................	1	0	1
Number of epileptics...............	1	2	3
Persons over seventy years old.......	4	6	10

SULLIVAN COUNTY ALMSHOUSE.

Monticello, N. Y.

M. C. STEWART, *Keeper.*

(Visited by the Commissioner September 19, 1901.)

The buildings of this almshouse are constructed of wood, and have an estimated value of $10,000. They will accommodate 80 inmates. The women's building is three stories high, and, in addition to the dormitory, contains the keeper's quarters and the offices. The old building used for men is three stories high, built into a hillside. Lately the former asylum building was renovated and prepared for the use of the men; it is a two-story structure, with a cellar underneath. The building devoted to the women is in a bad state of repair, and the old one used by the men is also in great need of repairs. The newly renovated building for men is in excellent condition, although its walls should be painted. It is expected that the women's building will be repaired the coming spring, the water supply be extended to the women's building, and bath tubs and flush water closets installed.

The new building for men is heated by steam, but the other buildings depend upon hot air and stoves. The laundry equipment is dilapidated and should be improved.

There are practically no precautions against fire, and there would be a serious danger to the inmates were one to get a start. The buildings were in general clean, although the bedding in the old building was found to be ragged and unfit for use, and the clothing of the inmates very poor. The food, however, was abundant and well cooked.

CENSUS.

The census was as follows:

	Males.	Females.	Total.
Number of inmates..................	28	18	46
Children under two years old........	0	1	1
Children between two and sixteen years...........................	0	0	0
Number of blind....................	1	1	2
Number of deaf-mutes...............	0	0	0
Number of feeble-minded...............	2	2	4
Number of idiots...................	5	1	6
Number of epileptics...............	1	0	1
Persons over seventy years old......	11	5	16

ULSTER COUNTY ALMSHOUSE.

New Paltz, N. Y.

ABRAM SAMMONS, *Superintendent.*

(Visited by the Commissioner September 12, 1900.)

This almshouse consists of two principal buildings, one the former asylum for the insane, and the other the almshouse proper. They are situated about three miles from the village of New Paltz. The main building is three stories high, has a basement, and contains the administration offices, together with the quarters for the superintendent and keeper, and has accommodation for 24 male inmates beside. The old almshouse is two stories high, with a cellar, and contains quarters for both men and women. It has in it also the kitchen, the laundry and the dining-room. A one-story building is used for tramps, and a two-story frame for isolating patients suffering from infectious diseases.

The buildings, at the time of inspection, were found in good repair. There have been no improvements recently, although, as indicated, the repairs are kept up.

The institution is lighted by kerosene oil lamps, which are a constant menace to the general safety. The laundry equipment is inadequate, and everything has to be done by hand.

In the matter of the care of the sick, there is no special hospital except the small structure used for isolating infectious cases. The patients suffering from non-infectious diseases are cared for in their own rooms, although the women have what is called a hospital ward, separated from the main dormitory. In this there are beds for six patients and one attendant. The isolation building has accommodations for six patients, with a large day room for each sex.

A number of times in previous reports it has been stated that it is an unwise practice to permit any of the male inmates to sleep in the cellar of the almshouse. During the year this has been continued, however, as some of the men seem to prefer such gloomy quarters to the more comfortable dormitories above. It is for the general safety of the institution that this practice should be discontinued.

The food seemed to be sufficient, and the inmates had no complaints to make as to their treatment.

CENSUS.

The census was as follows:

	Males.	Females.	Total.
Number of inmates..................	84	24	108
Children under two years old........	0	1	1
Children between two and sixteen years·............................	0	0	0
Number of blind.....................	1	1	2
Number of deaf-mutes...............	0	0	0
Number of feeble-minded...........	3	6	9
Number of idiots	3	0	3
Number of epileptics...............	2	1	3
Persons over seventy years old......	29	10	39

Statistical summary.

COUNTIES	INMATES			Children under 3 years.	Children between 3 and 16.	OVER 70 YEARS OLD.			Epileptics.	Feeble-minded.	Idiots.
	Male.	Female.	Total.			Male.	Female.	Total.			
Albany	125	66	191	0	0	26	25	51	0	19	0
Columbia	101	37	138	2	0	40	15	55	4	15	6
Greene	45	32	77	0	0	13	14	27	3	11	2
Kingston city	39	18	57	0	0	15	7	22	0	2	1
Rensselaer	209	67	276	0	0	40	22	62	0	4	0
Schoharie	19	15	31	1	1	4	6	10	3	6	1
Sullivan	28	18	46	1	0	11	5	16	1	4	6
Ulster	84	24	108	1	0	29	10	39	3	9	3
Total	650	277	927	5	1	178	104	282	14	70	19

REPORT

OF

Visitation of Almshouses in the Fourth Judicial District.

REPORT.

To the State Board of Charities:

During the fiscal year ending September 30, 1901, all the alms-houses of the Fourth Judicial District have been visited by the Commissioner, as well as regularly inspected from time to time by the Almshouse Inspectors and the Superintendent of State and Alien Poor.

IMPROVEMENTS.

The year has witnessed some improvement in each of the counties. The matter of repairs has received attention. In some instances new furniture has replaced old and worn-out material. In Clinton county the heating plant has been very much improved; three chute fire-escapes are attached to the building, and a cooler now enables the institution to properly care for the food supplies. Montgomery County Almshouse has also added a cold-storage room and a milk house to its equipment. Saratoga county is about to introduce electric light.

NEW ALMSHOUSE.

Schenectady county has made a contract for the erection of a new almshouse. The old buildings which served the county for so many years are to be abandoned, and a new structure, modern in all respects, is already under way. It is to be regretted that the supervisors of the county did not complete their good work by relocating the almshouse. It is unfortunate that an institution of this character is located in the heart of a growing town. It is far better always when on a farm and at some distance from a town. This gives opportunity for employment of the inmates, and the farm will contribute materially to

When inspected the grounds and buildings were found in order. The inmates appeared contented and comfortable, and the food supplied was seen to be good.

It would be well if the use of kerosene oil lamps was rendered unnecessary by the introduction of a safer illuminant.

CENSUS.

The census was as follows:

	Males.	Females.	Total.
Number of inmates	31	20	51
Children under two years old	0	0	0
Children between two and sixteen years	0	0	0
Number of blind	2	0	2
Number of deaf-mutes	0	3	3
Number of feeble-minded	2	5	7
Number of idiots	2	0	2
Number of epileptics	2	2	4
Persons over seventy years old	11	4	15

FULTON COUNTY ALMSHOUSE, GLOVERSVILLE, N. Y.

Joseph Sherman, *Superintendent.*

This is the newest almshouse in the district. It has only been in occupancy three months, having been entered on the 4th of June, 1901. The buildings are of brick, built on the cottage plan, each two stories high, having cellar underneath. The boiler-room and laundry occupy the basement under the work and service building.

As this building is so new, it is being adjusted to meet conditions. The drainage system of the old almshouse was found inadequate for the new, and consequently changes were rendered necessary immediately upon occupancy. It is expected that all of the old buildings will be razed or removed.

This group is now heated by steam from a low-pressure Mercer boiler. It is lighted by electricity, and has very good ventilation, for in addition to the usual doors, windows and flues for the dormitories, there are open fireplaces in each of the day rooms.

The water supply remains as for the old almshouse. It comes from a spring-fed reservoir holding about 4,000 barrels, from which, by means of a two-inch pipe, it enters the house. Another small spring on the hillside delivers water to the kitchen.

As this almshouse is so new, it is described herein in some detail. Its equipment for bathing consists of one shower bath for each sex, and a porcelain-lined tub in the hospital for the use of the women. The laundry contains a steam washing equipment of an upright engine, a rotary washer, a centrifugal extractor, and eight steam drying racks. The precautions against fire consist of standpipes with connected hose in each building, and also a number of liquid chemical extinguishers. No outside iron fire-escapes have been constructed, as these are only two-story buildings, and there are three exits from each of the buildings used as dormitories.

It is intended that a room over the dining-rooms in the work and service building, which has a bath and toilet, shall serve as a hospital.

On inspection the food was found to be well cooked and well served and also abundant. This almshouse is a credit to Fulton county.

CENSUS.

The census was as follows:

	Males.	Females.	Total.
Number of inmates....................	26	15	41
Children under two years old..........	2	0	2
Children between two and sixteen years	0	0	0
Number of blind	0	0	0
Number of deaf-mutes	0	0	0
Number of feeble-minded	2	0	2
Number of idiots	1	1	2
Number of epileptics	3	1	4
Persons over seventy years old.........	9	5	14

FRANKLIN COUNTY ALMSHOUSE, MALONE, N. Y.

WORDEN A. DRAKE, *Keeper.*

Some changes have been made in this institution since last report. These pertain to the safety of the institution and to the conveniences of administration. The heating plant has been extended, and additional radiators have made the institution more comfortable. The fire-escapes are of the chute pattern and are made of canvas. They of course are better than none, but as canvas is inflammable a fire in the building might render them useless in a short time. However, as they contribute somewhat to the assurance of safety and would probably serve to get out the helpless inmates, it is a satisfaction to know that they have been added to the equipment.

The installation of a meat cooler in the cellar will conserve economy, while the new wash wheel and extractor for the laundry will add to the cleanliness. There is a good range in the institution kitchen, and all of these things are a great improvement over last year. In fact, it may be stated that this almshouse has greatly improved during the past year in the matter of conditions. Its order and cleanliness have improved and the discipline is better. Its chief need at the present time is in the way of better accommodations for the sick.

CENSUS.

The census was as follows:

	Males.	Females.	Total.
Number of inmates..................	28	14	42
Children under two years old..........	2	0	2
Children between two and sixteen years	0	0	0
Number of blind.....................	0	0	0
Number of deaf-mutes................	0	0	0
Number of feeble-minded.............	2	1	3
Number of idiots....................	3	1	4
Number of epileptics.................	1	1	2
Persons over seventy years old........	13	9	22

MONTGOMERY COUNTY ALMSHOUSE, PALATINE BRIDGE, N. Y.
WILLIAM B. SMEALLIE, *Superintendent.*

All the buildings of this institution are in excellent condition, having been occupied but a short time. On the 1st of September, 1900, the almshouse was opened. It is built on the cottage plan, and the general arrangement adds to ease of administration.

At the time of inspection the institution was found in a satisfactory condition. Everything is an improvement upon the conditions which prevailed under the former contract system, and the county poor are contented and happy since the change.

· CENSUS.

The census was as follows:

	Males.	Females.	Total.
Number of inmates	21	22	43
Children under two years old	0	0	0
Children between two and sixteen years	0	0	0
Number of blind	0	1	1
Number of deaf-mutes	1	1	2
Number of feeble-minded	3	4	7
Number of idiots	1	2	3
Number of epileptics	1	3	4
Persons over seventy years old	7	7	14

ST. LAWRENCE COUNTY ALMSHOUSE, CANTON, N. Y.
M. T. STOOKING, *Superintendent.*

The buildings of this almshouse are in fairly good repair, although the walls need attention. At the time of inspection everything was found clean and in good order. It is proposed during the year that the walls shall be covered with pressed steel. The furniture of this almshouse has been added to lately, and the wooden bedsteads which remained have been removed. This almshouse has a fine dairy. As a consequence all the inmates receive butter and milk in sufficient quantity. The food in general is satisfactory.

37

CENSUS.

The census was as follows:

	Males.	Females.	Total.
Number of inmates....................	47	32	79
Children under two years old..........	0	0	0
Children between two and sixteen years	0	0	0
Number of blind.......................	1	0	1
Number of deaf-mutes.................	1	2	3
Number of feeble-minded..............	6	6	12
Number of idiots.....................	3	1	4
Number of epileptics.................	2	4	6
Persons over seventy years old........	17	16	33

SARATOGA COUNTY ALMSHOUSE, BALLSTON, N. Y.
S. W. Pearse, *Superintendent*.

All the buildings of this almshouse have been painted and repaired during the year and the institution is now in very good condition. It is expected that electric light will be put in and the old kerosene oil lamp system be abolished. This institution has for hospital purposes the extension of a two-story L. The main floor is used for men who are sick, and the second floor for women. At the time of inspection the institution was found in perfect order throughout, and the inmates were apparently contented. As this county is close to Schenectady, some of the tramps who roam in the central section of the State find their way to this almshouse for entertainment.

CENSUS.

The census was as follows:

	Males.	Females.	Total.
Number of inmates....................	54	17	71
Children under two years old..........	0	1	1
Children between two and sixteen years	0	0	0
Number of blind.......................	1	1	2
Number of deaf-mutes.................	0	0	0
Number of feeble-minded..............	6	2	8
Number of idiots.....................	0	0	0
Number of epileptics.................	1	0	1
Persons over seventy years old.........	21	7	28

SCHENECTADY COUNTY ALMSHOUSE, SCHENECTADY, N. Y.

O. R. WESTOVER, *Superintendent*.

This is probably the last time in which reference will be made to the old buildings in the commissioner's annual report, as a new almshouse, built upon modern lines, is now contracted for. Of this old institution it is enough to say that it has outlived its usefulness in every way. For years Schenectady county has needed a new almshouse, and now that it has been decided by the county to erect new buildings it is a pleasure to note that they are to conform to the ideas of service which are approved by the State Board of Charities.

These new buildings will be ready for the installation of water, steam, lighting fixtures and equipment by the middle of May, 1902. To insure a fair start in the matter of cleanliness none of the present equipment of the old almshouse will be transferred to the new buildings. This is wise, for it would be exceedingly unfortunate were the new building to be filled with the vermin which it has been impossible to get rid of in the old almshouse.

One matter of serious concern remains to be spoken of in connection with this institution, viz: The policy of taking care of tramps at the almshouse is not wise; it is expensive and destructive of discipline. Over 7,000 meals and lodgings to wayfarers of this character were furnished during the year at the expense of the county, and in one night (that preceding the last inspection) there were 47 tramps who obtained supper, lodging and breakfast at the expense of the county. It is supposed that they render some equivalent in the way of sawing wood, but it can readily be understood that there is no possibility of employing such large numbers. As matters stand at present, Schenectady has become a Mecca for the tramps of the State. They have found it easy to secure accommodations at the expense of the county, and traveling up and down Central New York they have held Schenectady in view as an objective point where they could rest for such time as they might deem necessary. A radical change of policy is essential. An enforcement of the law which provides punishment for tramping will be efficacious and prove economical.

CENSUS.

The census was as follows:

	Males.	Females.	Total.
Number of inmates.....................	61	22	83
Children under two years old..........	0	1	1
Children between two and sixteen years	0	0	0
Number of blind	1	0	1
Number of deaf-mutes	1	0	1
Number of feeble-minded..............	0	2	2
Number of idiots	1	0	1
Number of epileptics	0	0	0
Persons over seventy years old........	34	6	40

WARREN COUNTY ALMSHOUSE, WARRENSBURGH, N. Y.
A. L. SOPER, *Superintendent.*

Recently an addition was made to the men's building by which the hospital extension has now a second floor, which gives ten more rooms to the general department. The buildings were found clean throughout, and are generally in good repair. A new inside staircase was built in the women's building during the year, so that it is not now necessary for them to pass through the superintendent's quarters. No improvements other than these have been provided for, although a telephone will soon connect the almshouse with the town.

This almshouse should have a laundry building equipped with proper machinery. Outside fire-escapes will add to its safety.

CENSUS.

The census was as follows:

	Males.	Females.	Total.
Number of inmates....................	48	22	70
Children under two years old..........	0	1	1
Children between two and sixteen years	0	0	0
Number of blind......................	2	1	3
Number of deaf-mutes.................	0	0	0
Number of feeble-minded..............	6	5	11
Number of idiots.....................	1	0	1
Number of epileptics..................	1	0	1
Persons over seventy years old........	20	8	28

WASHINGTON COUNTY ALMSHOUSE, ARGYLE, N. Y.

M. S. GRAHAM, *Superintendent.*

A considerable number of improvements have been made at this almshouse. At the time of inspection it was found in a clean and well-ordered condition. The buildings are all in good repair.

New window sashes and glass have been placed throughout the work and service building. A building for the storage of wood and tools was also erected, and the main floor of the old asylum building entirely rebuilt for hospital purposes. The telephone service has now connected the hospital with the nearest village.

At the time of inspection an examination was made of the food, which was found to be well cooked and served in abundance.

The great need of this almshouse is a better water supply. At times there is great scarcity, and it will be necessary to assure the institution such a certain and adequate quantity of water as will provide for all the needs of the almshouse.

CENSUS.

The census was as follows:

	Males.	Females.	Total.
Number of inmates....................	30	27	57
Children under two years old..........	1	1	2
Children between two and sixteen years	0	0	0
Number of blind......................	1	1	2
Number of deaf-mutes................	0	0	0
Number of feeble-minded..............	5	4	9
Number of idots......................	1	1	2
Number of epileptics.................	1	0	1
Persons over seventy years old........	14	7	21

Statistical Summary.

COUNTIES.	INMATES.			Children under 2 years.	Children between 2 and 16	OVER 70 YEARS OLD.			Epileptics.	Feeble-minded.	Idiots.
	Male.	Female.	Total.			Male.	Female.	Total.			
Clinton	46	22	68	0	0	16	9	25	4	6	7
Essex	31	20	51	0	0	11	4	15	4	7	2
Franklin	28	14	42	2	0	13	9	22	2	3	4
Fulton	26	15	41	3	0	9	5	14	4	2	2
Montgomery	21	22	43	2	0	7	7	14	4	7	8
St. Lawrence	47	32	79	0	0	17	16	33	6	12	4
Saratoga	54	17	71	1	0	21	7	28	1	8	0
Schenectady	61	22	83	1	0	34	6	40	0	2	1
Warren	48	22	70	1	0	20	8	28	1	11	1
Washington	30	27	57	2	0	14	7	21	1	9	2
Total	392	213	605	11	0	162	78	240	27	67	26

REPORT

OF

Visitation of Almshouses

IN THE

FIFTH JUDICIAL DISTRICT.

REPORT.

'To the State Board of Charities:

I. have the honor to submit my annual report upon the alms-houses and public hospitals in the Fifth Judicial District. In submitting the same I am glad to be able to state that these institutions in the several counties of the Fifth Judicial District have been personally visited by me; that they have been inspected also by the almshouse inspectors of the State Board of Charities, as well as by the Superintendent of State and Alien Poor.

In this district three types of institutions come within the general definition of "almshouse" as that term has been used in the past. One is the almshouse proper, which with its various buildings, serves as the home of the aged, infirm and disabled poor who have no other refuge. The second is the hospital maintained wholly at public expense, and intended to provide for the indigent sick who are not inmates of the almshouse, and who upon recovery will be able to undertake their own support again. The third type of institution is a new venture in the field of public charity—the municipal lodging house.

Only one institution of this character exists in the Fifth Judicial District. It has so far been an experiment, an attempt on the part of the city of Syracuse to provide temporary shelter and food for homeless men and women seeking employment.

CLASSIFICATION.

These three types of institutions are developments of the original almshouse, which served as a shelter for all classes of dependents upon public bounty. As the necessity for the classification of public dependents has gained recognition, the inmates

of the almshouses have been divided into groups for more
efficient administration, in order to secure to each group that
particular form of assistance of which it stands most in need.

This process of classification has freed the almshouse, to some
extent, of a number of objectionable groups of inmates—objectionable because of the peculiar nature of their infirmity, and
from the fact that their presence increased greatly the difficulty
of properly ministering to the interests of other inmates.

As classification in this district has progressed, the most of
the defectives have been removed, although in some of the almshouses inmates who belong to the defective groups still remain.
Children between the ages of two and sixteen years have been
entirely removed except in a single instance, to which reference
will be made in the part of this report which bears upon the
particular almshouse in which the child is kept. Epileptics are
not numerous in the public institutions of this district, and an
effort has been made to remove the sick from close association
with the well. But the idea of a better grouping of public
dependents has resulted in another advance—to organization
of public hospitals for the reception of such members of society
as are temporarily incapacitated by sickness, and who are unable
to pay for medical treatment from private funds. The establishment of these public hospitals relieves the almshouse of a
large number of cases which otherwise would have to be taken
care of therein. It also brings about a separation, morally beneficial, by which those temporarily disabled are neither associated nor classed with the great body of paupers who make up
the population of the almshouse. By this arrangement the fact
that an individual requiring medical attention receives treatment at public expense does not weaken his desire for indepen-
dence nor degrade his sense of self-respect, as would be the
result if he were sent to the almshouse and recorded as a common pauper.

The last development of the idea of classification, embodied
in the municipal lodging house, is an effort to assist worthy but
unfortunate persons who are willing to work. Formerly the
only refuge of the penniless unfortunate seeking employment
and struggling against falling into degradations of pauperism

was that assistance supplied by lodging in a police station. In this lodging all applicants for shelter were herded together. No discriminations were made except in the one matter of sex. The young, the old, the clean, the foul, the tramp, and honest workman, all were herded together and found place in the same lodging room. The practice was destructive of health and morals, and resulted in fostering crime, for these station lodging houses were schools of vice.

The municipal lodging house attempts to separate the worthy from the unworthy. It makes inquiry into the antecedents of applicants for relief, and exacts a price to be paid in labor for the relief extended. It also proposes to prevent the abuse of public charity by tramps and other members of the vicious and criminal classes. The one example of this type of public institution in this district, while still an experiment, has accomplished much good, and rightly managed it must prove a blessing to honest poverty.

ALMSHOUSES.

The chief improvement in almshouses during the year is in more ample provision for the care of the sick, and rearrangement of the dormitories so as to provide more comfortable quarters for the inmates. Credit should be accorded the boards of supervisors whose intelligent interest in the needs of the county dependents has led them to make large appropriations for these betterments.

The board of supervisors of Onondaga county has been working toward a general reconstruction of the county almshouse, and they have so far progressed as to make it safe to forecast that in a few years at the outside the county will possess an almshouse modern in all its appointments, equal to the requirements of the county, and managed in a way to reflect credit upon the community.

The matter of fire protection has received consideration in this district, and one of the almshouses is equipped with a model fire-escape, by means of which the most infirm inmates can be quickly and safely transferred from the upper stories of the almshouse to the ground. The operation of this tubular

fire-escape is so satisfactory, and it presents such a certainty
of safety for inmates in the event of fire, it is hoped other almshouses in the district may soon be equipped with a similar form
of escape.

The question of water has not been a pressing one in this
district during the past year. Most of the almshouses are now
supplied with water in sufficient quantities for general needs,
and where there is any danger of a failure of supply the authorities are making preparation to secure an increase. Thus
throughout the district the general tendency is toward betterment. Conditions are becoming more satisfactory, and, if progress continues, this district will soon represent advanced
methods of administration in public institutions.

The notes on the several counties, showing their condition and
needs at the time of their last inspection, follow:

HERKIMER COUNTY ALMSHOUSE.
Middleville, N. Y.

The buildings remain substantially the same as they were a
year ago, although recent improvements in plumbing and steam-
fitting have added greatly to their comfort and improved the
sanitation. The residence buildings are of brick and stone, the
barns are frame, and all are generally in good condition. They
are heated by steam, lighted by acetylene gas, and are fairly
well ventilated. This is one of the few almshouses in the district which have not a sufficient water supply, nor has it a large
enough reservoir to insure pressure and quantity in case of
an emergency.

The laundry work is done in the basement, where a power
laundry is located. This is an unfortunate location, as the
steam rising from the basement has a tendency to destroy the
plaster of the house, and in addition the odors incident to
laundry work penetrate to all portions of the building. There
should be a separate building wherein work of this character
can be done.

One defect in this almshouse is connected with the care of the sick. .At present the sick are cared for in their rooms. While there is a degree of isolation, the general work of the almshouse makes this form of care not only unsatisfactory but a menace to the health of all other inmates. For these two reasons, as well as to secure better attention to the sick, there should be a small separated hospital large enough to accommodate about twenty-five patients.

Another need is fire-escapes. The safety of the inmates is imperative, and while there is some chance of escape by means of stairways in the two wings, fire escapes attached to the building would be useful in case the stairways were cut off.

The third need is for a competent cook. For some years an inmate has attended to the cooking, but economy and health will both be subserved by the employment of a competent paid assistant to have charge of the work.

CENSUS.

The census was as follows:

	Males.	Females.	Total.
Number of inmates..................	58	24	82
Children under two years............	0	0	0
Children between two and sixteen years	0	0	0
Number of blind....................	2	1	3
Number of deaf-mutes...............	1	0	1
Number of feeble-minded............	4	5	9
Number of idiots....................	0	0	0
Number of epileptics................	1	1	2
Persons over seventy years old......	15	12	27

JEFFERSON COUNTY ALMSHOUSE.

Watertown, N. Y.

The extensive group of stone and brick buildings with frame outbuildings, which constitutes the Jefferson county almshouse, is located in a beautiful situation on the Black river.

At the time of inspection the buildings were found in very fair condition, clean and orderly, and recently improved by change in plumbing and the introduction of steam power for the laundry work. Beside this the water supply has been made satisfactory by the introduction of water from the city system; some of the rooms have been ceiled with steel, and, on the whole, a commendable degree of progress has been shown by the work accomplished during the year.

Extensive changes in the main building are still necessary. It is possible to utilize some of the space which now is of little service, and the repairs necessary to keep the the building in proper order will provide the opportunity to make the alterations herein suggested.

The superintendent of the poor for Jefferson county, who is the keeper of the almshouse, has had charge of this institution about twenty years. He is one of the superintendents whose efficiency has been recognized by re-election term after term, and this fact indicates administrative ability of a high order. Under his management an effective discipline is maintained. The grounds are kept in excellent condition, and the household work is done thoroughly and regularly.

It is possible in an institution having as much spare room as is found in the Jefferson county almshouse to make experiments in the matter of classification. Something has been accomplished in this direction, and with the improvement of the buildings through complete repairs more may be attempted.

This is especially desirable in the matter of the care of the sick. At the present time the part of the building equipped for hospital purposes does not provide that isolation which is essential to their treatment. If a hospital were arranged in one wing of the main building, separated entirely from the dormitories occupied by other inmates, and properly furnished, it would obviate the necessity of sending some patients to the city hospital. A paid hospital attendant is necessary in any case, as the keeper and matron have enough responsible work without being compelled to wait upon the sick at all hours of the day and night.

CENSUS.

The census was as follows:

	Males.	Females.	Total.
Number of inmates..................	52	39	91
Children under two years...........	0	0	0
Children between two and sixteen years	0	0	0
Number of blind...................	2	1	3
Number of deaf-mutes..............	1	1	2
Number of feeble-minded...........	6	9	15
Number of idiots..................	0	0	0
Number of epileptics...............	0	0	0
Persons over seventy years old......	23	13	36

LEWIS COUNTY ALMSHOUSE.

Lowville, N. Y.

The general renovation of the group of brick buildings which constitutes the almshouse of Lewis county has taken place within a short time, and as a consequence the inmates have been made very comfortable. One important improvement introduced in the buildings is a new method of heating. The old stove system has been abandoned, and all the buildings are now heated by steam. A steam laundry has been purchased since the last report, and is doing effective work.

The care of the sick is satisfactory, as one portion of the building formerly used for the insane has been fitted up as a hospital.

The only serious defect at the present time is the difficulty of escape, in the event of fire, from the attics, where some of the men sleep. To assure their safety a fire-escape should be arranged, or they should be given a dormitory on the lower floor.

At the last meeting of the board of supervisors it was voted to tear down the old barns and build new ones. This will be a great improvement, especially as the new buildings are to be erected at a considerable distance from the dormitories. When this improvement is accomplished, Lewis county will have one

of the best among the smaller almshouses in the State. While
the number of permanent inmates is not large, the county
authorities have taken pleasure in making ample provision for
their welfare, and have not hesitated to give all the money
required to carry out the suggestions of the State Board of
Charities.

CENSUS.

The census was as follows:

	Males.	Females.	Total.
Number of inmates..................	25	15	40
Children under two years...........	0	0	0
Children between two and sixteen years	0	0	0
Number of blind	1	0	1
Number of deaf-mutes...............	1	1	2
Number of feeble-minded............	3	2	5
Number of idiots....................	1	1	2
Number of epileptics................	1	1	2
Persons over seventy years old.......	13	7	20

ONEIDA COUNTY ALMSHOUSE.
Rome, N. Y.

Comparatively new, the Oneida county almshouse is one which
embodies modern ideas. In form it consists of a group of separate brick buildings so arranged that all are connected with the
central work and service building, while all the barns and outbuildings are at a considerable distance in the rear.

The drainage is into the Mohawk river, on the banks of which
the almshouse is located. Its water supply is drawn from the
Rome city water system, but its light and power are furnished
by its own power plant.

At the beginning of the present year a change was made in
superintendent and keeper, and with this change some new
methods in administration were adopted.

In spite of the fact that these buildings are comparatively
new, the work upon them was of such a character as to necessitate repairs. Among the most serious defects is that which
concerns the drainage. The sewer pipe intended to carry off
the ordinary drainage and storm water from the buildings is
only eight inches in diameter, entirely inadequate to the needs.
This matter has been brought to the attention of the supervisors by reports made in the past two years, but up to the time
of preparing this one nothing has been done to enlarge the
capacity of the drain pipes. As a consequence of this defective
drainage, the basements of the buildings have been flooded by
sewage and back water, and the floors and walls are greatly
decayed. The present board of supervisors is considering the
matter, and doubtless steps will be taken to enlarge the sewers.
Unless this be done, the health of the inmates and the safety
of the buildings will continue to stand imperilled.

One other improvement was suggested heretofore, and
arrangements apparently made to carry the suggestion into
effect. This concerned the safety of the inmates in the event of
fire. It was suggested that there is need of adequate fire-
escapes from the upper portions of the buildings. The board of
supervisors authorized the building committee to provide fire-
escapes, but the flimsy character of the structures attached to
the building prevents them from increasing the safety of the
inmates. On the contrary the fire-escapes themselves, in the
event of fire, would be a deadly menace to the inmates compelled to attempt their use. Even an athletic young man might
find it dangerous to descend them. Then, too, the method of
attachment to the walls renders them shaky, and on the whole
it may be stated that they are altogether unsatisfactory and
dangerous. All almshouses should be equipped with a safe form
of descent in times of fire. It is not the least possible degree
of safety which should be provided, but enough to make it
absolutely certain that the halt, the blind, the lame, the feeble
could be saved by timely aid in case of a conflagration. Anything short of this provision is unsatisfactory.

38

The ventilation has been greatly improved since the last report. The opening of a ventilating flue from the men's dormitory has improved the ventilation to such an extent that it has made the gallery dormitory comfortable. Further improvement can be made in the ventilation of the attic, which is now used for dormitory purposes whenever the other wards are full. As the ventilating flues from other rooms open into this attic and do not pass out of the roof, the attic is filled with the foul air carried through the flues from other dormitories. The result is that the attics are unfitted for sleeping purposes, and will so continue until the ventilating shafts pass through the roof and carry the impurities into the outer atmosphere.

One other serious defect in this almshouse is the insufficient accommodation for the sick. Its great need is an adequate hospital building, separate from the rest of the group, that the sick may receive the special care they require, and be relieved from contact with the other inmates. It is hoped that this building will be provided in a short time.

It is reported that the board of supervisors is making arrangements to increase the space now allotted to the laundry. As this part of the work is done in the basement of the women's building, it would be much better were the laundry installed in some part of the almshouse removed from the dormitories.

CENSUS.

The census was as follows:

	Males.	Females.	Total.
Number of inmates	168	89	257
Children under two years	0	0	0
Children between two and sixteen years	0	0	0
Number of blind	4	3	7
Number of deaf-mutes	1	1	2
Number of feeble-minded	7	8	15
Number of idiots	2	1	3
Number of epileptics	4	2	6
Persons over seventy years old	62	41	103

ONONDAGA COUNTY ALMSHOUSE.

Syracuse, N. Y.

During the past year many improvements have been made in this institution. The repairs begun during the previous year have continued, the interior has been renovated with paint and kalsomine, the furniture been added to, the water supply enlarged, and a new set of boilers installed in a new power house. Thus in many ways conditions have changed for the better, and the welfare and comfort of the inmates receive greater attention.

The most important improvement completed during the year has been the new hospital. While this was under way at the time of the last annual report and almost ready for occupancy, it was not furnished and put into service until this year. The grounds have been graded, the general equipment enlarged, and, with the electric light, the hospital and the almshouse entered upon a new and better service. The new hospital is largely due to the untiring work of Supervisor Moses D. Rubin and the other members of the building committee of the board of supervisors. Not only has their work expressed itself in the new hospital, but all the improvements in the main almshouse are in consequence of their persistence and energy. There is hope that the continuance in office of these men will soon give to Onondaga county an almshouse first-class in every respect, and fully equipped for the public needs.

The administration continues as at last report. The keeper and matron remain the same, and through their work the tone of the almshouse has greatly improved.

CENSUS.

The census was as follows:

	Males.	Females.	Total.
Number of inmates	136	69	205
Children under two years	0	4	4
Children between two and sixteen years	0	0	0
Number of blind	3	2	5
Number of deaf-mutes	0	1	1
Number of feeble-minded	5	4	9

	Males.	Females.	Total.
Number of idiots	5	3	8
Number of epileptics	5	4	9
Persons over seventy years old	53	15	68

OSWEGO COUNTY ALMSHOUSE.
Mexico, N. Y.

This almshouse consists of a new three-story brick building, having wings, and containing quarters for the administration as well as for the inmates. It is in fairly good condition except in the older part. This has been permitted to go without repairs for a number of years, and as a consequence is not in service at the present time. The responsibility for the destruction of public property must rest with those whose duty it is to make repairs. The keeper and the matron are in no wise responsible, for they have no authority to undertake repairs unless directed so to do by the superintendent and the board of supervisors. Doubtless the board of supervisors would make the necessary repairs were the county superintendent to insist that they are necessary for the safety of the property. That he has been in any way a consenting party to the dilapidation of the almshouse is a matter of astonishment, and it is hoped that the necessary repairs will be made as soon as possible.

During the past year a number of improvements have been made, although they are confined to the newer portion of the building. These have greatly bettered general conditions, and have added to the safety of the institution and the comfort of the inmates.

A new keeper and matron have been appointed, and they have taken up their work with energy and enthusiasm. As they were employed in the institution for several years in subordinate capacities, their appointment is in the line of promotion. If they are given authority to make repairs and permitted to do the things they deem necessary, this almshouse will soon lose any appearance of dilapidation and become a credit to Oswego county.

Compared with the other almshouse in the county, this institution is not modern in equipment. It should have a small power laundry located in a building outside the main structure, so as to diminish the danger from fire and steam.

The provisions for escape in the event of fire are inadequate. Some of the dormitories are so located that there will be no difficulty of escape, but others will prove exceedingly dangerous if a fire breaks out. A system of fire escapes should be provided as soon as possible.

One reason why the old portion of the building should be put in repair is that a hospital department is needed. At the present time the sick are cared for in their rooms. As inmates of almshouses are frequently afflicted with most distressing diseases, as well as forms which are filthy and contagious, a hospital department should be provided where the sick may be isolated from the rest of the inmates.

One other matter in connection with this almshouse deserves attention. For several years the poor crippled child, Benny Brown, has been kept in this almshouse. He is within the prohibited ages, and has been in great need of special surgical treatment. In spite of this fact he has been kept in the almshouse in close association with the old pauper inmates, upon whom he has relied for much of the attention given to him each day. This has been unjust to the child, as well as contrary to law, and deserves condemnation. It would have cost two or three times as much to have sent the boy to an institution where he would have received skilled attention, but such a course might have prolonged his life, and certainly would have alleviated his distress. There can be no doubt the people of Oswego county do not sympathize with a policy so penurious that it deprives a suffering child of his only chance for proper surgical assistance.

CENSUS.

The census was as follows:

	Males.	Females.	Total.
Number of inmates	31	28	59
Children under two years	0	0	0

Children between two and sixteen	Males.	Females.	Total.
years	1	0	1
Number of blind	1	0	1
Number of deaf-mutes	2	0	2
Number of feeble-minded	5	5	10
Number of idiots	3	0	3
Number of epileptics	2	4	6
Persons over seventy years old	9	8	17

OSWEGO CITY ALMSHOUSE.
Oswego, N. Y.

The city of Oswego may well be proud of its city almshouse. The fine brick structure, well equipped, is a testimony to the intelligent interest of the people in the unfortunate poor who require public assistance. The building is in perfect repair and admirably cared for. Since its erection and equipment the barns and outbuildings have received attention, so that now the entire group is in good order and recently painted.

The main building is heated by steam. It is well supplied with water for all purposes, and, from the fact that it possesses a tubular fire escape, is safe in the event of fire.

This almshouse is nearly self-supporting. It derives a large revenue from the sale of farm products. The superintendent has managed the farm as successfully and profitably as though he were its owner. In consequence of this the expense of maintenance does not involve a heavy tax upon the people of Oswego city.

The general condition of good order and cleanliness testifies to the efficiency of the matron, and, on the whole, it may be said that this almshouse is one of the best in the State.

The great need is a small power laundry to complete the equipment. This should be added soon, and with it a spray bath be installed.

CENSUS.

The census was as follows:

	Males.	Females.	Total.
Number of inmates..................	24	19	43
Children under two years...........	0	0	0
Children between two and sixteen years	0	0	0
Number of blind....................	1	2	3
Number of deaf-mutes..............	0	0	0
Number of feeble-minded...........	1	1	2
Number of idiots...................	1	0	1
Number of epileptics...............	0	1	1
Persons over seventy years old......	12	8	20

UTICA CITY HOSPITAL.
Utica, N. Y.

This institution has not been enlarged since last report, but the building has been altered somewhat by repairs and reconstruction. Through this the suggestions heretofore made have to a certain extent been incorporated. Considerable painting has been done, and the office has been altered. The large dormitory on the third floor is now divided into three rooms, two of which are used for patients, and the third for a bath room. An elevator has been installed in the angle of the rear porch where the main building joins the extension. By this arrangement it is accessible from the driveway. Steel ceilings have been put in the kitchen and all the dormitories; ultimately every room in the house will be so furnished. The dining rooms have been removed from the basement to the second floor, a very great improvement. In addition to these, the plumbing throughout the building has been overhauled, new flush watercloset and bath tubs have been placed, and changes made in the doctor's office and reception room, in the latter of which are now a fireplace and gas log.

These improvements have involved an expenditure of nearly $7,000, and the hospital is now in a condition to reflect credit upon the Board of Charities of the city of Utica, who have it in charge.

During the past year this board has done considerable work in the way of relieving individuals and families, which has been incorporated in the annual report concerning the operations of the hospital. From this report it appears that 479 families have been relieved, and 1,875 individuals, beside 376 non-resident poor persons who have been assisted by transportation. The total expenses for all this amounted to $7,515.39, of which $5,144 was disbursed for provisions, and $1,191.25 for fuel.

In connection with the hospital work the city employed thirteen ward physicians. They attended to the sick poor of the city who otherwise would have had to be removed to the city hospital or some other charitable institution. These physicians attended 612 patients and made 1,669 visits. The total expense of this form of medical relief was $10,695.45.

The expenses of the city hospital amounted to $7,045.21, exclusive of the repairs to which attention has been called. During one year 368 patients were in the hospital, of whom 283 were discharged as recovered, 4 as improved, 3 unimproved, 36 died, and 14 were transferred to other institutions, mostly to the county almshouse.

This report, the last obtainable, is so interesting that, while it is not of recent date, it is appended as showing the methods and results of the work of the Board of Charities of the city of Utica.

ANNUAL REPORT

OF THE

CLERK OF THE BOARD OF CHARITIES

OF UTICA, N. Y.

From March 1, 1900, to March 1, 1901.

Number of families relieved..........................	479
Number of persons relieved	1,875
Number of non-resident poor persons assisted by transportation	376

Commissioners of Charities.

E. W. REUSSWIG, *Chairman.*   GEO. H. STACK, *Secretary.*

JOHN J. BARRY.

THOMAS O. COLE.   WILLIAM H. ROBERTS.

JOHN QUINN.

DISBURSEMENTS.

Provisions	$5,144 00	
Burials	787 00	
Shoes	113 50	
Medicine	4 87	
Meals	15 25	
Coal	1,154 45	
Wood	. 36 75	
Clothing	26 84	
Transportation	232 73	
		$7,515 39

OFFICE EXPENSES.

Clerk's and assistants' salary..........	$1,800 00
Telephone	43 11

Postage, telegrams, etc	$5 00	
Printing and stationery	55 65	
Cleaning and repairing office furniture.	4 50	
Census for county superintendent	25 00	
		$1,933 26

Ward Physicians.

Thirteen physicians were employed to attend the sick poor of the city at an expense of		1,325 00
Number of patients	612	
Number of prescriptions	2,301	
Number of visits	1,669	
Total outdoor relief		$10,773 65
Less amount received for non-resident poor		78 20
		$10,695 45

Expense of City Hospital—Indoor Relief.

Provisions	$894 85
Meat and fish	640 89
Flour and feed	190 84
Drugs and medicine	542 10
Coal and wood	481 70
Clothing and dry goods	161 79
Crockery	25 03
Tins and hardware	78 23
Gas	180 61
Ice	35 59
Soap	54 00
Furniture	37 40
Telephone	47 71
Disinfectant	3 00
Printing and papering	2 58
Laundry	80 00
Repairs and improvements	375 64
Printing and stationery	23 65
Horse shoeing, etc	25 00

Insurance	$162 00
Repairs to wagons, etc.	182 45
Horse and stock	191 00
Miscellaneous	43 13
Hospital physician's salary	600 00
Hospital keeper's salary	600 00
Hospital employes salaries	1,503 82
Total indoor relief	$7,163 01
Less amount received from patients	117 80
	$7,045 21

Number of patients remaining in hospital March 1, 1900.	23
Number admitted during year	345
Whole number of persons treated	368

Discharged recovered	283
Discharged improved	4
Discharged unimproved	3
Transferred	14
Died	36
	340

Remaining in hospital March 1, 1901	28
Number of days patients were in hospital	6,466

COMMITMENTS.

To the Utica Orphan Asylum	22
To St. John's Orphan Asylum	13
To House of Good Shepherd	11
To St. Vincent's Industrial School	7
To St. Joseph's Infant Home	17
	70

To the Oneida County Home:
  Males 40
  Females 27

                                                    67

Inmates returned to Oneida County Home:
  Males 29
  Females 7

                                                    36

Committed to Utica State Hospital:
  Males 15
  Females 11

                                                    26

CHILDREN RELEASED FROM INSTITUTIONS.

From Utica Orphan Asylum:
  Returned to relatives............................ 17
  Placed in homes.................................. 4
  Transferred to State Institute for Feeble-Minded
    Children 1

                                                    22

From St. Joseph's Infant Home:
  Returned to relatives............................ 13

From St. Vincent's Industrial School:
  Returned to relatives............................ 19
  Placed in homes.................................. 3

                                                    22

From St. John's Orphan Asylum:
  Returned to relatives............................ 23
  Placed in homes.................................. 3
  Transferred to other institutions................ 4

                                                    30

From House of Good Shepherd:

Returned to relatives............................ 7

CASH ACCOUNT.

Receipts.

Balance on hand March 1, 1900.................	$25 68
Received from Board of Charities for transporta-tion..	230 00
Received from county treasurer for conveying patients to County Home.....................	56 77
Received from sale of horse....................	65 00
Received from other towns for non-resident poor.	78 20
Received from patients at City Hospital.........	117 80
Received from parents for care of children......	1,167 50
	$1,740 95

Disbursements.

Paid transportation	$232 73
Paid postage, telegrams, etc....................	5 00
Paid Utica Orphan Asylum.....................	522 50
Paid St. John's Orphan Asylum.................	209 00
Paid St. Joseph's Infant Home.................	227 50
Paid St. Vincent's Industrial School.............	114 50
Paid House of Good Shepherd..................	94 00
Paid city treasurer............................	317 77
Cash on hand.................................	17 95
	$1,740 95

Summary.

Outdoor relief	$10,695 45
Indoor relief	7,045 21
	$17,740 66

Respectfully submitted,

J. W. MANLEY,

Clerk.

MUNICIPAL LODGING HOUSE.

113 and 115 Market street, Syracuse, N. Y.

The Municipal Lodging House of Syracuse remains in the same building in which it was first established. At the last inspection the difficulty of exit in case of fire was noted. During the interval since that inspection the arrangement of dormitories has not been altered for the better; on the contrary, two cells have been placed upon the second floor. These are intended for the confinement of persons suspected of insanity. They are furnished with bedding, and the doors are strongly barred.

The lavatory is not such as should be provided for an institution of this kind, nor are the baths of the best character. There is no method for sterilizing clothing, the laundry is rather primitive, and the roller towels in use may spread disease.

One serious defect in the equipment of the building is the provision made for homeless females. As has been said heretofore, it is not wise to have men and women kept in the same building. During the past year the number of night lodgings was 6,724. Many of these lodgings were furnished to women, so that there is evidently a necessity that provision be made for them, but it is not advisable to gather these dependents under one roof with men. Some more suitable arrangement should be made for the care of homeless women.

As was stated last year, the fire danger is greater for the women than for the men, owing to the fact that the rooms assigned to them are more secluded and separated by locked doors from the only stairway as well as the apartments of the men. The building has no fire-escapes, and in case of a fire in the building, unless the fire department were quick in the work of rescue, many of the inmates, especially the women, would be burned. Fortunately the fire department is located within a short distance of the building. This does not lessen the responsibility for making ample provision for safety.

The custody of the insane in cells is not the proper work of a municipal lodging house. If the city desires to establish a place for the temporary detention of those suspected of insanity, a pavilion should be erected in connection with some hospital, and certainly the care of the insane ought not to be made any part of the work of a home of this character. It were better to confine the cases of suspected insanity in the city hall itself, under the observation of police surgeons, than to associate them with the homeless men and women who depend upon the Municipal Lodging House for shelter. It is very doubtful if there be any legal warrant for making the Municipal Lodging House a place of detention for the insane, and, in fact, the association of the poor and the insane is in direct contravention of the spirit of our charity laws.

The furnishing of the Municipal Lodging House is well worn and requires renovation. The beds and tables need repairs, while the bedding should have mending.

The total expense for the maintenance of this institution for one year was $6,066.48. This money paid for rent, salaries, groceries, coal, light and other supplies. The county of Onondaga paid $621.75 for meals and lodging furnished to non-residents, and there was a further bill of $376.35 pending against the county.

Nine hundred and forty-six persons gave one hour's work each for the single meal they received from the lodging house. This, added to the work for night lodgings and meals, gave a total of 27,843 hours' work on the streets of the city of Syracuse. At the regular pay for eight hours' work per day, which is the time worked by city laborers, the labor of the lodgers amounted to $5,220.36, making the net expense to the city for the maintenance of the lodging house $846.12, provided the lodging house does not exact double pay from the county, that is, labor from the men and money from the county for the entertainment of non-residents. The city can well afford to pay $846.12 for the care of this class of temporary dependents.

The number of homeless men and women requiring shelter during the month of July, when the demand was lightest, was 252. The largest number in any one month was in December, when 848 persons applied for food and lodging; beside these, 49 persons in the same month applied for meals. From October to April the number did not fall below 600 persons per month, lodged and fed.

The question arises, "Does an institution of this kind have a
tendency to attract to Syracuse, tramps and other disreputable
characters for the sake of the shelter it gives?" Doubtless,
were there no restrictions upon the entertainment, Syracuse
would become the mecca of the tramps of the State, but the
fact that work is exacted in return for entertainment deters
very many from making application for help. Then, too, the
limited time during which shelter is given to any one ought to
weed out those who would otherwise remain in the lodging
house.

One feature of this work is that which pertains to an employment agency. The superintendent reports that he found employment for 982 persons during one year, and such a result is
highly gratifying, provided the employment was not of such a
temporary character as to have no real value. It is hardly
desirable to have the Municipal Lodging House become a
employment agency, and yet this work should not be discredited.

The Municipal Lodging House is still an experiment. There
is all probability that it will prove, as elsewhere, most successful, if it can be continued a charity and be managed strictly
upon business principles. The danger to these institutions is
that they are likely to fall into the control of politicians and
become agencies for colonizing voters.

Since the last inspection of this institution, the popular will,
as expressed by ballot, has decreed that the management of the
municipal affairs of Syracuse shall pass into new hands. The
political control of the city institutions was involved in the election, and some of the papers of Syracuse have published articles
intimating that as a measure of economy it may be desirable
to discontinue the Municipal Lodging House. Such discontinuance and consequent return to old methods of temporary relief
for homeless men and women would be a step backward. Enlightened philanthropy has no patience with methods of relief
which are vicious, nor with such provision for the homeless as
is destructive to self-respect.

The Municipal Lodging House of the city of Syracuse has been
in the experimental stage, as has been said, but during the time
it has been in service it has demonstrated the possibility of
great usefulness. Such an institution, properly managed, will

serve as the nexus between the worthy unemployed homeless workman and the opportunity by which he may improve his condition. In order to guard against the possibility of abuse it is not necessary to destroy an institution. Better prevent the possibility of abuse by careful regulation, systematic inspection, and competent management.

The chief difficulty the Municipal Lodging House has heretofore experienced has been due to the fact that its location does not give it the accommodation which its opportunity for usefulness demands. If it were located in a detached building, well located, and were equipped with the necessary conveniences, the Municipal Lodging House could accomplish a great work for the city of Syracuse. It is hoped that the new administration, taking advantage of the experience of other municipalities, will make arrangements for the equipment of this institution so that it may creditably represent the philanthropy of the city of. Syracuse.

It is interesting to know what Theodore Roosevelt had to say in this connection after serving as one of the four police commissioners of the city of New York during the years of 1895 and 1896. It will be remembered that he was appointed at that time by Mayor Strong, who in turn received his election as the result of a fusion movement, which succeeded in overthrowing the former administration. In September, 1897, a paper from Theodore Roosevelt appeared in the Atlantic Monthly in relation to the many reforms enacted by the police commissioners during his two years of office. In describing the reforms put into effect, among other things he says:

" One important bit of reform was, abolishing the tramp lodging houses which had originally been started in the police station in a spirit of unwise philanthropy. These tramp lodging houses, not being properly supervised, were mere nurseries for pauperism and crime, tramps and loafers of every shade thronging to the city every winter to enjoy their benefits. We abolished them, a municipal lodging house being substituted.

" Here all homeless wanderers were received, forced to bathe, given night clothes before going to bed and made to work next morning, and in addition were so closely supervised that habitual tramps and vagrants were speedily detected and apprehended."

The effects of this reform might justify us in the belief that the benefits obtained for New York might in an equal degree be of gain to us if carried on the same lines here.

If the existence of a municipal lodging house be accepted as a necessary means of providing for a certain element to be found in this and every other community, and if experience has demonstrated that its economical management has fallen far short of the ideal, may it not be pertinent to ask, Shall not a more economical management be had rather than the whole structure be destroyed?

A remedy can be applied to strengthen those parts showing the greatest weakness, and by so doing further build up the healthier parts, saving the whole in some such manner as the following:

Let there be a commission formed which shall be known as the Syracuse Municipal Lodging House Commission, which shall have entire supervision of the municipal lodging house, and whose members shall receive their appointment from the mayor, who shall also be of the number as an ex officio member. The qualifications should be good citizenship, together with the possession of such experience as will best fit them to intelligently administer such an institution. They should serve without compensation and be drawn largely, if not altogether, from the ranks of the various charity organizations of the city.

We may perhaps in this manner reach a more perfect administrative condition, and certainly by this means divorce the lodging house from politics, if merit alone be made the standard. The commission as far as is possible should be of such composition as to embrace all creeds. These conditions, I believe, would be acceptable to the taxpayer, who would recognize it as a long way in the right direction.

Respectfully submitted,

D. McCARTHY,

Commissioner, Fifth Judicial District.

Statistical summary.

COUNTIES.	INMATES.			Children under 2 years.	Children between 2 and 16.	OVER 70 YEARS OLD.			Epileptics.	Feeble-minded.	Idiots.
	Male.	Female.	Total.			Male.	Female.	Total.			
Herkimer	58	24	82	0	0	15	12	27	2	9	0
Jefferson	52	39	91	0	0	23	13	36	0	15	0
Lewis	25	15	40	0	0	13	7	20	2	5	2
Oneida	168	89	257	0	0	62	41	103	6	15	8
Onondaga	136	69	205	4	0	53	15	68	9	9	3
Oswego	31	28	59	0	1	9	8	17	6	10	3
Oswego city	24	19	43	0	0	12	8	20	1	2	1
Total	494	283	777	4	1	187	104	291	26	65	17

REPORT

OF

Visitation of Almshouses in the Sixth
Judicial District.

REPORT.

To the State Board of Charities:

I present herewith the annual report upon the almshouses in the Sixth Judicial District. In making this report it is gratifying to be able to state that the year has witnessed no backward movement in the management of these institutions; in fact, " progress " seems to be the general watchword, and as a consequence the outlook for our dependents is hopeful.

IMPROVEMENTS.

The improvements of the year are generally those which have to do with the care of the sick and protection of the population from the dangers of fire. It is generally understood that in making provision for the care of dependents it is necessary that the buildings be made safe. Many of the almshouses in this district were built years ago, at a time when the attention to sanitation and safety was not paid which is deemed essential to-day. As a consequence the older buildings were not equipped with fire-escapes, and the general sanitation was more or less neglected. These defects of construction are being overcome by repairs and improvements made from year to year. In some counties buildings have been torn down and replaced by more modern structures; in others buildings have been remodeled and the plumbing and drainage made satisfactory. In spite of these efforts to adjust the old buildings to present requirements some of our almshouses will not be made satisfactory until new structures replace those in use to-day, and the sooner this fact is recognized by boards of supervisors the better it will be for the public. It is not in the interest of economy to spend large sums of money in remodeling buildings which can never be made satisfactory.

THE CARE OF THE SICK.

It is gratifying to see the attention which is given to this part of the work of our almshouses. As a general thing the inmates of almshouses are old and infirm, with a pronounced tendency toward chronic disease. There are, however, in all the almshouses of the district certain inmates who are comparatively young, but prevented from self-support by defects or infirmities. It is not desirable that these inmates and others in the enjoyment of health should be imperiled by daily and nightly association with the sick. The erection of separate buildings for hospital purposes is a move in the right direction. Their use will take out of the ordinary dormitories the sick smells and germ-laden atmosphere which are always found where the sick are. The separate hospital will relieve those in ordinary health from the depressing influence of constant association with the sick. It will have a tendency to assure better care for the sick, as the hospital is usually much better equipped than the ordinary dormitory. It is hoped that the day is not far distant when each almshouse in the district will have its well-equipped hospital for the segregation of sick inmates.

WATER.

Next to the matter of protection from the dangers of fire, the matter of water supply is important. In fact, upon an abundant water supply the general safety of the institution depends, for without water fires will usually get beyond control, while with standpipes and hose, fires can be extinguished before they gain much headway. Besides this an abundant water supply assures domestic and personal cleanliness and the consequent health of the inmates in the institution. Attention is being paid to this matter in the several counties of the district, and where water has been scarce heretofore at certain seasons steps have been taken or are in contemplation which will secure an abundant supply for all purposes.

ADMINISTRATION.

Some changes have taken place in the list of officials charged with the management of our almshouses, but these changes are comparatively few. Consequently the administration remains substantially as heretofore. This is an advantage to the several counties. Where changes in the official staff are made frequently the discipline is more or less disturbed. Fortunately for the institutions the benefit of the continuance in service of capable officials. is recognized in the district. Kindliness has marked the intercourse of inmates and attendants.

In this district the food supply is usually abundant and varied, although the methods of cooking are not always satisfactory. In this matter of the preparation of food the attempt to economize results occasionally in waste and discontent. It is better to pay for a competent cook than to depend upon the services of the usually incompetent inmates.

The statistics will be found tabulated at the conclusion of the reports of the several counties.

Respectfully submitted,

PETER WALRATH,

Commissioner Sixth Judicial District.

BROOME COUNTY ALMSHOUSE, BINGHAMTON, N. Y.

JOHN MOSES, *Keeper.*

This almshouse has accommodations for about 150 inmates. The buildings are estimated to be worth about $40,000. There have been few improvements during the year outside of fencing and some new furnishing.

At the times of inspection the almshouse was found in good condition and the inmates appeared contented. The old wooden buildings are unsafe in the event of fire, and should therefore be removed entirely or relocated and converted to other purposes. A special building for a hospital for men ought to be built as soon as possible.

CENSUS.

The census was as follows:

	Males.	Females.	Total.
Number of inmates....................	84	33	117
Children under two years old..........	1	0	1
Children between two and sixteen years.	0	1	1
Number of blind.....................	2	0	2
Number of deaf-mutes................	0	0	0

	Males.	Females.	Total.
Number of feeble-minded..............	1	1	1
Number of idiots.....................	9	4	13
Number of epileptics.................	4	2	6
Persons over seventy years old........	36	14	50

CHEMUNG COUNTY ALMSHOUSE, BREESPORT, N. Y.

WILLIAM VAN DUZER, *Superintendent.*

This almshouse has been greatly improved since last report. A new administration building of brick, three stories high, has been built. A steam heating plant, furnishing warmth for the north building, was installed, and the laundry improved. Besides these improvements, some old structures which had outlived their usefulness were torn down. It is anticipated that a large cistern, which will receive the rainwater from the several buildings, will be constructed near the laundry. In addition to this, the reservoir upon the hillside is to be doubled in capacity. This will prove a good measure for the general safety of the institution.

There is ample space in some of the buildings connected with this almshouse to provide room for such of the county charges as now have to be cared for at Amityville and similar places. Pending the transfer to State care of the epileptics, idiots and feeble-minded persons who have to be supported by the county, it is proposed by the county superintendent and supervisors to domicile them in the available buildings. Such a step would result in considerable saving to the county, but it should only be taken to bridge over the time until the State institutions can receive all of these dependents.

An improvement in the water service in this institution is needed to secure its safety against the danger of fire. To render the water supply available, fire risers and connected hose should be placed in all the halls of the buildings.

The dietary is generally satisfactory and sufficient. A considerable supply for the table is raised by the labor of the inmates in the gardens, and consequently there is variety in the daily meals.

CENSUS.

The census was as follows:

	Males.	Females.	Total.
Number of inmates	49	29	78
Children under two years old	0	0	0
Children between two and sixteen years.	0	1	1
Number of blind	2	1	3
Number of deaf-mutes	0	0	0
Number of feeble-minded	6	3	9
Number of idiots	8	6	14
Number of epileptics	4	4	8
Persons over seventy years old	16	8	24

CHENANGO COUNTY ALMSHOUSE, PRESTON, N. Y.

RICHARD C. QUINN, *Superintendent*.

The group of buildings which constitutes the almshouse of Chenango county is located on high ground about four miles from the village of Norwich. The institution will accommodate about 100 inmates, and the estimated value of the property is $30,000. The main building is in good order.

Recently a masonry reservoir, holding about 750 barrels of water, was constructed, and a gas plant supplying 100 lights installed.

In this almshouse the dairy contains 20 cows giving milk, and the inmates are supplied with all the milk and butter they need.

The hospital is in the main building, a room with accommodations for eight patients being set apart for each sex. A small building in the rear of the main almshouse is used as a dormitory for the feeble-minded and idiotic. A number of this class should be sent to the State institutions as soon as possible.

CENSUS.

The census was as follows:

	Males.	Females.	Total.
Number of inmates	55	23	78
Children under two years old	0	0	0
Children between two and sixteen years.	0	0	0
Number of blind	0	1	1
Number of deaf-mutes	0	0	0
Number of feeble-minded	9	10	19

	Males.	Females.	Total
Number of idiots....................	2	1	3
Number of epileptics.................	0	1	1
Persons over seventy years old........	24	6	30

CORTLAND COUNTY ALMSHOUSE, CORTLAND, N. Y.

D. W. PORTER, *Keeper*.

Some minor repairs, especially to the asylum building, were made to this almshouse during the year, but the matter of fire protection by the provision of chemical fire extinguishers and increase of water storage and supply has been left unattended to by the supervisors. As this institution is lighted by kerosene oil lamps, there is greater necessity for special attention to safety in the event of fire. There are practically no precautions against fire, for the twenty hand grenades distributed about the buildings would be useless in case of an outbreak. The safety of the inmates is not assured by fire-escapes, and there is only one stairway from each upper floor in the buildings devoted to men and women. Escape from the second floor to the keeper's quarters and other parts of the buildings might be had across a tin roof, but the exit would be through a window and directly at the head of a stairway leading to the floor below, so that a fire breaking out in the lower part of the hall at the foot of the stairway would prevent the use of this window. Fortunately, the number of inmates is not large.

At the time of inspection everything was found clean and in good order. The food was seen to be well cooked, served in sufficient quantity and varied in its character. The inmates were apparently contented with their home and with the treatment they receive from the attendants.

CENSUS.

The census was as follows:

	Males.	Females.	Total.
Number of inmates..................	23	13	36
Children under two years old..........	1	0	1
Children between two and sixteen years.	0	0	0
Number of blind.....................	0	2	2
Number of deaf-mutes................	0	0	0

	Males.	Females.	Total.
Number of feeble-minded..............	1	1	2
Number of idiots	0	3	3
Number of epileptics..................	1	0	1
Persons over seventy years old.........	15	5	20

DELAWARE COUNTY ALMSHOUSE, DELHI, N. Y.

GEORGE B. SMITH, *Superintendent.*

This almshouse is pleasantly located. a short distance from Delhi, in a situation of great natural beauty. All the buildings are kept in good repair and are well painted inside and outside. Steel ceiling in the dining-room and a milk cooler are the recent improvements; and in addition material is now on hand for the extension of the steel ceiling to the other rooms.

A well kept dairy is connected with this institution, and as a consequence the inmates receive butter and milk at every meal. There are 42 cows which belong to the institution, and from these during the last year $1,000 worth of milk was sold to a neighboring creamery.

CENSUS.

The census was as follows:

	Males.	Females.	Total.
Number of inmates...................	30	12	42
Children under two years old..........	1	0	1
Children between two and sixteen......	0	0	0
Number of blind.....................	1	0	1
Number of deaf-mutes.................	0	1	1
Number of feeble-minded..............	3	0	3
Number of idiots.....................	5	1	6
Number of epileptics..................	1	1	2
Persons over seventy years old........	13	5	18

MADISON COUNTY ALMSHOUSE, EATON, N. Y.

S. A. CURTIS, *Superintendent.*

At the time of the last visitation the grounds and buildings were found in a commendable degree of cleanliness. Some use-less small buildings which had long encumbered the grounds near the building devoted to men were removed during the year, a new corn crib was erected, and the telephone at last installed.

It is expected that in the near future a new laundry with proper machinery will be purchased, as a committee of the board of supervisors has the matter under consideration.

Twenty-eight cows furnish milk for the institution, and all the products of the dairy are used for the benefit of the inmates, which is a proof that so far as diet is concerned the inmates are well cared for.

The former asylum building, which was renovated last year, was not occupied up to the time of the preparation of this report, but it is expected that soon it will be again put into service.

CENSUS.

The census was as follows:

	Males.	Females.	Total.
Number of inmates...................	59	38	97
Children under two years old..........	1	2	3
Children between two and sixteen years	0	0	0
Number of blind.....................	3	0	3
Number of deaf-mutes...............	1	0	1
Number of feeble-minded.............	1	7	8
Number of idiots....................	0	2	2
Number of epileptics.................	3	2	5
Persons over seventy years old........	25	15	40

OTSEGO COUNTY ALMSHOUSE, COOPERSTOWN, N. Y.

A. W. WEBER, Superintendent.

This institution is one of the oldest in the State. The main building is of stone and is two stories in height, with a basement. To the north of this main structure stands another stone building of the same height, used as the women's dormitory. The men have a three-story wooden building, with an addition. All the buildings are only in fair condition, needing many repairs to floors and walls.

A recent improvement was in the way of plastering in the men's buildings. Besides this a new shingle roof was put on one building.

The rooms in the stone building are generally low and dark. There is a lack of sufficient available space for the dining-room, and probably it would be economy to reconstruct the stone building so as to secure sufficient space for dining-room purposes. To do this, however, will require the erection of a suitable building for administrative purposes, as there is no room to be spared from the dormitories. By using the space occupied as quarters by the superintendent and family, and providing for him in a new building, a dining-room could be constructed. Some further improvement should also be made in the matter of fire protection.

CENSUS.

The census was as follows:

	Males.	Females.	Total.
Number of inmates	68	31	99
Children under two years old	1	1	2
Children between two and sixteen years	1	0	1
Number of blind	2	1	3
Number of deaf-mutes	0	0	0
Number of feeble-minded	1	0	1
Number of idiots	12	7	19
Number of epileptics	2	0	2
Persons over seventy years old	26	14	40

SCHUYLER COUNTY.

J. H. SHULENBURG, *Superintendent.*

Schuyler county continues to maintain its poor by arrangements with families as heretofore. There is neither town nor county almshouse, and as a consequence the poor maintained at public expense are scattered very widely. The county poor are supposed to be under the close and constant observation of the county superintendent, but owing to the fact that they are so widely distributed and cared for in so many different places, they are seen very seldom. This is apt to lead to neglect, for unless the persons who contract to board the poor are under observation and feel that they are likely to be visited frequently, their personal interest may lead them to save money at the expense of those placed under their care.

The reasons for the establishment of a county almshouse have been set forth at length many times. There is a growing feeling in Schuyler county that there should be no further delay in the matter. The board of supervisors has talked about a county almshouse on a number of occasions, but up to the present no official action has been taken. Perhaps the necessary steps will be taken in the year 1902.

TIOGA COUNTY ALMSHOUSE, OWEGO, N. Y.

DEWITT C. ORANGE, *Keeper*.

This almshouse is composed of a group of separated buildings, all of which are not in actual service. They are in fair repair, and some improvements to them have been made lately.

There is a small dairy in connection with the institution, and its products are given to the inmates. The general dietary is satisfactory, and the inmates were found at the time of inspection contented and well cared for. Among the inmates there are seven feeble-minded and idiotic persons.

The general order and cleanliness of the almshouse is deserving of mention. The greatest need is in the matter of better drainage and a safer illuminant.

CENSUS.

The census was as follows:

	Males.	Females.	Total.
Number of inmates	24	14	38
Children under two years old	1	0	1
Children between two and sixteen years	0	0	0
Number of blind	1	1	2
Number of deaf-mutes	0	0	0
Number of feeble-minded	2	3	5
Number of idiots	2	0	2
Number of epileptics	0	0	0
Persons over seventy years old	6	8	14

TOMPKINS COUNTY ALMSHOUSE, ITHACA, N. Y.

DAVID BOWER, *Superintendent.*

The main building of the group composing the almshouse of Tompkins county is of brick, the superintendent's house being in front of it and the women's building in the rear. Both of the latter are frame structures.

Recently a one-story building was erected for service as a morgue; an inmate did all the work upon this structure.

A steam pump is greatly needed for this institution so as to furnish lifting power for the water.

The hospital is in the brick building and contains accommodations for about 23 patients.

There is a large and fertile farm connected with the almshouse, and most of the work upon it is done by the inmates.

Great improvement was noted in the matter of cleanliness, but owing to the lack of sufficient help it is difficult to keep the institution in satisfactory condition. The board of supervisors does not allow a sufficient appropriation to pay for necessary help.

CENSUS.

The census was as follows:

	Males.	Females.	Total.
Number of inmates....................	40	14	54
Children under two years............	0	0	0
Children between two and sixteen years	0	0	0
Number of blind	1	0	1
Number of deaf-mutes	0	0	0
Number of feeble-minded	9	3	12
Number of idiots	3	1	4
Number of epileptics	1	0	1
Persons over seventy years old........	14	4	18

40

Statistical Summary.

COUNTIES.	INMATES.			Children, under 5 years.	Children between 5 and 16.	OVER 70 YEARS OLD.			Epileptics.	Feeble-minded.	Idiots.
	Male.	Female.	Total.			Male.	Female.	Total.			
Broome	84	33	117	1	1	36	14	50	6	2	13
Chemung	49	29	78	0	1	16	8	24	8	9	14
Chenango	55	23	78	0	0	24	6	30	1	19	3
Cortland	23	13	36	1	0	15	5	20	1	2	3
Delaware	30	12	42	1	0	13	5	18	2	3	6
Madison	59	38	97	3	0	25	15	40	5	8	2
Otsego	68	31	99	2	1	26	14	40	2	1	19
Tioga	24	14	38	1	0	6	8	14	0	5	2
Tompkins	40	14	54	0	0	14	4	18	1	12	4
Total	432	207	639	9	3	175	79	254	26	61	66

REPORT

OF

Visitation of Almshouses

IN THE

SEVENTH JUDICIAL DISTRICT.

627

REPORT.

To the State Board of Charities:

The almshouses in the Seventh Judicial District, which comprises the counties of Cayuga, Livingston, Monroe, Ontario, Seneca, Steuben, Wayne and Yates, have been visited and inspected by the officers of the Board at frequent intervals during the past year.

IMPROVEMENTS.

In two counties, Steuben and Wayne, considerable improvements have been made. In the former a new hospital as an addition to the women's building has been erected, which provides accommodations for the sick.

In Wayne county the fire which destroyed the old building gave opportunity for the erection of a new residence building for the keeper and a building for the women. The residence formerly occupied by the keeper has been removed to the rear of its former site, and is now an addition to the hospital. In this same county, since the close of the fiscal year, a fire has destroyed the barns. By this latest fire, all of the old group of farm buildings are removed, and an opportunity is now presented to relocate the outbuildings.

WATER.

The lack of sufficient water has been a serious handicap to the Wayne County Almshouse, and in other counties within the district a larger supply has also been required. It will bear frequent repetition that one of the first essentials in an almshouse or other public institution is an abundant supply of water. The health, comfort, cleanliness and safety of the inmates depend upon it, and unless such supply can be guaranteed where an almshouse is now located, it were better to remove to some place where an abundant supply of water can be assured.

THE CARE OF THE SICK.

This is a matter of prime importance, and, except in two or three instances, this district is not abreast with some of the other districts of the State. There are not adequate accommodations for the care of the sick in many of the almshouses. This matter has been pressed upon the attention of the boards of supervisors from time to time, and it is hoped each almshouse will soon be supplied with a separate hospital, adequately equipped, and large enough to provide for all the sick who are likely to require its accommodations.

MONROE ALMSHOUSE.

Monroe county has not yet decided to build a new almshouse. Its boards of supervisors have successively considered the removal question year after year, but, as in the famous parable of antiquity, "the labors of the mountain bring forth only a mouse." The matter has been referred to committee after committee. Visitations have been made of farms for the purpose of selection, but in the end nothing has been accomplished, while ever the difficulties of administration in the almshouse continue. The over-crowded hospital, the dormitories filled to overflowing, the difficulties of making proper provision in such cramped and crowded quarters, should spur the board of supervisors to speedy action. If the almshouse is not to be removed, then new buildings should be erected which could be equipped for hospital purposes.

ADMINISTRATION.

It may be stated in general that the administration of the almshouses in the several counties of the district has been satisfactory. The officials in charge are of high character, and take great interest in the work for which they are responsible. Cleanliness and good order are characteristic. The food supply is usually abundant and varied, and, in consequence, the inmates seem to be contented.

CONCLUSION

An examination of the census reports of the several almshouses shows that a large number of the inmates are over seventy years of age. A consideration of this fact leads to the conclusion that very little labor can be expected from them, and that from their age and infirmity more attendants are necessary to take proper care of them. In most of the almshouses of the district there is a sufficient number of helpers, but in one or two there is not enough of the right kind to look after these aged and infirm people.

Respectfully submitted,
ENOCH V. STODDARD, M. D.,
Commissioner, Seventh Judicial District.

CAYUGA COUNTY ALMSHOUSE.
Sennett, N. Y.
ANDREW J. TRIMBLE, *Keeper.*

Some new floors have been laid in this almshouse, and steel ceilings placed in many rooms. The matter of equipping the building with fire-escapes has been referred to a committee of the board of supervisors, and it may reasonably be expected that the buildings will soon be rendered much safer.

The water supply is obtained from a well located about 20 rods from the house. It is forced by steam pump to three tanks in the attics, which hold about 400 barrels. As the building is lighted by kerosene oil, in the event of a fire there is not sufficiency of water at command. However, stand pipes with connected hose are in the several halls, and a number of liquid chemical extinguishers are kept on hand. The inside stairways are not adequate as means of escape in the event of fire, for they are not favorably placed. The fire-escapes which are under consideration will be a great benefit.

For the sick, two rooms are set apart, one for each sex. The total accommodation thus provided is for five women and fifteen men. A small hospital building ought to be added to the equipment.

In general the premises at the time of inspection were found in good order.

CENSUS.

The census was as follows:

	Males.	Females.	Total.
Number of inmates....................	40	24	64
Children under two years old.........	0	0	0
Children between two and sixteen years.	0	0	0
Number of blind.....................	1	0	1
Number of deaf-mutes.................	0	0	0
Number of feeble-minded..............	3	5	8
Number of idiots.....................	1	2	3
Number of epileptics.................	1	1	2
Persons over seventy years old........	18	12	30

LIVINGSTON COUNTY ALMSHOUSE.
Geneseo, N. Y.
HYDE D. MARVIN, *Superintendent.*

There have been no recent improvements to this almshouse. The three brick buildings stand substantially in the same condition as at the time of last report, needing repairs and alterations. A year ago it was supposed that the supervisors would take steps to remodel the former asylum building and convert it into a hospital, and then have the superintendent redistribute and classify the inmates of the institution. The chairman of the building committee was very much in favor of such steps being taken as would promote the health and comfort of the inmates, but apparently the board of supervisors did not coincide with his view, for nothing has been done. Until some such change is made, this almshouse will not be in a satisfactory condition. It is ill-ventilated, and as the inmates are at present distributed, they are compelled to remain in small ill-ventilated rooms wherein the difficulties of administration are greatly increased by their segregation, and where their safety is not assured in case of a fire. Something should be done as soon as possible in order to separate the sick from the well. Some exceedingly offensive cases are now necessarily kept in the main dormitory building, and the health of all the inmates is imperiled as a consequence.

As the grounds have been cleared up and freed from rubbish, many old fences have disappeared, and the dilapidated outbuildings are now removed. Generally the buildings were clean and in order, but the changes heretofore suggested should be made as soon as possible.

CENSUS.

The census was as follows:

	Males.	Females.	Total.
Number of inmates.....................	42	14	56
Children under two years old..........	0	0	0
Children between two and sixteen years.	1	0	1
Number of blind......................	3	1	4
Number of deaf-mutes.................	0	0	0
Number of feeble-minded..............	8	2	10
Number of idiots.....................	1	1	2
Number of epileptics..................	3	3	6
Persons over seventy years old.........	17	4	21

MONROE COUNTY ALMSHOUSE.

Rochester, N. Y.

C. V. LODGE, *Superintendent.*

With the exception of some minor improvements, there have been no changes in the Monroe County Almshouse during the year. All improvements and changes are held in abeyance pending the final determination, by the supervisors, of the question of removal. There can be no doubt that a rural location for the almshouse will be an improvement. A large tract of land can be purchased, new buildings erected thereon, and the products of the farm will help pay the expense of maintenance. But in addition to this economical argument for a change, are the moral and humanitarian reasons. The crowded condition of the almshouse, the impossibility of giving suitable care to the many sick inmates, the temptations which are due to the contiguity to the city, all are good reasons why immediate action should be taken. The necessity for such removal has been urged by the commissioner in his annual report for several years past. The present board of supervisors seems to be fully impressed with the necessity for a change, but as yet no action has been taken which gives promise of the removal of the almshouse at an early date.

It may prove of interest to place here, in chronological order, the proceedings of the Monroe County Board of Supervisors since 1897, in this matter of removing the institution.

"December 4, 1897.—Committee on visiting county buildings reports that more room is needed in the almshouse for sleeping apartments, and that if a hospital could be built outside, the crowded condition would be relieved. Report agreed to.

"December 13, 1897.—Committee on almshouse and superintendent of poor accounts recommends the building of a hospital at the almshouse to relieve the overcrowded condition. Laid on the table under rules.

"December 14, 1897.—Above report unanimously adopted.

"December 17, 1897.—Resolution introduced by Supervisor Bareham, to the effect that the almshouse has insufficient capacity to properly accommodate the number of unfortunate dependents to be cared for by the county, and since the rapidly growing population of the county calls for immediate action the committee on almshouses should be directed to procure plans and specifications and estimated cost of a two-story hospital building. Laid on table under the rules.

"December 31, 1897.—Above resolution adopted.

"February 15, 1898.—Resolution introduced by Supervisor Oberlies, to the effect that since the erection of a hospital at the almshouse would probably cost $100,000 or more, and the county has not in proximity with the almshouse sufficient land to meet the requirements of such a building, and since it would be a great saving to the county to purchase a suitable farm site for the erection of a new almshouse on the cottage plan and use the existing structure for a hospital, the almshouse committee should be instructed to postpone plans for the hospital and look for available farming sites. Laid on the table under the rules.

" February 17, 1898.—Above resolution laid indefinitely on the table by vote of 26 to 10.

" May 17, 1898.—Almshouse committee reports that plans for almshouse have been submitted by five architects, and agreement entered into with one of those architects to prepare a full set of plans, specifications and estimated cost. Almshouse committee also introduces resolution that it be directed to build a hospital at the almshouse at a cost not to exceed $110,000. Laid on the table under the rules. State Board of Charities presents a report to the effect that it approves of the plans for a hospital submitted it by the committee.

" May 18, 1898.—Board goes into committee of the whole, with Supervisor Briggs in the chair, for the purpose of visiting the almshouse to see if proposed improvements are necessary.

" May 23, 1898.—Supervisor Briggs reports that after careful examination of proposed plans, and of site, the committee carried away the conviction that the present accommodations are inadequate, and that a hospital is necessary. Leave granted to sit again.

" May 25, 1898.—Supervisor Wellington moves that a report of Commissioner Enoch V. Stoddard, to the State Board of Charities, concerning and opposed to the proposed hospital, be referred to the committee of the whole, having the matter under consideration. Resolution adopted. Supervisor Wellington offers substitute to report of committee of the whole to the effect that present accommodations are grossly inadequate, stating that the board is not in favor of erecting the proposed hospital, but is in favor of securing suitable farm property not less than four miles from the city line, where the almshouse and hospital should be located. Substitute report agreed to.

" May 26, 1898.—Supervisor Wellington introduces resolution providing that committee on almshouse shall secure information about farm sites. Laid on the table under the rules.

" November 22, 1898.—Committee on almshouse reports its line of work in pursuance of instructions regarding farm sites, and says it has received 107 options, although it had expected less than half a dozen. The aggregate of the possible sites in the lot was 44. Full particulars as to the water supply, drainage, acreage, location and prices of the 44 farms were submitted. It was also reported that bids for the purchase of the present almshouse and adjacent land had been advertised for, but no offers were received. The committee particularly recommended seven of the offered sites. The report was received and ordered printed.

"November 28, 1898.—Law committee was requested to report at once as to the legislative steps necessary to sell the existing almshouse and erect another on a different site.

"January 19, 1899.—Almshouse committee reports that the time has come when definite action of some sort is necessary, that no time should be lost in settling the question of a new location or of providing the present site with buildings. The committee states that there is no remedy but to do one or the other, and it is inclined to favor the latter course. Since it would be necessary to use the present building for several years the committee does not recommend that any steps be taken immediately toward selling it. Laid on the table under the rules.

"January 20, 1899.—Above report adopted. Resolution introduced that it is the sense of the board that the county should purchase not less than 400 acres of land for the purposes of a county farm and remove the almshouse to such site with all reasonable dispatch. Laid on the table under the rules.

"January 24, 1899.—Resolution introduced stating that since the winter weather came so early that examination of the sites proposed by the almshouse committee was impracticable, all further discussion of these reports should be postponed until a more favorable season. Laid on the table under the rules.

"January 26, 1899.—Above resolution adopted by vote of 36 to 1, Supervisor Redman dissenting.

"January 27, 1899.—Members of State Board of Charities, and city and county superintendents of the poor invited to accompany the board when it makes its trips of inspection of sites for the poor farm.

"February 1, 1899.—Report submitted . November 22, 1898, adopted by unanimous vote. Law committee reports that board has right to change site to any place not more than a mile from the present location, and that a vote of the people would be necessary to make any further changes.

"February 2, 1899.—Report of law committee adopted, and an amending resolution introduced looking toward the settlement of the law so that board of supervisors could change site without securing consent of the people. Laid on the table under the rules.

"February 6, 1899.—Above resolution amended so as to strike out words 'without a vote of the people,' and adopted as amended.

June 2, 1899.—Report submitted to the effect that the Erie, Lehigh Valley and Rome, Watertown and Ogdensburg Railroads will provide special trains for the supervisors to visit farm sites, free of cost, if the board will accept them, or at any price up to $50 that the board may name. Resolutions included in the report that the trains be accepted at $50 each, and that Clerk Bastable see that sufficient luncheon is provided. Laid on the table under the rules.

"June 5, 1899.—Above report unanimously carried. Resolution that the county should acquire a farm for the almshouse site, provided it can be obtained in a suitable location and at a reasonable price. Laid on the table under the rules.

"June 5, 1899.—Board inspects almshouse sites.

"June 6, 1899.—Board inspects almshouse sites.

"June 7, 1899.—Board inspects almshouse sites.

"June 8, 1899.—Board inspects almshouse.

"June 10, 1899.—Board inspects almshouse sites.

"June 13, 1899.—Board inspects almshouse sites.

"June 15, 1899.—Board inspects almshouse sites.

"June 16, 1899.—Board inspects almshouse sites.

"June 19, 1899.—Decided to visit no more almshouse sites than those already agreed upon. Board inspects some sites again."

"June 21, 1899.—Communication received from State Board of Charities, reminding the board of supervisors that recommendations regarding the importance of changing the location of the almshouse to a rural section have been made for four years past, and that the Board is therewith instructed that such change is immediately necessary. Referred to committee on the whole on inspecting sites for an almshouse. Said committee reports that it is desirable that the board purchase a farm and build a new county almshouse upon it, that a competent engineer and a competent chemist be requested to examine each site and report as to the water and drainage facilities."

" June 22, 1899.—Above report adopted."

" September 20, 1899.—Clipping from a local newspaper read and ordered printed to the effect that Commissioner Stoddard again urges that the board of supervisors take immediate steps to provide a farm and transfer the inmates of the almshouse to the new site as soon as possible. William C. Gray, engineer, and Professor S. A. Lattimore, chemist, present their reports on the almshouse sites, which are laid on the table."

" September 22, 1899.—Board decides to have each man write on a card the four sites which he prefers out of the thirteen which were visited, and the four sites receiving the most votes would be the ones from which subsequent choice must be made. Sites Nos. 5, 29, 37 and 38 were designated as the ones. No. 5, is in Rush, No. 29 in Gates, No. 37 in Greece, and No. 38 in East Henrietta."

" October 24, 1899.—Lengthy report received from State Board of Charities, calling detailed attention to evils and defects in almshouse and asking that they be remedied as soon as possible. Referred to committee on almshouse."

" November 25, 1899.—Petition received from property owners on Beach avenue, Charlotte, protesting against removal of almshouse to lake front. Referred to committee on site for almshouse farm."

" November 27, 1899.—Resolution introduced that site No. 38 be purchased as an almshouse farm, including options Nos. 82, 83, 84 and 103."

" November 28, 1899.—Communication received from owners of above options reducing their price considerably. Resolution introduced and laid on the table providing that a contract be entered into with these men."

"December 5, 1899.—Resolution introduced that sites Nos. 29 and 37 be the ones to be purchased. No. 29 was lost by a vote of 12 to 29, and a resolution favoring the purchase of Nos. 5 and 8 was introduced."

"December 6, 1899.—Last resolution of previous day defeated, 8 to 29. Decided to revert to original plan and build an addition on south side of almshouse, to provide less crowded quarters for the inmates."

"December 29, 1899.—Architect Foote explains to board the plans for the addition to the almshouse."

"May 11, 1900.—Electrical workers, lathers, and street and building laborers' unions ask that union help and materials be employed in the contemplated almshouse."

"May 24, 1900.—Resolution that special almshouse committee present detailed report at next meeting carried by vote of 20 to 16."

"June 11, 1900.—Special almshouse committee reports that it is gratified to at last be able to say something which should lead to prompt and decisive action on the part of the honorable body. Five sites have been considered for the hospital, all of which were disapproved by the State Board of Charities, which did not want any building to be erected on the county's property. Hon. W. A. Sutherland delivered a legal opinion to the effect that the statutes do not give the State Board of Charities any right to coerce the county into building new county buildings on a farm which must be purchased for the purpose. He said that the powers of the State Board are of a visitorial nature, and although the statutes say that no almshouse shall be constructed without the consent of that Board, there is no mention of the location. Since the Board of Charities approved of plans submitted to them in April, 1898, there should be no valid objection to building on those plans. A communication from Secretary Robert W. Hebberd of the State Board of Charities was inclosed, which criticised the dilatory tactics of the successive boards of supervisors rather severely. The report goes on to say that the committee has been very greatly delayed by the tardy action of the State Board and alleges that the State Board has insisted on building a most expensive structure. The report says that the committee is not in favor of moving into the country, since the present site is sufficient for ten or fifteen years yet. It closes with resolutions to the effect that since the State Board has been stubborn, but after having Attorney Sutherland's opinion, did finally approve of a plan, the county should build an infirmary or addition on the south side of the present almshouse at a cost not to exceed $50,000. There is another resolution attached providing that if the State Board fails to agree to this, legal measures should be taken to force it to give the taxpayers their just consideration. This report was laid on the table under the rules, and a minority report, presented by Supervisor Webster, was treated likewise. The minority report stated that the purchase of a farm and removing to it all the inmates capable of manual labor, retaining the present buildings for hospital purposes, are the only practical solutions. A resolution stating that it was the sense of the Board that an almshouse farm of 200 or 300 acres be purchased within a reasonable distance of the present buildings, and that the inmates of the present almshouse capable of working should be removed to it, was included in the minority report. A communication from the Chamber of Commerce, asking for a conference on the subject of the almshouse, was read and accepted."

"August 14, 1900.—Decided to postpone all discussion of the whole affair until September session."

"November 14, 1900.—H. B. Hathaway, of the Chamber of Commerce, states the position of the Chamber of Commerce on the question of the almshouse."

"November 19, 1900.—Special committees appointed to visit the almshouse farms of Orleans, Cattaraugus, Genesee and Wyoming counties, and the committee of the whole was authorized to visit Craig Colony. It was decided to have a special committee visit the poor farms of Ontario and Allegany counties."

"November 20, 1900.— Proposition to appoint special committees to visit the almshouse farms of Orleans, Cattaraugus, Genesee and Wyoming counties adopted, and November 28th fixed as date of visiting. Supervisor Wellington added to all special visiting committees."

"November 27, 1900.—Board visits Craig Colony."

" December 1, 1900.—Report of visit is presented and laid on the table. Committee visiting Wyoming county poor farm reports."

" December 4, 1900.—Committee visiting Allegany county poor farm reports, as does committee visiting Cattaraugus county farm."

"December 10, 1900.—Committees visiting Orleans and Ontario county poor farms report. Almshouse questions made a special order for December 12th."

" December 12, 1900.—Both the majority and minority reports on the almshouse question, submitted June 11, 1900, were referred to a special committee with directions to obtain an option on the Crittenden farm in Brighton on the road from Rochester to East Henrietta."

" December 13, 1900.—Committee reports having secured option, and says it is well pleased with itself. Committee visiting Genesee county poor farm submits report.

" December 19, 1900.—Report of committee securing option on Crittenden property received and committee discharged. Minority report of committee submitted on June 11th, lost by a vote of 23 to 14. Majority report carried by a vote of 22 to 15.

" December 20, 1900.—Vote to reconsider adoption of majority report defeated by a vote of 20 to 16.

" February 9, 1901.—Resolution introduced that all labor done by the appropriation of $50,000 for the addition to the almshouse be by union workmen. Laid on the table under the rules.

" March 14, 1901.—Resolution introduced that the chair appoint a special committee of five to construct fireproof additions to the almshouse at a cost not to exceed $49,000. Laid on the table under the rules. Resolution introduced that the Crittenden farm be purchased for almshouse purposes. Laid on the table under the rules. Resolution that work on almshouse be done by union labor carried by vote of 20 to 15.

"March 14, 1901.—Resolution introduced to the effect that a committee of five be appointed to carry out the wishes of the board in regard to the additions to the almshouse. Laid on the table under the rules.

41

"March 25, 1901.—Above resolution debated without result.

"April 8, 1901.—Above resolution slightly amended and adopted.

"April 10, 1901.—Committee provided for in above resolution appointed.

"May 13, 1901.—Special almshouse committee reports that the Crittenden farm in not for sale.

"June 11, 1901.—Committee reports option may be secured on Hondorf-Patten property. Resolution introduced and laid on the table that the special almshouse committee secure plans for an addition to the almshouse.

"July 1, 1901.—Resolution authorizing committee to buy Hondorf-Patten farm for similar purpose laid on table.

"July 9, 1901.—Hondorf-Patten resolution lost.

"August 1, 1901.—Resolution of June 11th discussed and placed on table again.

"February 10, 1902.—Moved to elect member of special almshouse committee to succeed member from Nineteenth ward. Supervisor Sackett raised point of order that since committee was appointed by former board its tenure of office died with the board. Point decided to be well taken. Moved to elect new special almshouse committee.

"February 11, 1902.—Motion to elect new almshouse committee laid indefinitely on the table."

ADMINISTRATION.

The excellent record of this institution for many years past has been sustained during the period covered by this report. Cleanliness and order are noticeable in the institution, and the general contentment of the inmates speaks in favor of the officials. The food is as a general thing sufficient in quantity, at times varied, and always well cooked.

With so large a proportion of old and feeble inmates, this almshouse would be exceedingly dangerous in case of a fire, as the means of escape are very deficient. Loss of life would certainly occur, especially if the fire occurred at night.

The hospital facilities are altogether inadequate. This matter has been noted from year to year in the reports of inspection and the special reports of the commissioner, but all suggestions of enlargement are met by the statement that no improvements can be made until the question of removal is finally settled.

RECOMMENDATIONS.

The recommendations of the past five years are renewed. They are:

1. The removal of this almshouse from the city limits, and its establishment upon a large farm, one probably of not less than 500 acres, having thereon proper buildings and facilities for the care and classification of all of the inmates.

2. The establishment of a suitable hospital by which there may be a separation of the acutely sick from those inmates who are merely old and feeble, and by which also there may be a complete isolation of all tuberculous cases.

3. Some provision by which occupation will be found for all inmates who are capable of work. The crowded condition of the almshouse at the present time precludes work, and, in consequence, the inmates are compelled to spend a large portion of the time in idleness. For the sake of mental and bodily health, employment should be found, and this can best be secured when the almshouse is located upon a farm.

CENSUS.

The census was as follows:

	Males.	Females.	Total.
Number of inmates	249	110	359
Children under two years old	1	2	3
Children between two and sixteen years.	0	0	0
Number of blind	4	1	5
Number of deaf-mutes	1	1	2
Number of feeble-minded	13	7	20
Number of idiots	4	2	6
Number of epileptics	5	3	8
Persons over seventy years old	64	36	100

ONTARIO COUNTY ALMSHOUSE.

Canandaigua, N. Y.

RALPH S. WISNER, *Keeper.*

No improvements have been made to this institution recently. The main building is in good repair at the present time, but the addition should give place to a modern work and service building. During the year an acetylene-gas-lighting system was installed, which conduces to the safety of the institution. There are no outside fire-escapes, and the inside stairs would be inadequate in the event of a rapidly spreading fire. To make repairs to the present building would be to do a work which should be undone in a short time. There is no reason why this almshouse should not be remodeled and made to correspond with the trend of the times.

The administration of this almshouse is excellent. The inmates are cheerful and contented, always well fed, and the discipline, kindly but firm, has kept them employed as far as it is possible. The county superintendent, who is at the institution two or three days every week, the keeper, and the matron, are deeply interested in the welfare of the inmates, and the work which they have done during the years of their service has always been of a high order.

It is hoped that the supervisors of Ontario county will decide to make such changes in the building as will give to the county a model almshouse. The main building would probably form the nucleus of the new group, and, by taking away the long extensions which from their construction are dangerous, space would be found upon which to locate the new buildings.

CENSUS.

The census was as follows:

	Males.	Females.	Total.
Number of inmates	62	18	80
Children under two years old	0	0	0
Children between two and sixteen years.	0	0	0
Number of blind	0	3	3
Number of deaf-mutes	0	1	1
Number of feeble-minded	1	0	

	Males.	Females.	Total.
Number of idiots....................	0	0	0
Number of epileptics.................	0	0	0
Persons over seventy years old.........	24	8	32

SENECA COUNTY ALMSHOUSE.
Seneca Falls, N. Y.
OGDEN WHEELER, *Superintendent.*

At the time of inspection the institution was found in good order; the grounds clean. No improvements have been made during the year and none are in contemplation. The buildings are still heated by coal stoves and lighted by kerosene oil lamps. Both of these are dangerous in a public institution, but especially so in one which is ceiled from basement to roof with beaded pine.

This is one of the almshouses which has an inadequate supply of water. There is a well 150 feet deep, situated to the west of the house, from which water is raised by windmill to small tanks. Not only is the supply inadequate for purposes of protection, but insufficient for ordinary domestic use. A change should be made to equip the almshouse with sufficient wells and a steam pump. The steam necessary to run this pump could also be used for a power laundry.

Improvement should be made in the matter of the care of the sick. The basement floor room at the south end of the main building, containing nine beds, is used for men, while the women are cared for in the ordinary dormitories. As nearly one-half of the inmates are over seventy years of age there is a necessity for better hospital accommodations.

The food was found to be good and abundant but the cooking is not satisfactory.

CENSUS.

The census was as follows:

	Males.	Females.	Total.
Number of inmates....................	33	13	46
Children under two years old..........	2	0	2
Children between two and sixteen years.	0	0	0

	Males.	Females.	Total.
Number of blind....................	0	0	0
Number of deaf-mutes................	0	1	1
Number of feeble-minded.............	0	0	0
Number of idiots....................	2	0	2
Number of epileptics................	0	0	0
Persons over seventy years old........	14	6	20

STEUBEN COUNTY ALMSHOUSE.

Bath, N. Y.

WILLIAM C. ACKER, *Superintendent.*

Recently a hospital addition 19 x 30 feet has been added to the women's building. Another addition to the same building, 12 feet square, is arranged as a lavatory. Steam boilers have been put in, from which the steam to heat four buildings is derived. New plumbing throughout has been installed and a general improvement has taken place. It is expected that an icehouse and meat cooler will be built in the spring, as the superintendent has been empowered by the supervisors to arrange for its construction.

This almshouse is equipped with an abundant water supply, under good pressure, from the Bath water service.

At the time of inspection the institution was found in a very satisfactory condition, the dormitories and service rooms clean and in good order and the grounds and outbuildings well cared for. Some of the outbuildings are old and should be removed, which will doubtless be done in time.

There are a large number of idiotic and feeble-minded persons in this almshouse (18), and 33 persons are over seventy years of age. There are 6 blind and 2 epileptics.

Mr. Ezra Chatfield, the keeper, has general charge, and from the contentment of the inmates it is apparent that he takes a personal interest in their welfare. The food served was found abundant and well cooked.

CENSUS.

The census was as follows:

	Males.	Females.	Total.
Number of inmates	64	19	83
Children under two years old	1	0	1
Children between two and sixteen years.	0	0	0
Number of blind	6	0	6
Number of deaf-mutes	0	0	0
Number of feeble-minded	7	8	15
Number of idiots	2	1	3
Number of epileptics	0	2	2
Persons over seventy years old	27	6	33

WAYNE COUNTY ALMSHOUSE.

Lyons, N. Y.

JOHN S. JORDAN, *Keeper.*

Two new buildings are nearly completed to take the place of those destroyed by fire. One of these buildings is to be the keeper's residence and the other the women's dormitory. The building formerly used as the keeper's home has been moved back to and adjoins the hospital, which serves to give further accommodations to the sick. Thirty-two hundred dollars has been appropriated for improvement of this institution and for a new water supply.

The necessity of increase in water supply was made manifest, since the close of the fiscal year, by the destruction of all the barns and outbuildings by fire, there being no water on hand to save them. It is proposed that a 15-foot well shall be sunk near the canal, with a steam pump to draw water from the same. Perhaps the institution may be able to secure a sufficient supply in this manner.

Steps are being taken to purify the supply of water taken from the canal and designed for flushing and fire purposes, as well as to render the supply certain. The officials believe that a filtration through the intervening earth will purify the water, but this is exceedingly doubtful. The experience of the city of New Haven is a warning against depending upon such filtration.

The lighting is at present by kerosene oil lamps, and for an institution where there are no adequate means to fight fire— kerosene oil is a dangerous illuminant. Chemical fire-extinguishers are needed in all of the buildings and these should be put in as soon as possible.

At the time of inspection the food supply was found abundant and well cooked.

CENSUS.

The census was as follows:

	Males.	Females.	Total
Number of inmates	78	28	106
Children under two years old	1	0	1
Children between two and sixteen years.	0	0	0
Number of blind	0	3	3
Number of deaf-mutes	0	0	0
Number of feeble-minded	0	0	0
Number of idiots	1	5	6
Number of epileptics	0	2	2
Persons over seventy years old	24	8	32

YATES COUNTY ALMSHOUSE.

Penn Yan, N. Y.

HENRY TOWNSEND, *Superintendent.*

The almshouse of Yates county, the last in the district to be passed in review, is also the smallest. It has a capacity of 75 inmates and the estimated value of the buildings is $25,000. The main building is of concrete, three stories high, with a basement. At the time of inspection the building was clean, the walls well painted and all was found in good repair. Only a few minor repairs have been made recently and none are in contemplation. Money has been appropriated to purchase new iron beds for the dormitories.

The building is lighted by kerosene oil lamps and the water supply is drawn from wells and cisterns. The gasoline engine which operates the laundry furnishes power for the pumping.

The means of escape in event of fire are not adequate. There are three inside stairways, but outside fire-escapes are needed, and as another measure of protection liquid chemical fire-extinguishers should be supplied.

This almshouse has a small dairy, and the products are used for the inmates, so that they are supplied with milk and butter. The other food is generally ample and the inmates seem to be contented.

One improvement which should be made to this institution is a better provision for the sick. A small building, to be used exclusively for the sick, should be added to the group.

CENSUS.

The census was as follows:

	Males.	Females.	Total.
Number of inmates	29	8	37
Children under two years old..........	0	0	0
Children between two and sixteen years.	0	0	0
Number of blind......................	0	0	0
Number of deaf-mutes.................	1	0	1
Number of feeble-minded..............	2	2	4
Number of idiots	0	0	0
Number of epileptics..................	1	0	1
Persons over seventy years old........	14	6	20

Statistical summary.

COUNTIES.	INMATES.			Children under 2 years.	Children between 2 and 16.	OVER 70 YEARS OLD.			Epileptics.	Feeble-minded.	Idiots.
	Male.	Female.	Total.			Male.	Female.	Total.			
Cayuga	40	24	64	0	0	18	12	30	2	8	8
Livingston	42	14	56	0	1	17	4	21	6	10	2
Monroe	249	110	359	3	0	64	36	100	8	20	6
Ontario	62	18	80	0	0	24	8	33	0	1	0
Seneca	33	13	46	2	0	14	6	20	0	0	2
Steuben	64	19	83	2	0	27	6	33	2	15	8
Wayne	78	28	106	1	0	24	8	33	2	0	6
Yates	29	8	37	0	0	14	6	20	1	4	0
Total	597	234	831	7	1	202	86	288	21	58	32

REPORT

OF

Visitation of Almshouses

IN THE

EIGHTH JUDICIAL DISTRICT.

REPORT.

To the State Board of Charities:

I present herewith a report of the condition of the almshouses in the Eighth Judicial District.

IMPROVEMENTS.

The inspections made of the public institutions of this district during the year show that there is a decided tendency toward betterment. Some new buildings are about ready for occupancy, and repairs were made in almost every almshouse. In Erie county the long-debated question of removal has been finally settled in the negative, and the board of supervisors has determined on many changes and improvements in the present group of buildings.

THE CARE OF THE SICK.

In Erie county the hospital is an important part of the almshouse system. This has received special attention, and within the last year a new tuberculosis pavilion was opened. The new building is a decided improvement upon the one destroyed by fire some time ago and is much better located. It will probably prove the first of a number of pavilions, which are proposed as extensions of the hospital.

In Chautauqua county the care of the sick has always been considered a matter of prime importance. Eight thousand dollars was appropriated in 1901 for an addition to the front of the hospital in order that there may be better accommodations for the infirm inmates.

Niagara county also has a separate hospital, and, generally speaking, much better care is now taken of the sick throughout the district than heretofore. The erection of hospitals separated from other buildings is a move in the right direction. The additional expense for maintenance is counterbalanced by the better facilities which the separate buildings provide for the care of the sick, to say nothing of the decided gain in health of all other inmates due to the removal of the sick from the general dormitories. The depressing influence of bed-ridden people upon other aged persons compelled to associate with them cannot be overestimated, and the pollution of the atmosphere must necessarily promote disease. The hospital is a necessary part of the almshouse, and it is a sign of progress that the counties of the district are making such large provision for the care of the sick and infirm.

INDIANS.

In this district large numbers of the Indians of the State are resident. All the reservations are hemmed in by thriving communities, and the Indians feel the influence of daily contact with their white neighbors. This influence is both good and bad. In one way it is uplifting; in another way it is degrading; and it is sometimes difficult to know whether the net result at any given time is for the welfare of the Indians. The red man assimilates more readily the white man's vices than he does his virtues, and, as a consequence, upon the reservations in this district there are marked evidences of diseases and weakness directly traceable to vice. At the same time, to counterbalance, on all the reservations in the district there are centers of uplifting influence which are doing much to hold in check and overcome the tendency toward evil. The schools and the churches are at work, and from them we expect such assistance as will save the Indian from the many perils which surround him. These people, in the main, depend upon the products of their farms; they have not acquired the thrift and energy of their white neighbors, but they manage to raise enough farm products to sustain them from year to year.

Compared with the total number of the population, we have not a very large number of Indian paupers in this district. The State is compelled to give temporary relief to individuals or families from time to time, but few have to be cared for in the almshouses. It is only when diseased and helpless they are willing to leave their friends and kindred and consent to removal to the almshouse. It is fortunate that this is so. Were all who require temporary relief to insist upon going to the almshouse the expense of their maintenance would amount to a large sum each year.

Education has done a great deal for the Indians. Not the least of the educational influences at work in their behalf is the Thomas Asylum, which cares for orphan and destitute Indian children. The course of study mapped out is intended to develop habits of self-support. while the general influence of the asylum is promotive of sobriety and morality.

ADMINISTRATION.

The administration of the almshouses in this district continues to deserve commendation. The general order and cleanliness are matters of note, while the food and care result in the contentment of the inmates.

The statistics of the district will be found tabulated at the end of this report.

Respectfully submitted,
W. H. GRATWICK,
Commissioner Eighth Judicial District.

ALLEGANY COUNTY ALMSHOUSE.
Angelica, N. Y.

D. C. GRUNDER, *Superintendent and Keeper.*

This almshouse is built entirely of wood and is typical of the cottage plan. Although it has stood for eighteen years, all the buildings are in excellent condition and kept in thorough repair. Open corridors connect the dormitory buildings with the one devoted to work and service, and the atmosphere of the institution is that of cheerfulness and contentment.

One important feature of this institution is the dairy. The barns and outbuildings are maintained in a very satisfactory way, and from the dairy a large income is received.

The food given to the inmates was found by inspection to be well cooked, varied in character, and abundant in quantity. This is one of the almshouses which permits the use of table cloths in the inmates' dining-rooms.

The recent improvements are two low-pressure boilers for heating purposes. Natural gas has been found available and is used both for heating and illuminating purposes. A new barn and silo was built during the year, and it is proposed to put steel ceilings upon four rooms of the main building. and make further provision for extinguishing fire.

This almshouse is one of the very best in the State in the matter of its care and provision for the inmates.

CENSUS.

The census was as follows:

	Males.	Females.	Total.
Number of inmates...................	40	31	71
Children under two years old.........	0	0	0
Children between two and sixteen years.	0	0	0
Number of blind.....................	2	1	3
Number of deaf-mutes...............	0	0	0
Number of feeble-minded.............	0	7	7
Number of idiots....................	1	0	1
Number of epileptics................	0	0	0
Persons over seventy years old........	18	7	25

CATTARAUGUS COUNTY ALMSHOUSE.

Machias. N. Y.

JOHN LITTLE, *Keeper.*

This is another of the almshouses planned upon the cottage system. It has six wooden buildings, each two stories high. with attic and cellar, besides a number of older structures which are not now in use for dormitories. These older buildings are out of repair, and some of them, like the laundry building and the two-story frame building in the rear of the stone house, should be replaced by new ones.

An appropriation of $800 has been made for repairs to the barn, but other than that no improvements are in contemplation.

This almshouse has an excellent water supply. Its greatest need is a properly equipped hospital. One of the four cottages in the main group could be arranged for that purpose.

CENSUS.

The census was as follows:

	Males.	Females.	Total.
Number of inmates	58	17	75
Children under two years old	0	0	0
Children between two and sixteen years.	0	0	0
Number of blind	2	0	2
Number of deaf-mutes	1	1	2
Number of feeble-minded	4	1	5
Number of idiots	5	0	5
Number of epileptics	1	0	1
Persons over seventy years	27	7	34

CHAUTAUQUA COUNTY ALMSHOUSE.

Dewittville, N. Y.

MERVIN E. SMITH, *Keeper*.

This almshouse is large enough to accommodate 200 inmates, and the property is estimated to be worth $90,000. All the buildings are of brick and in good repair, and when inspected were found clean and in order.

The recent improvements are two silos, each of which has a capacity for seventy-five tons of ensilage. A well 150 feet deep has been sunk to supply additional water to the institution.

For some time the hospital facilities have been inadequate for the needs of the almshouse. The supervisors in recognition of this fact, appropriated $8,000 for an addition. This is to take the place formerly occupied by the old asylum which was removed last year. It will make a fitting front for the present hospital, and will give ample accommodations for the sick. The supervisors have always taken great interest in the care of the public dependents, and have not hesitated to make appropriations whenever the same were required for the well-being of the poor.

The food furnished the inmates at the time of inspection was found to be of excellent quality and in abundance. The

42

hospital has its own kitchen where the special diet of the sick is prepared.

One improvement which would add to the safety of the inmates and be a necessary precaution for their safety is a proper fire escape upon the hospital.

CENSUS.

The census was as follows:

	Males.	Females.	Total.
Number of inmates.....................	104	46	150
Children under two years.............	0	0	0
Children between two and sixteen.....	1	0	1
Number of blind...................,....	5	1	6
Number of deaf-mutes.................	0	0	0
Number of feeble-minded..............	5	5	10
Number of idiots.....................	3	3	6
Number of epileptics..................	1	1	2
Persons over seventy years............	44	22	66

ERIE COUNTY ALMSHOUSE.
Buffalo, N. Y.
JOHN A. STENGEL, *Keeper.*

The description of this almshouse as a "long stone building," which was made years ago, still holds good, but this stone building has a capacity for the accommodation of 600 inmates, besides the number who can be taken care of in the Erie County Hospital, which is practically a part of the almshouse.

The fact that the building is old may be taken as indicative of the fact that it needs many alterations and repairs. Great consideration is given to the order and cleanliness of the almshouse, and the large population taxes the watchfulness and attention of the officials.

During the year some sheds were built to take the place of those burned, and the roads and grades were labored upon. One advantage over former conditions is that due to the introduction of steam in the new barn. The former barn was burned down, in all probability because a stove was used to heat the harness room.

The matter of dietary is considered of prime importance in this institution, and the food served to the inmates, in consequence, is varied and well cooked, as well as abundant.

It is a matter of congratulation that this almshouse is in such good condition and under such excellent management.

THE CARE OF THE SICK.

Among the public hospitals of the State, the Erie County Hospital deserves a prominent place. During the last few years many important changes have been made in the building. A large amount of money was spent to adapt the original building to hospital purposes. In addition to this, the pavilion system now adopted will provide a group of separated pavilions by means of which a proper classification of the sick can be made.

Although regarded as a great misfortune at the time, the burning of the building formerly used for tuberculosis patients was really a benefit to the hospital. It gave an opportunity to remove this class of patients to a greater distance, and freed the main hospital from the proximity of an exceedingly dangerous structure. The new tuberculosis pavilion, now put in occupancy, is a very satisfactory building. Its equipment is up-to-date, and the patients committed to it will find their surroundings all they can reasonably desire. It is located at some distance in rear of the main building, and gives a sufficient separation from the other patients whose weakened condition might invite phthisis if associated with consumptive patients.

It is expected that other similar pavilions will be added from time to time until this hospital be adequately fitted to render ample medical and surgical service to the great city of Buffalo. Like the almshouse, it is in good hands. Its administration has proven competent and satisfactory.

CENSUS.

The census of the almshouse was as follows:

	Males.	Females.	Total.
Number of inmates...................	320	89	409
Children under two years.............	0	0	0
Children between two and sixteen.....	0	0	0

	Males.	Females.	Total.
Number of blind	5	4	9
Number of deaf-mutes	0	0	0
Number of feeble-minded	8	7	15
Number of idiots	1	1	2
Number of epileptics	3	2	5
Persons over seventy years old	132	66	198

The census of the almshouse was as follows:

	Males.	Females.	Total.
Number of inmates	232	106	338
Children under two years old	19	12	31
Children between two and sixteen	8	3	11
Number of blind	2	0	2
Number of deaf-mutes	1	0	1
Number of feeble-minded	0	4	4
Number of idiots	2	3	5
Number of epileptics	1	5	6

GENESEE COUNTY ALMSHOUSE.

Linden, N. Y.

THURMAN A. HART, *Keeper.*

The buildings which compose the almshouse group of Genesee county are valued at about $20,000, and are mostly frame structures. They are in good repair, although no improvements have been made recently. It is expected that some ditching and tiling will be accomplished on the farm this spring, as an appropriation of $500 has been made for that purpose.

The use of kerosene oil for illuminating purposes, and stoves and hot air furnaces, makes the necessity for precautions against fire apparent. At the present time these are not sufficient, and should be added to until the safety of the inmates is assured. Fortunately the third floor of the men's building is not now used for dormitory purposes, but an increase in population might require it, hence outside fire-escapes may well be added.

This almshouse is supplied with an excellent dairy, and as a consequence the inmates have plenty of milk and butter as well as other good food. During the summer season, when the garden is productive, the inmates are furnished with fresh vegetables in such variety as is desirable.

The main need of this almshouse is for a hospital. A separate building should be provided, in order that the dormitories be relieved of the presence of the sick. At the present time the sick are quartered in two rooms, each containing three beds. A small addition serves as an isolation room for infectious diseases; in this are two beds. It is fortunate that the total number of inmates is not large, but as one-half of them are over seventy years of age, a separate hospital building is a necessity.

CENSUS.

The census was as follows:

	Males.	Females.	Total.
Number of inmates	42	20	62
Children under two years	0	0	0
Children between two and sixteen	1	1	2
Number of blind	2	2	4
Number of deaf-mutes	0	1	1
Number of feeble-minded	5	2	7
Number of idiots	2	1	3
Number of epileptics	0	0	0
Persons over seventy years old	22	9	31

NIAGARA COUNTY ALMSHOUSE.

Lockport, N. Y.

ALBERT H. LEE, *Superintendent and Keeper.*

The Niagara County Almshouse is located about three miles from Lockport. The principal building is a stone structure three stories high and of L shape. The main front is 180 feet in length and has a depth of 60 feet. The L extension is 150 feet in length with a width of 60 feet, and has two wings each

30 feet square. Besides the main building there is a frame hospital, lately erected, 60x40 feet in dimension.

All the buildings are in good repair. Recently the hospital cellar was improved by putting down a cement floor. Three fire-escapes are now on the main building, and two on the hospital.

It is expected that a new power plant will be installed, and also that the water supply will be improved. For many years the subject of water has been under consideration. It is hoped the board of supervisors will take such action as will assure a satisfactory supply. It is dangerous to health and safety to permit a large institution like this to depend upon a meagre and uncertain supply of water.

The present method of lighting the almshouse is by the use of kerosene oil, but with the introduction of a new power plant it is expected that a dynamo and motor will furnish electric light.

The general condition of the almshouse, as indicated by the contentment of the inmates, is satisfactory. The food supply was found sufficient, and matters indicated attention to the details of administration.

As the main building is quite old, many alterations will be required before it represents the standard of care which should be provided for the poor. Little by little these changes are being made, and in time the whole almshouse will be remodeled.

CENSUS.

The census was as follows:

	Males.	Females.	Total.
Number of inmates	96	36	132
Children under two years old	0	0	0
Children between two and sixteen	0	1	1
Number of blind	1	2	3
Number of deaf-mutes	1	0	1
Number of feeble-minded	6	4	10
Number of idiots	1	0	1
Number of epileptics	0	0	0
Persons over seventy years old	32	13	45

ORLEANS COUNTY ALMSHOUSE.

Albion, N. Y.

V. D. LUDINGTON, *Superintendent and Keeper.*

About three miles from Albion, the Orleans County Almshouse stands in a prominent position, surrounded by a fine farm. It has a capacity sufficient to accommodate 125 inmates, and is generally well equipped. The buildings are in good repair at the present time. Each year the supervisors of the county were in the habit of making special appropriations to cover repairs, but unfortunately at the last annual session the board forgot this appropriation, and, in consequence, the institution must get along for a time as well as possible without repairs. Fortunately the almshouse is now in such good condition that it can probably do so for the current year, as it needs no special additions or improvements.

The sick are cared for in a small two-story frame cottage adjoining the main building, and connected with it on the second floor. Of this building, only the main floor is used as a hospital. This has thirteen beds for men. The women when sick are looked after in their ordinary rooms instead of being removed.

One necessary improvement has been deferred from year to year, and as a result there is a considerable annual loss. The coal supply is piled in the rear yard exposed to the weather, owing to lack of storage room in the building. The coal deteriorates in quality as a result, and, in all probability, were the loss of heating power carefully calculated it would be found that the exposure of the supply for the last few years has resulted in a loss which would more than pay for the erection of a storage building of considerable size. It has been suggested heretofore that the old frame building now used as a hospital for men be removed to some distance from the main structure and be adapted for the storage of the fuel. This building is not suitable for a hospital. As has been stated, it has no accommodations for the women, and should give way to a brick structure properly equipped. Its removal would solve the storage problem, and result in an economy which would go far toward paying for the new hospital in a short time.

CENSUS.

The census was as follows:

	Males.	Females.	Total.
Number of inmates......................	54	19	73
Children under two years old...........	0	0	0
Children between two and sixteen years.	0	0	0
Number of blind........................	5	0	5
Number of deaf-mutes..................	0	0	0
Number of feeble-minded...............	3	4	7
Number of idiots.......................	5	2	7
Number of epileptics...................	3	0	3
Persons over seventy years old........	24	10	34

WYOMING COUNTY ALMSHOUSE.
Varysburg, N. Y.
Edward C. Stanley, *Keeper*.

This is another representative of the cottage group alms-houses. Its buildings are all connected by open corridors, and the dormitories are completely separated from the work and service building. All are in good repair and kept well painted. It is expected that the general safety will be provided for by the erection of outside iron fire-escapes upon the men's building. A new ice house and cooler is also provided for.

The inmates are well cared for and abundantly supplied with milk and butter, as there is a large dairy connected with the almshouse.

It would be well were some safer and better illuminant used than the kerosene oil lamps which now serve for lighting purposes. This almshouse is perhaps near enough to the natural gas belt to have the gas introduced, but if that be impossible it may be well to install an acetylene gas plant.

CENSUS.

The census was as follows:

	Males.	Females.	Total.
Number of inmates......................	35	20	55
Children under two years old...........	0	0	0
Children between two and sixteen years.	0	0	0

	Males.	Females.	Total.
Number of blind......................	0	0	0
Number of deaf-mutes..................	0	1	1
Number of feeble-minded..............	8	4	12
Number of idiots.....................	2	2	4
Number of epileptics..................	1	0	1
Persons over seventy years old.........	19	8	27

Statistical Summary.

COUNTIES.	INMATES.			Children under 2 years.	Children between 2 and 16.	OVER 70 YEARS OLD.			Epileptics.	Feeble-minded.	Idiots.
	Male.	Female.	Total.			Male.	Female.	Total.			
Allegany	40	31	71	0	0	18	7	25	0	7	1
Cattaraugus	58	17	75	0	0	27	7	34	1	5	5
Chautauqua	104	46	150	0	1	44	22	66	2	10	6
Erie	552	195	747	31	11	132	66	198	11	19	7
Genesee	42	20	62	0	2	22	9	31	0	7	3
Niagara	96	36	132	0	1	32	13	45	0	10	1
Orleans	54	19	73	0	0	24	10	34	3	7	7
Wyoming	35	20	55	0	0	19	8	27	1	12	4
Total	981	384	1,365	31	15	318	142	460	18	77	34

Compliance with the Public Health Law

(Chapter 661, Laws of 1893, as Amended by Chapter 667 of
the Laws of 1900, Relative "to Institutions for Orphans,
Destitute or Vagrant Children or Juvenile Delinquents.")

In Institutions Under Private Control but in Receipt of Public Moneys.

PART I.

Compliance with the Public Health Law.

CHAPTER 661, LAWS OF 1893,

As amended by Chapter 667 of the Laws of 1900,

Relative " To Institutions for Orphans, Destitute or Vagrant Children or
Juvenile Delinquents," under Private Control but in Receipt
of Public Moneys.

The provisions of the Public Health Law which relate to children's institutions were first enacted in 1886. They were the
outgrowth of several years of agitation on the part of individual
physicians and of medical and charitable societies to remedy the
unsanitary and dangerous conditions which prevailed in many
of the children's institutions of the State.

The first definite demand that the State should fix by law
certain requirements for cubic air space, food, ventilation and
drainage, and that both children and institutions should be
regularly subjected to expert medical examination, is contained
in a paper by Dr. Cornelius R. Agnew, read before the New
York State Medical Society in 1882. The immediate cause of
this agitation was the appalling prevalence of contagious
ophthalmia.

In 1885 the committee on hygiene of the New York State
Medical Society, Dr. E. V. Stoddard, chairman, presented a
paper by Dr. Richard H. Derby upon "Contagious Ophthalmia
in Some of the Asylums in New York City." This was read
also before the New York County Medical Society and the New
York Academy of Medicine. The conditions therein described
aroused such a conviction of the necessity for action that the

Academy of Medicine called a joint committee of the State
Board of Charities, the State Charities Aid Association and the
Society for the Prevention of Cruelty to Children to confer with
the council of the Academy.* This committee was appointed
on June 23, 1885. Abstracts from the report prepared by this
committee, together with a proposed act as presented by Dr.
Derby, are printed in the Transactions of the New York State
Medical Society for 1886. Still more exhaustive statistics of
existing conditions are contained in this report.

On June 14th of this year the proposed act, with some modifications, became chapter 633 of the Laws of 1886, taking effect
October 1st. The modifications were such as to give discretionary powers to the attending physician as to the length of
quarantine, and to the local health board in the matter of air
space in the dormitories.

The laws of 1893 embodied this chapter in the general Public
Health Law. Certain sections were consolidated, and the arrangement and wording of some phrases were altered. Practically the only change in its provisions was the omission of the
section:

" No child suffering from any contagious or infectious disease, especially of the eyes or skin, shall be allowed to enter
or remain in any such institution in contact with any children
not so afflicted, unless it shall immediately be isolated or placed
in a proper room or infirmary which shall be provided for that
purpose by the officers of the institution under the direction of
said physician."

This provision is practically covered by regulations of the
local boards of health.

An amendment in 1900 merely renumbers the sections.

INQUIRY INSTITUTED BY THE BOARD.

For the purpose of ascertaining how great a degree of compliance had been accorded this law in the fifteen years of its
operation, 148 of the children's institutions of the State were

---

* See New York Medical Record June 14, 1885.

visited. In each institution note was made under each of the several specifications. The figures in the appended tables (Table I.) show that the degree of compliance is greatest in institutions receiving commitments from New York city and least in the scattering institutions of the Western district.

Where lack of compliance has not been due to ignorance of the law, or to a misunderstanding of its provisions, certain difficulties have been cited by officials, or objections have been urged by them. These will be considered under the various sections.

EXAMINATIONS AND QUARANTINE OF NEWCOMERS.

"Section 213. Examinations and quarantine of children admitted to institutions for orphans, destitute or vagrant children or juvenile delinquents.—Every institution in this state, incorporated for the express purpose of receiving or caring for orphan, vagrant or destitute children or juvenile delinquents, except hospitals, (1) shall have attached thereto a regular physician of its selection duly licensed under the laws of the state and in good professional standing, whose name and address shall be kept posted conspicuously within such institution near its main entrance. The words 'juvenile delinquents' here used shall include all children whose commitment to an institution is authorized by the penal code. (2) The officer of every such institution upon receiving a child therein, by commitment or otherwise, shall, before admitting it to contact with the other inmates, cause it to be examined by such physician (3) and a written certificate to be given by him, stating whether the child has diphtheria, scarlet fever, measles, whooping-cough or any other contagious or infectious disease, especially of the eyes and skin, which might be communicated to other inmates and specifying the physical and mental condition of the child, the presence of any indication of hereditary or other constitutional disease, and any deformity or abnormal condition found upon the examination to exist. No child shall be so admitted until such certificate shall have been furnished, (4) which shall be filed with the commitment or other papers on record in the case, by the officers of the institution, (5) who shall, on receiving such child, place it in strict quarantine thereafter from the other inmates, until discharged from such quarantine by such physician, (6) who shall thereupon indorse upon the certificate the length of quarantine and the date of discharge therefrom."

(The six provisions are indicated by figures for convenience.)

1. ATTENDING PHYSICIAN.

A regular physician is employed in every instance. In 30 institutions, the name and address were not posted. In 27 others either the name was posted with no address, or name and address were not "within such institution near its main entrance."

2. PHYSICIAN'S EXAMINATION.

But 17 institutions admit children without examination by a physician. Eleven others do so under "special circumstances," or when the child and its previous surroundings are personally known to the admitting officer, who has then considered it unnecessary to call the physician before his regular visiting time. If the physician lives at some distance from the institution, and a strict quarantine is observed until the child is examined, the spirit of this provision is not violated; but instances of exposure occurring without the knowledge of the child's own mother, or infection having been introduced from this source against all likelihood, serve to emphasize the necessity for literal compliance with the law.

3. PHYSICIAN'S CERTIFICATE.

The law enumerates certain specifications which must be stated in the certificate furnished at the child's admission. A large number of institutions make use of the form furnished by the State Board of Charities, or have similar printed forms specially prepared for their own use. Certain of the commitment papers in use have a certificate form printed thereon. Those of Erie county and those on Department of Charities commitments of the borough of Manhattan have no place for indicating "length of quarantine and date of discharge therefrom."

Certificates, when written out by the physician, usually state only that the child is "all right," or "may be admitted." The use of certificates of this character, or of an oral statement of fitness, defeats the purpose of the law, viz.: to preserve a complete official certificate of the child's condition at the time of admission to institution life.

Mental condition.—Two objections given by officials to stating " mental condition " have weight. (a) In the case of young infants it is practically impossible to be determined. (b) Older children may appear actually stupid through excessive shyness and homesickness, and afterwards prove to be normal, while others, seemingly quick and bright under the stimulus of novelty, are found later to lack memory and power of attention to a degree of feeble-mindedness. This difficulty may be met by wait-ing, in cases of reasonable doubt, and inserting the item a few weeks later.

4. FILING OF CERTIFICATES.

The wording of the law apparently has in view a system by which the " commitment or other papers on record " in each case shall be kept together for ready access. That 57 institutions do not file the certificates with the commitment papers is partly due to the fact that some officers commit children by lists, or in some cases orally. There is no such explanation, however, for the fact that only 49 institutions comply with the law in the matter of filing the certificates with the " other papers." (See Table I., 5 (a) and (b).)

In numerous instances the practice of filing physicians' cer-tificates (on separate forms) by themselves is adhered to because of the frequent handling of the commitment papers required by the rules of the Department of Charities. In Brooklyn several institutions formerly filed them as specified in section 213, but have changed to the other method " since the Comptroller requires each child's commitment with each month's bill."

The envelope system of record keeping has been found by some institutions a practical solution of these difficulties, and is wor-thy of general adoption.

5. QUARANTINE AT ENTRANCE.

One-third of the entire number of institutions (see Table I.) failed to comply, or complied but partially, with the law requir-ing each child to be placed in " strict quarantine from the other inmates, until discharged from such quarantine by such physi-

43

cian." Two or three institutions having separate cottages available for the purpose do not quarantine newcomers, as they consider it " useless when the children are so well known," or else on account of the added expense of heat and service.

Lack of facilities.—The reasons most frequently assigned for non-compliance, however, are lack of suitable room, and an insufficient number of attendants. Where the only institution in a community is taxed to the extent of its capacity in caring for children who cannot well be sent elsewhere, the problem of place is a real one. It is not infrequently the case that this added source of danger of introduction of contagion is coupled with lack of suitable means of isolation in the event of the outbreak of any infectious disease. The probability of one case causing an epidemic is thus increased.

Various methods.—Where additional building is possible, a plan that has been found to work satisfactorily and that offers the advantage of economy is as follows: A detached cottage or an attached wing with separate outside access is fitted with bath, toilet, attendants' room and means of heating water or food. Here newly admitted children are quarantined. If contagion occurs, admissions are suspended, and the quarantine is available for isolation. Another method, rarely pursued, is to board the child for the observation period in some reliable home near enough the institution for supervision, and where there are no children. When this can be done for the price paid the institution for maintenance, it meets the difficulty of increased cost for an additional attendant.

Infants not quarantined.—Some institutions which care for infants maintain no quarantine for babies less than six months old when admitted. Most of these little ones have been since birth under medical supervision, either in the hospital or in the maternity department of the institution, but some have not been. The serious results which may follow the admission to the babies' ward of one child who has been exposed to any contagious or infectious disease are a strong argument for the provision of facilities for the quarantine of children of all ages.

Loneliness in quarantine.—It has been urged that the isolation of a child (especially when through fewness of attendants it must be left much alone in the quarantine room), at the time when it is lonely and strange and often miserably homesick, is a species of cruelty. "Besides, a new child demands and gets more attention than those that are wonted to the institution life, and there is plenty of opportunity for observation." To this it may be said that boarding out in the right kind of a home should insure the child's happiness, while the risk to other children from possible contagion is too great not to be avoided.

Quarantining truants.—One really knotty problem is that of quarantining children committed for truancy. "They must go to school; that is what they are sent here for, and we cannot give them a special teacher or a separate classroom," said one perplexed official. Truants are usually among the oldest of the inmates at an institution, and are less likely themselves to develop contagion. For this reason physicians seem customarily to depend for protection upon examination and thorough disinfection in bathing and clothing, and so shorten the quarantine to a day or two.

MONTHLY EXAMINATIONS AND REPORTS.

"Section 214. Monthly examination of inmates and reports.—Such physician shall at least once a month (1) thoroughly examine and inspect the entire institution, and (2) report in writing, in such form as may be approved by the State Board of Health, to the board of managers or directors of the institution, and to the local board of the district or place where the institution is situated, its condition, especially as to its plumbing, sinks, water-closets, urinals, privies, dormitories, the physical condition of the children, the existence of any contagious or infectious disease, particularly of the eyes or skin, their food, clothing and cleanliness, and whether the officers of the institution have provided proper and sufficient nurses, orderlies, and other attendants of proper capacity to attend to such children, to secure to them due and proper care and attention as to their personal cleanliness and health, with such recommendations for the improvement thereof as he may deem proper. (3) Such boards of health shall immediately investigate any complaint against the management of the institution or of the existence of anything therein dangerous to life or health, and, if proven to be well founded, shall cause the evil to be remedied without delay."

1. MONTHLY EXAMINATION.

One hundred and ten institutions report that the attending physician examines at least once a month the buildings throughout as to their sanitary condition, and the physical condition of each child. The examination of children varies greatly in method. In large institutions the inmates may be sent to the office one by one on an appointed day or days. In other places, the physician sees them all much more frequently.

Non-compliance varies from "examinations made, but not so often as once a month," to instances where "the doctor never comes unless he is sent for to attend a sick child." As the written report presupposes the examination, objections and difficulties are noted under the next heading.

2. MONTHLY MEDICAL REPORTS.

Reference to the appended tables shows that 55 of the 148 institutions included in this examination fail to comply, or comply only partially, with that provision of the Public Health Law requiring reports of the attending physicians' examinations of buildings and inmates to be filed each month with the board of managers and with the local board of health. "Ignorance of the law" on the part of institution officers, attending physicians and local health boards was found in great part the cause of this failure. In some cases the supply of report forms had run out, and a new official was at a loss how to secure more. About half the remaining institutions had been filing these reports only since 1900. Many of those not complying at the time the inquiry was made have since begun doing so. The loss of valuable data occasioned by the attitude of some local health boards, who considered the matter entirely "perfunctory," will be referred to again in another portion of this report.

Opinions of attending physicians.—It was occasionally objected that as the attending physicians—men at the head of their profession and exceedingly busy—gave their services without compensation, they could not be asked to do the writing entailed, or even be called to the institution once each month if no child were ill. The physicians themselves when conversed with almost unanimously expressed themselves convinced that, aside from the obvious wisdom of a thorough examination each month such as the law contemplates, such a record, far from being " another piece of red-tapeism," would be of great scientific value. Suggestions given by them for enhancing the value of such records will be discussed later in this report. Some declared themselves too busy to attend to the matter, but said the reports ought to be made and suggested the wisdom of detailing a younger or less busy man to the work.

Recommendations.—" Recommendations made " are seldom on the blanks provided in the report form for that purpose. The great majority of physicians make them orally, or if of a nature requiring special action by the governing board, in a separate and formal communication to that body. " Not complying," therefore, means that recommendations have not been made, either orally or in writing, and may be modified by the explanation made in numerous instances that " none were necessary."

3. INVESTIGATION BY LOCAL HEALTH BOARDS.

In very few instances were there records of " complaints." The figures given in Table I. under this heading refer rather to whether or no general sanitary inspections are made by the local board.

DORMITORY REQUIREMENTS.

" Section 215. Beds, ventilation.—(1) The beds in every dormitory in such institution shall be separated by a passageway of not less than two feet in width, and so arranged that under each the air shall freely circulate and there shall be adequate ventilation of each bed, and such dormitory shall be furnished with such means of ventilation as the local board of health shall prescribe. (2) In every dormitory six hundred cubic feet of air space shall be provided and allowed for each bed or occupant, (3) and no more beds or occupants shall be permitted than are thus provided for, unless free and adequate means of ventilation exist approved by the local board of health, and a special permit in writing therefor be granted by such board, specifying the number of beds or cubic air space which shall under special circumstances be allowed, which permit shall be kept conspicuously posted in such dormitory. (4) The physician of the institution shall immediately notify in writing the local board of health and the board of managers or directors of the institution of any violation of any provision of this section."

1. LATERAL SPACING.

Referring again to Table I., it will be seen that 63 institutions observe the proper spacing in all dormitories, 66 in part of the dormitories, and 19 have all beds too closely crowded. Of the latter 16 are in the Eastern District (with 10 in New York city), and three in the Western District.

In a few instances dormitories would admit of the proper distance between beds with a different arrangement. In one institution where beds were properly spaced elsewhere those in the nursery dormitory were shoved side to side in rows of six or eight, and the largest or quietest of the children were placed in the end beds " to keep the others from rolling out."

Floor crowding.—Numerous dormitories have permits for a larger number of beds than could be placed in the room were they " separated by a passageway of not less than two feet in width." It is to be noted in connection with this fact that the provision for permits for an increased number of beds refers only to the lessening of the cubic space per bed, while no authority is given for floor crowding.

2. AIR SPACE.

Of the 148 institutions 9 have dormitories allowing 600 cubic feet or more of air space for each occupant. Ten others have less than the required amount in some dormitories, but the high ceilings or larger space in others make the average 600 cubic feet or more. The subjoined tables (Table II. and Summary) show the amount of air space per capita in institutions in different parts of the State.

A discussion of the apparent effect of these conditions on the health of the inmates will be found in Part III. of this report.

3. POSTING OF PERMITS.

Where non-compliance in posting of permits was not due to ignorance of the law it was found that perhaps more difficulty has been experienced by institutions in securing proper permits from the local health boards than in complying with any other provision of these sections.

The borough of Manhattan has had for years a printed form, giving dimensions and otherwise identifying the dormitory for which the permit is intended. In other boroughs permits posted previous to the unification under the laws of 1899 are usually of the "blanket" variety, giving on one sheet the number of beds allowed in each dormitory, but with no dimensions. Frequently but one such permit is provided, and that is in a hall, not "kept conspicuously posted in such dormitory." These blanket permits were found in many institutions outside of New York city, in both districts. Occasionally they were of so ancient a date that remodeling or rearrangement had made them wholly inapplicable to present conditions. In other places pen or typewritten permits were provided for each dormitory, but without dimensions or other means of determining for which particular dormitory each was meant. After a housecleaning these might be pretty thoroughly confused. It actually happened that some rooms showed permission for more beds than could possibly have been placed on the floor. This was true also in one institution (with unusually high ceilings) where it was apparently the custom of the local board of health to divide the number of cubic feet by 300 and grant beds accordingly, regardless of floor space.

Lack of proper forms.—Printed forms similar to those now provided for New York city have been recently furnished by the city of Troy. Some institutions report having made repeated requests for permits, but "nothing done about it." Officers of some of these and other local boards when interviewed requested instruction as to the proper form. In some of the cities of the Western District the local health boards were not aware that they had the right of examining dormitories and granting such permits. In one city was found an institution having instead of a permit a framed statement from the health department to the effect that there was no reason why a permit should not be granted. Two others had in several of the dormitories a neatly framed compliment from the town health officer, with no reference either to the number of beds or to dimensions.

A help to uniformity and accuracy in this matter would be a printed form specifying essential details, and like the monthly medical report and physicians' examination certificates, to be obtained from the Albany office on request. A form embodying such necessary features will be found at the conclusion of this report.

4.   NOTIFICATION BY PHYSICIAN.

In most instances of non-compliance, the attending physician's attention was called to the last clause of section 215.

PART II.

Preventive and Protective Measures

Employed by Institutions for Children Under Private Control, But in Receipt of Public Moneys.

In the course of years of actual management of children's institutions intelligent and earnest officials accumulate a fund of experience as to the most effective measures for preserving the health of inmates. To render the results of this experience available, both for the benefit of those dealing with similar problems in different localities and of those who from time to time begin the work, answers to a series of questions covering as many of these problems as possible have been collated. The information presented has been obtained by means of the cordial co-operation of superintendents, attending physicians and others dealing at first hand with institution child life. Frank statements have been made of objections to existing rules, together with criticisms and suggestions for improvement. The material thus gathered has been reduced to tabular form so far as practicable. The following pages contain more detailed statements and conclusions based upon the tables, together with a discussion of present practices and of certain problems involved.

1. PREVENTION.

Quarantine.—Section 213 of the Public Health Law requires that "the officers of the institution * * * shall, on receiving such child (by commitment or otherwise) place it in strict quarantine thereafter from the other inmates until discharged from such quarantine by such (regular attending) physician." To prevent confusion as well as to avoid the association with the idea of contagion which the word " quarantine " has in most minds, the term " observation period " would perhaps be preferable.

The reasons offered by institutions for non-compliance with this provision and their objections to its principle, are considered in Part I. of this report. The variety of usages in institutions which do comply is indicated in Table III.

Explanation of Table III.—The figures in this table will not give a total of " 148 " under each item. To make all columns tally would require much duplication of such headings as " Does not apply." Therefore the numbers refer only to the positive aspect of each practice, e. g., the item " Prohibited localities or times * * * (total) 39," means that this number specified such prohibition. The remaining 109 institutions either had not encountered conditions making such a rule necessary, or failed to specify their practice in this particular.

Length of quarantine.—It will be noted that the wording of the law makes the length of quarantine dependent upon the discretion of the attending physician. In most institutions practice has crystallized into a definite period, with a minimum limit. It is this limit which is indicated in the table. The statistics show that the largest number of institutions make this minimum either ten or fourteen days. This term corresponds approximately to the popular idea of the length of the period of incubation of contagious diseases. In not a few instances quarantine has been lengthened from ten to fourteen days after a child just dismissed had developed an infectious disease on the eleventh or twelfth day. Similarly the fourteen-day period has been lengthened to twenty-one. Reference to Table V. shows that while in forty-four institutions contagion has developed in less than one week from the child's admission, in thirty-five between one and two weeks' time has elapsed. At least twelve additional instances were cited of the appearance of contagion in a newly admitted child after an incubation of from sixteen to thirty days. In one case diphtheria occurred on the sixteenth day, the child's second day in school. More than 150 cases in the institution resulted. Obvious deductions from these facts point to the wisdom of the longer time for initial observation. Discretion and common sense make the length of absolute quarantine variable. It is desirable that the period of detention from school be as brief as seems wise when all circumstances are considered. A close watch for an extended time after dismissal from quarantine, insuring prompt detection of heightened temperature or other suspicious symptoms, lessens the danger of communication of contagion should exposure before admission be followed by such unusually long incubation period.

Facilities for quarantining.—Facilities for quarantine vary greatly. Of the forty-four institutions indicated in Table III. as having a separate building, several use a larger or smaller portion of such separate building for administration or hospital purposes. In the fifty-eight homes using some part of the institution building proper the amount of space devoted to quarantine depends upon (1) the average number of admissions, (2) whether one or both sexes are received, and (3) whether or no the total capacity of the institution is exceeded. Where there are but two or three admissions in a month one room may prove sufficient. While entrance quarantine and quarantine for contagion may be provided for in the same suite of isolation rooms without mutual interference, an attempt to combine either or both of these with a general infirmary, even where there is seldom a case of illness, sooner or later proves impracticable. Separate rooms for boys and girls, a place of detention for newcomers until the physician has made his examination, and, where admissions are more frequent, additional rooms, that the last week of quarantine may be spent without coming in contact with later arrivals—these are the essentials for compliance with the spirit of the above quoted provision of the Public Health Law. But four institutions making any attempt at quarantine separate the children in the dormitory only, and ten others permit them to use the same dining-room or to mingle at once in school or outdoor play. Their practice is the exception to the general understanding that by "strict quarantine" is meant separation both by day and by night, which is the custom in 94 institutions.

VISITING DAYS.

In the matter of visiting, each institution is a law unto itself; experience and convenience are the only guides.

Frequency of visits.—It may be said in explanation of the second part of Table III. that the two homes allowing no visits are reception houses only. For convenience in tabulating certain other data, these homes have been entered in the various lists as separate institutions. The "restrictions" to unlimited visiting, spoken of in the footnote, were too numerous to be easily summarized. "Any day except during school hours," "Any day but Sunday," "Any day but Saturday and Sunday," "Any day, but each visitor not more than once a fortnight" (month, etc., as the case might be), are phrases showing the general purport of these restrictions.

An analysis of the individual reports from which these summaries were made shows that the stringency of limitations to visiting is pretty generally in inverse proportion to the distance of the institution from the place where the children's friends reside and in direct proportion to the poverty and squalor of the homes of such visitors. The largest institutions situated in New York or easily accessible from that city have on the permitted days hundreds and even thousands of visitors, necessitating in three cases a separate pavilion or shelter for their reception.

Precautions against infection from visitors.—The danger of visiting day as a source of infection is discussed in Part III. of this report. Thirty-nine institutions distinctly specified that visits are suspended during the prevalence of any epidemic in the locality. Several of this number, with others that made no sweeping prohibitions, are careful at all times to ascertain the exact locality from which each visitor comes, and as far as possible the probability of exposure to contagion. Many institutions avail themselves of the bulletins of the Board of Health for this purpose. The reception room, or the play hall, dining-room or other place set apart for visitors, is usually disinfected afterwards.

Articles brought.—City institutions have perhaps the most to contend with in dealing with ignorant and obstinate visitors. When excluded they " raise fury," having more than once made it necessary to summon police assistance. They are certain that " something dreadful is going on," if they are not permitted to see their children. Their apparent conviction that the children need more to eat, and their ideas of suitable delicacies are equally vexatious, amusing and pathetic. One mother brought a cup of water and a stale roll, and a father had some cakes of chocolate for a four-months-old baby. Much vigilance is required to prevent overfeeding, even of permitted fruit and candies, and even where strict prohibition of edibles is enforced there is always danger of smuggling. Unwholesome and poisonously colored candies, tobacco and liquors are frequently confiscated. In all but a very few institutions distribution is carefully supervised. Packages are left at the door with an attendant who marks upon each the child's name and afterwards distributes them at her discretion, or a limited quantity is allowed to be given during the visit and the remainder is saved for future distribution. A few of the smallest institutions have found it a sufficient precaution to give instruction on the first visit as to the kind and amount of delicacies that are wholesome. Two or three institutions buy pure candy in quantity and allow the children to spend pennies given them for it. Others encourage ice cream, or fruit that can be washed.

In more than half the institutions clothing brought with the child is laid aside. This is done not always for fear of contagion, but because of the fact that when a child is taken away the parent usually demands every article ever brought to it, without considering the possibility of its having been worn out. Clothing is, however, a recognized source of danger. It is a common practice to destroy all that the child has on, and to open and fumigate all packages of clothing before they are taken into the house. Instances showing the wisdom of such action will be cited later.

Child visitors.—Twenty-six institutions allow no little children to visit, and a few place the minimum age limit as high as twelve or sixteen years. Others having no rule about the matter " discountenance " child visitors. A rather large proportion state . that "no children come," so that the problem has not arisen with them. Where small brothers and sisters live near enough to visit, it is the general experience that they are more liable to bring infection than are the parents. This is believed to be because they are apt to be fondled by other children.

Visitors' reception rooms.—Visitors are not permitted to go farther than the reception room in sixty-nine of the institutions. In the seventy-five where it was stated that parents are allowed to go through the building, it is usually only upon the first visit to show what the child's surroundings are to be, and almost without exception the visitor is accompanied by an official of the house.

Moral considerations.—The great problem involved in the whole subject of "visiting day" is the conflict between the moral and the physical welfare of the child. Although more than half the institutions report no trouble from this source, about one out of every five outbreaks of contagion in the whole number of institutions has been traced to visitors or suspected to have come from them. In some institutions it is positively declared that all contagion has been so introduced, and that total exclusion of visitors would practically mean total freedom from disease.

The danger of the other course is thus expressed by an official in one of the largest institutions for boys: "There is a great outcry against institution children being made machine-like, but what will go farther toward destroying the individuality of the child, as well as his home love and all finer feelings, than to prevent his visiting with his relatives? Much is said about this means of introducing contagion, but there is really less chance of contracting contagion in an institution than out, as the child is better fortified. I would rather allow them to run the risk than to lose the moral effect of home ties."

The attending physician of a large asylum for girls, at the same time that he described the evils and annoyances of visiting days and stated that it was practically the sole source of infection, added: "Still, the results of treatment are so good as to warrant running this risk, rather than the moral risk of totally alienating the child from her family."

Another far-reaching result is the effect on the parent. With rare visits interest wanes, and with it ceases the effort to become able to take the child back to its home.

Restrictions and sanitary regulations there must be. The foregoing pages indicate some of the means that have been found effective in lessening physical danger, and in reducing the friction with institution routine caused by unlimited interruptions. Total exclusion is a step that the most radical hesitate to take.

MINGLING WITH THE WORLD OUTSIDE.

Visits to parents or friends, attendance at church, Sunday school and public school, lectures and entertainments, excursions and picnics, involve a problem similar to that of " visiting day." Officials are generally agreed that the danger of institutionalizing the child by depriving him of such means of mingling in the life of the community far outweighs that from the relatively few cases of serious illness thus introduced. The largest number of cases of contagion in proportion to possible chances of this kind have been traced to visits to friends or relatives. These visits are customarily requested in case of death or illness in the family. Most institutions think the giving of permission for such visits unwise. Where circumstances seem to warrant it, experience emphasizes the necessity of quarantine on return as at first admission.

2. CARE OF CONTAGION.

(See Table IV.)

Place.—The practice of removing all cases of contagious diseases to a hospital depends somewhat on convenience of location and somewhat on the institution's own facilities for isolation.

Many that care for cases of "mild contagion" send away the three diseases commonly classified as "serious." The figures given show pretty clearly the relative fear with which each of the three is regarded. The caption "separate room for each disease" in Table IV. refers to these three, and means that the twenty institutions have means of caring for and isolating each from the other should all three occur at the same time. In most of these the scarlet fever room is kept solely for scarlet fever, and so on. "One room or suite of rooms for all contagion" indicates that after an epidemic is over the rooms are disinfected and utilized for whatever may next occur. Institutions on the cottage plan find it comparatively easy in an emergency to rearrange one cottage for hospital use. The advantages of a building wholly detached are appreciated by most workers, and the use of such a separate building is by no means confined to large institutions.

The phrase "outside access or separable hall" covers a variety of devices, from a wing close partitioned from the rest so as to be practically a separate but adjoining building, to an attic or top floor reached by stairs from which well children can be kept away. In some cases this stairway and the isolating rooms can be shut off by double doors. A number have outside stairways or utilize a suitably constructed fire-escape. Of the twenty-four institutions obliged to use the general infirmary for contagious diseases also, some have means of making isolation reasonably complete, and their greatest apprehension is lest contagious and non-contagious diseases should occur at the same time. Others have the infirmary so placed that well children must pass it on their way to dormitories, school and dining-room. Even the bath and toilet used by the sick must sometimes be reached through this common hall. Although comparative freedom from epidemics sometimes exists where such deplorable lack of isolation facilities is combined with an utter absence of initial quarantine, it seems, as one official expressed it, to be "attributable to Providence, not to precaution on our part."

Some institutions having a room set apart solely for use in contagion have with it no convenience for bath or toilet, or no means of ingress or egress without the possibility of coming in contact with well children.

The contagion quarantine, if in the institution building, is usually on the top floor. In two or three instances where a room on the first or second floor had been used, even with the greatest precaution, the disease had broken out among children in the rooms above, and the only assignable cause was the carrying of germs by upward currents of air.

ISOLATION OF QUARANTINE ATTENDANTS.

As the figures given in this table (Table IV.) show, usage and experience endorse the greatest strictness. The attendant is usually quarantined with the case and all meals sent to the room. In scarlet fever and diphtheria, and with increasing frequency in measles also, food is by some arrangement transferred to dishes which are kept in the sick room, and all dishes sent out are first scalded or rinsed in disinfectant solutions. Bed linen may be disinfected and washed separately, or where the equipment is more complete, washed in the quarantine hospital. Some institutions are careful to avoid having laundry and sweepings carried through the halls at all, but have the disinfected packages dropped from a window to some one who immediately cares for them.

The infectious as well as contagious character of measles is coming to be more widely recognized. An instance in point may be cited: During an epidemic of measles the attendants came down for their meals to the officers' dining-room, and the children detailed to wait on this table contracted the disease.

LENGTH OF QUARANTINE.

As to the custom in individual cases the figures in Table IV., 5, are self-explanatory. It is usual in a few institutions to quarantine all cases until the recovery of the last one. In general, results confirm the wisdom of the longer periods of quar-

44

antine. The practice of allowing contagion to "run through" an institution without quarantine will be considered in Part III.

Other precautions mentioned by officials are: The use of antiseptic gargles, sprays and mouth washes by the entire institution population during existence of contagion; a "throat-line" for daily examination; the administration of "immunizing doses of antitoxin;" a free use of disinfectant and antiseptic solutions at all times; and,(more frequently emphasized than any other) the prompt isolation of any child in the least degree ailing.

METHODS OF DISINFECTION (TABLE IV., II.).

Material.—Fumigation is generally employed after all outbreaks of contagion. The use of formaldehyde is increasing. Several institutions use both sulphur and formaldehyde, employing the former for general disinfection and for the " milder " diseases (such as chicken pox), and the latter for scarlet fever, diphtheria and measles. One institution used burning tar and another chlorine gas. The attending physician of the latter institution gave the following as a reason for his disbelief in the efficacy of sulphur: Some years before he had seen a pair of doves fall into a hop kiln where an enormous quantity of sulphur was being used to bleach the hops. As soon as possible after the fumes subsided the doves were taken out apparently dead, but in a short time they revived and were soon as well as ever. Another physician after attending a case of malignant infection, fumigated the clothing he had worn in his barn. As soon as he was able to enter the place he noticed a swarm of gnats dancing briskly where the sulphur fumes had been thickest.

On the other hand, one institution after experimenting with formaldehyde returned to the use of sulphur.

Quantity.—The rules given by the boards of health of different cities for the quantity of sulphur is from three to four and one-half pounds per 1,000 cubic feet. Although a large number of institutions use a smaller quantity, medical attendants generally were inclined to doubt the efficiency of less than three pounds per 1,000 cubic feet in cases of diseases that are infectious as well as contagious. Two institutions use from five to eight pounds per 1,000 cubic feet, and three others did not weigh it, but used " enough to burn continuously " for from 24 to 72 hours. Those with the most experience insist upon the use of steam in connection with sulphur fumigation. Rules for the use of formaldehyde vary from six to twelve ounces (by measure) of forty per cent. solution. When used in candle or pastil form the printed directions are followed. Different rules accompany the different forms of generators for producing the gas directly from wood alcohol. In Syracuse no generator of any kind is used, but sheets are suspended and the fluid is poured over them.

Disinfection of walls, floors and furniture.—In considering the use of disinfectants on walls, floors and furniture, it should be noted in connection with the number of institutions (88) given (Table IV.), as employing such means that many others send all infectious cases away as soon as diagnosed and consider that thorough fumigation is then a sufficient precaution. Solutions most frequently in use are carbolic acid and bichloride of mercury (each 1:1000 to 1:5000), Platt's chlorides and Wilson's tablets. The use of fluid formaldehyde for all disinfecting purposes had been found advantageous by a number of institutions because of its harmlessness to paint and fabrics. Other preparations whose name is legion are in use. These are effective in so far as they are disinfectants and not merely deodorants.

Owing to the impossibility of cleaning papered or rough plastered walls, and the improbability of effectively fumigating them, rooms used for the care of contagion are frequently enamel painted. Of the eighteen institutions specifying " repainting or whitewashing " after each outbreak, but two or three use whitewash.

Mattresses, if not destroyed, are frequently sterilized by steam heat. Methods described for disinfection of blankets are: steaming or dry-sterilizing for several hours at a high temperature; boiling; airing for several hours (after fumigating) in the sunshine, on fresh earth. Whatever can be boiled is usually so treated, frequently in some disinfectant solution.

LOCAL HEALTH BOARD REGULATIONS.

Regulations by local boards of health in regard to diseases which must be reported, placing responsibility for such reporting, length of quarantine and methods of disinfection, show considerable variance.

Diseases which attending physicians may or may not be required to report to the local health authorities are: chicken pox, whooping-cough, mumps, German measles, erysipelas, cerebrospinal meningitis and tuberculosis. Membranous croup, if not specified, is usually included under diphtheria in the list of contagious diseases which must be reported. Many cases of the four diseases first named are never brought to the attention of a physician, even though local ordinances require them to be reported. As one health officer said: "The trouble is, people are not afraid of those diseases, and it is hard to enforce quarantine. Many cases occur which we never hear of."

Responsibility for reporting contagion.—The ordinances of all cities make the attending physician responsible for required reports. Most cities have an additional clause or section requiring the nurse or attendant to make such report if no physician is employed, and some make it the duty of "any person knowing of or having reason to believe of the existence of a case of infectious or contagious disease not reported, or concealed, to report the same to the department."

Quarantine of measles.—Strictness of quarantine varies most in regard to measles. In some localities there seems to be no law which can be enforced to prevent visitors to such cases from mingling on the streets or in public conveyances with those susceptible to the disease. One health officer gave it as his opinion that measles could not be considered a "pestilential" disease, and therefore could not be placed under the rule that "no person shall enter or depart from a house in which a case of smallpox or other *pestilential* disease exists without permission from the health commissioner * * * ." This same city distinctly specifies that "no person suffering from any of the diseases named * * * (including measles), and no person *in charge of* such patient shall attend any public, private, or Sunday school or any public place, or enter any public convey-ance * * * ."

Length of quarantine specified by the local board of health is usually, for diphtheria, dependent upon certification of sterile culture; for scarlet fever, from 30 to 45 days. No ordinance was found specifying the length of quarantine for measles.

Disinfection is in some localities required to be performed by the health authorities. In others the rules are furnished by the authorities to be followed out by physician, family or insti-tution.

These differences account in part for the variations of regula-tions in institutions, and for the presence or absence in differ-ent institutions of certain assigned causes for the introduction and spreading of contagion. Further discussion of questions here indicated will be found under appropriate sections of Part III.

3. CARE OF CONTAGIOUS EYE, SKIN AND SCALP DISEASES.

Comparatively few of these maladies require the same methods of control as are followed in other contagious diseases. Some acute forms of such disease may make a child actually ill. These cases are usually placed promptly under the care of a specialist. are cured or removed for special treatment, and the outbreak is soon " over with."

Danger of relaxing vigilance.—The real problems occur in con-nection with chronic troubles of this kind. The child so affected may feel perfectly well. Aside from the danger of contagion there is no reason for his separation from the rest of the insti-tution population. The long continuance of the disease is apt to breed carelessness in the child himself, if not in the attend-ant. Once even a single case of such contagion is admitted eternal vigilance is the price of eradication, as many an institution has found to its sorrow. In some instances where the officer in charge had not met with the disease before and failed to appreciate the virility of the contagion, a small ringworm or apparently slight case of sore eyes has infected an entire institution before the danger was scarcely suspected. Years of fighting have followed to free the institution from the infection.

Many institutions positively refuse to accept any child having eye, skin or scalp disease. However, such children must be cared for. In some localities hospital treatment is not available. Methods found by institutions to be relatively efficient for the protection of uninfected children include the following precautions:

INDIVIDUAL TOILET ARTICLES, CLOTHING, TOWELS AND PILLOW CASES.

It has been found that the mere provision of these articles is not sufficient without vigilant insistence upon their proper use. Some institutions which do not mark towels for individual use provide a small, fresh one for each ablution, and wash all in some germicide solution. Pillow cases, mixed in the general laundry, may more frequently than is suspected cause ringworm to become endemic in an institution. Many institution officials testify that spray baths and running water in the lavatory are valuable aids in keeping free from contagion of this kind.

COVERING THE INFECTIOUS SURFACE.

The wearing of caps in ringworm of the scalp is a common practice. "Children will wear each other's hats in the play yard, or get their heads close enough together to infect each other," is the common experience. The caps or bandages also keep the local applications from being rubbed off.

Segregation has been employed where in spite of other precautions a disease seemed to be getting the upper hand. Such separation may amount to a complete quarantine. More commonly the infected children have separate dormitories and a special table in the dining-room. Total isolation has most frequently to be resorted to in eye diseases.

It is interesting to note that the immediate cause of the enactment of this portion of the Public Health Law was the wide prevalence of contagious eye diseases. The present freedom of the majority of institutions from eye diseases in particular is a forceful comment on the results of its enforcement.

PART III.

Occurrences of Contagious Diseases

In Institutions Under Private Control but Receiving Children as Public Charges, for the Three Years, May 1, 1898, to May 1, 1901.

1. GENERAL DEDUCTIONS FROM STATISTICAL TABLES.

Sources of information.—The statistics on which the following comparisons are based have been obtained from the monthly medical reports or other official records filed in the institutions or in the offices of the local health boards where such records exist. These records were frequently missing for the whole or a part of the time covered by this inquiry. Where monthly medical reports have been regularly made it sometimes occurred that those filed previous to some change in institution administration were not to be found. Visits were made to the offices of local health departments to supplement information from their duplicate files. In one large city it was learned that such reports were considered " merely perfunctory; if they were sent in, all right, and if not, no matter;" in another that it had been the custom of the clerk employed previous to January, 1900, to open the reports, glance through them, and if no action were called for, file them in the waste basket; while in a third the department had moved from one office to another two weeks before the request for information was made, and all reports on file had been destroyed to save the labor of moving them.

In some institutions private memoranda of infirmary attendants or attending physicians furnished reliable figures. In others the memory of officers or attendants was the only source

of information. In such instances, if there had been more than
a few outbreaks, the informant hesitated to give farther statement
than that a disease had or had not occurred within the
specified time, mistrusting the accuracy of any figures he might
furnish.[*] In more than one instance the records contained
such entries as " a few cases of chicken pox;" " a number of
slight cases of German measles." Chronic eye, skin and scalp
diseases, reported each month, frequently made a total several
times as large as the actual number of cases.

Verification.—Comparatively few institutions could give more
than an approximation to the number of cases of non-contagious
illness. Figures based on such estimates have been furnished
and verified by institution officials and attending physicians as
" fair." Where such verification could not be obtained the entry
is " no record."

Great courtesy has been shown by all officials and frequently
much patient labor has been expended by them in gathering from
obscure or confused data the information requested.

Death records, it is believed, are substantially accurate. It
is possible that in some cases where inquiry blanks were filled
by non-medical attendants deaths from typhoid, contagious
cerebro-spinal meningitis and general tuberculosis may have
been placed under the heading " deaths from all other diseases."

Statistics of population have been obtained by adding to the
number shown by the records in the Albany office to have been
present on May 1, 1898, the number of admissions for each of
the succeeding thirty-six months to April 30, 1901.

Such then are the statistical data obtained. It was hoped
they might prove of sufficient accuracy for an inductive study
of real value to those interested in the problems " relating to
the better preservation of the health of children in institutions."
Owing to the incompleteness of the figures but few of the questions
suggesting themselves for consideration could be answered
with any degree of satisfaction by statistical comparisons.

---

[*] It sometimes occurred that records, found later by the official, showed that in figures thus
given from memory several cases, and even one or more outbreaks of considerable extent, had
been omitted

It is believed that the following conclusions are based upon sufficiently accurate data to be valid:

1. *Does the observance of a period of quarantine at entrance lessen the amount of contagion?*

Following is a comparison of the totals given for the different boroughs of New York city, where quarantine is most strict, and for the remainder of the State, where it is least observed:

	Deaths		Cases	
	Contagious. Per cent.	Non-contagious. Per cent.	Contagious. Per cent.	Non-contagious. Per cent.
Boroughs of Manhattan and the Bronx................	.84	6.36	11.88	53.63
Boroughs of Brooklyn, Richmond and Queens	.72	2.14	15.63	22.37
Eastern Inspection District, outside Greater New York. .	.51	1.38	21.66	10.28
Western Inspection District.	.51	3.39	12.80	7.38

Study of the individual institutions in the tables named verifies the deduction from the above figures, that where entrance quarantine is maintained, the amount of contagion is less than that of other illness; where there is no quarantine the reverse is true, namely, the amount of contagion exceeds that of non-contagious illness.

2. *Does an insufficient allowance of air space in the dormitories impair the health of the children?*

As the results of overcrowding dormitories would naturally show as much in the amount of other illness as in the amount of contagion, only institutions having records of other illness also were selected for this comparison. Complete statistics were obtainable for 15 institutions having in their dormitories an average amount of air space per occupant of less than 330 cubic feet, and from 38 having more than 450 cubic feet per occupant. These lists exclude infant asylums; the number of city and country institutions in each is fairly proportionate, and all other conditions are such as to make the comparison just and fair.

Following are the totals and comparisons:

	15 institutions average dormitory air space 250 to 320 cubic feet.	38 institutions average dormitory air space 453 to 814 cubic feet.
Total population (May 1, 1898, to May 1, 1901)	5,822	13,681
Total cases contagious diseases	942	1,725
Total deaths contagious diseases	22	28
Total cases non-contagious diseases	5,474	1,625
Total deaths non-contagious diseases	72	93
Proportion of cases to population, contagious diseases, per cent	16.18	12.61
Proportion of cases to population, non-contagious diseases, per cent	94.02	11.88
Proportion of all cases to population, per cent	110.20	24.49
Proportion of deaths to population, contagious diseases, per cent	.38	.20
Proportion of deaths to population, non-contagious diseases, per cent	1.23	.68
Proportion of all deaths to population, per cent	1.61	.88

An examination of the general percentages for the individual institutions compared with the air space of each verifies the conclusion inevitable from the above figures. There are exceptions which are to be explained by unusual circumstances in the case, but in general the rule holds good. Insufficient air space in dormitories results in increased susceptibility to all kinds of diseases, and diminished power of resistance in combating them.

Air space and eye, skin and scalp diseases.—There appears also a marked connection between dormitory air space and diseases of the eyes, skin and scalp. Statistics of these diseases were, in general, incomplete. The records of 29 institutions having most trouble of this kind show that 17 have an average allowance of less than 400 cubic feet per occupant in the dormitories, while four of these have less than 300. But five of the remainder have 500 cubic feet or more.

3. *Is the danger from contagion as great as that from non-contagious diseases?*

All the institutions, except infant asylums, giving statistics for non-contagious diseases are included in this comparison. Following are the totals and percentages:

Total population (May 1, 1898, to May 1, 1901)	38,551
Total cases contagious diseases	3,892
Total deaths from contagious diseases	84
Total cases non-contagious diseases	10,392
Total deaths from non-contagious diseases	335
Proportion of cases to population, contagious, per cent.	10.09
Proportion of cases to population, non-contagious, per cent.	26.96
Proportion of deaths to population (from contagion), per cent.	.22
Proportion of deaths to population (from non-contagion), per cent.	.87

Had complete reports been obtainable from all institutions, the absolute percentages might vary somewhat from those here given. The slight variance between the death-rates just given and those in which *all* deaths are compared with the total population shows that the relative proportion of all percentages would probably not differ materially.

The total population of 148 institutions for the three years under consideration is 73,718; deaths from contagious diseases, 543; deaths from all other diseases, 3,413. Or in the same form as before:

	Per cent.
Proportion of deaths to population from contagious diseases	.74
Proportion of deaths to population from non-contagious diseases	4.63

That is, there is one chance of a child's dying from a contagious disease to from four to six that he will die from some *other illness.*

In considering the number of cases of either class of illness the figures above given show that the chance of contracting a contagious disease is about one-third as great as that of developing some other illness. On the other hand, by referring to the percentages quoted under the question of efficacy of quarantine, and to the general percentages of individual institutions, it is found that this statement must be modified by two considerations: (a) The danger from contagion is least where strict quarantine is maintained. (b) The danger from other diseases is least in small institutions, especially if located in the country.

The foregoing conclusions are justified by statistics obtained. Among other questions naturally suggesting themselves were:

Does the greater amount of contagion occur in large or in small institutions?

Does the greater amount of contagion occur in institutions located in the city, or in those located in the country?

Is the danger from contagious diseases increased by attendance at public school?

An attempt was made at securing an answer to these questions. This proved impossible for the following reasons:

1. The incompleteness of statistics precluded fair comparison between institutions when divided into the above categories.

2. A more strict age classification prevails among urban institutions and those with the largest population than among small institutions and those located in the country. While the largest death-rate occurs, of course, in infant asylums, elimination of these leaves an institution population of older children almost wholly. This makes comparison with the small and country institutions unfair, as these have inmates of all ages, and the greater proportion of deaths occur among the babies and little children. Present methods of keeping statistics afford no means of making the necessary age division for just comparison.

3. Many of the institutions sending children to public schools are those in which the custom most largely obtains of letting "mild contagion" run through the institution population with-

out quarantine. In several instances the children attending public school contracted a contagious disease prevalent in the community, and as no quarantine was established, "all took it who had not had it before." If this chanced to occur in an institution more than once during the three years covered by this inquiry, the proportion rose as high as 35 per cent. or 40 per cent., and in one instance reached 70 per cent. of the total population.

It is also true that most of the institutions having the best equipment for prompt and thorough isolation of suspects are on one side of the line in certain of these divisions for comparison.

4. Those institutions which have kept the best records because of that very fact compare unfavorably in statistical showing with those whose figures are incomplete. One institution complied with the Public Health Law in every particular. The excellent records it furnished gave a percentage of illness (both contagious and otherwise) many times as large as that of another institution very similar as to number, age and condition of children admitted. The other institution could furnish no figures but from the memory of officers and attendants. Any comparison placing the two in contrast would be manifestly as worthless as it would be unfair.

2. INTRODUCTION AND COMMUNICATION OF CONTAGIOUS DISEASES.

(See Table V.)

Sources of information.—Besides the general deductions to be gathered from statistical tables, the actual cause of a particular outbreak or epidemic of contagious disease was frequently to be ascertained. Those named in Table V. have in every instance been verified by the officer in charge, or by the attending physician, and frequently by both.

Explanation of table.—As explained in the footnote to Table V., the figures refer in each case to the number of institutions by which a given cause has been assigned. Many of these causes have occurred several times in one institution, as for instance:

Introduction through visitors, "Always," or "No other cause known."

1. CIRCUMSTANCES OF INTRODUCTION.

The first four causes named have already been discussed at some length in Part II.

Infection before admission.—Infection before admission is the chief source assigned according to the numerical showing of this table. In twenty-five of the forty-four institutions in which a contagious disease developed in a child in less than one week after its admission the child was still in quarantine detention. The inmates of the remaining nineteen were unprotected from this source of exposure. The infected children had been already discharged from quarantine in thirteen of the thirty-five institutions in which eight to fourteen days elapsed before the appearance of the disease. In one or more instances in several institutions, however, infection so introduced has been prevented from spreading farther.

School attendance.—Twenty-seven institutions have sent their children to public or parochial schools during the time covered by this inquiry. Such attendance has been assigned as a source of infection in twenty-four of these, and in one other where one older child was sent outside to school. In some cases the outbreak has been confined to the one or more children first contracting the disease. Other institutions have made no effort to prevent exposure of other inmates, thinking it better to let the children " have it over with."

Visitors.—If the cases " suspected but not traced" are included, this source ranks numerically next to " infection before admission." The problems involved in the subject of " visiting days" are stated in Part II. It has frequently been found that visiting parents had children ill with an infectious disease, either at home or in another institution. In some instances they concealed the fact when questioned, and the harm was done before the truth was found out. Others in the long car ride through the thickly populated parts of the city may have gathered the germs of infection entirely unknown to them-

selves. It is believed that germs are also carried by articles
which visitors bring to the children.

Excursions, attendance at church, etc.—Any large concourse of
people is liable to include individuals capable of infecting others
who may be susceptible to disease. Attendance at such a
gathering is therefore always a possible source of danger to a
company of children. Perhaps because this fact is so widely
recognized, contagion from this source is found to occur in relatively few instances. Care is usually exercised to prohibit such
attendance when any contagious disease is prevalent. On excursions to widely patronized pleasure resorts the institution
children are usually kept by themselves.

Walking, errands, etc.—Sometimes the only place for outdoor
exercise for children in city institutions is in the streets or
public parks. This means naturally some risk, as other children
play there also. It is the custom, too, in some institutions to
send children on errands to various places as a part of their
training in self-reliance. It is possible in this way to encounter
contagion of some kind. These causes were named in but eight
of the 148 institutions questioned.

Infection from surrounding premises.—One of the most baffling
problems presented to certain institutions is the danger from
infection in neighboring premises. In the tenement district of
New York city scores of cases of scarlet fever, measles and even
smallpox are not reported to any physician. They are concealed
with great cunning from the inspectors sent from the board of
health. Clothing full of scales from desquamation is hung
upon the pulley lines in courts upon which open the windows
from the homes of numerous families. The epidemic becomes
so widespread that the quarantine hospitals are taxed beyond
their limit and reported cases are not removed. After convalescence, mattresses and bedding are aired on the fire-escapes
overhanging the street. The disease-laden air can scarcely be
prevented from entering the institution.

In smaller cities and towns carelessness of neighboring families as to maintenance of quarantine and the place and mode of

disinfection may combine with the inquisitiveness of children to effect an exposure.

Visits to home or friends.—The fact that visits to home or friends are usually requested because of illness or death in the family suggests the danger from this source. Comparatively few institutions permit the inmates to make such visits. In those which have done so the experience frequently is that " the child comes back sick every time we allow it to go."

Other causes.—Still other causes were assigned by forty-one institutions. Although many of these have occurred but once, they are of interest as affording explanation of some of the figures given elsewhere.

1. *Probable exposure on journey by train* from reception house to main institution. This cause was cited by two institutions in which a child, quarantined for the full period in the reception house, developed a contagious disease in eight to fourteen days after the transfer.

2. *Children admitted near the end of the desquamation period,* and desquamation unnoticed at first. This also occurred in the case of children who had been placed out and readmitted.

3. *Hereditary predisposition to tuberculosis.*

4. *Clothing:* (a) *Clothing smuggled in by a visitor.* This was strongly suspected but not positively proved. (b) *Clothing brought by a new child.* Four instances of contagion from this cause were cited.

5. *Children returned from a hospital* after treatment for a contagious disease brought germs (a) of the same disease in clothing or hair (two institutions), or (b) of another contagious disease with which they came down in due time (three institutions).

6. *Recrudescence* of eye and scalp diseases after return of children from special hospital as cured.

7. *Defective plumbing,* or general tearing out and repairing of the plumbing system, were considered responsible for four epidemics of diphtheria.

8. *General repairs of the building are believed to have unearthed old infection,* producing one outbreak of scarlet fever.

45

9. *Polluted drinking water* was given as the cause of four epidemics of typhoid.

10. *Garbage and refuse dumped on vacant lots adjoining* the institution property were assigned as probable sources of typhoid and diphtheria, respectively, in two institutions.

11. *Milk from cows pasturing in a field where a cesspool overflowed* is thought to have been the cause of an epidemic of typhoid.

12. *Flies coming from this place of overflow to the kitchen* of the institution are supposed to have carried the infection to the same institution the following summer.

13. *Letters from a child's family* were once the suspected cause.

14. *Toys sent by the parents of a child, after its death,* introduced contagion into one institution; in another a similar gift was sent under suspicious circumstances and the toys were destroyed before harm was done.

15. *An attendant visited a relative ill with diphtheria,* contracted the disease and concealed the fact until every inmate of the institution had been exposed. Another attendant received a visitor who had mumps and thus exposed the inmates.

16. *An institution receiving day children* had an epidemic of measles introduced by them. (This is analogous to attendance at public schools.)

17. Three physicians stated the possibility that they themselves might have introduced infection through germs on their clothing.

18. *The theory of spontaneous generation of the bacilli* of some diseases was thought by three institutions to be the only explanation for certain outbreaks. So far as could be learned from institution officers these outbreaks were entirely sporadic in origin.

19. *Eye diseases are sometimes self induced* by the introduction of foreign substances, or other means of irritation. Three institutions stated that this had frequently occurred when a child wished to avoid some task by getting into the infirmary.

20. *Eye diseases in newly admitted children* have been traced to contact with such infection encountered in the public baths.

2. CIRCUMSTANCES OF COMMUNICATION.

Wherever an outbreak had not been confined to one case, careful inquiry was made as to the manner of its communication to other inmates. In general, of the more serious infection, diphtheria is most often confined to the first cases appearing, and outbreaks of measles are most widespread.

Common source of infection.—In one or more outbreaks in 71 institutions the first two or more cases have appeared within a few hours of each other. Such outbreaks are usually traced to a common source, such as a visiting day a week or two before, or common exposure in public school.

Communicated before diagnosis.—The infection of a large number of other children before the first case is sufficiently pronounced to determine its nature is assigned as a reason for spreading contagion more often than any other. This occurs most frequently with measles. This disease is especially contagious and infectious in its catarrhal stages when it is impossible to distinguish it from a common cold. Unless institution officials are aware of the presence of the disease in the community and are therefore especially watchful a whole dormitory may be "doomed" before danger is suspected. It has also happened that a child was affected with so mild a form of chicken pox or scarlet fever that it did not even complain of feeling ill. Discovery of its condition was made only when a warm bath revealed the rash or when desquamation began. Whooping-cough may exhibit its distinctive characteristics late in the course of the disease. The difficulty with dealing with the disease under such circumstances was thus expressed by one official: "If a physician says a child has a bad temper and a cold, and two or three days later it *whoops*, what are you to do?"

Confined to one dormitory.—An attempt was made to determine whether infection spreads more rapidly among children sleeping in the same dormitory. In sixty-nine institutions the whole population mingles in school, dining or play rooms, so that the question could not be answered. Forty-five institutions had succeeded in confining one or more outbreaks to the dor-

mitory or " set " of children in which it first appeared.　One
physician said his experience seemed to invalidate all theories
as to the communication of disease.　While an outbreak of diphtheria would not exceed three or four cases, these never occurred in the same room, but usually one on each floor of the institution building and one in a separate building used as a general
hospital.

Carried by quarantine attendants.—As has been noted in Part
II. (Table IV.) exceeding care is used in most institutions
to quarantine attendants of children affected with diseases
that are infectious as well as contagious.　In nine institutions spread of contagion had been traced to contact of
quarantine attendants with well children.　This was due in
some instances to lack of knowledge of the infectious character of the disease (e. g. in measles), and in others to alleged carelessness on the part of special nurses hired for the
emergency.　Such communication was suspected in six other
institutions.

Other causes.—Nineteen other causes of the spread of contagion were named by 29 institutions.　They are as follows:

1. *Inadequate quarantine facilities.*—Lack of separate toilet and
bath, or of separable means of access to the isolating room,
have made it practically impossible to institute effective quarantine in at least four institutions.

2. *Overlapping quarantine.*—In recognition of the possibility
that a child admitted in an early stage of incubation might
infect a child whose detention period was about completed,
especial pains were taken to gather information on this point.
But three institutions are recorded as having contagion spread
from quarantine in this way.

3. *Surreptitious visits by well children.*—In one institution it
was discovered that several children had watched their opportunity to elude attendants and steal up to the quarantine rooms
in order to satisfy their curiosity as to " what was going on."
In another, a boy with athletic inclinations climbed the fire-

escape to the open window of the quarantine room and effectually exposed himself.

4. *Toys thrown down by children in quarantine* were picked up by
children in the play yard below and caused a wider spread of one
epidemic.

5. *A visiting mother disobeyed instructions* and instead of *looking*
at her child, convalescent from scarlet fever, and departing by
the outside exit, took her in her arms and afterwards passed
through a group of well children in another room on her way
out of the building.

6. *Conveyance of germs by upward currents from quarantine* on a
lower floor and through a dumb-waiter shaft opening into the
sick room were assigned respectively in two institutions.

7. *Children who ran to see a bonfire* in which the infected bedding and garments from a scarlet fever patient were destroyed
came down with the disease at the expiration of the usual time.

8. *Conveyance of germs through the air*, perhaps through open
windows, is thought to be the only explanation in some instances where succeeding cases appear in a different wing of the
building or in another cottage.

9. *The carrying of sweepings and laundry packages* from the
quarantine room through the halls is believed to have spread
infection in one instance.

10. *A mother contracting a disease from her baby* (in an institution where mothers also are cared for), exposed other children
after her own had recovered.

11. *A newly admitted child contracted diphtheria from another
inmate long after the patient had recovered.*

12. *The return of nurslings* from homes where they have been
wet-nursed is mentioned by the New York Foundling Hospital as
a frequent medium of contagion.

13. *Difficulty of diagnosis* with young infants is named by two
infant asylums. "Diagnosis must be from objective symptoms
only. If the child does not complain of some characteristic pain,
mumps might appear to be adenoids or swollen lymphatics; even
the parotid glands may swell and become inflamed from a cold.

A baby is subject to many skin eruptions and feverish conditions which may be merely from stomach trouble or teething. Marasmus and rachitic cases are frequently tubercular. Tuberculosis and syphilis are the more difficult to determine, as it is not easy to obtain from the parents information which might be of aid."

14. *An untrained child, convalescent from typhoid fever, left stools exposed.*

15. *Eye diseases purposely communicated.* Either from malicious intent or pure mischief, a child would convey matter from its own eye to the eye of another child.

16. *Using the same towels,* either through carelessness of the children in "mixing them up" or through lack of a sufficient supply, is a means of communicating eye, skin and scalp diseases.

17. *Flies carried the secretion,* in eye diseases, to the eyes of well children in another cottage.

18. *Drinking from the same dipper* during school hours spread ringworm of the face.

19. *Medicine applied with the same brush to the eyelids of a number of children* during the absence of the regular physician is assigned as the cause of an epidemic of trachoma.

The *practice of allowing "light infection" to go unquarantined* was found to have some advocates. The arguments advanced in favor of the practice are: (1) It is better for a child to have children's diseases while young, as it will "have them lighter and will have them over with." (2) The child has better care in an institution than it might in its own home. (3) If once an epidemic is started, attempt at quarantine only prolongs the time, for all who are susceptible "will have it anyway."

The majority of institutions, however, are not in favor of this practice. They give as their reasons: (1) "One never can tell what children it may go hard with," and it too certainly weeds out the weaklings. (2) Whooping-cough and measles, in particular, have very undesirable consequences with children in any way inclined to lung trouble. Fatal pneumonia frequently follows measles. (3) "Without considering the welfare of the children, to have so much sickness is altogether too much trouble for the officers."

Study of the introduction and spread of contagion and of the prevalence of other illness in institutions brings into great clearness the fact of the organic connection of these small and half isolated groups with the rest of the world. The most scrupulous attention to the laws of health on the part of an institution is not sufficient to counterbalance the effects of ignorance and disease in the parents and of defective sanitary measures in the local community. As the attending physician of a New York city institution put it: "We shall never be able to fight contagion in the institution with much success until tenement reform is enlarged and enforced, and until the city has adequate appropriation for sanitary precautions properly and scientifically carried out."

Because of the comparatively small numbers affected, the truth has not been so generally recognized that the problems relating to the health of these institution children are of vital concern to the community at large. Cleanliness, food that is both cheap and wholesome, regular habits of eating and sleeping, emphasis of the importance of strict quarantine of contagious diseases—all these are object lessons given in the most impressionable stage of the child's development. Their influence upon the life of the larger community, to which the child will one day be restored, is hardly to be overestimated.

The problems discussed above are at least suggestive. Comparative tables and deductions from figures would have had greatly increased value had complete statistics been obtainable. From the acquaintance with institution records acquired in the course of this study the following considerations are suggested as a possible means of lightening the labor of record-keeping, and at the same time increasing the value of the data.

MONTHLY MEDICAL REPORTS.

Duplication in reports.—The law requires that every case of contagious or infectious disease existing in an institution during the month be enumerated in the monthly medical report of the attending physician. The result is, the same cases of chronic eye, skin and scalp diseases, tuberculosis, whooping-cough and scarlet fever are frequently entered on two or more successive reports. The sum of cases so reported therefore may exceed the number actually existing during any given period.

Records of other illness.—The lack of records of non-contagious illness was the greatest difficulty experienced in computing comparative statistics. The use of the following modified form of the medical report blank would ensure the preservation of complete data:

As to the physical condition of the inmates, existence of any contagious diseases (especially of eyes and skin) I find:

DISEASES.	Number of new cases.	Cases previously reported.	Cases of non-contagious illness.
Diphtheria	....	....	....
Scarlet fever	....	....	....
Pertussis	....	....	....
Eye diseases	....	....	....
Skin diseases	....	....	....
Other contagious diseases.....	....	....	....

Recording cause of death.—In order to ascertain the mortality as compared with the extent of any epidemic it was frequently necessary to go to the book of discharges and compare the names there checked as " died " with some other record, or perhaps to trust the memory of an attendant for information concerning the cause of death. It would be a great convenience for ready reference if an entry " Causes " were introduced in the " census " column of the present form of the monthly report blank·

CENSUS.

Admitted during month ....

Discharged during month ....

Died during month ....

Causes of death................................

....

....

Present at date ....

Filing reports in the institution.—Where the officers of a charitable society are changed frequently, or live at some distance from the institution, the practice of placing the monthly medical reports in a permanent file in the office of the institution, both safeguards their preservation and facilitates ready reference.

Files to be made permanent.—The provision of section 214 of the Public Health Law requiring the monthly medical reports to be filed in duplicate with the board of managers and with the local health board seems to have two objects: (1) To make sure that the result of the monthly examination by a competent authority on sanitary matters is presented to those responsible for enforcing improvements necessary for the preservation of the health of the inmates. (2) To keep valuable records in two places, so that accidental loss of one set should not mean total destruction of the data. Instances cited in the introductory pages of Part III. show that this second object has all too frequently been lost sight of. A true appreciation of the value of these reports would lead to adequate care in their preservation as permanent records of the institution.

Physician's record book.—A plan is followed by some institutions which is worthy of general adoption. The attending physician, at the close of each visit, jots down in a blank book the results of his observation. Many successive entries may be " all well." When sickness occurs a note is made of how many children are affected, and their condition is entered from day to day. Such a record would afford the basis for entries in the monthly medical report, or might be an alternative for the entry therein of non-contagious diseases suggested in a foregoing paragraph. A book of this kind affords a place to record all information regarding the introduction of contagion and cause of its spreading. Some physicians have made for their personal use memoranda of the results of experimental treatment. For example, in one epidemic of diphtheria half the cases were treated with antitoxin and half without. As in this instance all the children recovered, the results were disappointingly inconclusive. Records of this nature made in such a book would furnish information of scientific value in a form easy of preservation and convenient of access.

DORMITORY PERMITS.

Attention has been called to difficulties experienced by institution officials in securing permits of proper form, and to the desire expressed by health officers for a model. It might be of assistance in securing full compliance with section 215 of the Public Health Law if a form embodying the following essentials were, like the monthly medical reports, obtainable on application to the State Board of Charities:

This is to certify that the board of health of the (city, town) of .... of .... county has measured the .... dormitory on the ...... floor of the .... (institution). It is .... feet in length by .... feet in width by...... feet in height, and contains ....feet of floor space and .... cubic feet of air space.

Pursuant to section 215 of the Public Health Law (chapter 661 Laws of 1893 as amended by section 2, chapter 667, Laws of 1900), permission is hereby given to place single beds for .... occupants in this dormitory.

(Dated)............   (Signed)...................

Institutions might with advantage post such permits in all dormitories. In those having the required 600 cubic feet or more per occupant, the permits would serve as certificates to the fact.

CONCLUSION.

The foregoing pages have given a statement of the degree of compliance with the Public Health Law in 148 of the children's institutions of the State, together with an account of their practices in other matters concerning the preservation of the health of the children under their care.

In conclusion the attention of the State Board of Charities is invited to the following considerations suggested in the course of this study:

1. The quarantine at admission, required by section 213 of the Public Health Law, was not observed by thirty-six institutions and but partially observed by twelve others. The advantages of compliance and the necessity for such precaution are emphasized under appropriate headings in the preceding text.

2. In a considerable number of institutions a certificate embodying complete official statements of the physical and mental condition of the child at the time of its entrance upon institution life was not written and filed with the commitment or other papers on record in the case.

3. More than one third of the entire number of institutions were found to have filed no monthly medical report as required by section 214 of the Public Health Law, either with the governing board or with the local board of health. In a still larger number of institutions such reports have been made for a short time only, or records have not been placed in a permanent file. The resulting incompleteness of data has rendered it impossible to secure trustworthy information for purposes of comparison. A general compliance with this section and with the suggestions made in the course of this report would furnish complete and reliable data for a future study of great interest and value.

4. The amount of air space per occupant specified in section 215, was found to be allowed in the dormitories of but few of the institutions included in this inquiry. A larger proportion complied with the provision of this section requiring a space between beds of not less than two feet in width. Although many of the institutions having the lowest average allowance of air space per occupant had obtained from the local board of health permits for the number of beds placed in the dormitories, the figures and comparisons elsewhere show the advantage of the larger allowance which it is the evident intent of the law to secure.

5. The lack of permits from the local board of health in a large percentage of institution dormitories requiring them is noted in Table I. and in the pages of this report. Attention

is called to the advantage of a form embodying the essentials of information suggested by section 215, such as is given above.

6. The varying causes assigned by institution officials for the introduction and communication of contagious diseases, and the methods employed by them for prevention and control, cannot be summarized in a single sentence. A study. of the details above presented shows a growing appreciation of the need of ceaseless vigilance and of great strictness. in precautionary measures.

Respectfully submitted,

MARY E. MOXCEY,

Inspector.

To the State Board of Charities, the Capitol, Albany, N. Y.

MAY 23, 1902.

TABLE I., A.

COMPLIANCE WITH THE PUBLIC HEALTH LAW.

Institutions Under Private Control to Which Children Are Committed as Public Charges from New York City.

	Complying.	Not complying.	Partially complying.	Does not apply.	Total.
Section 213:					
1. Regular physician	73	0	0	0	73.
2. Name and address near entrance	54	15	4	0	73.
3. Examined before admission	70	3	0	0	73
4. Written certificate	66	5	1	1	73.
5. Filed with—					
(a) Commitment papers	46	18	1	8	73.
(b) Other papers	27	37	4	5	73.
6. Quarantine at entrance	68	4	1	0	73
7. Date and length endorsed on certificate.	44	17	11	1	73.
Section 214:					
8. Monthly examination—					
(a) Buildings, throughout	63	7	3	0	73.
(b) Inmates, individually	64	9	0	0	73
9. Report filed—					
(a) With governing board	58	15	0	0	73.
(b) With local board	55	17	1	0	73.
10. Recommendations made	51	20	0	0	a71
11. Investigation by local board of health.	52	19	0	0	a71
Section 215:					
12. Beds separated by passageway of not less than two feet	24	10	39	0	73
13. Cubic space of 600 feet	3	51	19	0	73
14. Permits from local health board posted.	48	12	10	3	73.

a Two not reporting.

TABLE I, B.

Compliance with the Public Health Law.

Institutions Under Private Control to Which Children are Committed as Public Charges from New York State, Not Including Such as Receive Public Charges from the City of New York (Table A).

	Complying.	Not complying.	Partially complying.	Does not apply.	Total.
Section 213:					
1. Regular physician	75	0	0	0	75
2. Name and address near entrance......	36	15	a23	1	75
3. Examined before admission...........	48	14	11	2	75
4. Written certificate	38	21	14	2	75
5. Filed with—					
(a) Commitment papers	23	39	b11	2	75
(b) Other papers	22	41	b10	2	75
6. Quarantine at entrance..............	29	32	c11	3	75
7. Date and length endorsed on certificate.	16	52	5	2	75
Section 214:					
8. Monthly examination—					
(a) Buildings, throughout	47	28	0	0	75
(b) Inmates, individually	47	28	0	0	75
9. Report filed—					
(a) With governing board	38	35	1	1	75
(b) With local board................	37	36	1	1	75
10. Recommendations made	49	22	0	2	d73
11. Investigation by local board of health.	48	27	0	0	75
Section 215:					
12. Beds separated by passageway of not less than two feet..................	39	9	27	0	75
13. Cubic space of 600 feet..............	6	28	41	0	75
14. Permits from local health board posted.	12	55	5	3	75

a Either not near main entrance or address not posted.
b Together under separate file
c Usually, "except young infants."
d Two not reporting.

TABLE I., C.

Compliance with the Public Health Law.

Institutions in New York State Under Private Control to Which Children are Committed as Public Charges.

	Com-plying.	Not com-plying.	Par-tially com-plying.	Does not apply.	To-tal.
Section 213:					
1. Regular physician	148	0	0	0	148
2. Name and address near entrance......	90	30	a27	1	148
3. Examined before admission...........	118	17	11	2	148
4. Written certificate	104	26	15	3	148
5. Filed with—					
(a) Commitment papers	69	57	b12	10	148
(b) Other papers	49	78	b14	7	148
6. Quarantine at entrance...............	97	36	c12	3	148
7. Date and length endorsed on certificate.	60	69	16	3	148
Section 214:					
8. Monthly examination—					
(a) Buildings, throughout...........	110	35	3	0	148
(b) Inmates, individually...........	111	37	0	0	148
9. Report filed—					
(a) With governing board...........	96	50	1	1	148
(b) With local board...............	92	53	2	1	148
10. Recommedations made...............	100	42	0	2	d144
11. Investigation by local board of health.	100	46	0	0	e146
Section 215:					
12. Beds separated by passageway of not less than two feet....................	63	19	66	0	148
13. Cubic space of 600 feet..............	9	79	60	0	148
14. Permits from local health board posted.	60	67	15	6	148

a Either not near main entrance or address not posted.
b Together under separate file.
c Usually, "except young infants."
d Four not reporting.
e Two not reporting.

TABLE II., A.

Cubic Air Space Per Occupant in Dormitories of Institutions Under Private Control to Which Children are Committed as Public Charges from the Boroughs of Manhattan and The Bronx.

[Dimensions from posted permits, from figures furnished by officials, and from personal measurements.]

	Lowest.	Highest.	Actual average.
American Female Guardian Society	308	589	325
Asylum of St. Vincent de Paul	303	822	314
Asylum of the Sisters of St. Dominic	367	598	454
Brace Farm School	256	372	330
Children's Fold (boys)	294	367	309
Children's Fold (girls)	252	340	294
Colored Orphan Asylum	304	744	453
Dominican Convent of Our Lady of the Rosary	303	391	326
Five Points House of Industry	300	322	317
German Odd Fellows' Home and Orphan Asylum	327	540	404
Good Counsel Reception House	306	323	321
Good Counsel Farm and Training School	309	484	378
Hebrew Benevolent and Orphan Asylum Society	600	797	676
Hebrew Infant Asylum	237	326	272
Hebrew Sheltering Guardian Society	264	441	345
Hebrew Sheltering Guardian Society (Reception House)	365	609	478
Institution of Mercy (girls)	306	398	369
Institution of Mercy (boys)	415	976	512
Mission of the Immaculate Virgin	424	466	464
Mission of the Immaculate Virgin, Mt. Loretto	371	881	549
Mission of the Immaculate Virgin, St. Benedict's	264	511	418
Missionary Sisters, Third Order, St. Francis	283	474	391
Missionary Sisters, Third Order, St. Francis (Reception House)	436	450	444
New York Catholic Protectory (boys)	297	718	404
New York Catholic Protectory (girls)	327	816	514
New York Foundling Hospital	308	634	458
New York Foundling. House of Nazareth	206	314	249
New York Infant Asylum	395	455	428
New York Infant Asylum (Country House)	340	546	496
New York Juvenile Asylum	301	658	373
Nursery and Child's Hospital	750	1,000	887
Nursery and Child's Hospital (Country Branch)	320	1,656	646
St. Ann's Home for Destitute Children	267	496	345
St. Ann's Home for Destitute Children (Mt. Florence)	521	568	544
St. Elizabeth's Industrial School	300	319	312
St. James' Home	302	315	305
St. Joseph's Orphan Asylum	201	346	288
St. Michael's Home	302	377	336
St. Agatha's Home	254	504	412
Sacred Heart Orphan Asylum	300	400	353

TABLE II., B.

Cubic Air Space Per Occupant in Dormitories of Institutions Under Private Control to Which Children are Committed as Public Charges from the Boroughs of Brooklyn, Richmond and Queens.

[Dimensions from posted permits, from figures furnished by officials, and from personal measurements.]

	Lowest.	Highest.	Actual average.
Brooklyn Children's Aid Society.................	459*	574†	574
Brooklyn Howard Colored Orphan Asylum......	382	506	448
Brooklyn Industrial Association and Home for Destitute Children	383	484	445
Brooklyn Nursery and Infant's Hospital........	215	356	209
Brooklyn Training School and Home for Young Girls	278	376	322
Convent of the Sisters of Mercy...............	192	449	336
Convent of the Sisters of Mercy (Angel Guardian Asylum)	406	652	492
Convent of the Sisters of Mercy (St. Mary's of the Angels)	250	815	298
Hebrew Orphan Asylum Society, etc............	470	583	506
House of St. Giles the Cripple.................	195	445	351
Industrial School Association of Brooklyn, E. D..	288	345	356
Orphan Asylum Society of the City of Brooklyn..	868	961	460
Ottilie Orphanage	248	422	304
Orphan Home	405	608	426
Orphan Home (Annunciation of the Blessed Virgin)	288	645	341
Orphan Home of the Sorrowful Mother.........	356	356	356
Orphan Home of the Most Holy Rosary.........	360	855	363
Orphan Home, Nazareth Trade School..........	496	624	556
Orphan Home, Sacred Heart of Jesus...........	287	287	287
Orphan Home (St. Dominic's).................	670	670	670
Orphan Home (St. Joseph's)...................	298	418	351
Orphan Home of Church Charity Foundation....	589	621	560
St. John's Home for Boys.....................	246	447	396
St. John's Roman Catholic Protectory..........	221	235	227
St. Joseph's Female Orphan Asylum............	347	487	421
St. Malachy's Home...........................	213	458	268
St. Malachy's Seaside Home...................	268	704	327
St. Malachy's Star of the Sea.................	297	684	418
St. Mary's Maternity and Infant Hospital.......	282	405	344
St. Paul's Industrial School...................	366	411	407
Sheltering Arms Nursery......................	218	588	388
Society for Aid of Friendless Women and Children	262	362	326
Temporary Home for Children, Mineola.........	390	585	474

*Figures on permit. †Figures by measurement.

46

TABLE II, C.

Cubic Air Space Per Occupant in Dormitories of Institutions Under Private Control to Which Children are Committed as Public Charges from the Eastern Inspection District (Exclusive of Greater New York. Tables A. and B.)

[Dimensions from posted permits, from figures furnished by officials, and from personal measurements.]

	Lowest.	Highest.	Actual average.
Albany Orphan Asylum..........................	560	817	589
Children's Home, Amsterdam..................	325	404	373
*Children's Home of Middletown...............	250	414	349
*Children's Home of Newburgh.................	257	1,084	470
Children's Home, Schenectady.................	612	706	708
Fairview Home Friendless Children, Watervliet.	361	616	565
Home for Friendless of North. N. Y., Plattsburg.	321	1,280	480
Hudson Orphan and Relief Association.........	365	668	582
Industrial Home of the City of Kingston........	177	300	246
Lathrop Memorial, Albany......................	290	404	333
Ogdensburg City Hospital and Orphan Asylum..	290	616	326
Poughkeepsie Orphan Home, etc................	289	987	495
St. Colman's Industrial School, etc., Watervliet..	579	886	690
St. Francis de Sales Orphan Asylum, Albany...	429	491	456
St. John's Orphan Home, Rensselaer...........	241	758	407
St. Joseph's Infant Home, Troy................	357	726	419
St. Margaret's House, Albany..................	282	582	402
St. Mary's Orphan Asylum, Port Jervis.........	252	357	313
St. Vincent's Female Orphan Asylum, Albany...	626	880	642
St. Vincent's Female Orphan Asylum, Troy.....	313	496	349
St. Vincent's Male Orphan Asylum, Albany......	487	655	554
Saratoga Home for Children....................	256	360	328
Society of the United Helpers, Ogdensburg......	397	637	434
*Suffolk County Children's Home, Yaphank....	308	552	363
Troy Catholic Male Orphan Asylum.............	415	920	456
Troy Orphan Asylum..........................	269	1,177	671
Westchester Temporary Home. White Plains....	390	779	469

* Under public control.

TABLE II., D.

Cubic Air Space Per Occupant in Dormitories of Institutions Under Private Control to Which Children are Committed as Public Charges from the Western Inspection District.

[Dimensions from posted permits, from figures furnished by officials, and from personal measurements.]

	Lowest.	Highest.	Actual average.
Auburn Orphan Asylum.........................	177	582	308
Asylum of Our Lady of Refuge, Buffalo.........	327	463	387
Buffalo Children's Aid Society...................	432	522	460
Buffalo Orphan Asylum.........................	234	582	341
Cayuga Asylum for Destitute Children, Auburn.	391	675	546
Charity Foundation of P. E. Church, Buffalo...	401	666	529
Evang'l Luth. St. John's Orphan Home, Buffalo.	419	763	607
George Junior Republic, Freeville..............	204	991	480
German Roman Catholic Orphan Asylum, Buffalo	297	702	502
Gustavus Adolphus Orphans' Home, Jamestown.	318	528	433
Home for the Friendless, Lockport.............	380	563	434
House of Providence of Onondaga Co., Syracuse	509	977	636
House of the Good Shepherd, Utica.............	282	373	330
Ithaca Children's Home........................	261	357	307
Jewish Orphan Asylum, Rochester.............	360	618	501
Jefferson County Orphan Asylum, Watertown...	450	626	557
*Madison County Orphan Asylum, Peterboro....	194	403	276
Onondaga County Orphan Asylum, Syracuse....	424	858	621
Orphan House and Industrial School of the Holy Saviour, Cooperstown.........................	230	396	311
Orphanage and Home, Free Meth. Church, Gerry	396	675	498
Ontario Orphan Asylum, Canandaigua..........	567	811	587
Oswego Orphan Asylum.........................	376	668	534
Protestant Episcopal Church Home, Rochester..	368	764	494
Rochester Orphan Asylum......................	450	675	517
Rochester Benevolent Industrial and Scientific School, Sisters of Mercy (Crèche).............	227	564	317
Sacred Heart of Mary Asylum, Buffalo.........	222	330	264
St. Francis Home, Oswego......................	333	567	372
St. John's Female Orphan Asylum, Utica.......	311	618	402
St. Joseph's Infant Home, Utica................	291	416	367
St. Joseph's Male Orphan Asylum, West Seneca.	438	569	511
St. Joseph's Orphan Asylum, Corning..........	1,680	1,680	1,680
St. Joseph's Orphan Asylum Society............	433	827	503
St. Mary's Boys' Orphan Asylum, Rochester....	319	735	633
St. Mary's Catholic Orphans' Home, Binghamton	352	787	496
St. Mary's Home and School, Dunkirk..........	455	744	620
St. Mary's Infant Asylum and Maternity Hospital, Buffalo	434	774	601
St. Mary's Maternity & Infant Hospital, Syracuse	330	790	462
St. Patrick's Orphanage, Watertown...........	472	867	648
St. Patrick's Orphan Girls' Asylum, Rochester..	446	529	473
St. Vincent's Female Orphan Asylum, Buffalo..	441	609	521
St. Vincent's Industrial School, Utica...........	384	925	597
St. Vincent's Orphan Asylum, Syracuse.........	585	1,010	772
Society for the Protection of Destitute Roman Catholic Children, West Seneca.............	396	776	539
Southern Tier Orphans' Home, Elmira..........	620	1,505	814
Susquehanna Valley Home, Binghamton........	228	720	455
Utica Orphan Asylum..........................	376	924	582
Western New York Society for the Protection of Homeless and Destitute Children, Randolph...	205	474	297
Syracuse Hospital for Women and Children.....	882	1,000	937

* Under public control.

SUMMARY OF TABLE II.

Showing the number of institutions in which the average cubic air space per occupant is:

CUBIC FEET.	In institutions receiving commitments from New York city.	In other institutions of the State.	Total.
200–250	2	1	8
250–300	7	8	10
300–350	20	12	82
350–400	11	5	16
400–450	12	7	19
450–500	9	14	23
500–550	5	11	16
550–600	3	7	10
600– +	5	14	19
	74	74	148

	N. Y. city.	E. I. D.[*]	W. I. D.[†]	Total[*]
I. Initial quarantine:				
1. Length:				
0 days	2	11	21	34
1 to 5 days	3	4	3	10
7 to 8 days	1	1	5	7
9 days	4	0	2	6
10 days	25	4	5	34
14 days	29	6	4	39
15 days	6	1	0	7
21 days	3	0	0	3
Indefinite	0	0	8	8
	73	27	48	148
2. Facilities for quarantine:				
Separate building	36	6	2	44
Separate suite of rooms	25	8	25	58
Entire time	60	13	21	94
Dormitory only	2	0	2	4
Same dining, school or play room	3	1	6	10
Does not apply	10	13	21	44
II. Visiting:				
1. Frequency:				
No visiting	2	0	0	2
No limit[‡]	11	8	28	47
Three times a week	1	1	2	4
Twice a week	2	0	6	8
Once a week	5	1	6	12
Twice a month	13	3	5	21
Once a month	24	11	1	36
Once in two to three months	3	0	0	3
Not ascertained	12	3	0	15
	73	27	48	148
2. Place:				
Separate building	3	0	0	3
Special room	35	15	32	82
Play, dining or other common room	33	12	16	61
Living rooms, admitted	19	20	36	75
Living rooms, prohibited	50	7	12	69
Infirmary (non-contagious), admitted	59	22	38	119
Infirmary (non-contagious), prohibited	6	2	10	18
No information, or does not apply	8	3	0	11
3. Restrictions:				
Prohibited localities or times	12	12	15	39
Age limit	19	3	4	26
Food prohibited	19	1	5	25
Fruit prohibited	13	1	1	15
Candy prohibited	19	2	5	26
Clothing prohibited or sterilized	21	1	32	54
Clothing, only new accepted	16	7	3	26
Distribution supervised	67	23	41	131

[*]Eastern Inspection District, exclusive of Greater New York.
[†]Western Inspection District.
[‡]In many cases restricted as to days or hours.

TABLE IV.

Methods of Control.

	N. Y. city.	E. I. D.*	W. I. D.†	Total.
I. During prevalence:				
1. Cases removed to hospital:				
Scarlet fever	24	4	12	40
Diphtheria	24	4	15	43
Measles	15	4	7	26
2. Separate room for each disease	15	2	3	20
3. One room or suite for all contagion	59	28	41	123
(a) Separate pavilion	25	13	8	46
(b) Outside access or separable hall	36	18	24	78
(c) General infirmary	13	5	6	24
(d) Attendants strictly isolated from other inmates only	4	3	12	19
(e) Attendants strictly isolated from other attendants	61	23	27	111
4. No provisions for quarantine:				
(a) Dormitory set aside	2	2	3	7
(b) Not quarantined:				
Measles	3	2	6	11
Mumps	1	1	1	3
Chicken pox	2	2	4	8
Whooping-cough	1	2	5	8
5. Length of quarantine, individual cases:				
Scarlet fever { 21 days	8	4	3	15
{ 42 days	1	0	0	1
Desquamation ceased	16	3	5	24
Desquamation ceased+7-14 days	6	1	0	7
Decided by doctor or board of health	2	1	2	5
{ 6-7 days	1	1	0	2
14 days	2	1	1	4
Diphtheria, { 21 days	5	2	2	9
30 days	1	2	1	4
{ 42 days	3	0	0	3
Sterile culture	12	3	4	19
Sterile culture+7-14 days	3	0	1	4
Decided by doctor or board of health	2	1	2	5
{ 6-7 days	4	0	3	7
14 days	5	1	1	7
Measles, { 21 days	10	4	4	18
30 days	4	0	2	6
{ 42 days	1	1	0	2
Desquamation or catarrhal symptoms ceased, or longer	12	1	5	18
Decided by doctor or board of health	9	7	2	18
II. Disinfection:				
1. Fumigation:				
Material:				
Sulphur only	59	14	29	102
Formaldehyde	7	4	11	22
Both	17	3	5	25
Quantity per 1,000 cubic feet:				
Sulphur:				
Less than 1 pound	11	5	11	27
One to three pounds	10	3	4	17
Three to five pounds	12	2	4	18
Not stated	10	1	8	19
Board of health	4	6	3	13

* Eastern Inspection District, exclusive of Greater New York.
† Western Inspection District.

TABLE IV—(*Continued*).

METHODS OF CONTROL.

	N.Y.city.	E. I. D.*	W. I. D.†	Total.
Formaldehyde, in general, according to formula with generator.				
2. Walls and floors:				
Disinfectant solutions	45	15	28	88
Repainting, whitewashing, etc.......	5	6	7	18
3. Bedding and clothing:				
Destroyed	27	8	7	42
Fumigated only	4	1	1	6
Sterilized	54	17	39	110

*Eastern Inspection District, exclusive of Greater New York.
†Western Inspection District.

TABLE V.

Outbreaks of Contagion.

I. Circumstances of first appearance:	N. Y. city.	E. I. D.*	W. I. D.†	Total.‡
1. Introduced by new child...............	44	14	28	86
Less than one week..................	22	6	16	44
In quarantine	15	3	7	25
Less than two weeks................	22	4	9	35
In quarantine	15	2	5	22
2. Introduced through public schools......	9	9	7	25
School in institution.................	56	17	35	108
3. Introduced through visitors............	18	3	7	28
Also suspected but not traced........	15	5	7	27
4. Introduced through excursions, entertainments, church, Sunday school, etc.	1	3	4	8
5. Walking in streets or parks or going on errands	2	1	5	8
6. "Germs in air" from cases in neighboring tenements or on adjoining premises	3	1	7	11
7. Visits to home or friends..............	0	1	7	8
8. Other causes	20	9	12	41
II. Circumstances of spreading:				
1. Apparently common source of infection.	30	13	28	71
2. Communicated before diagnosis........	37	18	29	84
3. Confined to one dormitory or "set" of children	26	8	11	45
All mingle in school or play..........	28	10	31	69
4. Contact of infirmary attendants with well children	2	4	3	9
Contact of infirmary attendants with well children, suspected only........	2	0	4	6
5. Other causes	14	4	11	29
Institutions in which no disease has spread	10	3	4	17

*Eastern Inspection District, exclusive of Greater New York.
†Western Inspection District.
‡The figures in this table refer, not to the total number of times, but to the number of institutions in which each cause has occurred.

Manual Containing the Constitutional Provisions and the Laws which Have Relation to the Work of the State Board of Charities, and the Rules and the By-Laws of the Board.

THE STATE BOARD OF CHARITIES.*

By article VIII. of the Constitution of the State of New York, adopted in 1894, the State Board of Charities, created in 1867, became a constitutional body January 1, 1895. Such Constitution provides that the Board shall visit and inspect all institutions, whether State, county, municipal, incorporated or not incorporated, which are of a charitable, eleemosynary, correctional or reformatory character, including institutions for epileptics and idiots, and all reformatories (save those in which adult males, convicted of felony, shall be confined), and excepting institutions for the care and treatment of the insane, and for the detention of adults charged with or convicted of crime, or detained as witnesses and debtors.

The Constitution also provides that the members of the Board shall be appointed by the Governor, by and with the advice and consent of the Senate, and all existing laws relating to institutions above mentioned, and to their supervision and inspection, in so far as such laws are not inconsistent with the provisions of the Constitution, shall remain in force, and that the Legislature may confer upon the Board any additional powers. It further provides that while payments by counties, cities, towns and villages to charitable, eleemosynary, correctional or reformatory institutions, wholly or partly under private control, for care, support and maintenance, may be authorised but shall not be required by the Legislature, no such payments shall be made for any such inmate of such institution who is not received and retained therein pursuant to rules established by the State Board of Charities.

The Commissioners comprising the Board are twelve in number, and are appointed for the term of eight years, one from each judicial district of the State, one additional member from the county of Kings, and three additional members from the county of New York. The Commissioners are required to reside in the districts from which they are respectively appointed, and no Commissioner can act as such while a trustee, director or other administrative officer of any of the institutions subject to the visitation and inspection of the Board.

The principal duties of the Board are to visit, inspect and maintain a general supervision of all institutions, societies or associations which are of a charitable, eleemosynary, correctional or reformatory character, whether State or municipal, incorporated or not incorporated, made subject to its jurisdiction by the Constitution and the statutes. Other duties are to frame rules for the reception and retention of inmates and to approve or disapprove the organisation and incorporation of all institutions which are or shall be subject to the supervision and inspection of the Board.

The chief officers of the Board are a President and a Vice-President, elected annually from its members.

Each Commissioner receives as compensation ten dollars for each day's attendance at meetings of the Board or any of its committees, not to exceed $800 in a year to any commissioner, and is also paid his expenses while engaged, and his outlay for any aid or assistance rendered, in the performance of his duties. The Board is required to report to the Legislature annually. The seal of the office is the Arms of the State surrounded by the inscription, " State of New York — The State Board of Charities."

*From the Legislative Manual of 1902.

THE COMMISSIONERS AND OFFICERS

OF THE

State Board of Charities.

1902.

COMMISSIONERS APPOINTED BY THE GOVERNOR. NAMES AND
RESIDENCES.

First Judicial District.—WILLIAM R. STEWART, 31 Nassau
street, New York.

New York County.—STEPHEN SMITH, M. D., 640 Madison
avenue, New York.

New York County.—ANNIE G. DE PEYSTER, 101 West Eighty-
first street, New York.

New York County.—MICHAEL J. SCANLAN, 56 Pine street,
New York.

*Second Judicial District.**

Kings County.—JOHN NOTMAN, 136 Joralemon street, Brooklyn.

Third Judicial District.—SIMON W. ROSENDALE, 57 State
street, Albany.

Fourth Judicial District.—NEWTON ALDRICH, Gouverneur,
St. Lawrence county.

Fifth Judicial District.—DENNIS McCARTHY, 219 South
Salina street, Syracuse.

*Sixth Judicial District.**

Seventh Judicial District.—ENOCH VINE STODDARD, M. D.,
62 State street, Rochester.

Eighth Judicial District.—WILLIAM H. GRATWICK, 877 Elli-
cott square, Buffalo.

---

*Vacant.

OFFICERS.

WILLIAM RHINELANDER STEWART, President.

ENOCH VINE STODDARD, M. D., Vice-President.

ROBERT W. HEBBERD, Secretary.

BYRON M. CHILD, Superintendent of State and Alien Poor.

WALTER S. UFFORD, Superintendent of Inspection.

GENERAL OFFICES OF THE BOARD.

THE CAPITOL, Albany, N. Y.

     Hours: 9 A. M. to 5 P. M. On Saturdays to 12 M.

ROBERT W. HEBBERD, Secretary.

The Secretary has general supervision of the employes and of all branches of the Board's work.

EMPLOYES OF THE GENERAL OFFICE.

WELLINGTON D. IVES, Chief Clerk.

ELLEN L. TENNEY, Statistician.

WILLIAM C. HINCKLEY, Stenographer.

LILIAN SCHLESINGER, Clerk.

DEPARTMENT OF STATE AND ALIEN POOR.

This department has supervision of the State, Alien and Indian dependent classes, and performs the duties required by law or prescribed by the Board for their final care and settlement; it is also charged with the inspection of the State charitable and reformatory institutions, the almshouses and other municipal institutions which report to the Board, and the foster homes of children placed out in families.

BYRON M. CHILD, Superintendent, The Capitol, Albany, N. Y.

HENRY D. KERR, Deputy Superintendent, 287 Fourth avenue, New York city.

ROBERT W. HILL, Inspector of State Institutions, The Capitol, Albany, N. Y.

CYRUS C. LATHROP, Inspector of Almshouses, The Capitol, Albany, N. Y.

EBEN P. DORR, Inspector of Almshouses, The Capitol, Albany, N. Y.

GEORGE McLEOD, Agent, Eastern Department, Blackwell's Island Almshouse, New York city.

SEWARD WIKOFF, Agent, Western Department, 241 Terrace, Buffalo, N. Y.

GEORGIA L. FANNING, Private Secretary to Superintendent of State and Alien Poor.

ANNA MITCHELL, Stenographer.

DEPARTMENT OF INSPECTION.

This department has charge of the visitation and inspection of all institutions, societies or associations which are of a charitable, eleemosynary, correctional or reformatory character, excepting state and municipal institutions and those having the custody of State, Alien and Indian poor.

WALTER S. UFFORD, Superintendent of Inspection, The Capitol, Albany, N. Y.

JULIA S. HOAG, Clerk.

IONA KARKER, Stenographer.

CHARLES L. GEHNRICH, Clerk.

FANNIE G. SCHLESINGER, Junior Clerk.

EASTERN INSPECTION DISTRICT.
Office, 287 Fourth avenue, New York city.
Hours: 9 A. M. to 5 P. M. On Saturdays to 12 M.

FRANK KUNZMANN, Superintendent.

HENRY M. LECHTRECKER, Inspector.

JOHN B. PREST, Inspector.

MARY S. OPPENHEIMER, Inspector.

L. ELIZABETH THACHER, Inspector.

KATE F. CAHILL, Stenographer.

CHARLES E. MUHLEISER, Page.

WESTERN INSPECTION DISTRICT.
Office, 853 Powers Building, Rochester, N. Y.
Hours: 9 A. M. to 5 P. M. On Saturdays to 12 M.

WILLIS L. WEEDEN, Superintendent.

KATHARINE M. RULISON, Stenographer.

EXTRACTS FROM THE CONSTITUTION

Of the State of New York Relating to the State Board of Charities.

ARTICLE VIII.

•　　•　•　　•　　•　　•　　•　　•　　•

§ 11. The legislature shall provide for a state board of charities, which shall visit and inspect all institutions, whether state,
county, municipal, incorporated or not incorporated, which are
of a charitable, eleemosynary, correctional or reformatory character, excepting only such institutions as are hereby made subject to the visitation and inspection of either of the commissions
hereinafter mentioned, but including all reformatories except
those in which adult males convicted of felony shall be confined;
a state commission in lunacy, which shall visit and inspect all
institutions, either public or private, used for the care and treatment of the insane (not including institutions for epileptics or
idiots); a state commission of prisons which shall visit and inspect all institutions used for the detention of sane adults
charged with or convicted of crime, or detained as witnesses or
debtors.

1. CORPORATIONS—WHEN CHARITABLE IN NATURE—CAPACITY TO TAKE
CHARITABLE GIFTS. The capacity of a corporation to take and administer charitable gifts does not imply that the corporation must necessarily
be of a charitable nature.

2. EXEMPTION FROM TAXATION AS INDICATION OF CHARITABLE NATURE
OF CORPORATION. The exemption from taxation given by chapter 553 of
the Laws of 1890 to societies for the prevention of cruelty to children
does not show that the New York Society for the Prevention of Cruelty
to Children is of the class designated as charitable, since charitable institutions were already exempt, and the statute was not necessary if this
corporation belonged to that class, and, moreover, exemption from taxation is a privilege frequently conferred by the legislature upon corporations with no charitable features whatever.

3. CORPORATION RECEIVING MONEY FROM CITY TREASURY. In receiving
and disbursing the money which is annually given from the city treasury
to the New York Society for the Prevention of Cruelty to Children that
corporation does not receive or administer any charity, but only takes an
allowance from the city for doing work that otherwise would devolve
upon the police department.

4. NEW YORK SOCIETY FOR THE PREVENTION OF CRUELTY TO CHILDREN—PURPOSE AND CHARACTER OF—NOT SUBJECT TO VISITATION BY STATE BOARD OF CHARITIES. The New York Society for the Prevention of Cruelty to Children, organized under chapter 130 of the Laws of 1875, for the prevention of cruelty to children and the enforcement by all lawful means of the laws relating to or in any wise affecting children, is not a charitable institution within the scope of sections 11 to 14 of article 8 of the Constitution, chapter 771 of the Laws of 1895 and chapter 546 of the Laws of 1896, giving to the State Board of Charities the right of visitation with respect to all charitable institutions, since it receives no public money for charitable uses and administers no charity in any legal sense, but exists for the sole purpose of enforcing the criminal laws to prevent cruelty to children, although the corporation, as a mere incident of its work, feeds, clothes and cares for children temporarily while detained as witnesses or victims of cruelty pending the prosecution of the offenders in the courts.

5. STATE SUPERVISION OF CHARITABLE INSTITUTIONS—EXTENT OF. The scheme of state supervision of charitable institutions under the Constitution and statutes was not intended to apply to every institution engaged in some good or commendable work for the relief of humanity from some of the various ills with which it is afflicted, but only to those corporations, public or private, maintained in whole or in part by the state, or some of its political divisions, through which charity, as such, is dispensed by public authority to those having a claim upon the generosity or bounty of the state. *People ex rel. State Board of Charities v. New York Society for Prevention of Cruelty to Children*, 16 N. Y. (42 App. Div. 83, reversed).

1. CORPORATIONS, WHEN CHARITABLE. A charitable institution, within the meaning of sections 11 to 14 of article 8 of the Constitution, chapter 771 of the Laws of 1895, and chapter 546 of the Laws of 1896, giving to the State Board of Charities the right of visitation with respect to all charitable institutions, is one that in some form or to some extent receives public money for the support and maintenance of indigent persons, and by public money is meant money raised by taxation not only in the State at large, but in any city, county or town. *People ex rel. State Board of Charities v. The New York Society for the Prevention of Cruelty to Children*, 162 N. Y., 429.

2. PRIVATE CHARITABLE INSTITUTION NOT SUBJECT TO STATE INSPECTION. A purely private institution, which, without any compensation from the public, cares for or maintains indigent adults or children who voluntarily seek it as a home, or who remain there voluntarily, is not subject to State inspection or regulation. *Id.*

In that case (161 N. Y. 233) the only question before the court was whether the defendant was an institution of "charitable, eleemosynary, correctional or reformatory" character within the nomenclature of section 11, article VIII of the Constitution, and, therefore, subject to the visitation of the State Board of Charities, a question not at all involved in this case. *For v. Mohawk and Hudson River Humane Society*, 165 N. Y. 517.

§ 12. The members of the said board and of the said commissions shall be appointed by the governor, by and with the advice and consent of the senate; and any member may be removed from office by the governor for cause, an opportunity having been given him to be heard in his defense.

§ 13. Existing laws relating to institutions referred to in the foregoing sections and to their supervision and inspection, in so far as such laws are not inconsistent with the provisions of the constitution, shall remain in force until amended or repealed by the legislature. The visitation and inspection herein provided for, shall not be exclusive of other visitation and inspection now authorized by law.

§ 14. Nothing in this constitution contained shall prevent the legislature from making such provision for the education and support of the blind, the deaf and dumb, and juvenile delinquents, as to it may seem proper; or prevent any county, city, town or village from providing for the care, support, maintenance and secular education of inmates of orphan asylums, homes for dependent children or correctional institutions, whether under public or private control. Payments by counties, cities, towns and villages to charitable, eleemosynary, correctional and reformatory institutions, wholly or partly under private control, for care, support and maintenance, may be authorized, but shall not be required by the legislature. No such payments shall be made for any inmate of such institutions who is not received and retained therein pursuant to rules established by the state board of charities. Such rules shall be subject to the control of the legislature by general laws.

PRIVATE CHARITABLE INSTITUTIONS—EFFECT OF NEW CONSTITUTION UPON STATUTORY LOCAL AID FROM PUBLIC MONEYS. The Constitution of 1894 did not of itself annul and render inoperative mandatory provisions in existing statutes requiring the payment by localities of public moneys to private charitable institutions, by force of the new provision (art. 8, § 14), that such payments "may be authorized, but shall not be required by the Legislature;" but its effect was to leave such statutory provisions in force until superseded by subsequent legislation. *People ex rel. The Inebriates' Home for Kings County v. The Comptroller of the City of Brooklyn,* 152 N. Y., 399.

LIMITATION ON FUTURE LEGISLATION. The above provision of the Constitution is a mere limitation on future legislative action, and was not intended to forbid the operation of existing laws. *Id.*

NON-ABROGATION OF ADMINISTRATIVE DUTY OF PAYMENT OF PUBLIC MONEYS TO PRIVATE CHARITABLE INSTITUTION. The above provision of the Constitution did not abrogate the purely administrative duty imposed upon the comptroller of the city of Brooklyn by chapter 169, Laws of 1877, of paying a portion of the excise moneys to the Inebriates' Home for Kings County, a private charitable and reformatory institution. *Id.*

REQUIREMENT OF COMPLIANCE WITH RULES OF STATE BOARD OF CHARITIES. The new provision of the Constitution of 1894 (art. 8, § 14), that no payments of public moneys by localities to private charitable institutions shall be made for any inmate who is not received and retained "pursuant to rules established by the State Board of Charities," operated presently, so that from the time rules should be established by the State Board on the subject, no payments would be justified for inmates received or retained, in contravention of the rules of the board. *Id.*

FAILURE OF PRIVATE CHARITABLE INSTITUTION TO EARN PUBLIC MONEYS. The courts will not compel the payment to a private charitable institution of public moneys authorized to be paid only for the current support of inmates during the period when the fund accrued, where it appears that the institution had to a great extent ceased its operations and had not, except to a limited extent, performed the service which was the consideration of the payment to be made out of the public funds. *Id.*

People ex rel. Inebriates' Home v. Comptroller (11 App. Div. 114), affirmed.

CHARITABLE INSTITUTIONS—SUPERVISION OF STATE BOARD OF CHARITIES. It is not necessary that an institution should be wholly charitable to fall within the provisions of the Constitution (art. 8, §§ 11–15) and the statutes (L. 1895, chaps. 754, 771) placing charitable institutions under the supervision and rules of the State Board of Charities. It is enough if the institution is partly charitable in its character and purpose. *People ex rel. the New York Institution for the Blind v. Fitch, Comptroller of the City of New York,* 154 N. Y., 14.

EDUCATIONAL AND CHARITABLE INSTITUTION. The mere fact that an institution is partly educational does not exclude it from the provisions of the Constitution and statutes placing charitable institutions under the supervision and rules of the State Board of Charities. If an institution is both educational and charitable, it falls within those provisions. *Id.*

INSTITUTIONS FOR INSTRUCTION OF THE BLIND. The fact that institutions for the instruction of the blind are subject to the visitation of the Superintendent of Public Instruction (L. 1894, chap. 556, tit. 15, art. 14) does not prevent such an institution from being charitable in its character and purpose, and, hence, also subject to the visitation of the State Board of Charities (Const., art. 8, § 13). *Id.*

MEANING OF "CHARITABLE." The word "charitable," as used in the provisions of the Constitution and the statutes subjecting charitable institutions to the supervision and rules of the State Board of Charities, is to be given only its usual and ordinary meaning. *Id.*

INSTITUTION FOR THE BLIND—CHARITABLE IN PART. The New York Institution for the Blind, an institution under private control, organized in 1831 (chap. 214) for the special education of the blind, is to be regarded as a charitable institution so far as it clothes, educates and maintains indigent pupils at public expense or by donations from individuals; and as to such pupils, it is subject to the supervision and rules of the State Board of Charities. *Id.*

INSTITUTION EDUCATIONAL IN PART. Such institution, so far as it educates pupils who pay for their tuition, board and maintenance, is not to be regarded as a charitable, but only as an educational institution, and as to those pupils the Board of Charities has no jurisdiction or power of supervision.

INSTITUTION OF CHARITABLE CHARACTER. Such institution, being to an extent charitable as well as educational, falls within the provisions of the Constitution and statutes as an institution of a charitable character or design. *Id.*

STATE MAINTENANCE OF FREE EDUCATION. The provision of the Constitution (art. 9, § 1), that "the Legislature shall provide for the maintenance and support of a system of free common schools, wherein all the children of this State may be educated," relates only to the public or common schools of the State, and has no application to appropriations made by the State to an institution for the education of the blind, wholly or partly under private control. *Id.*

STATE AID TO PRIVATE EDUCATION OF THE BLIND. Appropriations by the Legislature to a local or private institution, for the education and support of the blind, are based upon and authorized by the provisions of the Constitution (art. 8, § 10 of 1874; § 9 of 1894) which prescribe that the prohibition of State aid to any association, corporation or private undertaking shall not prevent the Legislature from making such provision for the education and support of the blind as to it may seem proper. *Id.*

PAST APPROPRIATIONS NOT VIOLATIVE OF THE CONSTITUTION. It does not follow that, if the New York Institution for the Blind is charitable, appropriations made to it in the past by the State for the education and support of pupils, and appropriations made by the counties of New York and Kings (under L. 1870, chap. 166, § 3) of the sums required for clothing the indigent pupils who were residents of the county making the appropriation were violative of the Constitution (art. 8, §§ 8, 11, of 1874). *Id.*

MANDATORY APPROPRIATION. The charitable character of the New York Institution for the Blind is not changed if the provisions of the statute (L. 1870, chap. 166, § 3) requiring the counties of New York and Kings to appropriate money to clothe indigent pupils is mandatory, and hence in conflict with the Constitution of 1894 (art. 8, § 14), which is not decided. *Id.*

PARTICIPATION IN PUBLIC SCHOOL FUND. It does not follow from the fact that the charter of Greater New York (L. 1897, chap. 378, § 1161), authorizes the board of education to distribute a ratable proportion of the school fund to every pupil in the New York Institution for the Blind, that the institution must be regarded as purely educational and not charitable. *Id.*

PUBLIC PAYMENTS TO CHARITABLE INSTITUTIONS. The Legislature can not now authorize a locality to pay, nor can a locality in any case pay its money to a charitable institution, wholly or partly under private control, for the care, support and maintenance of inmates who are not received and retained pursuant to the rules established by the State Board of Charities. (Const. 1894, art. 8, § 14.) *Id.*

PAYMENT DEPENDENT UPON OBSERVANCE OF RULES OF BOARD OF CHARITIES. The New York Institution for the Blind being, to an extent, a charitable institution and, so far as it is charitable, subject to the visitation and rules of the State Board of Charities, no payment can be properly made to it from the moneys of the city and county of New York for the maintenance or support, including clothing, of any indigent inmate not received and retained by it pursuant to the rules of that board. *Id.*

People ex rel. Inst. for the Blind v. *Fitch*, 12 App. Div. 581, reversed.

CHARITABLE INSTITUTIONS—PAYMENTS OF PUBLIC MONEYS TO INSTITUTIONS WHOLLY OR PARTLY UNDER PRIVATE CONTROL—RULES OF THE STATE BOARD OF CHARITIES. A municipal corporation is prohibited by the Constitution (art. 8, § 14) and the statutes (L. 1895, ch. 754; L. 1896, ch. 546, § 9, subd. 8) from paying public moneys to a charitable institution wholly or partly under private control, for the care, support and maintenance of inmates who are not received and retained therein pursuant to the rules established by the State Board of Charities for the purpose of determining whether such inmates are properly a public charge. In re application of New York Juvenile Asylum, appellant, for a writ of mandamus, John W. Keller, as commissioner of public charities in the city of New York, respondent, 172 N. Y., 50.

NEW YORK JUVENILE ASYLUM—CHARTER PROVISION REQUIRING PAYMENT BY THE CITY AND COUNTY OF NEW YORK FOR THE SUPPORT OF INMATES NOT COMMITTED TO IT IN ACCORDANCE WITH RULES OF STATE BOARD OF CHARITIES, SUPERCEDED BY THE CONSTITUTION. The fact that the New York Juvenile Asylum, a private charitable institution, was authorized by its charter (L. 1851, ch. 332) to take under its care the management of such children as should by consent, in writing, of their parents or guardians, be voluntarily surrendered and intrusted to it, and by section 28 of chapter 245 of the Laws of 1866 might require the county of New York to pay annually a specified sum for the support of children so committed to it, which section was incorporated into the charter of Greater New York (L. 1897, ch. 378, § 230) and has not in terms been repealed, amended or modified, does not authorize the city and county of New York to pay for the support and maintenance of any inmate not received and retained therein pursuant to the rules of the State Board of Charities, since such payment is prohibited, not by the rules affecting the repeal or amendment of the statute conferring the right thereto, but by the Constitution itself, which superseded the statute and operated presently from the time the rules were established. *Id.*

Matter of New York Juvenile Asylum, 69 App. Div. 615, affirmed.

§ 15. Commissioners of the state board of charities and commissioners of the state commission in lunacy, now holding office, shall be continued in office for the term for which they were appointed, respectively, unless the legislature shall otherwise provide. The legislature may confer upon the commissions and upon the board mentioned in the foregoing sections any additional powers that are not inconsistent with other provisions of the constitution.

STATUTE LAWS.

AN ACT relating to State Charities, constituting chapter 26 of the General Laws.

Chapter 546 of the Laws of 1896, as amended by chapters 437 of the Laws of 1897; 359 and 536 of the Laws of 1898; 368, 504 and 632 of the Laws of 1899; 49 of the Laws of 1900, and 252 and 356 of the Laws of 1902.

STATE CHARITIES LAW.

ARTICLE I.

STATE BOARD OF CHARITIES.

Section 1. Short title.—This chapter shall be known as the state charities law.

§ 2. Definitions.—The term state charitable institutions, when used in this chapter, shall include all institutions of a charitable, eleemosynary, correctional or reformatory character, supported in whole or in part by the state, except institutions for the instruction of the deaf and dumb and the blind, and such institutions which, by section eleven, article eight of the constitution, are made subject to the visitation and inspection of the commission in lunacy or the prison commission, whether managed or controlled by the state or by private corporations, societies or associations.

§ 3. State board of charities.—There shall continue to be a state board of charities, composed of twelve members, who shall be appointed by the governor, by and with the advice and consent of the senate, one of whom shall be appointed from and reside in each judicial district of the state, one additional member from the county of Kings, and three additional members from the county of New York, who shall respectively reside in such counties. They shall be known as commissioners of the state board of charities, and hold office for eight years. No commissioner shall qualify or enter upon the duties of his office, or remain therein, while he is a trustee, manager, director or other administrative officer of an institution subject to the visitation and inspection of such board. The commissioners in office at the time this chapter takes effect, shall continue in office for the terms for which they were respectively appointed. (As amended by chapter 437 of the Laws of 1897.)

§ 4. Officers of the board.— The board may elect a president, and vice-president from its own members, and shall appoint and continue to have a secretary, and may appoint such other officers, inspectors and clerks as it may deem necessary or proper and fix their compensation, who shall respectively hold their office during the pleasure of the board.

§ 5. Compensation and expenses of commissioners.— The compensation of each commissioner, in recognition of the provisions of the constitution, is fixed at ten dollars for each day's attendance at meetings of the board or of any of its committees, not exceeding in any one year the sum of five hundred dollars. The expenses of each commissioner, necessarily incurred while engaged in the performance of the duties of his office, and his outlay for any assistance that may have been required in the performance of such duties, on the same being paid out and certified by the commissioner making the charge, shall be paid by the treasurer, on the warrant of the comptroller.

§ 6. Meetings and effect of non-attendance.—The board may adopt rules and orders, regulating the discharge of its functions and defining the duties of its officers. It shall, by rule, provide for holding stated and special meetings. Six members regularly convened shall constitute a quorum. The failure on the part of any commissioner to attend three consecutive meetings of the board during any calendar year, unless excused by a formal vote of the board, may be treated by the governor as a resignation by such non-attending commissioner and the governor may appoint his successor. The annual reports of the board shall give the names of commissioners present at each of its meetings.

§ 7. Office room and supplies.—The trustees of public buildings shall furnish and assign to such board, in the capitol, at Albany, suitably furnished rooms for its office and place of holding meetings, and the comptroller shall furnish it with all necessary journals, account books, blanks and stationery.

§ 8. Official seal, certificates and subpœnas.—The board shall cause a record to be kept of its proceedings by its secretary or other proper officer, and it shall have and use an official seal; and the records, its proceedings and copies of all papers and documents in its possession and custody may be authenticated in the usual form, under such seal and the signature of its president or secretary, and shall be received in evidence in the same manner and with like effects as deeds regularly acknowledged or proven; it may issue subpœnas, which, when authenticated by its president and secretary, shall be obeyed and enforced in the same manner as obedience is enforced to an order or mandate made by a court of record.

§ 9. General powers and duties of board.—The state board of charities shall visit, inspect and maintain a general supervision of all institutions, societies or associations which are of a charitable, eleemosynary, correctional or reformatory character, whether state or municipal, incorporated or not incorporated, which are made subject to its supervision by the constitution or by law; and shall,

1. Aid in securing the just, humane and economic administration of all institutions subject to its supervision.

2. Advise the officers of such institutions in the performance of their official duties.

3. Aid in securing the erection of suitable buildings for the accommodation of the inmates of such institutions aforesaid.

4. Approve or disapprove the organisation and incorporation of all institutions of a charitable, eleemosynary, correctional or reformatory character which are or shall be subject to the supervision and inspection of the board.

5. Investigate the management of all institutions made subject to the supervision of the board, and the conduct and efficiency of the officers or persons charged with their management, and the care and relief of the inmates of such institutions therein or in transit.

6. Aid in securing the best sanitary condition of the buildings and grounds of all such institutions, and advise measures for the protection and preservation of the health of the inmates.

7. Aid in securing the establishment and maintenance of such industrial, educational and moral training in institutions having the care of children as is best suited to the needs of the inmates.

8. Establish rules for the reception and retention of inmates of all institutions which, by section fourteen of article eight of the constitution, are subject to its supervision.

People ex rel. Inebriates' Home for Kings County v. Comptroller of the City of Brooklyn, 152 N. Y. 399. *People ex rel. New York Institution for the Blind v. Comptroller of the City of New York,* 164 N. Y. 14; *In re application of the New York Juvenile Asylum, appellant, for a writ of mandamus, John W. Keller, as commissioner of public charities in the city of New York,* respondent, 172 N. Y. 50. For notes on these cases see pages 736, 737, 738, 739 and 740.

9. Investigate the condition of the poor seeking public aid and advise measures for their relief.

10. Administer the laws providing for the care, support and removal of state and alien poor and the support of Indian poor persons.

11. Collect statistical information in respect to the property, receipts and expenditures of all institutions, societies and associations subject to its supervision, and the number and condition of the inmates thereof, and of the poor receiving public relief.

§ 10. Visitation, inspection and supervision of institutions.—
All institutions of a charitable, eleemosynary, reformatory or

correctional character or design, including reformatories (except those now under the supervision and subject to the inspection of the prison commission), but including all reformatories, except those in which adult males convicted of felony shall be confined, asylums and institutions for idiots and epileptics, almshouses, orphan asylums, and all asylums, hospitals and institutions, whether state, county, municipal, incorporated or not incorporated, private or otherwise, except institutions for the custody, care and treatment of the insane, are subject to the visitation, inspection and supervision of the state board of charities, its members, officers and inspectors. Such institutions may be visited and inspected by such board, or any member, officer or inspector duly appointed by it for that purpose, at any and all times.

People ex rel. State Board of Charities v. New York Society for the Prevention of Cruelty to Children, 161 N. Y. 233; 162 N. Y. 429; 165 N. Y. 517. For notes on these cases see pages 734 and 735.

Such board or any member thereof may take proofs and hear testimony relating to any matter before it, or before such member, upon any such visit or inspection.

Any member or officer of such board, or inspector duly appointed by it, shall have full access to the grounds, buildings, books and papers relating to any such institution, and may require from the officers and persons in charge thereof, any information he may deem necessary in the discharge of his duties. The board may prepare regulations according to which, and provide blanks and forms upon which, such information shall be furnished, in a clear, uniform and prompt manner, for the use of the board. No such officer or inspector shall divulge or communicate to any person without the knowledge and consent of said board any facts or information obtained pursuant to the provisions of this act; on proof of such divulgement or communication such officer or inspector may at once be removed from office. The annual reports of each year shall give the results of such inquiries, with the opinion and conclusions of the board relating to the same. Any officer, superintendent or employe of any such institution, society or association who shall unlawfully refuse to admit any member, officer or inspector of the board, for the purpose of visitation and inspection, or who shall refuse or neglect to furnish the information required by the board or any of its members, officers or inspectors, shall be guilty of a misdemeanor, and subject to a fine of one hundred dollars for each such refusal or neglect. The right and powers hereby conferred may be enforced by an order of the supreme court after notice and hearing, or by indictment by the grand jury of the county or both.

§ 11. Powers and duties of the board on visits and inspections.— On such visits, inquiry shall be made to ascertain:

1. Whether all parts of the state are equally benefited by the institutions requiring state aid.

2. The merits of any and all requests on the part of any such institution for state aid, for any purpose, other than the usual expenses thereof; and the amount required to accomplish the object desired.

3. The sources of public moneys received for the benefit of such institution, as to the proper and economical expenditure of such moneys and the condition of the finances generally.

4. Whether the objects of the institution are being accomplished.

5. Whether the laws and the rules and regulations of this board, in relation to it, are fully complied with.

6. Its methods of industrial, educational and moral training, if any, and whether the same are best adapted to the needs of its inmates.

7. The methods of government and discipline of its inmates.

8. The qualifications and general conduct of its officers and employes.

9. The condition of its grounds, buildings and other property.

10. Any other matter connected with or pertaining to its usefulness and good management.

§ 12. **Investigations of institutions.**—The board, may direct an investigation, by a committee of one or more of its members, of the affairs and management of any institution, society or association, subject to its supervision, or of the conduct of its officers and employes. The commissioner or commissioners designated to make such investigation are hereby empowered to issue compulsory process for the attendance of witnesses and the production of papers, to administer oaths, and to examine persons under oath, and to exercise the same powers in respect to such proceeding as belong to referees appointed by the supreme court.

§ 13. **Orders of board directed to institutions.**—If it shall appear, after such investigation, that inmates of the institution are cruelly, negligently or improperly treated, or inadequate provision is made for their sustenance, clothing, care, supervision, or other condition necessary to their comfort and well being, said board may issue an order, in the name of the people, and under its official seal, directed to the proper officers or managers of such institution, requiring them to modify such treatment or apply such remedy, or both, as shall therein be specified; before such order is issued, it must be approved by a justice of the supreme court, after such notice as he may prescribe and an opportunity to be heard, and any person to whom such an order is directed who shall willfully refuse to obey the same, shall, upon conviction, be adjudged guilty of a misdemeanor.

§ 14. **Correction of evils in administration of institutions.**— The state board of charities shall call the attention of the trustees, directors or managers of any such institution, society or association, subject to its supervision, to any abuses, defects or evils which may be found therein, and such officers shall take proper action thereon, with a view to correcting the same, in accordance with the advice of such board.

§ 15. **Duties of the attorney-general and district attorneys.**— If, in the opinion of the board or any three members thereof, any matter in regard to the management or affairs of any such institution, society or association, or any inmate or person in any way connected therewith, requires legal investigation or action of any kind, notice thereof may be given by the board, or any three members thereof, to the attorney-general, and he shall thereupon make inquiry and take such proceedings in the premises as he may deem necessary and proper. It shall be the duty of the attorney-general and of every district attorney when so required to furnish such legal assistance, counsel or advice as the board may require in the discharge of its duties.

§ 16. State, non-resident and alien poor.—A poor person shall not be admitted as an inmate into a state institution for the feeble-minded, or epileptics, unless a resident of the state for one year next preceding the application for his admission.

The state board of charities, and any of its members or officers, may, at any time, visit and inspect any institution subject to its supervision to ascertain if any inmates supported therein at a state, county or municipal expense are state charges, non-residents, or alien poor; and it may cause to be removed to the state or country from which he came any such non-resident or alien poor found in any such institution.

§ 17. Reports of state board of charities.—The state board of charities shall annually report to the legislature its acts, proceedings and conclusions for the preceding year, with results and recommendations, which report shall include the information obtained in its inquiries and investigations, and from the reports made to it as in this chapter provided, giving a complete and itemized statement of expenditures for state poor, and of such other matters relating to the institutions subject to its visitations, as it may deem necessary or proper. The board shall collect, and so far as it shall deem advantageous, embody in its annual reports, such information as it may deem proper relating to all institutions, subject to the visitation of the board and respecting the best manner of dealing with those who require assistance from the public funds, or who receive aid from private charity, and represent its views as to the best methods of caring for the poor and destitute children who may be distributed through the various institutions of the state, or who may be with-

with which a dispensary shall manage or conduct its work or
determine the kind of medical or surgical treatment to be provided by any dispensary.

§ 22. Revocation of licenses.—The state board of charities or
any of its members may at any and all times visit and inspect
licensed dispensaries. They may examine all matters in relation
to such dispensaries, and ascertain how far they are conducted
in compliance with this law and the rules and regulations of the
board. After due notice to a dispensary, and opportunity for
it to be heard, the board may, if public interest demands, and
for just and reasonable cause, revoke a license by an order signed
and attested by the president and secretary of the board. Such
order shall state the reason for revoking such license, and shall
take effect within such time after the service thereof upon the
dispensary as the board shall determine. The said board is
hereby directed to apply to the supreme court to revoke the
license and annul the incorporation of any dispensary legally
incorporated, or conducted in connection with an incorporated
institution at the time of the passage of this act, for wilful
violation of the rules and regulations made by said board.

§ 23. Drug store or tenement house not to be used by dispensary; unlawful display of signs.—After the taking effect of this
act, no dispensary shall make use of any place commonly known
as a drug store, or any place or building defined by law or by an
ordinance of·the board of health as a tenement house; nor after
such time shall any person, corporation, institution, society, association, or agent thereof, except a duly licensed dispensary, display or cause to be displayed a sign or other thing which could
directly or indirectly or by suggestion indicate the existence of
the equivalent, in purpose and effect, of a dispensary.

§ 24. Any person who willfully violates any of the provisions of
this act, or any of the rules and regulations made and published
under the authority of this act, shall be guilty of a misdemeanor,
and on conviction thereof, shall be punished by a fine of not less
than ten dollars and not more than two hundred and fifty dollars.

§ 25. Any person who obtains medical or surgical treatment on false representations from any dispensary licensed under the provisions of this act shall be guilty of a misdemeanor, and on conviction thereof shall be punished by a fine of not less than ten dollars and not more than two hundred and fifty dollars.

§ 26. All acts or parts of acts inconsistent with the provisions of this act are hereby repealed.

§ 27. This act shall take effect on the first day of October, eighteen hundred and ninety-nine.

(*Sections* 19 *to* 27 *added by chapter* 368 *of the Laws of* 1899.)

ARTICLE II.

STATE CHARITIES AID ASSOCIATION.

Section 30. Visits by the state charities aid association.

31. Duties of officers in charge of institutions; enforcement of orders.

32. Annual reports.

Section 30. Visits by the state charities aid association.— Any justice of the supreme court, on written application of the state charities aid association, through its president or other officers designated by its board of managers, may grant to such person as may be named in such application, orders to enable such persons, or any of them, as visitors of such association to visit, inspect and examine, in behalf of such association any of the public charitable institutions and state hospitals for the insane owned by the state, and the county, town and city poor-houses and almshouses within the state. The persons so appointed to visit, inspect and examine such institutions shall reside in the counties from which such institutions receive their inmates, and such appointments shall be made by a justice of the supreme court of the judicial district in which such visitors reside. Each order shall specify the institution to be visited, inspected and examined and the name of each person by whom such visitation, inspection and examination shall be made, and shall be in force for one year from the date on which it shall have been granted, unless sooner revoked.

§ 31. Duties of officers in charge of institutions; enforcement of orders.—All persons in charge of any such institution shall admit each person named in any such order into every part of such institution, and render such person every possible facility to enable him to make in a thorough manner such visits, inspection and examination, which are hereby declared to be for a public purpose, and to be made with a view to public benefit. Obedience to the orders herein authorized shall be enforced in the same manner as obedience is enforced to an order or mandate by a court of record.

§ 32. Annual reports.—Such association shall make an annual report to the state board of charities upon matters relating to the institutions subject to the visitation of such board; and to the state commission in lunacy upon matters relating to the institutions subject to the inspection and control of such commission. Such reports shall be made on or before the first day of November for each preceding fiscal year.

ARTICLE III.

REGULATION OF STATE CHARITABLE INSTITUTIONS AND REPORTS TO AND ACCOUNTS AGAINST MUNICIPALITIES.

(As amended by chapter 252 of the Laws of 1902.)

Section 52. Reports by officers of certain institutions to clerks
of supervisors and cities.

53. Verified accounts against counties, cities and towns.

Section 40. Fiscal supervisor of state charities.—The office of
fiscal supervisor of state charities is hereby created. On or
before April fifteenth, nineteen hundred and two, the governor
shall appoint, by and with the advice and consent of the senate,
a fiscal supervisor of state charities. A successor to such supervisor shall be appointed in like manner. The term of office of
the fiscal supervisor of state charities shall be five years, and he
shall be paid by the state an annual salary of six thousand dollars, and his actual and necessary expenses. If a vacancy shall
occur, otherwise than by expiration of term, in the office of fiscal
supervisor of state charities, a fiscal supervisor of state charities shall be appointed in the manner provided by this section
for the unexpired term of his predecessor.

§ 41. Office and clerical force of fiscal supervisor.—The fiscal
supervisor of state charities shall be provided by the proper
authorities with a suitably furnished office in the state capitol.
He may employ a secretary, a stenographer and such other
employees as may be needed. The salaries and reasonable expenses of the fiscal supervisor and the necessary clerical assistants shall be paid by the treasurer of the state, on the warrant
of the comptroller, out of any moneys appropriated therefor.

§ 42. Powers and duties of fiscal supervisor.—The fiscal supervisor shall, as to the state charitable institutions, the New York
state school for the blind and the Elmira reformatory;

1. Visit each of such institutions at least twice in each calendar year.

2. Examine into the condition of all buildings, grounds and
other property connected with any such institution, and into
all matters relating to its financial management, and for such
purpose he shall have free access to the grounds, buildings, and
all books, papers, property and supplies of any such institution;
and all persons connected with any such institution shall give
such information and afford such facilities for such examination
or inquiry as the supervisor may require.

3. Appoint, in his discretion, a competent person to examine the books, papers and accounts of any institution to the extent deemed necessary.

4. Annually report to the legislature his acts and proceedings for the year ending September thirtieth last preceding, with such facts in regard to the condition of the buildings, grounds and property, and the financial management of the state charitable institutions, the New York state school for the blind and the Elmira reformatory as he may deem necessary for the information of the legislature, including estimates of the amounts required for the use of such institutions and the reasons therefor. The fiscal supervisor shall also on the first days of January and July in each year report to the governor the condition of the buildings, grounds and property on such date, together with such suggestions in regard to the financial management of such institutions as he deems proper. He shall also, on request of the governor or of any committee of either house of the legislature, make a special report in relation to the condition of the buildings, grounds and property, or the financial management of such institutions or of any of them.

§ 43. Removals by governor.—A fiscal supervisor of state charities, or the superintendent or the steward of any institution, subject to the provisions of this article, may be removed by the governor for cause, an opportunity having been given him to be heard in his defense.

§ 44. Fiscal year.—The fiscal year of all state charitable institutions, of the New York state school for the blind and of the Elmira reformatory shall commence with the first day of October in each year, and close with the thirtieth day of September, next succeeding; and the annual reports of such institutions required by this chapter, shall be made for the fiscal year as herein named.

§ 45. Monthly estimates of expenses; contingent fund.—The superintendent or other managing officer of each of the state charitable institutions, of the New York state school for the blind at Batavia and of the Elmira reformatory shall, on or before the fifteenth day of each month, cause to be prepared triplicate estimates in minute detail, of the expenses required for the institution of which he has the supervision, for the ensuing month. He shall countersign and submit two of such triplicates to the fiscal supervisor, and retain the other to be placed on file in the office of the institution. The fiscal supervisor may cause such estimates to be revised either as to quantity or quality of supplies and the estimated cost thereof, and shall certify that he has carefully examined the same and that the articles contained in such estimate, as approved or revised by him, are actually required for the use of the institution, and shall thereupon present such estimate and certificate to the comptroller. Upon the revision and approval of such estimate, the comptroller shall authorize the boards of managers, trustees or other managing officers of such institutions to make drafts on him, as the money may be required for the purposes mentioned in such estimates, which drafts shall be paid on his warrant, out of the funds in the treasury of the state appropriated for the support of such institutions. In every such estimate, there shall be a sum named, not to exceed two hundred and fifty dollars, as a contingent fund, for which no minute detailed statement need be made. No expenditures shall be made from such contingent fund, except in case of actual emergency, requiring immediate action, and which can not be deferred without loss or danger to the institution, or the inmates thereof. The treasurer of any such institution shall not pay accounts for goods furnished, salaries of officers or employees, unless they are contained in the estimate provided in this section, and duly approved by the fiscal supervisor. Nor shall the treasurer of any institution named or referred to in this section pay accounts for supplies furnished to officers or employees, unless the same be drawn from the ordinary supplies provided for the general use of the institution. No persons, other than the officers and employees of such institutions, and the families of the superintendents, medical officers, adjutants, quartermasters or stewards, necessarily residing therein, shall be allowed rooms and maintenance, except at a

rate fixed by the state comptroller and the fiscal supervisor
with the approval of the governor. The officers and employes
in the office of the state comptroller on April first, nineteen hundred and two, performing duties under section forty-one of the
state charities law, in relation to the estimates of the state charitable institutions, of the New York state school for the blind,
and of the Elmira reformatory are hereby continued in office and
transferred to the office of the fiscal supervisor subject to his
direction and control.

§ 46. Monthly statements of receipts and expenditures.—The
treasurer of each state charitable institution, of the New
York state school for the blind and of the Elmira reformatory
shall, on or before the fifteenth day of each month, make to the
fiscal supervisor a full and perfect statement of all the receipts
and expenditures, specifying the several items, for the last
preceding calendar month. Such statement shall be verified by the affidavit of the treasurer attached thereto, in
the following form: I,................treasurer of the......
.............do solemnly swear that I have deposited in the
bank designated by law for such purpose all the moneys received by me on account of such..............during the last
month; and I do further swear that the foregoing is a true
abstract of all the moneys received, and expenditures made by
me or under my direction as such treasurer during the month
ending on the.............day of..............nineteen......

§ 47. Affidavit of steward; vouchers.—There shall be attached to such treasurer's statement, the affidavit of the
steward or other officer having like powers, to the effect that
the goods and other articles therein specified were purchased
and received by him or under his direction at the institution,
that the goods were purchased at a fair cash market price and
paid for in cash, and that he or any person in his behalf had
no pecuniary or other interest in the articles purchased; that
he received no pecuniary or other benefit therefrom in the way
of commission, percentage, deductions or presents, or in any
other manner whatever, directly or indirectly; that the articles

contained in such bill were received at the institution; that they conformed in all respects to the invoiced goods received and ordered by him, both in quality and quantity. Such statement shall be accompanied by the voucher showing the payment of the several items contained in the statement, the amount of such payment and for what the payment was made. Such vouchers shall be examined by the fiscal supervisor and compared with the estimates made for the month for which the statement is rendered, and if found correct shall be endorsed and forwarded by the fiscal supervisor, with the statement, to the comptroller, who shall have the power of final audit in accordance with the estimate. If any voucher is found objectionable, the fiscal supervisor or the comptroller shall endorse his disapproval thereon, with the reason therefor, and return it to the treasurer, who shall present it to the board of managers for correction and immediately return it. All vouchers shall be filed in the office of the comptroller.

§ 48. Purchases.—All purchases for the use of the state charitable institutions, of the New York state school for the blind or of the Elmira reformatory shall be made for cash and not on credit or time; every voucher shall be duly filled up at the time it is taken, and with every abstract of vouchers paid, there shall be proof on oath that the voucher was filled up and the money paid at the time it was taken. The board of managers or trustees shall make all needful rules and regulations to enforce the provisions of this section. The fiscal supervisor, a member or officer of the state board of charities or manager or officer of any such institution, shall not be interested, directly or indirectly, in the furnishing of materials, labor or supplies for the use of any of such institutions nor shall any manager or trustee act as attorney or counsel for the board of managers or trustees thereof. The fiscal supervisor may arrange with the board of managers or trustees of the institutions mentioned in this section for the purchase by joint contract, of such staple articles of supplies as it may be found feasible to purchase for the use of such institutions, or any of them. Such contracts shall be executed by the stewards, under the direction of the boards of managers or trustees, and subject to the approval of the fiscal supervisor. Such contracts shall not be let except in conformity with the provisions of this act in relation to estimates. All goods for the use of such institutions except those furnished pursuant to law by some other institution of the state shall be bought, as far as practicable, of manufacturers or their immediate agents. All contracts, if let, shall, subject to the provisions of this article relating to estimates, be awarded to the lowest responsible bidder. Each of such institutions may manufacture such supplies and materials to be used in the institution as can be economically made therein. When requested by the fiscal supervisor, the superintendents of such institutions, or any of them, shall meet at the office of the fiscal supervisor at Albany, for the purpose of considering the feasibility of joint contracts.

§ 49. Plans and specifications; contracts.—The governor, the president of the state board of charities, and comptroller, or a majority of such officers, shall approve or reject plans and specifications for new buildings for any state charitable institution or for the New York state school for the blind and also for unusual repairs or improvements to existing buildings of such institutions or school; and no such building shall be erected or such repairs or improvements made until the plans and specifications therefor have been so approved. Contracts for such erection, repairs or improvements may be let by the board of managers or trustees, with the approval of the governor, the president of the state board of charities and comptroller, or a majority of such officers, for the whole or any part of the work to be performed, and in the discretion of the managers or trustees, and, subject to such approval, such contracts may be sublet. The comptroller and the board of managers or trustees shall determine to what extent and for what length of time advertisements are to be inserted in newspapers for proposals for the erection, repairs or improvements of state charitable institutions, the New York state school for the blind or the

Elmira reformatory. A preliminary deposit or certified check drawn upon some legally incorporated bank or trust company of this state shall in all cases be required as an evidence of good faith, upon all proposals for buildings, repairs or improvements, to be deposited with the superintendent of the institution for which the work is to be performed, in an amount to be determined by the state architect. All contracts for the erection, repairs or improvements to state charitable institutions, the New York state school for the blind or the Elmira reformatory shall contain a clause that the contract shall only be deemed executory to the extent of the moneys available, and no liability shall be incurred by the state beyond the moneys available for the purpose.

§ 50. Visitations and reports by managers or trustees.—The board of managers or trustees of each of the state charitable institutions, of the New York state school for the blind and of the Elmira reformatory, in addition to their other duties now required by law, shall, by a majority of its members, visit and inspect the institution for which it is appointed at least monthly, and shall make a written report in duplicate to the governor and the state board of charities within ten days after each visitation, to be signed by each member making such visitation. Such report shall state in detail the condition of the institution visited and of its inmates, and such other matters pertaining to the management and affairs thereof as in the opinion of the board should be brought to the attention of the governor or the state board of charities, and may contain recommendations as to needed improvements in the institution or its management.

§ 51. Reports to supervisors of appointments and committals to charitable institutions.—Every judge, justice, superintendent or overseer of the poor, supervisor or other person who is authorized by law to make appointments or commitments to any state charitable institution, except almshouses, in which the board, instruction, care or clothing is a charge against any county, town or city, shall make a written report to the clerk of the board of supervisors of the county, or of the county in which any town is situated, or to the city clerk of any city, which are liable for any such board, instruction, care or clothing, within ten days after such appointment or commitment, and shall therein state, when known, the nationality, age, sex and residence of each person so appointed or committed and the length of time of such appointment or commitment.

§ 52. Reports by officers of certain institutions to clerks of supervisors and cities.—The keeper, superintendent, secretary, director or other proper officer of a state charitable institution to which any person is committed or appointed, whose board, care, instruction, tuition or clothing shall be chargeable to any city, town or county, shall make a written report to the clerk of such city or to the clerk of the board of supervisors of the county, or of the county in which such town is situated, within ten days after receiving such person therein. Such report shall state when such person was received into the institution, and, when known, the name, age, sex, nationality, residence, length of time of commitment or appointment, the name of the officer making the same, and the sum chargeable per week, month or year for such person. If any person so appointed or committed to any such institution shall die, be removed or discharged, such officers shall immediately report to the clerk of the board of supervisors of the county, or of the county in which such town is situated, or to the city clerk of the city from which such person was committed or appointed, the date of such death, removal or discharge.

§ 53. Verified accounts against counties, cities and towns.— The officers mentioned in the last section shall annually, on or before the fifteenth day of October, present to the clerk of the board of supervisors of the county, or of the county in which such town is situated, or to the city clerk of a city from which any such person is committed and appointed, a verified report and statement of the account of such institution with such county, town or city, up to the first day of October, and in case of a claim for clothing, an itemized statement of the same; and if a part of the board, care, tuition or clothing has been paid by any person or persons, the account shall show what sum has been so paid; and the report shall show the name, age, sex, nationality and residence of each person mentioned in the account, the name of the officer who made the appointment or commitment, and the date and length of the same, and the time to which the account has been paid, and the amount claimed to such first day of October, the sum per week or per annum charged, and if no part of such account has been paid, the report shall show such fact. Any officer who shall refuse or neglect to make such report shall not be entitled to receive any compensation or pay for any services, salary or otherwise, from any town, city or county affected thereby. The clerk of the board of supervisors who shall receive any such report or account shall file and present the same to the board of supervisors of his county on the second day of the annual meeting of the board next after the receipt of the same.

§ 2. Subdivision twelve of section nine of chapter four hundred and forty-six of the laws of eighteen hundred and ninety-six, entitled "An act relating to state charities, constituting chapter twenty-six of the general laws," as added by chapter five hundred and four of the laws of eighteen hundred ninety-nine, in relation to approval of plans, and sections eleven to fourteen, both inclusive, of chapter three hundred and seventy-eight of the laws of nineteen hundred, entitled "An act to revise, consolidate and amend the several acts relating to the New York state reformatory at Elmira," in relation to estimates, are hereby repealed. *(As amended by chapter 252, Laws of 1902.)*

ARTICLE IV.

SYRACUSE STATE INSTITUTION FOR FEEBLE-MINDED CHILDREN.

Section 60. Institutions for idiots or feeble-minded children.

61. Powers and duties of boards of directors.

62. Salaries of officers.

63. Directors may hold donations in trust.

64. By-laws.

Section 60. Institution for idiots or feeble-minded children.—The management of the Syracuse State Institution for Feeble-Minded Children at Syracuse shall continue to be in a board of managers, which shall hereafter consist of the superintendent of public instruction and eight other persons, who shall continue to be appointed by the senate upon the recommendation of the governor, as often as vacancies shall occur therein, and shall hold office for eight years, and until their successors are severally appointed, subject to removal by the governor for cause, after an opportunity given them to be heard in their defense. The managers now in office shall hold their offices until the expiration of the term for which they were respectively appointed.

§ 61. General powers and duties of boards of managers.—Five members of the board shall constitute a quorum for the transaction of business. The board shall have the general direction and control of all the property and concerns of the institution, and shall take charge of its general interests and see that its general design is carried into effect, according to law and the by-laws, rules and regulations of the institution. It shall appoint a superintendent, who shall be a well-educated physician, and a treasurer, who shall reside in the city of Syracuse, and shall give an undertaking to the people of the state for the faithful performance of his trust, in such sum and with such sureties as the comptroller shall approve. Such board shall, annually, on or before the first day of February, report to the legislature the condition of the institution.

§ 62. Salaries of officers.— The board shall, from time to time, determine the annual salaries and allowances of the resident officers of the institution.

Such salaries and allowances shall be paid monthly by the treasurer of the institution in the same manner as other claims against the institution.

§ 63. **Managers may hold donations in trust.**— The managers may take, and hold in trust for the state, any grant or devise of land, or any donation or bequest of money or other personal property, to be applied to the maintenance and education of feeble-minded children and the general use of the institution.

§ 64. **By-laws.**—The managers may establish by-laws regulating the appointment and duties of officers, teachers, attendants and assistants; fixing the conditions of admission, support and discharge of pupils; and for conducting in a proper manner the business of the institution; and ordain and enforce a suitable system of rules and regulations for the internal government, discipline and management of the institution.

§ 65. **Duties of superintendent.**— The superintendent shall be the chief executive officer of the institution. He shall, subject to the provision of the board of managers and the by-laws and regulations established by them,

1. Have the general superintendence of the buildings, grounds and farm, with their furniture, fixtures and stock, and the direction and control of all persons employed in and about the same;

2. Appoint a steward, a medical assistant and a matron, who, with the superintendent, shall constantly reside in the institution or upon premises adjoining, and shall be termed the resident officers thereof;

3. Employ such teachers, attendants and assistants as he may think proper and necessary to economically and efficiently carry into effect the design of the institution; prescribe their several duties and places, fix their compensation, and discharge any of them;

4. Give, from time to time, such orders and instructions as he may deem best calculated to induce good conduct, fidelity and economy, in any department of labor and expense.

5. Maintain salutary discipline among all who are in the employ of the institution, and enforce strict compliance with his

instructions, and uniform obedience to all the rules and regulations of the institution;

6. Cause full and fair accounts and records of all his doings, and of the entire business and operations of the institution, with the condition and prospects of the pupils to be kept regularly, from day to day, in books provided for the purpose;

7. See that such accounts and records shall be fully made up to the first days of April and October in each year, and that the principal effects and results, with his report thereon, be presented to the board at its semi-annual meetings;

8. Conduct the official correspondence of the institution and keep a record of the applications received, and the pupils admitted;

9. Prepare and present to the board at its annual meetings, when required, an inventory of all personal property and effects belonging to the institution;

10. Account, when required, for the careful keeping and economical use of all furniture, stores and other articles furnished for the institution;

11. Enter in a book to be provided and kept for that purpose, at the time of the admission of each pupil to the institution, a minute, with the date, name, residence of the pupil, and of the persons on whose application he is received; with a copy of the application, statement, certificate, and all other papers accompanying such pupil; the originals of which he shall file and carefully preserve.

§ 66. Duties of treasurer.— The treasurer shall,

1. Have the custody of all moneys, notes, mortgages and other securities and obligations belonging to the institution;

2 Keep a full and accurate account of all receipts and payments, as directed in the by-laws, and such other accounts as shall be required of him by the managers.

3. Balance all the accounts on his book on the first day of each October, and make a statement thereof, and an abstract of all the receipts and payments of the past year; and. within three days thereafter, deliver the same to the auditing committee of

the managers, who shall compare the same with his books and vouchers, and verify the same by a further comparison with the books of the superintendent. and certify the correctness thereof to the managers at their annual meeting;

4. Render a quarterly statement of his receipts and payments to such auditing committee, who shall, in like manner as above, compare, verify, report and certify the result thereof to the man-agers at their annual meeting, who shall cause the same to be recorded in one of the books of the institution;

5. Render a further account of the state of his books and of the funds and other property in his custody, whenever required by the managers;

6. Receive for the use of the institution any and all sums of money which may be due upon any notes or bonds in his hands, belonging to the institution, any and all sums charged and due to the institution for the support of any pupil therein, or for actual disbursements made in his behalf for necessary, clothing and traveling expenses;

7. Prosecute an action in his name as such treasurer, to recover any sum of money that may be due or owing to the institution;

8. Execute a release and satisfaction of a mortgage, judgment or other lien, in favor of the institution, when paid, so that the same may be discharged from record.

§ 67. Semi-annual meetings and records of board of man-agers.— The board of managers shall maintain an effective in-spection of the affairs and management of the institution, for which purpose they shall meet at the institution twice in each year, at such times as the by-laws shall provide. The resident officers shall admit the managers into every part of the institu-tion, and shall exhibit to them on demand the books, papers, accounts and writings belonging to the institution, and shall furnish copies, abstracts and reports whenever required by the managers.

A committee of three managers to be appointed by the board at the annual meeting thereof, shall visit the institution once in every month, and perform such other duties and exercise such other powers as shall be prescribed in the by-laws, or the board may direct. The board shall keep in a bound book, to be provided for the purpose, a fair and full record of all its doings, which shall be open at all times to the inspection of its members, and all persons whom the governor and either house of the legislature may appoint to examine the same.

§ 68. Manner of receiving pupils.—There shall be received and gratuitously supported in the institution one hundred and twenty feeble-minded children, as state pupils, who shall be selected from those whose parents or guardians are unable to provide for their support, in equal numbers as far as may be, from each judicial district. Such additional number of feeble-minded children as can be conveniently accommodated shall be received into the institution on such terms as shall be just. .

If the number of feeble-minded children admitted shall not equal the capacity of the institution, such additional number of non-teachable idiots may be admitted as can be conveniently accommodated.

Feeble-minded children shall be received into the institution upon the written request of the person by whom they are sent, stating the name in full, age, place of nativity, if known, the town, city or county in which each resides, and whether such child, his parents or guardian, are able to provide for his support, in whole or in part, and if in part only what part, the degree of relationship or other circumstances of connection between him and the person requesting his admission, which statement must be verified by the affidavit of two disinterested persons, residents of the same county as the child and acquainted with the facts and circumstances stated, and certified to be credible by the county judge of the county.

Such judge must also further certify that such child is an eligible and proper candidate for admission to such institution.

Feeble-minded children may also be received into such institution upon the official application of a county superintendent of the poor, or the commissioners of charity of a city of the state having such officers.

In the admission of feeble-minded children, preference shall be given to poor or indigent children over all others, and to such as are able or have parents able to support them only in part, over those who are or who have parents who are able to wholly support such children.

§ 69. **Discharge of state pupils and payment of expenses.** —When the manager shall direct a state pupil to be discharged from the institution, the superintendent thereof may return him to the county from which he was sent, and deliver him to the keeper of the almshouse thereof, and the superintendent of the poor of the county shall audit and pay the actual and reasonable expenses of such return. If any town, county or person is legally liable for the support of such pupil, such expenses may be recovered by action in the name of the county by such superintendent of the poor. If the superintendent of the poor neglect or refuse to pay such expenses on demand, the treasurer of the institution may pay the same and charge the amount to the county; and the treasurer of the county shall pay the same with interest after thirty days, out of any funds in his hands not otherwise appropriated; and the supervisors shall raise the amount so paid as other county charges.

§ 70. **Expense of clothing state pupils.**—The supervisors of any county from which state pupils may have been received shall cause to be raised annually, while such pupils remain in the institution, the sum of thirty dollars for each pupil, for the purpose of furnishing suitable clothing, which shall be paid to the treasurer of the institution on or before the first day of April.

The superintendent may agree with the parent, guardian or committee of a feeble-minded child, or with any person, for the support, maintenance and clothing of such a child at the institution, upon such terms and conditions as may be prescribed, in the by-laws, or approved by the managers. Every parent, guardian, committee, or other person applying for the admission into the institution of a feeble-minded child who is able, or whose parents or guardians are of sufficient ability to provide for his maintenance therein, shall at the time of his admission, deliver

49

to the superintendent an undertaking, with one or more sureties, to be approved by the managers, conditioned for the payment to the treasurer of the institution of the amount agreed to be paid for the support, maintenance and clothing of such feeble-minded child, and for the removal of such child from the institution without expense thereto, within twenty days after the service of the notice hereinafter provided. If such child, his parents or guardians are of sufficient ability to pay only a part of the expense of supporting and maintaining him, such undertaking shall be only for his removal from the institution as above mentioned; and the superintendent may take security by note or other written agreement, with or without sureties, as he may deem proper, for such part of such expenses as such child, his parents or guardians are able to pay, subject, however, to the approval of the managers in the manner that shall be prescribed in the by-laws. Notice to remove a pupil shall be in writing, signed by the superintendent and directed to the parents, guardians, committee or other person upon whose request the pupil was received at the institution, at the place of residence mentioned in such request, and deposited in the post-office at Syracuse with the postage prepaid.

If the pupil shall not be removed from the institution within twenty days after service of such notice, according to the conditions of the agreement and undertaking, he may be removed and disposed of by the superintendent as herein provided, in relation to state pupils, and the provisions of this article respecting the payment and recovery of the expenses of the removal and disposition of a state pupil, shall be equally applicable to expenses incurred under this section.

ARTICLE V.

STATE CUSTODIAL ASYLUM FOR FEEBLE-MINDED WOMEN.

Section 80. Established as a corporation.

     81. Board of managers.

     82. Officers.

     83. Treasurer to give undertaking.

Section 80. Established as a corporation.—The asylum established at Newark, Wayne county, for feeble-minded women is hereby continued as a body corporate and shall be known as the State Custodial Asylum for Feeble-Minded Women.

§ 81. Board of managers.—Such asylum shall continue to have a board of nine managers, three of whom shall be women, and shall be appointed by the governor, by and with the consent of the senate, for six years, except appointments to fill vacancies, which shall be for the unexpired term. The board of managers shall have the custody and control of all property and power to make all rules for the management and control of the effects of the asylum.

§ 82. Officers.—The board of managers shall appoint, of their number, a president, a secretary and a treasurer. They shall appoint a superintendent, a matron, and employ all assistants that may be necessary for the proper management of the asylum.

§ 83. Treasurer to give undertaking.—The treasurer shall, before he receives any money, give an undertaking to the people of the state, with such sureties and in such amount as the board of managers shall require and to be approved by the comptroller, to the effect that he faithfully perform his trust as such treasurer.

ARTICLE VI.

ROME STATE CUSTODIAL ASYLUM.

Section 90. Asylum for unteachable idiots.

    91. Appointment of managers.

    92. Powers and duties of managers.

    93. Superintendent, qualifications, powers and duties.

    94. Commitments to asylums, maintenance.

Section 90. Asylum for unteachable idiots.—The asylum established at Rome for the support, maintenance and custody of unteachable idiots is hereby continued and shall be known as the Rome State Custodial Asylum.

§ 91. Appointment of managers.—Such asylum shall be under the control and management of a board of eleven managers, appointed by the governor, by and with the advice and consent of the senate and whose term of office shall be six years.

The managers now in office shall hold their offices until the expiration of the terms for which they were respectively appointed, or until their successors are appointed and have qualified. They may be removed by the governor, upon charges preferred against them in writing, after an opportunity given them to be heard thereon.

They shall appoint one of their number as president and another as secretary.

§ 92. Powers and duties of managers.—The board of managers shall,

1. Have the general direction and control of all the property and concerns of the asylum, take charge of its general interests and see that its design is carried into effect, according to law, and its by-laws, rules and regulations.

2. Establish by-laws, rules and regulations, subject to the approval of the state board of charities, for the internal government, discipline and management of the asylum.

3. Maintain an effective inspection of the asylum for which purpose, a majority of the managers shall visit the asylum at least once in every three months, and at such other times as may be prescribed in the by-laws.

The superintendent or other officer in charge shall admit such managers into every part of the asylum and its buildings and exhibit to them on demand all the books, accounts and writings belonging to the asylum and pertaining to its interest, and furnish copies, abstracts and reports whenever required by them.

4. Annually report to the legislature for the preceding fiscal year, the affairs and conditions of the asylum, with full and detailed estimates of the next appropriation required for maintenance and ordinary uses and repairs, and of special appropriations, if any, needed for extraordinary repairs, renewals, extensions, improvements, betterments or other necessary objects.

5. If lands are required for the use of the asylum, acquire the same by purchase, gift or condemnation.

§ 93. Superintendent, qualifications, powers and duties.—The superintendent shall be a resident of this state, a well-educated physician and a graduate of an incorporated medical college, of at least five years' actual experience in an institution for the cure and treatment of the insane. He shall be the chief executive officer of the asylum, and shall manage the institution in conformity to rules and regulations adopted by the board of managers. He shall appoint the assistant physicians, steward, clerk, a bookkeeper, matron and all subordinate employes, and he may discharge them, when, in his judgment, it may be necessary to do so, for the good of the institution.

§ 94. Commitments to asylum; maintenance.—The superintendents of the poor of the various counties of the state may commit to such asylum, if vacancies exist therein, such unteachable idiots residing in their respective counties, who are indigent or inmates of county almshouses, according to the by-laws and regulations of the asylum. All commitments shall be in the form prescribed by the board of managers. Insane idiots or epileptics shall not be committed to such asylum.

Unteachable idiots other than the poor and indigent may be admitted to the asylum, if vacancies exist, after providing for the care and custody of the poor and indigent idiots, at a rate which shall not exceed the weekly per capita cost of maintaining all inmates as determined yearly by the board of managers.

The maintenance of the institution and the poor and indigent inmates thereof shall be a charge upon the state.

ARTICLE VII.

THE CRAIG COLONY FOR EPILEPTICS.

Section 100. Establishment and objects of colony.—The colony for epileptics established at Sonyea, Livingston county, is hereby continued, and shall be known as the Craig Colony for Epileptics, in honor of the late Oscar Craig, of Rochester, New York, whose efficient and gratuitous public services in behalf of epileptics and other dependent unfortunates, the state desires to commemorate.

The object of such colony shall be to secure the humane, curative, scientific and economical care and treatment of epileptics, exclusive of insane epileptics.

§ 101. Managers of the colony.—There shall be a board of twelve managers of the Craig colony, all of whom shall be citizens of the state, appointed by the governor, by and with the advice and consent of the senate, one from each judicial district and one additional member from each of the fifth, sixth, seventh and eighth judicial districts. The term of office of each manager hereafter appointed to succeed a manager whose term has expired shall be three years, and the term of office of four of such managers shall expire annually. The managers in office when this chapter takes effect shall continue in office until the expiration of the term for which they were appointed and until their successors are appointed and have qualified. Appointments to fill vacancies occurring by death, removal or resignation, shall be made without unnecessary delay for the unexpired term. Failure of any manager to attend in each year the whole of two stated meetings of the board shall be a sufficient cause for removal by the governor. Any manager may be removed by the governor upon written charges preferred against him, after an opportunity to be heard in his defense. The managers shall receive no compensation for their services, but shall be allowed their reasonable traveling and official expenses, to be paid as other charges against the institution.

§ 102. **Buildings and improvements.**—The board of managers shall put the premises conveyed to the state for the use of the colony into proper condition for the reception of patients and shall receive patients gradually and as rapidly as the condition of the colony will admit. They shall utilize all buildings and improvements on the land so conveyed, and construct such additional buildings and make further improvements upon plans adopted by them and approved by the state board of charities and for which appropriations are made by the legislature.

There shall be provided for such colony an abundant supply of wholesome water, sufficient means for drainage and the disposal of sewage in a proper sanitary system. All of which shall be done under the direction of the board of managers in accordance with plans adopted by them, and approved by the state board of charities.

§ 103. **Powers and duties of managers.**—Six members of the board of managers shall constitute a quorum for the transaction of business. The board shall:

1. Elect from their number a president and secretary, and may adopt a seal for the use of the colony.

2. Have the government, direction and control of the patients, officers and employes of the colony and of all the property and concerns thereof.

3. Purchase supplies for the use of the colony and such raw materials as may be necessary for the trades and industries pursued therein, and provide for the disposal of the manufactured products and the product of the land.

4. Employ the assistants necessary for the government of the colony, and to educate and properly use the labor of the patients.

5. Establish such by-laws, rules and regulations as they may deem necessary regulating the appointment, powers and duties of officers, teachers, attendants and assistants, fixing the condition of admission, treatment, education, support, custody, dis-

cipline and discharge of patients, conducting in a proper manner
the business of the colony, and regulating the internal government, discipline and management of the colony.

6. Maintain an effective inspection of the affairs and management of the colony, for which purpose they shall meet at the
institution at least four times in each year and at such other
times as the by-laws shall prescribe. Their annual meeting shall
be held on the second Tuesday of October.

7. Appoint at its annual meeting, a committee of three managers, who shall visit the colony at least once in every month, and
perform such other duties and exercise such other powers as are
prescribed in the by-laws, or directed by the board.

8. Copy in a bound book, a fair and full record of all its proceedings, which shall be open at all times to the inspection of its
members and officers of the state board of charities, and all persons whom the governor or either house of the legislature may
appoint to examine the same. *(As amended by chapter 359 of
the Laws of 1898.)*

§ 104. Annual report; state board of charities.—The board
of managers of the Craig colony shall annually, on or before the
first day of November, for the preceding fiscal year, report to the
state board of charities the affairs and conditions of the colony,
with full and detailed estimates of the next appropriation required for maintenance and ordinary uses and repairs, and of
special appropriations, if any, needed for extraordinary repairs,
renewals, extensions, improvement, betterments or other necessary objects, as also for the erection of additional buildings
needed by reason of overcrowding, and in order to prevent the
same, or to meet the need of sufficient accommodations for patients seeking admission to the colony; and the state board of
charities shall, in its annual report to the legislature, certify
what appropriations are, in its opinion, necessary and proper.
The said colony shall be subject to the visitation and to the general powers of the state board of charities.

§ 105. Donations in trust.—The managers may take and
hold in trust for the state any grant or devise of land, or any gift

or bequest of money or other personal property, or a
to be applied, principal or income, or both, to the
and education of epileptics and the general uses of tl

§ 106. Officers of the colony.—The board of ma
appoint a superintendent of the colony, who shal
educated physician and a graduate of a legally chart
college, with an experience of at least five years i
practice of his profession, and who shall be certified
by the civil service commission, after a competitive
and a treasurer, who shall reside in the county of Liv
shall give an undertaking to the people of the state
ful performance of his trust, in such sum and form a
sureties as the comptroller shall approve. Such off
discharged or suspended at any time by such boar
cretion. The superintendent shall constantly resid
ony. The board shall determine the annual salarie
ances of the superintendent, steward and matron, n
in addition to maintenance supplies, the following
aries: Four thousand dollars to the superintendent
dred dollars to the steward; one thousand dollars to
and the board shall determine the annual salary of
of the colony, not exceeding fifteen hundred dollars.
ries and allowances shall be paid quarterly, on the
October, January, April and July, each year, by the
the colony, on presentation of bills therefor, audited,
certified, as prescribed in the by-laws.

§ 107. Duties of the superintendent.—The su
shall be the chief executive officer of the colony, an
the supervision and control of the board of managers

1. Oversee and secure the individual treatment
care of each and every patient of the colony wl
therein and the proper oversight of all the inhabitan

2. Have the general superintendence of the buildi
and farm, with their furniture, fixtures and stock, a
tion and control of all persons employed in and abo

3. Give, from time to time, such orders and instructions as he may deem best calculated to induce good conduct, fidelity and economy in any department of labor or education or treatment of patients.

4. Appoint a steward and a matron and employ a bookkeeper and such teachers, assistants and attendants as he may think necessary to economically and efficiently carry into effect the design of the colony; prescribe their duties and places, and, subject to the approval of the board of managers, fix their compensation. The steward and matron shall reside in the colony.

5. Maintain salutary discipline among all employes, patients and inhabitants of the colony, have the custody and control of every patient admitted to the colony until properly discharged, and subject to the regulations of the managers, restrain and discipline any patient in such manner as he may judge is for the welfare of the patient and the proper conduct of the colony, and enforce strict compliance with the instructions and uniform obedience to all the rules and regulations of the colony.

6. Cause full and fair accounts and records of the entire business and operations of the colony, with the conditions and prospects of the patients, to be kept regularly, from day to day, in books provided for that purpose.

7. See that such accounts and records shall be fully made up to the first days of January, April, July and October, in each year, and that the principal facts and results, with his report thereon, be presented to the board of managers at its quarterly meetings.

8. Conduct the official correspondence of the colony, and keep a record or copy of all letters written by himself and by his clerks and agents, and files of all letters received by him or them.

9. Prepare and present to the board, at its annual meeting, a true and perfect inventory of all the personal property and effects belonging to the colony, and account, when required by the board, for the careful keeping and economical use of all furniture, stores and other articles furnished for the colony.

10. Keep a record of all applications for admission of patients, and enter in a book to be provided and kept for that purpose, at the time of admission of each patient to the colony, a minute, with the date, name, residence of the patient, and of the persons on whose application he is received, with a copy of the application, statement, certificate, and all other papers received relating to such epileptic patient, the originals of which he shall file and carefully preserve, and certified copies whereof he shall forthwith transmit to the state board of charities. (As amended by chapter 359 of the Laws of 1898.)

§ 108. Duties of treasurer.—The treasurer, among his other duties, shall:

1. Have the custody of all moneys received on account of the monthly estimates made to the comptroller by the superintendent as provided by this chapter, and all other money, notes, mortgages and other securities and obligations belonging to the colony.

2. Keep a full and accurate account of all receipts and payments, in the form prescribed by the by-laws, and such other accounts as shall be required of him by the managers.

3. Balance all the accounts on his books on the first day of each October, and make a statement thereof, and an abstract of all the receipts and payments of the past year; and within five days thereafter deliver the same to the auditing committee of the managers, who shall compare the same with his books and vouchers, and verify the same by a comparison with the books of the superintendent, and certify the correctness thereof to the managers at their annual meeting.

4. Render a quarterly statement of his receipts and payments to such auditing committee who shall, in like manner as above, compare, verify, report and certify the result thereof, to the managers at their annual meeting, who shall cause the same to be recorded in one of the books of the colony.

5. Render a further account of the state of his books, and of the funds and other property in his custody, whenever required by the managers.

6. Receive for the use of the colony, money which may be paid upon obligation or securities in his hands belonging to the colony; and all sums paid to the colony for the support of any patient therein, or, for actual disbursements made in his behalf for necessary clothing and traveling expenses; and money paid to the colony from any other source.

7. Prosecute an action in the name of the colony to recover money due or owing to the colony, from any source; including the bringing of suit for breach of contract between private patients or their guardians and the managers of the colony.

8. Execute a lease and satisfaction of a mortgage, judgment, lien or other debt when paid.

9. Pay the salaries of the superintendent, treasurer, matron, steward, and of all employes of the colony, and the disbursements of the officers and members of the board as aforesaid. The treasurer shall have power to employ counsel, subject to the approval of the board of managers.

10. Deposit all moneys received for the care of private patients and all other revenues of the colony, in a bank designated by the comptroller, and transmit to the comptroller a statement showing the amount so received and deposited and from whom, and for what received, and the dates on which such deposits were made. Such statement of deposit shall be certified by the proper officer of the bank receiving such deposit or deposits. The treasurer shall verify by his affidavit that the sum so deposited is all the money received by him from any source of income for the colony up to the time of the last deposit appearing on such statement. A bank designated by the comptroller to receive such deposits shall, before any such deposit be made, execute a bond to the people of the state in a sum and with sureties to be approved by the comptroller, for the safe keeping of such deposits.

§ 109. Designation and admission of patients.—There shall be received and gratuitously supported in the colony, epileptics residing in the state, who, if of age, are unable, or, if under age, whose parents or guardians are unable to provide for their support therein; and who shall be designated as state patients. Such

additional number of epileptics as can be conveniently accommodated shall be received into the colony by the managers on such
terms as shall be just, and shall be designated as private patients.
Epileptic children shall be received into the colony only upon the
written request of the persons desiring to send them, stating the
name, age, place of nativity, if known, the town, city or county in
which such children respectively reside, and the ability of their
respective parents, or guardians or others to provide for their support in whole or in part, and if in part only, stating what part;
and stating also the degree of relationship or other circumstances
of connection between the patients and the persons requesting
their admission; which statement in all cases of state patients
must be verified by the affidavits of the petitioners and of two disinterested persons, and accompanied by the opinion of a qualified
physician, all residents of the same county with the epileptic
patient, and acquainted with the facts and circumstances stated,
and who must be certified to be credible by the county judge or
surrogate of the county; and such judge or surrogate must also
certify, in each case, that such state patient, in his opinion, is an
eligible and proper candidate for admission to the colony. State
patients may also be received into the colony upon the official application of a county superintendent of the poor, or of the poor
authorities of any city.

It shall be the duty of the superintendent of the poor in every
county and of the poor authorities of every city to furnish annually
to the state board of charities, a list of all epileptics in their respective jurisdictions, so far as the same can be ascertained, with
such particulars as to the condition of each epileptic as shall be
prescribed by the said state board. Whenever an epileptic shall
become a charge for his or her maintenance on any of the towns,
cities or counties of this state, it shall be the duty of all poor
authorities of such city, and of the county superintendents of the
poor, and of the supervisors of such county, to place such epileptic
in the said colony. Any parent, guardian or friend of an epileptic
child within this state may make application to the poor authorities of any city, or the superintendent of the poor of any county
or the board of supervisors or any supervisor of any town, ward

cipline and discharge of patients, conducting in a proper manner
the business of the colony, and regulating the internal government, discipline and management of the colony.

6. Maintain an effective inspection of the affairs and management of the colony, for which purpose they shall meet at the
institution at least four times in each year and at such other
times as the by-laws shall prescribe. Their annual meeting shall
be held on the second Tuesday of October.

7. Appoint at its annual meeting, a committee of three managers, who shall visit the colony at least once in every month, and
perform such other duties and exercise such other powers as are
prescribed in the by-laws, or directed by the board.

8. Copy in a bound book, a fair and full record of all its proceedings, which shall be open at all times to the inspection of its
members and officers of the state board of charities, and all persons whom the governor or either house of the legislature may
appoint to examine the same. *(As amended by chapter 359 of
the Laws of 1898.)*

§ 104. Annual report; state board of charities.—The board
of managers of the Craig colony shall annually, on or before the
first day of November, for the preceding fiscal year, report to the
state board of charities the affairs and conditions of the colony,
with full and detailed estimates of the next appropriation required for maintenance and ordinary uses and repairs, and of
special appropriations, if any, needed for extraordinary repairs,
renewals, extensions, improvement, betterments or other necessary objects, as also for the erection of additional buildings
needed by reason of overcrowding, and in order to prevent the
same, or to meet the need of sufficient accommodations for patients seeking admission to the colony; and the state board of
charities shall, in its annual report to the legislature, certify
what appropriations are, in its opinion, necessary and proper.
The said colony shall be subject to the visitation and to the general powers of the state board of charities.

§ 105. Donations in trust.—The managers may take and
hold in trust for the state any grant or devise of land, or any gift

or bequest of money or other personal property, or any donation, to be applied, principal or income, or both, to the maintenance and education of epileptics and the general uses of the colony.

§ 106. Officers of the colony.—The board of managers shall appoint a superintendent of the colony, who shall be a well-educated physician and a graduate of a legally chartered medical college, with an experience of at least five years in the actual practice of his profession, and who shall be certified as qualified by the civil service commission, after a competitive examination; and a treasurer, who shall reside in the county of Livingston, and shall give an undertaking to the people of the state for the faithful performance of his trust, in such sum and form and with such sureties as the comptroller shall approve. Such officers may be discharged or suspended at any time by such board, in its discretion. The superintendent shall constantly reside in the colony. The board shall determine the annual salaries and allowances of the superintendent, steward and matron, not exceeding, in addition to maintenance supplies, the following sums for salaries: Four thousand dollars to the superintendent; fifteen hundred dollars to the steward; one thousand dollars to the matron; and the board shall determine the annual salary of the treasurer of the colony, not exceeding fifteen hundred dollars. Such salaries and allowances shall be paid quarterly, on the first day of October, January, April and July, each year, by the treasurer of the colony, on presentation of bills therefor, audited, allowed and certified, as prescribed in the by-laws.

§ 107. Duties of the superintendent.—The superintendent shall be the chief executive officer of the colony, and subject to the supervision and control of the board of managers; he shall:

1. Oversee and secure the individual treatment and personal care of each and every patient of the colony while resident therein and the proper oversight of all the inhabitants thereof.

2. Have the general superintendence of the buildings, grounds and farm, with their furniture, fixtures and stock, and the direction and control of all persons employed in and about the same.

3. Give, from time to time. such orders and instructions as he may deem best calculated to induce good conduct. fidelity and economy in any department of labor or education or treatment of patients.

4. Appoint a steward and a matron and employ a bookkeeper and such teachers. assistants and attendants as he may think necessary to economically and efficiently carry into effect the design of the colony; prescribe their duties and places. and. subject to the approval of the board of managers. fix their compensation. The steward and matron shall reside in the colony.

5. Maintain salutary discipline among all employes. patients and inhabitants of the colony, have the custody and control of every patient admitted to the colony until properly discharged, and subject to the regulations of the managers, restrain and discipline any patient in such manner as he may judge is for the welfare of the patient and the proper conduct of the colony, and enforce strict compliance with the instructions and uniform obedience to all the rules and regulations of the colony.

6. Cause full and fair accounts and records of the entire business and operations of the colony. with the conditions and prospects of the patients. to be kept regularly. from day to day. in books provided for that purpose.

7. See that such accounts and records shall be fully made up to the first days of January. April, July and October, in each year, and that the principal facts and results, with his report thereon, be presented to the board of managers at its quarterly meetings.

8. Conduct the official correspondence of the colony, and keep a record or copy of all letters written by himself and by his clerks and agents, and files of all letters received by him or them.

9. Prepare and present to the board, at its annual meeting, a true and perfect inventory of all the personal property and effects belonging to the colony, and account, when required by the board, for the careful keeping and economical use of all furniture, stores and other articles furnished for the colony.

10. Keep a record of all applications for admission of patients, and enter in a book to be provided and kept for that purpose, at the time of admission of each patient to the colony, a minute, with the date, name, residence of the patient, and of the persons on whose application he is received, with a copy of the application, statement, certificate, and all other papers received relating to such epileptic patient, the originals of which he shall file and carefully preserve, and certified copies whereof he shall forthwith transmit to the state board of charities. *(As amended by chapter 359 of the Laws of 1898.)*

§ 108. Duties of treasurer.—The treasurer, among his other duties, shall:

1. Have the custody of all moneys received on account of the monthly estimates made to the comptroller by the superintendent as provided by this chapter, and all other money, notes, mortgages and other securities and obligations belonging to the colony.

2. Keep a full and accurate account of all receipts and payments, in the form prescribed by the by-laws, and such other accounts as shall be required of him by the managers.

3. Balance all the accounts on his books on the first day of each October, and make a statement thereof, and an abstract of all the receipts and payments of the past year; and within five days thereafter deliver the same to the auditing committee of the managers, who shall compare the same with his books and vouchers, and verify the same by a comparison with the books of the superintendent, and certify the correctness thereof to the managers at their annual meeting.

4. Render a quarterly statement of his receipts and payments to such auditing committee who shall, in like manner as above, compare, verify, report and certify the result thereof, to the managers at their annual meeting, who shall cause the same to be recorded in one of the books of the colony.

5. Render a further account of the state of his books, and of the funds and other property in his custody, whenever required by the managers.

or city where such child resides, showing by satisfactory affidavit
or other proof that the health, morals, comfort or welfare of such
child may be endangered or not properly cared for if not placed
in such colony; and thereupon it shall be the duty of such officer
or board to whom such application may be made to place such
child in said colony. The board of supervisors shall provide for
the support of such patients, except those properly supported by
the state, and may recover for the same from the parents or guardians of such children. In the admission of patients preference
shall always be given to poor or indigent epileptics, or the epileptic children of poor or indigent persons, over all others; and preference shall always be given to such as are able to support themselves only in part, or who have parents able to support them only
in part, over those who are able or who have parents who are able
wholly to furnish such support.

§ 110. Support of state patients.— State patients shall be
provided with proper board, lodging, medical treatment, care and
tuition; and the managers of the colony shall receive for each state
patient supported therein a sum not exceeding two hundred and
fifty dollars per annum; which payments, if any, shall be made by
the treasurer of the state, on the warrant of the comptroller, to the
treasurer of the said colony, on his presenting the bill of the actual
time and number of patients in the colony, signed and verified by
the superintendent and treasurer of the colony and by the president and secretary of its board of managers. The supervisors of
any county from which such patients may have been received into
the colony shall cause to be raised annually while such patients
remain in the colony, the sum of thirty dollars for each of such
state patients for the purpose of furnishing suitable clothing, and
the same shall be paid to the treasurer of the colony on or before
the first day of April of each year.

§ 111. Apportionment of state patients.— Whenever applications are made at one time for admission of more state patients
than can be properly accommodated in the colony, the managers
shall so apportion the number received, that each county may be
represented in a ratio of its dependent epileptic population to the

dependent epileptic population of the state, as shown by statistics furnished by the state board of charities.

§ 112. The support of private patients.— The superintendent of the colony may agree with any epileptic who may be of age, or his committee or guardian, or with the parents, guardian or committee of any epileptic child, or with any person for the entire or partial support, maintenance, clothing, tuition, training, care and treatment of such epileptic in the colony, on such terms and conditions as may be prescribed in the by-laws or approved by the managers. Every patient, guardian, committee or other person applying for the admission into the colony of an epileptic who is, or whose parents or guardians are of sufficient ability to provide for his support and maintenance therein, shall at the time of his admission, execute a bond to the treasurer of the colony with one or more sureties, to be approved by the superintendent and treasurer, in such sum as the managers shall prescribe, to the effect that the obligers will pay to the treasurer of the colony all sums of money at such time or times as shall be so agreed upon, and remove such epileptic from the colony free of expense to the managers within twenty days after the service of the notice hereinafter provided for. If such epileptic, his parents or guardian are of sufficient ability to pay only a part of the expenses of supporting and maintaining him at the institution, such undertaking shall be only for such partial support and maintenance and for removal from the institution as above mentioned; and the treasurer may take security by such obligation or in his discretion by note or other written agreement, with or without sureties, as he may deem proper for such part of such expenses as the epileptic, his parents or guardians are able to pay; but such exercise of discretion shall be with the approval of the superintendent and a committee of the managers in a manner that shall be prescribed in the by-laws. Notice to remove a patient shall be in writing, signed by the superintendent and directed to the epileptic, his parents, guardian, committee or other person upon whose request the patient was received at the colony, at the place of residence mentioned in such request, and deposited in the post-office at Sonyea or any post-office in Livingston county, with the postage prepaid.

6. Receive for the use of the colony, money which may be paid upon obligation or securities in his hands belonging to the colony; and all sums paid to the colony for the support of any patient therein, or, for actual disbursements made in his behalf for necessary clothing and traveling expenses; and money paid to the colony from any other source.

7. Prosecute an action in the name of the colony to recover money due or owing to the colony, from any source; including the bringing of suit for breach of contract between private patients or their guardians and the managers of the colony.

8. Execute a lease and satisfaction of a mortgage, judgment, lien or other debt when paid.

9. Pay the salaries of the superintendent, treasurer, matron, steward, and of all employes of the colony, and the disbursements of the officers and members of the board as aforesaid. The treasurer shall have power to employ counsel, subject to the approval of the board of managers.

10. Deposit all moneys received for the care of private patients and all other revenues of the colony, in a bank designated by the comptroller, and transmit to the comptroller a statement showing the amount so received and deposited and from whom, and for what received, and the dates on which such deposits were made. Such statement of deposit shall be certified by the proper officer of the bank receiving such deposit or deposits. The treasurer shall verify by his affidavit that the sum so deposited is all the money received by him from any source of income for the colony up to the time of the last deposit appearing on such statement. A bank designated by the comptroller to receive such deposits shall, before any such deposit be made, execute a bond to the people of the state in a sum and with sureties to be approved by the comptroller, for the safe keeping of such deposits.

§ 109. Designation and admission of patients.—There shall be received and gratuitously supported in the colony, epileptics residing in the state, who, if of age, are unable, or, if under age, whose parents or guardians are unable to provide for their support therein; and who shall be designated as state patients. Such

additional number of epileptics as can be conveniently accommodated shall be received into the colony by the managers on such terms as shall be just, and shall be designated as private patients. Epileptic children shall be received into the colony only upon the written request of the persons desiring to send them, stating the name, age, place of nativity, if known, the town, city or county in which such children respectively reside, and the ability of their respective parents, or guardians or others to provide for their support in whole or in part, and if in part only, stating what part; and stating also the degree of relationship or other circumstances of connection between the patients and the persons requesting their admission; which statement in all cases of state patients must be verified by the affidavits of the petitioners and of two disinterested persons, and accompanied by the opinion of a qualified physician, all residents of the same county with the epileptic patient, and acquainted with the facts and circumstances stated, and who must be certified to be credible by the county judge or surrogate of the county; and such judge or surrogate must also certify, in each case, that such state patient, in his opinion, is an eligible and proper candidate for admission to the colony. State patients may also be received into the colony upon the official application of a county superintendent of the poor, or of the poor authorities of any city.

It shall be the duty of the superintendent of the poor in every county and of the poor authorities of every city to furnish annually to the state board of charities, a list of all epileptics in their respective jurisdictions, so far as the same can be ascertained, with such particulars as to the condition of each epileptic as shall be prescribed by the said state board. Whenever an epileptic shall become a charge for his or her maintenance on any of the towns, cities or counties of this state, it shall be the duty of all poor authorities of such city, and of the county superintendents of the poor, and of the supervisors of such county, to place such epileptic in the said colony. Any parent, guardian or friend of an epileptic child within this state may make application to the poor authorities of any city, or the superintendent of the poor of any county or the board of supervisors or any supervisor of any town, ward

6. Receive for the use of the colony, money which may be paid upon obligation or securities in his hands belonging to the colony; and all sums paid to the colony for the support of any patient therein, or, for actual disbursements made in his behalf for necessary clothing and traveling expenses; and money paid to the colony from any other source.

7. Prosecute an action in the name of the colony to recover money due or owing to the colony, from any source; including the bringing of suit for breach of contract between private patients or their guardians and the managers of the colony.

8. Execute a lease and satisfaction of a mortgage, judgment, lien or other debt when paid.

9. Pay the salaries of the superintendent, treasurer, matron, steward, and of all employes of the colony, and the disbursements of the officers and members of the board as aforesaid. The treasurer shall have power to employ counsel, subject to the approval of the board of managers.

10. Deposit all moneys received for the care of private patients and all other revenues of the colony, in a bank designated by the comptroller, and transmit to the comptroller a statement showing the amount so received and deposited and from whom, and for what received, and the dates on which such deposits were made. Such statement of deposit shall be certified by the proper officer of the bank receiving such deposit or deposits. The treasurer shall verify by his affidavit that the sum so deposited is all the money received by him from any source of income for the colony up to the time of the last deposit appearing on such statement. A bank designated by the comptroller to receive such deposits shall, before any such deposit be made, execute a bond to the people of the state in a sum and with sureties to be approved by the comptroller, for the safe keeping of such deposits.

§ 109. Designation and admission of patients.—There shall be received and gratuitously supported in the colony, epileptics residing in the state, who, if of age, are unable, or, if under age, whose parents or guardians are unable to provide for their support therein; and who shall be designated as state patients. Such

. dependent epileptic population of the state, as shown by statistics furnished by the state board of charities.

§ 112. The support of private patients.— The superintendent of the colony may agree with any epileptic who may be of age, or his committee or guardian, or with the parents, guardian or committee of any epileptic child, or with any person for the entire or partial support, maintenance, clothing, tuition, training, care and treatment of such epileptic in the colony, on such terms and conditions as may be prescribed in the by-laws or approved by the managers. Every patient, guardian, committee or other person applying for the admission into the colony of an epileptic who is, or whose parents or guardians are of sufficient ability to provide for his support and maintenance therein, shall at the time of his admission, execute a bond to the treasurer of the colony with one or more sureties, to be approved by the superintendent and treasurer, in such sum as the managers shall prescribe, to the effect that the obligers will pay to the treasurer of the colony all sums of money at such time or times as shall be so agreed upon, and remove such epileptic from the colony free of expense to the managers within twenty days after the service of the notice hereinafter provided for. If such epileptic, his parents or guardian are of sufficient ability to pay only a part of the expenses of supporting and maintaining him at the institution, such undertaking shall be only for such partial support and maintenance and for removal from the institution as above mentioned; and the treasurer may take security by such obligation or in his discretion by note or other written agreement, with or without sureties, as he may deem proper for such part of such expenses as the epileptic, his parents or guardians are able to pay; but such exercise of discretion shall be with the approval of the superintendent and a committee of the managers in a manner that shall be prescribed in the by-laws. Notice to remove a patient shall be in writing, signed by the superintendent and directed to the epileptic, his parents, guardian, committee or other person upon whose request the patient was received at the colony, at the place of residence mentioned in such request, and deposited in the post-office at Sonyea or any post-office in Livingston county, with the postage prepaid.

§ 113. Discharge of patients.— The superintendent of the colony, with the approval of the managers or of a committee thereof, shall have power to discharge patients, but no epileptic patient shall be returned to any poor-house, directly through a superintendent of the poor, or otherwise. In case a patient, not an epileptic, shall be sent to the colony, through mistaken diagnosis of his disease, or other cause, and there received, such patient shall be returned to and the traveling expenses of such return shall be paid by the person who sent him or her to the colony. Should an epileptic become insane, such patient, if a state patient, shall be sent to the state hospital of the district of which he was a resident just prior to his admission to the colony in the manner prescribed by law. The bills for the reasonable expenses incurred in the transportation of state patients to and from the state hospitals after they have been approved in writing by the state commission in lunacy, shall be paid by the treasurer of the state on the warrant of the comptroller from the funds provided for the support of the state hospitals. In case the relatives, guardians or friends of such an insane patient desire that he become an inmate of any state hospital situated beyond the limits of the district of which he was formerly a resident, and there be sufficient accommodations in such state hospital, he shall be received there in the manner provided by law for the transfer of other insane persons. Private patients, who may become insane, shall be committed, as prescribed by law, subject to the regulations of the state commission in lunacy, to such institution for the insane as may be designated by the relatives, guardians or friends of such insane person, all traveling and other expenses of removal to be paid by them. After any patient has been delivered to the managers or officers of such hospital or institution, the care and custody of the managers of the colony over such insane person shall cease; and after any patient shall, as aforesaid, be so certified to be insane as prescribed by law, such patient shall come under the supervision of the state commission in lunacy.

§ 114. Notice of opening of colony.—So soon as the colony shall be ready for the reception of patients, it shall be the duty of the board of managers officially to send notice of such fact to the county clerks and the clerks of the boards of supervisors of the respective counties of the state, and the secretary of the state board of charities; and to furnish such clerks of counties and boards of supervisors with suitable blanks for the commitment of epileptics to such colony.

§ 115. Reimbursement for maintenance expenses.—The board of managers of such colony may appoint an agent, whose duty it shall be to secure from relatives or friends who are liable therefor, or who may be willing to assume the cost of maintenance of any inmate therein, who is not maintained as a private patient, reimbursement in whole or in part of the money expended by the state for such purpose. Such agent shall perform such other duties as the board of managers may prescribe. The compensation of such agent shall be fixed by the board of managers at not more than five dollars per day, and he shall be allowed his necessary expenses, payable from the money appropriated for the support of such institution. If the board of managers believes that any inmate of such colony, not maintained therein as a private patient, has any property, or that any relative who would be liable for his support if he were not an inmate of such institution is of sufficient ability to wholly or partly provide for his maintenance therein, such board of managers may apply to a justice of the supreme court of the judicial district in which such institution is located for an order directing the application of the property of such inmate to his maintenance in such institution, or requiring the relatives so liable for his support to pay to such institution at the time specified in such order a stated amount for such maintenance. At least ten days notice of the application of such order shall be given to such persons and in such manner as such justice shall direct, and such order shall be granted only after a hearing of parties interested who appear and desire to be heard. The relatives against whom such proceeding is instituted and who are served with the notice of the application for the order shall be deemed to be of sufficient ability, unless the contrary shall affirmatively

appear to the satisfaction of such justice. If more than one relative is liable for the support of such inmate and is of sufficient ability to contribute to the expense of his maintenance in such institution, such order shall determine the portion of the expense of his maintenance to be paid by each. If the property of such inmate is not applied as directed in such order, or the relatives liable for the support of such inmate refuse or neglect to comply with such order, the board of managers of such colony may bring an action in the name of such institution to recover the amount due such institution by virtue of such order. (*Added by Chapter* 356 *of the Laws of* 1902.)

ARTICLE VIII.

*INSTITUTIONS FOR JUVENILE DELINQUENTS.

Section 120. State industrial school; managers.

    121. Managers of House of Refuge for Juvenile Delinquents in New York city.

    122. Powers and duties of managers.

    123. Superintendent.

    124. Commitment of children.

    125. Register.

    126. Discipline and control of inmates.

    127. Military drill.

    128. Transfer of inmates to penitentiary or Elmira Reformatory.

    129. Confinement of juvenile delinquents under sentences by the courts of the United States.

    130. Effects of alcoholic drinks and narcotics to be taught.

Section 120. State industrial school; managers.—The State Industrial School, at Rochester, is hereby continued for the reception of all male and female children, under the age of sixteen years, who shall be legally committed to such school as vagrants or on a conviction for any criminal offense by any court having authority to make

*See also chapter 470 of the Laws of 1893, page 804.

such commitment.   Such school shall be under the control
and management of a board of fifteen managers appointed
by the governor, by and with the advice and consent of the
senate.   Their term of office shall be three years, and they shall
be so appointed that the terms of one-third shall expire on the
first Tuesday of February in each year.   All vacancies shall be
filled by the governor and the person appointed to fill a vacancy
shall hold office for the remainder of the term of the person
whom he succeeds.   In the discretion of the governor, persons
of either sex may be appointed as managers of such school.
Such managers shall serve without compensation.   (*As amended
by Chapter 536 of the Laws of* 1898.)

§ 121. Managers of House of Refuge for Juvenile Delinquents in New York city.—The Society for the Reformation of
Juvenile Delinquents in the city of New York shall continue to
be a corporation by the name of " the managers of the Society
for the Reformation of Juvenile Delinquents in the city of New
York," with all the powers conferred upon it by its act of incorporation and the acts amendatory thereof.   There shall continue
to be thirty managers of such society, each of whom shall hold
office for the term of three years; and the managers in office
when this chapter takes effect shall continue in office for the
terms for which they were chosen respectively.   The members
of such society residing in the city of New York shall annually
on the third Monday in November, by a plurality of votes, elect
ten managers of such society.   If a vacancy shall occur in the
office of any manager, the board of managers may appoint a person to fill the vacancy for the remainder of the unexpired term.

§ 122. Powers and duties of managers.— The managers of
such house of refuge, established by the society for the reformation of juvenile delinquents, in the city of New York, and of such
state industrial school shall have the general control of such
institutions and shall make all such rules, regulations, ordinances
and by-laws for the government, discipline, employment, management and disposition of the officers thereof, and of the children
while in such institution or in the care of such managers, as to

them may appear just and proper. They shall appoint a superintendent and such other officers as they may deem necessary
for the conduct and welfare of the institution under their charge.
They shall report in detail annually to the legislature on or before the fifteenth day of January, the number of children received
by them into the institution, the disposition thereof, their receipts
and expenditures, their proceedings during the preceding year,
and all other matters which they deem advisable to be brought to
the attention of the legislature.

§ 123. Superintendent.— The superintendent so appointed shall
be the chief executive officer of such school, or house of refuge,
and subject to the by-laws, rules and regulations thereof and the
powers of the board of managers, shall have control of the internal affairs and shall maintain discipline therein and enforce a
compliance with, and obedience to, all rules, by-laws, regulations
and ordinances adopted by said board for the government, discipline and management of such school or house of refuge.

Under direction of such managers, he shall receive and take
into such institution all children legally committed thereto by
any court having authority to make such commitment.

§ 124. Commitment of children.— Children under the age of
sixteen years may be committed from the rural counties of this
state as vagrants, or on the conviction of any criminal offense
by any court having authority to make such commitments, to the
state industrial school or the house of refuge established by the
society for the reformation of juvenile delinquents; but such children in the counties of New York and Kings shall be committed
to the house of refuge in New York city, established by such
society. But no child under the age of twelve years shall be
committed or sentenced to either of such institutions for any
crime or offense less than felony. The courts of criminal jurisdiction in the several counties shall ascertain by such proof as
may be in their power, the age of every delinquent committed to
either of such institutions, and insert such age in the order of
commitment and the age thus ascertained shall be deemed and
taken to be the true age of such delinquent. If the court shall

omit to insert in the order of commitment the age of any delinquent committed to such school or house of refuge, the managers shall as soon as may be after such delinquent shall be received by them, ascertain his age by the best means in their power, and cause the same to be entered in a book to be designated by them for that purpose, and the age of such delinquent thus ascertained shall be deemed and taken to be the true age of such delinquent.

§ 125. Register.— Upon the commitment of a delinquent to such industrial school or house of refuge, the superintendent thereof shall cause to be entered in the register kept for that purpose, the date of admission, name, sex, age, place of birth, nationality, residence and such other facts as may be ascertained, relating to the origin, condition, peculiarity or inherited tendencies of such delinquent.

§ 126. Discipline and control of inmates.— The managers of the state industrial school shall receive and detain during minority, every delinquent committed thereto in pursuance of law, or to the western house of refuge for juvenile delinquents, or to the house of refuge for juvenile delinquents in western New York. The managers of the house of refuge for juvenile delinquents in the city of New York, may receive and detain during minority all delinquents committed thereto. The managers of each institution shall cause the children detained therein or under their care to be instructed in such branches of useful knowledge, and to be regularly and systematically employed in such lines of industry as shall be suitable to their years and capacities, and shall cause such children to be subjected to such discipline, as in the opinion of such board, is most likely to effect their reformation. The managers of each institution, with the consent of any child committed thereto, may bind out as an apprentice or servant, such child during the time they would be entitled to retain him or her, to such persons and at such places to learn such trade and employment as in their judgment will be for the future benefit and advantage of such child.

§ 127. Military drill.— The superintendent of the state industrial school, and the superintendent of the house of refuge, established by the society for the reformation of juvenile delinquents, with the approval of the respective boards of managers thereof, may institute and establish a system of rules and regulations for uniforming, equipping, officering, disciplining and drilling in military art, the male inmates of such institutions, and for the exercise and drill of such inmates according to the most approved tactics, such number of hours daily as such superintendent may deem advisable.

§ 128. Transfer of inmates to penitentiary or Elmira reformatory.—If a delinquent confined in the state industrial school or the house of refuge established by the society for the reformation of juvenile delinquents is guilty of attempting to set fire to any building belonging to either of such institutions, or to any combustible matter for the purpose of setting fire to any such building or of openly resisting the lawful authority of an officer thereof, or of attempting to excite others to do so, or shall by gross or habitual misconduct exert a dangerous and pernicious influence over the other delinquents, the board of managers of the institution wherein such case arises shall submit a written statement of the facts to a justice of the supreme court, or if the case arises within the state industrial school, to the county judge of the county of Monroe, and apply to him for an order authorizing a temporary confinement of such delinquent, in the Monroe county penitentiary, or if over sixteen years of age in the Elmira reformatory; and if the case arises within the house of refuge, established by the society for the reformation of juvenile delinquents in the city of New York, in the county jail or penitentiary of the county of New York, or if the delinquent be over sixteen years of age, to the Eastern New York reformatory, when completed, and until then to the Elmira reformatory. Such judge shall forthwith inquire into the facts, and if it appear that the statement is substantially true, and that the ends desired to be accomplished by the institution wherein the case has arisen will be best promoted thereby, he shall make an order authorizing the confinement of such delinquent in such penitentiary, county jail or reformatory for the limited time expressed in the order, and the keeper or superintendent of such penitentiary, county jail or reformatory shall receive such delinquent and detain him during the time expressed in such order. At the expiration of the time limited by such order, or sooner, if the board of managers of either of such institutions shall direct, the superintendent or keeper of such reformatory, county jail or penitentiary shall return such delinquent to the custody of the superintendent of the institution from which such delinquent shall have been received.

§ 129. Confinement of juvenile delinquents under sentences by the courts of the United States.—The superintendents of the house of refuge, established by the society for the reformation of juvenile delinquents in the city of New York, and the state industrial school at Rochester, shall receive and safely keep in their respective institutions, subject to the regulations and discipline thereof, and the provisions of this article, any criminal under the age of sixteen years convicted of any offense against the United States, under sentences of imprisonment in any court of the United States, sitting within this state, until such sentences be executed, or until such delinquent shall be discharged by due course of law, conditioned upon the United States supporting such delinquent and paying the expenses attendant upon the execution of such sentence.

§ 130. Effects of alcoholic drinks and narcotics to be taught.— The nature of alcoholic drinks and other narcotics and their effects on the human system shall be taught in the schools connected with such house of refuge established by the society for the reformation of juvenile delinquents in the city of New York and in the State Industrial school at Rochester, for not less than four lessons a week for ten or more weeks in each year. All pupils who can read shall study this subject from suitable text books, but pupils unable to read shall be instructed in it orally by teachers using text books adapted for such oral instruction as a guide and standard, and these text books shall be graded to the capacities of the pupils pursuing such course of study.

ARTICLE IX.

HOUSES OF REFUGE AND REFORMATORIES FOR WOMEN.

Section 140. Names and locations of houses of refuge and reformatories for women.—The houses of correction for women located at Hudson and Albion are continued and shall be known respectively as the House of Refuge for Women at Hudson, and the Western House of Refuge for Women. The reformatory for women located at Bedford is also continued and shall be known as the New York State Reformatory for Women.

§ 141. Appointment of managers.—Each such institution shall be under the control of its present board of managers, until others are appointed. Such boards shall consist of six managers to be appointed by the governor, by and with the advice and consent of the senate. All such managers shall be residents of the state, two shall be women and one a physician who has practiced his profession for ten years. The terms of the managers hereafter appointed shall be six years, except that the managers appointed to fill vacancies shall hold office for the unexpired terms of the

managers whom they succeed. The term of office of one of such
managers shall expire each year. If in any such institution there
be less than six managers in office when this act takes effect, the
governor shall appoint additional managers to make up the number of six, who shall be so classified by him that the term of one
manager shall expire each year. Where the term of office of a
manager of any such institution expires at a time other than the
last day of December in any year, the term of office of his successor is abridged so as to expire on the last day of December,
preceding the time when such term would otherwise expire, and
the term of office of each manager thereafter appointed shall
begin on the first day of January.

The governor may remove any manager, at any time, for cause,
on giving to such manager a copy of the charges against him and
an opportunity to be heard in his defense.

Such managers shall receive no compensation for their time or
services; but the actual expenses necessarily incurred by them in
the performance of their official duties shall be paid in the same
manner as other expenses of such institution. Nothing contained
in this section shall abridge the term of any manager now in office.

§ 142. General powers and duties of managers.—Each board
of managers shall have the general superintendence, management and control of the institution over which it is appointed;
of the grounds and buildings, officers and employes thereof; of
the inmates therein, and of all matters relating to the government, discipline, contracts and fiscal concerns therof, and may
make such rules and regulations as may seem to them necessary
for carrying out the purposes of such institutions.

§ 143. Appointment and removal of officers and employes;
compensation.—The board of managers of each of such institutions shall appoint from among its members a president, secretary
and treasurer, who shall hold office for such length of time as such
board may determine.

They shall appoint a female superintendent, who shall hold
office during the pleasure of the board.

Such boards of managers shall fix the compensation of the officers and employes of the institution under their charge.

§ 144. General powers of superintendents.—The superintendent of each such institution shall, subject to the direction and control of the board of managers thereof:

1. Have the general supervision and control of the grounds and
buildings of the institution, the subordinate officers and employes
and the inmates thereof, and of all matters relating to their government and discipline.

2. Make such rules, regulations and orders, not inconsistent
with law or with the rules, regulations or directions of the board
of managers, as may seem to her proper or necessary for the government of such institution and its officers and employes; and for
the employment, discipline and education of the inmates thereof.

3. Exercise such other powers and perform such other duties
as the board of managers may prescribe.

Such superintendent shall also have power to appoint and remove all subordinate female officers and employes, subject to the
approval of the board.

§ 145. Oaths and bonds.—Each manager and superintendent
of such institutions shall take the constitutional oath of office
and each superintendent shall execute a bond to the people of
this state in the sum of five thousand dollars with sureties
approved by the state comptroller, which shall be filed in the
office of the comptroller. The manager appointed as treasurer
of such institution shall give a bond in such amount as the
comptroller may direct. The comptroller may require other
officers of such institutions to give a bond if in his opinion the
interests of the state demand it. (*As amended by Chapter* 49 *of
the Laws of* 1900.)

§ 146. Commitments; papers furnished by committing magistrates.

Subdivision 1. A female, between the ages of fifteen and thirty
years, convicted by any magistrate of petit larceny, habitual
drunkenness, of being a common prostitute, of frequenting disorderly houses or houses of prostitution, or of a misdemeanor,
and who is not insane, nor mentally or physically incapable of
being substantially benefited by the discipline of either of such

institutions, may be sentenced and committed to the House of
Refuge for Women at Hudson, or to the Western House of
Refuge for Women, at Albion, or the New York State Reformatory for Women, at Bedford. The term of such sentence and
commitment shall be three years, but such female may be sooner
discharged therefrom by the board of managers. Such commitments to the House of Refuge for Women, at Hudson, until
the New York State Reformatory for Women, at Bedford, is
completed and ready for the reception of inmates shall be from
the first, second, third, fourth, and fifth judicial districts, and
the counties of Delaware and Otsego; to the Western House of
Refuge, at Albion, from the other counties in the sixth and from
the seventh and eighth judicial districts. On the completion of
the New York State Reformatory for Women, at Bedford, commitments thereto shall be made from the first judicial district
and the counties of Westchester, Kings, Queens, Nassau, Suffolk
and Richmond.

2. The board of managers of each such institution shall furnish
the several county clerks of the state with suitable blanks for the
commitment of women thereto. Such county clerks shall immediately notify the magistrates of their respective counties of the
reception of such blanks and that upon application they will be
furnished to them.

3. The magistrate committing a female, pursuant to this section, shall immediately notify the superintendent of the institution to which the commitment is made of the conviction of such
female, and shall cause a record to be kept of the name, age,
birthplace, occupation, previous commitments, if any, and for
what offenses; the last place of residence of such female, and the
particulars of the offense for which she is committed. A copy of
such record shall be transmitted, with the warrant of commitment, to the superintendent of such institution, who shall cause
the facts stated therein, and such other facts as may be directed
by the board of managers, to be entered in a book of record.

4. Such magistrate shall, before committing any such female,
inquire into and determine the age of such female at the time

of commitment, and her age as so determined shall be stated in the warrant. The statement of the age of such female in such warrant shall be conclusive evidence as to such age, in any action to recover damages for her detention or imprisonment under such warrant, and shall be presumptive evidence thereof in any other inquiry, action or proceeding relating to such detention or imprisonment. (*As amended by Chapter 632 of the Laws of* 1899.)

§ 147. Return of females improperly committed.—Whenever it shall appear to the satisfaction of the board of managers of any such institution, that any person committed thereto is not of proper age to be so committed or is not properly committed, or is insane or mentally incapable of being materially benefited by the discipline of any such institution, such board of managers shall cause the return of such female to the county from which she was so committed. Such female shall be so returned in the custody of one of the persons employed by such boards of managers to convey to such institutions women committed thereto, who shall deliver her into the custody of the sheriff of the county from which she was committed. Such sheriff shall take such female before the magistrate making the commitment, or some other magistrate having equal jurisdiction in such county, to be by such magistrate re-sentenced for the offense for which she was committed to any such institution and dealt with in all respects as though she had not been so committed.

The cost and expenses of the return of such female, necessarily incurred and paid by any such board of managers shall be a charge against the county from which such female was committed, to be paid by such county to such board of managers in the same manner as other county charges are collected.

§ 148. Disposition of children of women so committed.— If any woman committed to any such institution, at the time of such commitment is a mother of a nursing child in her care under one year of age, or is pregnant with child which shall be born after such commitment, such child may accompany its mother to and remain in such institution until it is two years of age and must then be removed therefrom.

The board of managers of any such institution may cause such child to be placed in any asylum for children in this state and pay for the care and maintenance of such child therein at a rate not to exceed two and one-half dollars a week, until the mother of such child shall have been discharged from such institution, or may commit such child to the care and custody of some relative or proper person willing to assume such care.

If such woman, at the time of such commitment, shall be the mother of and have under her exclusive care a child more than one year of age, which might otherwise be left without proper care or guardianship, the magistrate committing such woman shall cause such child to be committed to such asylum as may be provided by law for such purposes, or to the care and custody of some relative or proper person willing to assume such care.

§ 149. Conveyance of women committed.—The board of managers of each of such institutions shall employ suitable persons to be known as marshals, to convey from the place of conviction to such institution, all women legally committed thereto, and such marshals shall have the power and authority of deputy sheriffs in respect thereto. All expenses necessarily incurred in making such conveyance shall be paid by the treasurer of the board of managers. In case of the commitment of a woman, who, at the time thereof, is the mother of a nursing child or is pregnant, the board of managers shall designate a woman of suitable age and character to accompany the person so committed, along with the officer or representative, authorized in this section to be employed by such managers.

§ 150. Detentions and rearrests in cases of escapes.—The board of managers of any such institution may detain therein, under the rules and regulations adopted by them, any female legally committed thereto, according to the terms of the sentence and commitment, and conditionally discharge such female at any time prior to the expiration of the term of commitment.

If an inmate escape or be conditionally discharged from any such institution, the board of managers may cause her to be rearrested and returned to such institution, to be detained therein for the unexpired portion of her term, dating from the time of her escape or conditional discharge. A person employed by the board of managers of any such institution to convey to such institution, women committed thereto, may arrest, without a warrant, an escaped inmate in any county in this state, and shall forthwith convey her to the institution from which she escaped; and a magistrate may cause an escaped inmate to be arrested and held in custody, until she can be removed to such institution, as in the case of her first commitment thereto.

A person conditionally discharged from any such institution may be arrested and returned thereto, upon a warrant issued by its president and secretary. Such warrant shall briefly state the reason for such arrest and return, and shall be directed and delivered to a person employed by such board of managers to convey to such institutions, women committed thereto, and may be executed by such person in any such county of this state.

§ 151. Employment of inmates.—The board of managers of each institution shall determine the kind of employment for women committed thereto and shall provide for their necessary custody and superintendence. The provisions for the safe keeping and employment of such women shall be made for the purpose of teaching such women a useful trade or profession and improving their mental and moral condition.

Such board of managers may credit such women with a reasonable compensation for the labor performed by them, and may charge them with the necessary expenses of their maintenance and discipline, not exceeding the sum of two dollars per week. If any balance shall be found to be due such women at the expiration of their terms of commitment, such balance may be paid to them at the time of their discharge.

To secure the safe keeping, obedience and good order of the women committed to any such institution, the superintendent thereof, has the same power as to such women, as keepers of jails and penitentiaries possess as to persons committed to their custody.

§ 152. Clothing and money to be furnished discharged inmates.—The board of managers of any such institution may,

in their discretion, furnish to each inmate of such institution
who shall be discharged therefrom, necessary clothing not exceeding twelve dollars in value, or if discharged between the first
day of November and the first day of April to the value of not
exceeding eighteen dollars, and ten dollars in money, and a ticket
for the transportation of one person from such institution to the
place of conviction of such inmate, or to such other place as
such inmate may designate, at no greater distance from such
institution than the place of conviction.

§ 153. Board of managers of Bedford reformatory to
notify county clerks of completion thereof.—As soon as the
Bedford Reformatory for Women is completed and ready for
the reception of inmates, the board of managers thereof shall
notify the county clerks of Westchester and New York counties
and furnish such clerks with suitable blanks for the commitment
of women to such institution.   Such county clerks, on the reception of such notification, shall transmit a copy thereof to the
several magistrates of such counties.

ARTICLE X.

THOMAS ASYLUM FOR ORPHAN AND DESTITUTE INDIAN CHILDREN.

Section 160. Establishment of asylum.

    161. Board of managers.

    162. Powers and duties of the board.

    163. Officers; salaries.

    164. Superintendent, powers and duties.

    165. Treasurer, powers and duties.

Section 160. Establishment of asylum. --The Thomas Asylum
for Orphan and Destitute Indian Children, established on the Cattaraugus reservation in the county of Erie, is hereby continued.

Such asylum may sue and be sued in the corporate name of
" Thomas Asylum for Orphan and Destitute Indian Children,"
and service of process and papers may be made upon the superintendent or any manager of such asylum.

§ 161. Board of managers.—Such asylum shall be under the
control and management of a board of managers, consisting

of ten members. three of whom shall be Seneca Indiana. Such managers and their successors shall be appointed by the governor, by and with the advice and consent of the senate. and shall hold their office for six years. and until others are appointed in their stead. subject to removal for cause by the governor. If any manager fails. without being excused by vote of the board. for one year. to attend the regular meeting of the board of which he is a member. his office shall become vacant. A certificate of every such failure shall forthwith be transmitted by the board to the governor. and all vacancies caused by removal or expiration of office or otherwise shall be filled by the governor, by and with the consent of the senate.

§ 162. Powers and duties of board of managers.—The board of managers shall have the general direction and control of all the property and concerns of such asylum, not otherwise provided for by law. They may acquire and hold, in the name of and for the people of the state of New York, property, by grant, gift, devise or bequest, except reservation lands, which may be held by those managers who are Seneca Indians, to be applied to the maintenance of orphan and destitute Indian children, and the general use of the asylum. They shall not receive any compensation for their services, but shall receive actual and necessary traveling expenses for attending the regular meetings of the board. as prescribed by the by-laws of said asylum. They shall:

1. Adopt, with the approval or consent of the state board of charities. by-laws for the regulation and management of said asylum, and regulating the appointment and duties of officers, assistants and employes of the asylum, and ordain and enforce a suitable system of rules and regulations for the internal government, discipline and management of the same.

2. Take care of the general interests of the asylum, and see that its design is carried into effect according to law, and its by-laws, rules and regulations. They shall, on application, receive destitute and orphan Indian children from any of the several reservations located within this state, and shall furnish them such care, moral training, and education, and such instruction

in husbandry, and the arts of civilization as shall be prescribed
by their by-laws, rules and regulations.

3. Keep in a book provided for that purpose, a fair and full
record of their doings, which shall be open at all times to the
inspection of the governor, the state board of charities or any
person appointed to examine the same by the governor, the state
board of charities, or either house of the legislature.

4. Maintain an effective inspection of the asylum, for which purpose a committee of the board, consisting of at least four members
thereof, shall visit the asylum at least bi-monthly, and the whole
board at least twice a year, and at such other times as may be prescribed by the by-laws.

5. Enter in a book kept by them for that purpose, the date of
each visit, the condition of the asylum and the children therein,
and its property, and all such managers present shall sign such
entries.

6. Make, annually, on or before the fifteenth day of January, a
report to the legislature of the condition of said asylum, including
a true account, in detail, of the receipts and disbursements of all
moneys that shall come into their hands, or under their control,
the number, age and sex of such destitute orphan children in said
asylum, with the name of the reservation to which they belong,
and the proportion of the year each has been maintained and instructed in said asylum, and such suggestions and recommendations as they may deem proper, or which may be required of them
by the state board of charities.

§ 163. Officers; salaries.—Such board shall appoint for the asylum, as often as necessary, and for cause, after an opportunity to
be heard, remove:

1. A superintendent, a matron, and a well-educated physician,
who shall be a graduate of an incorporated medical college.

2. A treasurer, who shall give a bond to the people of the state
for the faithful performance of his trust, with such sureties, and
in such amount as the comptroller of the state shall approve.

The superintendent, matron, and other assistants shall constantly reside in the asylum, or on the premises, and shall be
designated the resident officers of the asylum. The physician

shall visit said asylum at such times, and perform such duties as shall be prescribed by the by-laws, rules and regulations of the asylum. Such board shall also, from time to time. with the approval of the state board of charities, fix the annual salaries and allowances of such officers. Such salaries shall be paid in equal monthly installments by the treasurer on the warrant of the board of managers, countersigned by the superintendent thereof. and certified as correct.

§ 164. Superintendent, powers and duties.—The superintendent shall be the chief executive officer of such asylum, and in his absence or sickness, the matron shall perform the duties. and be subject to the responsibilities of the superintendent. Subject to the by-laws, rules and regulations established by the board of managers, such officer shall have the general superintendence of the buildings. grounds, and farm, together with their furniture, fixtures and stock, and shall:

1. Daily ascertain the condition of all the children and prescribe their conduct.

2. Appoint, with the approval of the board of managers. the other resident officers, assistants and employes not otherwise provided for, that he may think necessary for the economical and efficient performance of the business of the asylum, and prescribe their duties, and he may discharge them at his discretion.

3. Cause full and fair accounts and records of all his doings. and of the entire business and operation of the asylum to be kept regularly, from day to day, in books provided for that purpose.

4. See that all such accounts and records are justly made up for the annual report to the legislature, as required by this act, and present the same to the board of managers, who shall incorporate them into their report to the legislature.

5. Keep in a book, in which he shall cause to be entered, at the time of the reception of any child, his name, age, residence, and the names of his parents (if any), to what reservation and tribe he belongs, and the date of such reception, and by whom brought, and the condition of the general health of such child.

§ 165. Treasurer, powers and duties.— The treasurer shall have the custody of all moneys, obligations and securities belonging to the asylum. He shall:

1. Open with some good and solvent bank, conveniently near the asylum, an account in his name as such treasurer, and deposit all moneys, upon receiving the same, therein, and draw from the same in the manner prescribed by the by-laws, specifying the object of payment.

2. Keep a full and accurate account of all receipts and payment in the manner directed by the by-laws, and such other accounts as the board of managers shall prescribe, render a statement to the board of managers whenever required by them.

ARTICLE XI.

Section 170. Laws repealed.

171. When to take effect.

Section 170. Laws repealed.— Of the laws enumerated in the schedule hereto annexed, that portion specified in the last column is repealed.

§ 171. When to take effect.—This chapter shall take effect on October first, eighteen hundred and ninety-six.

SCHEDULE OF LAWS REPEALED.

Laws of—	Chapter.	Sections.
1846	143	All.
1850	24	All.
1851	502	All.
1852	387	All.
1853	159	All.
1853	608	All.
1855	163	All.
1861	306	All.
1862	220	All.
1867	739	All.
1867	951	All.
1873	571	All.
1875	228	All.
1878	72	All.
1879	109	All.

Laws of—	Chapter.	Sections.
.1881	187	All.
1885	281	All.
1886	539	All.
1888	404	All.
1890	238	All.
1891	51	All.
1891	216	All.
1891	375	All.
1892	637	All, except § 5.
1892	704	All.
1893	635	All.
1894	363	All.
1895	13	All.
1895	38	All, except § 9.
1895	59	All.
1895	253	All.
1895	439	All.
1895	771	All.

THE STATE INDUSTRIAL SCHOOL, ROCHESTER.

AN ACT to amend chapter five hundred and thirty-nine of the laws of eighteen hundred and eighty-six, entitled "An act changing the name of the 'Western House of Refuge for Juvenile Delinquents in Western New York,' to 'The State Industrial School,' and relating to discipline and instruction therein, and commitments thereto, and making an appropriation therefor."

Chapter 470 of the Laws of 1893.

Section 1. Section three of chapter five hundred and thirty-nine of the laws of eighteen hundred and eighty-six is hereby amended to read as follows:

§ 3. It shall be lawful for the board of managers of the State Industrial School to receive into said school all children who have heretofore been, or who may hereafter be, sentenced to the Western House of Refuge for Juvenile Delinquents, or to the House of Refuge for Juvenile Delinquents in Western New York or to the State Industrial School, and to retain the same. subject to the rules and regulations of said institution, and said board of managers shall have the right, and it shall be their duty to receive and detain all such persons committed to their custody, and such right and duty shall not be affected, prejudiced or impaired by reason of, or in consequence of, any technical defect or clerical error in the warrant of commitment. The several courts having criminal jurisdiction and who shall hold criminal courts in all the counties of this state, except the counties of New York and Kings, are hereby authorized to sentence juvenile delinquents convicted in any of such courts to such State Industrial School.

NEW YORK STATE SOLDIERS AND SAILORS' HOME.

THE PUBLIC BUILDINGS LAW.
Chapter 227 of the Laws of 1893.

ARTICLE IV.
NEW YORK STATE SOLDIERS AND SAILORS' HOME.
Section 40. Trustees.
>   41. Powers of trustees.
>   42. Admission to home.
>   43. Transfer of inmates to state hospital.
>   44. Annual report.

Section 40. Trustees.—The property heretofore conveyed to the state by the corporation known as the Grand Army of the Republic Soldiers' Home of New York, and all property heretofore or hereafter acquired by the state for the same purpose, shall continue to be known as the New York State Soldiers and Sailors' Home, and shall continue to be under the management and control of a board of trustees consisting of eleven members, of which the governor and attorney-general shall be ex-officio members; and the remaining nine members shall be reputable citizens of the state appointed by the governor, by and with the advice and consent of the senate, and each shall hold office for three years. No trustee shall receive any compensation for his services as such trustee or otherwise, except the trustee elected to act as secretary who may receive a reasonable annual compensation for his services, to be fixed by the board, with the approval of the comptroller, not exceeding the sum of two hundred and fifty dollars. The board shall annually elect by ballot a president, secretary, treasurer and executive committee, but the offices of secretary and treasurer may be held by one trustee or separately as the board may determine. The board shall be known as the board of trustees of the New York State Soldiers and Sailors' Home.

§ 41. Powers of trustees.—The board of trustees shall have possession of all property belonging to or constituting such home and may complete the buildings therein already commenced or hereafter to be erected, and keep them in readiness for occupation with any funds appropriated therefor or that may come into their hands for such purpose, and may pay any existing indebtedness of such corporation which shall be or might become a lien upon such property or any part thereof. The board may make contracts in its name, subject to the approval of the comptroller, for work and materials for the completion of the buildings on such property, the furnishing thereof and of supplies for use and consumption therein, but shall spend no money and incur no indebtedness for such purpose beyond the appropriation previously made therefor by the legislature. It may adopt rules and regulations, subject to like approval, specifying the duties of the officers of the home, the government of its inmates, fixing the terms and conditions of admission thereto and the cause and manner of expulsion therefrom. The board may require and take in its name any security by way of bond or otherwise from any person appointed or elected by it, for the faithful performance of his duties, and for truly accounting for all moneys or property received by him, for or on account of the board of trustees or in the performance of such duties.

§ 42. Admission to home.—Every honorably discharged soldier or sailor who served in the army or navy of the United States during the late rebellion, who enlisted from the state of New York, or who shall have been a resident of this state for one year preceding his application for admission, and who shall need the aid or benefit of such home in consequence of physical disability or other cause within the scope of the regulations of the board, shall be entitled to admission thereto, subject to the conditions, limitations and penalties prescribed by the rules and regulations of the board.

§ 43. Transfer of inmates to state hospital.—Any soldier or sailor regularly admitted into the home found to be insane, may be transferred by an order of the president and secretary of the board of trustees and the superintendent of the home to any state hospital for the insane, there to remain at the expense of the home until legally discharged, and such expense shall be paid out of the maintenance fund of the home, at the same rate as is charged for the support of the county insane.

§ 44. Annual report.—Such board shall, annually, on or before January fifteenth, make to the legislature a detailed report of all its receipts and expenditures and of all its proceedings for the previous year, with full estimates for the coming year verified by the president and treasurer.

(*This chapter repealed chapter 48 of the laws of 1878; also chapter 407 of the laws of 1879.*)

SALE OF ALE AND BEER AT THE NEW YORK STATE SOLDIERS AND SAILORS' HOME.

AN ACT authorizing the sale of ale and beer upon the premises of the New York State Soldiers and Sailors' Home of Bath, New York, and providing for the expenditure of the net proceeds therefrom.

Chapter 900 of the Laws of 1896.

Section 1. The trustees of the New York Soldiers and Sailors' Home at Bath, New York, upon complying with the provisions of chapter one hundred and twelve, laws of eighteen hundred

and ninety-six, of the state of New York, are hereby authorized
to sell ale and beer to the members of said home, upon the premises of said home, under such rules and regulations as said trustees shall prescribe, and the provisions of clause one, section
twenty-four and clause six of section thirty of said chapter one
hundred and twelve of the laws of eighteen hundred and ninety-
six shall not apply to such New York State Soldiers and Sailors'
Home.

§ 2. The said trustees shall expend the net proceeds of such
sales for the support of the library and reading-room of said
home and for such other purposes as they shall deem best for the
comfort and amusement of the members of said home.

§ 3. All acts and parts of acts inconsistent with this act are
hereby repealed.

EXEMPTED FROM THE MANAGEMENT AND CONTROL OF STATE BOARD OF CHARITIES.

AN ACT relating to the state board of charities and their control and management of the New York State Soldiers and
Sailors' Home.

Chapter 769, Laws of 1900.

Section 1. Soldiers and sailors' home exempted.—The New
York state soldiers and sailors' home is hereby exempted from
the management and control of the state board of charities and
in respect to said institution said board are hereafter only to
exercise their constitutional right to visit and inspect.

§ 2. Repeal.—All acts and parts of acts inconsistent with the
provisions of this act are hereby repealed.

NEW YORK STATE WOMAN'S RELIEF CORPS HOME, OXFORD.

AN ACT to provide for the establishment of a home for the aged
and dependent veteran and his wife, veterans' mothers, widows, and army nurses, residents of New York.

Chapter 468 of the Laws of 1894.

Section 1. Establishment of home.—There shall be established
in this state a home for the aged dependent veteran and his wife,

veterans' mothers, widows, and army nurses, which shall be located within the state at a point which shall be determined as hereinafter provided, said home to be known as " New York State Woman's Relief Corps Home." *(As amended by chapter 47 of the Laws of 1897.)*

§ 2. Board of managers.—It shall be the duty of the governor within thirty days after the passage of this act, by and with the advice and consent of the senate, to appoint nine residents of the state, six of whom shall be women and three men, to constitute a board of managers of said home who shall hold office, three for two, three for four, and three for six years, respectively, as shall be indicated by the governor on making the appointment, and thereafter all appointments except to fill vacancies in said board shall be for six years and shall be made by the governor with the advice and consent of the senate. Whenever a vacancy occurs in said board after the expiration of a term of office or by resignation or removal or otherwise, the governor shall appoint a resident of the state to fill such vacancy, but when an appointment shall be made to fill an unexpired term, the governor shall so indicate at the time of making the appointment, and the person so appointed shall hold office only until the close of the unexpired term, and appointments shall be so made that there will be at all times six women and three men as members of said board. The male members of said board shall be at the time of their appointment members of the Grand Army of the Republic of the department of New York, and the female members shall be members of the women's relief corps, auxiliary to the Grand Army of the Republic, department of New York.

§ 3. Official oath.—Before entering on their duties the said managers shall respectively take and subscribe to the usual oath of office, which oath may be taken and subscribed before the judge of any court of record of this state, or any notary public having a seal, and shall be filed in the office of the secretary of state.

§ 4. Compensation and expenses.—Said managers shall receive no compensation for their time of services, but the actual and necessary expenses of each of them while engaged in the performance of his or her office, and any expenses of said board incurred in the performance of the duties imposed by this act, on being presented in writing and verified by affidavit, shall be paid by the treasurer of said board of managers.

§ 5. Organization of board.—It shall be the duty of said board of managers immediately after their appointment to meet and organize by the election of a president, secretary and treasurer from their number. Said board when organized are directed to confer with the trustees of the New York Soldiers and Sailors' Home to ascertain whether any of the land now used by the said New York Soldiers and Sailors' Home can be made available for the purpose of erecting the home established by this act, and whether such lands, if any there be, are suitable for the purposes of said home. Said board is also directed to examine and make inquiry as to any other location within the state that may be available or suitable for the purposes of the home established by this act. And the said board is hereby empowered to contract for the purchase of any site that they may determine suitable, which said contract, however, shall be subject to the approval of the next legislature of this state; no contract for such purpose, however, shall be valid and binding on the state until the same shall have been duly approved by the next legislature.

§ 6. Report to legislature.—Said board of managers shall report the action which they have taken under the provisions of this act to the senate and assembly within ten days after the organization of the legislature in the year eighteen hundred and ninety-five, and they shall also prepare and submit with such report, for the consideration of the legislature, a statement of the cost of location or grounds required and a general plan for the construction of said home, together with an estimate of the cost of the same, and the cost and expense of maintaining the same.

§ 7. **Purchase of site and erection of building.**—Whenever any site shall have been selected, and contract for the purchase of same made and approved by the legislature, and an appropriation for the payment thereof, and the erection of the buildings thereon made by the legislature of this state, it shall be the duty of said board of managers to purchase such site and to erect suitable buildings thereon for the care, maintenance and relief of aged dependent veterans and their wives, veterans' mothers, widows, and army nurses who, from any cause, need the care and benefits of a home, and to do all things necessary and requisite in the premises.

§ 8. **Admission to home.**—Whenever said lands shall have been purchased, buildings erected, and said home ready for occupancy, every honorably discharged soldier or sailor who served in the army or navy of the United States during the late rebellion, or who enlisted from the state of New York, or who shall have been a resident of this state for one year preceding the application for admission, and the wives, widows and mothers of any such honorably discharged soldier or sailor, and army nurses who served in said army or navy and whose residence was at the time of the commencement of such service or whose residence shall have been for one year preceding his or her application for admission to said home, within the state of New York, or who shall need the aid or benefit of said home in consequence of physical disability or other cause within the scope of the regulations of the board, shall be entitled to admission to said home, subject to the conditions, limitations and penalties prescribed by the rules and regulations adopted by said board. Provided, however, said soldier or sailor shall be a married man and shall be accompanied or attended by his wife during the time he may be an inmate of said home, but no wife or widow of a soldier or sailor shall be admitted as an inmate of said home unless due and sufficient proof is presented of her marriage to such soldier or sailor prior to the year eighteen hundred and eighty.

THOMAS ASYLUM FOR ORPHAN AND DESTITUTE INDIAN CHILDREN.

AN ACT to authorize the transfer of Indian children from the Thomas Asylum for Orphan and Destitute Indian Children to other asylums, hospitals or institutions for the custody and care of orphan, dependent or sick children, and to provide for their care, support and treatment therein.

Chapter 242 of the Laws of 1896.

Section 1. Transfers.—Whenever the number of Indian children in the Thomas Asylum for Orphan and Destitute Indian Children, on the Cattaraugus Reservation, duly admitted thereto, shall be in excess of its proper capacity or the applications for admission of such Indian children to such asylum shall exceed its proper accommodations therefor, or whenever, in the opinion of the trustees of such asylum, the comfort and well-being of any such Indian children therein will likely be promoted by their removal to other asylums, hospitals or institutions for the custody, care and treatment of orphan, dependent or sick children, they may, with the approval of the state board of charities, contract with the managers or other authorities of such asylums, hospitals or institutions as they may deem desirable for the reception, care and treatment of such Indian children, as may, from time to time, be transferred thereto, at a fixed weekly per capita rate not exceeding two dollars, except in the case of sick children requiring hospital treatment and care, when the fixed weekly per capita rate shall not exceed three dollars. The sum of two thousand dollars or so much thereof as may be necessary is hereby appropriated out of any moneys in the state treasury, not otherwise appropriated, for the purpose of this act.

NEW YORK STATE INSTITUTION FOR THE BLIND, BATAVIA (NOW THE NEW YORK STATE SCHOOL FOR THE BLIND).

AN ACT to authorize the establishment of the New York State Institution for the blind.

Chapter 587 of the Laws of 1865.

Section 10. Trustees.—As soon as suitable accommodations shall be provided, the governor shall, by and with the consent of the senate, appoint nine trustees, two from the first judicial district and one from each of the other judicial districts, who shall take charge of said institution. Such trustees shall serve without pay, and shall hold their offices for three years and until others are appointed.

§ 11. Admissions to asylums.—Application for admission into such institution shall be made to a justice of the supreme court or of the court of common pleas or to a county judge in the county where such applicant shall reside. Such justice or judge shall hear the application and make due inquiry into the pecuniary circumstances of such applicant, or of the parents or guardians thereof, and if it shall be proved to his satisfaction that such person or the parents or guardians of such person are unable to pay for the support thereof, and that such county is entitled to send such person to such institution, he may make his order to that effect, and thereupon such person shall be sent to and admitted into such institution for a term not exceeding seven years.

§ 12. Preference to soldiers' children.—The persons who shall be entitled to the benefits of this institution shall be admitted in the order of their application for admission, except that the blind children of those who shall have died in the military service of the United States, or from wounds or injuries received therein during the present rebellion, shall in all cases have a preference; except however that each county shall be entitled to admission for its blind population in indigent circumstances in the same proportion which the whole number of its blind population shall bear to the whole blind population of the state, which proportion shall be determined by the trustees; provided however, that for each person sent by any county, such county shall pay the annual sum of fifty dollars towards the support of such person.

§ 13. Power of trustees.—Said trustees shall, as soon after their appointment as may be. meet and organize by choosing one of their number as president and appointing a secretary. They shall have power to make by-laws and rules and regulations for the transaction of their business, and for the regulation and management of said institution, which institution shall be wholly under their control; and as soon as may be necessary, they shall appoint some suitable person as superintendent, and such other officers and employees as may be necessary to properly carry on the business of said institution, and fix the compensation thereof.

§ 14. Records to be kept.—Said trustees shall keep full and complete records of all their proceedings, and also of the business and daily transactions of such institution, in books to be provided for that purpose; and shall annually make report thereof to the legislature, in and during the month of January.

Objects and Management.

AN ACT to define the objects of the New York State Institution for the Blind, and to provide for its management.

Chapter 744 of the Laws of 1867.

Section 1. Persons entitled to privileges of the institution.— All blind persons of suitable age and capacity for instruction, who are legal residents of the State, shall be entitled to the privileges of the New York State Institution for the Blind, without charge, and for such a period of time in each individual case as may be deemed expedient by the board of trustees of said institution; provided, that whenever more persons apply for admission at one time than can be properly accommodated in the institution, the trustees shall so apportion the number received, that each county may be represented in the ratio of its blind population to the total blind population of the state: and provided further, that the children of citizens who died in the United States service, or from wounds received therein during the late rebellion, shall take precedence over all others.

§ 2. Non-residents.—Blind persons from without the state may be received into the institution upon the payment of an adequate sum, fixed by the trustees, for their boarding and instruction; provided that such applicant shall in no case exclude those from the state of New York.

§ 3. Applications for admission, how made; certificate required.—Applications for admission into the institution shall be made to the board of trustees in such manner as they may direct, but the board shall require such application to be accompanied by a certificate from the county judge or county clerk of the county or the supervisor or town clerk of the town, or the mayor of the city where the applicant resides, setting forth that the applicant is a legal resident of the town, county and state claimed as his or her residence. (As amended by chapter 616 of the Laws of 1872.)

§ 4. Object of the institution.—The primary object of the institution shall be, to furnish to the blind children of the state the best known facilities for acquiring a thorough education, and train them in some useful profession or manual art, by means of which they may be enabled to contribute to their own support after leaving the institution; but it may likewise, through its industrial department, provide such of them with appropriate employment and boarding accommodations as find themselves unable after completing their course of instruction and training, to procure these elsewhere for themselves. It shall, however, be in no sense an asylum for those who are helpless from age, infirmity, or otherwise, or a hospital for the treatment of blindness.

§ 5. Successors of present board of trustees.—Upon the expiration of the term of office of the present board of trustees, the governor shall, by and with the consent of the senate, appoint their successors, two of whom shall reside in the county wherein said institution is located, and a majority of whom shall reside within fifty miles of said institution, and at the first

meeting of said board, after their appointment as aforesaid they
shall divide themselves by lot into three equal classes, who shall
serve for two, four and six years, respectively, from the date of
their appointments, and until their successors shall have been
appointed, and every alternate year thereafter the governor
shall, by and with the consent of the senate, appoint three trustees to fill the places of those whose term of service will have
expired, in accordance with the provisions of this section.

§ 6. Declination.—In case of the declension of any member of
said board of trustees to act under his appointment, or of the
occurrence of any other casual vacancy in the board, the governor shall forthwith appoint some suitable person to fill such
vacancy, and the member so appointed shall serve out the time
of his predecessor.

§ 7. Trustees to receive no compensation, except mileage.—
The trustees shall receive no compensation as such, but they
may allow themselves mileage, at the same rate as that paid
to members of the legislature, for any distance actually traveled in the service of the institution. Nor shall any trustee be
pecuniarily interested in any contract for buildings pertaining
to the institution, or in furnishing supplies therefor.

§ 8. Powers of board of trustees.—The board of trustees shall
have charge of all the affairs of the institution, with power to
make all necessary by-laws and regulations for their government and the proper management of the institution, as well as
for the admission of pupils, and to do all else which may be
found necessary for the advancement of its humane design.

§ 9. Adoption of seal.—They shall elect from their own number a president, treasurer and secretary, together with such
standing committees as they may deem necessary, and adopt a
common seal for the institution.

§ 10. Treasurer.—The treasurer shall have the custody of all
the funds of the institution, and pay out the same only upon
properly authenticated orders of the board or its executive committee. Before entering upon the duties of his office he shall
give a bond with at least two sureties to be approved as herein-

after stated, to the people of the state of New York in the penal sum of twenty-five thousand dollars, conditioned for the faithful discharge of his trust, which bond shall be approved by the state treasurer of this state, in whose office the same shall be filed.

§ 11. Superintendent.—The trustees shall have power to appoint a competent and experienced superintendent, who shall be the chief executive officer of the institution, together with an efficient corps of instructors and other subordinate officers; prescribe the duties and terms of service of the same; fix and pay their salaries and for just cause, remove any or all of them from office. They shall likewise employ the requisite number of servants and other assistants in the various departments of the institution, and pay the wages of the same.

§ 12. Furniture.—They shall purchase all furniture, apparatus and other supplies necessary to the equipment and carrying on of the institution in the most efficient manner.

§ 13. Provision of clothing for those admitted to institution.— When any blind person shall, upon proper application, be admitted into the institution, it shall be the duty of his or her parents, guardians or other friends, to suitably provide such person with clothing at the time of entrance and during continuance therein, and likewise to defray his or her traveling expenses to and from the institution at the time of entrance and discharge, as well as at the beginning and close of each session of the school, and at any other time when it shall become necessary to send such person home on account of sickness or other exigency. And whenever it shall be deemed necessary by the trustees to have such person permanently removed from the institution, in accordance with the by-laws and regulations thereof, the same shall be promptly removed upon their order, by his or her parents, guardians or other friends.

§ 14. Neglect to provide the same.—If the friends of any pupil from within the state of New York shall fail, through neglect or inability, to provide the same with proper clothing or with funds to defray his or her necessary traveling expenses to

52

and from the institution, or to remove him or her therefrom, as required in the preceding section, the trustees shall furnish such clothing, pay such traveling expenses, or remove such pupil to the care of the overseers of the poor of his or her township, and charge the cost of the same to the county to which the pupil belongs; provided that the annual amount of such expenditures on account of any one pupil shall not exceed the sum of sixty dollars. And in case of the death of any pupil at the institution, whose remains shall not be removed or funeral expenses borne by the friends thereof, the trustees shall defray the necessary burial expenses, and charge the same to his or her county as aforesaid. Upon the completion of their course of training in the industrial department, the trustees may furnish to such worthy poor pupils as may need it, an outfit of machinery and tools for commencing business, at a cost not exceeding seventy-five dollars each, and charge the same to the proper county as aforesaid. *(As amended by chapter 463 of the Laws of 1873, §1.)*

§ 15. Itemized accounts against respective counties.—On the first day of October in each year, the trustees shall cause to be made out against the respective counties concerned, itemized accounts, separate in each case, of the expenditures authorized by the preceding section of this act, and forward the same to the board of supervisors chargeable with the account. The board shall thereupon direct the county treasurer to pay the amount so charged to the treasurer of the Institution for the Blind, on or before the first day of March next ensuing.

§ 16. And payment of the same.—The counties against which the said accounts shall be made out as aforesaid shall cause their respective treasurers, in the name of their respective counties, to collect the same, by legal process, if necessary, from the parents or estate of the pupils who have the ability to pay, on whose account the said expenditures shall have been made; provided that at least five hundred dollars' value of the property of such parents or estate shall be exempt from the payment of the accounts aforesaid.

§ 17. **Books gratuitously distributed by state.**—The institution shall be entitled to receive copies of all books and other publications which are distributed gratuitously by the state to township or county libraries, common schools, academies, colleges and societies. It may also receive, in the name of the state, bequests or donations of money or any kind of property, but such money or property shall in all cases belong to the state, and be subject to its control; provided that the same shall not be diverted from the particular object for which it shall be bequeathed or donated.

§ 18. **Records of proceedings of board of trustees.**—The board of trustees shall keep full and complete records of their proceedings, and make an annual report of the same to the legislature, at the commencement of the regular session thereof, strictly accounting in detail for their expenditures, on account of the institution, during the preceding fiscal year, of the state, setting forth the progress and condition of the several departments of the institution, making such suggestions concerning its future management as they may deem essential, and submitting proper estimates of the funds needed for its support, as well as for building and all other purposes.

§ 19. **Payment of appropriations.**—The state treasurer is hereby directed to pay over to the board of trustees, upon the warrant of the comptroller, all moneys which shall hereafter be appropriated on account of the New York State Institution for the Blind; the general appropriations for the current support of the institution to be paid in equal quarterly installments, and specific appropriations for building and other purposes, to be paid when needed by the trustees.

§ 20. **Drafts upon the state.**—All drafts upon the state treasury on behalf of the institution shall be based upon orders of the board of trustees, signed by the president and secretary of the same, and attested by the common seal of the institution.

§ 21. **Sections construed.**—Sections nineteen and twenty of this act shall not be construed to alter, impair or affect the powers or duties of the building commissioners appointed under the provisions of chapter five hundred and eighty-seven, of the laws of eighteen hundred and sixty-five; and nothing in this act shall be construed to interfere with the erection by said building commissioners of the State Institution for the Blind, in accordance with the plans heretofore approved by the governor, secretary of state and comptroller; and all moneys now or hereafter to be appropriated for the building of said institution, shall be paid to said building commissioners for that purpose.

§ 22. Further powers of the institution.—The New York Institution for the Blind shall continue to have the custody, charge, maintenance and education of all such pupils as are now intrusted to them by the state, and of any others who may be appointed prior to the opening of the state institution at Batavia; and shall receive compensation from the state for the maintenance, education and support of said pupils in the same manner as is now, or has heretofore been provided, and shall receive the same amount per capita from the counties from which said pupils are respectively appointed as is now paid, for their clothing, until such period as the New York State Institution for the Blind shall be ready to receive such pupils, and shall then, without reference to the term of years for which said pupils have been appointed under existing laws, and received by said New York Institution for the Blind, transfer said pupils to said state institution; provided however, that they shall retain and continue to receive all pupils heretofore appointed or hereafter to be appointed, from the counties of New York and Kings under the appointment of the superintendent of public instruction, in like manner as is now provided by law, to be received, maintained and educated by the said New York Institution for the Blind, which shall be compensated for their maintenance and education by the state; and for their clothing by the counties from which they are appointed, in like manner as is now done.

§ 23. Repeal.—All acts and parts of acts, inconsistent with the provisions of this act, are hereby repealed.

CHANGE OF NAME.

AN ACT changing the name of the New York State Institution for the Blind.

Chapter 563 of the Laws of 1895.

§ 1. Name changed.—The New York State Institution for the Blind as the same was authorized to be established by chapter five hundred and eighty-seven of the laws of eighteen hundred and sixty-five and the acts supplemental thereto shall hereafter be known and designated as the "New York State School for the Blind."

NEW YORK INSTITUTION FOR THE BLIND, NEW YORK CITY.

AN ACT to amend an act entitled "An act to continue in force 'An act to incorporate the New York Institution for the Blind,' passed April 21, 1831, and to extend the benefits of said institution," passed April 16, 1862.

Chapter 166 of the Laws of 1870.

§ 1. Reception of state pupils; powers of superintendent of public instruction; extension of terms.—The managers of the New York Institution for the Blind are hereby authorized to receive, upon the appointment of the superintendent of public instruction, made for a term not exceeding five years, all blind persons, residents of the counties of New York and Kings, Queens and Suffolk, between eight and twenty-five years of age, who, in the judgment of the board of managers of said institution, shall be of suitable character and capacity for instruction, and shall have charge of their maintenance, education and support, and shall receive compensation therefor from the state in the same manner as is now provided by law. The term of such appointments may be extended, from time to time by the superintendent of public instruction, on the recommendation of the board of managers of the said New York Institution for the Blind, for such further period as they may deem advantageous in each individual case. (*As amended by chapter 166 of the Laws of 1871.*)

§ 2. *Applications for admission.*—Application for admission
into the institution shall be made to the board of managers,
and each application shall set forth the age, the fact of blindness, and that the applicant is a legal resident of the town,
county and state claimed as his or her residence, with such
other information as the board may require; and each application shall be sworn to by the applicant, or his or her parents or
guardian, and shall be signed by at least one member of the
board of supervisors of the county in which the applicant may
reside, and also be recommended by the president and superintendent of the said institution, and transmitted by the said
institution to the superintendent of public instruction.

§ 3. *Supervisors of New York and Kings counties to furnish
clothing; to pay fifty dollars for each indigent pupil.*—The supervisors of the county of New York or Kings, Queens and Suffolk,
from which state pupils shall be sent to and received in the
said institution, whose parents or guardians shall, in the opinion
of the superintendent of public instruction, be unable to furnish
them with suitable clothing, are hereby authorized and directed,
in every year while such pupils are in said institution, to raise
and appropriate fifty dollars for each of said pupils from said
counties respectively, and to pay the sum so raised to the said
institution, to be by it applied to furnishing such pupils with
suitable clothing while in said institution. (*As amended by
chapter 166 of the Laws of 1871.*)

§ 4. *Disposition of surplus.*—If in any year hereafter there
shall be any surplus of the amount above required to be paid
yearly by the said counties for clothing for pupils from said
counties, respectively, then such surplus shall be deducted pro
rata the ensuing year from the amount above required to be
paid by the said counties respectively.

THE DEAF AND DUMB.

AN ACT in relation to the New York Institution for the Instruction of the Deaf and Dumb.

Chapter 272 of the Laws of 1854.

Section 1. Selection of pupils.—Every indigent, deaf and dumb person, resident of this state, between twelve and twenty-five years of age, whose parent or parents, or, if an orphan, whose nearest friend, shall have been a resident of this state for three years, and who may make application for that purpose, shall, until provision be made by law for his or her instruction in some other institution or school, be received into the New York Institution for the Instruction of the Deaf and Dumb, provided his or her application for that purpose be first approved of by the superintendent of public instruction.

§ 2. How supported.—Each indigent pupil, so received into the institution aforesaid, shall be provided with board, lodging and tuition; and the directors of the institution shall receive for each pupil so provided the sum of one hundred and fifty dollars per annum, in quarterly payments, to be paid by the treasurer of the state, on the warrant of the comptroller to the treasurer of the said institution, on his presenting a bill of the actual time and number of pupils attending the institution, and which bill shall be signed and verified by the oath of the president and secretary of the institution. The regular term of instruction for such pupils shall be five years. The indigent pupils, provided for in this act, shall be designated state pupils, and all the existing provisions of law, applicable to state pupils now in said institution, shall apply to pupils herein provided for.

§ 3. Superintendent may continue pupils for studies in higher branches.—It shall be lawful for the superintendent of public instruction to continue at the said institution, for a period not exceeding three years, for the purpose of pursuing a course of studies in the higher branches of learning, such pupils, not exceeding thirty-six in number, as may have completed their full term of instruction, and who may be recommended by the directors of said institution. *(As amended by chapter 58 of the Laws of 1885, and chapter 197 of the Laws of 1890.)*

CARE AND EDUCATION.

AN ACT to provide for the care and education of indigent deaf-mutes under the age of twelve years.

Chapter 325 of the Laws of 1863.

Section 1. Deaf-mutes to be placed in state institutions.—Whenever a deaf-mute child, under the age of twelve years, shall become a charge for its maintenance on any of the towns or counties of this state, or shall be liable to become such charge, it shall be the duty of the overseers of the poor of the town, or of the supervisors of such county, to place such child in the New York Institution for the Deaf and Dumb, or in the Institution for the Improved Instruction of Deaf-mutes, or in the LeCouteulx St. Mary's Institution for the Improved Instruction of Deaf-mutes, in the city of Buffalo, or in the Central New York Institution for Deaf-mutes, in the city of Rome, or in any institution of the state for the education of deaf-mutes. *(As amended by chapter 213 of the Laws of 1875.)*

§ 2. Deaf-mute children, placing of, upon application of parents, etc., in certain institutions.—Any parent, guardian or friend of a deaf-mute child, within this state, over the age of five years and under the age of twelve years, may make application to the overseer of the poor of any town or to any supervisor of the county where such child may be, showing by satisfactory affidavit or other proof, that the health, morals or comfort of such child may be endangered, or not properly cared for, and thereupon it shall be the duty of such overseer or supervisor to place such child in the New York Institution for the Deaf and Dumb, or in the Institution for the Improved Instruction of Deaf-mutes, or in the LeCouteulx Saint Mary's Institution for the Improved Instruction of Deaf-Mutes in the City of Buffalo, or in the Central New York Institution for Deaf-mutes in the city of Rome, or in the Albany Home School for the Oral Instruction of the Deaf at Albany, or in any institution of the state, for the education of deaf-mutes, as to which the board of state charities shall have made and filed with the superintendent of public instruction a certificate to the effect that said institution has been duly organized and is prepared for the reception and instruction of such pupils. *(As amended by chapter 213 of the Laws of 1875, and chapter 36 of the Laws of 1892.)*

§ 3. Expense.—The children placed in said institutions, in pursuance of the foregoing sections, shall be maintained therein at the expense of the county from whence they came, provided that such expense shall not exceed three hundred dollars each per year, until they attain the age of twelve years, unless the directors of the institution to which a child has been sent shall find that such child is not a proper subject to remain in said insitution. *(As amended by chapter 213 of the Laws of 1875.)*

§ 4. Id.—The expenses for the board, tuition and clothing for such deaf-mute children, placed as aforesaid in said institutions, not exceeding the amount of three hundred dollars per year, above allowed, shall be raised and collected as are other expenses of the county from which said children shall be received; and the bills therefor, properly authenticated by the principal or one of the officers of the institution, shall be paid to said institution by the said county; and its county treasurer or chamberlain, as the case may be, is hereby directed to pay the same on presentation, so that the amount thereof may be borne by the proper county. *(As amended by chapter 213 of the Laws of 1875.)*

NEW YORK INSTITUTION FOR THE INSTRUCTION OF THE DEAF AND DUMB.

AN ACT to amend an act entitled "An act in relation to the New York Institution for the Instruction of the Deaf and Dumb," passed April eighteenth, eighteen hundred and thirty-eight.

Chapter 386 of the Laws of 1864.

§ 1. Amendment.—The third section of the act entitled "An act in relation to the New York Institution for the Instruction of the Deaf and Dumb," passed April eighteenth, eighteen hundred and thirty-eight, is hereby amended so as to read as follows:

§ 2.* **Money may be raised to clothe indigent pupils.**—The supervisors of any county in this state from which county pupils may be selected, whose parents or guardians are unable to furnish them with suitable clothing, are hereby authorized and required to raise in each year for this purpose, for each such pupil from said county, the sum of thirty dollars.

AN ACT relative to the care and education of deaf-mutes.
Chapter 180 of the Laws of 1870.

§ 2. **Expenses.**—All provisions of law now existing, fixing the expense of the board, tuition and clothing of children under twelve years placed in the New York Institution for the Instruction of the Deaf and Dumb, shall apply to children who may, from time to time, be placed in the said institution for the improved instruction of deaf-mutes, in the same manner, and with the like effect, as if said last-mentioned institution had also originally been named in the acts fixing such compensation, and as if said acts had provided for the payment thereof to the institution last-mentioned, and the bills therefor properly authenticated by the principal or one of the officers of the said last-mentioned institution shall be paid to said institution by the counties respectively from which such children were severally received, and the county treasurer or chamberlain, as the case may be, is hereby directed to pay the same on presentation, so that the amount thereof may be borne by the proper county.

SUPERVISORS MAY GRANT PERMISSION TO ATTEND SCHOOLS FOR DEAF.

AN ACT relative to the care and education of deaf-mutes.
Chapter 253 of the Laws of 1874.

Section 1. **Application by parent, guardian, etc.; duty of supervisor.**—Any parent, guardian or friend of any deaf-mute child within this state, over the age of six years and under the age of twelve years, may make application to the supervisor of the town or city where such child may be for a permit or order

---

*So in the original.

to place such child in the New York Institution for the Deaf
and Dumb or in the Institution for the Improved Instruction of
Deaf-Mutes, or in any of the deaf-mute institutions of this state,
and it shall be the duty of such supervisor, if in his judgment
the means of the child, or the parents or parent of such child,
will not enable them to defray the expense in a public institution, to grant such permit or order and to cause said child to be
received and placed in such one of the institutions of this state
for the education of deaf-mutes, as the said supervisor shall
select. ·

WESTERN NEW YORK INSTITUTION FOR DEAF-MUTES.

AN ACT in relation to the Western New York Institution for Deaf-Mutes.

Chapter 331 of the Laws of 1876.

Section 1. Reception of pupils.—The Western New York
Institution for Deaf-Mutes, at Rochester, is hereby authorized
to receive deaf and dumb persons between the ages of twelve
and twenty-five years, eligible to appointment as state pupils,
and who may be appointed to it by the superintendent of public
instruction, and the superintendent of public instruction is authorized to make appointments to said institution in the same
manner and upon the same conditions as to the New York Institution for the Instruction of the Deaf and Dumb.

§ 2. Powers of supervisors, etc.—Supervisors of towns and
wards and overseers of the poor are hereby authorized to send
to the Western New York Institution for Deaf-Mutes, deaf and
dumb persons between the ages of six and twelve years, in the
same manner and upon the same conditions as such persons
may be sent to the New York Institution for the Instruction of
the Deaf and Dumb, under the provisions of chapter three hundred and twenty-five of the laws of eighteen hundred and sixty-
three.

NORTHERN NEW YORK INSTITUTION FOR DEAF-MUTES.

AN ACT in relation to the Northern New York Institution for
Deaf-Mutes, at Malone, New York.

Chapter 275 of the Laws of 1884.

Section 1. Institutions may receive pupils, etc.—The Northern
New York Institution for Deaf-Mutes, at Malone, is hereby
authorized to receive deaf and dumb persons, between the ages
of twelve and twenty-five years, eligible to appointment as state
pupils, and who may be appointed to it by the superintendent of
public instruction, and the superintendent of public instruction
is authorized to make appointments to the aforesaid institution.

§ 2. Supervisors, etc., may send pupils under provisions of
law named.—Supervisors of towns and wards and overseers of
the poor are hereby authorized to send to the Northern New
York Institution for Deaf-Mutes, deaf and dumb persons between the ages of six and twelve years, under the provisions of
chapter three hundred and twenty-five of the laws of eighteen
hundred and sixty-three, as amended by chapter two hundred
and thirteen of the laws of eighteen hundred and seventy-five.
Provided that before any pupils are sent to said institution the
board of state charities shall have made and filed with the
superintendent of public instruction a certificate to the effect
that said institution has been duly organized and is prepared
for the reception and instruction of such pupils.

NEW YORK STATE HOSPITAL FOR THE CARE OF CRIPPLED AND DEFORMED CHILDREN.

Chapter 369 of the Laws of 1900.

Section 1. Establishment of the New York state hospital for
the care of crippled and deformed children.
2. Board of managers, appointment of.
3. Powers and duties of board of managers.
4. Powers and duties of the surgeon-in-chief.
5. Salaries and compensation for services.
6. Powers and duties of the treasurer.
7. Official oath.

Section 1. Establishment of the New York state hospital for the care of crippled and deformed children.—A state hospital, to be known, as the New York state hospital for the care of crippled and deformed children, that shall be for the care and treatment of any indigent children who may have resided in the state of New York for a period of not less than one year, who are crippled or deformed or are suffering from disease from which they are likely to become crippled or deformed, shall be established in the city of New York or within a reasonable distance of said city of New York. No patient suffering from an incurable disease shall be admitted to said hospital. Said hospital shall provide for and permit the freedom of religious worship of said inmates to the extent and in the manner required in other institutions, by chapter three hundred and ninety-six of the laws of eighteen hundred and ninety-two entitled "An act to provide for the better security of freedom of worship in certain institutions."

§ 2. Board of managers, appointment of.—The governor by and with the advice and consent of the senate, shall appoint five citizens of this state who shall constitute the board of managers of the New York state hospital for the care of crippled and deformed children. The full term of office of each manager shall be five years, and the term of office of one of such managers shall expire annually. To effect such order of expiration of the term of office of the managers, the first appointment shall be made for the respective terms of five, four, three, two and one years. Appointments of successors to fill vacancies occurring by death, resignation or other cause, shall be made for the unexpired term. Other appointments shall be for the full term. Failure of any manager to attend the regular meetings of the board for the period of one year, shall be considered as a resignation therefrom, and his office shall be declared vacant by resolution of the board. A certified copy of such resolution shall forthwith be transmitted by the board to the governor. The managers shall receive no compensation for their services, but shall be allowed their reasonable traveling and other expenses. Such expenses shall be duly verified and paid by the treasurer of the board on the audit of the comptroller. Any of said new trustees may be removed from office by the governor for any cause that he may deem sufficient, after an opportunity to be heard in his defense, and the vacancy may be filled as herein provided. Three members of the board shall constitute a quorum for the transaction of business.

§ 3. Powers and duties of board of managers.—The board of managers shall have the general direction and control of the property and affairs of said hospital, which are not otherwise specially provided by law, subject to the inspection, visitation and powers of the state board of charities. They may acquire and hold, in the name of and for the people of the state of New York, by grant, gift, devise or bequest, property to be applied to the maintenance of indigent children who are crippled or deformed or are suffering from diseases through which they are likely to become crippled or deformed in and for the general use of the hospital. They shall,

1. Take care of the general interests of the hospital and see that its design is carried into effect according to law and its by-laws, rules and regulations.

2. Keep in a book provided for that purpose a fair and full record of their doings, which shall be open at all times to the inspection of the governor of the state, the state board of charities, or any person appointed by the governor, the state board of charities, or either house of the legislature, to examine the same.

3. Make a detailed report to the state board of charities, in each month of October, in such form as said state board of charities may require, and with such recommendations as said managers may deem expedient, together with a statement of all moneys received by them and of the progress made in the erec-

tion of buildings for hospital purposes, if any, for the year ending on the thirtieth day of September preceding the date of such report.

4. Establish such by-laws as they may deem necessary or expedient for regulating the duties of officers, assistants and employes of the hospital and make and enforce rules and regulations for the internal government, discipline and management of the same.

5. They shall appoint a surgeon-in-chief who shall be a person of suitable experience in the care and treatment of disabling and deforming diseases, and may for cause at any time remove him and appoint his successor. They shall also appoint a treasurer who shall have the custody of all moneys, obligations and securities belonging to the hospital.

§ 4. Powers and duties of the surgeon-in-chief.—The surgeon in chief shall be the superintendent of the hospital. He shall appoint and may remove the steward, matron and such assistant physicians and surgeons, assistants and attendants as may be necessary for the proper treatment of the patients under the care of the hospital, and shall have power to fill vacancies as often as they occur. Subject to the by-laws and regulations established by the board of managers, he shall have the general superintendence of the property, buildings, grounds, fixtures and effects, and control of all persons therein. He shall also,

1. Provide for ascertaining daily the condition of all the patients and proper prescription for their treatment.

2. Keep a book in which he shall cause to be entered at the time of the reception of any patient, his or her name, residence and occupation, and the date of such reception, by whom brought and by what authority committed, and an abstract of all orders, warrants, requests, certificates and other papers accompanying such person.

3. On or before the fifteenth of each month cause to be prepared by the steward, estimates in duplicate of the amount required for the expenses of the hospital for the current month, including salaries and compensation of employes, which esti-

mates shall be certified by him to be required for the hospital.
When approved by the board of managers, one of said estimates
shall be transmitted to the comptroller who shall, if he approve
of the same, issue his warrant for the amount thereof and transmit the same to the treasurer of the hospital.

§ 5. Salaries and compensation for services.—All surgical and
medical officers of the hospital, except the surgeon in chief, shall
render their services gratuitously. All salaries and compensation of officers and employees shall be fixed by the board of
managers with the approval of the comptroller, president of the
state board of charities and the governor, within the appropriation made therefor.

§ 6. Powers and duties of treasurer.—The treasurer shall have
the custody of all moneys, obligations and securities belonging
to the hospital. He shall,

1. Open with some good and solvent bank conveniently near
the hospital, to be selected with the approval of the comptroller
of the state, an account in his name as such treasurer, for the
deposit therein of all moneys, immediately upon receiving the
same, and drawing from same only for the use of the hospital,
in the manner prescribed in the by-laws, upon the written order
of the steward specifying the object of the payment, approved
by the surgeon in chief and subject to audit by the board of
managers.

2. Keep a full and accurate account of all receipts and payments in the manner directed by the by-laws, and such other
accounts as the managers shall prescribe.

3. Balance all accounts on his books annually on the last day
of September and make a statement thereof and an abstract of
the receipts and payments of the past year, and deliver the same
within thirty days to the auditing committee of the managers
who shall compare the same with the books and vouchers and
verify the results upon further comparison with the books of
the steward and certify to the correctness thereof to the managers at their next meeting.

4. Render statements quarterly in each year of his receipts and payments for the three months then next preceding to such auditing committee, who shall compare, verify and certify in regard to the same in the manner provided in the last preceding subdivision, and cause the same to be recorded in one of the books of the hospital.

5. Render a further account of the state of the books, and of the state of the funds and of the property in his hands, whenever required by the managers. Execute any necessary release and satisfaction of mortgage, judgment or other lien in favor of the hospital.

6. Such treasurer shall give an undertaking to the people of the state for the faithful performance of his duties, with such sureties and in such amount as the comptroller of the state shall approve.

§ 7. Official oath.—The surgeon in chief, treasurer and steward, before entering upon their duties as such, shall take the constitutional oath of office and file the same in the office of the clerk of the county of New York.

§ 8. Who may receive treatment.—No patient shall be received except upon satisfactory proof made to the surgeon in chief by the next of kin, guardian or a state, town or county officer under rules to be established by the board of managers showing that the patient is unable to pay for private treatment. Such proof shall be by affidavit. If there was an attending physician before the patient entered the hospital, it shall be accompanied by the certificate of such physician giving the previous history and condition of the patient.

§ 9. Donations.—All donations made to the hospital may be received, retained and expended by the managers for the purposes for which they were given, or in such manner if unaccompanied by conditions, as the board deems advisable.

§ 10. Managers' report of receipts.—The managers shall make detailed report of all moneys received by them by virtue of this act, and the progress made in the erection of any buildings that may be hereafter from time to time erected, to the legislature, in January of each year, and also to the comptroller as often and in such manner as the comptroller shall or may from time to time require.

§ 11. Appropriation for maintenance of hospital.—There is hereby appropriated out of any moneys in the state treasury not otherwise appropriated, the sum of fifteen thousand dollars, or so much thereof as may be necessary, for the New York state hospital for the care of crippled and deformed children in carrying out the provisions of this act.

NEW YORK STATE HOSPITAL FOR THE TREATMENT OF INCIPIENT PULMONARY TUBERCULOSIS.

Chapter 416 of the Laws of 1900, as amended by chapter 108 of the Laws of 1902.

Section   1. Establishment and objects of hospital.
        2. Trustees.
        3. Lands.
        4. Powers and duties of trustees.
        5. Annual report; state board of charities.
        6. Donations in trust.
        7. Site of hospital.
        8. Buildings and improvements.
        9. Superintendent and treasurer.
      10. Duties of superintendent.
      11. Duties of treasurer.
      12. Medical assistants and examining physicians.
      13. Free patients.
      14. Private patients.
      15. Support of free patients.
      16. Support of private patients.
      17. Appropriation.
      18. When to take effect.

Section 1. Establishment and objects of hospital.—A state hospital in some suitable locality in the Adirondacks, for the treatment of incipient pulmonary tuberculosis is hereby established.

§ 2. Trustees.—The governor, by and with the advice and consent of the senate, shall appoint five citizens of this state, of whom two shall be physicians, who shall constitute the board of trustees of the New York state hospital for the treatment of incipient pulmonary tuberculosis. The full term of office of each trustee shall be five years, and the term of office of one of such trustees shall expire annually. To effect such order of expiration of terms of trustees, the first appointments shall be made for the respective terms of five, four, three, two and one years. Appointments of successors shall be for the full term of five years, except that appointment of persons to fill vacancies occurring by death, resignation or other cause, shall be made for the unexpired term. Failure of any trustee to attend in each year two stated meetings of the board shall cause a vacancy in his office, unless said absence be excused by formal action of the board. The trustees shall receive no compensation for their services, but shall be allowed their actual and necessary traveling and other expenses, to be paid on the audit and warrant of the comptroller. Any of said trustees may at any time be removed from office by the governor by and with the consent of the senate for any cause they may deem sufficient after an opportunity to be heard in his or her defense, and others may be appointed in their places as herein provided. Three members of the board of trustees shall constitute a quorum, but no business involving expenditure shall be transacted except by the affirmative vote of at least three members.

§ 3. Lands.—The lands to be held for the purposes herein mentioned shall not be taken for any street, highway or railway without leave of the legislature.

§ 4. Powers and duties of trustees.—For the purposes of this act the said trustees and their successors shall be a body corporate with all the powers necessary to carry into effect the purposes of this act, together with the following powers, duties and obligations. They shall,

1. Take care of the general interests of the hospital and see that its design is carried into effect, according to law, and its by-laws, rules and regulations.

2. Establish such by-laws, rules and regulations as they may deem necessary and expedient for regulating the appointment and duties of officers and employees of the hospital, and for the internal government, discipline and management of the same.

3. Maintain an effective inspection of the affairs and management of the hospital, for which purpose the board shall meet at the hospital at least once in every three months, and at such other times as may be prescribed in the by-laws. The annual meeting of the board of trustees shall be held on the second Saturday of January.

4. Keep in a book provided for that purpose, a fair and full record of the doings of the board, which shall be open at all times to the inspection of its members, the governor of this state, and officers of the state board of charities, or any person appointed by the governor or either house of the legislature to examine the same.

5. Cause to be typewritten within ten days after each meeting of such trustees or of a committee thereof, the minutes and proceedings of such meeting, and cause a copy thereof to be sent to each member of such board.

6. Enter in a book kept by them for that purpose, the date of each of their visits, and the condition of the hospital and patients and all such trustees present shall sign the same.

7. Make to the legislature in January of each year, a detailed report of the results of their visits and inspection, with suitable suggestions and such other matter as may be required of them by the governor, for the year ending on the thirty-first day of December, preceding the date of such report. The resident officers shall admit such trustees into every part of the hospital and its buildings, and exhibit to them on demand all the books, papers, accounts and writings belonging to the hospital or pertaining to its business management, discipline or government, and furnish copies, abstracts and reports whenever required by them.

§ 5. Annual report; state board of charities.—The board of trustees of the hospital shall annually, on or before the first day

of November for the preceding fiscal year, report to the state
board of charities the affairs and conditions of the hospital,
with full and detailed estimates of the next appropriation required for maintenance and ordinary uses and repairs, and of
special appropriations, if any, needed for extraordinary repairs,
renewals, extensions, improvement, betterments or other necessary objects, as also for the erection of additional buildings;
and the state board of charities shall, in its annual report to the
legislature, certify what appropriations are, in its opinion,
necessary and proper. The said hospital shall be subject to the
visitation and to the general powers of the state board of
charities.

§ 6. Donations in trust.—The trustees may take and hold in
trust for the state any grant or devise of land, or any gift or
bequest of money or other personal property, or any donation,
to be applied, principal or income, or both, to the maintenance
and the general uses of the hospital.

§ 7. Site of hospital.—The said trustees are hereby empowered
to select a site for the establishment of said state hospital, such
site to be subject to the approval of the state board of health
and the forest preserve board. The said trustees are empowered to contract for the purchase of, to acquire title to and to
hold a tract of land not exceeding one thousand acres in extent
for the establishment of such hospital, or at the request of the
said trustees, subject to the approval of the state board of
health, the forest preserve board may set apart a like amount
of land now owned by the state for the purposes of said hospital.

§ 8. Buildings and improvements.—The trustees to be appointed under the provisions of this act are authorized, empowered and required as soon as the site for such hospital is
selected and approved to proceed with the construction and
equipment of all necessary and suitable buildings including
heating, lighting, plumbing, laundry fixtures and water supply
therefor, and with the construction of roads thereto, upon plans
adopted by them, to be approved by the state architect, and the
state board of charities at an expense not to exceed one hundred

and fifty thousand dollars, which buildings shall furnish accommodations for at least two hundred patients beside the officers, employees and attendants of said institution. The said trustees shall have power to select plans approved as above and to make and award contracts for the erection and construction of said buildings, and the equipment above provided; but no part of the several sums herein appropriated shall be available for any construction, improvement or purchase unless a contract or contracts shall have first been made for the completion or purchase within the appropriation therefor and the performance thereof secured by a satisfactory bond approved by the comptroller.

§ 9. Superintendent and treasurer.—The trustees shall also have power to appoint a superintendent of the hospital, who shall be a well-educated physician, not a member of the board of trustees, a graduate of a legally chartered medical college, with an experience of at least six years in the actual practice of his profession, including at least one year's actual experience in a general hospital, and a treasurer, who shall give an undertaking to the people of the state for the faithful performance of his trust in such penal sum and form and with such sureties as the comptroller shall approve. Said officers may be discharged or suspended at any time by the said board of trustees in its discretion.

§ 10. Duties of superintendent.—The superintendent shall

1. Appoint such employees as are necessary and proper for the due administration of the affairs of such institution, prescribe their duties and places and, subject to the approval of the trustees, fix their compensation, within the appropriation fixed therefor.

2. Oversee and secure the individual treatment and personal care of each and every patient of the hospital while resident therein, and keep a proper oversight over all the inhabitants thereof.

3. Have the general superintendence of the buildings and grounds with their furniture and fixtures and the direction and control of all persons employed in and about the same.

4. Give from time to time such orders and instructions as he may deem best calculated to induce good conduct, fidelity and economy in any department for the treatment of patients.

5. Maintain salutary discipline among all employees, patients, and inmates of the hospital, and enforce strict compliance with his instructions, and obedience to all the rules and regulations of the hospital. He shall, under the supervision and control of the board, discharge such patients as are sufficiently restored to health, or such as are found to be unsuitable patients for the hospital.

6. Cause full and fair accounts and records of the conditions and prospects of the patients to be kept regularly, from day to day, in books provided for that purpose.

7. See that such accounts and records shall be fully made up to the first days of January, April, July and October, in each year, and that the principal facts and results with the report thereon be presented to the trustees at their regular meetings.

8. Conduct the official correspondence of the hospital, and keep a record or copy of all letters written, and files of all letters received.

9. Prepare and present to the board, at its annual meeting. a true and perfect inventory of all the personal property and effects belonging to the hospital, and account, when required by the board, for the careful keeping and economical use of all furniture, stores and other articles furnished for the hospital.

§ 11. Duties of treasurer.—The treasurer, among his other duties, shall

1. Have the custody of all moneys received and all money, notes, mortgages and other securities and obligations belonging to the hospital.

2. Keep a full and accurate account of all receipts and payments, in the form prescribed by the by-laws, and such other accounts as shall be required of him by the trustees.

3. Balance all the accounts on his books on the first day of each January, and make a statement thereof, and an abstract of all the receipts and payments of the past year; and within five

days thereafter deliver the same to the auditing committee of the trustees, who shall compare the same with his books and vouchers, and verify the same by a comparison with the books of the superintendent, and certify the correctness thereof to the trustees at their annual meeting.

4. Render a quarterly statement of his receipts and payments to such auditing committee who shall, in like manner as above, compare, verify, report and certify the result thereof, to the trustees at their annual meeting, who shall·cause the same to be recorded in one of the books of the hospital.

5. Render a further account of the state of his books, and of the funds and other property in his custody, whenever required by the trustees.

6. Receive for the use of the hospital, money which may be paid upon obligations or securities in his hands belonging to the hospital; and all sums paid to the hospital for the support of any patient therein or for actual disbursements made in said patient's behalf for necessary clothing and traveling expenses; and money paid to the hospital from any other source.

7. Prosecute an action in the name of the hospital to recover money due or owing to the hospital, from any source; including the bringing of suit for breach of contract between private patients or their representatives and the trustees of the hospital.

8. Execute a release and satisfaction of a mortgage judgment, lien or other debt when paid.

9. Pay the salaries of the superintendent and of all employees of the hospital, and the disbursements of the officers and members of the board as aforesaid. The treasurer shall have power to employ counsel, subject to the approval of the board of trustees.

10. Deposit all moneys received for the care of private patients and all other revenues of the hospital, in a bank designated by the comptroller, and as often as the comptroller may require, transmit to the comptroller a statement showing the amount so received and deposited and from whom, and for what re-

ceived, and the dates on which such deposits were made. Such
statement of deposit shall be certified by the proper officer of
the bank receiving such deposit or deposits. The treasurer
shall make affidavit that the sum so deposited is all the money
received by him from any source of income for the hospital up
to the date of the latest deposit appearing on such statement.
A bank designated by the comptroller to receive such deposits
shall, before any deposit be made, execute a bond to the people
of the state in a sum and with sureties to be approved by the
comptroller, for the safe keeping of such deposits.

§ 12. Medical assistants and examining physicians.—All medical assistants shall be appointed by the superintendent. No
medical assistant shall be appointed who is not a well-educated
physician and a graduate of a legally chartered medical college,
and with an experience of at least two years in the actual practice of his profession, including at least one year's actual experience in a general hospital. Said trustees shall also appoint in
all the cities of the state reputable physicians, citizens of the
state of New York, who shall examine all persons applying for
admission to said hospital for treatment. There shall be not
less than two nor more than four of such examining physicians
appointed in cities of the first class, and two each in cities of the
second and third class. Said examining physicians shall have
been in the regular practice of their profession for at least five
years, and shall be skilled in the diagnosis and treatment of
pulmonary diseases. Their fee or compensation for each patient
examined shall be three dollars. Not more than one-half of all
the physicians to be appointed under this section shall belong
to the same school of medicine or practice.

§ 13. Free patients.—The trustees of said hospital to be appointed under and pursuant to the provisions of this act, and
their successors, are hereby given power and authority to receive
therein patients who have no ability to pay, but no person shall
be admitted to the hospital who has not been a citizen of this
state for at least one year preceding the date of application.
Every person desiring free treatment in said hospital shall apply

to the local authorities of his or her town, city or county having charge of the relief of the poor, who shall thereupon issue a written request to the superintendent of said hospital for the admission and treatment of such person. Such request shall state in writing whether the person is able to pay for his or her care and treatment while at the hospital, which request and statement shall be kept on file by the superintendent of the hospital. Such requests shall be filed by the superintendent in a book kept for that purpose in the order of their receipt by him. When said hospital is completed and ready for the treatment of patients, or whenever thereafter there are vacancies caused by death or removal, the said superintendent shall thereupon issue a request to an examining physician, appointed as provided for in section twelve, in the same city or county, and if there be no such examining physician in said city or county then to the nearest examining physician, for the examination by him of said patient. Upon the request of such superintendent said examining physician shall examine all persons applying for free admission and treatment in said institution, and determine whether such persons applying are suffering from incipient pulmonary tuberculosis. No person shall be admitted as a patient in said institution without the certificate of one of said examining physicians certifying that such applicant is suffering from incipient pulmonary tuberculosis, and if upon the reception of a person at such hospital, it is found by the authorities thereof that he is not suffering from incipient pulmonary tuberculosis, or is suffering from pulmonary tuberculosis in such an advanced stage as to prevent his deriving any benefit from care and treatment at such hospital, he shall be returned to the place of his residence, and the expense of transportation to and from the hospital shall be paid by said local authorities. Admissions to said hospital shall be made in the order in which the names of applicants shall appear upon the application book to be kept as above provided by the superintendent of said hospital, in so far as such applicants are subsequently certified by the said examining physician to be suffering from incipient pulmonary

tuberculosis. Every person who is declared as herein provided
to be unable to pay for his or her care or treatment shall be
transported to and from the hospital at the expense of said
local authorities, and cared for, treated and maintained therein
at the expense of the municipality which would otherwise be
chargeable with the support of such poor or indigent person;
and the expense of transportation, treatment and maintenance
shall be a county, city or town charge, as the case may be.

§ 14. Private patients.—Applicants for admission to this institution who are able to pay for their care and treatment are
not required to obtain a written request from the local authorities having charge of the relief of the poor, but shall apply in
person to the superintendent who shall enter the name of such
applicant in the book to be kept by him, for that purpose, as
provided in section thirteen; and when there is room in said
hospital for the admission of such applicant, without interfer-
ing with the preference in the selection of patients, which shall
always be given to the indigent, such patient shall be admitted
to the hospital upon the certificate of one of the examining
physicians, which certificate shall be kept on file by the said
superintendent.

§ 15. Support of free patients.—At least once in each month
the superintendent of the hospital shall furnish to the comptroller a list countersigned by the treasurer of the hospital of
all the free patients in the hospital, together with sufficient
facts to enable the comptroller to collect from the proper local
official having charge of the relief of the poor such sums as
may be owing to the state for the examination, care, treatment
and maintenance of the patients who have been received by the
hospital and who are shown by the statement of such local
official to be unable to pay for their care, treatment and maintenance. The comptroller shall thereupon collect from the said
local official the sums due for the care, treatment and maintenance of each such patient at a rate not exceeding five dollars
per week for each patient. (As amended by chapter 108, Laws
of 1902.)

§ 16. Support of private patients.—The trustees shall have
power and authority to fix the charges to be paid by patients
who are able to pay for their care and treatment in said hospital
or who have relatives bound by law to support them, who are
able to pay therefor.

§ 17. Appropriation.—The sum of fifty thousand dollars is
hereby appropriated for the purpose of purchasing a site and of
erecting, constructing and equipping the hospital and buildings
as herein provided. The treasurer of the state shall, on the
warrant of the comptroller, and on the certificate of the state
architect pay to the treasurer of the trustees of said hospital
the above named sum in such amounts as may, from time to
time, in the judgment of the trustees, be necessary.

THE STATE FINANCE LAW.

Chapter 413 of the Laws of 1897, as amended by Chapter 383 of 1899 and Chapters 432 and 457 of 1901.

Section 10. Deposit of moneys by state officers.
      11. Deposit of money by charitable and benevolent
         institutions.
      12. Proofs required on audit by the comptroller.
      13. Regulations for the transmission of public moneys.
      17. Itemized and quarterly accounts of public officers.
      18. Inspection of supplies and entry in books.
      19. Deposit in banks of moneys received by State insti-
         tutions.
      20. Annual inventory and report of institutions.
      21. Rendition of accounts.
      22. Statements of accounts not rendered.
      23. Statements of accounts rendered.

Section 10. Deposit of moneys by state officers.—Every state
officer or other person except the state treasurer, receiving or
disbursing moneys belonging to the state, shall deposit and keep
all the moneys received by him, deposited to his official credit in
some responsible bank or banking house, to be designated by
the comptroller, until such moneys are paid out or disbursed

according to law. Every such bank or banking house, when required by the comptroller, shall execute and file in his office an undertaking to the state in such sum and with such sureties as are required and approved by him, for the safe keeping and prompt payment on legal demand therefor of all such moneys held by or on deposit in such bank or banking house, with interest thereon, on daily or monthly balances at such rate as the comptroller may fix. Every such undertaking shall have indorsed thereon, or annexed thereto, the approval of the attorney-general as to its form.

§ 11. **Deposit of moneys by charitable and benevolent institutions.**—All moneys received from the state by any charitable or benevolent institution, supported wholly or partly by moneys received from the state, shall be deposited in such national or state bank or trust company, as the comptroller may designate. Every such bank or trust company shall give an undertaking, as provided in the last section. The treasurer of such institution shall keep all the funds thereof which come into his possess'on from the state, deposited in his name as such treasurer in such bank or trust company.

§ 12. **Proofs required on audit by the comptroller.**—The comptroller shall not draw his warrant for the payment of any sum appropriated, except for salaries and other expenditures and appropriations, the amounts of which are duly established and fixed by law, until the person demanding the same presents to him a detailed statement thereof in items and makes all reports required of him by law. If such statement is for services rendered or articles furnished, it must show when, where, to whom and under what authority they were rendered or furnished. If for traveling expenses, the distance traveled, between what places, the duty or business for the performance of which the expenses were incurred, and the dates and items of each expenditure. If for transportation, furniture, blank and other books purchased for the use of offices, binding, blanks, printing, stationery, postage, cleaning and other incidental expenses, a bill duly receipted must be attached to the statement. Each

statement of accounts must be verified by the person presenting
the same to the effect that it is just, true and correct, that no
part thereof has been paid, except as stated therein, and that
the balance therein stated is actually due and owing. No pay·
ment shall be made to any salaried state officer or commissioner
having an office established by law, for personal expenses incurred by him while in the discharge of his duties as such officer
·or commissioner at the place where such office is located. No
manager, trustee or other officer of any state charitable or other
institution, receiving moneys from the state treasury in whole
or in part for the maintenance or support of such institution
shall be interested in any purchase or sale by any of such
·officers.

§ 13. Regulations for the transmission of public moneys.—
The comptroller may make such regulations and give such directions from time to time, respecting the transmission to the treasury of moneys belonging to the state from the several county
treasurers and other public officers as in his judgment is most
conducive to the interests of the state. He may, in his discretion, audit, allow and cause to be paid the expenses necessarily
incurred under or in consequence of such regulations and directions or so much thereof as he deems equitable and just.

§ 17. Itemized and monthly accounts of public officers.—The
proper officer of each state hospital, asylum, charitable or
reformatory institution, the state commission in lunacy, the
state board of charities, the state board of health, the commissioners of fisheries, game and forests and all other state commissions, commissioners and boards, shall, on or before the fifteenth day of each month, render to the comptroller a detailed
and itemized account of all receipts and expenditures of such
hospital, asylum, institution, commission, board of commissioners during the month next preceding. Such accounts shall give
in detail the source of all receipts, including the sums received
from any county, and be accompanied by original and proper
vouchers for all funds paid from the state treasury, unless such
vouchers have been previously filed with the comptroller and

have appended or annexed thereto the affidavit of the officer making the same to the effect that the goods and other articles therein specified were purchased and received by him or under his direction or that the indebtedness was incurred under his direction; that the goods were purchased at a fair cash market price and that neither he, nor any person in his behalf, had any pecuniary or other interest in the articles purchased or in the indebtedness incurred; that he received no pecuniary or other benefit therefrom, nor any promises thereof; that the articles contained in such bill were received by him, and that they conformed in all respects to the goods ordered by him or under his direction, both in quality and quantity. The state comptroller and the president of the state board of charities, subject to the approval, in writing, of the governor, shall from time to time classify into grades the officers and employes of the various charitable and reformatory institutions required by law to report to the comptroller, and shall fix the salaries and wages to be paid such officers and employes. Differences in the expense of living and rates of wages in the localities in which such institutions are situate may be considered. The comptroller shall have the power of audit subject to such classification. *(As amended by chapter 383 of the Laws of 1899, and chapter 432 of the Laws of 1901.)*

§ 18. Inspection of supplies and entry in books.—The steward, clerk or bookkeeper in every such institution, board or commission shall receive and examine all articles purchased or received for the maintenance thereof, compare them with the bills for the same, ascertain whether they correspond in weight, quality or quantity, and inspect the supplies thus received. Such steward, clerk or bookkeeper shall enter each bill of goods thus received in the books of the institution or department at the time of receipt thereof. He shall make a full memorandum in the book of accounts of such institution of any difference in weight, quality or quantity of any article received from the bill thereof, and no goods or other articles of purchase or manufacture or farm or garden production of land of the institution shall be received unless so entered in such book with the proper bill, invoice or statement, according to the form of accounts and record prescribed by the comptroller. In accounts for repairs or new work, the name of each workman, the number of days employed and the rate and amount of wages paid to him shall be given. If contracts are made for repairs or new work, or for supplies, a duplicate thereof, with specifications, shall be filed with the comptroller. The steward of every such institution or other officer performing the duties of a steward under whatever name, shall take, subscribe and file with the comptroller, before entering on his duties, the constitutional oath of office, and may administer oaths and take affidavits concerning the business of, such institution.

§ 19. Deposit in banks of moneys received by state institutions.—Every state institution supported, in whole or in part, by the state, shall deposit at interest, all its funds received from sources other than the state in a bank or trust company, which shall give a bond with sufficient sureties for the security of such deposit, to be approved by the comptroller. (As amended by chapter 457 of the Laws of 1901.)

§ 20. Annual inventory and report of institutions.—Every state charitable institution, state hospital, reformatory, house of refuge and industrial school shall file with the comptroller annually, on or before October twentieth, a certified inventory of all articles of maintenance on hand at the close of the preceding fiscal year, stating the kind and amount of each article. Every state charitable institution, state hospital, reformatory, house of refuge, state agricultural experiment station, and the quarantine commissioners, required by law to report annually to the legislature, shall state an inventory of each article of property, stating its kind and amount, except supplies for maintenance, belonging to the state and in their possession on October first of each year.

§ 21. Rendition of accounts.—The comptroller, from time to time, shall require all public officers and other persons receiving moneys or securities, or having the care and management of any property of the state, of which an account is or is required'to be kept in his office, to render statements thereof to him; and all such officers or persons shall render such statements at such time and in such form as he requires, and at all times when required by law. He may require any one presenting to him an account or claim for audit or settlement, to be examined upon oath before him touching such account or claim, as to any facts relating to its justness or correctness. He may issue a notice to any person receiving moneys of the state for which he does not account or to the legal representatives of such a person, requiring an account and vouchers for the expenditure of such moneys to be rendered at a time to be fixed not less than thirty nor more than ninety days from the date of the service of the notice. Such notice shall be served by delivering a copy thereof to such person or representative or leaving such copy at his usual place of abode; and if such service is made by the sheriff of the county, where the person served resided, the certificate of such sheriff, and if made by any other person, the affidavit of such other person, shall be presumptive evidence of such service.

§ 22. Statements of account not rendered.—The comptroller shall state an account against every person who receives moneys belonging to the state for which he does not account when required, charging him with the amount received according to the best information which the comptroller may have in regard thereto, with interest at six per centum per annum from the time when the same was due and payable, and shall deliver a certified copy of such account to the attorney-general for prosecution, and such certified copy shall be presumptive evidence of the indebtedness of such person to the state for the amount stated therein. The person against whom an action is brought by the attorney-general on any such account, shall be liable for and pay the costs of the action whether final judgment therein shall be against him or in his favor, unless he is sued as the representative of the person originally accountable for such moneys.

54

§ 23. Statements of account rendered.—The comptroller shall immediately examine the accounts rendered by every public officer or other person receiving moneys belonging to the state, with the vouchers, and audit, adjust and make a statement thereof. If any necessary vouchers are wanting or defective, he shall give notice to such person to furnish proper vouchers within not less than thirty nor more than ninety days, and at the expiration of such time he shall audit, adjust and make a statement of such accounts on the vouchers and proofs before him. He shall transmit a copy of every account as settled to such persons, and if any balance is stated therein to be due the state, and is not paid to the treasurer within ninety days after its transmission to such person, the comptroller shall deliver a certified copy of such account to the attorney-general for prosecution. Such certified copy shall be presumptive evidence of the indebtedness of such person to the state for the balance so certified, and if on the trial of any action brought thereon, the defendant gives any evidence other than such as was produced to the comptroller before the statement of such accounts, and by means thereof, the balance so stated is reduced or no balance is found to be due, the defendant shall be liable for and pay the costs of such action.

§ 35. Indebtedness not to be contracted without appropriation.—A state officer, employe, board, department or commission shall not contract indebtedness on behalf of the state, nor assume to bind the state, in an amount in excess of money appropriated or otherwise lawfully available. (*Added by chapter 580 of the Laws of 1899.*)

§ 36. Specific appropriation not to be used for other purposes.—Money appropriated for a specific purpose shall not be used for any other purpose; and the comptroller shall not draw a warrant for the payment of any sum appropriated, unless it clearly appears from the detailed statement presented to him by the person demanding the same as required by this chapter, that the purposes for which such money is demanded are those for which it was appropriated. The comptroller shall not audit any claim for salary, labor or wages, unless an appropriation applicable thereto has been already made specifying the amount thereof appropriated for such purpose. (*Added by chapter 580 of the Laws of 1899.*)

§ 37. Monthy payments to state treasurer.—Every state officer, employe, board, department or commission receiving money for or on behalf of the state from fees, penalties, costs, fines, sales of property, or otherwise, except the health officer of the port of New York, shall on the fifth day of each month, pay to the state treasurer all such money received during the preceding month and on the same day file a detailed verified statement of such receipts with the comptroller, who shall keep an account thereof in his office. This section shall not apply to the manufacturing fund of the state prisons, known as the capital fund; nor to the convict deposit and miscellaneous earning fund, so called, of the state prisons and Eastern New York reformatory; nor to the proceeds of sales of manufactures or other products of the state hospitals for the insane. This section shall be deemed to supersede any other provisions of this chapter or of any other general or special law inconsistent therewith. (*Added by chapter 580 of the Laws of 1899, and amended by chapter 715 of the Laws of 1899, chapter 326 of the Laws of 1900, and chapter 457 of the Laws of 1901.*)

§ 38. Contracts in pursuance of appropriations.—A contract or contracts made in pursuance of an appropriation by the state for a specific object shall be for the completion of the work contemplated by the appropriation, and in the aggregate shall not exceed the amount of such appropriation. A contract for a part of such work shall not be binding upon the state until contracts are also made covering the entire work contemplated by such appropriation, except where it is expressly provided by such appropriation that a part of the work may be done by day's labor. Every such contract shall be accompanied by a bond for the completion of the work specified in the contract, within the amount stipulated therein, which bond shall be filed in the office of the state comptroller. (*Added by chapter 479 of the Laws of 1899.*)

PURCHASE OF SUPPLIES.

AN ACT requiring preference to be given in the purchase of
supplies for state institutions to products raised within this
state.

Chapter 32 of the Laws of 1899.

Section 1. The officers, boards, commissions and departments
whose duty it is to purchase supplies for the maintenance of
inmates of state institutions, shall, in purchasing such supplies, give preference to products raised within the state, price
and quality being equal.

PROTECTION OF INMATES AND PUBLIC BUILDINGS.

AN ACT to protect the lives of the inmates of public buildings
of state institutions and to protect said buildings against
destruction by fire.

Chapter 535, Laws of 1895.

Section 1. It shall be the duty of each superintendent or chief
executive officer of each of the public institutions of the state,
supported wholly or partly by the funds of the state, to provide
that the following regulations for the protection of the inmates
of said buildings and the buildings be complied with: There
shall be provided a sufficient number of stand-pipes, with connections or outlets on each floor, to which a length of fire hose
shall be attached, to properly protect the entire floor surface.
All fire hose must be tested at least once in three months under
the direction of the engineer, and employes must be trained in
its use. Not less than six portable fire-extinguishers for each
floor of each building, hand grenades and fire-pails kept constantly filled with water and used for no other purpose shall be
provided. Bath-tubs shall be kept filled with water during the
night and pails ready for use placed near them. Suitable steps
must be provided under windows used as exits to fire-escapes and
all fire-escapes must be properly inclosed with wire netting.
Wards of the state, if physically and mentally able, must be required to occasionally go up and down the outside iron stairways
which must be provided in order to become accustomed to their

use. If gas is used, the pressure shall be regulated by governor that the flow may be as nearly uniform as possible. All swinging gas jets in closets, clothes-rooms, employes' rooms and in rooms occupied by wards of the state must be protected by wire screens. Gas stoves must be used only when absolutely necessary, and if used must be suitably inclosed with metal. Kerosene oil must not be used for lighting purposes unless the institution is not fully provided with gas or electric lights; and if such oil is used it must be of the highest fire test commercially obtainable. Candles must only be used in an emergency, and on the express authorization of the superintendent or chief executive officer. None but safety matches, or those which can be used only on a specially prepared surface, must be allowed in or about the institution, and, so far as possible, matches should be dispensed with and electric torches be supplied. All lanterns must be kept outside the buildings used for sleeping purposes, in charge of one person, who must regularly clean, replenish and distribute them. Painters' supplies and inflammable liquids of all kinds must not be stored in buildings occupied by wards of the state or employes. When oil or other inflammable substance is applied to floors, it must be applied only by persons skilled in its application, and all articles used in applying such inflammable material must be carefully destroyed after use. All attics and basements must be constantly kept free from rubbish or articles not necessary to the proper conduct of the institution, and must be regularly swept, cleaned and all broken or needless articles promptly removed.

§ 2. The moneys necessary to carry out the provisions of this act shall be supplied from the moneys annually appropriated for the maintenance of the above-described institutions.

COMMITTEE FOR INCOMPETENT PERSONS.

AN ACT to amend the code of civil procedure, relating to the appointment of committees for incompetent persons who are inmates of state institutions.

Chapter 149, Laws of 1897.

Section 1. Section twenty-three hundred and twenty-three-a of the code of civil procedure, is hereby amended to read as follows:

§ 2323-a. Application when incompetent person is in a state institution; petition, by whom made; contents and proceedings upon presentation thereof.—Where an incompetent person has been committed to a state institution in any manner provided by law, and is an inmate thereof, the petition may be presented on behalf of the state by a state officer having special jurisdiction over the institution where the incompetent person is confined or the superintendent or acting superintendent of said institution; the petition must be in writing and verified by the affidavit of the petitioner or his attorney, to the effect that the matters therein stated are true to the best of his information or belief; it must show that the person for whose person or property, or both, a committee is asked has been legally committed to a state institution over which the petitioner has special jurisdiction, or of which he is superintendent or acting superintendent, and is at the same time an inmate thereof; it must also state the institution in which he is an inmate, the date of his admission, his last known place of residence, the name and residence of the husband or wife, if any, of such person, and if there be none, the name and residence of the next of kin of such person living in this state so far as known to the petitioner; the nature, extent and income of his property, so far as the same is known to the petitioner, or can with reasonable diligence be ascertained by him. The petition may be presented to the supreme court at any special term thereof, held either in the judicial district in which such incompetent person last resided, or in the district in which the state institution in which he is committed is situated, or to a justice of the supreme court at chambers within such judicial district. Notice of the presentation of such petition shall be personally given to such person, and also to the husband or wife, if any, or if none to the next of kin named in the petition, and to the officer in charge of the institution in which such person is an inmate. Upon the presentation of such petition, and proof of the service of such notice, the court or justice may, if satisfied of the truth of the facts required to be stated in such petition, immediately appoint a committee of the person or property, or both, of such incompetent person, or may require any further proof which it or he may deem necessary before making such appointment.

DEPOSIT OF FUNDS OF CHARITABLE INSTITUTIONS.

AN ACT to regulate the deposit of funds received by charitable and benevolent institutions supported in whole or in part by public moneys.

Chapter 415, Laws of 1884.

Section 1. Board of trustees to designate depository of funds. —It shall be the duty of the board of trustees or managers of each charitable or benevolent institution in this state, supported in whole or in part by moneys received from the state, or by any county, city or town thereof, to designate by resolution, to be entered upon their minutes, some duly incorporated national or state bank or trust company as the depository of the funds of such institution.

§ 2. Treasurer to deposit moneys in same.—After such designation, it shall be the duty of the treasurer of each such charitable or benevolent institution immediately to deposit in the bank or trust company so designated, in his name as treasurer of the institution, naming it, all funds of the institution which may come into his possession.

INVESTIGATION OF COMPLAINTS AGAINST CHARITABLE INSTITUTIONS.

AN ACT to provide for taking testimony in certain matters relating to state charitable institutions.

Chapter 699, Laws of 1871.

Section 1. Investigation of complaints, etc.; power to administer oaths and compel attendance of witnesses; production of papers.—Whenever the state board of commissioners of public charities, or the managers, directors or trustees of any asylum, hospital, or other charitable institution, the managers, directors or trustees of which are appointed by the governor and senate, or by the legislature, shall deem it necessary or proper to investigate and ascertain the truth of any charge or complaint made or circulated respecting the conduct of the superintendent, assistants, subordinate officers or servants, in whatever capacity or duty employed by or under the official control of any such board, managers, directors or trustees, it shall be lawful for the presiding officer for the time being of any such board, managers, directors or trustees, to administer oaths to all witnesses coming before them respectively for examination, and to issue compulsory process for the attendance of any witness within the state whom they may respectively desire to examine, and for the production of all papers that any such witness may possess, or have in his power, touching the matter of such complaint or investigation; and wilful false swearing by any witness who may be so examined is hereby declared to be perjury.

§ 2. Fees of witnesses.—All persons examined as witnesses under the first section of this act shall be paid the same fees as are now paid to witnesses in the supreme court by the said board, managers, directors or trustees, authorizing the issue of such compulsory process.

REPORT OF PERSONS IN STATE INSTITUTIONS.

AN ACT to provide for the reporting of persons in the various state benevolent institutions of this state.

Chapter 54, Laws of 1876.

Section 1. Officers to report.—It shall be the duty of the superintendent, warden or other proper officer in charge of each of the benevolent institutions of this state, in which are persons whose maintenance, treatment, tuition or clothing is a charge against any county of this state, to make a report on or before the fifteenth day of September, in each year, to the clerk of the board of supervisors of the county to which such maintenance, treatment, tuition or clothing is chargeable, which report shall show the name, age, sex, color and nationality of every person in such institution, chargeable to such county; also, when each person was received into such institution, from what town sent, for what term 'received, to what time the expense of each such person has been paid, and the amount chargeable to such county for each such person for the ensuing year, which report shall be verified by the oath or affirmation of the person making the same.

THE POOR LAW.

An act in relation to the Poor, constituting chapter 27 of the General Laws.

Chapter 225, Laws of 1896, as amended by chapters 48, 222 and 507 of the Laws of 1897; 337 and 536 of the Laws of 1898; 83 and 462 of the Laws of 1899; 24, 345 and 475 of the Laws of 1900; 103 and 664 of the Laws of 1901; and 117 of the Laws of 1902.

ARTICLE I.

COUNTY SUPERINTENDENTS OF THE POOR.

Section 1. Short title.—This chapter shall be known as the poor law.

§ 2. Definitions.—A poor person is one unable to maintain himself, and such person shall be maintained by the town, city, county or state, according to the provisions of this chapter. In counties having but one superintendent of the poor, the term " superintendent " or " superintendents of the poor," when used in this chapter, means such superintendent; and in towns or cities having but one overseer of the poor, the term " overseers " or " overseers of the poor," when used in this chapter, means a town or city overseer of the poor. An "almshouse" is a place where the poor are maintained at the public expense.

The popular meaning of the word " almshouse " is, of course, well under-stood, but the revisers and the legislature have not confined us to the popular meaning. They have given to the word a much wider and more comprehensive definition than it has in popular usage. That may properly be termed the statutory definition which is found in the second section of the Poor Law. It is there defined as a "place where the poor are maintained at the public expense." It is not necessary that it should be a public building or that there should be but one place. *The People ex rel. John B. French as Overseer of the Poor of the City of Ithaca, respondent, v. James S. Lyke, as Superintendent of the Poor of the County of Tompkins, appellant, 159 N. Y., 149.*

The town poor are such persons as are required by law to be relieved or supported at the expense of the town or city; the county poor are such persons as are required by law to be relieved or supported at the expense of the county; and the state poor are such persons as are required by law to be relieved or supported at the expense of the state.

§ 3. County superintendents of the poor.—The county superintendents of the poor shall:

1. Have the general superintendence and care of poor persons who may be in their respective counties.

2. Provide and keep in repair suitable almshouses when directed by the board of supervisors of their county.

3. Establish rules and by-laws for the government and good order of such almshouses, and for the employment, relief, management and government of the poor therein; but such rules and regulations shall not be valid until approved by the county judge of the county, in writing.

4. Unless a keeper be appointed by the board of supervisors, employ suitable persons to be keepers of such houses, and physicians, matrons and all other necessary officers and servants, and vest such powers in them for the government of such houses, and the poor therein, as shall be necessary, reserving to such poor persons who may be placed under the care of such keepers, matrons, officers or servants, the right of appeal to the superintendents.

5. Purchase all necessary furniture, implements, food and materials for the maintenance of the poor in such houses, and for their employment in labor, and use, sell and dispose of the proceeds of such labor as they shall deem expedient.

6. Prescribe the rate of allowance to be made for bringing poor persons to the county almshouse, subject to such alterations as the board of supervisors may by general resolution make.

7. Authorize the keepers of such houses to certify the amount due for bringing such poor persons; which amount shall be paid by the county treasurer on the production of such certificate, countersigned and allowed by the county superintendents of the poor.

8. Summarily decide any dispute that shall arise concerning the settlement of any poor person, upon a hearing of the parties, and for that purpose may issue subpoenas to compel the attendance of witnesses, with the like powers to enforce such process, as is given to a justice of the peace in an action pending before him; their decisions shall be filed in the office of the county clerk within thirty days after they are made, and shall be conclusive and final upon all parties interested, unless an appeal therefrom shall be taken, as provided in this chapter.

9. Direct the commencement of suits by any overseer of the poor who shall be entitled to prosecute for any penalties, or upon any recognizance, bonds, or securities taken for the indemnity of any town or of the county; and in case of the neglect of any such overseer, to commence and conduct such suits, without the authority of such overseer, in the name of such superintendents.

10. Draw on the county treasurer for all necessary expenses incurred in the discharge of their duties, which draft shall be paid by such treasurer out of the moneys placed in his hands for the support of the poor.

11. Audit and settle all accounts of overseers of the poor, justices of the peace, and all other persons, for services relating to the support, relief or transportation of the county poor; and draw on the county treasurer for the amount of the accounts which they shall so audit and settle.

12. Furnish necessary relief to such of the county poor as may require only temporary assistance, or are so disabled that they cannot be safely removed to the county almshouse, or to the county poor who can be properly provided for elsewhere than at the county almshouse at an expense not exceeding that of their support at such almshouse.

13. Render to the board of supervisors of their county, at their annual meeting, a verified account of all moneys received and ex-

pended by them, or under their direction, and of all their proceedings in such manner and form as may be required by the board.

14. Pay over all moneys remaining in their hands, within fifteen days after the expiration of their terms of office, to the county treasurer, or their successors.

15. Administer oaths and take affidavits in all matters pertaining to their office, and elicit, by examination under oath, statements of facts from applicants for relief.

Expenditures by the superintendent of the poor in the administration of his department are subject to the following limitations: The board of supervisors, at its annual meeting, may fix the maximum sum which may be expended by the superintendent, at his discretion, during the next ensuing year, and may provide that expenditures in excess of that sum shall be made only with the written approval of the chairman of the board of supervisors, or of a committee of the board, composed of not exceeding three members. If such limitation is fixed and such provision made, the county treasurer shall not pay any draft or order of the superintendent in excess of the sum so fixed by the board, unless it is accompanied with the written approval of such chairman or committee. (*As amended by chapter 507 of the Laws of 1897.*)

The board of supervisors of a county has no power to direct the county treasurer not to pay, out of the poor funds, any draft drawn by the superintendents of the poor to their own order, or to the order of either of them, nor to direct him not to pay any draft unless the object for which the money is to be paid be specified therein. *People ex rel. Severn v. Demarest, 16 Hun, 123.*

As to whether the statute (chap. 26, Laws of 1832) authorizing superintendents of the poor to "audit and settle all accounts * * * for services relating to the support, relief or transportation of county paupers" confers upon those officers power to audit claims under contracts made with them, *quaere.*

The claim of an attorney for services rendered by him on the employment of superintendents of the poor in bastardy proceedings is not one "relating to the support, relief or transportation" of paupers within the meaning of that statute, and no power is conferred upon the superintendents to audit such a claim.

Said officers have power to employ an attorney to conduct such proceedings; they are responsible to the attorney for his services and he may enforce his claim against them by action.

It seems that every expense they incur by such employment is a county charge, subject to the audit of the board of supervisors.

It seems also that where bastardy proceedings are successful and indemnity secured, the attorneys fees with other expenses incurred may be charged upon the putative father (1 R. S. 644, §§ 13, 14). *Neary v. Robinson, 98 N. Y., 81; Neary v. Robinson (27 Hun, 145), reversed.*

It was more than intimated in *Hayes v. Symonds (9 Barb. 260)*, that purchases of material and employment of labor by the superintendents, for which they were authorized to contract, were not the class of accounts to which the statute cited had reference. It would seem to be the more reasonable interpretation that their auditing power does not extend to their own contracts, and so make them sit as judges upon questions relating to their own conduct and their own corporate liability. *Neary v. Robinson, 98 N. Y. 84.*

Superintendents of the poor are not bound to audit the accounts of physicians and others for services rendered to county paupers by request of the overseers of the poor of the several towns; and this though the services were rendered in pursuance of orders for temporary relief. It is the duty of the overseers to adjust such accounts and charge them in their bills against the county. The employment of a physician by the superintendents of the poor of a county does not supersede the right of the overseers of the several towns to employ other physicians to attend county paupers entitled to temporary relief. *Ex parte Green & Brown, 4 Hill, 558.*

The provisions of subdivision 11 have no reference to services performed by the servants and laborers who are employed at the county poorhouse. *Hayes v. Symonds, 9 Barb. 260.*

Superintendents of the poor have capacity to contract a liability for supplies furnished for the county poorhouse; which liability may be enforced by suit. *Id.*

But where it appears that the credit for supplies thus furnished was given to a *fund*, in the county treasury, raised by virtue of the 50th section of the act for the relief of indigent persons, called the poorhouse fund, instead of to the superintendents, and on the supposition that the goods would be paid for by a draft on the treasurer, no action will lie against the superintendents until an application has been made to them for an order on the fund, and they have refused to give it. *Id.*

The office of superintendent of the poor, though invested with corporate powers, is, notwithstanding, a mere agency of the county, and the relation between the county and its superintendent is that of principal and agent. *People v. Bennett, 37 N. Y. 117.*

Where a person sells to superintendents of the poor, provisions for the poorhouse, upon an agreement that it is to be a cash sale, or if an order shall be given that it shall answer as cash, whereupon the superintendents give him an order upon the treasurer of the county, for the amount, and upon presentment of such order to the treasurer payment is refused, for want of funds, the vendor is remitted to his original right of action against the superintendents and may recover of them the value of the supplies.

In such a case the county is liable on the contract made by its authorized agents in the business specially committed to them by the statute. *Paddock v. Symonds, 11 Barb. 117.*

The acts of a majority of the superintendents is binding upon the whole board. *Johnson r. Dodd, 56 N. Y. 76.*

The statutes relating to the support of the poor at county poorhouses furnish no authority for a discrimination between county and town poor, in respect to the application of the income of the poorhouse farm. On the contrary the legislature intended the income should be applied to the support of the poor of the county generally at the poorhouse, without distinction.

The statutory provisions obviously contemplate that the benefits resulting from the poorhouse and farm shall be common to the county and towns, in respect to the support of the poor at the poorhouse, without any regard whatever to the general obligation of each to support its own poor.

The occupancy of the property, the products of the farm consumed thereon and in the poorhouse, the labor of the poor in carrying on the farm and the business of the poorhouse, the avails of sales of products of the farm and the labor of the poor, are all to go, and be applied, to reduce the expenses of the support of the poor generally, at the poorhouse, without any discrimination.

Thus, where the city of Rochester was, by law, in the condition of a town, in respect to the mode of supporting its poor at the county poorhouse, it was held that the income of the poorhouse farm in Monroe county ought to be applied to the support, indiscriminately, of the county, town and city poor, kept at the county poorhouse on said farm. *City of Rochester v. Supervisors of Monroe, 22 Barb. 248.*

The overseer of the poor cannot incur for the county a liability beyond the sum of $10, for relief in a single case, without the consent of one of the superintendents of the poor.

But with this restriction, his power of giving temporary relief is independent of the control of the superintendents of the poor. *Gere v. Supervisors of Cayuga, 7 How. 255.*

The superintendents of the poor are not authorized to receive paupers into the county poorhouse to be supported at the expense of the county, unless an order to that effect has been made by the overseer of the poor; or a warrant has been issued for the removal of the pauper to the county poorhouse as a lunatic. *Pomeroy v. Wells, 8 Paige, 405.*

The court of sessions has no power in a proceeding under title 8 of part 6 of the Code of Criminal Procedure to prescribe the place where the poor person shall be supported, nor any of the conditions of such support, except that the manner of it shall be such as shall be approved by the superintendent of the poor. The provisions of the Revised Statutes requiring the removal to the county house of all persons requiring permanent relief or support do not apply to such a case. *In re Weaver, Supt., 45 St. Rep. 95.*

An account of moneys expended for the support of a pauper, in a county having a poorhouse, need not be audited by town auditors. *People v. Supervisors of Washington, 1 Wend. 75.*

An action cannot be maintained against the superintendents of the poor upon an account for services relating to the support of county paupers.

Should the superintendents refuse to audit such an account, the proper remedy is by *certiorari. Vedder r. Superintendents of Schenectady County, 5 Den. 564.*

Chapter 169 (sec. 4) of the Laws of 1877 is not violative of the provision of § 11, article 8 of the Constitution forbidding the giving by a city of its money or property in aid of persons or corporations, save as excepted; it comes within the exception allowing such gifts by a city "in aid or support of its poor as may be authorized by law." *White v. Inebriates' Home, 141 N. Y. 123; s. c. 56 St. Rep. 665; s. c. 56 St. Rep. 194; affirmed.*

No implied obligation rests upon an overseer of the poor to compensate a person, who has, voluntarily and without request from him, relieved a pauper. *Smith v. Williams, 13 Misc. 761; s. c. 69 St. Rep. 611.*

If the person directed by an order of the court of sessions to pay a certain sum of money per week, payable monthly to a superintendent of the poor, to be applied exclusively to the support of her daughter, desires to relieve herself from the effect thereof, she should apply to the court of sessions under the provisions of sec. 918 of the Code of Civil Procedure. for its modification, but so long as the order remains unchanged, she is by force of the statute liable to pay the sum therein prescribed; such an order is not void because it gives no option to such person either to support her daughter or to pay the amount provided, and if it is irregular or improper the remedy is by appeal, and the question of its irregularity or impropriety cannot be raised in an action brought to collect the amount directed to be paid. *Aldridge v. Walker, 73 Hun, 281; s. c. 57 St. Rep. 272.*

§ 4. Appointment of superintendent as keeper of almshouse.

— The board of supervisors of any county may, by resolution, appoint as keeper of its county almshouse one of the superintendents of the poor of such county, who shall hold such office until the expiration of his term as superintendent or until the board of supervisors, by resolution, shall determine that he shall no longer act in such capacity. The board of supervisors may fix the compensation such superintendent shall receive for acting as such keeper, and such compensation shall be a county charge. While a resolution of the board of supervisors directing such superintendent to act as keeper of the county almshouse is in force, the superintendents shall not employ a keeper thereof.

For work, labor and services rendered to the keeper of a county poorhouse by an inmate thereof and his wife, for the benefit of such keeper and in his business, and upon his promise to pay therefor, he is liable.

The keeper of a county poorhouse is not entitled, any more than a stranger, to the labor and services of the paupers therein, for his own advantage, without compensation; and any contract or promise he may make to pay for such labor will be obligatory upon him. *Bergin v. Wemple, 30 N. Y. 319.*

Laws of 1896, c. 225, § 4, providing that the county superintendents of the poor, one of whom is elected annually, shall "employ" a keeper of the almshouse unless a keeper be "appointed" by the board of supervisors, does not authorize the superintendents of the poor to employ an almshouse keeper for a term of years.

A keeper of an almshouse "employed" by the superintendents of the poor on the failure of the board of supervisors to "appoint" a keeper (Laws 1896, c. 225, § 4) is not an officer within constitution 1895, art. 10, § 3, providing that an office, the duration of which is not fixed by the constitution or by statute shall be held during the pleasure of the body making the appointment. *Abrams v. Horton, 18 App. Div. 208; s. c. 45 N. Y. Supp. 887.*

§ 5. When they may direct overseers of the poor to take charge of the county poor.—Whenever the county superintendents take charge of the support of any county poor person, in counties where no almshouse is provided, they may authorize the overseers of the poor of the town in which such poor person may be, to continue to support him, on such terms and under such regulations as they shall prescribe; and thereafter no moneys shall be paid to such overseers for the support of such poor person, without the order of the superintendents; or the superintendents may remove such poor person to any other town, and there provide for his support, in such manner as they shall deem expedient.

§ 6. Idiots and lunatics.—The superintendents of the poor shall provide for the support of poor persons that may be idiots or lunatics, at other places than in the almshouse, in such manner as shall be provided by law for the care, support and maintenance of such poor persons.

Where the property of a father consists solely of pension moneys, and property purchased therewith, he cannot be compelled, under sections 915 and 916 of the criminal code, to support his pauper insane son. *Matter of St. Lawrence State Hospital, 15 Misc. 159; s. c. 57 N. Y. Supp. 12; affirmed in 13 App. Div. 436. See also s. c. 15 Misc. 165.*

§ 7. **Pestilence in almshouse.**—Whenever any pestilence of infectious or contagious disease shall exist in any county almshouse or in its vicinity, and the physician thereof shall certify that such pestilence or disease is likely to endanger the health of the persons supported thereat, the superintendents of the poor of such county shall cause the persons supported at such almshouse or any of them, to be removed to such other suitable place in the same county as shall be designated by the board of health of the city, town or village, within which such almshouse shall be, there to be maintained and provided for at the expense of the county, with all necessary medical care and attendance, until they can be safely returned to the county almshouse from which they were taken, or otherwise discharged.

§ 8. **Accounts of county treasurer with towns.**—In counties where there are town poor, the county treasurer thereof shall open and keep an account with each town, in which the town shall be credited with all the moneys received from the same, or from its officers, and shall be charged with the moneys paid for the support of its poor. If there be a county almshouse in such county, the superintendents of the poor shall, in each year, before the annual meeting of the board of supervisors, furnish to the county treasurer a statement of the sums charged by them as herein directed, to the several towns for the support of their poor, which shall be charged to such towns, respectively, by the county treasurer in his account.

The actual expense to towns for the support of their poor in the county almshouse must be determined by what has really been paid for such support by the county. There shall be no discrimination between town and county poor, in respect to the application of products from the poor farm, or the products derived from the labor of the poor. *City of Rochester v. Supervisors of Monroe Co., 22 Barb. 248.*

§ 9. **Annual apportionment of town expenses.**—In counties having an almshouse, and where there are town poor, the superintendents shall annually, and during the week preceding the annual meeting of the board of supervisors, make out a statement of all the expenses incurred by them the preceding year for the support of town poor, and of the moneys received therefor, exhibiting the deficiency, if any, in the funds provided for defraying such expenses, and they shall apportion the deficiency among the several towns in proportion to the number and expenses of the town poor of such towns respectively, who shall have been provided for by the superintendents, and shall charge the towns with such proportion; which statement shall be by them delivered to the county treasurer.

§ 10. Tax levy on towns.—At the annual meeting of the board of supervisors, the county treasurer shall lay before them the account kept by him; and if it shall appear that there is a balance against any town, the board shall add the same to the amount of taxes to be levied and collected upon such town, with the other contingent expenses thereof, together with such sum for interest as will reimburse and satisfy any advances that may be made, or that may have been made, by the county treasurer for such town, which moneys, when collected, shall be paid to the county treasurer.

§ 11. Expense of county poor.—The superintendents of the poor shall annually present to the board of supervisors, at their annual meeting, an estimate of the sum which, in their opinion, will be necessary during the ensuing year for the support of the county poor; and such board of supervisors shall cause such sum as they may deem necessary for that purpose, to be assessed, levied and collected, in the same manner as other contingent expenses of the county, to be paid to the county treasurer and to be by him kept as a separate fund, distinct from the other funds of the county.

Superintendents of the poor have capacity to contract a liability for supplies for the county almshouse. *Hayes v. Symonds*, 9 Barb. 260.

§ 12. Superintendents' report to the state board of charities.—The superintendents of the poor of every county shall, on or before the first day of December in each year, make reports covering the year ending September thirtieth, to the state board of charities in such form as the board shall direct, showing the number of the town poor and of the county poor that have been re-

lieved or supported in their county the year preceding October
first; the whole expense of such support, the amount paid for
transportation of poor persons, and any other items not part of the
actual expenses of maintaining the poor, and the allowance made
to superintendents, overseers, justices, keepers, matrons, officers
and other employes of the superintendents; the actual value of
the labor of the poor persons maintained, and the estimated
amount saved in the expense of their support in consequence of
their labor; the sex and native country of every such poor person,
with the causes, either direct or indirect, which have operated to
render such persons poor, so far as the same can be ascertained;
and shall include in such report a statement of the name and age
of, and of the names and residence of the parents of, every poor
child who has been placed by them in a family during the year,
with the name and residence of the family with whom every such
child was placed, and the occupation of the head of the family,
together with such other items of information in respect to their
character and condition as the state board of charities shall direct.

§ 13. Supervisors and members of town boards may direct as
to temporary or outdoor relief to the poor.—The board of supervisors of any county may make such rules and regulations as it
may deem proper in regard to the manner of furnishing temporary or outdoor relief to the poor in the several towns in said
county, and provided the board of supervisors shall have failed
to make any such rules and regulations the town board of any
town may make such rules and regulations as it may deem
proper in regard to furnishing temporary or outdoor relief to the
poor in their respective towns, by the overseer or overseers of the
poor thereof, and also in regard to the amount such overseer or
overseers of the poor may expend for the relief of each person
or family, and after the board of supervisors of any county,
or the town board of any town, shall have made such rules
and regulations, it shall not be necessary for the overseer
of the poor of the towns in said county, where such rules and
regulations were made by the board of supervisors, or if in a
town by the said town board, to procure an order from the

supervisor of the town, or the sanction of the superintendent of the poor to expend money for the relief of any person or family, unless the board of supervisors of such county or the town board of such town shall so direct; but this section shall not apply to the counties of New York and Kings. (*As amended by chapter* 48 *of the Laws of* 1897.)

§ 14. **Penalty for neglect or false report.**—Any superintendent of the poor or other officer or person having been an officer, who shall neglect or refuse to render any account, statement or report required by this chapter, or shall willfully make any false report, or shall neglect to pay over any moneys within the time required by law, shall forfeit two hundred dollars to the town or county of which he is or was an officer, and shall be liable to an action for all moneys which shall be in his hands after the time the same should have been paid over, with interest thereon at the rate of ten per centum per annum from the time the same should have been paid over. The state board of charities shall give notice to the district attorney of the county of every neglect to make the report required to be made to that board, and every officer or board to whom any such account, statement, report or payment should have been made, shall give notice to such district attorney of every neglect or failure to make the same; and such district attorney shall, on receiving such notice or in any way receiving satisfactory evidence of such default, prosecute for the recovery of such penalties or moneys in the name of the town or county entitled thereto, and the sum recovered, if for the benefit of the town, shall be paid to the overseer of the poor thereof, and if for the benefit of the county, shall be paid into the county treasury, to be expended by the overseer or superintendent of the poor for the support of the poor of such town or county.

ARTICLE II.

OVERSEERS OF THE POOR.

Section 20. Relief in counties having almshouse.
  21. Expense of removal, and temporary relief.
  22. How supported, and when discharged.

Section 23. Temporary relief to persons who can not be removed
to almshouse.

    24. Relief in counties having no almshouse.

    25. Overseer to make monthly examinations and audit
accounts.

    26. Overseers to keep books of account.

    27. Annual report of overseers.

    28. Accounts of town officers.

    29. Overseers of the poor in cities.

    30. Certain poor persons to be sent to hospitals.

Section 20. Relief in counties having almshouse.—When
any person shall apply for relief to an overseer of the poor, in a
county having an almshouse, such overseer shall inquire into the
state and circumstances of the applicant; and if it shall appear
that he is a poor person, and requires permanent relief and support, and can be safely removed, the overseer shall, by written
order, cause such poor person to be removed to the county almshouse, or to be relieved and provided for, as the necessities of
the applicant may require. If the county be one where the
respective towns are required to support their own poor, the
overseer shall designate in such order of removal, whether such
person be chargeable to the county or not; and if no such designation be made, such person shall be deemed to belong to the
town whose overseer made such order.

A person receiving aid as a poor sick person from the officers of the
poor in a city or county, in the absence of any representations on his part
as to his responsibility or physical condition, incurs no liability to repay
the amount expended on his behalf.

It seems the question as to the propriety of granting relief asked is confided to the discretion of said authorities, and if they grant it, the presumption is that they made such investigations as they deemed necessary
and determined the question as to the right of the party to relief, their
determination cannot be reviewed.

Such aid once furnished must thereafter be regarded as a charity extended by the authorities without expectation of reimbursement, and their
misjudgment as to the necessities of the person relieved raises no implied
promise on his part to repay moneys expended in his behalf.

Money voluntarily paid out by one person for another cannot be recovered back. To maintain an action to recover moneys paid out and expended, it is essential to prove a request to make the payment on the part of the person benefited, either expressed or fairly to be implied from the circumstances.

Every person has a natural right to choose the mode and manner of his life, and so long as he does not violate any positive provision of law, to follow it; and money voluntarily furnished by the charitable and credulous, without deception, to aid him cannot be recovered back.

The possession of some property by a person does not always and necessarily preclude such person from a just claim for charitable relief. *City of Albany v. McNamara, 117 N. Y. 168.*

A poor person has no right to choose the place or manner of his support, but must take it in the way the law confers it.

There is no implied obligation upon an overseer or superintendent of the poor to compensate a person who has voluntarily relieved a pauper without a request from the overseers of the poor.

One B having met with an accident was received by the plaintiff into his house, and there nursed and cared for. Notice was given to the overseer of the poor, who offered to remove B to the poorhouse and there care for him, but B refused to be removed and remained with the plaintiff. *Held* that these facts were insufficient to create a liability on the part of the overseer to compensate plaintiff for the care and nursing provided by him for B. *Smith v. Williams, 13 Misc. 761.*

In counties where the poor are a county and not a town charge, money paid for either the permanent, or temporary, support of a pauper is the money of the county and not of the town. Hence the town can have no color of right to recover it back from a person alleged to have obtained it fraudulently.

In counties where there is no county poorhouse, and the towns are severally liable for the support of their own poor, moneys raised for the support of the poor are placed in the hands of the overseers of the poor; and when an overseer pays out money for the support of a pauper or contracts for his support, he is entitled to appropriate the money, in the first case, and retain it in his own hands in the other. He has absolute control of the fund and is liable only for moneys not lawfully appropriated.

If an overseer of the poor, having money for the support of the poor, in his hands, makes a contract with another for the support of a pauper, that is within the amount which he has a right to furnish, he may properly charge it in account, and retain it, in his settlement with the board of town auditors.

If he becomes personally liable, upon such contract, by reason of his not having obtained an *order* for the support of the pauper, it is not fraudulent for him to protect himself against such personal liability upon his contract, by retaining the amount thereof out of moneys in his hands. *Robbins v. Woolcott, 66 Barb. 63.*

Where overseers of the poor relieved and supported paupers belonging to another town, at the request of the overseer of the poor of the town in which the paupers belonged, and the latter overseer, after such support had been furnished, on the presentation of the bill therefor, agreed to pay the same, it was *held* that he was not personally liable on the contract; it appearing from the facts and circumstances that he was acting in his official character, and did not intend to bind himself personally.

Held also, that he was not liable in his official character; the proper remedy for the plaintiffs being that pointed out by statute, viz., to get the claim for the maintenance allowed by the superintendents of the poor, and to lay the same, when thus allowed, before the board of supervisors, in order that they might add the same to the tax list of the town in which the paupers belonged. *Holmes v. Brown. 13 Barb. 599.*

Where a person has at the request of an overseer, and on his promise to see him paid, boarded a pauper and furnished him with necessaries, he may maintain an action of *assumpsit* against the overseer, although no order had ever been made for relief of the pauper. *King v. Butler, 15 Johns. 281.*

They are subject to an action for debts contracted by their predecessors, as overseers. *Todd v. Birdsell, 1 Cow. 260; Grant v. Fancher, 5 Id. 309.*

Overseers are not liable, in their individual capacities, for the fraud of their predecessors. Overseers cannot be held individually for the fraudulent acts of their predecessors. *Gregory v. Reeve, 5 Johns. ch. 232.*

Overseers may make contracts, within the scope of their authority, which are binding upon them in their official capacity, and upon their successors in office; which successors are liable to be sued for a non-performance of such contracts. *Palmer v. Vandenbergh, 3 Wend. 193; Paddock v. Symonds, 11 Barb. 117.*

A contract for the support of a pauper, for an indefinite period, may be rescinded by the overseers. *Id.*

An overseer of the poor cannot contract with the poor officers of another town, for the maintenance of paupers then temporarily residing in the latter. The account must be audited by the superintendents of the poor, and the amount levied by the supervisors against the town responsible for the support of the paupers. *Overseers of Norwich v. Overseers of Pharsalia, 15 N. Y. 341.*

§ 21. Expense of removal, and temporary relief.—Unless such poor person is properly chargeable to the town, the overseer, in addition to the expense of such removal, shall be allowed such sum as may have been necessarily paid out, or contracted to be paid, for the relief or support of such poor person, previous to such removal and as the superintendent shall judge was reasonably expended while it was improper or inconvenient to remove such poor person, which sum shall be paid by the county treasurer, on the order of the superintendent.

§ 22. How supported and when discharged.—The person so removed shall be received by the superintendents, or their agents, and be supported and relieved in a county almshouse until it shall appear to them that such person is able to maintain himself, or, if a minor, until he is bound out or otherwise cared for, as hereinafter provided, when they may, in their discretion, discharge him.

One who is an inmate of the poorhouse at the expense of the county, although not committed as a pauper, is amenable to the rules and regulations of the institution so long as he remains. *Spence v. Brown, 17 Weekly Dig. 518.*

§ 23. Temporary relief to persons who can not be removed to almshouse.—If it shall appear that the person so applying requires only temporary relief, or is sick, lame or otherwise disabled so that he can not be conveniently removed to the county almshouse, or that he is a person who should be relieved and cared for at his home under article five of this chapter, the overseers shall apply to the supervisor of the town, who shall examine into the facts and circumstances, and shall, in writing, order such sum to be expended for the temporary relief of such poor person, as the circumstances of the case shall require, which order shall entitle the overseer to receive any sum he may have paid out or contracted to pay, within the amount therein specified, from the county treasurer, to be by him charged to the county, if such person be a county charge, if not, to be charged to the town where such relief was afforded; but no greater sum than ten dollars shall be expended or paid for the relief of any one poor person, or one family, without the sanction, in writing, of one of the superintendents of the poor of the county, which shall be presented to the county treasurer, with the order of the supervisor, except when the board of supervisors has made rules and regulations as prescribed in section thirteen of this chapter.

The overseer of the poor cannot incur for the county liability beyond the sum of ten dollars, for relief in a single case, without the consent of one of the superintendents of the poor.

But with this restriction, his power of giving temporary relief is independent of the control of the superintendents of the poor. *Gere v. Supervisors of Cayuga Co.*, *7 How. Pr. 255.*

The question as to the propriety of granting relief asked is confided to the discretion of the poor authorities, and if they grant it, the presumption is that they made such investigations as they deemed necessary, and determined the question as to the right of the party to relief, their determination cannot be reviewed. *City of Albany v. McNamara, 117 N. Y. 168.*

An action will not lie against overseers of the poor for omitting to apply to a justice to obtain an order for the relief of a pauper settled in their town, at the suit of one who, after giving them notice, and requiring them to provide for the pauper, supports him at his own expense, voluntarily, and without request from the overseers of the poor. The appropriate remedy is by mandamus in behalf of the pauper. *Minklaer v. Rockfeller, 6 Cow. 276.*

An order of a justice of the peace (supervisor), authorizing an allowance for the relief of a pauper, is authority sufficient for an overseer to contract for the support of such pauper. A formal adjudication of the settlement of the pauper in such case is not necessary. *Palmer v. Vandenbergh et al., 3 Wend. 193.*

If no fraud be shown and no injury resulted to the taxpayers no action by the taxpayers can be maintained against an overseer of the poor under the taxpayers act of 1881, chapter 531, for expending more than ten dollars for the relief of a pauper or poor family without the written consent of a supervisor. *Cobb v. Ramsdell, 57 St. Rep. 457.*

" In those counties in which there is no poorhouse an overseer (§ 43) is authorized to make an order for the allowance of such sum, weekly or otherwise, as the necessities of the poor person may require. If such pauper (§ 44) has a legal settlement in the town where the application is made, or in any other town of the same county, the overseer is required to apply the money to the relief of such pauper. The money paid by the overseer or contracted to be paid pursuant to such order, shall be drawn by him from the county treasurer on producing the order. If such pauper has not a legal settlement in some town of the county in which the application is made, then notice is to be given to the superintendent of the poor, and the overseer may support the pauper after such notice and until the superintendent assumes his support, and the overseer is to be paid therefor from the county treasury." *Robbins v. Woolcott, 66 Barb. 67.*

§ 24. Relief in counties having no almshouse.—If application for relief be made in any county where there is no county almshouse, the overseer of the poor of the town where such application is made shall inquire into the facts and circumstances of the case, and with the written approval of the supervisor of such town, make an order in writing for such allowance, weekly or otherwise, as they shall think required by the necessities of such poor person. If such poor person has a legal settlement in such town, or in any other town in the same county, the overseer shall apply the moneys so allowed to the relief and support of such poor person. The money so paid by him, or contracted to be paid, when the poor person had no legal settlement in the town, and charged to the town in which he had a legal settlement, shall be drawn by such overseer from the county treasurer on producing such order. If such person has no legal settlement in such county, the overseer shall, within ten days after granting to him any relief, give notice thereof, and that such person has no legal settlement in such county, to one of the county superintendents, and until the county superintendents shall take charge of the support of such poor person, the overseer shall provide for his relief and support, and the expense thereof from the time of giving such notice shall be paid to such overseer by the county treasurer, on the production of such order and of proof by affidavit of the time of the giving of such notice, and shall be by him charged to the county.

§ 25. Overseer to make monthly examinations and audit accounts.—The overseer of the poor of a town or city shall, at least once each month, examine into the condition and necessities of each person supported by the town or city out of the county almshouse, and provide within the provisions of this chapter for such allowances, weekly or otherwise, as the circumstances may in his judgment require. All accounts for care, support, supplies or attendance, connected with the maintenance of such poor person or family, shall be settled once in three months, and paid if there be funds for that purpose. No bill, claim or account for care, support, supplies or attendance, furnished to poor persons, by order of the overseer of the poor, or otherwise, shall be audited or allowed by the overseer, unless such bill, claim, or account be verified by the claimant, to the effect that such care, support, supplies or attendance have been actually furnished for such poor persons, that such poor persons have actually received the same, and that the prices charged therefor are reasonable, and not above the usual market rates.

Overseers of the poor may make contracts within the scope of their authority, which are binding upon them in their official capacity, and upon their successors in office; which successors are liable to be sued for a non-performance of the contracts of their predecessors. *Palmer r. Vandenbergh, 3 Wend. 193.*

Where a person has, at the request of an overseer of the poor, and on his promise that he would see him paid, boarded a pauper, and furnished him with necessaries, he may maintain an action of *assumpsit* against the overseer, although no order had ever been made for the relief of the pauper. *King r. Butler. 15 Johns. 281.*

But *in re Olney v. Wickes. 18 Johns. 122,* the court said: " There is no longer any question as to the rule of law, that, where a public agent acts ostensibly in the line of his duty, his contracts are public and not personal. It is also clear that a known public agent, acting within the scope of his authority and contracting for the use of the public, may, by special agreement, superadd his personal responsibility so as to render himself indi-vidually liable; but, as was correctly remarked by *Ch. J. Marshall,* in *Hogsden v. Dexter,* ' Under these circumstances, the intent of the officer to bind himself personally must be very apparent to induce such a construc-tion of the contract.' " *See also King v. Butler, supra,* and *Holmes v. Brown, 13 Barb. 599.* In the latter case the court said: " The cases where an action has been held to lie against an overseer of the poor for the support of paupers, are placed upon the ground that the credit was given to the person individually, in his private capacity, and not as the officer or agent of the town."

In re The Overseers of the Poor of Norwich v. Overseer of Pharsalia, 15 N. Y. 341, the town of Pharsalia being liable for the support of certain paupers, at the time being in the town of Norwich, the defendant as overseer of the poor of Pharsalia promised the plaintiffs, overseers, etc., of Norwich, that, if they would provide for such paupers, he would pay the expenses incurred. It was held that it was not within the official power of the defendant to make such a contract, and that the plaintiffs are confined to the remedy given by statute, viz., the audit of the account by the super-intendents of the poor, and the levying of the amount by the board of supervisors on the town of Pharsalia for the benefit of Norwich.

§ 26. Overseers to keep books of account.—Overseers of the poor, who receive and expend money for the relief and support of the poor in their respective towns and cities, shall keep books to be procured at town or city expense, in which they shall enter the name, age, sex and native country of every poor person who shall be relieved or sup-ported by them, together with a statement of the causes, either direct or indirect, which shall have operated to ren-

der such relief necessary, so far as the same can be ascertained.
They shall also enter upon such books a statement of the name
and age, and of the names and residences of the parents of every
child who is placed by them in a family, with the name and address of the family with whom every such child is placed, and the
occupation of the head of the family. They shall also enter upon
books so procured, a statement of all moneys received by them,
when and from whom, and on what account received, and of all
moneys paid out by them, when and to whom paid and on what
authority, and whether to town, city or county poor; also a statement of all debts contracted by them as such overseers, the names
of the persons with whom such debts were contracted,.the amount
and consideration of each item, the names of the persons for whose
benefit the debts were contracted, and if the same have been paid,
the time and manner of such payment.

The overseers shall lay such books before the board of town
auditors, or the common council of the city, at its first annual
meeting in each year, and, upon being given ten days' notice
thereof, at any adjourned or special meeting of such board or
council, together with a just, true and verified itemized account,
of all moneys received and expended by them for the use of the
poor since the last preceding annual meeting of said board, and a
verified statement of debts contracted by them as such overseer
and remaining unpaid. The board or council shall compare said
account with the entries in the book, and shall examine the vouchers in support thereof, and may examine the overseers of the poor,
under oath, with reference to such account. They shall thereupon audit and settle the same, and state the balance due to or
from the overseer, as the case may be. Such account shall be
filed with the town or city clerk, and at every annual town meeting the town clerk shall produce such town account for the next
preceding year, and read the same, if it be required by the meeting.
The overseers of the town shall have such books present each year
at the annual town meeting, subject to the inspection of the voters
of the town, and the entries thereon for the preceding year shall
there be read publicly at the time reports of other town officers
are presented, if required by a resolution of such meeting.

No credit shall be allowed to any overseers for moneys paid,
unless it shall appear that such payments were made necessarily
or pursuant to a legal order. (*As amended by chapter* 222 *of the
Laws of* 1897.)

§ 27. Annual report of overseers.— Such overseer shall make
to the town board, at its second annual meeting in each year, a
written report, stating their account as provided in the last section, continued to that date, and any deficiency that may then exist
in the town poor fund, with their estimate of the sum which they
shall deem necessary for the temporary and outdoor relief and
support of the poor in their town for the ensuing year, and in
counties where there is no county almshouse, their estimate of
such sum as they shall deem necessary to be raised and collected
therein for the support of the poor for the ensuing year. If such
board shall approve the statement and estimate so made or any
part thereof, they shall so certify in duplicate, one of which certificates shall be filed in the office of the town clerk, and the other
shall be laid by the supervisor of the town, before the board of
supervisors of the county, on the first day of its next annual meeting. The board of supervisors shall cause the amount of such
deficiency and estimates, as so certified, together with the sums
voted by such town for the relief of the poor therein to be levied
and collected in such town, in the same manner as other town
charges, to be paid to the overseers of the poor of such town, and
the warrants attached to the tax-rolls in such county shall direct
accordingly. The moneys so raised shall be received by such overseers, and applied toward the payment of such deficiency, and for
the maintenance and support of the poor, for whose relief such
estimates were made. The town board shall also, on or before the
first day of December, annually certify to the county superintendents, the name, age, sex and native country, of every poor person
relieved and supported by such overseers during the preceding
year, with the causes which shall have operated to render them
such poor persons, the amount expended for the use of each person, as allowed by the board, and the amount allowed to each
      rseer for services rendered in relation to temporary or town

The town board shall include in such annual statement to the county superintendents and the county superintendents shall include in their own report to the state board of charities a statement of the name and age, and of the names and residence of the parents of every child who has been placed by such overseers in a family during the preceding year, with the name and address of the family with whom each child is placed, and the occupation of the head of the family.

The supervisors are not obliged to allow any charge for services relative to a pauper, unless a previous order has been obtained, or the services have been performed at the request of the overseers of the poor, and the account presented to them for adjustment. *Hull v. Supervisors of Oneida,* *19 Johns. 259.*

See *Osterhoudt v. Rigney, 98 N. Y. 222, under § 29 post.*

§ 28. Account of town officers.—The accounts of any town officer for personal or official services rendered by him, in relation to the town poor, shall be audited and settled by the town board and charged to such town. But no allowance for time or services shall be made to any officer for attending any board solely for the purpose of having his account audited or paid.

§ 29. Overseers of the poor in cities.—This chapter shall apply to overseers of the poor in cities, except where otherwise specially provided by law. In the absence of such special provision, overseers of the poor in each city shall make their report to the auditing board of such city, by whatever name known, at the beginning of the fiscal year of such city, if such time be fixed, otherwise on the first day of January in each year; the common councils of such cities as shall be liable for the support of their own poor shall yearly determine the sum of money to be appropriated for the ensuing year, and a certified copy of such determination shall be laid before the board of supervisors of the county, who shall cause the same to be assessed, levied, collected and paid to the county treasurer.

Where overseers of the poor in a county which had adopted, pursuant to the act of 1846 (chapter 245, Laws of 1846), the provisions of the act of 1845 (chapter 334, Laws of 1845), for the relief of the poor, instead of pursuing the system provided by the act, procured supplies upon their own credit, and presented their accounts annually to the board of audit for allowance, the amount audited being put into the schedule of accounts and levied by the board of supervisors with other town charges. *Held*, that the failure to fill the requirements of the act did not deprive the overseers of any power to provide for the relief of the poor, and the advances so made were properly audited and charged against the town; that while the overseers were not bound to furnish supplies upon their own credit, and the act contemplates that they shall be put in funds in advance, under the provision therein (§ 7), authorizing the town board of audit to include in the estimate such sum as shall be necessary " to supply any deficiency in the preceding year," it had power to audit all sums fairly expended where no provision had been made therefor the preceding year. *Osterhoudt v. Rigney et al*, 98 N. Y. 222.

The omission of an overseer of the poor to bring the overseer's book before the town board and an audit of his account without a comparison of the items in the account with those in the book, are irregularities merely and do not render the audit invalid. *Id.*

Where audited claims of an overseer of the poor were included in the general schedule of town accounts, and in the warrant of the supervisors the amount was directed to be paid to the supervisor of the town, with direction to him to pay to the overseer—*Held*, that this was equivalent to a direction to pay to the overseer and so was a substantial compliance with the act. *Id.*

Also *held*, that orders drawn at the request of the overseer by the board of audit upon the supervisors and accepted by them, created no liability against the town or any of its officers; that at most they operated only as assignments *pro tanto* of any moneys he was entitled to receive upon the audit. *Id.*

Where in a claim presented to the board of audit by an overseer of the poor there was included a portion of a claim presented and rejected the previous year, and the audit was for less than the whole amount, but for more than the amount of the claim, deducting the amount so improperly included—*Held*, that a judgment vacating the whole audit was proper, as it could not be ascertained what amount of the illegal claim was allowed, or whether the deduction was made therefrom, or from the items which the board had jurisdiction to audit. *Id.*

Also *held*, that assignees of the overseer stood in the same position with and were bound by the result reached in respect to him. *Id.*

This action was brought by the plaintiff, a corporation organized under the laws of this state, for the care, education and support of poor orphan children, to recover the amount due it for supporting certain children between the age of two and sixteen years, residents of Long Island City, and whom it had received, cared for and supported, on the authority of written orders given by the overseer of the poor of the defendant city.

Held, that the plaintiff was entitled to recover, as it had acted under the direction of an officer who had full power to give such direction, and who was compelled by law to furnish the support for such children outside of the poorhouse, and in an incorporated orphan asylum.

That, as the relief of the children was permanent and not temporary, the ten dollar limitation imposed by section 42 of 2 Revised Statutes (7th ed., p. 1801), did not apply to them. *Nuns of St. Dominick v. Long Island City, 48 Hun 306.*

The overseer of the poor cannot incur a liability beyond the $10 for relief in a single case without the consent of one of the superintendents of the poor. But with this restriction, his power of giving temporary relief is independent of the control of the superintendents of the poor. *Gere v. Supervisors, 7 How. 255.*

In re Robbins v. Woolcott, 66 Barb. 71, the court said: "By section *fifty-one* it is provided that in those counties where there are no county poorhouses the overseers of the towns shall enter in books an account of all matters transacted by them relating to their official duties; of all moneys received by them; of all moneys laid out and disbursed by them.

By section *fifty-two* these books must be laid before the board of town auditors, with an account of moneys received and paid out. The board is required to compare such accounts with the entries in the book; examine the vouchers, and audit and settle the same; and state the balance due from such overseers, or to them, as the case may be. No credit shall be allowed to any overseer for moneys paid, unless it shall appear that such payment was made pursuant to a legal order. It seems to have been supposed that the account of the overseer must be audited and allowed before he can be paid. But clearly this cannot be the meaning of the section. The money for the support of the poor, whether it is paid into the county treasury and paid out by the superintendent, or is paid over to the overseer, is raised in advance of the expenditure, and is, or is supposed to be, in the hands of the treasurer or overseer. The overseer presents his account to the board of auditors, so as to determine, not what he shall be paid, but whether he is entitled to keep what he has taken. It is not true, doubtless, that in all instances the money required is actually in his hands. He may issue orders or make contracts when there are no funds with which to pay. He must render an account of these also, and in such case the board audits before payment; and if he receives the money allowed for such expenditures it is in order to pay debts actually due to himself, or to other persons holding the orders, or to whom he is liable for support rendered upon a contract made with him. If an overseer, under such circumstances, should charge for moneys paid, or claim allowance for liabilities incurred, which had no existence in fact, and obtain the money, he would be guilty of fraud."

§ 30. In all counties of this state in which there are not adequate hospital accommodations for indigent persons requiring medical or surgical care and treatment, or in which no appropriations of money are made for this specific purpose, it shall be the duty of county superintendents of the poor, upon the certificate of a physician approved by the board of supervisors, or of the overseers of the poor in the several towns of such counties, upon the certificate of a physician approved by the supervisor of the town, as their jurisdiction over the several cases may require, to send all such indigent persons requiring medical or surgical care and treatment to the nearest hospital, the incorporation and management of which have been approved by the state board of charities, provided transportation to such hospital can be safely accomplished. The charge for the care and treatment of such indigent persons in such hospitals, as herein provided, shall not exceed one dollar per day for each person, which shall be paid by the several counties or towns from which such persons are sent, and provision for which shall be made in the annual budgets of such counties and towns. (*Added by chapter* 103, *Laws of* 1901.)

ARTICLE III.

SETTLEMENT AND PLACE OF RELIEF OF POOR PERSONS.

Section 40. Settlements, how gained.
    41. Qualification of last section.
    42. Poor persons not to be removed, and how supported.
    43. Proceedings to determine settlement.
    44. Hearing before superintendents.
    45. How to compel towns to support poor persons.
    46. Proceedings to determine who are county poor.
    47. In counties without almshouse.
    48. Decisions to be entered and filed.
    49. Appeal to the county court.
    50. Penalty for removing.
    51. Proceedings to compel support.
    52. Liability, how contested.
    53. Neglect to contest.
    54. Actions, when and how to be brought.
    55. Penalty for bringing foreign poor into this state.
    56. Poor children under sixteen years of age.
    57. Persons having real or personal property.

§ 10. Settlements, how gained.—Every person of full age, who shall be a resident and inhabitant of any town or city for one year, and the members of his family who shall not have gained a separate settlement, shall be deemed settled in such town or city, and shall so remain until he shall have gained a like settlement in some other town or city in this state, or shall remove from this state and remain therefrom one year. A minor may be emancipated from his or her father or mother and gain a separate settlement:

1. If a male, by being married and residing one year separately from the family of his father or mother.

2. If a female, by being married and having lived with her husband; in which case the husband's settlement shall be deemed that of the wife.

3. By being bound as an apprentice and serving one year by virtue of such indentures.

4. By being hired and actually serving one year for wages, to be paid such minor.

The place of birth of an infant pauper is, *prima facie*, his place of settlement, but it may be removed to the last legal settlement of the parents when discovered. *Overseers of Vernon v. Overseers of Smithville, 17 Johns. 89;* and see, also, *Delavergne v. Noxon, 14 Johns. 333; Overseers of Berne v. Overseers of Knox, 6 Cow. 433; Niskayuna v. Albany, 2 Cow. 537; Vernon v. Smithville, 17 Johns. 89.*

If it do not appear that one has gained a settlement in his own right, his settlement follows that of his father:

But a change in the settlement of the father will not affect that of the son, if the father's settlement is obtained after the emancipation of the son.

To acquire settlement by apprenticeship, the servant must be under an indenture, or a deed, contract or writing not indented; a parole binding is not sufficient.

The place of birth is, *prima facie*, the place of settlement; but if the father's settlement be in another place, the settlement of the child follows his. *Overseers of Niskayuna v. Overseers of Albany, 2 Cow. 537.*

A father, who has acquired a legal settlement in a town, cannot by any deed, release or act of emancipation, devest his son, who has not arrived at 21 nor acquired a settlement for himself, of his right of settlement derived from his father; though the son, since such deed of emancipation, had not resided in his father's family, but had acted in all things for himself and worked entirely for his own benefit. *Adams v. Foster, 20 Johns. 452.*

Until a poor person acquires a settlement in his own right, his settlement is that of his father or mother. *Stillwell v. Kennedy, 51 Hun, 114.*

Italian laborers, who come to the United States in search of work, leaving their families in Italy, are employed in constructing railroads, liable to be discharged at any time, and free to leave their employment when they see fit and living in rough shanties built by the railroad contractors, do not give a settlement in a town in which they work for a year, under 3 Rev. St. (Banks 8th ed.) p. 2111, § 29, providing that every person of full age, who shall be " a resident and inhabitant of any town one year," shall be deemed settled in said town. *In re Town of Hector, 24 N. Y. Supp. 475.* See *Smith v. Williams, 13 Misc. 761; s. c., 69 St. Rep. 611.*

The overseer is the sole judge as to who are paupers in his town, and should be relieved by him, and the exercise of that power cannot be reviewed collaterally either in the supreme court or by the town auditors. *Christman v. Phillips, 58 Hun, 282; s. c., 34 St. Rep. 444.*

The town is charged with the support of the poor when there is no action taken by the supervisors to abolish the distinction between town and county poor. The city stands under the Poor Law in the place of the town. *Nuns v. L. I. City, 48 Hun 306.*

A person living on and working a farm on shares for two years or more gains a settlement. *Overseers v. Overseers, 14 Johns. 365.*

An estate situate in a town without residence there, does not gain the owner a settlement in that town. *Sherburne v. Norwich, 16 Johns. 186.*

A bastard child is settled in the town where it was born until it acquires a settlement for itself. *Delavergne v. Noxon, 14 Johns. 333.*

Where a town is divided by an act of the legislature into two towns, and the poor are also directed to be divided between the two, those who afterwards become paupers, are to be considered as settled in the towns within which they were respectively born, and not where they happened to reside at the time of the division. *Washington v. Stanford, 3 Johns. 193.*

A person cannot gain a settlement in any town until he shall have resided there for at least one year, whether such person be a pauper or not. When a settlement is once legally gained in any town it must necessarily remain there until one is subsequently established in some other town or county. *Sitterly v. Murray, 63 How. Pr. 367.*

An adjudication as to the settlement of paupers for whose relief expenditures have been incurred by a town, may be made subsequent to such expenditures. *People v. Supervisors of Oswego, 2 Wend. 291.*

The question of settlement cannot be tried in an action on a bond given to indemnify the town for the support of a bastard: the obligor is estopped by his bond from contesting that question. *Falls v. Belknap, 1 Johns. 486.*

If a pauper having no settlement, be removed to another town to relieve the overseers from the burden of supporting him, and the overseers of the town to which he is removed are compelled to support him, the latter may recover by an action for reimbursement, against the overseers of the town which improperly removed him. *Pittstown v. Plattsburgh, 15 Johns. 436.*

An overseer or superintendent of the poor who finds a pauper in his county or town, has no right to remove such pauper to another town or county where he believes he belongs; but he must provide for the pauper and then pursue the remedy afforded by the laws. *Smith v. Brundage, 17 Weekly Dig. 266.*

A day laborer, who supported his family in one county, until immediately after moving into another county he becomes disabled and a county charge, is not a pauper as intended by the statutes. *Wood v. Simmons, 51 Hun 325; s. c. 21 St. Rep. 390; 4 N. Y. Supp. 368.*

Rev. St. N. Y, pt 1, tit. 1, c. 20, § 59, as amended by chap. 546, L. 1885, provides that, when a pauper strays or is removed from one municipality to another, the county superintendents of the poor shall give the overseers of the poor of the pauper's town notice of such improper removal, and require them to take charge of the pauper. *Held,* that a notice which does not state that the pauper was a pauper while in the town from which he came, nor that his voluntary change of residence was improper was insufficient. *McKay v. Walsh, 6 N. Y. Supp. 358; 2 Sil. s. c. 463.*

It is not necessary that a written denial of responsibility for the support of pauper by an overseer or superintendent should follow the exact language of the statute. *Stillwell v. Coons, 122 N. Y. 242; affirming s. c. 12 St. Rep. 745.*

Appeal is debarred from an order of removal which has not been executed owing to the death of the pauper. *Adams v. Foster, 20 Johns. 452.*

Though an overseer abandon the appeal from an order of removal and takes back the pauper, yet the unreversed order is not conclusive evidence of settlement in the appellate town. *Vernon v. Smithville, 17 Johns. 89.* See also *People v. Supervisors of Cayuga County, 2 Cow. 530.*

On appeal from an order of removal of a pauper, the order is no evidence of the facts it contains; but the respondents are bound to begin *de novo;* and make out their case independent of the order. *Otsego v. Smithfield, 6 Cow. 760.*

The sessions may allow costs on appeals to them, from orders of removal. *Newburg v. Plattekill, 1 Johns. 330.*

. The force of an order requiring a relative to pay a certain sum per week to the county superintendent of the poor, for the support of an alleged dependent poor person, until the further order of the court, is terminated by the termination of the person's dependency upon the public for support, as, by a discharge from the poorhouse followed by self-support; the doctrine of *res adjudicata* does not preclude the defendant, against whom such an order has been made, from setting up such a defence. *Aldridge v. Walker, 151 N. Y. 527; reversing s. c. 82 Hun, 614.*

A widow with children, who has a little personal property and is sick and unable to work, and whose husband's funeral expenses were paid by the town, and who has received aid from the town without objection from the overseer, is a poor and indigent person, within the meaning of the statute against the removal of poor persons from one town or county to another, with the intent to charge such town or county with their support. *Bartlett v. Ackerman, 49 St. Rep. 296; s. c. 66 Hun, 629.*

The individual, under whose roof a poor person dies, is bound to carry the body, decently covered, to the place of burial. *Griffin v. Condon, 18 Misc, 236; s. c. 41 N. Y. Supp. 380.*

Where a man and his wife resided for some years in Cattaraugus county, when they removed to Chemung, where the wife became insane and was taken to the asylum in Cattaraugus county, and the husband then moved to Buffalo and procured his wife's discharge and took her to his home, but shortly afterwards he took her back to the asylum, it was *held,* that when the wife was removed from the asylum, she ceased to be an insane pauper, that the husband acquired a settlement in Erie county, and his settlement became that of his wife, and an action for her support at the asylum could be maintained against Erie county. *Superintendent of Cattaraugus v. Superintendent of Erie, 50 St. Rep. 347; s. c. 66 Hun, 636.*

§ 41. Qualifications of last section.—A woman of full age, by marrying, shall acquire the settlement of her husband. Until a poor person shall have gained a settlement in his or her own right, his or her settlement shall be deemed that of the father, if living, if not, then of the mother; but no child born in any almshouse shall gain any settlement merely by reason of the place of such birth; neither shall any child born while the mother is such poor person, gain any settlement by reason of the place of its birth. No residence of any such poor person in any almshouse, while such person, or any member of his or her family is supported or relieved at the expense of any other town, city, county or state, shall operate to give such poor person a settlement in the town where such actual residence may be.

§ 42. Poor person not to be removed, and how supported.— No person shall be removed as a poor person from any city or town to any other city or town of the same or any other county, nor from any county to any other county except as hereinafter provided; but every poor person, except the state poor, shall be supported in the town or county where he may be, as follows:

1. If he has gained a settlement in any town or city in such county, he shall be maintained by such town or city.

2. If he has not gained a settlement in any town or city in the county in which he shall become poor, sick or infirmed, he shall be supported and relieved by the superintendents of the poor at the expense of the county.

3. If such person be in a county where the distinction between town and county poor is abolished, he shall, in like manner, be supported at the expense of the county, and in both cases, proceedings for his relief shall be had as herein provided.

4. If such poor person be in a county where the respective towns are liable to support their poor, and has gained a settlement in some town of the same county other than that in which he may then be, he shall be supported at the expense of the town or city where he may be, and the overseers shall, within ten days after the application for relief, give notice in writing to an overseer of the town to which he shall belong, requiring him to provide for the support and relief of such poor person.

The penalty given by statute for bringing a poor or indigent person, not having a settlement, into any city or town within this State without legal authority, is incurred as well by bringing such person from one town to another town within the State, as by bringing him from without the State. *Thomas v. Ross, 8 Wend. 672.*

To subject a party to the penalty, it must be shown that he acted *mala fide;* it seems, that carriers of passengers are within the letter, but not within the spirit of the act, and cannot be charged, unless in bringing poor and indigent persons into a city or town, and leaving them there, they act fraudulently.

Proof by an inhabitant long a resident in the town, that he had never known the pauper is *prima facia* sufficient evidence that the pauper has not a legal settlement in the town. *Id.*

It is no defence that the pauper had formerly a legal settlement in the place to which he was brought, and had not subsequently gained one elsewhere. *Winfield v. Mapes, 4 Den. 571.*

§ 43. Proceedings to determine settlement.—If, within ten days after the service of such notice, the overseer to whom the same was directed, shall not proceed to contest the allegation of the settlement of such poor person, by giving the notice hereinafter directed, he or his successors, and the town which he or they represent, shall be precluded from contesting or denying such settlement. He may, within the time mentioned, give written notice to the overseer of the town where such person may be, and from whom he has received the notice specified in the last section, that he will appear before the county superintendents, at a place and on a day therein to be specified, which·day shall be at least ten days and not more than thirty days from the time of the service of such notice of hearing, to contest the alleged settlement. If the county superintendents fail to appear at the time and place so appointed, they shall, at the request of the overseers of either town appoint some place, and some other day, for the hearing of such allegations, and cause at least five days' notice thereof to be given to such overseers; and no poor person shall· be deemed to have gained a settlement, when the proper notices to contest the settlement have been served, until there has been a hearing before the superintendent thereof, and an order by them made and filed in the office of the county clerk, fixing the settlement of such poor person.

In *Stfterly v. Murray 63 How. Pr. 370*, the court said, "the object and scheme of the statute seem to be to provide for the settlement of all persons under the poor laws, no matter what their previous financial condition may have been, and whether they were ever paupers before or not. and to fix the liability of the proper town for their support and maintenance, whenever by misfortune or otherwise they should become a charge upon the public. This is the reasonable and natural conclusion to be drawn from the various provisions of the statute and from the language of these particular sections."

§ 44. Hearing before superintendents.—The county superintendents shall convene whenever required by any overseer pursuant to such notice, and shall hear and determine the controversy, and may award costs, not exceeding fifteen dollars, to the prevailing party, which may be recovered in an action in a court of competent jurisdiction. Witnesses may be allowed fees as in courts of record. The decision of the superintendent shall be final and conclusive, unless an appeal therefrom shall be taken as provided by this chapter.

§ 45. How to compel towns to support poor persons.—The overseers of the poor of the town in which it may be alleged any poor person has gained a settlement, may, at any time after receiving such notice requiring them to provide for such person, take and receive such poor person to their town, and there support him; if they omit to do so, or shall fail to obtain the decision of the county superintendents, so as to exonerate them from the maintenance of such poor person, the charge of giving such notice, and the expense of maintaining such person, after being allowed by the county superintendents, shall be laid before the board of supervisors at their annual meetings from year to year, as long as such expenses shall be incurred, and the supervisors shall annually add the amount of such charges to the tax to be laid upon the town to which such poor person belongs, together with such sum in addition thereto, as will pay the town incurring such expense, the interest thereon, from the time of expenditure to the time of repayment, which sum shall be assessed, levied and collected in the same manner as other charges of such town.   Such moneys when collected shall be paid to the county treasurer and be by him credited to the account of the town which incurred the expenses.

See *Overseers of Norwich v. Overseers of Pharsalia, 15 N. Y. 341.* The town of Pharsalia being liable for the support of certain paupers, at the time being in the town of Norwich, the defendant, as overseer of the poor of Pharsalia, promised the plaintiffs, overseers, etc., of Norwich, that if they would provide for such paupers, he would pay the expenses incurred; *Held,* that it was not within the official power of the defendant to make such a contract, and that the plaintiffs are confined to the remedy given by the statute, viz., the audit of the account by the superintendents of the poor, and the levying of the amount by the board of supervisors on the town of Pharsalia for the benefit of Norwich. Chief Justice Denio, writing the opinion, says:

"It was not contended, on the argument, that the defendant was personally liable, on the alleged promise, to reimburse the town of Norwich. The action was brought to enforce an alleged liability of the town, which the defendant represents, in favor of the town represented by the plaintiffs. But an examination of the statutes will show that the alleged contract of the defendant was not within the scope of his official power, and hence, that no action against the town can be maintained upon it. The Revised Statutes provide that paupers shall not be removed from one town to another, as they might have been under the former statutes; but they declare that every poor person shall be supported in the town or county where he may be. In counties where the respective towns are liable to support their poor (which was the case in Chenango), if a pauper has

gained a settlement in a different town, in the same county, from the one
where he may be when he requires relief, 'he shall be supported at the
expense of the town where he may be, and the overseers shall give notice,
in writing, to the overseers of the town in which such pauper shall belong.
or to one of them, requiring them to provide for the support and relief of
such pauper.' The two following sections provide for trying the question
as to the settlement of the pauper before the county superintendents of
the poor, in cases where the overseer of the poor, on whom the notice is
served, shall contest that point; and it is declared that, if he do not institute the proceedings authorized to be taken for that purpose, he and his
town shall be forever precluded from denying that the settlement was in
that town. The next section shows the manner in which the expenses.
incurred by the town of Norwich, in this case, might have been recovered,
as follows: 'The overseers of the poor of the town in which it may be
alleged any pauper has gained a settlement, may, at any time, after receiving such notice, requiring them to provide for such pauper, take and receive
such pauper to their town, and there support him. If they omit to do so,
or shall fail to obtain the decision of the county superintendents so as to
exonerate them from the maintenance of such pauper, the charge of giving
such notice, and the expense of maintaining such pauper, after being
allowed by the county superintendents, shall be laid before the board of
supervisors at their annual meetings, from year to year, as long as such
expenses shall be incurred; and the supervisors shall annually add the
amount of such charges to the tax to be levied upon the town to which
such pauper belongs, together with such sum, in addition thereto, as will'
pay the town incurring such expenses the lawful interest thereon, from the
time of expenditure to the time of repayment, which sum shall be assessed,
levied and collected in the same manner as the other contingent expenses
of such town. The said moneys, when collected, shall be paid to the
county treasurer, and be by him credited to the account of the town which
incurred the said expenses.'

" Now assuming that the defendant, as overseer of Norwich, made the
promise alleged in the complaint, he did not bind his town more strongly
for the payment of these expenses than it was bound by the statute; and
he could not, by making such a promise, change the mode which the law
had provided for the auditing, collecting and paying over the money. The
overseers of Pharsalia, on receiving the notice from the plaintiff's town,
could do one of two things. They could contest the allegation of settlement in their town by a proceeding before the superintendents. If they
believed this could not be successfully done, they might take the pauper
home to their own town, and provide for his support under their own
superintendence. If they do neither, then the law takes charge of the
case, and declares that the pauper shall be supported (in the first instance)
at the expense of the town where he may be, and that such expense, after
being audited by the county superintendents, shall be collected like the
other town charges, out of the town which is chargeable, through the

agency of the board of supervisors. The defendant elected neither to contest the settlement in his town, nor to bring the pauper there, to be supported under his direction; but it is said he bound his town, by an express
promise, that it should reimburse the plaintiff's town. This is just what
the statute declared should be done, and that obligation was not increased
or diminished by the making of such promise. Nor can the fact of the
making of such an undertaking authorize the town entitled to be reimbursed to pass by the agencies which the law has provided for the ascertainment of the amount of the expenses before they are levied upon the
taxpayers, and sue the town, or its representative, in the courts. The
alleged official promise of the defendant was void for want of authority,
on his part, to make it. If he did not choose to adopt one or the other of
the causes which I have mentioned, he had no further agency in the case.
The promise, therefore, was officious, and did not affect his town in any
manner. The decision of the referee was right, and his judgment should
be affirmed."

§ 46. **Proceedings to determine who are county poor.**—The support of any poor person shall not be charged to the county, without the approval of the superintendents. If a poor person be sent
to the county almshouse as a county poor person, the superintendents, in counties where there are town poor, shall immediately
inquire into the facts, and if they are of opinion that such person
has a legal settlement in any town of the county, they shall within
thirty days after such poor person shall have been received, give
notice to the overseers of the poor of the town to which such poor
person belongs that the expenses of such support will be charged
to such town, unless the overseers within such time as the superintendents shall appoint, not less than twenty days thereafter,
show that such town ought not to be so charged. On the application of the overseers, the superintendents shall re-examine the
matter and take testimony in relation thereto, and decide the question; which decision shall be conclusive, unless an appeal therefrom shall be taken in the manner provided in this chapter.

§ 47. **In counties without almshouse.**—In counties having
no almshouse, no person shall be supported as a county poor person, without the direction of at least one superintendent. In such
cases the overseers of the poor, where such person may be, shall,
within ten days after granting him relief, give notice thereof and
that such person is not chargeable to their town, to one of the

superintendents who shall inquire into the circumstances, and if satisfied that such poor person has not gained a legal settlement in any town of the county, and is not a state poor person, he shall give a certificate to that effect, and that such poor person is chargeable to the county. He shall report every such case to the board of superintendents at their next meeting, who shall affirm such certificate, or, on giving at least eight days' notice to the overseers of the poor of the town interested may annul the same. After hearing the allegations and proofs in the premises, if the superintendent to whom the overseers have given such notice shall neglect or refuse to give such certificate, the overseers may apply to the board of superintendents, who shall summarily hear and determine the matter, and whose decision shall be conclusive, unless an appeal therefrom shall be taken in the manner provided in this chapter. Such appeal may also be taken from the refusal of one superintendent to grant such certificate when there is but one superintendent in the county.

§ 48. Decisions to be entered and filed.— The decisions of county superintendents in relation to the settlement of poor persons, or to their being a charge upon the county, shall be entered in books to be provided for that purpose, and certified by the signature of such of the superintendents as make the same; and a duplicate thereof, certified in the same manner, shall be filed in the office of the county clerk within thirty days after making such decision.

§ 49. Appeal to the county court.—Any or either of the parties interested in a decision of the superintendent of the poor. or in any dispute that shall arise concerning the settlement of any poor person, may appeal from such decision to the county court of the county in which such decision shall be made, by serving upon the other parties interested therein, within thirty days after service upon the appellant of a notice of the same, a notice of appeal. which shall be signed by the appellant or his attorney, and which shall specify the grounds of the appeal. The hearing of such appeal may be brought on by either party in or out of term, upon notice of fourteen days. Upon such appeal a new trial of the matters in dispute shall be had in the county court without a jury, and a decision of the county court therein shall be final and conclusive, and the same costs shall be awarded as are allowed on appeals to said court.

For the purposes of this chapter the county court shall be deemed open at all times.

§ 50. Penalty for removing.—Any person who shall send, remove or entice to remove, or bring, or cause to be sent, removed or brought, any poor or indigent person, from any city, town or county, to any other city, town or county, without legal authority, and there leave such person for the purpose of avoiding the charge of such poor or indigent person upon the city, town or county from which he is so sent, removed or brought or enticed to remove, shall forfeit fifty dollars, to be recovered by and in the name of the town, city or county to which such poor person shall be sent, brought or removed, or enticed to remove, and shall be guilty of a misdemeanor.

To make a person liable, under the statutes, for removing, without legal authority a poor and indigent person to another county, it must be alleged, and proved to be, *with intent*, to make such county chargeable with the support of such pauper.

The same intent must also be established, where the action is to make the county from which the pauper was removed liable under such provisions.

The intent with which the removal is affected, is the gravamen of criminal offense. An action will not lie by the superintendents of the poor of one county against the superintendents of another county for the maintenance of a pauper removed from the county of the latter *without legal authority*, into the county of the former, where the removal is made *at the request of the pauper*, so that he may be under the care of his family and friends, and *without any intent on the part of the person removing him to make the county into which he is removed chargeable with his support.* It *seems*, that the bringing of a pauper into this state, will not subject the person bringing him to the penalties of the act on this subject, unless it be done *with the intent* of subjecting some particular town or county to the charge of supporting such pauper. *Foster v. Cronkhite, 35 N. Y. 139.* A party may testify directly to the intent with which he did an act, when the intent is a fact material to the issue. *Cortland County v. Herkimer County, 44 N. Y. 22.*

In the latter case it was held that the superintendent might testify directly as to the intent with which he did an act when the intent is a fact material to the issue.

§ 51. Proceedings to compel support.—A poor person so removed, brought or enticed, or who shall of his own accord come or strayed from one city, town or county into any other city, town or county not legally chargeable with his support, shall be maintained by the county superintendents of the county where he may be. They may give notice to either of the overseers of the poor of the town, or city from which he was brought or enticed, or came as aforesaid, if such town or city be liable for his support, and if there be no town or city in the county from which he was brought or enticed or came liable for his support, then to either of the county superintendents of the poor of such county, within ten days after acquiring knowledge of such improper removal, informing them of such improper removal, and requiring them forthwith to take charge of such poor person. If there be no overseers or superintendents of the poor in such town, city or county, such notice shall be given to the person, by whatever name known, who has charge and care of the poor in such locality.   ·

In *Bellows v. Counter*, 6 N. Y. *Supp.* 73, it was held that an action will not lie for the support of a pauper by a county into which he had voluntarily removed, at a time when he was not a pauper, against the county from which he had so removed.

An overseer or superintendent of the poor who finds a pauper in his county or town, has no right to remove him to another town or county where he believes he belongs; but he must provide for his support and then pursue his remedy afforded by the laws. *Smith v. Brundage*, 17 *Wkly. Dig.* 266.

In *McKay v. Welch*, 6 N. Y. *Supp.* 358, it was *Held*, that a notice which does not state that the pauper was a pauper while in the town from which he came nor that his voluntary change of residence was improper, was insufficient.

§ 52. Liability, how contested.—The county superintendents, or overseers, or other persons to whom such notice may be directed, may, after the service of such notice, take and remove such poor person to their county, town or city, and there support him, and pay the expense of such notice, and of the support of such person; or they shall, within thirty days after receiving such notice, by a written instrument under their hands, notify the county superintendents from whom such notice was received, or either of them, that they deny the allegation of such improper enticing or removal, or that their town, city or county is liable for the support of such poor person.

It is not necessary to follow the language of the statute in a denial of liability for the support of a pauper. *Stillwell v. Coons, 122 N. Y. 242.*

Personal service of a notice is not necessary to enable a town, city or county to contest its liability. *Stillwell v. Kennedy, 51 Hun, 114.*

When a poor person removes, or is removed from a town in one county to a town, not chargeable with his support, in another county, and is there necessarily relieved by the overseer of the poor of the town the expense incurred and the burden of thereafter maintaining the person is, as between that town and its county, a charge on the county, provided the overseer gives the superintendent of the poor of his county notice of the circumstances of the case, as provided by the statute. *Stillwell v. Coons, 122 N. Y. 242-4.*

If such denial be served by mail, received and retained by the plaintiff without objection, the service is sufficient. *Id., Stillwell v. Kennedy, 51 Hun, 114.*

Revised Statutes N. Y., pt. I, ch. 20, tit. I, § 31, provides that no person shall be removed as a pauper from any city or town to any city or town of the same or any other county, or from any county to any other county, but every poor person shall be supported in the county where he may be; that if he has gained a settlement in any town in such county he shall be maintained by such town; and that if he has not gained a settlement in the county in which he shall become poor, sick or infirm, he shall be supported and relieved by the superintendent of the poor at the expense of the county. Such statutes, as amended by Laws of New York, 1885, ch. 546, provide that any pauper, who shall, of his own accord, come or stray from one city, town or county, into any other city, town or county not legally chargeable with his support, shall be maintained by the superintendent of the county where he may be, and that by taking certain proceedings the liability of the county or town from whence he came for his support may be fixed, if such county is so liable. Held, that one who had always been able to support himself and family by manual labor, though the wages earned by him were not more than sufficient for that purpose, was not a pauper, within the meaning of the statute; and where, having been a resident of the city and county of New York he went to another county, and there met with an accident, which rendered him unable to support himself, the county from whence he came is not liable for his support. *Wood v. Simmons, 4 N. Y. Supp. 368; s. c. 51 Hun, 325.*

§ 53. Neglect to contest.—If there shall be a neglect to take and remove such poor person, and to serve notice of such denial within the time above prescribed, the county superintendents and overseers, respectively, whose duty it was so to do, their successors, and their respective counties, cities or towns, shall be deemed to have acquiesced in the allegations contained in such first notice, and shall be forever precluded from contesting the same, and their counties, cities and towns, respectively, shall be liable for the expenses of the support of such poor person, which may be recovered from time to time, by county superintendents incurring such expenses, in the name of their county in actions against the county, city or town so liable.

§ 54. Actions, when and how to be brought.—Upon service of any such notice of denial, the county superintendents upon whom the same may be served, shall, within three months, commence an action in the name of their county, against the town, city or county so liable for the expenses incurred in the support of such poor person, and prosecute the same to effect; if they neglect to do so, their town, city or county, shall be precluded from all claim against the town, city or county to whose officers such first notice was directed.

§ 55. Penalty for bringing foreign poor into this state.— Any person who shall knowingly bring or remove, or cause to be brought or removed, any poor person from any place without this state, into any county, city or town within it, and there leave or attempt to leave such poor person, with intent to make any such county, city or town, or the state, wrongfully chargeable with his support, shall forfeit fifty dollars, to be recovered by an action in a court of competent jurisdiction in the county, and in the name of the county, city or town into which such poor person shall be brought, and shall be obliged to convey such person out of the state, or support him at his own expense, and shall be guilty of a misdemeanor, and the court or magistrate before whom any person shall be convicted for a violation of this section shall require of such person satisfactory security that he will within a reasonable time, to be named by the court or magistrate, transport such person out of the state, or indemnify the town, city or county for all charges and expenses which may be incurred in his support; and if such person shall refuse to give such security when so required, the court or magistrate shall commit him to the common jail of the county for a term not exceeding three months.

Overseers of the poor, who have expended money, under an order for the maintenance of a pauper, cannot maintain an action on the case against the person who brought the pauper into the town, having no legal settlement in the state, for the amount so expended; but their remedy is under the statute to recover the penalty given in such case. *Orouse v. Mabbett et al., 11 Johns. 167.*

The penalty given by statute for bringing a poor, or indigent person, not having a settlement, into any city or town within this state without legal authority, is incurred as well by bringing such person from one town to another town within the state, as by bringing him from without the state. To subject a party to the penalty, it must be shown that he acted *mala fide; it seems*, that carriers of passengers are within the letter, but not within the spirit of the act, and cannot be charged, unless in bringing poor and indigent persons into a city or town, and leaving them there, they acted fraudulently. Proof by an inhabitant long a resident in the town, that he had never known the pauper, is *prima facie* sufficient evidence that the pauper has not a legal settlement in the town. *Thomas v. Ross & Shaw, 8 Wend. 672.*

§ 56. **Poor children under sixteen years of age.**—No justice of the peace, board of charities, police justice, or other magistrate, or court, shall commit any child under sixteen years of age, as a vagrant, truant or disorderly person, to any jail or county almshouse, but to some reformatory, or other institution, as provided for in the case of juvenile delinquents; and when such commitments are made, the justice of the peace, board of charities, police justice, or other magistrate or court making the same, shall immediately give notice to the superintendents of the poor or other authorities having charge of the poor of the county in which the commitment was made, giving the name and age of the person committed, to what institution, and the time for which committed; nor shall any county superintendents, overseers of the poor, board of charity, or other officer, send any child under the age of sixteen years, as a poor person, to any county almshouse, for support and care, or retain any such child in such almshouse, but shall provide for such child or children in families, orphan asylums, hospitals, or other appropriate institutions for

57

the support and care of children as provided by law, except that a child under two years of age may be sent with its mother, who is a poor person, to any county almshouse, but not longer than until it is two years of age. The board of supervisors of the several counties, and board of estimate and apportionment of the county of New York, and the appropriate board or body in the county of Kings shall take such action in the matter as may be necessary to carry out the provisions of this section. When any such child is committed to an orphan asylum or reformatory, it shall, when practicable, be committed to an asylum or reformatory that is governed or controlled by persons of the same religious faith as the parents of such child.

This action was brought by the plaintiff, a corporation organized under the laws of this state for the care, education and support of poor orphan children, to recover the amount due it for supporting certain children between the age of two and sixteen years, residents of Long Island City, and whom it had received, cared for and supported, on authority of written orders given by the overseer of the poor of the defendant city.

Held, that the plaintiff was entitled to recover, as it had acted under the direction of an officer, who had full power to give such direction, and who was compelled by law to furnish the support for such children outside of the poorhouse, and in an incorporated orphan asylum.

That, as the relief of the children was permanent and not temporary, the $10 limitation imposed by section 42 of 2 Revised Statutes (7th ed., page 1861), did not apply to them. *Nuns of St. Dominick v. Long Island City,* 58 Hun, 306.

Relator was a charitable institution incorporated under chap. 319 of 1848, and having the approval of the state board of charities under chap. 446, of 1883. Under the statutes and by commitments not in all respects perfect, children were sent to relator and its bills therefor audited by the supervisors; the defendant, county treasurer, refused to pay. Held, that the bills were a county charge and that the court would not here scrutinize the commitments with that care which it would exercise if the proceeding were a habeas corpus and the commitment were claimed to be illegal or insufficient. *People ex rel. Mt. Magdalen School v. Dickson,* 32 St. Rep. 495; 57 Hun, 312; See In re Jurisdiction, 3 How. Pr. 39, 43, 44.

§ 57. If it shall at any time be ascertained that any person, who has been assisted by or received support from any town, city or county, has real or personal property, or if any such person shall die, leaving real or personal property, an action may be

maintained in any court of competent jurisdiction, by the overseer of the poor of the town or city, or the superintendent of
the poor of any county which has furnished or provided such
assistance or support, or any part thereof, against such person
or his or her estate, to recover such sums of money as may
have been expended by their town, city or county in the assistance and support of such persons during the period of ten years
next preceding such discovery or death. (*Added by chapter* 664
of the Laws of 1901.)

ARTICLE IV.

SUPPORT OF BASTARDS.

Section 73. When mother and child to be removed to county
almshouse.

    74. Compromise with father of bastard; when mother
may receive money.

    75. Compromise with putative fathers in New York.

Section 60. Penalty for removing mother of bastard; how
supported after removal.— If the mother of any bastard, or of
any child likely to be born a bastard, shall be removed, brought or
enticed into any county, city or town from any other county, city
or town of this state, for the purpose of avoiding the charge of
such bastard or child upon the county, city or town from which
she shall have been brought or enticed to remove, the same penal
ties shall be imposed on every such person so bringing, removing
or enticing such mother to remove, as are provided in the case of
the fraudulent removal of a poor person. Such mother, if unable
to support herself, shall be supported during her confinement and
recovery therefrom, and her child shall be supported, by the
county superintendents of the poor of the county where she shall
be, if no provision be made by the father of such child.

In bastardy cases the mother and child are deemed paupers, and the
fact that the mother or child are likely to become chargeable to the county
as paupers, gives the superintendents of the poor authority to institute
these proceedings. *Neary v. Robinson, 27 Hun, 145.*

§ 61. Mother and child poor persons; proceedings against
county or town from which she was removed.—Such mother
and her child shall, in all respects, be deemed poor persons; and
the same proceedings may be had by the county superintendents
to charge the town, city or county from which she was removed
or enticed, for the expense of supporting her and her child, as are
provided in the case of poor persons fraudulently or clandestinely
removed; and an action may be maintained in the same manner
for said expenses and for all expenses properly incurred in appre-
hending the father of such child, or in seeking to compel its support by such father or its mother.

§ 62. Mother and bastard; how to be supported.— The
mother of every bastard, who shall be unable to support herself
during her confinement and recovery therefrom, and every bastard,

after it is born, shall be supported as other poor persons are required to be supported by the provisions of this chapter, at the expense of the city or town where such bastard shall be born, if the mother have a legal settlement in such city or town, and if it be required to support its own poor; if the mother have a settlement in any other city or town of the same county, which is required to support its own poor, then at the expense of such other city or town; in all other cases, they shall be supported at the expense of the county where such bastard shall be born.

§ 63. Mother and child not to be removed without her consent.—The mother and her child shall not be removed from any city or town to any other city or town in the same county, nor from one county to any other county, in any case whatever, unless voluntarily taken to the county, city or town liable for their support, by the county superintendent of such county or the overseers of the poor of such city or town.

§ 64. Overseers to notify superintendents of cases of bastardy; when county chargeable.—The overseers of the poor of any city or town where a woman shall be pregnant with a child, likely to be born a bastard, or where a bastard shall be born, which child or bastard shall be chargeable, or likely to become chargeable to the county, shall, immediately on receiving information of such fact, give notice thereof to the county superintendents, or one of them.

§ 65. Duty of superintendents to provide for mother and child.—The county superintendents shall provide for the support of such bastard and its mother, in the same manner as for the poor of such county.

§ 66. Until taken charge of by superintendents, to be supported by overseers.—Until the county superintendents take charge of and provide for the support of such bastard and its mother so chargeable to the county, the overseers of the poor of the city or town shall maintain and provide for them; and for that purpose, the same proceedings shall be had as for the support of a poor person chargeable to the county, who can not be conveniently removed to the county almshouse.

§ 67. Overseers of towns to support bastard and mother whether chargeable or not.—Where a woman shall be pregnant with a child likely to be born a bastard, or to become chargeable to a city or town, or where a bastard shall be born chargeable, or likely to become chargeable to a city or town, the overseers of the poor of the city or town where such bastard shall be born, or be likely to be born, whether the mother have a legal settlement therein or not, shall provide for the support of such child and the sustenance of its mother during her confinement and recovery therefrom, in the same manner as they are authorized by this chapter to provide for and support the poor of their city or town.

§ 68. Moneys received by overseers from parents of bastard, how applied and accounted for.—Where any money shall be paid to any overseer, pursuant to the order of any two justices, by any putative father, or by the mother of any bastard, the overseers may expend the same directly, in the support of such child, and the sustenance of its mother as aforesaid, without paying the same into the county treasury. They shall annually account, on oath, to the board of town auditors, or to the proper auditing board of a city, at the same time that other town or city officers are required to account for expenditures of all moneys so received by them, and shall pay over the balance in their hands, and under like penalties, as are provided by this chapter, in respect to the poor moneys in their hands.

§ 69. When moneys received on account of bastard chargeable to county; how to be disposed of.—All moneys which shall be ordered to be paid by the putative father, or by the mother of a bastard chargeable to any county, shall be collected for the benefit of such county; and all overseers of the poor, superintendents, sheriffs, and other officers, shall within fifteen days after the receipt of any such moneys, pay the same into the county treasury. Any officer neglecting to make such payment shall be liable to an action by and in the name of the county, for all moneys so received and withheld, with interest from the time of receipt, at the rate of ten per centum; and shall forfeit a sum equal to that so withheld to be sued for and recovered by and in the name of the county.

§ 70. Disputes concerning settlement of bastard, how determined.—When a dispute shall arise concerning the legal settlement of the mother of a bastard, or of a child born or likely to
be born a bastard, in any city or town, the same shall be determined by the county superintendents of the poor, upon a hearing
of the parties interested, in the same manner and with the same
effect as they are authorized to determine the settlement of a poor
person under this chapter.

(See notes under section 40, ante.)

§ 71. Proceedings when bastard is chargeable to another
town.—When a bastard shall be born, or be likely to be born in a
town or city, when the legal settlement of the mother is in another
town or city of the same county, which is required by law to support its own poor, the overseers of the poor of the town or city
where such bastard shall be born, or be likely to be born, shall
give the like notice to the overseers of the town or city where the
mother's settlement may be, as is required in the case of a person
becoming a poor person, under the like circumstances, and the
same proceedings shall be had, in all respects, to determine the
liability of such town or city as in the case of poor persons.

The overseers of the town or city to which the mother of such
bastard belongs may, before the confinement of such mother, or at
any time after the expiration of two months after her delivery,
if her situation will permit it, take and support such mother and
her child.

If they omit to do so, and fail to obtain the determination of
the county superintendents in their favor on the question of settlement, the town or city to which the mother belongs shall be
liable to pay all the expenses of the support of such bastard, and
of its mother during her confinement and recovery therefrom;
which expenses, after being allowed by the county superintendents, shall be assessed, together with the lawful interest on the
moneys expended, on the town or city to which such mother belongs, and shall be collected in the same manner as provided for
poor persons supported under the same circumstances, and the

moneys so collected, shall be paid to the county treasurer, for the benefit of, and to be credited to, the town which incurred such expenses.

§ 72. Mode of ascertaining sum to be allowed for support of bastard.— When any town is required to support a bastard, and its mother, whether the mother have a settlement in such town or not, and no moneys shall be received from the putative father or from the mother, to defray the expense of such support, the overseers of the poor shall apply to the supervisor of the town and obtain an order for the support of such bastard, and the sustenance of its mother during her confinement and recovery therefrom, and the sum to be allowed therefor, in the same manner as is required in the case of poor persons, and the moneys paid or contracted to be paid by the overseer, pursuant to such order, shall be paid by the county treasurer in the same manner as for poor persons, and be charged to the town to whose officers such payment shall be made.

§ 73. When mother and child to be removed to county almshouse.—If there be a county almshouse in any county where the towns are required to support their own poor, the overseers of the poor of a town where a bastard shall be born, or shall be likely to be born, may, with the approval of the county superintendents or any two of them, and when the situation of the mother will allow it, remove the mother of such bastard, with her child, to such almshouse, in the same manner as poor persons may be removed; the expenses of which removal shall be defrayed in like manner, and such mother and her child shall be considered as poor of the town so liable for their support, and the expense shall in like manner be estimated and paid.

§ 74. Compromise with father of bastard; when mother may receive money.— Superintendents and overseers of the poor may make such compromise and arrangements with the putative father of any bastard child within their jurisdiction, relative to the support of such child, as they shall deem equitable and just, and thereupon discharge such putative father from all further liability for the support of such bastard.

Whenever a compromise is made with the putative father of bastard child, the mother of such child, on giving security for the support of the child, and to indemnify the city and county or the town and county, from the maintenance of the child, to the satisfaction of the officers making the compromise, shall be entitled to receive the moneys paid by such putative father as the consideration of such compromise. If the mother of such child shall be unable to give the security, but shall be able and willing to nurse and take care of the child, she shall be paid the same weekly allowance for nursing and taking care of the child, out of the moneys paid by the father on such compromise, as he shall have been liable to pay by the order of filiation; such weekly sum to be paid the mother, may be prescribed, regulated or reduced, as in the case of an order of filiation.

An action will not lie by the county superintendents of the poor against the putative father of a bastard child on a promise to indemnify the county, made by him to the supervisor of the town in which the child was born, where it is not shown that the supervisor, in obtaining the promise, acted in the premises at the request or with the privity of the county superintendents. *Birdsall v. Edgerton et al., 25 Wend. 619.*

Money paid by a person charged as the father of an unborn bastard to the superintendent of the poor, upon a compromise, under the statutes, it may be recovered back upon its appearing that the supposed mother was not in fact pregnant. It is no defense by the superintendent that he paid the money into the county treasury, no expense having been incurred in the support of the expected child or mother. *Rheel v. Hicks, 25 N. Y. 289.*

§ 75. **Compromise with putative fathers in New York.**— The commissioners of public charities of the city of New York, or any two of them, may make such compromise and arrangements with the putative fathers of bastard children in said city, relative to the support of such children, as they shall deem equitable and just, and thereupon may discharge such putative fathers from all further liability for the support of such bastards.

ARTICLE V.

SOLDIERS, SAILORS AND MARINES.

Section 80. Relief to soldiers and their families.

81. Post to give notice that it assumes charge.

82. Poor or indigent soldiers, et cetera, without families.

Section 83. Burial of soldiers, sailors or marines.

    84. Headstones to be provided.

Section 80. **Relief to soldiers and their families.**—No poor or indigent soldier, sailor or marine who has served in the military or naval service of the United States, nor his family nor the families of any who may be deceased, shall be sent to any alms-house but shall be relieved and provided for at their homes in the city or town where they may reside, so far as practicable, provided such soldier, sailor or marine or the families of those deceased, are, and have been residents of the state for one year and the proper auditing board of such city or town in those counties where the poor are a county charge, the superintendent, if but one, or superintendents of the poor, as such auditing board in those counties shall provide such sum or sums of money as may be necessary to be drawn upon by the commander and quartermaster of any post of the Grand Army of the Republic of the city or town, made upon the written recommendation of the relief committee of such post; or if there be no post in a town or city in which it is necessary that such relief should be granted, upon the like request of the commander and quartermaster and recommendation of the relief committee of a Grand Army post located in the nearest town or city, to the town or city requested to so furnish relief, and such written request and recommendation shall be a sufficient authority for the expenditures so made. (*As amended by chapters 83 of the Laws of 1899, and 475 of the Laws of 1900.*)

    The power to determine who are the indigent persons and families, the necessity for their relief, the measure thereof, the place where and the circumstances under which the same shall be administered, is not vested exclusively in a relief committee of a Grand Army post, but the proper officers of a town, city or county, having jurisdiction to raise and appropriate money for the relief of the poor, have jurisdiction and control over the same, and may determine the amount of money necessary.

    The Grand Army post may apply to the auditing board of the municipality for such sum of money as it deems necessary for the purpose of the act, and that board must exercise its judgment and discretion as to the amount to be appropriated; where it has so done its determination is final, and not subject to review by any court. *People ex rel. Crammond v. The Common Council, 136 N. Y. 489.*

§ 81. Post to give notice that it assumes charge.—The commander of any such post which shall undertake to supervise relief of poor veterans or their families, as herein provided, before his acts shall become operative in any town, city or county, shall file with the clerk of such town, city or county, a notice that such post intends to undertake such supervision of relief, which notice shall contain the names of the relief committee, commander and other officers of the post; and also an undertaking to such city, town or county, with sufficient and satisfactory sureties for the faithful and honest discharge of his duties under this article; such undertaking to be approved by the treasurer of the city or county, or the supervisor of the town, from which such relief is to be received. Such commander shall annually thereafter, during the month of October, file a similar notice with said city or town clerk, with a detailed statement of the amount of relief requested by him during the preceding year, with the names of all persons for whom such relief shall have been requested together with a brief statement in each case, from the relief committee, upon whose recommendation the relief was requested, provided, however, that in cities of the first class said notice and said detailed statement shall be filed with the comptroller of such city, and said undertaking shall be approved by him, and provided further that in any city of the first class which is now or may hereafter be divided into boroughs, a duplicate of such notice and of such detailed statement shall be filed with the commissioner of charities for the borough in which the headquarters of such post is situated, and it shall be the duty of such commissioner to annually include in his estimate of the amount necessary for the support of his department such sum or sums of money as may be necessary to carry into effect the provisions of sections eighty, eighty-one, eighty-two, eighty-three and eighty-four of this act and the proper officers charged with the duty of making the budget of any such city shall annually include therein such sum or sums of money as may be necessary for that purpose. Moneys actually laid out and expended by any such post for the relief specified in section eighty of this act shall be reimbursed quarterly to such post by the comptroller on vouchers duly verified by the commander and quartermaster of said post, showing the date and amount of each payment, the certificate of the post relief committee, signed by at least three members, none of whom shall have received any of the relief granted by the post for which reimbursement is asked, showing that the person relieved was an actual resident of such city, and that they recommended each payment, and the receipt of the recipient for each payment, or in case such receipt could not be obtained, a statement of such fact, with the reason why such receipt could not be obtained. Such vouchers shall be made in duplicate on blanks to be supplied by the comptroller and shall be presented to the commissioner of charities for the borough in which the headquarters of the post is situated, and if such commissioner is satisfied that such moneys have been actually expended as in said voucher stated, he shall approve the same, and file one of said duplicates in his office and forward the other to the comptroller, who shall pay the same by a warrant drawn to the order of the said commander. And provided further, that in any city, county or borough in which Grand Army posts have organized or may organize a memorial and executive committee, the latter shall be regarded as a post of the Grand Army of the Republic. And the chairman, treasurer or almoner and bureau of relief or relief committee referred to, shall exercise the same privileges and powers as the commander, quartermaster and relief committee of a post, on complying with the requirements of this and the preceding section. Wilful false swearing to such voucher shall be deemed perjury and shall be punishable as such.

2. Within thirty days after the passage of this act, any memorial and executive committee in any city, county or borough may file with the proper officers the notice mentioned in the preceding section and such officers are hereby empowered and it is hereby made their duty to estimate for, provide and raise, in the same manner as other local expenditures are estimated for, provided and raised, such sum or sums of money as may be neces-

sary to carry into effect the provisions of this act during the year eighteen hundred and ninety-nine, and such bureau of relief or relief committee shall be reimbursed for moneys expended by it upon compliance with the terms of this act. (*As amended by chapter 462 of the Laws of 1899.*)

A claim for relief, furnished to an indigent soldier, upon the recommendation of the relief committee of a Grand Army post, and the order of the officer of such post, was properly disallowed by the board of town auditors, where the alleged relief was furnished by two members of such relief committee. *People ex rel. Hovey v. Leavenworth, 90 Hun, 48; s. c. 69 St. Rep. 853.*

§ 82. Poor and indigent soldiers, et cetera, without families.—Poor or indigent soldiers, sailors or marines provided for in this article, who are not insane, and who have no families or friends with whom they may be domiciled, may be sent to a soldiers' home. Any poor or indigent soldier, sailor or marine provided for in this chapter, or any member of the family of any living or deceased soldier, sailor or marine, who may be insane, shall, upon recommendation of the commander and relief committee of such post of the Grand Army of the Republic, within the jurisdiction of which the case may occur, be sent to the proper state hospital for the insane.

§ 83. Burial of soldiers, sailors or marines.—The board of supervisors in each of the counties shall designate some proper person or authority, other than that designated for the care of poor persons, or the custody of criminals, who shall cause to be interred, the body of any honorably discharged soldier, sailor or marine, who has served in the military or naval service of the United States, who shall hereafter die without leaving means sufficient to defray his funeral expenses, but such expenses shall in no case exceed thirty-five dollars. If the deceased has relatives or friends who desire to conduct the burial, but are unable or unwilling to pay the charges therefor, such sum shall be paid by the county treasurer upon due proof of the claim, and of the death and burial of the soldier, sailor or marine to the person so conducting such burial.

Such interment shall not be made in a cemetery or cemetery plot used exclusively for the burial of poor persons deceased. (*As amended by chapter 24 of the Laws of* 1900.)

§ 84. Headstones to be provided.—The grave of any such deceased soldier, sailor or marine shall be marked by a headstone containing the name of the deceased, and, if possible, the organization to which he belonged, or in which he served; such headstone shall cost not more than fifteen dollars, and shall be of such design and material as shall be approved by the board of supervisors, and the expense of such burial and headstone as provided for in this article, shall be a charge upon, and shall be paid by the county in which the said soldier, sailor or marine shall have died; and the board of supervisors of such county is hereby authorized and directed to audit the account and pay the expense of such burial in the same manner as other accounts against said county are audited and paid; provided, however, that in case such deceased soldier, sailor or marine shall be at the time of his death an inmate of any state institution, including state hospitals and soldiers' homes, or any institution supported by the state and supported at public expense therein, the expense of such burials and headstones shall be a charge upon the county of his legal residence.

ARTICLE VI.

STATE POOR.

Section 90. Who are state poor, and how relieved.

91. Notice to be given to county clerks of location of state almshouse.

92. State poor to be conveyed to state almshouses.

93. Punishment for leaving almshouse.

94. Expenses for support.

95. Duties of keeper; superintendent of state and alien poor to keep record of names.

96. Visitation of almshouses.

97. Insane poor.

98. Care of and binding out of state poor children.

99. Transfer to other states or countries.

§ 90. Who are state poor, and how relieved.—Any poor person who shall not have resided sixty days in any county in this state within one year preceding the time of an application by him for aid to any superintendent or overseer of the poor, or other officer charged with the support and relief of poor persons, shall be deemed to be a state poor person, and shall be maintained as in this article provided. The state board of charities shall, from time to time, on behalf of the state, contract for such time, and on such terms as it may deem proper, with the authorities of not more than fifteen counties or cities of this state, for the reception and support, in the almshouses of such counties or cities respectively, of such poor persons as may be committed thereto. Such board may establish rules and regulations for the discipline, employment, treatment and care of such poor persons, and for their discharge. Every such contract shall be in writing, and filed in the office of such board. Such almshouses, while used for the purposes of this article, shall be appropriately designated by such board and known as state almshouses. Such board may, from time to time, direct the transfer of any such poor person from one almshouse to another, and may give notice from time to time to counties, to which almshouses they shall send poor persons.

§ 91. Notice to be given to county clerks of location of state almshouses.—Such board shall give notice to the county clerks of the several counties of the location of each of such almshouses, who thereupon shall cause such notice to be duly promulgated to the superintendents and overseers of the poor, and other officers charged with the support and relief of poor persons in their respective counties. A circular from the superintendent of state and alien poor, appointed by such board shall accompany such notice, giving all necessary information respecting the commitment, support and care of the state poor in such almshouses, according to the provisions of this article.

§ 92. State poor to be conveyed to state almshouses.—County superintendents of the poor, or officers exercising like powers, on satisfactory proof being made that the person so applying for relief as a state poor person, as defined by this chapter, is such poor person, shall, by a warrant issued to any proper person or officer, cause such person, if not a child under sixteen years of age, to be conveyed to the nearest state almshouse, where he shall be maintained until duly discharged, but a child under two years of age may be sent with its mother, who is a state poor person, to such state almshouse, but not longer than until it is two years of age. All testimony taken in any such proceeding shall be forwarded, within five days thereafter, to the superintendent of state and alien poor, and a verified statement of the expenses incurred by the person in making such removal, shall be sent to such superintendent. Such board shall examine and audit the same, and allow the whole, or such parts thereof, as have been actually and necessarily incurred; provided that no allowance shall be made to any person for his time or service in making such removal. All such accounts for expense, when so audited and allowed, shall be paid by the state treasurer, on the warrant of the comptroller, to the person incurring the same.

§ 93. Punishment for leaving almshouse.—An inmate of a state almshouse, who shall leave the same without being duly discharged, and within one year thereafter is found in any city or town of this state soliciting public or private aid, shall be punished by confinement in the county jail of the county in which he is so found, or in any workhouse of this state in such county, for a term not exceeding three months, by any court of competent jurisdiction; and it shall be the duty of every superintendent and overseer of the poor and other officers charged with the support and relief of poor persons, to cause, as far as may be, the provisions of this section to be enforced.

94. Expenses for support.—The expenses for the support, treatment and care of all poor persons who shall be sent as state

poor to such almshouses, shall be paid quarterly, on the first day
of January, April, July and October in each year, to the treasurer
of the county, or proper city officers incurring the same, by the
treasurer of the state, on the warrant of the comptroller; but no
such expenses shall be paid to any county or city, until an account
of the number of persons thus supported, and the time that each
shall have been respectively maintained, shall have been rendered
in due form and approved by the state board of charities.

§ 95. Duty of keepers; superintendent of state and alien poor
to keep record of names.—The keeper or principal officer in charge
of such almshouse shall enter the names of all persons received
by him pursuant to this article, with such particulars in reference
to each as the board, from time to time may prescribe, together
with the name of the superintendent by whom the commitment
was made, in a book to be kept for that purpose. Within three
days after the admission of any such person, such keeper or principal officer shall transmit the name of such person, with the particulars hereinbefore mentioned, to the superintendent of state and
alien poor; and notice of the death, discharge or absconding of
any such person shall in like manner and within the time above
named, be thus sent to such superintendent. Such superintendent
shall cause the names of such persons in each such almshouse furnished as above provided for, to be entered in a book to be kept for
that purpose in the office of such board, and he shall verify the correctness thereof by comparison with the books kept in such almshouse, and by personal examination of the several inmates thereof,
and in any other manner the board may from time to time direct;
and he shall furnish the board, in tabulated statements, on or
before the second Tuesday in January, annually, the number of
inmates maintained in each and all of such almshouses during the
preceding year, the number discharged, transferred to other institutions, bound out or removed from the state, and the number
who died or left without permission during the year, with such
other particulars and information as the board may require.

§ 96. Visitation of almshouses.—The superintendent of state
and alien poor shall visit and inspect each of such almshouses at

58

and if satisfied that such removal was proper, and that the expenses thereof were actually and necessarily incurred, shall audit and allow the amount of such expenses, which when so audited and allowed, shall be paid by the state treasurer, on the warrant of the comptroller, to the person incurring the same.

If, however, it shall appear to the satisfaction of such superintendent that the Indian poor person making application for relief is in such physical condition as to make it improper to remove him to the almshouse, the superintendent may, subject to such rules and regulations as may be prescribed by the state board of charities, provide for the care and support of such Indian poor person, without removing him to the almshouse, and the expenses incurred in such care and support shall be paid by the state treasurer on the warrant of the comptroller, upon the order and allowance thereof by the state board of charities as in cases of support of Indian poor persons in almshouses.

§ 102. Contracts for support of Indian poor persons.—The state board of charities, shall from time to time, on behalf of the state, contract with the proper officers of the county within which such Indians who are poor persons reside, on such terms and for such times as it may deem proper, for the reception and support in the almshouse of such counties of such Indians who are poor persons as may be committed thereto. Such board may establish rules and regulations for the discipline, treatment and care of such Indians and provide for their discharge. Every such contract shall be in writing and filed in the office of such board.

§ 103. Expenses for support of Indian poor persons.—The expenses for the support, treatment and care of all Indians who are poor persons and shall be sent to such county almshouse pursuant to this chapter, shall be paid quarterly on the 1st day of January, April, July and October in each year, to the treasurer of the county wherein such Indians are supported, by the state treasurer, on the warrant of the comptroller, but no such expenses shall be paid until an account of the number of Indians thus supported, and the time that each shall have been respectively maintained shall have been rendered in due form and approved by the state board of charities.

§ 104. Duty of keepers; superintendent of state and alien poor to keep record.—The keeper or principal officer in charge of such almshouse shall enter the names of all Indians committed thereto, with such particulars in relation thereto as the state board of charities may prescribe. Immediately upon the admission of any such Indian, such keeper or principal officer shall transmit by mail the names of such Indians, with the particulars hereinbefore mentioned, to the superintendent of state and alien poor; and notice of the death, discharge or absconding of any such Indian shall in like manner be transmitted to such superintendent. Such superintendent shall cause the names of such Indians in such county almshouse to be entered in a book to be kept for that purpose in the office of such board, and he shall verify the correctness thereof by comparison with the books kept in the almshouse by personal examination of such Indians or in such other manner as the board may direct; and he shall furnish the board in tabulated statements, annually on or before the second Tuesday in January, the number of Indians maintained in all such county almshouses during the preceding year, the number discharged, bound out, removed from the state, and the number who died or left without permission during the year, with such other information as the board may require.

ARTICLE VII.

DUTIES OF STATE BOARD OF CHARITIES; POWERS OF STATE CHARITIES AID ASSOCIATION.

Section 115. Duties of the State Board of Charities relating to the poor.—The State Board of Charities shall:

1. Investigate the condition of the poor seeking public aid and devise measures for their relief.

2. Administer the laws providing for the care, support and removal of state and alien poor and the support of Indian poor persons.

3. Advise the officers of almshouses in the performance of their official duties.

4. Collect statistical information in respect to the property, receipts and expenditures of all almshouses, and the number and condition of the inmates thereof.

§ 116. Visitation and inspection of almshouses.—Any commissioner or officer of the State Board of Charities, or any inspector duly appointed by it for that purpose, may visit and inspect any almshouse in this state. On such visits inquiry shall be made to ascertain:

1. Whether the rules and regulations of the board, in respect to such almshouse, are fully complied with.

2. Its methods of industrial, educational and moral training, if any, and whether the same are best adapted to the needs of its inmates.

3. The condition of its finances generally.

4. The methods of government and discipline of its inmates.

5. The qualifications and general conduct of its officers and employes.

6. The condition of its grounds, buildings and other property.

7. Any other matter connected with, or pertinent to, its usefulness and good management.

Any commissioner or officer of the board, or inspector duly appointed by it, shall have free access to the grounds, buildings, books and papers relating to such almshouse, and may require from the officers and persons in charge, any information it may deem necessary. Such board may prepare regulations according to *age, and provide blanks and forms upon which such informa-

*As in the original.

tion shall be furnished, in a clear uniform and prompt manner for the use of the board; any such officer or inspector who shall divulge or communicate to any person without the knowledge and consent of such board, any facts or information obtained in pursuance of the provisions of this chapter, shall be guilty of a misdemeanor, and shall at once be removed from office. The annual reports of each year shall give the results of such inquiry, with the opinion and conclusions of the board relating to the same. Any officer, superintendent or employe of any such alms-house who shall willfully refuse to admit any member, officer or inspector of the board, for the purpose of visitation and inspection, and who shall refuse or neglect to furnish the opinion required by the board, or any of its members, officers or inspectors, shall be guilty of a misdemeanor, and subject to a fine of one hundred dollars for each such refusal or neglect. The rights and powers hereby conferred may be enforced by an order of the supreme court after such notice as the court may prescribe, and an opportunity to be heard thereon, or by indictment by the grand jury of the county, or both.

§ 117. Investigations by board of committee; orders thereon.— The board may, by order, direct an investigation by a committee of one or more of its members, of the officers and managers of any almshouse, or of the conduct of its officers and employes; and the commissioner or commissioners so designated to make such investigation may issue compulsory process for the attendance of witnesses and the production of books and papers, administer oaths, examine persons under oath, and exercise the same powers in respect to such proceeding as belong to referees appointed by the supreme court.

If it shall appear, after such investigation, that the inmates of the almshouse are cruelly, negligently or improperly treated, or inadequate provision is made for their sustenance, clothing, care and supervision, or other condition necessary to their comfort and well being, such board may issue an order in the name of the people, and under its official seal, directed to the proper officer of such almshouse, requiring him to modify such treatment or apply

such remedy, or both, as shall therein be specified. Before such order is issued it must be approved by a justice of the supreme court, after such notice as he may subscribe, and an opportunity to be heard thereon, and any person to whom such an order is directed who shall willfully refuse to obey the same shall, upon conviction, be deemed guilty of a misdemeanor.

§ 118. Almshouse construction and administration.—No almshouse shall be built or reconstructed, in whole or in part, except on plans and designs approved in writing by the state board of charities. It shall be the duty of such board to call the attention, in writing or otherwise, of the board of supervisors and the superintendent of the poor, or other proper officer, in any county, of any abuses, defects or evils, which, on inspection, it may find in the almshouse of such county, or in the administration thereof, and such county officer shall take proper action thereon, with a view to proper remedies, in accordance with the advice of such board.

§ 119. Duties of the attorney-general and district attorneys.—If, in the opinion of the state board of charities, or any three members thereof, any matter in regard to the management or affairs of any such almshouse, or any inmate or person in any way connected therewith, require legal investigation or action of any kind, notice thereof may be given by the board, or any three members thereof, to the attorney-general, who shall thereupon make inquiry and take such proceedings in the premises as he may deem necessary and proper. It shall be the duty of the attorney-general and of every district attorney when so required to furnish such legal assistance, counsel or advice as the board may require in the discharge of its duties under this chapter.

§ 120. State, nonresident and alien poor.—The State board of charities, and any of its members or officers, may, at any time, visit and inspect any almshouse to ascertain if any inmates are state charges, nonresidents, or alien poor; and it may cause to be removed to the state or country from which he came, any such nonresident or alien poor found in any such almshouse.

§ 121. Visit by the State Charities Aid Association.—Any justice of the supreme court, on written application of the state charities aid association, through its president or other officer designated by its board of managers, may grant to such persons as may be named in such application, orders to enable such persons, or any of them, as visitors of such association, to visit, inspect and examine, in behalf of such association, any almshouse within the state. The person so appointed to visit, inspect and examine such almshouse and almshouses, shall reside in the county or counties from which such almshouse or almshouses receive their or some of their inmates, and such appointment shall be made by a justice of the supreme court of the judicial district in which such visitors reside. Each order shall specify the almshouse to be visited, inspected and examined, and the name of each person by whom such visitation, inspection and examination shall be made. and shall be in force for one year from the date on which it shall have been granted, unless sooner revoked.

All persons in charge of any such almshouse shall admit each person named in any such order into every part of such almshouse, and render to such person every possible facility to enable him to make in a thorough manner such visit, inspection and examination, which are hereby declared to be for a public purpose and to be made with a view to public benefit. Obedience to the orders herein authorized shall be enforced in the same manner as obedience is enforced to an order or mandate of a court of record.

Such association shall make an annual report to the state board of charities upon matters relating to the almshouse subject to its visitation. Such reports shall be made on or before the first day of November for each preceding fiscal year.

ARTICLE VIII.

MISCELLANEOUS PROVISIONS.

Section 130. Superintendents and overseers may redeem on sheriff's sale.

131. Redemption, how made.

Section 130. Superintendents and overseers may redeem on sheriff's sale.—County superintendents and overseers of the poor may redeem real property, which may have been seized by them pursuant to sections nine hundred and twenty-one to nine hundred and twenty-six of the code of criminal procedure, the same as judgment-creditors under section fourteen hundred and thirty to fourteen hundred and seventy-eight of the code of civil procedure. No such redemption shall be made, unless at the time of such redemption the seizure of the property sought to be redeemed, shall have been confirmed by the county court of the county where the premises may be situated, nor unless such property shall, at the time of making such redemption, be held by the superintendents or overseers, under and by virtue of such seizure.

§ 131. Redemption, how made.—To entitle such superintendents or overseers to acquire the title of the original purchaser, or to be substituted as purchaser from any other creditor, they shall present to and leave with such purchaser or creditor, or the officer who made the sale, the following evidence of their right:

1. A copy of the order of the county court, confirming the warrant and seizure of such property, duly verified by the clerk of the court;

2. An affidavit of one of the superintendents or overseers that such property is held by them under such warrant and seizure,

and that the same have not been discharged, but are then in full
force.

§ 132. Moneys therefor, and how paid.—The superintendent or overseers of the poor may, for the purpose of making such
redemption, use any moneys in their hands belonging to the poor
funds of their respective towns or counties, which moneys shall
be replaced, together with the interest thereon, out of the first
moneys which may be received by them from the rent or sale of
the premises so redeemed.

§ 133. When warrant of seizure may be discharged.—
If such redemption shall be made, and the person against whom
the warrant was issued and seizure made shall apply to have
the warrant discharged, he shall, before such warrant and seizure are discharged, in addition to the security required to be
given by section nine hundred and twenty-four of the code of
criminal procedure, pay to such superintendents or overseers the
sum paid by them to redeem such property, together with interest thereon, from the time of such redemption.

§ 134. Boards of supervisors may abolish or revive distinction between town and county poor.—The board of supervisors of any county may, at an annual meeting or at a special
meeting called for that purpose, by resolution, abolish or revive
the distinction between town and county poor of such county, by
a vote of two-thirds of all the members elected to such board,
and until such abolition or revival, such county, or the towns
therein, shall continue to maintain and support their poor as at
the time when this chapter shall take effect. The clerk of the
board shall, within thirty days after such determination, serve,
or cause to be served, a copy of the resolution upon the clerk of
each town, village or city within such county, and upon each of
the superintendents and overseers of the poor therein. Upon
filing such determination to abolish the distinction between
town and county poor, duly certified by the clerk of the board,
in the office of the county clerk, the poor of the county shall
thereafter be maintained, and the expense thereof defrayed, by
the county; and all costs and charges attending the examina-

tions, conveyance, support and necessary expenses of poor persons therein, shall be a charge upon the county. Such charges and expenses shall be reported by the superintendent of the poor, to the board of supervisors, and shall be assessed, levied and collected the same as other county charges.

In order to render the expense of maintaining all the poor of the county a county charge pursuant to the above section, the board of supervisors must not only determine to abolish the distinction between county and town poor, but must file such determination with the county clerk. Until such determination be filed, the duties of the officers arising out of such change in the poor system do not attach. The service of the resolution of the board of supervisors on the town clerks is not essential to effect a change of system; the provision respecting such service is only directory. *Thompson v. Smith, 2 Den. 177.* .

In order to abolish the distinction between town and county poor, in a particular county, a resolution to that effect must be passed by the board of supervisors, and the same must be filed in the county clerk's office. *Baldwin v. McArthur, 17 Barb. 414.*

The town is charged with the support of the poor, when there is no action taken by the supervisors to abolish the distinction between town and county poor, and a city stands under the poor laws in place of the town *Nuns of St. Dominic v. Long Island City, 48 Hun, 306.*

The act of 1882, ch. 28, making the town of Oswegatchie a separate and distinct poor district, did not operate as a repeal of the privilege extended to the supervisors of St. Lawrence county by the act of 1846, ch. 245, to adopt the " Livingston County Act " chap. 334, of 1845. *People v. Supervisors of St. Lawrence, 103 N. Y. 541.*

§ 135. Overseers, when to pay money to county treasurer.—Within three months after notice shall have been served upon the overseers of the poor, that the distinction between town and county poor has been abolished, they shall pay over all moneys which shall remain in their hands as overseers for the use of their town, after discharging all demands against them, to the county treasurer, to be applied by him toward the future taxes of such town; and all moneys thereafter received by them, as such overseers, for the use of the poor of their town, shall be paid by them to the county treasurer within three months after receiving the same, and by him credited to the town whose overseer shall have paid the same. It shall be the duty of all officers or persons to pay to the county treasurer all moneys which shall

be received for, or owing by them to the overseers of the poor of
any such town, for the use of the poor thereof, pursuant to any
law or obligation requiring the same to be paid to such overseers, and credited by such county treasurer to the town for
whose use such moneys were received or owing. Any overseer
or other person having received or owing such moneys, who shall
neglect or refuse to pay the same within thirty days after demand
thereof, shall be liable to an action therefor, with interest at the
rate of ten per cent thereon, by such county treasurer, in the
name of his county.

In counties where the poor are a county and not a town charge, money
paid for either the permanent or temporary support of a pauper is the
money of the county, and not of the town. Hence the town can have no
right to recover it back from a person alleged to have obtained it
fraudulently. *Robbins v. Woolcott, 60 Barb. 63.*

§ 136. Invested town money.—When any town shall have any
moneys raised for the support of the poor, invested in the name
of the overseers of the poor of such town, such overseers shall
continue to have the control thereof, and shall apply the interest
arising therefrom to the support of the poor of their town, so
long as such town shall be liable to support its own poor, but
when relieved from such liability by a vote of the supervisors of
the county, the money so raised and invested shall be applied
to the payment of such taxes upon the town, as the inhabitants
thereof shall at an annual town meeting, or a special town meeting called for that purpose determine.

§ 137. Report by supervisors.—The supervisor of every town
in counties where all the poor are not a county charge, shall report to the clerk of the board of supervisors, within fifteen days
after the accounts of the overseers of the poor have been settled
by the town board at its first annual meeting in each year, an
abstract of all such accounts, which shall exhibit the number
of poor persons that have been relieved or supported in such
town the preceding year, specifying the number of county poor,
and town poor, the whole expense of such support, the allowance
made to overseers, justices, constables or other officers, which
shall not comprise any part of the actual expenses of maintaining the poor.

§ 138. **Register of sex and age.**—In addition to the general register of the inmates of the various almshouses, there shall be kept a record of the sex, age, birthplace, birth of parents, education, habits, occupation, condition of ancestors and family relations, and cause of dependence of each person at the time of admission, with such other facts and particulars in relation thereto as may be required by the state board of charities, upon forms prescribed and furnished by such board. Superintendents and overseers of the poor, and other officers charged with the relief and support of poor persons, shall furnish to the keepers or other officers in charge of such almshouses, as full information as practicable in relation to each person sent or brought by them to such almshouse, and such keepers or other officers, shall record the information ascertained at the time of the admission of such person, on the forms so furnished. All such records shall be preserved in such almshouses, and the keepers and other officers in charge thereof shall make copies of the same on the first day of each month, and immediately forward such copies to the state board of charities.

§ 139. **Care of poor persons not to be put up at auction.**—No officer or persons whose duty it may be to provide for the maintenance, care or support of poor persons at public expense, shall put up at auction or sale, the keeping, care or maintenance of any such poor person to the lowest bidder, and every contract which may be entered into in violation of this provision shall be void.

§ 140. **Reports of certain other officers.**—The provisions of this chapter, relating to reports by superintendents of the poor, to the state board of charities, and the penalties applicable thereto, are hereby extended to, and made applicable to the commissioners of public charities for the city and county of New York, the superintendent of the almshouse of the county of Albany, the keeper of the almshouse of the county of Putnam, the commissioners of the almshouse elected in the cities of Newburgh and Poughkeepsie, and all poor officials elected or appointed in other cities of this state, under general or special acts of the legislature.

§ 141. **Almshouse commissioners to report.**—The commissioners of the almshouse of the cities of Newburgh and Poughkeepsie, and the poor officers of other cities chosen under special acts of the legislature, shall annually, on the first day of December, report to the superintendent of the poor of their respective counties such statistics as, from time to time, may be required to be reported in the other cities and towns under the provisions of this chapter.

§ 142. Report of state board of charities.—The state board of charities shall include in its annual report to the legislature the results of the information obtained from the reports to be made to it as herein provided. It shall also, from time to time, furnish to the officials so required to report to it, necessary forms, blanks and instructions required in making up such reports.

§ 143. The supervisor of a town may as such official accept a deed or conveyance of real property or mortgage thereon in behalf of the town, and sell and convey such real property or mortgage the same after the expiration of one year from the date of such conveyance or mortgage for the care and maintenance of a poor person. No such deed or conveyance shall be accepted by him, unless by the written consent of the town board given at any regular meeting thereof. Such consent shall be filed in the office of the town clerk. The person or persons giving such deed or mortgage may within one year from the date of such conveyance or mortgage secure a conveyance or cancellation of said deed or mortgage upon payment to said supervisor of the expense incurred by such town for taxes and necessary repairs on said property and also in maintaining such person or persons. (*Added by chapter* 117 *of the Laws of* 1902.)

A bequest to a town in trust in perpetuity for the benefit of the poor of the town generally, not confined to those for whose support the town is under statutory liability, is invalid for want of an ascertained beneficiary. *Fosdick v. Hempstead.* 125 *N. Y.* 581; *s. c.* 35 *St. Rep.* 863; *reversing s. c.* 29 *St. Rep.* 545; 8 *N. Y. Supp.* 772; *see s. c.* 126 *N. Y.* 651.

ARTICLE IX.

LAWS REPEALED; WHEN TO TAKE EFFECT.

Section 150. Laws repealed.

151. When to take effect.

Section 150. Laws repealed.—Of the laws enumerated in the schedule hereto annexed, that portion specified in the last column is repealed.

§ 151. When to take effect.—This chapter shall take effect on the first day of October, eighteen hundred and ninety-six.

SCHEDULE OF LAWS REPEALED.

Revised Statutes, part I, ch. 20, tit. I .... All.

Revised Statutes, part I, ch. 20, tit. VI .... All.

Laws of—	Chapter.	Sections.
1828	6	All.
1830	320	8, 9.
1831	277	All.
1832	26	All.
1834	236	All.
1838	202	All.
1842	214	All.
1845	334	All.
1846	245	All.
1848	176	All.
1849	100	All.
1851	532	All.
1853	70	All.
1854	188	All.
1855	269	All.
1862	473	All.
1870	424	All.
1872	38	All.
1872	48	All.
1873	661	All.
1874	464	All.
1875	140	All.
1875	173	All.
1875	308	All.
1876	266	All.
1878	404	All.

Laws of—	Chapter.	Sections.
1879	240	All.
1881	203	All.
1881	398	All.
1881	574	All.
1883	247	All.
1884	319	All.
1885	34	All.
1885	546	All.
1887	216	All.
1887	655	All.
1887	706	All.
1888	261	All.
1888	486	All.
1890	420	All.
1892	698	All.
1893	42	All.
1894	436	All.
1894	663	All.
1895	783	All.

LOCATION OF COUNTY BUILDINGS.

AN ACT to amend section thirty-one of chapter six hundred and eighty-six of the laws of eighteen hundred and ninety-two known as the county law, relative to location of county buildings.

* Chapter 133, of the Laws of 1899.

Section 1. Section thirty-one of chapter six hundred and eighty-six of the laws of eighteen hundred and ninety-two, known as the county law, is hereby amended so as to read as follows:

§ 31. Location of county buildings.—The board of supervisors may, except in the county of Kings, by a majority vote of all the members elected thereto, fix or change the site of any county building, and the location of any county office; but the site or location of no county building or office shall be changed when the change shall exceed one mile, and

59

shall be beyond the boundaries of the incorporated village or city, where already situated, except upon a petition of at least twenty-five freeholders of the county, describing the buildings or office, the site or location of which is proposed to be changed, and the place at or near which it is proposed to locate such new buildings or office; which petition shall be published once in each week for six weeks immediately preceding an annual or special meeting of such board, in three newspapers of the county, if there be so many, otherwise, in all the newspapers published in the county as often as once a week. With such petition shall also be published a notice, signed by the petitioners, to the effect that such petition will be presented to the board of supervisors at the next meeting thereof. The board of supervisors of any county may acquire a new site or location for the county almshouse, erect suitable buildings thereon, and remove the inmates of the existing almshouse thereto, upon a majority vote of all the members elected to said board at a regular session thereof or at a special session called for that purpose, in any case where the state board of charities shall have certified to said board of supervisors that in the opinion of a majority of said state board of charities such change is necessary to the proper care of the inmates of such institution; in which case it shall not be necessary to receive or publish the petition hereinbefore provided or to submit the question of change or removal to the electors of such county as provided in sections thirty-two and thirty-three of the act hereby amended; provided, however, that no site or location shall be selected or acquired by such board of supervisors which shall not have been approved by said state board of charities.

Proceedings respecting the support of poor persons.

TITLE VIII OF PART VI OF THE CODE OF CRIMINAL PROCEDURE.

Section 914. Who may be compelled to support poor relatives.

915. Order to compel a person to support a poor relative, etc.

Section 914. Who may be compelled to support poor relatives. —The father, mother and children, of sufficient ability, of a poor person who is insane, blind, old, lame, impotent or decrepit, so as to be unable by work to maintain himself, must at their own charge, relieve and maintain him in a manner to be approved by the overseers of the town where he is, or in the city of New York, by the commissioners of public charities. If such poor person be insane, he shall be maintained in the manner prescribed by the insanity law. The father, mother, husband, wife, or children of a poor insane person, legally committed to and confined in an institution supported in whole or in part by the state, shall be liable if of sufficient ability for the support and maintenance of such insane person from the time of his reception in such institution. (As amended, chapter 399 of the Laws of 1898.)

Where a son requests the superintendent of the poor to take proceedings to have his father committed to an asylum, and promises to pay a certain sum towards his future support he is liable therefore. 49 Hun, 53.

A grandchild is liable to support grandparents. *Ex parte Hunt, 5 Cow., 284.*

A husband is not bound to maintain his wife's illegitimate children born before their marriage. *Minden v. Cox, 7 Cow., 235.*

Persons having relatives within prescribed degrees and whom they have sufficient ability to support are under an absolute duty, at their own charge. to support the persons described, not in the poorhouse, nor even through the agency of, but only in a manner to be approved by, the poor authorities of town or county. *Matter of Weaver v. Benjamin, 45 St. Rep., 97; 18 N. Y. Supp., 630, 631.* This scheme is outside of the general provisions of the statute for the care and relief of the poor, who are, or who become, a public charge. *Id.* Its purpose is to prevent these persons from becoming a public charge. *Id.* It is not the intent that they are to be made and marked as public paupers by being consigned to the poorhouse of the county. *Id.*

The order for support goes beyond the power of the court when it attaches to the liability of a party to support his mother, the condition that she shall receive such support in the county poorhouse. *Id.*

The court has no power to prescribe the place where the poor person shall be supported, nor any of the conditions of such support, except that the manner of it shall be such as is approved by the overseers or superintendents of the poor. *Id.*

Whatever power there is over that support is vested in the overseers or superintendents of the poor; the court can only declare the duty to support, and in default to fix the sum to be paid. *Id.*

The wife of a man who is bound by law to support her, and who is abundantly able to do so, cannot be regarded as a pauper. *Norton v. Rhodes, 18 Barb. 100.*

In *Stevens v. Cheney, 36 Hun, 1,* the court said: " Under this statute (§ 914) the child is bound to aid in the support of a parent if he is a poor person and unable to defend himself, and, if he fails to do so, the court of sessions may compel him. If the child recognizes the duty laid upon him by statute to care for his indigent parent and voluntarily assumes it without waiting to be compelled by the court of sessions, what right have third persons or wrongdoers to interfere and prevent? The law affords the same protection to those who perform their duty voluntarily as it does to those who reluctantly act under compulsion, and we are of opinion that if the parent is a poor person within the provisions of the statute, it was the duty of the son to aid in his support, and if he voluntarily did that and the plaintiff has been deprived of his means of support by reason of the intoxication, that then he may recover, even though his child is over the age of twenty-one years." See, also, *De Puy v. Cook, 90 Hun, 43.*

Where two or more persons are equally liable to support an indigent person but are unequally able to grant such support, contribution may be

ordered and all may be made to pay in accordance with their means.
Stone v. Burgess, 47 N. Y. 521; 2 Lans. 439.

The common law affords no means of compelling a husband to support
his wife otherwise than by making him liable to third persons who have
supplied her with necessaries after he has improperly refused to do so
and the statute providing for the compulsory support of indigent relatives
does not extend to husband and wife. *People ex rel. Kehlbeck v. Walsh,
11 Hun, 292.*

The wife of a man who is abundantly able to provide for her cannot
be deemed a poor person. Superintendents of the poor cannot, as such,
maintain an action against a husband for boarding, clothing and medical
aid furnished to his wife as a pauper. *Norton et al. v. Rhodes. 18 Barb. 100.*

§ 915. Order to compel a person to support a poor relative,
etc.—If a relative of a poor person fail to relieve and maintain
him, as provided in the last section, the overseers of the poor
of the town where he is, or in the city of New York, the commissioners of public charities may apply to the county court
where the relative dwells for an order to compel such relief,
upon at least ten days' written notice, served personally, or by
leaving it at the last place of residence of the person to whom
it is directed, in case of his absence, with a person of suitable
age and discretion. If such poor person be insane and legally
committed to and confined in an institution supported in whole
or in part by the state, and his relatives refuse or neglect to pay
for his support and maintenance therein, application may be
made by the treasurer of such institution in the manner provided in this section for an order directing the relatives liable
therefor to make such payment. (*As amended by chapter 399 of
the Laws of 1898.*)

The overseers are the proper parties to begin proceedings to compel a
father to support his poor and infirm son. *Tillotson v. Smith, 12 St. Rep.
331.* See also *Stone v. Burgess, 2 Lans. 439.*

§ 916. Court to hear the case and make order of support.—
At the time appointed in the notice, the court must proceed
summarily to hear the allegations and proofs of the parties,
and must order such of the relatives of the poor person mentioned in section nine hundred and fourteen, as were served
with the notice and are of sufficient ability, to relieve and

maintain him, specifying in the order the sum to be paid weekly for his support, and requiring it to be paid by the father, or if there be none, or if he be not of sufficient ability, then by the children, or if there be none, or if they be not of sufficient ability, then by the mother. If the application be made to securing an order compelling relatives to pay for the maintenance of insane poor persons committed to and confined in an institution supported in whole or in part by the state, such order shall specify the sum to be paid for his maintenance by his relatives liable therefor, from the time of his reception in such institution to the time of making such order, and also the sum to be paid weekly for his future maintenance in such institution. The relatives served with such notice shall be deemed to be of sufficient ability, unless the contrary shall affirmatively appear to the satisfaction of the court. *(As amended by chapter 399 of the Laws of 1898.)*

§ 917. Support; when to be apportioned among different relatives.—If it appear that any such relative is unable to wholly maintain the poor person or to pay for his maintenance if confined in a state institution for the insane, but is able to contribute toward his support, the court may direct two or more relatives of different degrees, to maintain him or pay for his maintenance in such an institution if insane, prescribing the proportion which each must contribute for that purpose; and if it appear that the relatives are not of sufficient ability wholly to maintain him, or to pay for his maintenance in such an institution, if insane, but are able to contribute something, the court may direct the sum, in proportion to their ability, which they shall pay weekly for that purpose. If it appear that the relatives who are liable for the maintenance of an insane poor person confined in a state institution for the insane are not able to pay the whole amount due for such maintenance from the time of such poor person's admission to such institution, the court must direct the sum to be paid for such maintenance, in proportion to the ability of the relatives liable therefor. *(As amended by chapter 399 of the Laws of 1898.)*

Two out of five children may be ordered to support an indigent parent, and those two in unequal amounts. *Stone v. Burgess, 2 Lans. 439.*

The liability of the children charged by the order is several, and either is liable on default, in an action to recover the payment required of him by the order. *Id.*

Where the poor are a charge upon the county, the action to enforce such support is properly brought by the superintendent of the poor. *Id.*

See *Herendeen v. DeWitt, 17 St. Rep. 298; 1 N. Y. Supp. 469; 49 Hun, 55.*

§ 918. Order to prescribe time during which support is to continue, or may be indefinite; when and how order may be varied.—The order may specify the time during which the relatives must maintain the poor person, or during which any of the sums directed by the court are to be paid, or it may be indefinite or until the further order of the court. If the order be for the payment of a weekly sum for the maintenance of an insane poor person in a state institution, the order shall specify that such sum shall be paid as long as such insane poor person is maintained in such institution. The court may from time to time vary the order, as circumstances may require, on the application of either of any relative affected by it, or of any officer on whose application the order was made, upon ten days' written notice. *(As amended by chapter 399 of the Laws of 1898.)*

So long as an order, made by a court of sessions, directing the relative of a poor person to pay a specified sum periodically to the superintendent of the poor for the support of such poor person, remains unchanged, such relative is liable to pay the sum therein prescribed. If he or she desires to be relieved therefrom application to amend the order should be made. If the person directed by an order of the Court of Sessions to pay a certain sum of money per week, payable monthly to a superintendent of the poor, to be applied exclusively to the support of her daughter, desires to relieve herself from the effect thereof, she should apply to the Court of Sessions under the provisions of this section for its modification, but so long as the order remains unchanged such person is, by force of the statute, liable to pay the sum therein prescribed. *Aldridge v. Walker, 73 Hun, 281; 57 St. Rep. 273; 26 N. Y. Supp. 296.*

Such an order is not void because it gives no option to such person either to support her daughter or to pay the amount provided, and if it is irregular or improper the remedy is by appeal, and the question of its irregularity or impropriety cannot be properly raised in an action brought to collect the amount directed to be paid by such person and unpaid by her. *Id.*

While the determination provided for by this title is denominated an order, it was a final determination of the matter, and in effect a judgment. *Id.*

See matter of *Weaver v. Benjamin, 45 St. Rep. 97; 18 N. Y. Supp. 631; Herendeen v. DeWitt, 17 St. Rep. 298; 49 Hun, 55; 1 N. Y. Supp. 469.*

§ 919. **Costs, by whom to be paid, and how enforced.**—The costs and expenses of the application must be ascertained by the court, and paid by the relatives against whom the order is made; and the payment thereof, and obedience to the order of maintenance, and to any order for the payment of money, may be enforced by attachment.

§ 920. **Action on the order on failure to comply therewith.**— If a relative, required by an order of the court, to relieve or maintain a poor person, neglect to do so in the manner approved by the officers mentioned in section nine hundred and fourteen, and neglect to pay them weekly the sum prescribed by the court, the officers may maintain an action against the relative, and recover therein the sum prescribed by the court, for every week the order has been disobeyed, to the time of the recovery, with costs, for the use of the poor. If the order directs a relative to pay for the maintenance of an insane poor person in a state institution, and such relative refuses or neglects to pay the amount specified therein, an action may be brought by the treasurer of such institution in its corporate name to recover the amount due to such institution by virtue of such order. *(As amended by chapter 399 of the Laws of 1898.)*

The relative may provide for the support of the pauper at such place, and in such manner, as he shall deem proper, provided the place and manner are approved by the proper officers. *Duel v. Lamb, 1 T. & C. 66.* It is not, until he has neglected or refused to do this, that he is liable for the sum directed to be paid. *Id.*

The court of sessions has no authority to prescribe the place or manner of support. *Id.* Whatever power there is over that support is vested in the overseers or superintendents of the poor. *Id.; Converse v. McArthur, 17 Barb. 410.*

If the pauper, of his own accord, leaves the supporting party who is ready and willing to take him back and support him upon the terms of the order, the duty of the supporting party is fully discharged. *Duel v. Lamb, 1 T. & C. 69; Converse v. McArthur, 17 Barb. 410.*

See *Herendeen v. DeWitt, 17 St. Rep. 298; 49 Hun, 55; 1 N. Y. Supp. 469.*

§ 921. Proceedings against absconding parents, leaving children chargeable to public, etc.—When the father, or the mother being a widow, or living separate from her husband, absconds from the children, or a husband from his wife, leaving any of them chargeable or likely to become chargeable upon the public, the officers mentioned in section nine hundred and fourteen may apply to any two justices of the peace or police justices in the county in which any real or personal property of the father, mother or husband is situated, for a warrant to seize the same. Upon due proof of the facts, the magistrate must issue his warrant, authorizing the officers so applying to take and seize the property of the person so absconding. Whenever any child shall be committed to an institution pursuant to any provision of the Penal Code, any magistrate may issue a warrant for the arrest of the father of the child, and examine into his ability to maintain such child in whole or in part; and if satisfied that such father is able to contribute towards the support of the child, then the magistrate shall, by order require the weekly payment by such father of such sum, and in such manner as such magistrate shall, in said order direct towards the maintenance of such child in such institution, which amount when paid shall be credited by the institution to the city, town, or county against any sums due to it therefrom on account of the maintenance of the child.

In cases of a commitment of a child to an institution under the Penal Code, the magistrate is authorized to order the father to pay a sum for the child's support which is to be credited by the institution to the city, town or county against any sum due for maintenance. *People ex rel. St. Magdalen School, etc., v. Dickson, 32 St. Rep. 496; 57 Hun, 315; 10 N. Y. Supp. 605.*

One of two overseers of the poor is authorized to institute and carry on proceedings for the seizure of property of one who has absconded, leaving his wife or child chargeable to the town. When only one overseer acts, the consent of the other will be presumed. *Downing v. Rugar, 21 Wend. 178.*

§ 922. Seizure of their property. Transfer thereof, when void.—The officers so applying may seize and take the property, wherever it may be found in the same county; and are vested with all the right and title thereto, which the person absconding

then had. The sale or transfer of any personal property, left in
the county from which he absconded, made after the issuing of
the warrant, whether in payment of an antecedent debt or for
a new consideration, is absolutely void. The officers must immediately make an inventory of the property seized by them, and
return it, together with their proceedings, to the next county
court of the county where they reside, there to be filed. (As
amended by chapter 880 of the Laws of 1895.)

§ 923. Warrant and seizure, when confirmed or discharged.
Direction of the court thereon.—The court, upon inquiring into
the circumstances of the case, may confirm or discharge the
warrant and seizure; and if it be confirmed, must, from time to
time, direct what part of the personal property must be sold,
and how much of the proceeds of the sale, and of the rents and
profits of the real property, if any, are to be applied toward the
maintenance of the children or wife of the person absconding.

§ 924. Warrant, in what cases to be discharged.—If the party
against whom the warrant issued, return and support the wife
or children so abandoned, or give security satisfactory to any
two justices of the peace, or police justices in the city, village or
town, to the overseers of the poor of the town, or in the city of
New York, to the commissioners of charities and corrections,
that the wife or children so abandoned shall not be chargeable
to the town or county, then the warrant must be discharged by
an order of the magistrates, and the property taken by virtue
thereof restored to the party.

§ 925. Sale of the property seized, and application of its proceeds.—The officers must sell at public auction the property
ordered to be sold, and receive the rents and profits of the real
property of the person absconding, and in those cities, villages
or towns which are required to support their own poor, the officers charged therewith must apply the same to the support of
the wife or children so abandoned; and for that purpose must
draw on the county treasurer, or in the city of New York, upon
the comptroller, for the proceeds as directed by special statutes.
They must also account to the county court of the county, for
all money so received by them, and for the application thereof,

from time to time, and may be compelled by that court to render that account at any time. *(As amended by chapter 880 of the Laws of 1895.)*

§ 926. Powers of superintendents of poor.—In those counties where all the poor are a charge upon the county, the superin·tendents of the poor are vested with the same powers, as are given by this title to the overseers of the poor of a town, in respect to compelling relatives to maintain poor persons, and in respect to the seizure of the property of a parent absconding and abandoning his family; and are entitled to the same remedies in their names, and must perform the duties required by this title, of overseers, and are subject to the same obligations and con·trol.

This section gives to the superintendents of the poor of those counties in which all the poor are a county charge the powers given to the over-seers of the towns by the preceding sections. *Matter of Wearer v. Ben-jamin, 45 St. Rep. 97; 18 N. Y. Supp. 831.*

An application to compel relatives to maintain poor persons should be made by the county superintendent, where all the poor are a charge upon the county. *Matter of Tillotson v. Smith, 12 St. Rep. 332.*

CARE OF AGED, DECREPIT AND FEEBLE-MINDED PERSONS.

AN ACT to provide for the care of aged, decrepit, and mentally enfeebled persons who are not insane.

Chapter 914 of the Laws of 1896.

Section 1. It shall be lawful for the state board of charities, within ten days after the passage of this act, to exercise super·vision over all aged, decrepit and feeble-minded persons who are not proper subjects for care and treatment in a hospital for the insane, but who, on application by themselves, or by their rela·tives, or if without relatives, then by their friends or legal guard·ians, seek to obtain admission into any homes, retreats, or other asylums which may be authorized under the provisions of this act, to receive and administer to their necessities in a safe and hu·mane manner.

§ 2. The state board of charities, in the exercise of such official supervision, is hereby empowered to license any home, retreat, or other asylum devoted to the sole purpose of keeping and caring for such aged, decrepit or mentally enfeebled persons whenever in the judgment of said board such home, retreat or asylum possesses the necessary equipment in officers and attendants, together with suitable domestic accommodations in all other respects, for the safe and humane maintenance of such patients. And the power of exercising supervision over such institutions by the state board of charities, and of visiting and inspecting them and their inmates at all times, shall be the same as now belongs to them in respect to the other institutions under their care.

§ 3. Any person not a minor may voluntarily enter such a licensed institution upon filing an application of his intention with the superintendent thereof, supported by the affidavits of two reputable physicians of the places of residence of such person, certifying to the fact that the said applicant, though aged, decrepit or mentally enfeebled, is not insane nor a proper subject for treatment in a hospital for the insane, and that he goes there with the consent of his relatives, friends, or legal guardians.

§ 4. In case such applicant be incompetent to act for himself, a similar application may be made in his behalf by any relative, friend or legal guardian in whose charge, or by whose assistance he is maintained, and the superintendent of such institution is hereby authorized to receive him in like manner as above stated.

§ 5. Any patient upon application made to the state board of charities by him, or his friends or legal guardians, may be discharged from any such home, retreat or asylum, and placed in the care of his friends or other suitable place as the said board, in their judgment, may deem best.

Pasteur Institute; Overseers of the Poor May Send Persons in Danger of Infection with Rabies or Hydrophobia.

AN ACT to provide for a permanent establishment for the cure and prevention of hydrophobia.

Chapter 770 of the Laws of 1895.

Section 1. Patients sent to Pasteur Institute.—Overseers of the poor or other officers having charge of the dispensation of public charity in the several counties of this state may here-after send to the Pasteur institute in the city of New York all persons duly certified by regular physicians to have been bitten by rabid animals, or otherwise put in danger of infection with rabies. (As amended by chapter 482 of the Laws of 1901.)

§ 2. Transportation, cost of.—The transportation of such persons, with necessary attendant or attendants, to and from the city of New York, shall be a charge upon the counties in which they reside. The sustenance, nursing and preventive treatment of such persons, for the time adjudged necessary, shall be provided by the Pasteur institute of the city of New York.

§ 3. Charges, how paid.—The charges for the services of the Pasteur institute of the city of New York shall be paid as is provided for the several poor persons by section forty-two of chapter two hundred and twenty-five of the laws of eighteen hundred and ninety-six, at a rate not exceeding one hundred dollars a patient. (As amended by chapter 482 of the Laws of 1901.)

§ 4. Institute open to inspection.—The Pasteur institute of the city of New York shall be at all times open to the inspection of the governor and of the state board of health or of the accredited representative of either, and shall annually, on or before the fifteenth of January of each year make its report to the legislature.

§ 5. All acts and parts of acts inconsistent with this act are hereby repealed.

Care of Indigent and Pauper Children.

AN ACT to revise and consolidate the statutes of the state relating to the custody and care of indigent and pauper children by orphan asylums and other charitable institutions.

Chapter 438, of the Laws of 1884.

Section 1. Guardianship of indigent children may be committed to any incorporated orphan asylum.—The guardianship of the person and the custody of any indigent child may be committed to any incorporated orphan asylum or other institu-

tion incorporated for the care of orphan, friendless or destitute
children, by an instrument in writing signed by the parents of
such child, if both such parents shall then be living, or by the
surviving parent, if either parent of such child be dead, or if
either one of such parents shall have, for the period of six
months then next preceding, abandoned such child, by the other
of such parents, or if the father of such child shall have
neglected to provide for his family during the six months then
next preceding, or if such child be a bastard, by the mother of
such child; or if both parents of such child shall then be dead,
by the guardian of the person of such child, legally appointed,
with the approval of the court or officer which appointed such
guardian to be entered of record; or if both parents of such
child shall then be dead and no legal guardian of the person of
such child shall have been appointed, and no guardian of such
child shall have been appointed by a last will and testament,
or by a deed by either parent thereof, or if the parents of such
child shall have abandoned such child for the period of six
months then next preceding, by the mayor of the city or by the
county judge of the county in which such asylum or such other
institution shall be located, upon such terms, for such time, and
subject to such conditions as may be agreed upon by the parties
to such written instrument. And such written instrument may
provide for the absolute surrender of such child to such corporation. But no such corporation shall draw or receive money
from public funds for the support of any such child committed
under the provisions of this section, unless it shall have been
determined by a court of competent jurisdiction that such
child has no relative, parent or guardian living, or that such
relative, parent or guardian, if living, is destitute and actually
unable to contribute to the support of such child.

§ 2. Children not to be sent to county poor-houses, etc.—It
shall not be lawful for any county superintendent or overseer
of the poor, board of charity or other officer, to send any child
between the ages of two and sixteen years, as a pauper, to any
county poor-house or alms-house for support and care, or to

detain any child between the ages of two and sixteen years in
such poor-house or alms-house; but such county superintendents, overseers of the poor, boards of charities or other officers
shall provide for such child or children, in families, orphan
asylums, hospitals, or other appropriate institutions, as provided by law. The boards of supervisors of the several counties
of the state are hereby directed to take such action in the
matter as may be necessary to carry out the provisions of this
section. When any such child shall be so provided for or placed
in any orphan asylum or such other institution, such child shall,
when practicable, be so provided for or placed in such asylum
or such other institution as shall then be controlled by persons
of the same religious faith as the parents of such child.

§ 3. Record to be kept by all institutions for reception of
minors, etc.—All institutions, public or private, incorporated or
not incorporated, for the reception of minors, whether as orphan,
or as pauper, indigent, destitute, vagrant, disorderly, or delinquent persons, are hereby required to provide and keep a record
in which shall be entered the date of reception, and the names
and places of birth and residence, as nearly as the same can
reasonably be ascertained, of all children admitted in such institutions, and how and by whom and for what cause such children
shall be placed therein, and the names, residence, birthplace and
religious denomination of the parents of such children so admitted, as nearly as the same can be reasonably ascertained;
and whenever any such child shall leave such institution, the
proper entry shall be made in such record, showing in what
manner such child shall have been disposed of, and if apprenticed to or adopted by any person or family, or otherwise
placed out at service or on trial, the name and place of residence of the person or head of the family to or with whom such
child shall have been so apprenticed, adopted or otherwise
placed out. The supreme court may, upon application by a
parent, relative or legal guardian of such child, after due notice
to the institution and hearing had thereon, by order direct the
officers of such institution to furnish such parent, relative or

legal guardian with such extracts from such record relating to such child as such court may deem proper. Nothing in this section shall be construed to prevent visitation by relatives and friends in accordance with the established rules of such institutions. (*As amended by chapter 54 of the Laws of 1894.*)

§ 4. Removal of children from one institution to another, etc. —While any child which shall have been placed in such asylum, or other institution, as a pauper, in pursuance of the second section of this act, shall remain therein at the expense of the county or town to which such pauper child is chargeable, the superintendents of the poor of such county, or the overseer of the poor of such town, may, in their discretion, remove such child from such asylum or other institution and place such child in some other such institution or make such other disposition of such child as shall then be provided by law. The name of no child shall be changed while in such institution as in this section aforesaid. But no parent of such pauper child, so in such asylum or other institution as in this section aforesaid, shall be entitled to the custody thereof except in pursuance of a judgment or order of a court or judicial officer of competent jurisdiction, adjudging or determining that the interests of such child will be promoted thereby, and that such parent is fit, competent and able to duly maintain, support and educate such child.

§ 5. Children may be bound out as apprentices, servants, etc. —Any corporation specified in the first section of this act may bind out any indigent or pauper child, if a male, for a period which shall not be beyond his twenty-first year, and if a female, for a period which shall not be beyond her eighteenth year, which shall have been absolutely surrendered to the care and custody of such corporation in pursuance of the provisions of the first section of this act, or which shall have been placed therein as a pauper in pursuance of the provisions of the second section of this act, or which shall have been left to the care of such corporation with no provision by the parent, relative or *legal* guardian of such child, for its support for a period of one

year then next preceding, to be a clerk, apprentice or servant.
(Balance of section repealed. See Domestic Relations Law.)

§ 7. Children may be placed by adoption with suitable persons.—Any child which a corporation specified in the first section of this act is, by the fifth section of this act, authorized to bind out may be placed by such corporation, by adoption. ·
(Balance of section repealed. See Domestic Relations Law.)

(§§ 6, 8, 9, 10, 11, 12, repealed by Domestic Relations Law.)

PAYMENTS OF PUBLIC MONEYS TO PRIVATE INSTITUTIONS.

AN ACT to authorize payments by counties, cities, towns and villages to charitable, eleemosynary, correctional and reformatory institutions wholly or partly under private control, for care, support and maintenance.

Chapter 754 of the Laws of 1895.

Section 1. Boards of estimate and apportionment, common councils, boards of aldermen, boards of supervisors, town boards, boards of trustees of villages, and all other boards or officers of counties, cities, towns and villages, authorized to appropriate and raise money by taxation and make payments therefrom, are hereby authorized in their discretion to appropriate and to raise money by taxation and to make payments from said moneys, and from any moneys received from any other source and properly applicable thereto, to charitable, eleemosynary, correctional and reformatory institutions wholly or partly under private control, for the care, support and maintenance of their inmates, of the moneys which are or may be appropriated therefor; such payments to be made only for such inmates as are received and retained therein pursuant to rules established by the state board of charities; except that boards of trustees of villages and town boards of towns in which there is no hospital located, and which are situated upon and adjoin the boundary line of a neighboring state, are hereby authorized in their discretion to appropriate and to raise money by taxation and to make payments from said moneys, and from any moneys received from any other source and properly applicable thereto, to hospitals in such adjoining state for the purpose of maintaining a bed or beds in such hospital for the benefit of and to be used exclusively by the inhabitants of such village or town. Boards of trustees of villages and town boards of towns situate upon the boundary line of a neighboring state, which have appropriated and raised money by taxation for the purpose of maintaining a bed or beds in a hospital in such adjoining state and have not paid the same are hereby authorized to use said money for the purpose for which it was appropriated and raised. Payments to such hospital in an adjoining state shall be made only for such inmates as are received and retained therein pursuant to rules established by the state board of charities. (*As amended by chapter 155 of the Laws of 1902.*)

PROPERTY AND FAMILIES OF ABSCONDING PERSONS.

AN ACT in relation to the property and families of absconding persons.

Chapter 304 of the Laws of 1878.

Section 1. Whenever the father, or the mother being a widow or living separate from her husband, has absconded, or shall abscond from his or her children or a husband from his wife, leaving any of such children or such wife chargeable, or likely to become chargeable upon the public for their support, and any real or personal estate of such father, or mother, or husband, has been or shall be seized by a superintendent of the poor or an overseer of the poor, or by a board of charities (or by other officers authorized to make such seizures), by warrant of the justices of the peace of the county where such real or personal property may be situated, and the court of sessions of the county wherein such superintendent or overseer of the poor or board of charities, or other officers authorized to make such seizure resides, has confirmed, or shall confirm said warrant and seizure and has heretofore directed, or shall hereafter direct what part of any of the said personal property shall be sold and how much if any of the proceeds of such sale and of the rents and profits of the real estate, if any, be applied toward the main-

tenance of the children or wife of the person so absconding, then
the said superintendent or overseer of the poor, board of charities or other officers so authorized and directed, shall apply the
said proceeds of sale of said personal property, or rents and
profits of the real estate (as the case may be): First, to the payment of such taxes and assessments as may be outstanding and
existing liens upon the said real estate, and repairs necessary to
be made upon said real estate; and premiums for insurance on
the buildings on said real estate, and the balance, if any, directly
to the maintaining, bringing up and providing for the wife, child
or children so left and abandoned, as the same may be required
from time to time; and for all of such expenditures they shall
take proper vouchers, and from the rents and profits thereafter
received from any real estate so seized they shall first pay all
legal taxes and assessments, as they shall be assessed against
said real estate and such premiums for insurances and expenses
for such repairs thereon as they may deem necessary for the protection and preservation of said real estate, and the balance of
said rents and profits shall be applied by said overseers, superintendents, boards of charities, or other persons authorized to
make such seizures, to the maintaining, bringing up, and providing for the wife, child, or children so left and abandoned, and
proper vouchers shall be taken thereof.

§ 2. Whenever any child or children, entitled to the benefits
provided by this act, shall be a minor or minors whose mother
is dead and whose father has absconded from his children, or
whose mother, being a widow or living apart from her husband,
has absconded from her children, and such minor or minors
shall have no guardian, the court of sessions having jurisdiction
of this matter shall appoint some suitable person guardian ad
litem or next friend of such minor or minors, whose duty it shall
be to see that the provisions of this act are carried into effect.
The proceeds of the sale of said personal property and the rents
and profits of said real estate shall not be mingled or placed
with any other funds held or owned by the officer or officers
receiving the same, but shall be kept separate and distinct.

Such superintendent, overseer of the poor, board of charities or other authorized officer shall give security for the faithful performance of the duties hereby imposed in such form and in such sum as the aforesaid court may direct, and shall account to the court of sessions for all moneys so received by them and for the application thereof from time to time and may be compelled by the said court to render such account at any time.

§ 3. Notice of such accounting shall be given to the wife or children, so left and abandoned, as the case may be, and to the guardian of such children, if any of them be minors. And in the event that no guardian or next friend has been appointed, as hereinbefore provided, the said court shall, prior to such accounting being had, appoint some suitable person to attend upon such accounting in behalf of said minors, and notice of such appointment and of such accounting shall be given to the persons so appointed.

§ 4. All penalties received from the prosecution of any recognizance given by any person who shall have abandoned or neglected his wife or children, or who shall have threatened to run away and leave his wife or children a burden on the public, shall be retained by the officer at whose instance such recognizance was prosecuted, and applied for the same purpose and in the same manner as in the first section of this act provided for the disposition of the proceeds of the sales of personal property and the rents and profits of real estate seized under the provisions of this act.

Proceedings Respecting Vagrants.

Title VI of Part VI of the Code of Criminal Procedure.

§ 887. Who are vagrants.—The following persons are vagrants:

* * * * * * * *

8. Any child between the age of five and fourteen, having sufficient bodily health and mental capacity to attend the public schools, found wandering in the streets or lanes of any city or incorporated village, a truant, without any lawful occupation.

§ 888. **Proceedings before magistrate.**—When complaint is made to any magistrate by any citizen or peace officer against any vagrant under subdivision eight of the last section, such magistrate must cause a peace officer to bring such child before him for examination, and shall also cause the parent, guardian or master of such child, if the child has any, to be summoned to attend such examination. If thereon the complaint shall be satisfactorily established, the magistrate must require the parent, guardian or master to enter into an engagement in writing to the corporate authorities of the city or village, that he will restrain such child from so wandering about, will keep him in his own premises, or in some lawful occupation and will cause him to be sent to some school at least four months in each year until he becomes fourteen years old. The magistrate may, in his discretion, require security for the faithful performance of such engagement. If the child has no parent, guardian or master, or none can be found, or if the parent, guardian or master refuse or neglect, within a reasonable time, to enter into such engagement, and to give such security, if required, the magistrate shall *make the like disposition of such child as is authorized to be made by section two hundred and ninety-one of the Penal Code, of children coming within the descriptions therein mentioned.* (As amended by chapter 220 of the Laws of 1888.)

Preservation of the Health of Children in Institutions.

PUBLIC HEALTH LAW.

Chapter 661 of the Laws of 1893.

Section 213. **Examination and quarantine of children admitted to institutions for orphans, destitute or vagrant children or juvenile delinquents.**—Every institution in this state, incorporated for the express purpose of receiving or caring for orphan, vagrant or destitute children or juvenile delinquents, except hospitals, shall have attached thereto a regular physician of its selection duly licensed under the laws of the state and in good professional standing, whose name and address shall be kept posted conspicuously within such institution near its main entrance. The words

"juvenile delinquents" here used shall include all children whose
commitment to an institution is authorized by the penal code.
The officer of every such institution upon receiving a child
therein, by commitment or otherwise, shall, before admitting it to
contact with the other inmates, cause it to be examined by such
physician, and a written certificate to be given by him, stating
whether the child has diphtheria, scarlet fever, measles, whooping
cough or any other contagious or infectious disease, especially of
the eyes and skin, which might be communicated to other inmates and specifying the physical and mental condition of the
child, the presence of any indication of hereditary or other constitutional disease, and any deformity or abnormal condition
found upon the examination to exist. No child shall be so admitted until such certificate shall have been furnished, which
shall be filed with the commitment or other papers on record in
the case, by the officers of the institution, who shall, on receiving
such child, place it in strict quarantine thereafter from the other
inmates, until discharged from such quarantine by such physician, who shall thereupon indorse upon the certificate the length
of quarantine and the date of discharge therefrom.

§ 214. Monthly examination of inmates and reports.—Such
physician shall at least once a month thoroughly examine and inspect the entire institution, and report in writing, in such form as
may be approved by the state board of health, to the board of
managers or directors of the institution, and to the local board of
the district or place where the institution is situated, its condition,
especially as to its plumbing, sinks, water-closets, urinals, privies,
dormitories, the physical condition of the children, the existence
of any contagious or infectious disease, particularly of the eyes or
skin, their food, clothing and cleanliness, and whether the officers
of the institution have provided proper and sufficient nurses.
orderlies, and other attendants of proper capacity to attend to
such children, to secure to them due and proper care and attention
as to their personal cleanliness and health, with such recommendations for the improvement thereof as he may deem proper. Such
boards of health shall immediately investigate any complaint

against the management of the institution or of the existence of anything therein dangerous to life or health, and, if proven to be well founded, shall cause the evil to be remedied without delay.

§ 215. Beds; ventilation.—The beds in every dormitory in such institution shall be separated by a passageway of not less than two feet in width, and so arranged that under each the air shall freely circulate and there shall be adequate ventilation of each bed, and such dormitory shall be furnished with such means of ventilation as the local board of health shall prescribe. In every dormitory six hundred cubic feet of air space shall be provided and allowed for each bed or occupant, and no more beds or occupants shall be permitted than are thus provided for, unless free and adequate means of ventilation exist approved by the local board of health, and a special permit in writing therefor be granted by such board, specifying the number of beds or cubic air space which shall, under special circumstances, be allowed, which permit shall be kept conspicuously posted in such dormitory. The physician of the institution shall immediately notify in writing the local board of health and the board of managers or directors of the institution of any violation of any provision of this section. *(As amended by chapter 667 of the Laws of 1900.)*

ANTI-BUTTERINE LAW.

AN ACT to prevent the use of butterine, oleomargarine or adulterated or imitation dairy products in certain institutions within this state.

Chapter 364, Laws of 1893.

Section 1. Expenditures for products, etc., forbidden.—No money appropriated by law for maintenance and support in whole or in part of a state institution; nor money received by a charitable, benevolent, penal or reformatory institution from the state, or from a county, city or town thereof, or appropriated by such county, city or town for the maintenance or support in whole or in part of such institution; nor money belonging to or used for the maintenance or support of such institution, shall be expended for the purchase of, or in payment for, butterine, oleo-

margarine, lard cheese, or articles or products in imitation or semblance of natural butter or cheese produced from pure un-adulterated milk or cream from the same, which articles or products have been rendered or manufactured in whole or in part from animal fats, or animal or vegetable oils not produced from unadulterated milk or cream from the same.

§ 2. Purchase, sale and use of products, etc., prohibited.—No officer, manager, superintendent or agent of an institution men-tioned in the first section of this act, shall purchase for the use of such institution articles or products for the purchase of which the money appropriated by law, or by a county, city or town, is forbidden to be used by this act, and no person shall sell to, or for the use of such institution, such articles or products. Nor shall such articles or products be used as articles of food or for cooking purposes in such institutions within this state.

THE DOMESTIC RELATIONS LAW.
Chapter 272 of the Laws of 1896.
ARTICLE VI.
THE ADOPTION OF CHILDREN.

Section 60. Definitions; effect of article.
     61. Whose consent necessary.
     62. Requisites of voluntary adoption.
     63. Order.
     64. Effect of adoption.
     65. Adoption from charitable institutions.
     66. Abrogation of voluntary adoption.
     67. Application in behalf of the child for abrogation of an adoption from a charitable institution.
     68. Application by a foster parent for the abrogation of such an adoption.

Section 60. Definitions; effect of article.—Adoption is the legal act whereby an adult takes a minor into the relation of child and thereby acquires the rights and incurs the responsi-bilities of parent in respect to such minor. Hereafter, in this article, the person adopting is designated the " foster parent."

A voluntary adoption is any other than that of an indigent child, or one who is a public charge from an orphan asylum or charitable institution. An adult unmarried person, or an adult husband or wife, or an adult husband and his adult wife together, may adopt a minor in pursuance of this article, and a child shall not hereafter be adopted except in pursuance thereof. Proof of the lawful adoption of a minor heretofore made may be received in evidence, and any such adoption shall not be abrogated by the enactment of this chapter and shall have the effect of an adoption hereunder. Nothing in this article in regard to an adopted child inheriting from the foster parent, applies to any will, devise or trust made or created before June twenty-fifth, eighteen hundred and seventy-three, or alters, changes or interferes with such will, devise or trust, and as to any such will, devise or trust, a child adopted before that date is not an heir so as to alter estates or trusts, or devises in wills so made or created.

§ 61. Whose consent necessary.—Consent to adoption is necessary as follows:

1. Of the minor, if over twelve years of age;

2. Of the foster parent's husband or wife, unless lawfully separated, or unless they jointly adopt such minor;

3. Of the parents or surviving parent of a legitimate child, and of the mother of an illegitimate child; but the consent of a parent who has abandoned the child, or is deprived of civil rights, or divorced because of his or her adultery or cruelty, or adjudged to be insane, or to be an habitual drunkard, or judicially deprived of the custody of the child on account of cruelty or neglect, is unnecessary.

4. Of a person of full age having lawful custody of the child, if any such person can be found, where the child has no father or mother living, or no father or mother whose consent is necessary under the last subdivision. If such child has no father or mother living, and no person can be found who has the lawful custody of the child, the judge or surrogate shall recite such facts in the order allowing the adoption.

§ 62. Requisites of voluntary adoption.—In adoption the following requirements must be followed:

1. The foster parents or parent, the minor and all the persons whose consent is necessary under the last section, must appear before the county judge or the surrogate of the county where the foster parent or parents reside, and be examined by such judge or surrogate, except as provided by the next subdivision.

2. They must present to such judge or surrogate an instrument containing substantially the consents required by this chapter, an agreement on the part of the foster parent or parents to adopt and treat the minor as his, her, or their own lawful child, and a statement of the age of the child as nearly as the same can be ascertained, which statement shall be taken prima facie as true. The instrument must be signed by the foster parent or parents and by each person whose consent is necessary to the adoption, and severally acknowledged by said persons before such judge or surrogate; but where a parent or person or institution having the legal custody of the minor resides in some other country, state or county, his or their written acknowledged consent, or the written acknowledged consent of the officers of such institution, certified as conveyances are required to be certified to entitle them to record in a county in this state, is equivalent to his or their appearance and execution of such instrument. (As amended by chap. 498 of 1899.)

§ 63. Order.—If satisfied that the moral and temporal interests of the child will be promoted thereby, the judge or surrogate must make an order allowing or confirming such adoption, reciting the reasons therefor, and directing that the minor shall thenceforth be regarded and treated in all respects as the child of the foster parent or parents. Such order, and the instrument and consent, if any, mentioned in the last section must be filed and recorded in the office of the county clerk of such county.

It is not required by the statute that the judge or surrogate shall witness by his signature the consent of the parties adopting the child; it is sufficient if the order recites that the parties appeared before him and that they signed the necessary consents. *People ex rel. Burns v. Bloedel, 42 N. Y. St. Rep. 453, 16 N. Y. Supp. 837.*

§ 64. Effect of adoption.—Thereafter the parents of the minor are relieved from all parental duties toward, and of all responsibility for, and have no rights over such child, or to his property by descent or succession. Where a parent who has procured a divorce, or a surviving parent, having lawful custody of a child, lawfully marries again, or where an adult unmarried person who has become a foster parent and has lawful custody of a child, marries, and such parent or foster parent consents that the person who thus becomes the stepfather or the stepmother of such child, may adopt such child, such parent or such foster parent, so consenting, shall not thereby be relieved of any of his or her parental duties toward, or be deprived of any of his or her rights over said child, or to his property by descent or succession. The child takes the name of the foster parent. His rights of inheritance and succession from his natural parents remain unaffected by such adoption. The foster parent or parents and the minor sustain toward each other the legal relation of parent and child and have all the rights, and are subject to all the duties of that relation, including the right of inheritance from each other, except as the same is affected by the provisions in this section in relation to adoption by a stepfather or stepmother, and such right of inheritance extends to the heirs and next of kin of the minor, and such heirs and next of kin shall be the same as if he were the legitimate child of the person adopting, but as respects the passing and limitation over of real or personal property dependent under the provisions of any instrument on the foster parent dying without heirs, the minor is not deemed the child of the foster parent so as to defeat the rights of remaindermen. (*As amended by chap. 408 of 1897, § 1.*)

§ 65. Adoption from charitable institutions.—Where an orphan asylum or charitable institution is authorized to place children for adoption, the adoption of every such child shall, when practicable, be given to persons of the same religious faith as the parents of such child. The adoption shall be effected by the execution of an instrument containing substantially the same provisions as the instrument provided in this article for voluntary adoption, signed and sealed in the corporate name of such corporation by the officer or officers authorized by the directors thereof to sign the corporate name to such. instruments, and signed by the foster parent or parents and each person whose consent is necessary to the adoption; and may be signed by the child, if over twelve years of age, all of whom shall appear before the county judge or surrogate of the county where such foster parents reside and be examined, except that such officers need not appear and such judge or surrogate may thereupon make the order of adoption provided by this article. Such instrument and order shall be filed and recorded in the office of the county clerk of the county where the foster parent resides and the adoption shall take effect from the time of such filing and recording.

§ 66. Abrogation of voluntary adoption.—A minor may be deprived of the rights of a voluntary adoption by the following proceedings only: The foster parent, the minor and the persons whose consent would be necessary to an original adoption, must appear before the county judge or surrogate of the county where the foster parent resides, who shall conduct an examination as for an original adoption. If he is satisfied that the abrogation of the adoption is desired by all parties concerned, and will be for the best interests of the minor, the foster parent, the minor, and the persons whose consent would have been necessary to an original adoption shall execute an agreement, whereby the foster parent and the minor agree to relinquish the relation of parent and child and all rights acquired by such adoption, and the parents or guardian of the child or the institution having the custody thereof, agree to reassume such relation. The judge or surrogate shall indorse, upon such agreement, his consent to the abrogation of the adoption. The agreement and consent shall be filed and recorded in the office of the county clerk of the county where the foster parent resides, and a copy thereof filed and recorded in the office of the county clerk of the county where the parents or guardians

reside, or such institution is located, if they reside, or such
institution is located, within this state. From the time of the
filing and recording thereof, the adoption shall be abrogated,
and the child shall reassume its original name and the parents
or guardians of the child shall reassume such relation. Such
child, however, may be adopted directly from such foster parents
by another person in the same manner as from parents, and as
if such foster parents were the parents of such child.

§ 67. Application in behalf of the child for abrogation of an
adoption from a charitable institution.—A minor who shall
have been adopted in pursuance of this chapter or of any act
repealed thereby, from an orphan asylum or charitable institution, or any corporation which shall have been a party to the
agreement by which such child was adopted, or any person on
the behalf of such child, may make an application to the county
judge or the surrogate's court of the county in which the foster
parent then resides, for the abrogation of such adoption, on the
ground of cruelty, misusage, refusal of necessary provisions or
clothing, or inability to support, maintain or educate such child,
or of any violation of duty on the part of such foster parent
toward such child; which application shall be by a petition
setting forth the grounds thereof, and verified by the person or
by some officer of the corporation making the same. A citation
shall thereon be issued by such judge or surrogate in or out of
such court, requiring such foster parent to show cause why the
application should not be granted. The provisions of the code
of civil procedure relating to the issuing, contents, time and
manner of service of citation issue out of a surrogate's court,
and to the hearing on the return thereof, and to enforcing the
attendance of witnesses, and to all proceedings thereon, and to
appeals from decrees of surrogate's courts, not inconsistent
with this chapter, shall apply to such citation, and to all proceedings thereon. Such judge or court shall have power to
order or compel the production of the person of such minor.
If on the proofs made before him, on the hearing on such citation, the judge or surrogate shall determine that either of the

grounds for such application exists, and that the interests of such child will be promoted by granting the application, and that such foster parent has justly forfeited his right to the custody and services of such minor, an order shall be made and entered abrogating the adoption, and thereon the status of such child shall be the same as if no proceedings had been had for the adoption thereof. After one such petition against a foster parent has been denied, a citation on a subsequent petition against the same foster parent may be issued or refused in the discretion of the judge or surrogate to whom such subsequent petition shall be made.

§ 68. Application of the foster parent for the abrogation of such an adoption.—A foster parent who shall have adopted a minor in pursuance of this chapter or of any act repealed thereby, from an orphan asylum or charitable institution, may apply to the county judge or surrogate's court of the county in which such foster parent resides, for the abrogation of such adoption on the ground of the willful desertion of such child from such foster parent, or of any misdemeanor or ill-behavior of such child, which application shall be by petition, stating the grounds thereof, and the substance of the agreement of adoption, and shall be verified by the petitioner; and thereon a citation shall be issued by such judge or surrogate in or out of such court, directed to such child, and to the corporation which was a party to such adoption, or, if such corporation does not then exist, to the superintendent of the poor of such county, requiring them to show cause why such petition should not be granted. Unless such corporation shall appear on the return of such citation before the hearing thereon shall proceed, a special guardian shall be appointed by such judge or court to protect the interests of such child in such proceeding, and the foster parent shall pay to such special guardian such sum as the court shall direct for the purpose of paying the fees and the necessary disbursements in preparing for and contesting such application on behalf of the child. If such judge or surrogate shall determine, on the proofs made before him, on the hearing of such citation, that the child has violated his duty toward such foster parent, and that due regard to the interests of both require that such adoption be abrogated, an order shall be made and entered accordingly; and such judge or court may make any disposition of the child, which any court or officer shall then be authorized to make of vagrant, truant or disorderly children. If such judge or surrogate shall otherwise determine an order shall be made and entered denying the petition.

ARTICLE VII.

APPRENTICES AND SERVANTS.

Section 70. Definitions; effect of article.—The instrument whereby a minor is bound out to serve as a clerk or servant in any trade, profession or employment, or is apprenticed to learn the art or mystery of any trade or craft, is an indenture.

Every indenture made in pursuance of the laws repealed by this chapter shall be valid hereunder, but hereafter a minor shall not be bound out or apprenticed except in pursuance of this article.

To entitle a master to recover from a stranger the value of work and services performed for and rendered to him by one alleged to be an apprentice, a valid contract of apprenticeship must be established by the plaintiff. *Barton v. Ford*, 35 Hun, 32.

§ 71. Consents to indenture.—Every indenture must contain:

1. The names of the parties;

2. The age of the minor as nearly as can be ascertained, which age on the filing of the indenture shall be taken prima facie to be the true age;

3. A statement of the nature of the service or employment to which the minor is bound or apprenticed;

4. The term of service or apprenticeship, stating the beginning and end thereof;

5. An agreement that the minor will not leave his master or employer during the term for which he is indentured;

6. An agreement that suitable and proper board, lodging and medical attendance for the minor during the continuance of the term shall be provided, either by the master or employer, or by the parent or guardian of the apprentice;

7. A statement of every sum of money paid or agreed to be paid in relation to the service;

8. If such minor is bound as an apprentice to learn the art or mystery of any trade or craft, an agreement on the part of the employer to teach, or to cause to be carefully and skillfully taught, to such apprentice, every branch of the business to which such apprentice is indentured, and that at the expiration of such apprenticeship he will give to such apprentice a certificate, in writing, that such apprentice has served at such trade or craft a full term of apprenticeship specified in such indenture;

9. If a minor is indentured by the poor officers of a county, city or town, or by the authorities of an orphan asylum, penal or charitable institution, an agreement that the master or employer will cause such child to be instructed in reading, writing and the general rules of arithmetic, and that at the expiration of the term of service he will give to such minor a new bible.

Every such indenture shall be filed in the office of the county clerk of the county where the master or employer resides. *(As amended by chapter 448, Laws of 1899.)*

§ 72. Indenture by minor; by whom signed.—Any minor may, by the execution of the indenture provided by this article, bind himself or herself:

1. As an apprentice to learn the art or mystery of any trade or craft for a term of not less than three nor more than five years; or,

2. As a servant or clerk in any profession, trade or employment for a term of service not longer than the minority of such minor, unless such indenture be made by a minor coming from a foreign country, for the purpose of paying his passage, when such indenture may be made for a term of one year although such term may extend beyond the time when such person will be of full age.

An indenture made in pursuance of this section must be signed,

1. By the minor;

2. By the father of the minor unless he is legally incapable of giving consent or has abandoned his family;

3. By the mother of the minor unless she is legally incapable of giving consent;

4. By the guardian of the person of the minor, if any;

5. If there be neither parents or guardians of the minor legally capable of giving consent, by the county judge of the county or a justice of the supreme court of the district, in which the minor resides; whose consent shall be necessary to the binding out or apprenticing in pursuance of this section of a minor coming from a foreign country or of the child of an Indian woman, in addition to the other consents herein provided;

6. By the master or employer.

§ 73. Indenture by poor officers; by whom signed.—The poor officers of a municipal corporation may, by an execution of the indenture provided by this article bind out or apprentice any minor whose support shall become chargeable to such municipal corporation.

In such case the indenture shall be signed,

1. By the officer or officers binding out or apprenticing the minor;

2. By the master or employer;

3. By the county judge of the county, if the support of such child was chargeable to the county, by two justices of the peace, if chargeable to the town, or by the mayor and aldermen or any two of them, if chargeable to the city.

The poor officers by whom a child is indentured and their successors in office, shall be guardians of every such child and shall inquire into the treatment thereof, and redress any grievance as provided by law.

The provision of the Revised Statutes (1 R. S. 617, § 15) declaring that a majority of the superintendents of the poor of a county " shall be at all times competent to transact business and to execute any powers vested in the board of superintendents " authorizes the majority to act, irrespective of and without consultation, with the minority.

The authority to bind minors as apprentices given to said superintendents (2 R. S. 134, § 5) may, therefore, be executed by a majority, without a meeting of or notice to all. *Johnson v. Dodd, 56 N. Y. 76.*

The government has the right to require the services of its citizens, minors as well as adults, for the public defense. It may dissolve the relation of master and apprentice existing by force of municipal regulations, and the obligation of service resulting from indentures executed under or sanctioned by local law.

The relation is dissolved by the acceptance of the apprentice into the military service of the government, although his enlistment was his voluntary act, not compelled by the government, and without the consent of the master; and the wages due the former for his service in the army as well as bounty money belong to him, to the exclusion of any claim thereto by the latter. *Id.*

A mother who has received temporary relief from the poor officers is not a person chargeable to the public, within the meaning of the statutes, allowing a child who, or whose parents, become chargeable, to be bound out. *People ex rel. Heilbronner v. Hoster, 14 Abb. Pr. N. S. 414.*

Abandonment of a child by the father is the surrender of his parental right to the child's custody. *People ex rel. Wehle v. Weissenbach, 60 N. Y. 385.*

§ 74. Indenture by a charitable corporation; by whom signed. —Where an orphan asylum or charitable institution is authorized to bind out or apprentice dependent or indigent children committed to its charge, every such child shall, when practicable, be bound out or apprenticed to persons of the same religious faith as the parents of such child, and the indenture shall in such case be signed,

1. In the corporate name of such institution by the officer or officers thereof authorized by the directors to sign the corporate name to such instrument, and shall be sealed with the corporate seal;

2. By the master or employer; and

3. May be signed by the child, if over twelve years of age.

§ 75. Penalty for failure of master or employer to perform provisions of indenture.—If a master or employer to whom a minor has been indentured shall fail, during the term of service, to perform any provision of such indenture, on his part, such minor or any person in his behalf, may bring an action against the master or employer to recover damages for such failure; and if satisfied that there is sufficient cause, the court shall direct such indenture to be canceled, and may render judgment against such master or employer for not to exceed one thousand nor less than one hundred dollars, to be collected and paid over for the use and benefit of such minor to the corporation or officers indenturing such minor, if so indentured, and otherwise, to the parents or guardian of the child.

§ 76. Assignment of indenture on death of master or employer.—On the death of a master or employer to whom a person is indentured by the poor officers of a municipal corporation, the personal representatives of the master or employer may, with the written and acknowledged consent of such person, assign such indenture and the assignee shall become vested with all the rights and subject to all the liabilities of his assignor; or if such consent be refused, the assignment may be made with like effect by the county judge of the county, on proof that fourteen days' notice of the application therefor has been given to the person indentured, to the officers by whom indentured, and to his parent or guardian, if in the country.

§ 77. Contracts with apprentices in restraint of trade void.— No person shall accept from any apprentice any agreement or cause him to be bound by oath, that after his term of service expires, he will not exercise his trade, profession or employment in any particular place; nor shall any person exact from any

apprentice. after his term of service expires, any money or other
thing, for exercising his trade, profession or employment in any
place. Any security given in violation of this section shall be
void; and any money paid, or valuable thing delivered, for the
consideration, in whole or in part, of any such agreement or
exaction, may be recovered back by the person paying the same
with interest; and every person accepting such agreement, causing such obligation to be entered into, or exacting money or
other thing, is also liable to the apprentice in the penalty of
one hundred dollars, which may be recovered in a civil suit.

PLACING OUT CHILDREN.

AN ACT to prevent evils and abuses in connection with the placing out of children.

Chapter 264 of the Laws of 1898.

Section 1. When used in this act the term destitute child means
an orphan, abandoned or destitute minor, under the age of sixteen years, who is an inmate of a public or private charitable
institution or is maintained by or dependent upon public or organized charity. The term place-out, when used in this act, means
the placing of a destitute child in a family, other than that of a
relative within the second degree, for the purpose of providing
a home for such child. The term board, when used in this act,
means the state board of charities.

§ 2. It is hereby made unlawful for any person or corporation,
other than a charitable or benevolent institution, society or association, or society for the prevention of cruelty to children, now
or hereafter duly incorporated under the laws of this state, or a
local officer charged with the relief of the poor and placing out in
the manner now provided by law, to place out any destitute child,
directly or indirectly, unless such person or corporation shall be
duly licensed, as hereinafter provided, by the state board of charities, to place out destitute children. Nor shall any local officer
charged with the relief of the poor, directly or indirectly, place
out any child or children in a family not residing within this

In *People ex rel. Charles W. Spaulding v. The Board of Supervisors of Sara-toga County, 66 App. Div. 117,* the court said: "That such resolution empowered the superintendent of the poor to employ Maybee to assist him in finding homes for indigent children, which was one of his official duties.

"That the duty of placing children in the homes found by Maybee devolved upon the superintendent of the poor and not upon Maybee, and, therefore, that the fact that Maybee was not licensed by the State Board of Charities to 'place out' children, as required by section 2 of chapter 264 of the Laws of 1898, did not render the contract of employment invalid."

Decision affirmed, *170 N. Y. 93,* but order based upon decision modified.

§ 3. The state board of charities is hereby authorized to issue licenses to such persons or corporations as apply therefor, and, in the judgment of said board, are proper to place out children, empowering such licensees to place out destitute children. Any such license may be revoked by said board, in its discretion, on reasonable notice to such licensee and after affording such licensee an opportunity to be heard before said board. The reason for not granting any such license within six months after application has been made therefor, or for revoking a license, shall be entered in full in the minutes of said board.

§ 4. Any person or corporation who shall place out a destitute child shall keep and preserve a record of the full name and actual or apparent age of such child, the names and residence of its parents, so far as known, and the name and residence of the person or persons with whom such child is placed. If such person or corporation shall subsequently remove such child from the custody of the person or persons with whom it was placed, the fact of such removal and the disposition made of such child shall be entered upon such record.

§ 5. The state board of charities, through any member, officer or duly authorized inspector of said board, is hereby authorized to visit, in its discretion, any child under the age of sixteen years, not legally adopted, placed out by any person or corporation mentioned in the second section of this act, or by any person licensed by said board to place out destitute children.

§ 6. In every case where practicable any child placed out shall be placed with individuals of like religious faith as the parents of the child.

§ 7. Whenever the state board of charities shall decide by the affirmative vote of a majority of its members that any person or corporation has placed out children for purposes of gain, or without due inquiry as to the character and reputation of the persons with whom such children are placed, and with the result that such children are subjected to cruel or improper treatment or neglect or immoral surroundings, the said board may issue an order prohibiting such person or corporation from thereafter placing out children. No such order shall be issued unless such person or corporation has had reasonable notice, with a copy of the charge, and an opportunity to be heard before said board, and a full record of the proceedings and decision on such hearings shall be kept by said board. Any such order issued by said board may be revoked by said board.

§ 8. Any person or corporation who may feel aggrieved by the decision of the state board of charities in issuing any order pursuant to the provisions of section seven of this act, may apply to any judge of the supreme court in the judicial district in which such person resides, or in which the chief office of such corporation is situated, for a writ of certiorari, and upon the return of such writ the reasonableness of such decision shall be subject to review by the supreme court of this state.

§ 9. Any person or corporation who shall willfully violate any of the provisions of this act or shall place out a child in violation of an order issued under the provisions of section seven of this act shall be guilty of a misdemeanor, and upon conviction thereof shall be punished by a fine of not less than fifty and of not more than two hundred and fifty dollars.

ABANDONMENT AND OTHER ACTS OF CRUELTY TO CHILDREN.
Chapter III of Title X of the Penal Code.

Section 287.   Abandonment of child under six years.

      288.   Unlawfully omitting to provide for child.

      289.   Endangering life, health or morals of child.

Section 290. Keepers of concert saloons, etc.

      291. Children not to beg, etc.   ·

      292. Certain employment of a child.

      292a. Penalty for sending messenger boys to certain places.

      292b. Taking apprentice without consent of guardian.

      293. Duty of officers of society.

Section 287. Abandonment of child under six years.—A parent, or other person having the care or custody, for nurture or education, of a child under the age of six years, who deserts the child in any place, with intent wholly to abandon it, is punishable by imprisonment in a state prison, for not more than seven years. *(Amended by chapter 325 of the Laws of 1892.)*

This amendment eliminated the statement of the minimum limit and place of punishment.

§ 288. Omitting to provide for child. A person who,

1. Willfully omits, without lawful excuse, to perform a duty by law imposed upon him to furnish food, clothing, shelter or medical attendance to a minor, or to make such payment toward its maintenance as may have been required by the order of a court or magistrate when such minor has been committed to an institution; or,

2. Not being a superintendent of the poor, or a superintendent of almshouses, or an institution duly incorporated for the purpose, without having first obtained a license in writing so to do from the board of health of the city or town wherein such females or children are received, boarded or kept, erects, conducts, establishes or maintains any maternity hospital, lying-in asylum where females may be received, cared for or treated during pregnancy, or during or after delivery; or receives, boards or keeps any nursing children, or any children under the age of twelve years not his relatives, apprentices, pupils or wards without legal commitment; or,

3. Being a midwife, nurse or other person having the care of an infant within the age of two weeks, neglects or omits to report immediately to the health officer or to a legally qualified

practitioner of medicine of the city, town or place where such
child is being cared for, the fact that one or both eyes of such
infant are inflamed or reddened whenever such shall be the case,
or who applies any remedy therefor without the advice, or
except by the direction of such officer or physician; or,

4. Neglects, refuses or omits to comply with any provisions
of this section, or who violates the provisions of such license, is
guilty of a misdemeanor. Every such license must specify the
name and residence of the person so undertaking the care of
such females or children, and the place and the number of
females or children thereby allowed to be received, boarded and
kept therein, and shall be revocable at will by the authority
granting it. Every person so licensed must keep a register
wherein he shall enter the names and ages of all such children
and of all children born on said premises, and the names and
residences of their parents, as far as known, the time of the
reception and discharge of such children and the reasons therefor, and also a correct register of the name and age of every
child under the age of five years who is given out, adopted,
taken away or indentured from such place to or by any one,
together with the name and residence of the person so adopting,
taking or indenturing such child; and shall cause a correct copy
of such register to be sent to the authority issuing such license
within forty-eight hours after such child is so given out, adopted,
taken away or indentured. It shall be lawful for the officers of
any incorporated society for the prevention of cruelty to children and of such board of health at all reasonable times to
enter and inspect the premises wherein such females and children are so boarded, received or kept, and also such license
register and the children.

5. No institution shall be incorporated for any of the purposes mentioned in this section except with the written consent
and approbation of a justice of the supreme court, upon the
certificate in writing of the state board of charities approving
of the organization and incorporation of such institution. The
said board of charities may apply to the supreme court for the

cancellation of any certificate of incorporation previously filed without its approval, and may institute and maintain an action in such court through the attorney-general to procure a judgment dissolving any such corporation not so incorporated and forfeiting its corporate rights, privileges and franchises. *(Added by chapter 171 of the Laws of 1894.)*

Unlawfully and feloniously suffering and permitting a child to die through willful negligence, without lawful excuse, to supply it with proper food, clothing and care, constitutes a misdemeanor. *People v. McDonald, 17 St. Rep., 494; 49 Hun, 68; 1 N. Y. Supp. 704.*

One failing to supply a child in his custody with proper food is guilty of an offence under the statute. *Crowley v. People, 21 Hun, 415.*

In same case on appeal, 83 N. Y. 464, it was held that one who, with no natural or legal duty, voluntarily seeks and assumes the care and custody of a child, is amenable to the statute, if he fails to perform the duty required, to the injury of the child. It is not requisite to aver or prove that he had means of support, but he must either perform his duty or surrender such care and custody.

§ 289. Endangering life, et cetera, of child.—A person who,

1. Willfully causes or permits the life or limb of any child actually or apparently under the age of sixteen years to be endangered, or its health to be injured, or its morals to become depraved; or,

2. Willfully causes or permits such child to be placed in such a situation or to engage in such an occupation that its life or limb is endangered, or its health is likely to be injured, or its morals likely to be impaired; is guilty of a misdemeanor. *(As amended by chapter 145 of the Laws of 1888.)*

§ 290. Permitting children to attend certain resorts.—A person who,

1. Admits to or allows to remain in any dance-house, concert saloon, theatre, museum, skating rink, or in any place where wines or spirituous or malt liquors are sold or given away, or in any place of entertainment injurious to health or morals, owned, kept or managed by him in whole or in part, any child actually or apparently under the age of sixteen years, unless accompanied by its parent or guardian; or

2. Suffers or permits any such child to play any game of skill
or chance in any such place. or in any place adjacent thereto, or
to be or remain therein, or admits to or allows to remain in
any reputed house of prostitution or assignation, or in any place
where opium or any preparation thereof is smoked, any child
actually or apparently under the age of sixteen years; or,

3. Sells or gives away. or causes or permits or procures to
be sold or given away to any child actually or apparently under
the age of sixteen years any beer. ale. wine. or any strong or
spirituous liquors; or.

4. Being a pawnbroker or person in the employ of a pawnbroker. makes any loan or advances or permits to be loaned or
advanced to any child actually or apparently under the age of
sixteen years any money. or in any manner directly or indirectly
receives any goods. chattels. wares or merchandise from any
such child in pledge for loans made or to be made to it or to
any other person or otherwise howsoever; or.

5. Sells. pays for or furnishes any cigar. cigarette or tobacco
in any of its forms to any child actually or apparently under the
age of sixteen years:

Is guilty of a misdemeanor. *(As amended by chapter 46 of the
Laws of 1884; 31 of 1886; and 170 of 1889.)*

7. No child actually or apparently under sixteen years of age
shall smoke or in any way use any cigar. cigarette or tobacco
in any form whatsoever in any public street. place or resort. A
violation of this subdivision shall be a misdemeanor. and shall
be punished by a fine not less than two dollars for each offense.
(Added by chapter 417 of the Laws of 1890.)

§ 291. Children not to beg. etc.—Any child actually or apparently under the age of sixteen years who is found:

1. Begging or receiving or soliciting alms, in any manner or
under any pretense; or gathering or picking rags. or collecting
cigar stumps, bones or refuse from markets; or

2. Not having any home or other place of abode or proper
guardianship; or who has been abandoned or improperly exposed
...ted, by its parents or other person or persons having it
e, or being in a state of want or suffering; or

3. Destitute of means of support, being an orphan, or living or having lived with or in custody of a parent or guardian who has been sentenced to imprisonment for crime, or who has been convicted of a crime against the person of such child, or has been adjudged an habitual criminal; or

4. Frequenting or being in the company of reputed thieves or prostitutes, or in a reputed house of prostitution or assignation, or living in such a house either with or without its parent or guardian, or being in concert saloons, dance-houses, theatres, museums or other places of entertainment, or places where wines, malt or other spirituous liquors are sold, without being in charge of its parent or guardian; or playing any game of chance or skill in any place wherein or adjacent to which any beer, ale, wine or liquor is sold or given away, or being in any such place; or

5. Coming within any of the descriptions of children mentioned in section two hundred and ninety-two, must be arrested and brought before a proper court or magistrate, who may commit the child to any incorporated charitable reformatory, or other institution, and when practicable, to such as is governed by persons of the same religious faith as the parents of the child, or may make any disposition of the child such as now is, or hereafter may be authorized in the cases of vagrants, truants, paupers or disorderly persons, but such commitment shall, so far as practicable, be made to such charitable or reformatory institutions. Whenever any child shall be committed to an institution under this code, and the warrant of commitment shall so state, and it shall appear therefrom that either parent, or any guardian or custodian of such child was present at the examination before such court or magistrate, or had such notice thereof as was by such court or magistrate deemed and adjudged sufficient, no further or other notice required by any local or special statute, in regard to the committal of children to such institution shall be necessary, and such commitment shall in all respects be sufficient to authorize such institution to receive and retain such child in its custody as therein directed.

Whenever any commitment of a child shall for any reason be adjudged or found defective, a new commitment of the child may be made or directed by the court or magistrate, as the welfare of the child may require. And no commitment of a child which shall recite therein the facts upon which it is based shall be deemed invalid by reason of any omission of the court or magistrate by whom such commitment is made to file any documents, papers or proceedings relating thereto, or by reason of any limitation as to the age of the child committed, contained in the act or articles of incorporation of the institution to which it may have been committed. *(As amended by chapter 31 of the Laws of 1886, and chapter 145 of the Laws of 1888.)*

6. Any magistrate having criminal jurisdiction may commit, temporarily, to an institution authorized by law to receive children on final commitment, and to have compensation therefor from the city or county authorities, any child under the age of sixteen years, who is held for trial on a criminal charge; and may, in like manner, so commit any such child held as a witness to appear on the trial of any criminal case; which institution shall thereupon receive the same, and be entitled to the like compensation proportionally therefor as on final commitment, but subject to the order of the court as to the time of detention and discharge of the child. Any such child convicted of any misdemeanor shall be finally committed to some such institution, and not to any prison or jail, or penitentiary, longer than is necessary for its transfer thereto. No child under restraint or conviction, actually or apparently under the age of sixteen years, shall be placed in any prison or place of confinement, or in any court-room, or in any vehicle for transportation in company with adults charged with or convicted of crime. *(As amended by chapter 217 of the Laws of 1892.)*

7. All cases involving the commitment or trial of children for any violation of the penal code, in any police court or court of special sessions, may be heard and determined by such court, at suitable times to be designated therefor by it, separate and apart from the trial of other criminal cases, of which session a

separate docket and record shall be kept.   *(Added by chapter 217 of the Laws of 1892.)*

By this section certain acts or conduct on the part of children render them liable to be arrested and dealt with as vagrants. *Matter of McMahon, 1 N. Y. Cr., 60; 64 How., 285.*

It is not necessary to show that the children were found wandering in the streets. *Matter of Moses, 1 N. Y. Cr., 512.*

To justify a commitment of a child under section 291, subd. 2 of the Penal Code, as being "abandoned or improperly exposed" such abandonment or improper exposure must be by the parents or the person or persons having it in charge. A child of good character who on a single occasion and while about to return to her home is found in the company of a reputed prostitute of whose character she is ignorant does not "frequent," nor is she in the company of, reputed prostitutes, within section 291, subd. 4, of the Penal Code. *People ex rel. Van Riper r. Catholic Protectory, 19 Abb. N. C., 142, 148; sub nomine, People ex rel. Van Riper v. Home of the Good Shepherd, 44 Hun, 529; 5 N. Y. Cr., 139, 504; 11 St. Rep., 155.*

Where the examining magistrate commits the child without summoning its guardian, if there be one, the child will be discharged on *habeas corpus. Matter of Maloney, 2 N. Y. Supp., 248; 4 id., 428.*

§ 292. Certain employments of child prohibited.—A person who employs or causes to be employed, or who exhibits, uses, or has in custody, or trains for the purpose of the exhibition, use or employment of, any child actually or apparently under the age of sixteen years; or who having the care, custody or control of such a child as parent, relative, guardian, employer, or otherwise sells, lets out, gives away, so trains, or in any way procures or consents to the employment, or to such training, or use, or exhibition of such child; or who neglects or refuses to restrain such child from such training, or from engaging or acting, either

.1. As a rope or wire walker, gymnast, wrestler, contortionist, rider or acrobat; or upon any bicycle or similar mechanical vehicle or contrivance; or,

2. In begging or receiving or soliciting alms in any manner or under any pretense, or in any mendicant occupation, or in gathering or picking rags, or collecting cigar stumps, bones or refuse from markets; or in peddling; or,

3. In singing; or dancing; or playing upon a musical instrument; or in a theatrical exhibition; or in any wandering occupation; or,

4. In any illegal, indecent or immoral exhibition or practice; or in the exhibition of any such child when insane, idiotic, or when presenting the appearance of any deformity or unnatural physical formation or development; or

5. In any practice or exhibition or place dangerous or injurious to the life, limb, health or morals of the child, is guilty of a misdemeanor. But this section does not apply to the employment of any child as a singer or musician in a church, school or academy; or in teaching or learning the science or practice of music; or as a musician in any concert or in a theatrical exhibition, with the written consent of the mayor of the city, or the president of the board of trustees of the village where such concert or exhibition takes place. Such consent shall not be given unless forty-eight hours previous notice of the application shall have been served in writing upon the society mentioned in section two hundred and ninety-three of the penal code, if there be one within the county, and a hearing had thereon if requested, and shall be revocable at the will of the authority giving it. It shall specify the name of the child, its age, the names and residence of its parents or guardians, the nature, time, duration and number of performances permitted, together with the place and character of the exhibition. But no such consent shall be deemed to authorize any violation of the first, second, fourth or fifth subdivisions of this section. (*As amended by chapter 46 of the Laws of 1884; 31 of 1886; and 309 of 1892.*)

This section is not unconstitutional as infringing on the rights of parents or those of the child. *People v. Ewer, 47 St. Rep., 501; 8 N. Y. Cr., 392.*

§ 292a. Penalty for sending messenger boys to certain places. —A corporation or person employing messenger boys who:

1. Knowingly places or permits to remain in a disorderly house, or in an unlicensed saloon, inn, tavern or other unlicensed place where malt or spirituous wines or liquors are sold, any instrument or device by which communication may be had

between such disorderly house, saloon, inn, tavern or unlicensed place, and any office or place of business of such corporation or person; or

2. Knowingly sends or permits any person to send any messenger boy to any disorderly house, unlicensed saloon, inn. tavern, or other unlicensed place, where malt or spirituous liquors or wines are sold on any errand or business whatsoever except to deliver telegrams at the door of such house, is guilty of a misdemeanor, and incurs a penalty of fifty dollars to be recovered by the district attorney. *(Added by chapter 692 of the Laws of 1893.)*

§ 292b. **Taking apprentice without consent of guardian.**—A person who takes an apprentice without having first obtained the consent of his legal guardian or unless a written agreement has been entered into as prescribed by law, is guilty of a misdemeanor. *(Added by chapter 692 of the Laws of 1893.)*

§ 293. **Arrests, by whom made.**—A constable or police officer must. and any agent or officer of any incorporated society for the prevention of cruelty to children may, arrest and bring before a court or magistrate having jurisdiction, any person offending against any of the provisions of this chapter and any minor coming within any of the descriptions of children mentioned in section two hundred and ninety-one, or in section two hundred and ninety-two. Such constable, police officer or agent may interfere to prevent the perpetration in his presence of any act forbidden by this chapter. A person who obstructs or interferes with any officer or agent of such society in the exercise of his authority under this chapter, is guilty of a misdemeanor. All fines, penalties and forfeitures imposed or collected for a violation of the provisions of this code or of any act relating to or affecting children, now in force or hereafter passed, must be paid on demand to the incorporated society for the prevention of cruelty to children in every case where the prosecution shall be instituted or conducted by such a society; and any such payment heretofore made to any such society may be retained by it.

SENTENCE OF MINOR.
Section 701 of the Penal Code.

House of refuge.—Where a person under the age of twelve years is convicted of a crime amounting to felony, or where a person of twelve years and under the age of sixteen years is convicted of a crime, or where a male person of the age of sixteen years and under the age of eighteen years is convicted of crime not amounting to a felony, the trial court may, instead of sentencing him to imprisonment in a state prison or in a penitentiary, direct him to be confined in a house of refuge under the provisions of the statute relating thereto. Where the conviction is had and the sentence is inflicted in the first, second or third judicial district, the place of confinement must be a house of refuge established by the managers of the Society for the Reformation of Juvenile Delinquents in the city of New York; where the conviction is had and the sentence inflicted in any other district, the place of confinement must be in the Western House of Refuge for Juvenile Delinquents. But nothing in this section shall affect any of the provisions contained in section seven hundred and thirteen. (*As amended by chapter 554 of the Laws of 1896.*)

Section 713 of the Penal Code.

Sentence of minor.—When a person under the age of sixteen is convicted of a crime, he may, in the discretion of the court, instead of being sentenced to fine or imprisonment, be placed in charge of any suitable person or institution willing to receive him, and be thereafter, until majority or for a shorter term, subjected to such discipline and control of the person or institution receiving him as a parent or guardian may lawfully exercise over a minor. A child under sixteen years of age committed for misdemeanor, under any provision of this Code, must be committed to some reformatory, charitable or other institution authorized by law to receive and take charge of minors. And when any such child is committed to an institution, it shall, when practicable, be committed to an institution governed by

persons of the same religious faith as the parents of such child.
(As amended by chapter 46 of the Laws of 1884.)

REFORMATORY PUPILS NOT TO BE EMPLOYED BY CONTRACT.

AN ACT relating to the employment of children by contract in houses of refuge, reformatories and other correctional institutions.

Chapter 470 of the Laws of 1884.

Section 1. It shall be unlawful for the trustees or managers of any house of refuge, reformatory or other correctional institution, to contract, hire, or let by the day, week, or month, or any longer period, the services or labor of any child or children under, now or hereafter committed to or inmates of such institutions.

THE CHILDREN'S COURT IN THE CITY OF NEW YORK.

AN ACT to amend the Greater New York charter, chapter three hundred and seventy-eight of the laws of eighteen hundred and ninety-seven entitled "An act to unite into one municipality under the corporate name of the city of New York, the various communities lying in and about New York harbor, including the city and county of New York, the city of Brooklyn and the county of Kings, the county of Richmond and part of the county of Queens, and to provide for the government thereof."

Chapter 466 of the Laws of 1901.

Section 1418. The justices of special sessions of the first division shall, as soon as a special court building can be put in readiness, assign a separate part for the hearing and disposition of cases heretofore within the jurisdiction of city magistrates involving the trial or commitment of children, which part shall be called the children's court; and in all such cases the justice or justices holding said court shall have all the powers, duties and jurisdiction now possessed by the city magistrates within said first division, and such other and further powers, duties and jurisdiction as are contained in the following section. Said children's court shall be held by one or more of the justices

62

of special sessions of the first division, as the circumstances require in such manner as the said justices shall by rule provide. Whenever, under any provision of law, after said separate part shall be assigned, a child under sixteen years of age, unless jointly charged with one or more persons above that age, is taken into custody, it shall be the duty of the officer having the child in charge, and at the earliest time when a justice will be present, to take such child before the children's court, and shall not take said child, knowingly, to any city magistrate's court, or before any city magistrate, except for the purpose of giving bail. If through inadvertence any such child shall be arraigned before a city magistrate, it shall be the duty of such magistrate, as soon as the age of such child is discovered, to transfer the case to the children's court, and if any papers have been prepared, to indorse the transfer thereon and to send the same with the officer to said court; and it is hereby made the duty of the officer to take such child with said papers to the children's court with all convenient speed, to be heard and disposed of, pursuant to law, by the justice there presiding. The justices of the court of special sessions for the first division shall appoint a clerk and a deputy clerk for the children's court, and such and so many officers and attendants, including a stenographer, as may be necessary, whose salaries, except the clerk, shall be fixed by the board of aldermen, on the recommendation of the board of estimate and apportionment. The salary of the clerk shall be three thousand dollars per year, payable in monthly installments, and the clerk, appointed by the board of civil magistrates, in office at the time this act shall go into effect, shall continue in office as clerk until removed therefrom by expiration of term, or by due process of law.

The said court shall be held in some building separate and apart from one used for the trial of persons above the age of sixteen charged with any criminal offense, and if practicable in the building which has been appropriated and set aside, by the sinking fund commissioners, as a children's court. Nothing herein contained shall affect any provisions of law with respect to the temporary commitment by magistrates of children as witnesses for the trial of any criminal case. For statistical purposes the clerk of said children's court, annually, at such time

and in such form as the board of city magistrates of the first
division may require, shall prepare, in duplicate, a report of
the arrests, commitments and dispositions, with such other data
as said board may require, of all persons arraigned in or
brought before such court during the year; one of which said
duplicates shall be transmitted to the board of city magistrates
to be included in its annual report; and the other shall be transmitted to the mayor and be printed in the city record.

§ 3. The said Greater New York charter as re-enacted by
chapter 466 of the said laws of nineteen hundred and one, is
hereby further amended by adding thereto a new section to be
known as section one thousand four hundred and nineteen and
which shall read as follows:

§ 1419. In addition to the powers, duties and jurisdiction heretofore conferred, the court of special sessions of the first division, and the justices thereof, shall supersede the city magistrates in the trial, determination and disposition of all cases
concerning children under sixteen years of age, unless upon a
criminal charge in which two or more persons are jointly
charged and some of them are above that age, and the said
court, and the justices thereof, shall have and exercise the
powers, duties and jurisdiction as follows:

1. The said court of special sessions of the first division shall
hear and adjudicate all charges of a criminal nature against
children under sixteen years of age, of the grade of, or, under
section six hundred and ninety-nine of the penal code, permitted
to be tried as misdemeanors, including all charges coming
within the summary jurisdiction of magistrates, and impose or
suspend sentence or remit to probation pursuant to law. But
all such hearings and trials shall, except as hereinafter provided, be had in a court room exclusively used for the hearing
and disposition of children's cases.

2. Such court, as provided in section one thousand four hundred and eighteen, shall be open each day, except Sundays and
legal holidays, during such hours as the justices of special sessions of the first division, by public rule shall determine, and
one of said justices shall be in attendance who shall possess and
exercise, as to all matters arising in said court, all the powers
and jurisdiction now conferred on city magistrates, and, unless

an objection shall be interposed by the prosecution or the defense at or before the time the defendant, or defendants, are called upon to plead to a charge graded, or permitted by law, as a misdemeanor, all the powers and jurisdiction of a court of special sessions.

3. If an objection be interposed, as provided for in the preceding subdivision, or thereafter if permitted by the justice presiding, the case shall be adjourned to some future day when, either in the same building or at the main court, as the justice of special sessions shall regulate, a trial may be had before three justices.

4. Any order, determination or judgment of one of said justices when sitting alone pursuant to the foregoing provisions, or any two of said justices when three are sitting, shall be the order, determination or judgment of said children's court sitting as a court of special sessions.

5. Section one thousand four hundred and twelve, as to the adoption of rules, is hereby extended so as to cover said children's court.

§ 4. Any unexpended balance of the appropriation made to the board of city magistrates for the year nineteen hundred and two for the construction and maintenance of a children's court shall be transferred to the justices of special sessions for the first division to continue said court as herein authorized, and any additional amount, including the salary of the additional justice, shall be determined under the provisions of the charter and shall be added to and included in the final estimate for the year nineteen hundred and two, and shall be collected by tax from the estates, real and personal, subject to taxation, in the city of New York.

§ 5. All acts and parts of acts not inconsistent with the provisions of this act shall apply to and govern the jurisdiction and proceedings in said children's court; and all acts and parts of acts inconsistent with the provisions of this act are hereby repealed so far as they or either of them affect a court exclusively for children.

§ 6. This act shall take effect immediately.

(As amended by chapter 590, Laws of 1902.)

PROBATIONARY OFFICERS.

AN ACT to amend the code of criminal procedure, relating to the appointment of probationary officers and defining their duties.

Chapter 372 of the Laws of 1901.

Section 1. Title one, part one of the code of criminal procedure is hereby amended by adding thereto a new section to be known as section eleven-a, to read as follows:

§ 11-a. 1. The justices of the courts having original jurisdiction of criminal actions in all cities of the state, shall from time to time appoint a person or persons to perform the duties of probation officers as hereinafter described, within the jurisdiction and under the direction of said court or justice, to hold such office during the pleasure of the court or justice making such appointment. Such probation officer may be chosen from among private citizens, male or female, clerks or assistants of the court making the appointment, or from the officers, deputies, assistants or clerks of the district attorney's office in the county wherein the court making the appointment is held. Any officer or member of the police force of any city or incorporated village who may be detailed to duty in such courts, or any constable or peace officer, may be employed as probation officer upon the order of any court or justice as herein provided. No probation officer appointed, under the provisions of this section shall receive compensation for his services as such probation officer, but this shall not be construed to deprive any court clerk or court assistant or any officer, deputy assistant or clerk of a district attorney's office, or any officer or member of the police force, or any constable or peace officer, appointed probation officer as herein provided, from receiving the salary or compensation attached to his said official employment.

2. Every probation officer so appointed shall when so directed by the court, inquire into the antecedents, character and offense of persons over sixteen years arrested for a crime within the jurisdiction of the court appointing him, and shall report the same to the court. It shall be his duty to make such report of all cases investigated by him, of all cases placed in his care by the court, and of any other duties performed by him in the discharge of his office, as shall be prescribed by the court or justice

making the appointment, or his successor, or by the court or justice assigning the case to him, or his successor, which report shall be filed with the clerk of the court, or where there is no clerk, with the justice thereof. He shall furnish to each person released on probation committed to his care, a written statement of the terms and conditions of his probation, and shall report to the courts or justice appointing him, any violation or breach of the terms and conditions imposed by said court, of the persons placed in his care. Such probation officers shall have, as to the persons so committed to their care, the powers of a peace officer.

§ 2. Sections four hundred and eighty-three, four hundred and eighty-seven, nine hundred and forty-one, nine hundred and forty-two, nine hundred and forty-three and nine hundred and forty-six of the code of criminal procedure, are hereby amended to read as follows:

§ 483. After a plea or verdict of guilty in a case where a discretion is conferred upon the court as to the extent of the punishment, the court, upon the suggestion of either party that there are circumstances, which may be properly taken into view, either in aggravation or mitigation of the punishment, may, in his discretion, hear the same summarily at a specified time, and upon such notice to the adverse party as it may direct. At such specified times, if it shall appear by the record and the circumstances of any person over the age of sixteen years convicted of crime, that there are circumstances in mitigation of the punishment, the court shall have power, in its discretion, to place the defendant on probation in the manner following:

1. If the sentence be suspended, the court upon suspending sentence, may direct that such suspension continue for such period of time, and upon such terms and conditions as it shall determine, and shall place such person on probation under the charge and supervision of the probation officer of said court during such suspension.

2. If the judgment is to pay a fine and that the defendant be imprisoned until it be paid, the court upon imposing sentence, may direct that the execution of the sentence of imprisonment be suspended for such period of time, and on such terms and

conditions, as it shall determine, and shall place such defendant on probation under the charge and supervision of the probation officer during such suspension, provided, however, that upon payment of the fine being made, the judgment shall be satisfied and the probation cease.

3. At any time during the probationary term of a person convicted and released on probation in accordance with the provisions of this section, the court before which, or the justice before whom, the person so convicted was convicted, or his successor, may, in its or his discretion, revoke and terminate such probation. Upon such revocation and termination, the court may, if the sentence has been suspended, pronounce judgment at any time thereafter within the longest period for which the defendant might have been sentenced, or, if judgment has been pronounced and the execution thereof has been suspended, the court may revoke such suspension, whereupon the judgment shall be in full force and effect for its unexpired term.

§ 487. If the judgment be imprisonment, or a fine and imprisonment until it be paid, the defendant must forthwith be committed to the custody of the proper officer, and by him detained, until the judgment be complied with. Where, however, the court has suspended sentence or where after imposing sentence, the court has suspended the execution thereof and placed the defendant on probation, as provided in section four hundred and eighty-three of the code of criminal procedure, the defendant if over the age of sixteen years, must forthwith be placed under the care and supervision of the probation officer of the court committing him, until the expiration of the period of probation and the compliance with the terms and conditions of the sentence or of the suspension thereof. Where, however, the probation has been terminated, as provided in paragraph four of section four hundred and eighty-three of the code of criminal procedure, and the suspension of the sentence or of the execution revoked, and the judgment pronounced, the defendant must forthwith be committed to the custody of the proper officer and by him detained until the judgment be complied with.

§ 941. Within ten days after the adjournment of any criminal court of record in this state, the district attorney of the county in which the court shall be held, shall furnish to the clerk of the county a certified statement containing the names of all persons convicted of crime in said court; the crime for which convicted; whether the conviction was upon a trial or upon a plea of guilty and whether sentence was suspended or the defendant placed on probation; the cases in which counsel were assigned by the court to defend the defendant; the sex, age, nativity, residence and occupation of the defendant; whether . married or single; the degree of education and religious instruction; whether parents are living or dead; whether temperate or intemperate, and whether before convicted or not of any crime, and any other information regarding them as may seem to him expedient. If necessary in order to obtain information of these facts, the defendant may be interrogated upon oath in court by the district attorney before judgment is pronounced. He shall also furnish to the clerk of the court a certified statement containing the names of all probation officers appointed by the court, with their address and date of appointment.

§ 942. The clerk or the deputy clerk of the court of special sessions in the city of New York shall on or before the first day of February, eighteen hundred and ninety-five, and quarterly thereafter, transmit to the secretary of state a tabulated and certified statement, in the form prescribed by the secretary of state, containing the name of every person convicted of a crime, of every person against whom sentence was suspended, and of every person placed on probation in such court, after October thirty-first, eighteen hundred and ninety-four, and since the date of the closing of each last preceding quarterly report; a description of the offense of which such person was convicted; whether the conviction was upon a trial or upon a plea of guilty; and the date of the conviction; and also a certified statement containing the names of all probation officers appointed by the court, with their address and date of appointment. The police clerks of the city magistrates of the city of New York, shall on or before February first, nineteen hundred and one, and annually thereafter, transmit to the secretary of state, a tabulated statement made from their records, showing the number of males and females convicted of crime during each month in the preceding quarter in the several courts of such city magistrates; the number convicted of each offense, the number sentenced, the number fined, the number of those against whom sentence was suspended, and the number placed on probation; and shall also furnish a certified statement containing the names of all probation officers appointed by the magistrates, with their address and date of appointment. Such statements shall be in the form prescribed by the secretary of state.

§ 943. On or before the first day of February, eighteen hundred and ninety-five, and quarterly thereafter, the clerk of each county shall transmit to the secretary of state a tabulated and certified statement, in the form prescribed by the secretary of state, of all the matters contained in the statements filed with such clerks by the district attorney of such county after October thirty-first, eighteen hundred and ninety-four; and of the name of each person shown to be convicted by a court of special sessions by the certificate of conviction filed with him by magistrates holding courts of special sessions after October thirty-first, eighteen hundred and ninety-four, and since the date of the closing of each last preceding quarterly report made after October thirty-first, eighteen hundred and ninety-four, and showing the offense for which each person was so convicted; whether the conviction was upon a trial or upon a plea of guilty; the sentence imposed, whether the sentence was suspended, and whether the defendant was placed on probation. Said certified statement shall also contain the names of all probation officers appointed by said courts of special sessions, with their address and the date of their appointment.

§ 946. The secretary of state shall cause this title to be published with forms and instructions for the execution of the duties therein prescribed, and copies thereof to be furnished annually to each county clerk. The forms furnished by the secretary of state as herein provided, shall contain in tabulated form, the nature of every offense upon which a conviction was had, the court before which the defendant was convicted, the character of the sentence imposed, the cases where defendant had been previously convicted, the cases where sentence was suspended, the cases where the defendant was placed upon probation, and the cases where probation was revoked, together with the age, sex, nativity and residence of the defendant. And a sufficient number of the copies of this title, and of such instructions, and of the forms to be used by the district attorney, or clerk or deputy clerk of the court of special sessions of the city and county of New York, shall also be furnished to each clerk to enable him to furnish at least one copy thereof annually to the district attorney, and the clerk of the court of special sessions of the city and county, of New York and the county clerk shall distribute the copies of this title and of such forms and instructions accordingly, and when said county clerk is not a salaried officer his disbursements and compensation for his services under this act shall be a county charge. The expense of the secretary of state in publishing this title and distributing copies thereof, and of such forms and instructions as are herein required, shall be paid by the treasurer of the state, upon the warrant of the comptroller, from moneys in the treasury not otherwise appropriated.

§ 3. All acts or parts of acts inconsistent with the provisions of this act, in so far as inconsistent therewith, are hereby repealed.

PROBATION OFFICERS IN THE CITY OF BUFFALO.

AN ACT to amend chapter one hundred and five of the laws of the year eighteen hundred and ninety-one, entitled "An act to revise the charter of the city of Buffalo," in relation to the police justice.

Chapter 627 of the Laws of 1901.

Section 1. Chapter one hundred and five of the laws of the year eighteen hundred and ninety-one, entitled "An act to revise the charter of the city of Buffalo," is hereby amended by adding therein after section three hundred and eighty-four-a two new sections to be known as sections three hundred and eighty-four-b and three hundred and eighty-four-c, to read as follows:

§ 384-b. Probation officers.—The police justice shall have authority to appoint or designate not more than five discreet persons of good character to serve as probation officers during the pleasure of the police justice; said probation officers to receive no compensation from the public treasury. Whenever any child under or apparently under the age of sixteen years shall have been arrested, it shall be the duty of said probation officers to make such investigation as may be required by the court, to be present in court in order to represent the interests of the child; when the case is heard to furnish to the police justice such information and assistance as he may require, and to take charge of any child before and after trial as may be directed by the court.

§ 384-c. Whenever any such child is found guilty or pleads guilty to the commission of any crime or misdemeanor before the police justice, the said police justice may in his discretion suspend sentence during the good behavior of the child so convicted. The child so convicted may be placed in the care of said probation officer for such time not to exceed three months and upon such conditions as may seem proper. Said probation officers shall have the power to bring the child so convicted before the police justice at any time within three months from the date of conviction for such disposition as may be just. When practicable said child shall be placed with a probation officer of the same religious faith as that of the child's parents.

Provisions of the Membership Corporations Law, being Chapter 559 of the Laws of 1895, Constituting Chapter 43 of the General Laws.

*   *   *   *   *   *   *

ARTICLE II.

CORPORATIONS FOR PURPOSES NOT ELSEWHERE AUTHORIZED.

§ 30. Purposes for which corporations may be formed under this article.— A membership corporation may be created under this article for any lawful purpose, except a purpose for which a corporation may be created under any other article of this chapter, or any other general law than this chapter.

§ 31. Certificates of incorporation.—Five or more persons may become a membership corporation for any of the purposes for which a corporation may be formed under this article or for any two or more of such purposes of a kindred nature, by making, acknowledging and filing a certificate, stating (a.) *The particular objects for which the corporation is to be formed*, each of which must be such as is authorized by this article;

(b.) *The name of the proposed corporation;*

(c.) *The territory in which its operations are to be principally conducted;*

(d.) *The town, village, or city in which its principal office is to be located, if it be then practicable to fix such location;*

(e.) *The number of its directors*, not less than three nor more than thirty; and

(f.) *The names and places of residence of the persons to be its directors until its first annual meeting.*

Such certificate shall not be filed without the written approval, indorsed thereupon or annexed thereto, of a justice of the supreme court. If such certificate specify among such purposes the care of orphan, pauper or destitute children, the establishment or maintenance of a maternity hospital or lying-in asylum where women may be received, cared for or treated during pregnancy or during or after delivery, or for boarding or keeping nursing children, the written approval of the state board of charities shall also be indorsed thereupon or annexed thereto, before the filing thereof.

On filing such certificate, in pursuance of law, the signers thereof, their associates and successors, shall be a corporation in accordance with the provisions of such certificate.

Any corporation heretofore or hereafter organized under this article for the purpose of gathering, obtaining and procuring information and intelligence, telegraphic or otherwise for the use and benefit of its members, and to furnish and supply the same to its members for publication in newspapers owned or represented by them may admit as members thereof, other corporations, limited liability companies, joint stock and other associations, partnerships and individuals engaged in the same business or in the publication of newspapers, periodicals or other publications, upon such terms and conditions, not inconsistent with law or with its certificate of incorporation. as may be prescribed in its by-laws. (*As amended by chapter 205 of the Laws of 1897, § 1, and chapter 436 of the Laws of 1901.*)

ARTICLE VI.

HOSPITAL CORPORATIONS.

Section 80. Certificate of incorporation.—Five or more persons may become a corporation for the purpose of erecting, establishing, or maintaining a hospital, infirmary, dispensary, or home for invalids, aged or indigent persons, by making acknowledging and filing a certificate, stating

. (a.) *The particular object for which the corporation is to be formed;*

(b.) *The name of the proposed corporation;*

(c.) *The town, village or city in which its principal office is to be located;*

(d.) *The number of directors,* not less than three nor more than forty-eight;

(e.) *The names and places of residence of the persons to be its directors until its first annual meeting;* and

(f.) *The time for holding its annual meetings.*

Such certificate may also specify the qualification of members of the corporation with respect to their adherence or non-adherence to a particular school or theory of medical or surgical treatment; and the systems of medical practice or treatment to be used or applied in such hospitals, infirmary, dispensary or home.

Such certificate shall not be filed without the written approval indorsed thereupon, or annexed thereto, of the state board of charities and of a justice of the supreme court of the district in which the principal office or place of business of such corporation shall be located.

On filing such certificate, in pursuance of law, the signers thereof, their associates and successors, shall be a corporation, in accordance with the provisions of such certificate. (*As amended by chapter 404 of the Laws of* 1900.)

Rules of State Board of Charities to be Observed by Persons Presenting Certificates of Incorporation for Approval.

The rules to be observed as to all certificates of incorporation presented to the state board of charities for its approval are as follows:

1. Such certificate shall be executed in duplicate and presented in due form, duly executed and acknowledged by the proper persons

before competent officers, as the special law may direct, and without erasures or interlineations; and should contain in full every statement directed by the statute. In the articles hereinbefore given these statements are italicized.

2. Each certificate shall state the law under which it is proposed to incorporate.

3. A copy of such certificate shall also be furnished for filing with the state board of charities.

Additional rules setting forth the duties of the commissioners and the officers of the board in regard to certificates of incorporation and application for approval are laid down in Article X. of the By-Laws.

Statutes and Rules Relating to Corporations.

STATUTES.

The written approval of the State Board of Charities is necessary —

1. For the incorporation of any institution for the purpose of receiving, boarding or keeping any nursing children, or any children under the age of twelve years, not pupils or wards.

(Chapter 171, Laws of 1894, referring to Penal Code, section 288.)

2. For the extension of the purposes of a membership corporation, if the care of orphan, pauper or destitute children be included.

(Chapter 559, Laws of 1895, article I, section 4.)

3. For the incorporation of any membership corporation mentioned in the third paragraph of section 31 of article II of the Membership Corporations Law, chapter 559 of the Laws of 1895, and of hospital corporations.

4. The State Board of Charities shall approve or disapprove the organization and incorporation of all institutions of a charitable, eleemosynary, correctional or reformatory character, which are or shall be subject to the supervision and inspection of the board. (Art. I, sec. 9, subd. 4, chap. 546, Laws of 1896.)

BY-LAWS OF THE BOARD.

(As amended to June 1, 1902.)

I.   ON THE MEETINGS OF THE BOARD.

1. Stated meetings of the Board shall be held on the second Wednesday in January, April, July and October, and unless otherwise ordered by the Board, at 3 o'clock p. m.

2. All stated meetings of the Board shall be held at the office of the Board at the Capitol in the city of Albany, unless otherwise specially ordered by the Board.

3. The Board, or the President, may direct special meetings to be called.

4. The President shall direct a special meeting to be called on the written request of two commissioners stating the particular purpose for which the meeting is desired.

5. Notice of meeting shall be given by mailing the notice to each commissioner at his last known place of address, and when practicable, such notice shall be given at least ten days in advance.

6. Notice of special meetings shall state the particular purposes for which the meetings are called.   •

II.   ON THE CONDUCT OF BUSINESS.

1. If at the time appointed for the meeting of the Board the President and Vice-President are both absent, any commissioner may call the meeting to order, and a chairman shall be chosen.

2. At the meetings of the Board the following order of business, unless otherwise ordered shall be observed:

Reading of the minutes of previous meetings.

Election of officers.

Reference of accounts.

Unfinished business of the last meeting.

Reports of Standing and Special Committees.

Reports on proposed incorporations.

Communications from Commissioners and officers.

Miscellaneous business.

3. At a special meeting, the object of the meeting shall be stated by the chair immediately after the minutes of the last meeting have been read, and no other business than that stated in the call shall be considered at such meeting, unless ordered by the concurrent vote of all the Commissioners present.

4. All resolutions shall be in writing and, with the name of the mover, shall be entered on the minutes.

5. On the demand of any Commissioner, the vote on any question shall be taken by ayes and noes, and entered on the minutes.

6. All questions of order and proceeding, not specially provided for in these By-Laws, shall be governed by Cushing's Manual.

7. The minutes of all meetings of the Board shall be printed as soon after adjournment as possible, and a copy furnished to each Commissioner.

III. ON THE ELECTION OF OFFICERS.

1. The stated meeting in April shall be the annual meeting of the Board.

2. At this meeting it shall elect by ballot a President and a Vice-President.

3. The President and Vice-President so elected shall hold their respective offices for one year and until their successors are elected.

4. All other officers or agents, unless their term of office be fixed by law, or by these By-Laws, shall hold office at the pleasure of the Board.

IV. ON THE PRESIDENT AND VICE-PRESIDENT.

1. The President shall have general supervision of the affairs of the Board, and shall preside at the meetings.

2. He shall represent the Board before the Governor, Executive Department and Legislative Committees, unless otherwise ordered by the Board and may request any Commissioner or officer to assist him or appear in his stead.

3. The Vice-President shall perform the duties of President whenever the President is unable to perform the duties assigned to him by these By-Laws.

V. ON THE SECRETARY.

1. The Secretary shall reside in the city of Albany, and shall be in attendance at the office of the Board during the hours of business, unless called elsewhere by official duties, or unless excused by the Board.

2. He shall have general supervision of employes and of all branches of the Board's work, and shall aid the Commissioners *and other* officers of the Board in the performance of their duties *whenever* required.

3. He shall submit to the Committee on Publication, on or before the second Wednesday of October in each year, the subjects of which it is proposed to treat in the annual report, and the text of the report shall be completed and submitted by him to said Committee on or before the first Wednesday of December.

4. He shall have general charge of the office; superintend the clerical business; and, except as otherwise provided by these By-Laws, conduct the correspondence of the Board, and be the medium of communication of its orders and requests under its direction.

5. He shall attend the meetings of the Board, and keep the records of the same.

6. He shall make examination of, and certify to, the correctness of all expense accounts presented for the audit of the Board, and attest the audit of all bills allowed by the Board.

7. He shall keep a record of all accounts audited by the Board, and report at each stated meeting the condition of the several appropriations.

8. He shall advise the Commissioners of any proposed legislation affecting institutions under the supervision of the Board, or which in any manner concerns its interests or its work, and furnish them with all legislative bills bearing on such subjects.

9. The Secretary shall bring to the attention of the appropriate committees of the Board any matter requiring their consideration or action, and shall also make a report thereof to the Board at the first meeting thereafter.

10. He shall perform such other duties as are especially assigned to him by these By-Laws, or which the board may from time to time direct.

VI.   ON THE SUPERINTENDENT OF STATE AND ALIEN POOR.

1. The Superintendent of State and Alien Poor shall have supervision of the State, Alien and Indian dependent classes, and shall perform all the duties required by law, or prescribed by the Board, for their care and final settlement.

2. He shall supervise and direct the work of the Inspectors of Almshouses, transmitting copies of their reports, through the Secretary, to the Commissioners of the respective districts; the work of the Inspector of State Charitable Institutions, trans-

mitting copies of his reports, through the Secretary, to the respective Committees of the Board having jurisdiction of such institutions; and the work of the other employes of his department, requiring each, with the exception of the clerks at the office in the Capitol, to file in his office a daily record of their work. He shall cause the State Institutions, within the Board's jurisdiction, to be inspected at least quarterly, and the other institutions within the Board's jurisdiction, which are in receipt of State moneys, and the almshouses and their auxiliary institutions, at least once in every six months.

3. He shall also supervise the work devolved upon the Board by chapter 264 of the Laws of 1898, "An act to prevent evils and abuses in connection with the placing out of children," and shall keep as full a record as practicable, of the cases of children placed out in this State, reporting, through the Secretary, to the Committee on Placing out of Children, any evils, defects or abuses discovered in connection with such work.

4. He shall preserve, in suitable form for reference, the records of each individual of the above classes who may come under his official care.

5. He shall examine all accounts pertaining to State, Alien and Indian poor, and, before said accounts are presented to the Board for audit, shall certify to their correctness.

6. He shall, in his visitations of State charitable and reformatory institutions and almshouses, examine and inquire into any violations of the laws in respect to the retention of children, epileptics, insane and feeble-minded in these institutions, and, also, as to the necessity of providing more suitable and better care for any of the inmates of such institutions, and report quarterly to the Board the results of his examinations and inquiries. It shall also be his duty to keep a register of all epileptics, idiots and feeble-minded persons committed to institutional care, in such manner as will show the status of each and every such epileptic, idiotic and feeble-minded inmate so committed.

7. He shall make quarterly reports of his work and shall prepare, for the annual reports of the Board, a full statement of the work performed in the bureau under his charge, with such suggestions and recommendations as he may deem important.

VII. ON THE SUPERINTENDENT OF INSPECTION.

1. The Superintendent of Inspection shall, subject to the pleasure of the Board, have charge of the visitation and inspection of all institutions, societies or associations which are of a charitable, eleemosynary, correctional or reformatory character, excepting State institutions and those having the custody of State, Alien and Indian poor.

2. He shall supervise and direct the work of the Superintendents, Inspectors and other employes of his department, requiring each, with the exception of the clerks in the office in the Capitol, to file in his office a daily record of their work.

.3. He shall organize and maintain such methods of visitation and inspection of the above classified institutions, societies or associations, as will furnish the Board reliable information as to the official conduct of trustees, directors and other officers and employes of the same; the success of the management in each in promoting the physical and moral well-being of the inmates; whether the objects of the several institutions, societies or associations are accomplished; whether the moneys appropriated for their aid are or have been economically and judiciously expended; whether the laws in relation to them and the rules of the Board governing the reception and retention of inmates have been fully complied with; and all other matters pertaining to their usefulness.

4. He shall have charge of the reports, provided in section 2, Rule III, of rules established by the Board pursuant to section 14, article VIII, of the Constitution, and shall maintain such a system of registration of the inmates of the institutions, societies or associations classified under said section 2, as will show the present status of each of said inmates.

5. He shall make quarterly reports of his work, and prepare for the annual reports of the Board a full statement of the work performed during the year in his bureau, with such suggestions and recommendations as he may deem important.

VIII. ON THE VISITATION AND INSPECTION BY COMMISSIONERS.

1. All the institutions of a District subject to the inspection of this Board shall be under the special supervision of the Com-

missioner or Commissioners resident in such District. It shall be
the duty of the Commissioners to visit and inspect said institutions as often as in their opinion the public interests require, and
whenever directed by the Board.

2. In case of inability, from any cause, of a Commissioner to
discharge the duty of supervision, visitation and inspection imposed by this By-Law, the Board shall assign it, in whole or in
part, to another Commissioner or to an officer of the Board. But
this By-Law shall not be construed to impair the right of the
Board to direct special investigations or examinations of the
affairs and management of any institution, society or association,
or to institute and pursue investigations on any subject germane
to its work in any district or county of the State.

3. The President may, during the recess of the Board, appoint
a committee of one or more Commissioners to make a preliminary
investigation into the affairs, management and conduct of any
institution, society or association subject to its supervision, with
the full powers conferred by law.

IX.   ON THE OBJECTS OF VISITATION AND INSPECTION.

The subjects of inquiry, inspection and examination of institutions, societies or associations under the supervision of the
Board, shall be as specified in chapter 546 of the Laws of 1896,
article I, section 11.

X.   ON THE APPROVAL OF CERTIFICATES OF INCORPORATION.

1. Whenever application is made to the State Board of Charities
for the approval of a certificate of incorporation, the application
shall first be sent to the Secretary of the Board, at the Capitol,
for record, and submission to the Attorney-General or to the
counsel of the Board for opinion as to legal form, and shall then
forthwith be referred by the Secretary to the Commissioner or
Commissioners resident in the district from which the application
is made.

In case of an application from a district in which there is
more than one resident Commissioner, such certificate shall be
sent to such Commissioner as may be appointed by the Commissioners resident in such district.

2. It shall be the duty of the Commissioner acting alone or with such Commissioner or Commissioners as he may invite, to inquire by personal examination or by a public hearing upon notice into the merits of the application, and specially to consider the following points:

(a) The necessity for the existence of such an institution as is proposed to be incorporated, at the time and place and under the circumstances set forth in the application and certificate.

(b) The character and standing, in the community, of the proposed incorporators.

(c) The financial resources of the proposed institution, and its sources of future revenue.

3. Such Commissioners shall report to the Board in writing, before final action upon the application, the result of the examination and the recommendation based thereon, and this report, together with all papers in the matter of the application, shall be filed in the office of the Board.

XI. ON THE ANNUAL REPORT.

1. The Committee on Publication shall have general supervision of the preparation of the report by the Secretary, and shall have power to select or reject matter, subject to the final action of the Board.

2. The annual report shall contain such statements, items and particulars as are specified in chapter 546 of the Laws of 1896, or in the acts amendatory thereof or supplemental thereto, and also such other matters relating to the institutions, societies or associations under the supervision of the Board, as the Committee may deem necessary or proper.

3. The title of each paper intended for publication with the annual report, shall be filed in the office of the Board on or before the second Wednesday of October, and no paper, report or document, the title of which is not so filed, shall be received or considered for the annual report of the Board, except on special leave of the Committee on Publication, nor shall any such report, paper or document be published in the appendix of the annual report, unless the same shall have been read through by at least one member of said Committee, reported favorably to and approved by the Board.

4. It shall be the duty of the Committee on Publication to submit the text of the report, in proper form for transmission to the Legislature, to the Board on or before the second Wednesday of December.

XII.   ON THE OFFICE OF THE BOARD.

1. The office of the Board, in the Capitol at Albany, is the authorized depository of all books, papers, records and documents, the property of the Board, and shall, so far as practicable, be the place for the transaction of its business.

2. The office shall be kept open on all secular days, except legal holidays, from 9 a. m., to 5 p. m.

XIII.   ON THE ACCOUNTS OF THE BOARD.

1. All bills or accounts made by virtue of any law whose execution is under the supervision of the Board, shall receive the audit of the Board or of the Finance Committee before presentation to the Comptroller for payment.

2. A copy of all accounts passed by the Board or Finance Committee shall be kept in the office.

3. No indebtedness chargeable to any appropriation, shall be incurred by any Commissioner or officer except on the order of the Board or Finance Committee, but this provision shall not apply to the personal expenses of Commissioners, expenses incurred by the Superintendent of State and Alien Poor, the Inspector of Charities, the Secretary, or the miscellaneous contingent expenses of the office.

4. All appropriations made by the Legislature for the use of the Board shall be entered in books prepared for that purpose, and in connection with each appropriation, every item of expenditure, duly authorized and made chargeable to said appropriation, shall be recorded, and these accounts shall be so kept as to show at all times the available balance of each appropriation remaining to the credit of the Board.

XIV.   ON THE COMMITTEES.

There shall be the following Standing Committees. which shall be appointed by the President-elect as soon as practicable after each annual meeting. The President may, subject to the pleasure of the Board, appoint such other or further Committees as the work of the Board may, from time to time, demand.

All the Committees shall report at each stated·meeting of the Board, or oftener when necessary, upon the matters coming under their jurisdiction or specially referred to them.

1. *On Publication.*

This Committee shall consist of five Commissioners, and shall have supervision of the preparation of the annual report of the Board.

2. *On Finance.*

This Committee shall consist of the President and two Commissioners, and shall have charge of the finances of the Board, and shall audit such bills in the intervals of the meetings of the Board as the Board may direct.

3. *On Inspection of Charities.*

This Committee shall consist of three Commissioners, and shall have supervision of the Bureau of Inspection of Charities.

4. *On State and Alien Poor.*

This Committee shall consist of three Commissioners, and shall have supervision of the Bureau of State and Alien Poor.

XV. ON THE DECLARATION OF THE OPINION AND POLICY OF THE BOARD.

The opinion and policy of the Board can be declared only by resolution adopted at a meeting regularly convened, and when so declared shall furnish a rule of official action to Commissioners and officers.

XVI. ON THE METHODS OF CHANGING THE BY-LAWS.

No alteration, addition or amendment to these By-Laws shall be made, unless upon notice at one meeting of intention to propose the same at the next stated or special meeting of the Board and upon a majority vote of all Commissioners at such next stated or special meeting.

RULES FOR THE RECEPTION AND RETENTION OF INMATES OF INSTITUTIONS.

[As amended January 14, 1903.]

I. RECEPTION OF INMATES.

The following classes of persons, and no others, may be received as public charges into charitable, eleemosynary, correctional, and reformatory institutions, wholly or partly under private control, authorized by law to receive payments from any county, city, town or village for the support, care or maintenance of inmates:

1. Children under the age of sixteen years, who have been convicted of crime and committed to such institution.

2. Persons who have been committed to such institutions by any court or magistrate having jurisdiction.

3. Persons who, pursuant to the provisions of existing laws, have been received or are retained in any such institution by the written order or permit of the superintendent of the poor of a county, or overseer of the poor of a town, or commissioner or commissioners of charities or other local officer or board legally exercising the powers of an overseer of the poor in the county, city, town or village sought to be charged with the support of such persons.

4. Persons who have been received into such institutions as, under special or existing laws or appropriations, are entitled to receive payments of money in gross sum or for specific purposes, from any county, city, town or village. No child between the ages of two and sixteen, unless convicted of a crime, shall be received into any such institution as a public charge, unless committed thereto, or placed therein, by a court or magistrate having jurisdiction, or by the superintendent of the poor of a county, or overseer of the poor of a town, or commissioner or commissioners of charities, or other local officer or board legally exercising the powers of an overseer in the county, city, town or village sought to be charged with the support of such child, and authorized by law to commit children to such institutions or to place them therein.

II. RETENTION OF INMATES.

1. No child under the age of sixteen years, unless convicted of crime, nor any destitute minor nor adult person, whether com-

mitted by any court or magistrate, or otherwise received, shall
be retained in any such institution, *as a public charge*, unless
accepted in writing as such by the officer charged with the support and relief of the poor of the county, city, town or village
upon which such child or destitute minor or adult person is
sought to be made a public charge, subject to such regulations as
the Board may from time to time prescribe, *and all acceptances
so made shall lapse and become void* unless renewed in writing
within thirty days of the expiration of one year from the time
of the first acceptance; said year to date from the period of said
acceptance. The reacceptance in writing shall be repeated each
year that the inmate remains in the institution and within thirty
days of the expiration of each successive year. Every such acceptance or renewal of acceptance, shall be based upon the results
of an investigation into the circumstances of the person accepted,
and into the circumstances of his parents, relatives or guardians,
if there be any. No destitute child shall be retained as a public
charge in any institution wholly or partly under private control,
which shall fail to keep a book in which shall be entered the name
and address of every person visiting such child, supported in
whole, or in part, by public funds in such institution, which name
and address shall be secured upon such visit.

2. *Children.*—No *minor* who is an inmate of any such institution, other than a person under the age of sixteen who has been
convicted of crime and duly committed, may be retained *at public
expense* in any such institution, if the State Board of Charities,
or a committee thereof, shall have notified such institution in
writing, that in the judgment of the Board, or of a committee of
the Board, it is for the interest of such minor that he or she should
be returned to his or her parents or guardians, or placed out in a
family by adoption or indenture or other agreement, except that
such minor may be retained at public expense, for a period not
exceeding two months after the service of the notice to the institution, at its request, for the purpose of enabling it to place out
such child.

3. In no case shall any *child*, supported in whole or in part
at public expense, in any such institution, be *transferred* to any
other institution except upon the written approval of the commissioner of the district or county in or from which the transfer is

proposed, or in case of his absence any other commissioner of the Board.

4. No *minor* shall remain as an inmate of any such institution which has not furnished evidence of having complied with the provisions of sections 213, 214 and 215 of article XII of chapter 25 of the general laws, called the Public Health Law, passed by the Legislature May 9, 1893, chapter 661. *(And amended by chapter 667, Laws of 1900.)*

5. *Destitute and other adults.*— No *adult inmate* of any such institution, who has been placed or permitted to remain therein by a proper officer, shall be retained therein *at public expense*, after a date fixed by a commissioner, resident in the district in which the institution is situated, and of which the proper authorities or superintendent or officer in charge thereof has been notified in writing.

6. No payment shall be made by any county, city, town or village to any charitable, eleemosynary, correctional or reformatory institution wholly or partly under private control, for care, support or maintenance, which shall fail within a reasonable time after notice to comply:

First. With any law affecting the health of the inhabitants of said county, city, town or village,

Second. With any rules or regulation of the local board of health passed pursuant to law,

Third. With any law regulating the erection of the buildings of said institutions, or

Fourth. With any law, or rules or regulation made pursuant to such law, enacted to protect the inmates thereof from fire, or requiring the erection of fire-escapes or additional means of egress.

7. The inmates of all charitable, correctional or reformatory institutions, wholly or partly under private control, who are retained therein as a charge upon any county, city, town or village, shall be humanely and suitably provided with food, lodging and clothing and whatever further may be necessary for their safety, reasonable comfort and well being.

8. Children of school age retained in any such institution as a charge upon any county, city, town or village, shall receive *regular* and suitable instruction in at least the common school

branches of reading, spelling, writing, arithmetic, English grammar and geography.

9. The commissioners, officers, inspectors and other representatives of the State Board of Charities shall at all reasonable times be allowed to examine such children with relation to their scholastic training, and also with respect to their fitness for placing in family homes, or with relation to any other matter pertaining to their care, comfort and general welfare, as may be directed by the board by resolution duly adopted and entered on its minutes.

III. REPORTS OF INSTITUTIONS.

1. *Annual Reports.*

Each and every charitable, eleemosynary, correctional and reformatory institution, wholly or partly under private control, whether incorporated or not incorporated, subject to the visitation and inspection of the State Board of Charities, pursuant to article VII, section 11 of the Constitution, shall, on or before the first day of November in each and every year, prepare and file with the Board, at its office in the Capitol at Albany, a report of the condition of the institution and its operations, for the preceding fiscal year ending September 30th, upon forms prescribed and furnished for the purpose, to wit:

First. The estimated value of the real and personal property of the institution and its assets and liabilities October 1st.

Second. The total amount and sources of the receipts of the institution and its total and classified expenditures for the fiscal year ending September 30th.

Third. The whole number of persons supported in the institution, and the changes in the population during the fiscal year ending September 30th, and the number and sex of those in its custody and care October 1st, with such other particulars as may, from time to time, be required by the Board.

2. *Reports of Institutions Having the Custody, Care and Training of Orphan, Destitute, Delinquent and Defective Children.*

Every charitable, eleemosynary, correctional or reformatory institution, wholly or partly under private control, having the custody, treatment, care and training of orphan, destitute, delinquent or defective children, excepting deaf and blind pupils, shall, on or before the 10th day of October, 1895, file with the Board, at its office in the Capitol at Albany, the name and sex of each and every child, inmate of such institution January 1, 1895, and the name and sex of each and every child who may have been received in such institution from January 1 to September 30, 1895, inclusive, on a separate blank to be prescribed and furnished by the Board for the purpose, including the following particulars in respect to each, viz.: Date of reception; age; color; birthplace; whether orphan, half-orphan, or both parents living; physical and mental condition; birthplace of parents; authority under which received; county, city, village or town upon which a charge; amount received from parent, relative or guardian, or other private source, or whether supported wholly by the institution; per capita amount received from public sources; authority under which payments are made; and, in the case of delinquents, the offense or crime for which committed; and, each and every such institution shall, on or before November 10, 1895, and on or before the tenth of each month thereafter, file at the office of the Board, as aforesaid, the name and sex of each and every child, with the particulars above enumerated, in relation thereto, who may have been received in such institution during the preceding month; and such institution shall give prompt notice to the Board, upon blanks furnished therefor, of any and all discharges, removals, escapes, transfers or deaths occurring in the institution during the month.

IV. ACCOUNTS OF INSTITUTIONS.

Each and every charitable, eleemosynary, reformatory and correctional institution, wholly or partly under private control, shall keep proper books of account which shall set forth all receipts and expenditures with the vouchers therefor, and be open for the inspection of the State Board of Charities, its commissioners, officers, inspectors and agents.

Rules to be observed by those submitting plans for buildings and additions thereto.

1. All plans for the building of almshouses or other institutions, or of structures connected therewith or additions thereto or of modifications of such buildings or structures, requiring the Board's approval, must be submitted to the Board with the specifi-

cations relating thereto, *both in duplicate* before being referred
to the Committee on Construction of buildings.

2. Such plans and specifications must in every case be accompanied by a statement specifying the building or buildings to be
erected in accordance therewith, the location or locations of such
building or buildings and the work otherwise covered by the
plans and specifications, naming the amount or amounts appropriated for such construction, certifying that said plans and specifications have been officially approved by the responsible authorities presenting them for the Board's approval, together with a
specific request for such approval by the Board.

3. One of such plans, and one of a duplicate modification of
such plans, if such shall be made and approved, shall be filed
among the archives of the Board.

4. No changes or modifications shall be permitted in such plans
without the approval of the Board and the filing of such modified
plans in the archives of the Board.

5. The Board may at any time appoint an inspector to examine
the work of construction to see that the plans as approved by the
Board are adhered to.

Rules of the State Board of Charities for granting a license
to institutions devoted to the sole purpose of keeping and
caring for aged, decrepit and feeble-minded persons, who
are not proper subjects for care and treatment in a hospital
for the insane, under the Laws of the State of New York,
known as chapter 914 of the Laws of 1896, entitled "An act
to provide for the care of aged, decrepit and mentally enfeebled persons who are not insane."

Rule 1. Every applicant for a license shall file in the office of
this Board accurately-drawn plans of every part of the building
or buildings to be employed for a home, retreat or asylum, together with the following verified statements in writing:

A. A succinct description of the building or buildings and of
the location and surroundings of the institution and of the conditions or accommodations provided for the safe and humane
maintenance of the patients.

B. The number and names of the officers, attendants and employes, with a statement of their respective duties and their

C. The financial resources of the institution, aside from its income derived from patients, and the scale of weekly charges for patients.

Rule 2. No license shall be granted until the Commissioner of the district, or, in case of his absence, of an adjoining district, has personally inspected the grounds, buildings and appurtenances of the proposed institution, and reported in writing that in his opinion, it possesses the necessary equipment in officers and attendants, together with suitable domestic accommodations in all other respects for the safe and humane maintenance of such patients, and the number which can be properly provided for at any one time.

Rules of the State Board of Charities governing the management of homes, retreats and asylums for the care and maintenance of aged, decrepit and mentally enfeebled persons who are not insane.

1. Such institution shall be devoted to the sole purpose of keeping and caring for such persons.

2. The Superintendent thereof shall transmit to the office of this Board, within three days after the reception of a patient, a certified copy of the application of said patient, or his or her relative, friend or guardian, as the case may be, together with copies of the affidavits of the physicians supporting said application.

3. Whenever any patient by him or his friends or legal guardians shall make application to the State Board of Charities to be discharged from such home, retreat or asylum, the Superintendent thereof shall forthwith forward such application to the office of this Board, together with such recommendations in regard to the further care of the patient as he may deem useful and necessary.

4. Said institution shall have, in regular attendance upon its patients, a reputable physician, resident of the vicinity, duly qualified by law to practice his profession in this State, and whose appointment is approved by the State Board of Charities.

5. No form of *injury to the person*, or deprivation of the necessaries of life shall be allowed in such institution for the purpose of punishment or discipline.

6. All the provisions of the laws of the State relative to the sanitary care of public institutions and the preservation and promotion of the health of the inmates shall be rigidly complied with.

7. Said institution shall make to this Board the quarterly reports required of hospitals and the annual reports required of all charitable institutions.

8. The forms of application for the admission of all patients to such institutions shall be such as are prescribed by the State Board of Charities.

9. Whenever any patient in such institution shall become so violent in conduct as to become uncontrollable without the aid of mechanical restraint or permanent seclusion, it shall be the duty of the Superintendent thereof to notify forthwith the State Board of Charities of the condition of such patient by means of a certificate signed by him and the resident physician, and pending the action of said Board upon such notice, it shall not be lawful to discharge or transfer said patient to any other custody.

Rules and regulations in accordance with which dispensaries shall furnish medical or surgical relief, advice or treatment, medicine or apparatus; adopted October 11, 1899, pursuant to the provisions of chapter 368, Laws of 1899, as amended October 10, 1900.

I. POSTING A PUBLIC NOTICE.

There shall be posted and permanently maintained in a conspicuous place in the reception room for applicants a notice as follows:

This dispensary has been licensed under the laws of the State of New York by the State Board of Charities, to furnish medical or surgical relief, advice or treatment, medicine or apparatus to the sick poor who are unable to pay for the same. The law provides as follows:

(Section 25, chapter 368, Laws of 1899.)

"Any person who obtains medical or surgical treatment on false representations from any dispensary licensed under the provision of this act shall be guilty of a misdemeanor, and on conviction thereof shall be punished by a fine of not less than ten dollars and not more than two hundred and fifty dollars."

(Imprisonment until fine be paid may be imposed. Code Crim. Pro., § 718.)

II. THE REGISTRAR.
(As amended October 10, 1900.)

There shall be an officer to be known as "The Registrar," whose duties shall be to supervise the work of the dispensary, and either personally, or by a competent deputy selected by him for that purpose, to make and preserve all records, receive all applicants, and see that all rules and regulations are enforced.

III. THE ADMISSION OF APPLICANTS.
(As amended October 10, 1900.)

1. It shall be the duty of the Registrar to examine all applicants to determine the question of their admission, and the following rules shall guide his actions: (a) All emergency cases shall be admitted and receive prompt treatment and care. (b) Every applicant who is, in the opinion of the Registrar, after examination and personal inquiry, poor and needy, shall be admitted. (c) Every applicant, either personally or by the parent or guardian of such applicant, in regard to whose ability to pay for medical or surgical relief, advice or treatment, medicine or apparatus, or either, in whole or in part, the Registrar is in doubt, shall be admitted to a first treatment on signing a card containing the "representation" or statement of the applicant, but the Registrar shall forthwith cause an investigation of his or her ability to pay either personally, or by parent or guardian; the results of such investigation shall be filed among the permanent records of the dispensary. Any such applicant who declines to sign the required "representation" or statement shall be refused admission.

2. Such "representation" or statement shall be in the following form:

Card of Admission on "Representation" or Statement of Patient.

Name....................................... Date..................

Dr...................................... No. in family...............

Nationality...................... Address...........................

Occupation, Man.................... Woman.......................

Income............................ Rent....................

This is my..........application to this Dispensary in the year......

I have been an applicant to no other Dispensary in the year..........

(or to the following Dispensaries: ....

....)

The foregoing statement is in all respects true.

Signature of applicant...........................

Admitted....................... Refused........................

---

3. The Registrar shall issue to every applicant who is admitted for treatment a pass card, on one side of which shall be printed the usual information in regard to attendance upon the class to which he or she is assigned, and on the other side the card shall be in the following form:

Penalty for False Representations.
Section 25, Chapter 368, Laws of 1899.
"Any person who obtains medical or surgical treatment on false representations from any dispensary licensed under the provisions of this act shall be guilty of a misdemeanor, and on conviction thereof shall be punished by a fine of not less than ten dollars and not more than two hundred and fifty dollars."
(Imprisonment until fine be paid may be imposed. Code Crim. Pro., § 718.)

IV. THE MATRON.

There shall be á Matron whose duty it shall be, under the direction of the Registrar, to preserve cleanliness and good order in all parts of the dispensary, and be present during gynæcological examinations and operations; no such examination shall be made of, or operation performed on, any female patient except in the presence of the Matron or of a woman detailed for such duty.

V. CONTAGIOUS DISEASES EXCLUDED.

The following contagious diseases shall not be treated in any dispensary not devoted to the treatment of contagious diseases, viz.: smallpox, scarlet fever, measles, diphtheria. When a person suffering from any one of these diseases shall apply for treatment to any dispensary, the Registrar shall take immediate measures to prevent the exposure of other persons in the dispensary, and shall forthwith report the case to the proper health authority.

VI. INSTRUCTIONS IN DISPENSARIES.

Managers may make needful rules and regulations for clinical, secular and religious instruction in their respective dispensaries, but in no instance shall any applicant be required to attend such instruction as a condition on which he or she may receive medical or surgical relief at the dispensary. No applicant shall be required to submit to an examination, oral or physical, for other purposes than his or her proper medical or surgical treatment without his or her full and free consent; in the case of an infant,

64

the consent of the father, mother or guardians must be obtained for the purpose above mentioned.

VII. THE APOTHECARY.

The Apothecary must be licensed under the laws of this State or be a graduate of a regularly incorporated medical college. If employed in public service the Apothecary must be appointed under Civil Service rules.

VIII. SANITARY INSPECTIONS.
(As amended October 10, 1900.)

The managers of dispensaries shall comply with the ordinances and orders of the local Board of Health, and shall annually make a minute showing compliance therewith, upon their official records on or before September 30th in each and every year.

IX. ARRANGEMENTS AND EQUIPMENT.

Each dispensary shall provide: 1. Seats for all applicants. 2. Arrangements for the separation of the sexes in both waiting and treatment rooms, except in cases of family groups or of infants. 3. Such equipment in the matter of rooms and supplies as will secure the best results of treatment.

*RULES FOR DISTRICT COMMITTEES.

For administration purposes the State shall be divided into two inspection districts, to be known as the Eastern District and the Western District. The Eastern District shall embrace the first, second, third and fourth judicial districts of the State. The Western District shall embrace the fifth, sixth, seventh and eighth judicial districts of the State.

The Committee in the Eastern District shall consist of the members of the Board resident therein. The work in the Eastern District may be carried on by a sub-committee of three of its members, to be appointed by the President.

The Committee in the Western District shall consist of the members of the Board resident therein. The work in the Western District may be carried on by a sub-committee of two of its members, to be appointed by the President. The President shall designate the Chairman of the said Committees.

---

*As adopted by the State Board of Charities at its meeting of May 11, 1899.

With the exception of the months of July and August, each of the Committees shall hold meetings at their respective district offices at least once a month, as the Committee may decide. Three members shall constitute a quorum in the Eastern District and two in the Western District. Special meetings may be called by the Chairman as often as he may deem the same necessary. The District Committees may, when in their judgment the work of inspection requires it, hold joint meetings.

The Committees may in their respective districts designate from time to time one of their members to supervise and direct the daily conduct of the work of the District.

The district offices shall be open for business from 9 A. M. to 5 P. M. on every week day, not a legal holiday, except on Saturdays, when they shall be open from 9 A. M. to 12 M.

In each district there shall be a Superintendent. to be appointed by the Board upon the nomination of the District Committee, who shall be subject to the said Committees, and shall have the immediate direction of the Inspectors in the said districts.

It shall be the duty of the Superintendent to see that the instructions of the District Committees are duly carried out and that the details of business of their offices receive prompt and suitable attention. The district offices shall be in their charge and they shall act as Secretary of their respective District Committees and keep a record of the Committee's proceedings.

They shall have the custody of the records of their respective offices and be responsible for the safe preservation of all papers, books, letters and documents.

In each district there shall be such number of inspectors and other employes as the Board may see proper to employ.

The inspectors may, as far as practicable, be classified as " auditing inspectors," " sanitary inspectors " and " general inspectors." The duties of the " auditing inspectors " may be specially directed to examination of the accounts, records and other matters relative to the financial affairs of institutions. The duties of " sanitary inspectors " may be specially directed to inspection of conditions affecting the sanitary status of institutions. The duties of " general inspectors " may be considered as connected with conditions not belonging specially to the departments of auditing and sanitary inspectors. All inspectors and other employes of the District shall perform such duties as may from time to time be designated by the District Committees.

The joint committee of the Eastern and the Western Districts may temporarily transfer inspectors from the Eastern to the Western District and *vice versa*. The reasons of such transfers shall be entered in the minutes of both of the District Committees.

The hours of duty of the said Superintendents, Inspectors and other employes shall be from 9 A. M to 5 P. M., with an hour's intermission for lunch, every week day, not a legal holiday, except on Saturdays, when the hours will be from 9 A. M. to 12 M.

Inspectors shall make full and complete records in such form as shall be prescribed by the Board or the District Committees of all visits, inspections and examinations, and shall file the same in the office of the proper inspection district.

If, in the opinion of either Committee, it appears that any institution is not complying with the rules adopted pursuant to Article VIII., Section 14 of the Constitution, said Committee shall promptly bring the matter to the attention of the Board in order that the proper financial officer of the county, city, town or village affected thereby may be duly notified.

On or about the 20th of each month, each District Committee shall send requisitions to the Secretary for such postage stamps, stationery and other supplies as may be required in the performance of their duties.

As soon after the first of each month as practicable, the said Committees shall send to the Secretary of the Board a full report of the inspection work of the district, during the month preceding, together with a separate account of the salary and disbursements of each employe of the District, certified by the Chairman of said respective Committees.

MANUAL FOR THE GUIDANCE OF THE INSPECTORS OF THE STATE BOARD OF CHARITIES.

THE OFFICE OF INSPECTOR.

An inspector of the State Board of Charities is a State officer appointed by that Board under the State Civil Service Rules. The statute confers important powers and requires of him the performance of certain duties in the visitation and inspection of institutions of a charitable, eleemosynary, reformatory or correctional character or design. These powers and duties are contained in the "State Charities Law" (chapter 546, Laws of 1896). With a view to familiarize inspectors with their statutory obligations and the instructions of the State Board of Charities in relation thereto, the provisions of law relating to their powers and duties have been collated in this manual, and such explanations, instructions and regulations have been added as were deemed necessary for their information and guidance.

I. PROVISIONS OF LAW RELATING TO THE POWERS AND DUTIES OF INSPECTORS.

1. *Institutions subject to inspection.*

Section 10. All institutions of a charitable, eleemosynary, reformatory or correctional character or design, including reformatories (except those now under the supervision and subject to the inspection of the prison commission), but including all reformatories, except those in which adult males convicted of felony, shall be confined, asylums and institutions for idiots and epileptics, almshouses, orphan asylums, and all asylums, hospitals and institutions, whether state, county, municipal, incorporated or not incorporated, private or otherwise, except institutions for the custody, care and treatment of the insane, are subject to the visitation, inspection and supervision of the state board of charities, its members, officers and inspectors.

The Court of Appeals has defined the meaning of the words "charitable institution," as used in the Constitution and the State Charities Law, as follows:

"A charitable institution, within the meaning of sections 11 to 14 of article 8 of the Constitution, chapter 771 of the Laws of 1895, and chapter 546 of the Laws of 1896, giving to the State Board of Charities the right of visitation with respect to all charitable institutions, is one that in some form or to some extent receives public money for the support and maintenance of indigent persons, and by public money is meant money raised by taxation, not only in the State at large, but in any city, county or town."

The important facts which should be noticed by inspectors are as follows:

1. Certain classes of institutions are excepted from inspection by the State Board of Charities, because they are not in receipt of public money, or are under the jurisdiction of other State authorities.

2. The language of the statute makes all institutions, with the exceptions given, subject to inspection, which in *character* or *design* are charitable, eleemosynary, reformatory or correctional. Managers and officers may object to an inspection, alleging that the institution is not a charity in character or design. It is important, therefore, that inspectors should inform themselves as accurately as possible, before visiting an institution with which they are unacquainted, as to its character and the objects which it was designed to accomplish, and whether or not the institution is in receipt of public money. This information may be obtained by examining the articles of incorporation and the annual reports.

3. Objection may be made to an inspection because the institution belongs to a county or city, or because it is unincorporated or is private, but the statute is very explicit in this respect, and includes all that come under the general definition, whatever may be the nature of their origin, their location or their control.

For decisions on this subject see

The People ex rel. Inebriate Home vs. Comptroller, 152 N. Y. 399.

The People ex rel. N. Y. Institution for the Blind vs. Fitch, 154 N. Y. 14.

The People ex rel. State Board of Charities vs. The New York Society for the Prevention of Cruelty to Children, 161 N. Y. 233 and 162 N. Y. 429.

Fox vs. Mohawk and H. R. Humane Society, 165 N. Y. 517.

2. *Inspections may be made at any and all times.*

Section 10 continued: Such institutions may be visited and inspected by such board, or any member, officer or inspector duly appointed by it for that purpose, at any and all times.

No examination of an institution can be made for the purpose of obtaining all of the information which the law requires when the inspector is limited as to the time of his inspection by any *rules* or regulations of the managers or officials. The everyday

working condition of all parts of an institution can most satisfactorily be determined only by the casual and unexpected visits
of the inspector. For example, unannounced visits must be made
at meal times to learn the kind, quality and quantity of foods
ordinarily served, and visits to the dormitories at night is the
only method of deciding as to their ventilation.

3. *Powers of inspectors during an inspection.*

Section 10 continued: Any member or officer of such board,
or inspector duly appointed by it, shall have full access to the
grounds, buildings, books and papers relating to any such institution, and may require from the officers and persons in charge
thereof, any information he may deem necessary in the discharge
of his duties.

The statutory powers of inspectors during an inspection enable them to obtain full and accurate knowledge of the entire
premises and of every feature of the institution and its management. They have the right to see personally every part of the
buildings and premises, every inmate, all of the books, records
and papers, and finally, they may require any additional information deemed necessary for the proper discharge of their duties.
In exercising these powers, inspectors should be courteous and
considerate towards officers of institutions, and whenever refused unlawfully they should use no force nor mandatory language, but discontinue the inspection and withdraw and report
the facts to the Board for its action.

4. *Relation of officers, superintendents and employes of institutions to inspectors of the Board.*

Section 10 continued: Any officer, superintendent or employe
of any such institution, society or association who shall unlawfully refuse to admit any member, officer or inspector of the
board, for the purpose of visitation and inspection, or who shall
refuse or neglect to furnish the information required by the
board or any of its members, officers or inspectors, shall be guilty
of a misdemeanor, and subject to a fine of one hundred dollars
for each such refusal or neglect. The right and powers hereby
conferred may be enforced by an order of the supreme court
after notice and hearing, or by indictment by the grand jury of
the county or both.

This clause of the section establishes the character of the offense committed by an officer, superintendent or employe of an institution, society or association who unlawfully refuses to admit an inspector for the purpose of inspection, or refuses or neglects to furnish information required. It also prescribes the method of enforcing the rights and powers of the inspector.

5. *Inspectors confidential agents of the Board.*

Section 10 continued: No such officer or inspector shall divulge or communicate to any person without the knowledge and consent of said board any facts or information obtained pursuant to the provisions of this act; on proof of such divulgement or communication such officer or inspector may at once be removed from office.

The necessity of this restriction upon inspectors grows out of the extraordinary powers of inquiry into the affairs of institutions given them by law in making inspections. Inspectors are peculiarly exposed to the temptation of giving information in regard to facts obtained in the performance of their duties. Officers of institutions are very liable to make inquiries of them as to the condition and management of other institutions of the same class. While much of the information thus sought might be given, not only without detriment, but even with benefit, the occasional scandals that might result render the legal restriction eminently wise and conservative.

No record, document or paper containing information considered confidential regarding the history and personality of any inmate, and sealed or kept under lock and key, by resolution duly adopted by the board of managers of any institution, shall be examined by any inspector, except by direction of the State Board of Charities.

11. PROVISIONS OF LAW RELATING TO THE SUBJECTS OF INQUIRY DURING INSPECTION.

Section 11. This section provides that "on such visits, inquiry shall be made to ascertain " the following information:

1. *Whether all parts of the State are equally benefited by the institution requiring State aid.*

To obtain this information the inspector must first learn from the act creating the institution the precise terms on which it is required to receive inmates from the several counties of the State or of the district to which its operations are confined. Then a census of the inmates must be taken and the residence of each noted. Finally, the population of each county entitled to representation in the institution must be taken as the basis of calculation as to the proper ratio of inmates from each county in the institution.

2. *The merits of any and all requests on the part of any such institution for State aid, for any purpose other than the usual expenses thereof, and the amount required to accomplish the object desired.*

Inquiries required by this section are to be made only when the managers of institutions make requests for State aid for some specific purpose. They are not subjects of inquiry, therefore, on every inspection, and should receive the attention of the inspector only when directed by the State Board of Charities.

3. *The sources of public moneys received for the benefit of such institution, as to the proper and economical expenditure of such moneys and the condition of the finances generally.*

The sources of public moneys received for the benefit of an institution, and the condition of the finances generally, are subjects for special inquiry under the direction of the Board; but inquiries as to the expenditure of moneys ought to be constantly in the mind of the inspector during his inspections, and accurate notes should be made whenever he discovers evidences of improper and uneconomical uses of the funds of an institution. Improper expenditures are more likely to be found in the purchase of luxuries, as in furniture, foods, implements, horses, carriages and in other directions. The lack of economy is found in the prices paid for the great variety of articles purchased, the cost of the erection and repair of buildings.

4. *Whether the objects of the institution are being accomplished.*

The inquiries required by this provision should be taken in their larger sense. The unit in every charitable institution is the individual inmate. For his welfare alone it was established and now exists. To relieve or mitigate the special disabilities which make him an object of charity, every matter or thing connected with the institution, whether lands, buildings, furniture, officers, management, should contribute to their fullest capacity.

The inspector must, therefore, in all the details of inspections, have in mind the ultimate objects of the institution and endeavor to determine how far they are accomplished by the existing conditions.

5. *Whether the laws and the rules and regulations of this Board, in relation to it, are fully complied with.*

To make the inquiries under this head, the inspector should first make himself thoroughly familiar with the laws and the rules and regulations of this Board in relation to the institution about to be inspected. The laws relating to it will be found in the State Charities Law, and other statutes,.and in the act of incorporation, and the amendments thereto. The rules of the Board will be found in its manual or in other form at the central office. Inquiry should be made as to whether a copy of the Board's manual is in the hands of the managers. Three classes of institutions are now operating under the rules of the Board, namely: 1. Institutions wholly or partly under private control, authorized by law to receive payments from any county, city,. town or village for the support, care or maintenance of inmates. (Chap. 546, Laws of 1896.) 2. Homes, retreats and asylums for the care and maintenance of aged, decrepit and mentally enfeebled persons who are not insane. *(Chap. 914, Laws 1896.)* 3. Dispensaries. *(Chap. 368, Laws of 1899, as amending Chap. 546 of the Laws 1896.)*

6. *Its methods of industrial, educational and moral training, if any, and whether the same are best adapted to the needs of its inmates.*

The methods of industrial, educational and moral training in practice in an institution can be learned by inquiry and observation, but it requires large experience and good judgment to determine whether they are best adapted to the needs of its inmates. Inspectors should make very accurate notes of the method of training in each of these branches, and report the facts, with such observations as they may have made as to the effects upon the inmates.

7. *The methods of government and discipline of its inmates.*

It is difficult to determine definitely the government and discipline of an institution, as in obtaining information the inspector is limited to inquiry, for by his observation he can determine only the most superficial facts. His inquiries must not be limited to officers and attendants, but must include such inmates as, in his opinion, will make truthful statements. Inquiries of inmates should be very judiciously made, in order not to prejudice them against attendants. In general, they should be examined singly and in private, that they may not be actuated by fear.

8. *The qualifications and general conduct of its officers and employes.*

The opinion of the inspector in regard to the qualifications and general conduct of officers and employes must be formed chiefly by observation and intercourse with them. In his examination of the different departments of an institution he should carefully discriminate as to the officer or employe who is personally responsible for the conditions found, and thus he can very accurately determine his qualifications and general conduct. In his intercourse with officers and employes, the Inspector can form a very accurate judgment as to their fitness for their position by the discussion of topics relating to their duties.

9. *The condition of its grounds, buildings and other property.*

This information is obtained only by personal inspection. It is very important that these inspections be made in a methodical manner, in order that nothing shall escape thorough examination. Each matter or thing undergoing inspection should be exhaustively examined before another is undertaken.

10. *Any other matter connected with or pertaining to its usefulness and good management.*

During an inspection many incidents will occur and many observations will be made bearing on the usefulness of the institution and its management. Ample notes and full reports should be made of everything that in any manner comes to the knowledge of the inspector illustrating its condition and management.

III. RULES AND REGULATIONS OF THE BOARD RELATING TO INSPECTORS AND INSPECTION.

1. *Relation of inspectors to District Committees.*

1. All inspectors will be under the special direction of the District Committee to which they are assigned by the Board, and will receive their orders either directly from the Chairman of

the District Committee or the Superintendent of Inspection, or through their District Superintendent.

2. All assignments of inspectors for ordinary inspections will be made by the District Committees, while special inspection duties may be assigned by the Board.

2. *The relation of inspectors to the institutions which they inspect.*

1. In all visitations and inspections, inspectors, while maintaining their statutory privileges, will so conduct their investigations as to avoid unnecessary friction on the part of the officers of institutions, or to disturb the usual daily routine of the service. The establishment of cordial coöperation on the part of the managers and officers of institutions will facilitate the work of inspection.

2. Inspectors must not criticise the management of institutions, either publicly or privately, but in their reports to the Board they shall accurately describe such defects as, in their opinion, require to be remedied; nor shall they direct or advise changes to be made of any matter or thing in any institution unless first specifically authorized by the Board, the District Committee, the Commissioner of the district, or, in his absence, some other Commissioner.

3. *The conduct of inspections.*

1. Special inspections.

A special inspection is a visit to an institution to inquire or examine as to some particular fact or condition. It may be made at any time, the hour selected being the best adapted to obtain the desired information.

For example, the inspector might wish to learn by his own observation of the kind of food served to the inmates at dinner. This information could be secured only by a personal visit unannounced at the dinner hour.

2. General inspections.

All general inspections should be made in accordance with a plan which, while it economizes the time of the inspector and officials, and creates the least possible disturbance of the ordinary details of daily management, will secure a thorough inquiry into the operations and condition of every department of an institution. The inspector should always carry a note-book and make an immediate entry of every observation. The following scheme of a general inspection is best adapted to secure reliable results:

1. Before visiting an institution, the inspector should familiarize himself, as far as possible, with the law relating to it, the objects it is designed to accomplish, as set forth in its charter and its previous history. This information can be obtained at the offices of the Board and will enable the inspector to anticipate the defects of management which may exist.

2. On entering the institution the inspector should first call on the chief officer and inform him of his intention to make a general inspection. If this officer volunteers to accompany him he should accept the offer, but the inspector should not be diverted from the plan of inspection proposed, unless the suggestions of such officer would manifestly facilitate the work or accomplish some other useful purpose.

3. In order to see the institution in its usual every-day working condition, the inspector should at once visit those parts where such changes may readily be made in existing conditions as will give false impressions if there is any delay. The changes more likely to be made are in the clothing, location or surroundings of certain troublesome inmates. The inspector should, therefore, first make a rapid tour of the institution and endeavor to see all of the inmates in whatever place and condition they may be found. He should next pass rapidly through the dormitories, the kitchen, the laundry and other departments. Having completed this preliminary survey, he should commence a detailed, exhaustive examination of the entire establishment. Every room in the entire building should be examined in regular succession, with the single exception of the chief officers' living rooms. No attendants' rooms, no closets or clothes room, no pantry or cupboard, no wardrobe or recess, no cellar or attic should be exempt from inspection. Every inmate should be seen, and those whose appearance indicates diseases of the eyes or scalp, or uncleanliness of person, or deficient clothing or any other evidences of neglect, should be made the subject of special inquiry. If there is a farm connected with the institution, inquiry should be made as to the crops raised and their value, the amount of labor of inmates, and the cost of hired labor, and the final disposition of the products of the farm. The inspection may close with the examination of the books, records and papers.

INDEX TO VOLUME ONE OF ANNUAL REPORT FOR 1901.

Lightning Source UK Ltd.
Milton Keynes UK
UKHW020659150219
337291UK00007B/655/P